DEDICATION

To Brian, Christine, and Paul, who lost their father to the computer during the making of this book.

ACKNOWLEDGMENTS

A special thanks to some of the many people who have helped make this guide possible:

John Wharton
Robert Sohl
Scott McAdam
Kim McLynn
Melaine Donovan
Mary Janaky
Rebecca Greason
Clif Erickson
Diane McCue
Linda Terpstra
Judy and Elmer Waldmann
Holly Everson

My wife, Charlotte, who has been very supportive with my collecting.

NOTE FROM THE AUTHOR

Any questions can be directed to the author either by e-mailing (LGBSteve@aol.com), visiting his web page (www.JPS.Net/LGBSTEVE), or by sending a letter with a self-addressed stamped envelope to:

Steve Santi
19626 Ricardo Ave.
Hayward, CA 04541

FOREWORD

I met Steve Santi in late 1987. Since then, I've come to know him as a man who cares… What I mean by that is golden books. What? Golden books? Yes. I'm not sure how long he has been collecting them… since who knows when. I don't consider him a collector, though, but a historian. Think back on how we have been raised on the little golden book—as much as we have been raised on the Disney animated film. He has taken of his time, energy, money, and knowledge to accumulate the history of a treasure—the Little Golden Book. Without him, not even the Golden Book people, Western Publishing, would know all about the Golden's recorded history.

It has been a pleasure to know Steve, a man with a golden vision… Thanks, Steve.

Ron Dias

Note:

Ron Dias has illustrated or collaborated on many of Disney children's books since getting his first job as an animator/illustrator for the Walt Disney Studios in the late 1950s. He is credited with illustrating 12 Little Golden Books, but he worked on many before Disney Studios started allowing illustrators to be given name credit. Ron received national attention in 1956 when he was invited to visit President Eisenhower in Washington, DC, as a result of winning a national contest on designing a "Children's Friendship" postal stamp. Ron is still very active in the animation industry.

Table of Contents

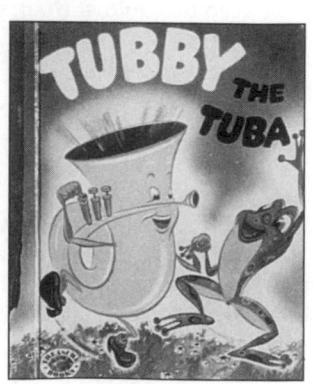

COLLECTING

LITTLE GOLDEN BOOKS

A COLLECTOR'S IDENTIFICATION AND PRICE GUIDE

4th
Edition

Steve Santi

Published by

700 East State St., Iola, WI 54990-0001
715-445-2214
www.krause.com

Please, call or write us for our free catalog of antiques and collectibles publications.
To place an order or receive our free catalog, call 800-258-0929. For editorial comment and further information,
use our regular business telephone at (715) 445-2214

Library of Congress Catalog Number: 00-101574
ISBN: 0-87341-872-7

Printed in the United States of America

The History of Little Golden Books

One of the largest printers of children's books in the world, Western Publishing Company, Inc., had its beginning in the basement of 618 State St. in Racine, WI. Edward Henry Wadewitz, the 30-year-old son of German immigrants, had been working two jobs—one at a paint store and the other for West Side Printing Company—while taking bookkeeping classes at night. When the owner of the printing company was unable to pay Wadewitz his wages, he offered to sell Wadewitz the business. With dreams of owning his own business, Wadewitz, with $2,504—some of it borrowed from his brother, Al—purchased the West Side Printing Company in 1907.

Wadewitz knew that if the printing company were to make it, he would need someone with more knowledge than he had. Roy A. Spencer, a printer with the Racine Journal Co., was one of the first people Wadewitz hired.

West Side Printing Company, with four employees, showed sales of $5,000 at the end of its first year. In 1908, with commercial job sales increasing, the company hired more employees. That year, it also left a $10-a-month rental building and moved into a larger one and purchased a new automatic cutting machine and three new presses.

In 1910, after the purchase of the company's first lithographic press, the name was changed to Western Printing and Lithographing Co.

Less than four years later, the company moved into an even larger building—the basement of the Dr. Clarendon I. Shoop Building located at State and Wisconsin Avenue in

Western's business started in 1907 in this basement print shop. "Pioneer employees" were (from the left) Roy A. Spencer, Catherine Bongarts Rutledge, E.H. Wadewitz, W.R. Wadewitz, and William Bell. The shop consisted of not much more than two battered presses, a few fonts of worn type, and a hand-powered cutting machine.

Racine. Dr. Shoop was famous for bottled medications and tonics. Western Printing and Lithographing Co. had become so successful that when Dr. Shoop retired in 1914, the company took over all six floors of the Shoop Building.

By its seventh year, sales had topped $127,000 and two new departments were formed: electrotyping and engraving. The company also purchased a new 28-inch by 42-inch offset press.

A major sign of growth was the 1929 move to the new main plant in Racine, Wisconsin.

Wadewitz was approached by the Hamming-Whitman Publishing Company of Chicago to print its line of children's books. What Wadewitz did not foresee was that Hamming-Whitman would soon be going out of business. Unable to pay its bills, Hamming-Whitman left Western with thousands of books in its warehouse and in production.

Trying to cut its losses, Wadewitz entered Western into the retail book market for the first time. It proved so successful that the remaining Hamming-Whitman books were liquidated.

After acquiring Hamming-Whitman on February 9, 1916, Western formed a subsidiary corporation called Whitman Publishing Company. Whitman employed two salesmen the first year and grossed more than $43,500 in children's book sales.

Sam Lowe, who later owned Bonnie Books, joined the Western team in 1916. Lowe sold Western and Whitman on the idea of bringing out a 10-cent children's book in 1918. Disaster almost followed when an employee misread a book order from S.S. Kresge Company, confusing dozens for gross, resulting in too many books being printed. Lowe was able to sell F.W. Woolworth Company and other chains the idea of having children's books on sale all year round. Until that time, stores usually treated children's books as Christmas items.

Toward the end of 1918, Western was outgrowing the Shoop Building, so another one was purchased—named Plant 2—to house the bookbinding and storage depart-

In 1910 West Side Printing Company changed its name to Western Printing & Litographing Co. and moved to the imposing building seen here, which was owned by Dr. Sharp's Laboratories.

ments. In order to print a 6-inch by 9-inch book, Western purchased a 38-inch by 52-inch Potter offset press in 1923. This same year, Western started producing games and puzzles.

With sales of more than $1 million in 1925, Western decided to add another product, playing cards, to its ever-growing line of merchandise. To be able to handle this, Western obtained the Sheffer Playing Card Company and formed another subsidiary corporation, the Western Playing Card Company.

By 1928, Western had built a new, modern, air-conditioned plant on Mound Avenue in Racine, and by 1929, sales were more than $2.4 million. The print run for children's books exceeded $10 million, playing cards $5 million, and games and puzzles $1 million. As a result, the company had to make plans to expand its new building.

In 1929, Western purchased Stationer's Engraving Company of Chicago, manufacturer of stationery and greeting cards. This was the second operation the company had outside of Racine.

Western was able to keep its plant operational during the Depression years (1929–1933) by introducing a couple of new products: the Whitman jigsaw puzzle became very popular during this time of uncertainty, and a new series of books called Big Little Books was marketed. Brought out in 1932, the 10-cent Little Big Books became very popular during the years when people were looking for inexpensive entertainment. The first Big Little Book title was The Adventures of Dick Tracy. With this line of books, Western was setting the stage for future inexpensive reading material like comic books and Little Golden Books. People love to copy success, and many publishers started bringing out their own books styled after the Big Little Book.

By the end of 1933, the Depression was coming to a close, Disney's Big Bad Wolf had been beaten by the Three Little Pigs, and Western and Walt Disney signed their first contract, giving Western exclusive rights to Disney's major characters.

Western, seeing a problem in having its plants and offices so far away from the rest of the publishing industry, purchased a plant in Poughkeepsie, NY, in 1934. This event marked the beginning of a close relationship with Dell Publishing Company and Simon & Schuster, Inc. Dell Publishing and Western produced Color Comics, which contained many of Western's licensed characters, from 1939 to 1962, and A Children's History was the first joint effort between Western and Simon & Schuster in 1938.

Western formed the Artists and Writers Guild Inc. in the 1930s to handle the development of new children's books. This company, located on Fifth Avenue in New York City, would later have an immense hand in the conception of Little Golden Books.

Western expanded its operations to the West Coast when it opened an office in Beverly Hills, CA, sometime in the early 1940s. Being closer to the movie capital of the world made it a lot easier to do business with the studios that owned the characters the company licensed.

During World War II, Western did its part to help with the war effort. The company had a contract with the U.S. Army Map Service to produce maps for American soldiers in the fields. Along with the maps and other projects it did for the military, Western also manufactured many of its own products that were sent to the soldiers and the Red Cross overseas, such as playing cards and books.

In 1940, Sam Lowe left the company and George Duplaix replaced him as head of the Artists and Writers Guild. While the guild and Simon & Schuster were collaborating on a book of Walt Disney's Bambi, Duplaix came up with the concept of a colorful children's book that would be durable and affordable to more American families than those being printed at that time. In 1941, children's books sold for between $2 and $3—a luxury for a lot of families. With the help of Lucile Olge, also of the guild, Duplaix contacted Albert Leventhal— a vice president and sales manager at Simon & Schuster—and Leon Shimkin, also of Simon & Schuster, with his idea.

The group decided on 12 titles to be released at the same time. Each title would have 42 pages, 28 in two color and 14 in four color. The book's binding was designed after a side-staple binding being done in Sweden. These books were to be called Little Golden Books.

The group originally discussed a 50-cent price for Little Golden Books, but Western did not want to compete with the other 50-cent books already on the market. The group did some more figuring and found that if it printed 50,000 copies of each book instead of 25,000, the books could be sold for 25 cents. In September 1942, the first 12 titles were printed and released to stores in October.

Little Golden Books, with their colorful, bright pages, were designed to be handled by children, and inexpensive enough that children could read or handle their books whenever they wanted. With these qualities and many more, the books became very popular with parents, but not with librarians in these early years, who felt these books did not contain the quality of literature a child should be reading. They did not consider that a book a child could handle was better than a book on a six-foot shelf or that an affordable book was better than not owning one, but this attitude has mellowed quite a bit since the 1940s.

The first ad to announce Little Golden Books was published in the September 19, 1942, edition of Publisher's Weekly. The ad listed the types of stories and the artists doing the first 12 books. The ad stated the books measured 8-1/4 inches by 6-1/4 inches and contained 44 pages—30 pages in black and white and 14 in full color. Whether it was because of the war, getting the price down to a quarter, or a printing error in the ad, the books were released with 42 pages, not 44.

The First 12 Little Golden Books

1   Three Little Kittens
2   Bedtime Stores
3   The Alphabet A-Z
4   Mother Goose
5   Prayers for Children
6   The Little Red Hen
7   Nursery Songs
8   The Poky Little Puppy
9   The Golden Book of Fairy Tales
10   Baby's Book
11   The Animals of Farmer Jones
12   This Little Piggy

Within five months, 1.5 million copies had been printed and the books were in their third printing. They became so popular with children that by the end of 1945, most of the first 12 books had been printed seven times. Simon & Schuster, Inc. published Little Golden Books, while the Artists and Writers Guild produced them and Western Printing and Lithographing did the printing.

When the books were first released, they were sold mainly in book and department stores. From there, they moved into variety, toy, and drug stores, and finally in the late 1940s to something new called the supermarket. Often, parents did not mind paying a quarter for a book, so, for the first time, a quality children's book was made available to children who normally couldn't have afforded one.

During World War II, there was a paper shortage in the United States. To help ease this shortage, in 1943 the War Production Board put restrictions on paper use. As a result, retailers were receiving only one of every 10 books they ordered. Some Little Golden Book titles were being printed with less than the original 42 pages. In some cases, the size of the book was also reduced slightly. Books that had been reduced to compensate for the paper shortage stated on the copyright page "First Printing this edition."

Most of the first 35 titles were released with blue bindings. Books that have this binding were published with dust jackets. Book No. 35, The Happy Family, was the last book published with the blue binding. The dust jackets of these early books mentioned on their back inside flap the purchasing of U.S. Savings Stamps. One of the characters of each of these books was also used to talk to the child about purchasing these stamps.

The following are some of these shorts:

THREE LITTLE KITTENS

*They found their mittens and they rushed out to say,
"Oh! Mother dear, see here, see here our mittens we have found."
"What! Found your mittens, you good little kittens!
I'll get you all War Stamps today!"
So, you be good kittens, hold on to your mittens, save your pennies the War Stamp way!*

BEDTIME STORIES

*One day Chicken Little strutted through the woods.
Behind her strutted Henny Penny and Ducky Lucky and Goosey Loosey. On the way they met Turkey Lurkey.
"Where are you going?" asked Turkey Lurkey.
"We are all going to buy War Savings Stamps, just as we do every week!"
So Turkey Lurkey joined them and they all hurried off to buy War Savings Stamps. And so should you!*

FROM A TO Z

***A** is for the airplanes which Jimmy's War Stamps buy.
B is for the Bond he'll get to keep them in the sky.
C is for children who save a bit each day.
D is for the dimes they save that help the U.S.A.
You can buy Stamps every week, like Jim.
Soon you'll be buying a Bond, like him.*

MOTHER GOOSE

*There was an old woman who lived in a shoe.
She had so many children,
She knew just what to do.
She gave them some broth without any bread,
Bought them all War Stamps*

And sent them to bed.
Soon she was able to buy them a War Bond.
If you buy War Stamps with your pennies, soon you
can buy a Bond too.

PRAYERS FOR CHILDREN

Today our country, which has given us so much, needs
our help. It asks all of us, children and grown-ups
alike, to put our savings into War Stamps and Bonds.
These Bonds will help to buy the ships and tanks and
planes and guns our country needs to win the war
quickly.
Then, too, we will get back all the money we invest,
and more, later on.
Surely we will all want to buy War Stamps or Bonds
every week to help our country!

THE LITTLE RED HEN

This year the Little Red Hen has a Victory Garden.
She has extra food to sell to the duck, the goose, the
cat and the pig who will not grow their own.
With the pennies she saves, she buys War Savings
Stamps every week. Soon she will have enough
stamps to buy a War Bond. If you buy War Stamps
every week, you will soon be able to buy a Bond too.

NURSERY SONGS

Mary buys War Savings Stamps, Savings Stamps,
Savings Stamps,
Mary buys War Savings Stamps
To help the U.S.A.
Soon she's going to have a Bond, Have a bond, Have
a Bond, Soon She's going to have a Bond.
Why not start yours today?

THE POKY LITTLE PUPPY

The poky little puppy sat near the bottom of the hill, look-
ing hard at something on the ground in front of him.
"What is he looking at?" the four little puppies asked
one another And down they went to see.
There was a War Savings Stamp lying on the grass.
And the poky little puppy hurried home faster than he
had ever run before, to paste the stamp in his War
Stamp Book. All the five little puppies buy War
Stamps every week.
So should you.

THE GOLDEN BOOK OF FAIRY TALES

While the wicked Old Giant was asleep, Jack tucked
the magic hen under his arm, and fled down the
beanstalk to his home.
Every day the hen laid a golden egg, and Jack sold the
gold to buy a War Savings Bond, which is much more
valuable.
Even if you don't have a magic hen, your pennies will
buy War Savings Stamps and soon you will be able
to buy a Bond too!

BABY'S BOOK

Where is Tommy?
Here he is.
He has a new War Stamp.
Soon he will buy a War Bond.
Do you buy War Stamps every week like Tommy?
Of course you do!

THE ANIMALS OF FARMER JONES

All the animals are hungry. But Farmer Jones has
gone to town. He is buying War Savings Stamps. He
buys War Savings Stamps every week. You should
buy War Stamps every week, too.
Soon you will be able to buy a War Savings Bond.

THIS LITTLE PIGGY AND OTHER COUNTING RHYMES

This little piggy goes to market.
What do you think he'll buy?
He's buying some War Savings Stamps.
So do I.
This little piggy cried, "Wee, wee, wee,
Boo! hoo! hoo!
I have no War Savings Stamps."
Is that you?

THE GOLDEN BOOK OF BIRDS

Robin Redbreast's beak is high and he is singing
proudly, he has just bought War Stamps for the
whole Robin Family.
If you save your pennies and buy War Stamps, you will
want to sing, too.

NURSERY TALES

You remember how the kind old shoemaker and his
wife made tiny shoes and tiny jackets and trousers
and hats for the good little elves who helped them.
(If you don't remember, you can read about them in
this very book.)
Well, one night the elves came back. They crept into the
shop and left a gift on the shoemaker's workbench.
What do you suppose that gift was? It was a War Sav-
ings Stamp Book half filled with War Savings
Stamps. These days, a War Savings Stamp is the
best gift of all!

A DAY IN THE JUNGLE

All the animals were on their way to visit the mouse.
The story had spread that he had something really
worth seeing, and all were anxious to find out what
this tiny animal could possibly have that was worth
looking at. But they all gasped when he showed it to
them-a brand new twenty-five-dollar War Bond!
"How," growled the lion, "did you manage to do that?"
"I just kept buying War Stamps," said the mouse,
"and pretty soon I had enough for a bond. It was
quite simple."
If a mouse can to it, can't you, too?

THE LIVELY LITTLE RABBIT

The red squirrel, was very wise, told all the animals
that buying War Stamps was a very fine thing to do.
All the rabbits hurried off to take his advice. And who
do you think was the first in line? The lively little rab-
bit, of course.
Then all the other little rabbits, and the squirrel, and
the owl, and yes, even the weasels, bought their War
Stamps.
And so should you!

THE GOLDEN BOOK OF FLOWERS

If Miss Petunia, The Rose, the shy Violet, the naughty
Daisy, the Water Lily, the Goldenrod and all our other

flower friends could come right out of this book to speak to you today they would all say: *"BUY MORE WAR STAMPS"*

HANSEL AND GRETEL

Hansel and Gretel have learned how to provide for the future. Each week they buy War Savings Stamps, and soon they are going to buy a Bond. It's a good way for you to save, too.

MY FIRST BOOK OF BIBLE STORIES

Just as Joseph asked the Egyptians to set aside part of their crop to provide for the years to come, so your Government is asking you to use part of your money to buy War Savings Stamps.

Once the paper shortage was over, the books were again printed in their original 42 pages. Backorders that had piled up during the shortage began being filled and the company found itself with thousands of new customers.

Sales of Little Golden Books were doing so well that in 1944, Simon & Schuster decided to create a new division headed by George Duplaix called Sandpiper Press. Duplaix hired Dorothy Bennett—who was formerly employed as the assistant curator at Museum of Natural History—as the general editor. She was responsible for many of the subjects used in Little Golden Books through the mid-1950s, and she authored numerous books, including The Giant Golden Book Encyclopedia. Bennett fought very hard to keep television and movies out of Little Golden Books; she felt the quality and context of the books would be weakened. She hated to see the book J. Fred Muggs printed and thought it poetic justice when the monkey bit the host and the television show was taken off the air. Bennett wanted the books to teach children something of the world they lived in, whether it was history, geography, science, or the experiences a child would have while growing up.

In the 1940s, Little Golden Books, dealing with good little boys and girls and their experiences of everyday things, were approved by Mary Reed, Ph.D., Assistant Professor of Education at the Teacher's College, Columbia University. Reed went on to supervise the subject matter of Little Golden Books until 1961.

Walt Disney Little Golden Books have been published since 1944, but it wasn't until 1947 that new stories were published quite regularly, and have been ever since. The first three books of the Disney series were published under Walt Disney's Little Library before being changed to A Little Golden Book. The first three stories originally came with dust jackets.

Doctor Dan, the Bandage Man, Little Golden Book No. 111, was released in January 1951. The first printing of the book was 1,750,000, the largest first printing on any Little Golden Book to date. Six Johnson & Johnson Band-Aids® were glued down the right side of the title page. Later, girls were given equal time with Nurse Nancy. As the Doctor Dan stories changed, so did the style of the Band-Aids included with the book—later there were circus and stars and stripes varieties.

In 1952, on the Little Golden Book's tenth anniversary, approximately 182,615,000 Little Golden Books had been sold. The Night Before Christmas alone sold more than 4 million copies! In their eleventh year, almost 300,000,000 Little Golden Books had been sold. More than half of the titles printed by 1954 had sold more than 1,000,000 copies each. Little Golden Books were now available almost everywhere in the world except the Soviet Union. No Little Golden Books, including The Poky Little Puppy—which had the distinction of being labeled a capitalistic story—were not allowed to be sold in the Soviet Union.

May 1, 1954, was the release date of Little Lulu and Her Magic Tricks, with a first printing of 2,250,000. The book had a small package of Kleenex in its front cover and directions for making tissue toys. Such an extensive advertising and promotional campaign was done for the book that it was even shown on the Arthur Godfrey Show in the month of the book's release.

Quite a few of the titles in the 1950s showed that children were starting to spend a lot of time in front of their television sets. By the mid-1950s, children's TV shows and westerns were top sellers in Little Golden Books, while in the early 1960s, the books were about Saturday morning cartoon shows. From 1965 to the early 1970s, though, Little Golden Books dropped TV and went back to printing original stories about growing up.

In 1955, Little Golden Books were released in the activity series, which ran until 1961. This series consisted of books with learning wheels, stamps, paper dolls, paper models, paint and coloring books, and even a calendar. This was not a new idea for Little Golden Books; back in the early 1950s, the company brought out books with masks, puzzles, stencils, decals, tape, tissue, and, as previously mentioned, Band-Aids.

In 1958, Little Golden Books were brought out in A Giant Little Golden Book. Most of these contained three Little Golden Books of the same subject in one volume.

In 1958, Western Publishing and Lithographing Co., Inc. and Pocket Books Inc. became joint publishers, and the company name then became Golden Press, Inc. But in 1960, Western Printing and Lithographing became Western Publishing Company, Inc. and Pocket Books' interest in Golden Press was acquired in 1964.

In 1959, a series of Little Golden Books called a Ding Dong School Book, written by Dr. Frances R. Horwich, was published by Golden Press (see Ding Dong School Books, page). Ding Dong School was a children's television show in the 1950s hosted by Miss Frances.

Boxed puzzles, made from cover art of Little Golden Books, were produced in the early 1950s. The boxes were a little smaller than the original books. There were four series. Value ranges from $35.00-$85.00.

The first series consisted of:
The Lively Little Rabbit
The Five Little Firemen
The Jolly Barnyard
The Poky Little Puppy
The Shy Little Kitten
Tootle
The second series consisted of:
The Alphabet from A to Z
A Year on the Farm
Johnny's Machines
The Wonderful House
The Marvelous Merry-Go-Round
Dr. Dan the Bandage Man

The third series consisted of:
- Busy Timmy
- Little Black Sambo
- When You Were a Baby
- Little Yip Yip and His Bark
- Happy Man and His Dump Truck
- A Day At The Playground

The fourth series consisted of:
- Katy the Kitten
- How Big
- Brave Cowboy Bill
- Little Golden ABC
- Day at the Beach
- Train in Timbuctoo

There was also a release of tray puzzles by Playskool. These puzzles came in a box of four and each set had to do with a certain subject. The pictures were of Little Golden Book covers or inside art. Each puzzle in the set had a different number of pieces for ages 4 to 8. Value per set is $25.00-$40.00.

Puzzle Sets:
- 80-1 Animal Babies
- 80-2 Ways to Travel
- 80-3 Horses and Colts
- 80-4 Fairy Stories
- 80-5 Life of a Cowboy
- 80-6 Indian Pals
- 80-7 Farms and Farming
- 80-8 Children and Religion
- 80-9 Funny Animals
- 80-10 Workers We Know
- 80-11 Dogs and Puppies
- 80-12 Children in Action

The Golden Hours Library was produced in 1967. This consisted of a box shaped like a clock, with moving hands, that contained 12 Little Golden Books in miniature. Value is $45.00.

The books were:
- How To Tell Time
- Heidi
- The Big Little Book
- Old MacDonald Had A Farm
- Four Little Kittens
- Rumpelstiltskin
- Hop Little Kangaroo
- Four Puppies
- The Littlest Raccoon
- Tommy's Camping Adventure
- Colors Are Nice
- Little Cotton Tail

In 1972, Golden produced an 11-1/2-inch by 14-inch four-tray puzzle boxed set. Each set contained four puzzles about a Little Golden Book, with the condensed story printed on the box's inside top flap. The two titles were The Poky Little Puppy and The Lively Little Rabbit. Scuffy the Tugboat Game was also produced in this series.

In 1974, Little Golden Books were published in the Eager Reader series. These books were printed with large type for beginning readers (see Eager Reader Series, page).

In 1977, Western Publishing developed A Little Golden Game for children ages 5 to 8, which were games based on Little Golden Books. The boxed covers were duplicates of the Little Golden Book the game depicted. Three books that were produced as games were Old MacDonald Had a Farm, Jack and the Beanstalk, and The Three Little Pigs.

Little Golden Books have been printed in more than 42 countries. Most of these countries release the same titles as the United States, although a few have had original titles of their own (see Foreign Little Golden Books, page).

In 1982, Little Golden Books were 40 years old and more than 800,000,000 books had been sold. On Nov. 20, 1986, the one billionth Little Golden Book was printed, The Poky Little Puppy. Australia celebrated the printing of the 200 millionth Little Golden Book in February 1988.

The Numbering System

Little Golden Books were originally numbered numerically, starting with No. 1, The Three Little Kittens, in 1942, and ending with 600, Susan in the Driver's Seat. But just because they were numbered does not mean they were published in sequential order. For instance, book 205 was published two years before 204, and some numbers never had a title. In 1971, new releases began to be numbered by going back to 105. Later, 102 through 104 were redone. One possibility for the renumbering not continuing past 600 could be that 615 through 630 had already been given to My First Golden Learning Library in 1965. This was a series of books, illustrated by William Dugan and written by Jane Werner Watson, with different colored foil spines and letters of the alphabet broken down in a dictionary-type format.

The books of the 1970s had no chronological order of publishing—the books were published in the 100, 200, 300, and 500 numbers. The only similarity I have noticed in these different numbers was that the two books redone in the 500s did not have to do with science fiction.

In 1979, Western changed its numbering again to the new numbering system; for example, 101-42, where 1 indicates assortment, 01 indicates category, and -42 indicates position in category. I recommend that if you are a collector trying to collect by book numbers, collect the first

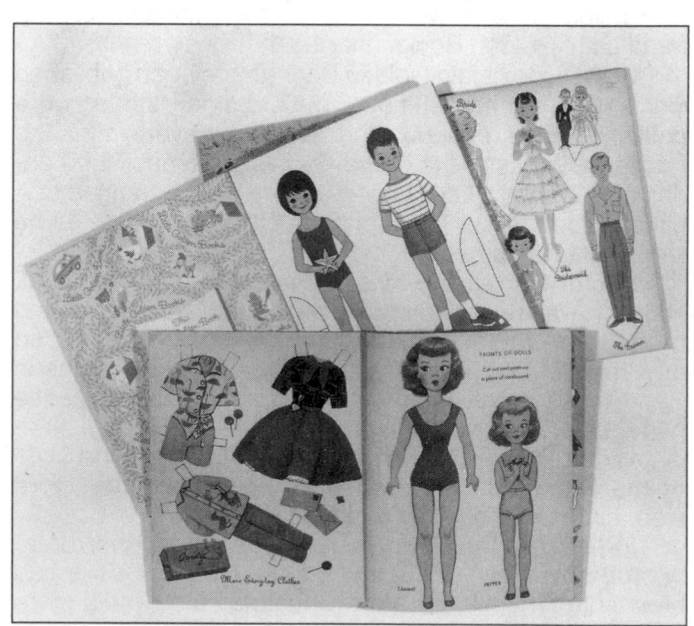

Examples of Little Golden Activity Books with paper dolls

Percentage of listed value	Condition	Comments
100%	Mint	No marks of any kind on book. Should look like it just came off the store shelf.
75%	Fine	Clean, tight book. May have some light pencil marks. Name may be written on inside cover in space provide. A little of the cover luster may be gone. Overall condition of the book should be one that was read but well cared for.
50%	Good	This is your average book. May have some light soiling or chipping on front cover. No tears or scrapes on the cover. The inside pages may have small creases or folded corners, could have small tears no more than 1/4 inch long. No tape. Some of the spine cover may be missing or chipping. The book is well read but still in complete condition.
25%	Fair	The spine is getting loose. The cover is soiled. No crayon scribbling or ink that distracts from any part of the book. There may be some tape on pages. A well-read and not taken care of copy.
0%-10%	Poor	A damaged book. Crayon, ink on pages, missing pages, chewed pages, missing activities. The book probably looks like it just came out of the trash.

Values on the following pages are for first editions in very fine + or better condition.

edition and forget the numbers because the categories' subject matter may change each year.

The year 1997 brought the latest change to the numbering system, when the book numbers became five numbers followed by a dash and one or two numbers. Most of these begin with a 9, but there a few beginning with an 8.

The Changing Price of Little Golden Books

The price of Little Golden Books has changed quite a bit since 1942, when they sold for 25 cents each. Twenty years later, the price increased to 29 cents. This was followed by 39 cents in 1968, 40 cents in 1974, 59 cents in 1977, 69 cents in 1979, 89 cents in 1982, and 99 cents in 1986. Books printed today no longer have a price printed on the cover and still sell for around $1.

How to Determine Editions

1. The edition number will be mentioned on the first or second page of the book.

2. Look on the last page of the book in the lower right hand corner by the spine. There will be a letter which tells the edition. For example, A=1st, Z=26th, AA=27th.

3. On the bottom of one of the first two pages, you will see something like A B C D E or a b c d e. The first letter to the far left is the edition.

4. Books printed since late 1991 no longer have the letters of the alphabet designating editions on the title page. Now, the books, besides having the copyright date, will also have a printing date in Roman numerals. If a book from this period does not have a Roman numeral date, it is a first printing, and it was left off by mistake. If the letter "A" precedes the Roman numerals, the book is a first edition, and if an "R" precedes the Roman numeral, the book is a (R)evised edition of an earlier Little Golden Book. If there is no letter preceding the Roman numeral, the numerals themselves state when the book was printed.

For those of you not familiar with Roman numerals, "MCMXCI" is 1991. When reading Roman numerals, you subtract the number on the left from the one the right when the one on the left is smaller: M=1000, C=100, X=10, VIII=8, VII=7, VI=6, V=5, IV=4 (or 5-1), III=3, II=2, I=1; so with the number "MCMXCI," you have "M"=1000,

"CM"=900 (1000-100), "XC"=90 (100-10), "I"=1 for 1000 + 900 + 90 + 1 = 1991.

5. If none of the above can be used, it is probably a first edition. You can also take the last book number listed on the back of the book and look up its copyright date in this guide and compare it with the copyright of the book you are not sure of.

How to Determine the Value and Condition of a Book

There isn't an easy way of putting a condition on a book. What is good to one might be fair to another. In this book, I will give you guidelines to assist you in putting a value and condition on your books. The prices given in this book are also only meant to assist you in valuing or paying a fair price. The prices listed in this book were compiled from dealings with different people throughout the United States. The prices may be a little high or low depending on the area in which you live. Dust jackets are not priced and add 25 to 200 percent to the value of the book.

How to Use This Book

Original copyright dates are printed without parenthesis. When a date is given in parentheses, it designates the approximate date of publication. A letter/number in quotations is what I consider the edition for book number or the numbers title variation.
For example,

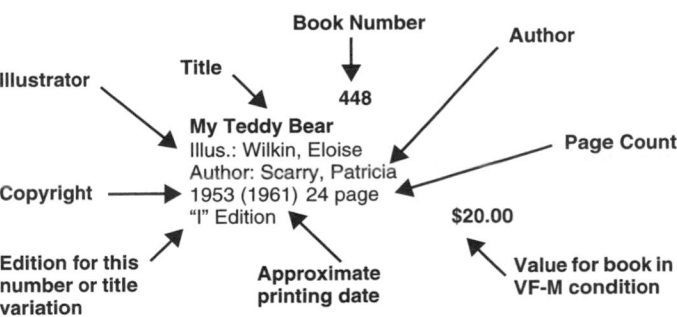

Little Golden Books—By Book Number

1
Three Little Kittens
Four Color and Black & White
Blue Spine w/ Dust Jacket **$50-$200**
Illus.: Masha
1942 42 Pages
1st Edition w/out Jacket **$40.00**

1
Four Color and Black & White
Blue Spine
Abridged for the War
"To Albert" no longer written above clothesline
Blue Spine w/ Dust Jacket **$40-$100**
(1946) 24 Pages
9th Edition **$30.00**

1
Four Color and Three Color
Golden Paper Spine
Song added to last page
(1951) 42 Pages
"Q" Edition **$20.00**

1
Four Color and Three Color
Foil Spine
Song on page 4
(1952) 28 Pages
"S" Edition **$12.00**

2
Bedtime Stories
Four Color and Black & White
Blue Spine w/ Dust Jacket **$50-$150**
5 Stories: Chicken Little, The Three Bears, The Three Little Pigs, Little Red Riding Hood, The Gingerbread Man
Illus.: Tenggren, Gustaf
1942 42 Pages
1st Edition w/out Jacket **$40.00**

2
Foil Spine
3 Stories: The Gingerbread Man, Chicken Little, Little Red Riding Hood
(1955) 28 Pages
"U" Edition **$12.00**

3
Alphabet From A-Z, The
Four Color and Black & White
Blue Spine w/ Dust Jacket **$50-$200**
Illus.: Blake, Vivienne Leah
1942 42 Pages
1st Edition w/out Jacket **$40.00**

3
Four Color and Black & White
Golden Paper Spine
Song added to last page
(1950) 42 Pages
"R" Edition **$16.00**

4
Mother Goose
Four Color and Black & White
Blue Spine w/ Dust Jacket **$50-$200**
Illus.: Elliott, Gertrude
Author: Fraser, Phyllis
1942 42 Pages
1st Edition w/out Jacket **$40.00**

4
Four Color and Black & White
Blue Spine
Abridged for the War
Blue Spine w/ Dust Jacket **$40-$100**
(1943) 24 Pages
4th Edition **$20.00**

4
Four Color and Three Color
Foil Spine
(1953) 28 Pages
"V" Edition **$12.00**

5
Prayers For Children
Four Color and Black & White
Blue Spine w/ Dust Jacket **$50-$200**
1942 42 Pages
1st Edition w/out Jacket **$40.00**

5
Four Color and Black & White
Golden Paper Spine
Prayer "Till the victory is ours changed" to "Good Night"
(1948) 42 Pages
"L" Edition **$15.00**

5
Four Color and Three Color
Golden Paper Spine
Song added to last page
(1950) 42 Pages
"R" Edition **$12.00**

5
Four Color and Three Color
Golden Paper Spine
Song given solid background
(1950) 42 Pages
"S" Edition **$10.00**

6
Little Red Hen, The
Four Color and Black & White
Blue Spine w/ Dust Jacket **$50-$200**
Illus.: Freund, Rudolf
1942 42 Pages
1st Edition w/out Jacket **$40.00**

6
Four Color and Three Color
Golden Paper Spine
(1949) 42 Pages
"L" Edition **$15.00**

6

Little Red Hen, The
(2nd Cover)
Four Color and Three Color
Foil Spine
Illus.: Freund, Rudolf
1942 (1952) 28 Pages
"M" Edition   **$22.00**

7

Nursery Songs
Four Color and Black & White
Blue Spine w/ Dust Jacket **$50-$200**
Illus.: Malvern, Corinne
Author: Gale, Leah
1942   42 Pages
1st Edition w/out Jacket   **$40.00**

7

Nursery Songs
(2nd Cover)
Four Color and Three Color
Golden Paper Spine
Illus.: Malvern, Corinne
Author: Gale, Leah
1942 (1949) 42 Pages
15th Edition   **$15.00**

8

Poky Little Puppy, The
Four Color and Black & White
Blue Spine w/ Dust Jacket **$50-$200**
Illus.: Tenggren, Gustaf
Author: Lowrey, Janet Sebring
1942   42 Pages
1st Edition w/out Jacket   **$40.00**

8

Golden Paper Spine
(1950)   42 Pages
"U" Edition   **$15.00**

8

Foil Spine
(1950)   28 Pages
"V" Edition   **$10.00**

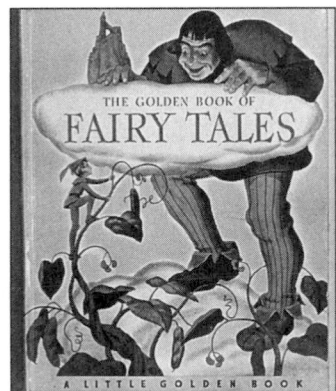

9

Golden Book Of Fairy Tales, The
Four Color and Black & White
Blue Spine w/ Dust Jacket **$50-$200**
4 Stories: Jack and the Beanstalk, Cinderella, Puss in Boots, Sleeping Beauty
Illus.: Hoskins, Winfield
1942   42 Pages
1st Edition w/out Jacket   **$40.00**

9

Four Color and Black & White
Blue Spine
Abridged for the War
3 Stories: Jack and the Beanstalk, Puss in Boots, Cinderella
Blue Spine w/ Dust Jacket **$40-$100**
(1943)   24 Pages
1st Edition w/out Jacket   **$22.00**

9

First Little Golden Book Of Fairy Tales, The
(2nd Cover)
Four Color and Black & White
Blue Spine w/ Dust Jacket   **$50-$100**
3 Stories: Jack and the Beanstalk, Puss in Boots, Sleeping Beauty
Illus.: Elliott, Gertrude
1946   24 Pages
1st Ed. (unstated) w/out Jacket **$20.00**

9

Four Color and Black & White
Golden Paper Spine
(1947)   42 Pages
"B" Edition   **$16.00**

10

Baby's Book
Four Color and Black & White
Blue Spine w/ Dust Jacket **$75-$300**
Illus.: Smith, Bob
Author: Smith, Bob
1942   42 Pages
1st Edition w/out Jacket   **$50.00**

10

My First Book
(2nd Cover)
Four Color and Black & White
Blue Spine w/ Dust Jacket   **$60-$150**
Illus.: Smith, Bob
Author: Smith, Bob
1942 (1943) 42 Pages
4th Ed. w/out Jacket   **$30.00**

10

My First Book (Third Cover)
Four Color and Black & White
Gold Paper Spine
Laddie the dog's name changed to "Bow-wow"
Illus.: Smith, Bob
Author: Smith, Bob
1942 (1947) 42 Pages
"H" Edition   **$20.00**

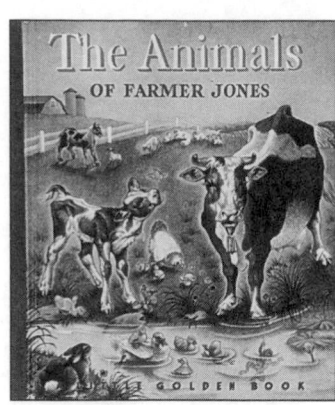

11

Four Color and Black & White
Blue Spine
Abridged for the War
Blue Spine w/ Dust Jacket **$40-$100**
W/out Dust Jacket   **$22.00**
(1943)   24 Pages
1st Edition w/out Jacket   **$22.00**

11

Four Color and Black & White
Golden Paper Spine
(1947)   42 Pages
"L" Edition   **$15.00**

11
Animals Of Farmer Jones, The
Four Color and Black & White
Blue Spine w/ Dust Jacket **$50-$200**
Illus.: Freund, Rudolf
Author: Gale, Leah
1942   42 Pages
1st Edition w/out Jacket   **$40.00**

12
This Little Piggy And Other Count-
ing Rhymes
Four Color and Black & White
Blue Spine w/ Dust Jacket **$60-$250**
Illus.: Paflin, Roberta
1942   42 Pages
1st Edition w/out Jacket   **$50.00**

12
Counting Rhymes
(2nd Cover)
Four Color and Black & White
Blue Spine w/ Dust Jacket **$50-$100**
Illus.: Malvern Corrine
1946   42 Pages
1st Edition w/out Jacket   **$20.00**

12
Golden Paper Spine
(1948)   28 Pages
"D" Edition   **$16.00**

13
Golden Book Of Birds, The
Four Color and Black & White
Blue Spine w/ Dust Jacket **$50-$150**
Illus.: Rojankovsky, Feodor
Author: Lockwood, Hazel
1943   42 Pages
1st Edition w/out Jacket   **$25.00**

13

Four Color and Black & White
Golden Paper Spine
(1948)   42 Pages
4th Edition   **$20.00**

14
Nursery Tales
Four Color and Black & White
Blue Spine w/ Dust Jacket **$50-$150**
Illus.: Masha
1943   42 Pages
1st Edition w/out Jacket   **$25.00**

14

Four Color and Black & White
Golden Paper Spine
Song added to last page
(1951)   42 Pages
"I" Edition   **$20.00**

15
Lively Little Rabbit, The
Four Color and Black & White
Blue Spine w/ Dust Jacket **$50-$150**
Illus.: Tenggren, Gustaf
Author: Ariane
1943   42 Pages
1st Edition w/out Jacket   **$35.00**

15

Four Color and Black & White
Blue Spine
War Edition
Blue Spine w/ Dust Jacket **$50-$100**
(1943)   24 Pages
1st Edition   **$22.00**

15

Four Color and Black & White
Golden Paper Spine
Sleeping owl picture dropped from
book
(1948)   42 Pages
10th Edition   **$15.00**

15

Foil Spine
Song added to last page
(1951)   42 Pages
14th Edition   **$14.00**

15
Lively Little Rabbit, The
(2nd Cover)
Foil Spine
Illus.: Tenggren, Gustaf
Author: Ariane
1943 (1954) 28 Pages
15th Edition   **$15.00**

16

Golden Book Of Flowers, The
Four Color and Black & White
Blue Spine w/ Dust Jacket **$50-$150**
Illus.: Hershberger
Author: Witman, Mabel
1943 42 Pages
1st Edition w/out Jacket **$30.00**

17

Hansel And Gretel
Four Color and Black & White
Blue Spine w/ Dust Jacket **$50-$150**
Illus.: Weihs, Erika
Author: Bros. Grimm
1943 42 Pages
1st Edition w/out Jacket **$30.00**

17

Hansel And Gretel
(2nd Cover)
Four Color and Three Color
Cover art by Eloise Wilkin
Illus.: Weihs, Erika
Author: Bros. Grimm
1943 (1952) 28 Pages
"H" Edition **$14.00**

18

Day In The Jungle, A
Four Color and Black & White
Blue Spine w/ Dust Jacket **$50-$150**
Illus.: Gergely, Tibor
Author: Lowrey, Janet Sebring
1943 42 Pages
1st Edition w/out Jacket **$35.00**

18

Four Color and Black & White
Blue Spine w/ Dust Jacket **$50-$125**
A couple pictures where modified
(1946) 42 Pages
3rd Edition **$27.00**

18

Four Color and Black & White
Golden Paper Spine
Pictures are back to original
(1951) 42 Pages
"I" Edition **$20.00**

19

My First Book Of Bible Stories
Four Color and Black & White
Blue Spine w/ Dust Jacket **$60-$175**
Illus.: Ferand, Emmy
Author: Walton, Mary Ann
1943 42 Pages
1st Edition w/out Jacket **$40.00**

20

Night Before Christmas, The
Blue Spine but never printed w/ Dust Jacket
Illus.: Dewitt, Cornelius
Author: Moore, Clement C.
1946 42 Pages
1st Edition **$25.00**

20

Four Color and Black & White
Golden Paper Spine
2 songs added
(1948) 42 Pages
"C" Edition **$22.00**

20

Night Before Christmas, The
(2nd Cover)
Gilded cover and pages
Illus.: Malvern, Corinne
Author: Moore, Clement C.
1949 28 Pages
"A" Edition **$15.00**

20

Night Before Christmas, The
(3rd Cover)
Foil Spine
Gilded cover and pages
Illus.: Malvern, Corinne
Author: Moore, Clement C.
1949 (1951) 28 Pages
"E" Edition **$18.00**

20

Foil Spine
Gilded cover only
(1951) 28 Pages
"F" Edition **$16.00**

20

Foil Spine
No Gilding
(1952) 24 Pages
"G" Edition **$15.00**

20

Night Before Christmas, The
Christmas Spine
(1963)   24 Pages
"O" Edition $8.00

20

Red Spine
Title lettering change
(1968)   24 Pages
"S" Edition $6.00

20

Foil Spine
Red cover background and title
lettering change.
(1970)   24 Pages
28th Edition $5.00

21

Tootle
Four Color and Black & White
Blue Spine w/ Dust Jacket $50-$175
Red title lettering
Illus.: Gergely, Tibor
Author: Crampton, Gertrude
1945   42 Pages
1st Edition w/out Jacket $30.00

21

Four Color and Black & White
Blue Spine w/ Dust Jacket $50-$150
Title in white lettering
(1945)   42 Pages
2nd Edition w/out Jacket $20.00

21

Four Color and Three Color
Foil Spine
(1951)   42 Pages
"N" Edition $15.00

21

Four Color and Three Color
Foil Spine
(1952)   28 Pages
"O" Edition $7.00

21

Four Color and Three Color
Foil Spine
(1957)   24 Pages
"Q" Edition $5.00

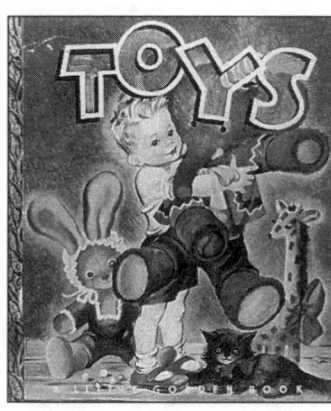

22

Toys
Four Color and Black & White
Blue Spine w/ Dust Jacket $50-$150
Illus.: Masha
Author: Oswald, Edith
1945   42 Pages
1st Edition w/out Jacket $25.00

22

Four Color and Three Color
Golden Paper Spine
(1949)   42 Pages
"I" Edition $16.00

23

Shy Little Kitten, The
Four Color and Black & White
(Unstated 1st)
Blue Spine w/ Dust Jacket $50-$150
Illus.: Tenggren, Gustaf
Author: Schurr, Kathleen
1946   42 Pages
1st Edition w/out Jacket $25.00

23

Golden Paper Spine
(1949)   28 Pages
"F" Edition $12.00

24

New House In The Forest, The
Four Color and Black & White
(Unstated 1st)
Blue Spine w/ Dust Jacket $50-$175
Illus.: Wilkin, Eloise
Author: Mitchell, Lucy Sprague
1946   42 Pages
1st Edition w/out Jacket $40.00

25

Taxi That Hurried, The
Four Color and Black & White
Blue Spine w/ Dust Jacket $50-$150
Illus.: Gergely, Tibor
Author: Mitchell, Lucy Sprague;
Simonton
1946   42 Pages
1st Edition w/out Jacket $25.00

25

Taxi That Hurried, The
Foil Spine
(1951)   28 Pages
"J" Edition $8.00

25

Foil Spine
(1963)   24 Pages
"M" Edition $5.00

26

Christmas Carols
Four Color and Black & White
(Unstated 1st)
Blue Spine w/ Dust Jacket $50-$125
Illus.: Malvern, Corinne
Author: Wyckoff, Marjorie
1946   42 Pages
1st Edition w/out Jacket $20.00

26

Foil Spine
(1955)   24 Pages
"J" Edition $6.00

26

Red Spine
(1968)   24 Pages
"P" Edition $8.00

26

Four Color and Three Color
Golden Paper Spine
(1949)   42 Pages
"F" Edition $15.00

26

Christmas Carols
(2nd Cover)
Foil Spine
Illus.: Malvern, Corinne
Author: Wyckoff, Marjorie
1946 (1952) 28 Pages
"G" Edition $9.00

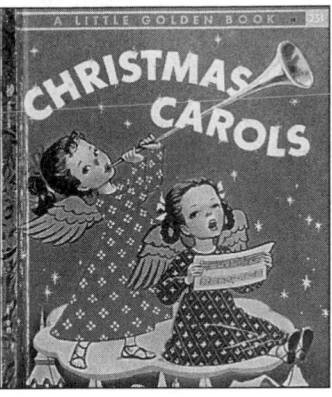

27

Story Of Jesus, The
Four Color and Black & White
(Unstated 1st)
Blue Spine w/ Dust Jacket $50-$150
Illus.: Lerch, Steffie
Author: Alexander, Beatrice
1946   42 Pages
1st Edition w/out Jacket $25.00

27

Four Color and Three Color
Golden Paper Spine
(1949)   42 Pages
"F" Edition $18.00

28

Chip Chip
Four Color and Black & White
Blue Spine w/ Dust Jacket $50-$150
Illus.: Carbe, Nino
Author: Wright, Norman
1947   42 Pages
1st Edition w/out Jacket $25.00

29

Noises And Mr. Flibberty-Jib
Four Color and Black & White
(Unstated 1st)
Gold Paper Spine
Illus.: Wilkin, Eloise
Author: Wilkin, Eloise
1947   42 Pages
"A" Edition $40.00

29

Four Color and Three Color
Golden Paper Spine
(1949)   42 Pages
"E" Edition $18.00

30

Scuffy The Tugboat
Four Color and Black & White
(Unstated 1st)
Blue Spine w/ Dust Jacket $50-$150
Illus.: Gergely, Tibor
Author: Crampton, Gertrude
1946   42 Pages
1st Edition w/out Jacket $25.00

30

Foil Spine
(1951)   42 Pages
"I" Edition $18.00

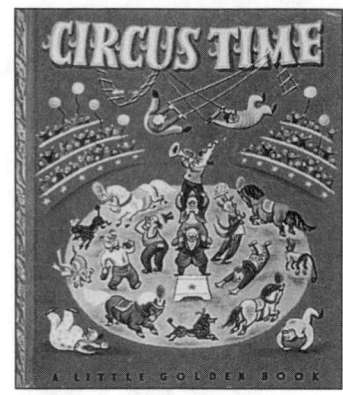

31
Four Color and Three Color
Golden Paper Spine
(1950)   42 Pages
"G" Edition $16.00

31
Foil Spine
(1952)   28 Pages
"I" Edition $12.00

31

Circus Time
Four Color and Black & White
Illus.: Gergely, Tibor
Author: Conger, Marion
1948   42 Pages
1st Edition $20.00

32

Fix It, Please
Four Color and Black & White
Gold Paper Spine
Illus.: Wilkin, Eloise
Author: Mitchell, Lucy Sprague
1947   42 Pages
1st Edition $35.00

33

Let's Go Shopping
Four Color and Black & White
Golden Paper Spine
Illus.: Combes, Lenora
Author: Combes, Lenora
1948   42 Pages
"A" Edition $17.00

33
Four Color and Three Color
Golden Paper Spine
(1949)   42 Pages
"E" Edition $15.00

33
Four Color and Three Color
Golden Paper Spine
Song added to last page
(1950)   42 Pages
"F" Edition $15.00

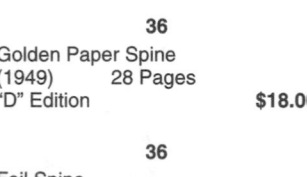

34

Little Golden Book Of Hymns, The
Four Color and Black & White
Golden Paper Spine
Illus.: Malvern, Corinne
Author: Werner, Elsa Jane
1947   42 Pages
"A" Edition $16.00

34
Golden Paper Spine
(1949)   28 Pages
"D" Edition $8.00

34
Golden Paper Spine
42 pages is correct
(1950)   42 Pages
"H" Edition $12.00

35

Happy Family, The
Four Color and Black & White
(Unstated 1st)
Blue Spine w/ Dust Jacket $50-$175
Last Title with a Dust Jacket
Illus.: Elliott, Gertrude
Author: Nicole
1947   42 Pages
1st Edition w/out Jacket $40.00

36

Saggy Baggy Elephant, The
Four Color and Black & White
(Unstated 1st)
Golden Paper Spine
Illus.: Tenggren, Gustaf
Author: Jackson, Kathryn & Byron
1947   42 Pages
1st Edition $25.00

36
Golden Paper Spine
(1949)   28 Pages
"D" Edition $18.00

36
Foil Spine
(1955)   28 Pages
"K" Edition $8.00

36
Foil Spine
11th Edition
Done with 28 & 24 pages
(1955)   24 Pages
"K" Edition $5.00

37

Year On The Farm, A
Four Color and Black & White
Golden Paper Spine
Illus.: Floethe, Richard
Author: Mitchell, Lucy Sprague
1948   42 Pages
"A" Edition $20.00

37
Four Color and Three Color
Golden Paper Spine
(1949)   42 Pages
4th Edition $15.00

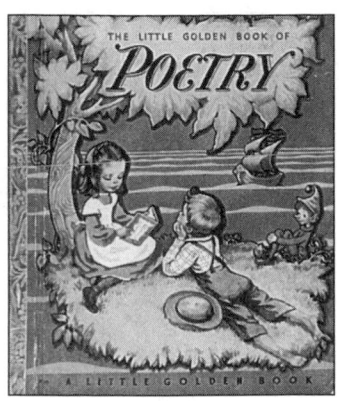

38
Golden Paper Spine
(1948)   28 Pages
"B" Edition $12.00

38
Little Golden Book Of Poetry, The
Four Color and Black & White
Golden Paper Spine
Illus.: Malvern, Corinne
1947   42 Pages
"A" Edition $16.00

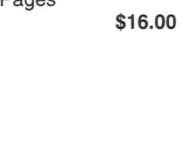

39
(1949)   28 Pages
"C" Edition $12.00

39
Animal Babies
Four Color and Black & White
Golden Paper Spine
Illus.: Werber, Adele
Author: Jackson, Kathryn & Byron
1947   42 Pages
"A" Edition $16.00

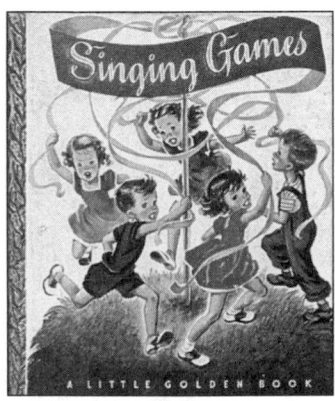

40
Little Golden Book Of Singing Games, The
Four Color and Black & White
Golden Paper Spine
Illus.: Malvern, Corinne
Author: Wessles, Katheryne Tyler
1947   42 Pages
"A" Edition $15.00

41
New Baby, The
Red title lettering
Four Color and Black & White
Golden Paper Spine
Illus.: Wilkin, Eloise
Author: Shane, Ruth & Harold
1948   42 Pages
"A" Edition $40.00

41
Four Color and Black & White
Golden Paper Spine
Blue title lettering
(1948)   42 Pages
"B" Edition $35.00

41
Four Color and Three Color
Golden Paper Spine
(1950)   42 Pages
"F" Edition $25.00

41
New Baby, The
(2nd Cover)
Foil Spine
Illus.: Wilkin, Eloise
Author: Shane, Ruth & Harold
1948 (1954) 28 Pages
"G" Edition $15.00

42
Little Red Riding Hood
Four Color and Black & White
Golden Paper Spine
Illus.: Jones, Elizabeth Orton
Author: Jones, Elizabeth Orton
1948   42 Pages
"A" Edition $40.00

42
Golden Paper Spine
(1949)   28 Pages
"D" Edition $15.00

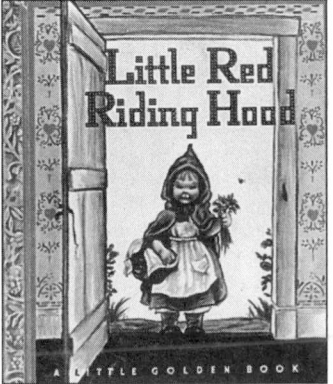

42
Foil Spine
(1957)   24 Pages
"U" Edition $8.00

42
Little Red Riding Hood
Puzzle Edition
Foil Spine
Illus.: Jones, Elizabeth Orton
Author: Jones, Elizabeth Orton
1948 (1951) 28 Pages
"G" Edition $150.00

42

Little Red Riding Hood puzzle

Without Puzzle   **$15.00**

43

Little Pond In The Woods
Four Color and Black & White
Golden Paper Spine
Illus.: Gergely, Tibor
Author: Ward, Muriel
1948   42 Pages
"A" Edition   **$30.00**

44

Come Play House
Four Color and Black & White
Golden Paper Spine
Illus.: Wilkin, Eloise
Author: Oswald, Edith
1948   42 Pages
"A" Edition   **$35.00**

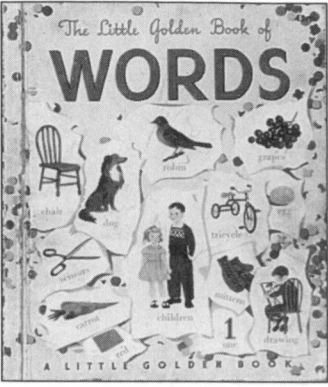

45

Little Golden Book Of Words, The
Yellow background
Four Color and Black & White
Golden Paper Spine
Illus.: Elliott, Gertrude
Author: Chambers, Selma Lola
1948   42 Pages
"A" Edition   **$18.00**

45

Red background
Four Color and Three Color
Golden Paper Spine
(1949)   42 Pages
"E" Edition   **$15.00**

45

Foil Spine
(1952)   28 Pages
"H" Edition   **$8.00**

45

Foil Spine
Title changed to "Word's"
(1955)   24 Pages
"L" Edition   **$5.00**

46

Golden Sleepy Book, The
Four Color and Black & White
Golden Paper Spine
Illus.: Williams, Garth
Author: Brown, Margaret Wise
1948   42 Pages
"A" Edition   **$25.00**

47

Three Bears, The
Four Color and Black & White
Golden Paper Spine
Illus.: Rojankovsky, Feodor
1948   42 Pages
"A" Edition   **$150.00**

47

Three Bears, The
(2nd Cover)
Four Color and Black & White
Golden Paper Spine
Illus.: Rojankovsky, Feodor
1948 (1948) 42 Pages
"B" Edition   **$25.00**

47

Four Color and Three Color
Golden Paper Spine
(1949)   42 Pages
"E" Edition   **$16.00**

47

Foil Spine
(1955)   28 Pages
"J" Edition   **$8.00**

47

Foil Spine
(1955)   24 Pages
"M" Edition   **$4.00**

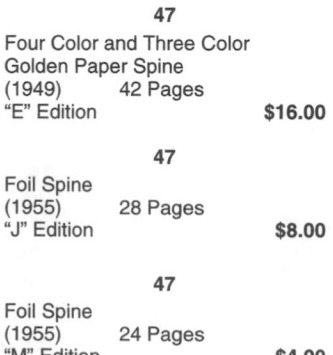

48

Year In The City, A
Four Color and Black & White
Golden Paper Spine
Illus.: Gergely, Tibor
Author: Mitchell, Lucy Sprague
1948   42 Pages
"A" Edition   **$25.00**

49

Mr. Noah And His Family
Golden Paper Spine
Illus.: Provensen, Alice & Martin
Author: Werner, Jane
1948   28 Pages
"A" Edition   **$18.00**

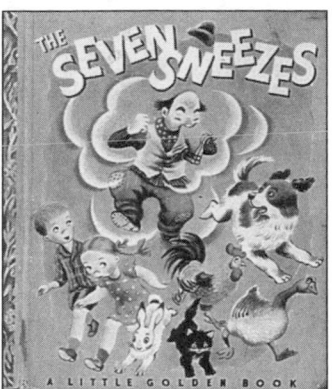

51
Golden Paper Spine
(1948)   28 Pages
"D" Edition $15.00

50

Busy Timmy
Golden Paper Spine
Illus.: Wilkin, Eloise
Author: Jackson, Kathryn & Byron
1948   28 Pages
"A" Edition $35.00

51

Seven Sneezes, The
Four Color and Black & White
Golden Paper Spine
Illus.: Gergely, Tibor
Author: Cabral, Olga
1948   42 Pages
"A" Edition $25.00

52

Little Peewee Or, Now Open The Box
Four Color and Black & White
Golden Paper Spine
Illus.: Miller, J.P.
Author: Kunhardt, Dorothy
1948   42 Pages
"A" Edition $17.00

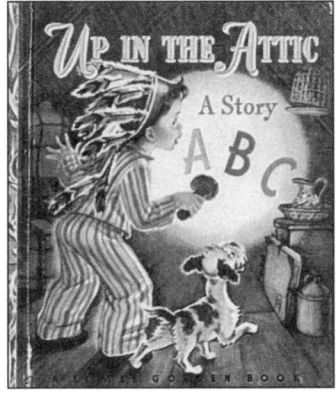

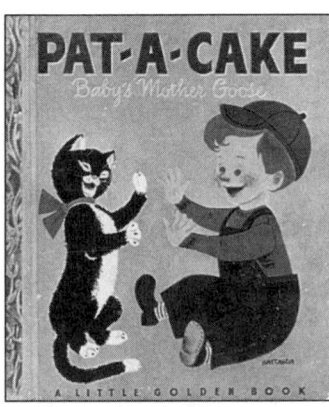

52

Little Peewee, The Circus Dog Or, Now Open The Box
Four Color and Three Color
Golden Paper Spine
Illus.: Miller, J.P.
Author: Kunhardt, Dorothy
1948 (1949) 42 Pages
"G" Edition $25.00

53

Up In The Attic
Four Color and Black & White
Golden Paper Spine
Illus.: Malvern, Corinne
1948   42 Pages
"A" Edition $18.00

54

Pat-A-Cake
Golden Paper Spine
Illus.: Battaglia, Aurelius
Author: Mother Goose
1948   28 Pages
"A" Edition $14.00

55

Name For Kitty, A
Golden Paper Spine
Illus.: Rojankovsky, Feodor
Author: Mcginley, Phyllis
1948   28 Pages
"A" Edition $14.00

57
Four Color and Three Color
Golden Paper Spine
(1949)   42 Pages
"E" Edition $125.00

56

Our Puppy
Golden Paper Spine
Illus.: Rojankovsky, Feodor
Author: Nast, Elsa Ruth
1948   28 Pages
"A" Edition $14.00

57

Little Black Sambo
Four Color and Black & White
Golden Paper Spine
Illus.: Tenggren, Gustaf
Author: Bannerman, Helen
1948   42 Pages
"A" Edition $175.00

57

Foil Spine
(1952)   28 Pages
"G" Edition $100.00

57

Little Black Sambo
Foil Spine
(1960)   24 Pages
"O" Edition   **$75.00**

58

What Am I?
Golden Paper Spine
Illus.: De Witt, Corneluis
Author: Leon, Ruthelius
1949   28 Pages
"A" Edition   **$14.00**

58

What Am I?
Puzzle Edition
Foil Spine
Illus.: De Witt, Corneluis
Author: Leon, Ruthelius
1949 (1951) 28 Pages
"E" Edition   **$150.00**

58

What Am I? puzzle

Without Puzzle   **$8.00**

59

Nursery Rhymes
Golden Paper Spine
Illus.: Elliott, Gertrude
1948   28 Pages
"A" Edition   **$14.00**

60

Guess Who Lives Here
Four Color and Black & White
Golden Paper Spine
Illus.: Wilkin, Eloise
Author: Woodcock, Louise
1949   42 Pages
"A" Edition   **$30.00**

60

Four Color and Three Color
Golden Paper Spine
(1949)   42 Pages
3rd Edition

61

Good Morning, Good Night
Four Color and Black & White
Golden Paper Spine
Illus.: Wilkin, Eloise
Author: Werner, Jane
1948   42 Pages
"A" Edition   **$35.00**

62

We Like To Do Things
Four Color and Three Color
Golden Paper Spine
Illus.: Lerch, Seffie
Author: Mason, Walter M.
1949   42 Pages
"A" Edition   **$14.00**

63

Tommy's Wonderful Rides
Four Color and Black & White
Golden Paper Spine
Illus.: Miller, J.P.
Author: Palmer, Helen
1948   42 Pages
"A" Edition   **$17.00**

63

Four Color and Three Color
Golden Paper Spine
(1950)   42 Pages
"F" Edition   **$15.00**

64

Five Little Firemen
Four Color and Black & White
Golden Paper Spine
Illus.: Gergely, Tibor
Author: Brown, Margaret Wise
1948   42 Pages
"A" Edition   **$30.00**

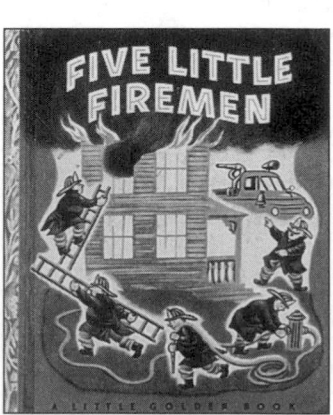

64

Five Little Firemen
Foil Spine
Picture with poem changed
(1951)   28 Pages
"H" Edition $15.00

65

Gaston And Josephine
Four Color and Black & White
Golden Paper Spine
Illus.: Rojankovsky, Feodor
Author: Duplaix, Georges
1949   42 Pages
"A" Edition $30.00

65

Four Color and Three Color
Golden Paper Spine
(1950)   42 Pages
"D" Edition $25.00

66

Two Little Miners
Four Color and Black & White
Golden Paper Spine
Illus.: Scarry, Richard
Author: Brown, Margaret Wise
1949   42 Pages
"A" Edition $30.00

66

Four Color and Three Color
Golden Paper Spine
(1949)   42 Pages
"B" Edition $25.00

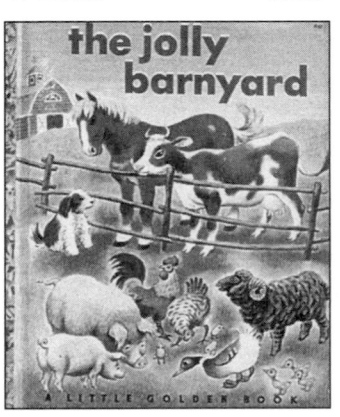

67

Jolly Barnyard, The
Illus.: Gergely, Tibor
Author: Bedford, Annie North
1950   28 Pages
"A" Edition $16.00

67

Foil Spine
(1965)   24 Pages
"D" Edition $6.00

67

Jolly Barnyard, The
Puzzle Edition
Illus.: Gergely, Tibor
Author: Bedford, Annie North
1950 (1951) 28 Pages
"B" Edition $100.00

Without Puzzle $10.00

68

Little Galoshes
Four Color and Three Color
Golden Paper Spine
Illus.: Miller, J.P.
Author: Jackson, Kathryn & Byron
1949   68 Pages
"A" Edition $25.00

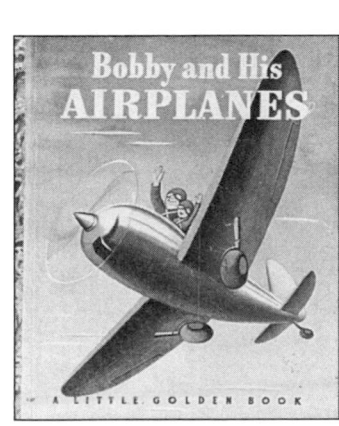

69

Bobby And His Airplanes
Four Color and Black and White
Golden Paper Spine
Illus.: Gergely, Tibor
Author: Palmer, Helen
1949   42 Pages
"A" Edition $20.00

70

When You Were A Baby
Four Color and Black & White
Golden Paper Spine
Illus.: Malvern, Corinne
Author: Eng, Rita
1949   42 Pages
"A" Edition $17.00

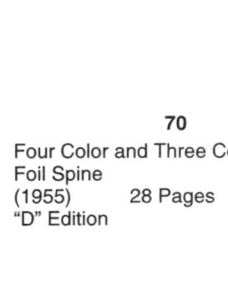

70

Four Color and Three Color
Foil Spine
(1955)   28 Pages
"D" Edition $15.00

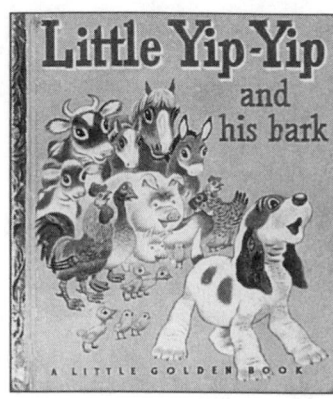

71

Johnny's Machines
Four Color and Three Color
Golden Paper Spine
Illus.: De Witt, Cornelius
Author: Palmer, Helen
1949   42 Pages
"A" Edition $16.00

72

Bugs Bunny
Four Color and Black & White
Golden Paper Spine
Illus.: Warner Bros.
Author: Mckimson, Tom
1949   42 Pages
"A" Edition $15.00

73

Little Yip-Yip And His Bark
Foil Spine
Illus.: Gergely, Tibor
Author: Jackson, Kathryn & Byron
1950   42 Pages
"A" Edition $16.00

74

Little Golden Funny Book, The
Golden Paper Spine
Illus.: Miller, J.P.
Author: Crampton, Gertrude
1950   42 Pages
"A" Edition $14.00

75

Katie The Kitten
Golden Paper Spine
Illus.: Provenson, Alice & Martin
Author: Jackson, Kathryn & Byron
1949   28 Pages
"A" Edition $15.00

75

Katie The Kitten
Puzzle Edition
Foil Spine
Illus.: Provenson, Alice & Martin
Author: Jackson, Kathryn & Byron
1949 (1950) 28 Pages
"E" Edition $125.00

75

Katie The Kitten puzzle

Without Puzzle $10.00

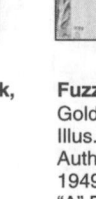

76

Wonderful House, The
Foil Spine
Illus.: Miller, J.P.
Author: Brown, Margaret Wise
1950   42 Pages
"A" Edition $17.00

77

Happy Man And His Dump Truck, The
Golden Paper Spine
Illus.: Gergely, Tibor
Author: Miryam
1950   28 Pages
"A" Edition $20.00

77

Happy Man And His Dump Truck, The
Puzzle Edition
Foil Spine
Illus.: Gergely, Tibor
Author: Miryam
1950   28 Pages
"B" Edition $100.00
Without Puzzle $15.00

78

Fuzzy Duckling, The
Golden Paper Spine
Illus.: Provenson, Alice & Martin
Author: Werner, Jane
1949   28 Pages
"A" Edition $15.00

79

Little Trapper, The
Golden Paper Spine
Illus.: Tenggren, Gustaf
Author: Jackson, Kathryn & Byron
1950   42 Pages
"A" Edition   **$18.00**

79

Foil Spine
(1950)   28 Pages
"B" Edition   **$16.00**

80

Baby's House
Golden Paper Spine
Illus.: Blair, Mary
Author: Mchough, Gelolo
1950   28 Pages
"A" Edition   **$20.00**

80

Baby's House
Puzzle Edition
Foil Spine
Illus.: Blair, Mary
Author: Mchough, Gelolo
1950 (1951) 28 Pages
"B" Edition   **$150.00**
Without Puzzle   **$18.00**

81

Duck And His Friends
Golden Paper Spine
Illus.: Scarry, Richard
Author: Jackson, Kathryn & Byron
1949   28 Pages
"A" Edition   **$14.00**

81

Foil Spine
(1954)   24 Pages
"D" Edition   **$10.00**

81

Foil Spine
Red title lettering
(1977)   24 Pages
7th Edition   **$5.00**

81

Duck And His Friends
Puzzle Edition
Foil Spine
Illus.: Scarry, Richard
Author: Jackson, Kathryn & Byron
1949 (1951) 28 Pages
2nd Edition   **$100.00**

81

Duck And His Friends puzzle

Without Puzzle   **$8.00**

82

Pets For Peter
Puzzle Edition
Foil Spine
Illus.: Battaglia, Aurelius
Author: Werner, Jane
1950   42 Pages
"A" Edition   **$100.00**

82

Pets For Peter puzzle

Without Puzzle   **$10.00**

82

Pets For Peter
Foil Spine
Illus.: Battaglia, Aurelius
Author: Werner, Jane
1950 (1950) 28 Pages
"B" Edition   **$14.00**

83

How Big
Golden Paper Spine
Illus.: Malvern, Corinne
Author: Malvern, Corinne
1949   28 Pages
"A" Edition   **$20.00**

83

How Big?
(2nd Cover)
Foil Spine
Illus.: Malvern, Corinne
Author: Malvern, Corinne
1949 (1970) 24 Pages
2nd Edition   **$6.00**

84

Surprise For Sally
Comes in Gold Paper and Foil Editions
Illus.: Malvern, Corinne
Author: Crowninshield, Ethel
1950   42 Pages
"A" Edition   **$22.00**

85

Susie's New Stove
Golden Paper Spine
Illus.: Malvern, Corinne
Author: Bedford, Annie North
1950   42 Pages
"A" Edition   **$35.00**

86

Color Kittens, The
Golden Paper Spine
Illus.: Provenson, Alice & Martin
Author: Brown, Margaret Wise
1949   28 Pages
"A" Edition   **$25.00**

86

Color Kittens, The
Puzzle Edition
Foil Spine
Illus.: Provenson, Alice & Martin
Author: Brown, Margaret Wise
1949 (1950) 28 Pages
"B" Edition   **$125.00**

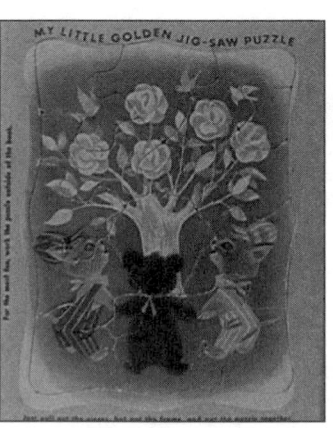

86

Color Kittens, The, puzzle

Without Puzzle   **$20.00**

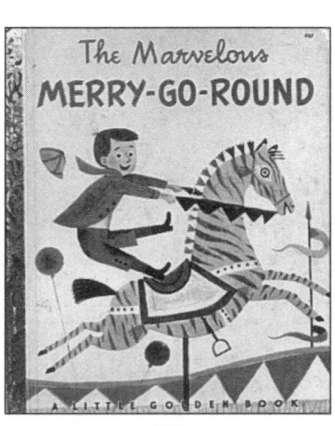

87

Marvelous Merry-Go-Round, The
Foil Spine
Illus.: Miller, J.P.
Author: Werner, Jane
1949   42 Pages
"A" Edition   **$15.00**

88

Day At The Zoo, A
Foil Spine
Illus.: Gergely, Tibor
Author: Conger, Marion
1950   42 Pages
(Unstated 1st)   **$14.00**

88

Foil Spine
(1952)   28 Pages
"B" Edition   **$12.00**

89

Big Brown Bear, The
Golden Paper Spine
Illus.: Tenggren, Gustaf
Author: Duplaix, Georges
1947   42 Pages
"A" Edition   **$25.00**

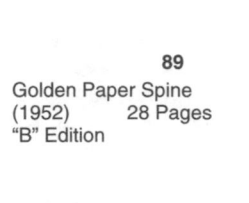

89

Golden Paper Spine
(1952)   28 Pages
"B" Edition   **$15.00**

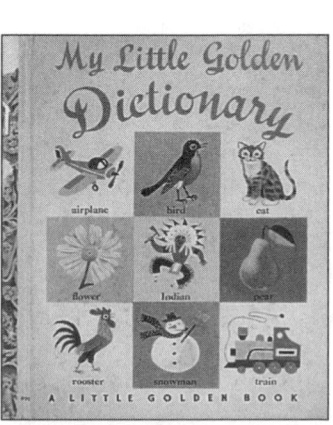

90

My Little Golden Dictionary
Golden Paper Spine
Illus.: Scarry, Richard
Author: Reed, Mary; Oswald, Edith
1949   56 Pages
"A" Edition   **$15.00**

91
(1951)   28 Pages
"B" Edition   **$14.00**

91
Little Fat Policeman, The
Illus.: Provenson, Alice & Martin
Author: Brown, Margaret Wise
1950   42 Pages
"A" Edition   **$12.00**

92
I Can Fly
Illus.: Blair, Mary
Author: Krauss, Ruth
1950   42 Pages
"A" Edition   **$25.00**

93
Brave Cowboy Bill
Both Editions had a puzzle
Illus.: Scarry, Richard
Author: Jackson, Kathryn & Byron
1950   42 Pages
"A" Edition   **$150.00**
"B" Edition   **$125.00**

93
Brave Cowboy Bill puzzle

93
Without Puzzle   **$20.00**

94
Jerry At School
Puzzle Edition
Illus.: Malvern, Corinne
Author: Jackson, Kathryn & Byron
1950   42 Pages
"A" Edition   **$100.00**

94
Jerry At School puzzle

Without Puzzle   **$12.00**

94
Jerry At School
Illus.: Malvern, Corinne
Author: Jackson, Kathryn & Byron
1950 (1951) 28 Pages
"B" Edition   **$15.00**

95
Christmas In The Country
Illus.: Worcester, Retta
Author: Collyer, Barbara; Foley,
John R.
1950   28 Pages
"A" Edition   **$20.00**

96
When I Grow Up
Puzzle Edition
Illus.: Malvern, Corinne
Author: Mace, Kay & Harry
1950   28 Pages
"A" Edition   **$100.00**

96
When I Grow Up puzzle

Without Puzzle   **$12.00**

96
When I Grow Up
Illus.: Malvern, Corinne
Author: Mace, Kay & Harry
1950 (1951) 28 Pages
"B" Edition   **$15.00**

97

Little Benny Wanted A Pony
(Unstated "A")
Illus.: Scarry, Richard
Author: Barnett, Olive O'connor
1950　　　42 Pages
"A" Edition　　　$60.00

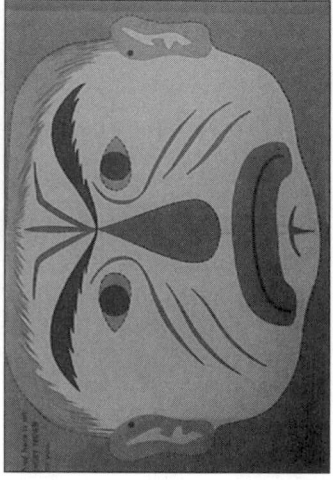

97

Little Benny Wanted A Pony mask

Without Mask　　　$15.00

98

Bugs Bunny's Birthday
Illus.: Warner Bros.
Author: Warner Bros.
1950　　　28 Pages
"A" Edition　　　$14.00

99

Howdy Doody's Circus
Illus.: Dauber, Liz
Author: Gormley, Don
1950　　　28 Pages
"A" Edition　　　$25.00

100

Little Boy With A Big Horn
Illus.: Battaglia, Aurelius
Author: Bezchdolt, Jack
1950　　　42 Pages
"A" Edition　　　$16.00

101

Little Golden ABC, The
Puzzle Edition
Illus.: De Witt, Cornelius
1951　　　28 Pages
"A" Edition　　　$100.00

101

Little Golden ABC, The, puzzle

Without Puzzle　　　$10.00

101

Little Golden ABC, The
Illus.: De Witt, Cornelius
1951 (1952) 28 Pages
"B" Edition　　　$8.00

101
(1955)　　　24 Pages
"F" Edition　　　$5.00

101
Red Spine
(1965)　　　24 Pages
"W" Edition　　　$3.00

102

Ukelele And Her New Doll
Puzzle Edition
Illus.: Grant, Campbell
Author: Grant, Clara Louise
1951　　　28 Pages
"A" Edition　　　$125.00

102

Ukelele And Her New Doll puzzle

102
Without Puzzle　　　$25.00

102

Daisy Dog's Wake-Up Book
(Unstated 1st)
Illus.: Vogel, Ilse-Margaret
Author: Vogel, Ilse-Margaret
1974　　　24 Pages
1st Edition　　　$10.00

103

Christopher And The Columbus
Illus.: Gergely, Tibor
Author: Jackson, Kathryn & Byron
1951   28 Pages
"A" Edition $12.00

103

Fritzie Goes Home
(Unstated 1st)
Illus.: Augistiny, Sally
Author: Emerypogue, Kate
1974   24 Pages
1st Edition $7.00

104

Just Watch Me!
(Unstated 1st)
Illus.: Aloisel, Frank
Author: Daly, Eileen
1975   24 Pages
1st Edition $6.00

105

Never Pat A Bear
(Unstated 1st)
Illus.: Seiden, Art
Author: Watts, Mabel
1971   24 Pages
1st Edition $6.00

106

Magic Next Door, The
(Unstated 1st)
Illus.: Stang, Judy
Author: Swetnam, Evelyn
1971   24 Pages
1st Edition $6.00

107

Kitten's Surprise, The
Illus.: Rojankovsky, Feodor
Author: Nina
1951   28 Pages
"A" Edition $12.00

107

Woodsy Owl And The Trail Bikers
(Unstated 1st)
Illus.: Mc Savage, Frank
Author: Graham, Kennon
1974   24 Pages
1st Edition $7.00

108

Two Little Gardners
Illus.: Elliott, Gertrude
Author: Brown, Margaret Wise
1951   28 Pages
"A" Edition $15.00

108

ABC Is For Christmas
(Unstated 1st)
Illus.: Augistiny, Sally
Author: Watson, Jane Werner
1974   24 Pages
1st Edition $6.00

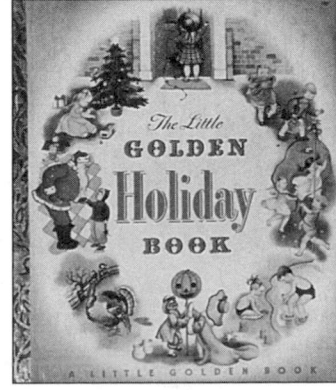

109

Little Golden Holiday Book, The
Illus.: Wilkin, Eloise
Author: Conger, Marion
1951   28 Pages
"A" Edition $25.00

109

Noah's Ark
(Unstated 1st)
Illus.: Gergely, Tibor
Author: Hazen, Barbara Shook
1969   24 Pages
1st Edition $6.00

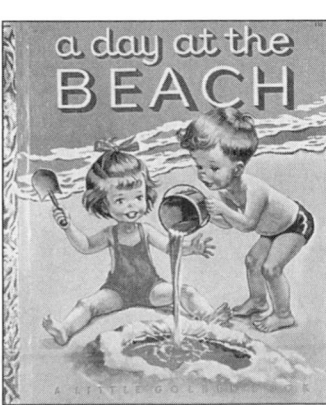

110

Day At The Beach, A
Illus.: Malvern, Corinne
Author: Jackson, Kathryn & Byron
1951   28 Pages
1st Edition $25.00

110

David And Goliath
(Unstated 1st)
Illus.: Lee, Robert J.
Author: Hazen, Barbara Shook
1974   24 Pages
1st Edition   **$6.00**

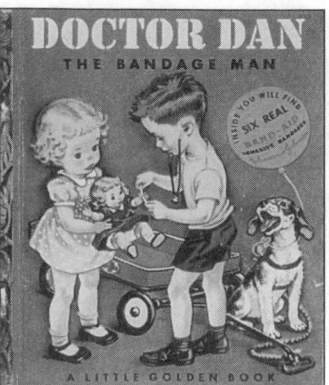

111

Dr. Dan The Bandage Man
Illus.: Malvern, Corinne
Author: Gaspard, Helen
1950   28 Pages
"C" Edition   **$100.00**

111

Dr. Dan The Bandage Man Title Page

111

W/out Band-Aids   **$18.00**

111

I Think About God Two Stories About My Day
Illus.: Cassan, Christine; Hyman
Author: Val, Sue; Smaridge, Norah
1974   24 Pages
1st Edition   **$6.00**

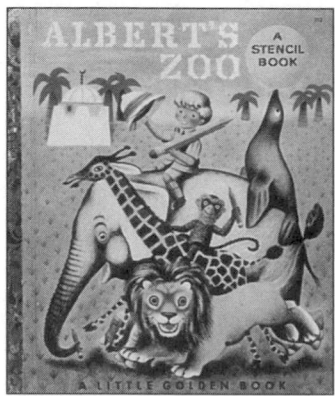

112

Albert's Zoo, A Stencil Book
Illus.: Scarry, Richard
Author: Werner, Jane
1951   28 Pages
"A" Edition   **$80.00**
W/out stencils   **$10.00**

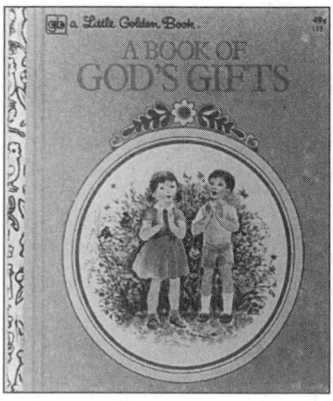

112

Book Of God's Gifts, A
Illus.: Schreter, Rick
Author: Hannh
1972   24 Pages
"A" Edition   **$6.00**

113

Little Golden Paper Dolls, The
Illus.: Miloche, Hilda; Kane, Wilma
Author: Miloche, Hilde; Kane, Wilma
1951   28 Pages
"A" Edition   **$125.00**
With cut-out clothes and dolls **$35.00**
Missing clothes and dolls   **$5.00**

113

Little Golden Paper Dolls, The
Does not have the dresser in the back of the book
Illus.: Miloche, Hilde; Kane, Wilma
Author: Miloche, Hilde; Kane, Wilma
1951 (1952) 28 Pages
"B" Edition   **$110.00**

113

Little Crow
(Unstated 1st)
Illus.: Aldrich, Andy
Author: Mcdermott, Caroline
1974   24 Pages
1st Edition   **$7.00**

114

Pantaloon
1st Edition can be found with cut and uncut window
Illus.: Weisgard, Leonard
Author: Jackson, Kathryn
1951   28 Pages
"A" Edition   **$25.00**

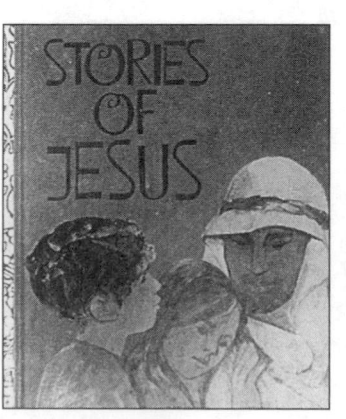

114

Stories Of Jesus
(Unstated 1st)
Illus.: Forberg, Ari
Author: Richards, Jean H.
1974   24 Pages
1st Edition   **$6.00**

115

My Home
(Unstated 1st)
Illus.: Rofry
Author: Bartowski, Renee
1971   24 Pages
1st Edition   **$6.00**

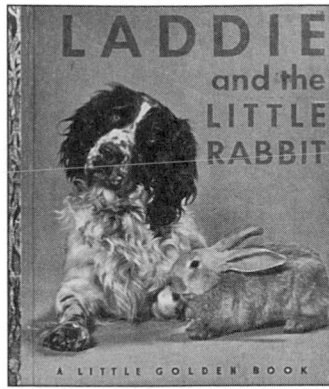

116

Laddie And The Little Rabbit
Purple title lettering
Illus.: Gottlieb, William
Author: Gottlieb, William P.
1952   28 Pages
"A" Edition   **$12.00**

116

Yellow title lettering
(1954)   28 Pages
"B" Edition   **$10.00**

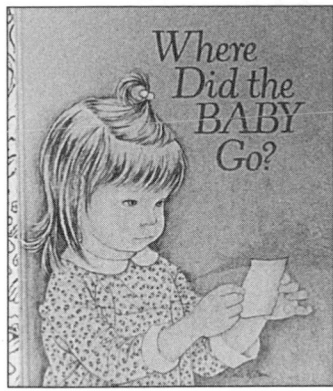

116

Where Did The Baby Go?
(Unstated 1st)
Illus.: Wilkin, Eloise
Author: Hayes, Sheila
1974   24 Pages
1st Edition   **$11.00**

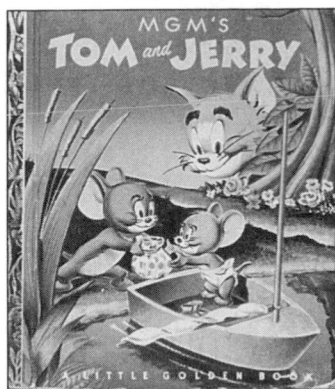

117

Tom And Jerry
Illus.: Eisenberg, Harvey; Maclaughlin, Don
Author: MGM
1951   28 Pages
"A" Edition   **$14.00**

117

Pano The Train
(Unstated 1st)
Illus.: Giannini
Author: Holvaes, Sharon
1975   24 Pages
1st Edition   **$7.00**

118

Train To Timbuctoo, The
Illus.: Seiden, Art
Author: Brown, Margaret Wise
1951   28 Pages
"A" Edition   **$20.00**

118

Title lettering style changed
(1972)   24 Pages
2nd Edition   **$7.00**

119

Day At The Playground, A
Illus.: Wilkin, Eloise
Author: Schlein, Miriam
1951   28 Pages
"A" Edition   **$25.00**

119

Wizard Of Oz, The
(Unstated 1st)
Illus.: Turner, Don; Jason Studios
Author: Carey, Mary
1975   24 Pages
1st Edition   **$8.00**

120

Bugs Bunny And The Indians
Illus.: Kelsey, Richard
Author: Bedford, Annie North
1951   28 Pages
"A" Edition   **$14.00**

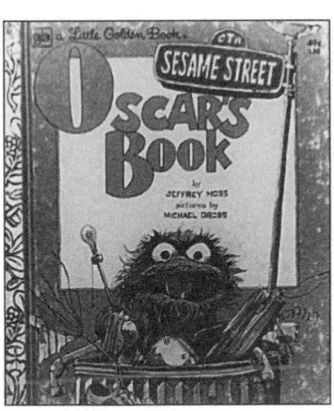

120

Oscar's Book
(Unstated 1st)
Illus.: Gross, Michael
Author: Moss, Jeffery
1975   24 Pages
1st Edition   **$6.00**

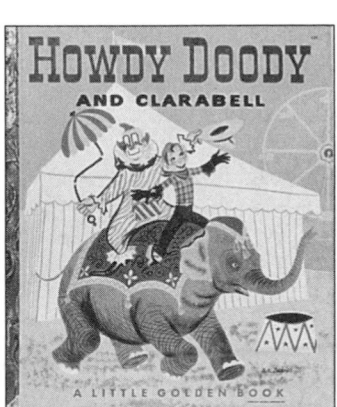

121

Howdy Doody And Clarabell
Illus.: Seiden, Art
Author: Kean, Edward
1951   28 Pages
"A" Edition   **$25.00**

121

Santa's Surprise Book
(Unstated 1st)
Illus.: Winship, Florence
Author: Elwart, Joan Rotter
1966   24 Pages
1st Edition   **$6.00**

122

Lucky Mrs. Ticklefeather
Illus.: Miller, J.P.
Author: Kunhardt, Dorothy
1951   28 Pages
"A" Edition   **$30.00**

122

Road Runner A Very Scary Lesson, The
(Unstated 1st)
Illus.: Delara, Phil; Totten, Bob
Author: Schroeder, Russel
1974   24 Pages
1st Edition   **$6.00**

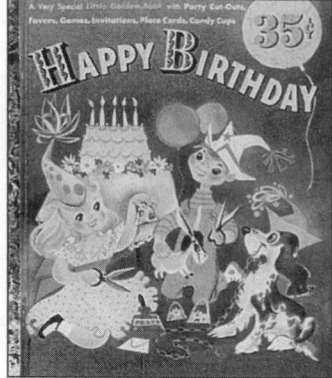

123

Happy Birthday
Uncut
Illus.: Worcester, Retta
Author: Nast, Elsa Ruth
1952   28 Pages
"A" Edition   **$40.00**
With activities cut out   **$3.00**

123

Remarkably Strong Pippy Longstocking, The
(Unstated 1st)
Illus.: Turner, Don; Jason Studios
Author: Hogan, Cecily
1974   24 Pages
1st Edition   **$14.00**

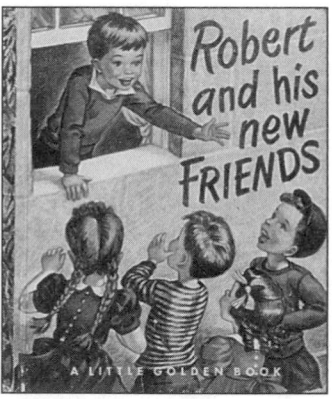

124

Robert And His New Friends
Illus.: Malvern, Corinne
Author: Schneider, Nina
1951   28 Pages
"A" Edition   **$15.00**

124

Tom And Jerry's Photo Finish
(Unstated 1st)
Illus.: Anderson, Al
Author: Lewis, Jean
1974   24 Pages
1st Edition   **$10.00**

125

Boats
Illus.: Combes, Lenora & Herber
Author: Lackman, Ruth Mabee
1951   28 Pages
"A" Edition   **$8.00**

125

Barbie
Illus.: Biesterveld, Betty
Author: Biesterveld, Betty
1974   24 Pages
1st Edition   **$9.00**

126

Gingerbread Shop, The
Illus.: Elliott, Gertrude
Author: Travers. P. L.
1952   28 Pages
"A" Edition   **$20.00**

126

Scooby Doo And The Pirate Treasure
(Unstated 1st)
Illus.: Lorencz, William; Arens, Michael
Author: Lewis, Jean
1974   24 Pages
1st Edition   **$12.00**

127

Bugs Bunny's Carrot Machine
(Unstated 1st)
Illus.: Totten, Bob
Author: Carlisle, Clark
1971   24 Pages
1st Edition   **$6.00**

128

Mister Dog
Illus.: Williams, Garth
Author: Brown, Margaret Wise
1952   28 Pages
"A" Edition $25.00

128

Tawney Scrawney Lion And The Clever Monkey, The
(Unstated 1st)
Illus.: Jancar, Milli
Author: Carey, Mary
1974   24 Pages
1st Edition $7.00

129

Tex And His Toys
Illus.: Malvern, Corinne
Author: Nast, Elsa Ruth
1952   28 Pages
"A" Edition $90.00
W/out tape and activities
        28 Pages
1st Edition $3.00

129

Bouncy Baby Bunny Finds His Bed, The
(Unstated 1st)
Illus.: Westerberg, Christine
Author: Bowden, Joan
1974   24 Pages
1st Edition $6.00

130

What If?
Illus.: Miller, J.P.
Author: Tanous, Helen & Henry
1951   28 Pages
"A" Edition $12.00

130

Poky Little Puppy Follows His Nose Home, The
(Unstated 1st)
Illus.: Miclat, Alex
Author: Holl, Adelaide
1975   24 Pages
1st Edition $6.00

131

Little Golden Book Of Dogs, The
Illus.: Gergely, Tibor
Author: Jones, Nita
1952   28 Pages
"A" Edition $8.00

131

New Friends For The Saggy Baggy Elephant
Illus.: Neely, Jan; Alvarado, Pet
Author: Holl, Adelaide
1975   24 Pages
1st Edition $7.00

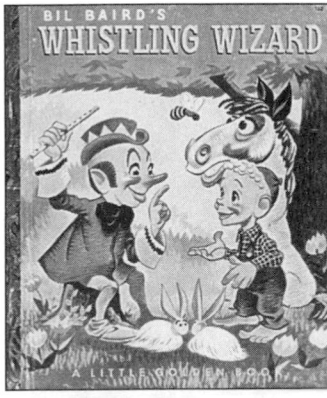

132

Whistling Wizard
(Unstated 1st)
Illus.: Crawford, Mel
Author: Stern, Alan; Pray, Rupert
1953   28 Pages
"A" Edition $18.00

133

Rainy Day Play Book, The
Illus.: Malvern, Corinne
Author: Pray, Rupert
1951   28 Pages
"A" Edition $18.00

133

Mr. Rogers Neighborhood 'Henrietta Meets Someone New'
(Unstated 1st)
Illus.: Jason Art Studios
Author: Rogers, Fred M.
1974   24 Pages
1st Edition $6.00

134

Seven Little Postmen
Illus.: Gergely, Tibor
Author: Brown, Margaret Wise
1952   28 Pages
"A" Edition $18.00

134

Waltons And The Birthday Present, The
(Unstated 1st)
Illus.: Godfry, Jane
Author: Godfry, Jane
1975   24 Pages
1st Edition   **$6.00**

135

Howdy Doody And The Princess
Illus.: Seiden, Art
Author: Kean, Edward
1952   28 Pages
"A" Edition   **$25.00**

135

Underdog And The Disappearing Ice Cream
(Unstated 1st)
Illus.: Jason Art Studios
Author: Fern, Mary
1975   24 Pages
1st Edition   **$15.00**

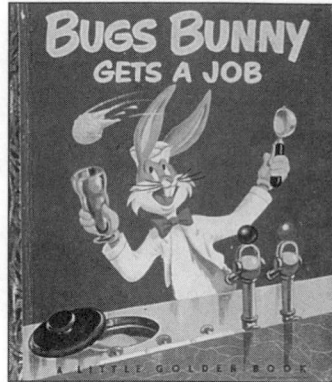

136

Bugs Bunny Gets A Job
Illus.: Strobel, Tony; Maclaughlin, Don
Author: Bedford, Annie North
1952   28 Pages
"A" Edition   **$12.00**

136

Land Of The Lost, The Surprise Guests
(Unstated 1st)
Illus.: Irvin, Fred
Author: Graham, Kennon
1975   24 Pages
1st Edition   **$10.00**

137

Puss In Boots
Illus.: Miller, J.P.
Author: Jackson, Kathryn
1952   28 Pages
"A" Edition   **$11.00**

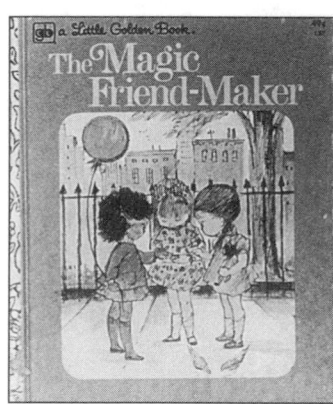

137

Magic Friend-Maker, The
Illus.: Nagel, Stina
Author: Bond, Gladys Baker
1975   24 Pages
1st Edition   **$15.00**

138

Tawny Scrawny Lion
Illus.: Tenggren, Gustaf
Author: Jackson, Kathryn
1952   28 Pages
"A" Edition   **$16.00**

138

Title lettering changed
(1970)   24 Pages
2nd Edition   **$5.00**

138

"Tenggren's" is removed from cover
(1974)   24 Pages
6th Edition   **$5.00**

139

Fun With Decals
Illus.: Malvern, Corinne
Author: Nast, Elsa Ruth
1952   28 Pages
"A" Edition   **$125.00**

139

Fun With Decals decal page

139

W/out decals
"A" Edition   **$15.00**

139

Raggedy Ann And Andy The Little Gray Kitten
(Unstated 1st)
Illus.: Goldsborough, June
Author: Curren, Polly
1975   24 Pages
1st Edition   **$6.00**

140

Mr. Wigg's Birthday Party
Illus.: Elliott, Gertrude
Author: Travers, P. L.
1952   28 Pages
"A" Edition   **$18.00**

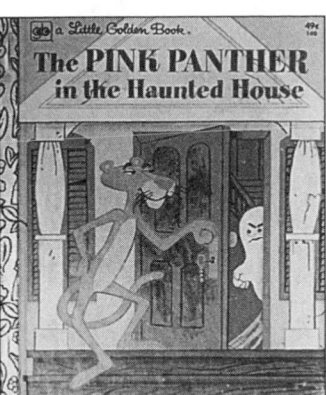

140

Pink Panther In The Haunted House, The
(Unstated 1st)
Illus.: Baker, Darrell; Jason Studios
Author: Graham, Kennon
1975   24 Pages
1st Edition   **$6.00**

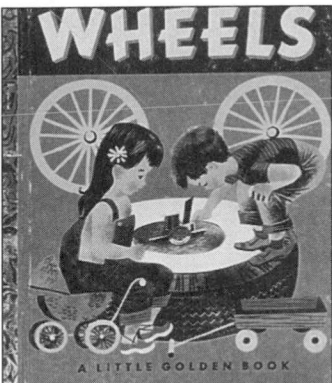

141

Wheels
Illus.: Weisgard, Leonard
Author: Jackson, Kathryn
1952   28 Pages
"A" Edition   **$14.00**

141

Tweety Plays Catch The Puddy Cat
(Unstated 1st)
Illus.: Alverado, Peter; Lorencz, William
Author: Daly, Eileen
1975   24 Pages
1st Edition   **$6.00**

142

Frosty The Snowman
Illus.: Malvern, Corinne
Author: Bedford, Annie North
1951   28 Pages
"A" Edition   **$15.00**

142

Christmas Spine
(1951)   24 Pages
"L" Edition   **$8.00**

142

Green Background
Red Spine
(1968)   24 Pages
"P" Edition   **$6.00**

142

Frosty The Snowman
(2nd Cover)
Illus.: Malvern, Corinne
Author: Bedford, Annie North
1951 (1972) 24 Pages
22nd Edition   **$6.00**

143

Here Comes The Parade
Illus.: Scarry, Richard
Author: Jackson, Kathryn
1950   28 Pages
"A" Edition   **$16.00**

143

Runaway Squash, The
(Unstated 1st)
Illus.: Bunky
Author: Wiersum, Gale
1976   24 Pages
1st Edition   **$6.00**

144

Road To Oz, The
Illus.: Mc Naught, Harry
Author: Baum, Frank L.
1951   28 Pages
"A" Edition   **$25.00**

144

My Christmas Treasury
(Unstated 1st)
Illus.: Emrich, Sylvia
Author: Wiersum, Gale
1976   24 Pages
1st Edition $6.00

145

Woody Woodpecker
Illus.: Thompson, Riley
Author: Lantz, Walter
1952   28 Pages
"A" Edition $11.00

145

Bugs Bunny, Too Many Carrots
(Unstated 1st)
Illus.: Alverado, Peter; Totten, Bob
Author: Lewis, Jean
1976   24 Pages
1st Edition $6.00

146

Magic Compass, The
Illus.: Elliott, Gertrude
Author: Travers, P.L.
1953   28 Pages
"A" Edition $20.00

146

Porky Pig And Bugs Bunny Just Like Magic!
(Unstated 1st)
Illus.: Totten, Bob
Author: Nathan, Stella Williams
1976   24 Pages
1st Edition $6.00

147

Hopalong Cassidy And The Bar 20 Cowboys
Illus.: Sahula-Dycke
Author: Mulford, E.M.
1952   28 Pages
"A" Edition $25.00

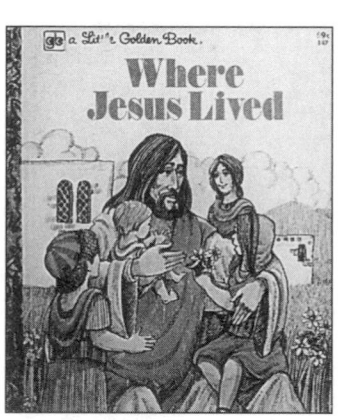

147

Where Jesus Lived
(Unstated 1st)
Illus.: Le Hew, Ronald
Author: Watson, Jane Werner
1977   24 Pages
1st Edition $6.00

148

Uncle Wiggily
Illus.: Crawford, Mel
Author: Garis, Howard R.
1953   28 Pages
"A" Edition $20.00

148

Ginghams The Backward Picnic, The
(Unstated 1st)
Illus.: Koenig, Jo Anne E.
Author: Bowden, Joan Chase
1976   24 Pages
1st Edition $6.00

149

Indian Indian
Illus.: Weisgard, Leonard
Author: Zolotow, Charlotte
1952   28 Pages
"A" Edition $16.00

149

Woody Woodpecker At The Circus
(Unstated 1st)
Illus.: Mc Savage, Frank
Author: Nathan, Stella Williams
1976   24 Pages
1st Edition $6.00

150

Rootie Kazootie
Illus.: Crawford, Mel
Author: Carlin, Steve
1953   28 Pages
"A" Edition $30.00

150

Cats
(Unstated 1st)
Illus.: Crawford, Mel
Author: French, Laura
1976   24 Pages
1st Edition $6.00

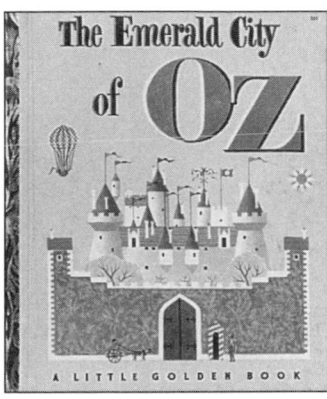

151

Emerald City Of Oz, The
Illus.: Mc Naught, Harry
Author: Archer, Peter
1952   28 Pages
"A" Edition $27.00

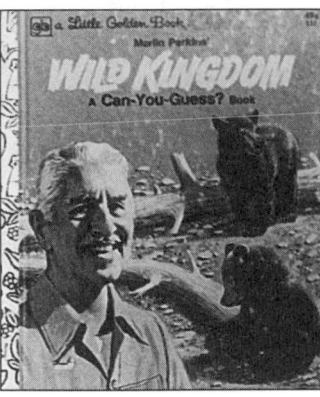

151

Wild Kingdom
Illus.: Seward, James; Creative Studios
(Unstated 1st)
Author: Meier, Esta
1976   24 Pages
1st Edition $6.00

152

All Aboard!
Illus.: Malvern, Corinne
Author: Conger, Marion
1952   28 Pages
"A" Edition $16.00

152

Big Enough Helper, The
(Unstated 1st)
Illus.: O'sullivan, Tom
Author: Hall, Nancy
1978   24 Pages
1st Edition $6.00

153

Thumbelina
Illus.: Tenggren, Gustaf
Author: Anderson, Hans Christian
1953   28 Pages
"A" Edition $14.00

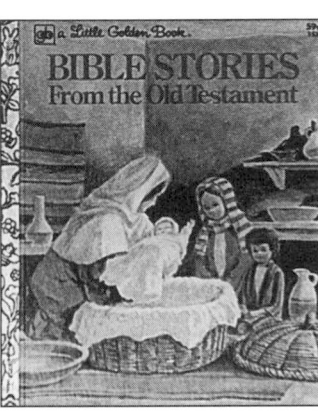

153

Bible Stories From The Old Testament
(Unstated 1st)
Illus.: Robison, Jim
Author: Lee, Sing
1977   24 Pages
1st Edition $6.00

154

Nurse Nancy
Illus.: Malvern, Corinne
Author: Jackson, Kathryn
1952   28 Pages
"A" Edition $110.00
W/out Band-Aids $40.00

154

Nurse Nancy title page

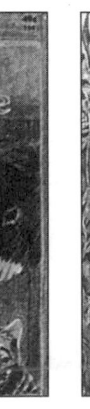

154

Animals' Christmas Eve, The
(Unstated 1st)
Illus.: Robison, Jim
Author: Wiersum, Gale
1977   24 Pages
1st Edition $6.00

155

Little Eskimo, The
Illus.: Weisgard, Leonard
Author: Jackson, Kathryn
1952   28 Pages
"A" Edition $16.00

155

Shazam!, A Circus Adventure
(Unstated 1st)
Illus.: Shafenburger, Kurt
Author: Ottum, Bob
1977   24 Pages
1st Edition $6.00

156

Sailor Dog, The
Illus.: Williams, Garth
Author: Brown, Margaret Wise
1953   28 Pages
"A" Edition $25.00

156

Raggedy Ann And Andy Help Santa Claus
(Unstated 1st)
Illus.: Goldsborough, June
Author: Curren, Plooy
1977   24 Pages
1st Edition $6.00

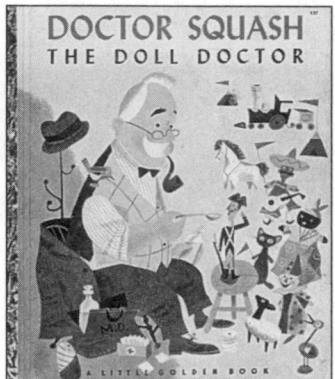

157

Doctor Squash
Illus.: Miller, J.P.
Author: Brown, Margaret Wise
1952   28 Pages
"A" Edition $20.00

157

Big Bird's Red Book
(Unstated 1st)
Illus.: Smollin, Michael J.
Author: Cert, Rosanne & Jonathon
1977   24 Pages
1st Edition $6.00

158

Christmas Story, The
Illus.: Wilkin, Eloise
Author: Werner, Jane
1952   28 Pages
"A" Edition $15.00

158

(1955)   24 Pages
"C" Edition $8.00

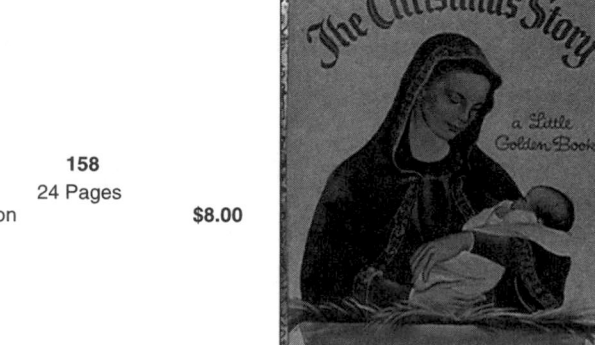

158

White cover background
(1969)   24 Pages
"F" Edition $4.00

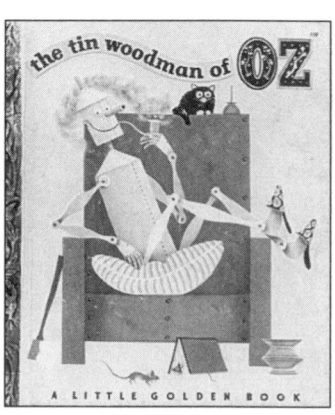

159

Tin Woodsman Of Oz, The
Illus.: Mc Naught, Harry
Author: Baum, Frank L.; Archer, Harry
1952   28 Pages
"A" Edition $25.00

159

Cookie Monster And The Cookie Tree
(Unstated 1st)
Illus.: Mathieu, Joe
Author: Korr, David
1977   24 Pages
1st Edition $6.00

160

Danny Beaver's Secret
Illus.: Scarry, Richard
Author: Scarry, Pat
1953   28 Pages
"A" Edition $15.00

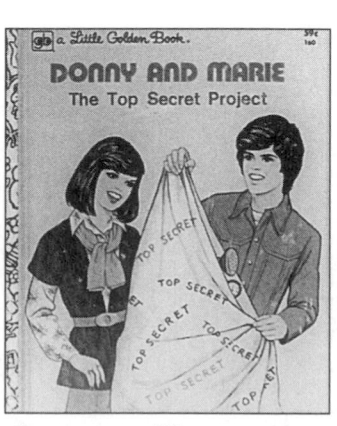

160

Donnie And Marie, The Top Secret Project
(Unstated 1st)
Illus.: Neely, Jan
Author: French, Laura
1977   24 Pages
1st Edition $8.00

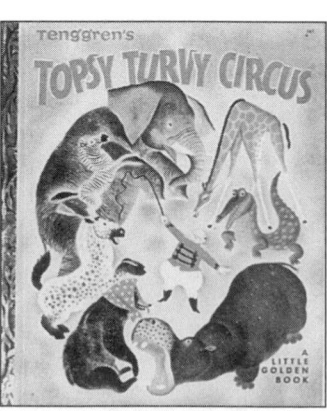

161

Topsy Turvy Circus
Illus.: Tenggren, Gustaf
Author: Duplaix, Georges
1953   28 Pages
"A" Edition $15.00

161

Bugs Bunny, Pioneer
(Unstated 1st)
Illus.: Baker, Darrell
Author: Brown, Fern G.
1977   24 Pages
1st Edition   **$6.00**

162

Little Red Caboose, The
Illus.: Gergely, Tibor
Author: Potter, Marion
1953   28 Pages
"A" Edition   **$12.00**

162

Superstar Barbie
(Unstated 1st)
Illus.: Robison, Jim; Irvin, Fred
Author: Foster, Anne
1977   24 Pages
1st Edition   **$7.00**

163

My Kitten
Illus.: Wilkin, Eloise
Author: Scarry, Patsy
1954   28 Pages
"A" Edition   **$18.00**

163

What Lily Goose Found
(Unstated 1st)
Illus.: Sumera, Anabelle
Author: Cawley, Lorinda Bryan
1977   24 Pages
1st Edition   **$6.00**

164

Bugs Bunny At The County Fair
Illus.: Beecher, Elizabeth
1954   28 Pages
"A" Edition   **$14.00**

164

Rabbit's Adventure, The
(Unstated 1st)
Illus.: Swanson, Maggie
Author: Wright, Betty Ren
1977   24 Pages
1st Edition   **$6.00**

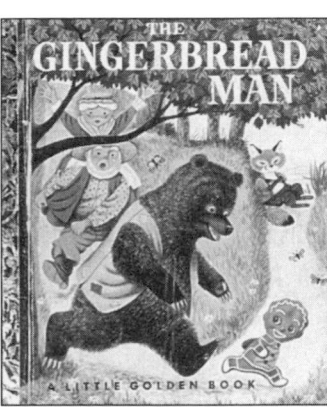

165

Gingerbread Man, The
Illus.: Scarry, Richard
Author: Nolte, Nancy
1953   28 Pages
"A" Edition   **$11.00**

165

Benji, Fastest Dog In The West
(Unstated 1st)
Illus.: Willis, Werner
Author: Ingoglia, Gina
1978   24 Pages
1st Edition   **$5.00**

166

Wiggles
Illus.: Wilkin, Eloise
Author: Woodcock, Louise
1953   28 Pages
"A" Edition   **$30.00**

167

Animal Friends
Illus.: Williams, Garth
Author: Werner, Jane
1953   28 Pages
"A" Edition   **$12.00**

168

My Teddy Bear
Illus.: Wilkin, Eloise
Author: Scarry, Patricia
1953   28 Pages
"A" Edition   **$25.00**

169
(1973)   24 Pages
2nd Edition $4.00

168

Circus Is In Town, The
(Unstated 1st)
Illus.: Ross, Larry
Author: Harrison, David L.
1978   24 Pages
1st Edition $5.00

169

Rabbit And His Friends
Illus.: Scarry, Richard
Author: Scarry, Richard
1953   28 Pages
"A" Edition   **$12.00**

170

Merry Shipwreck, The
Illus.: Gergely, Tibor
Author: Duplaix, Georges
1953   28 Pages
"A" Edition   **$15.00**

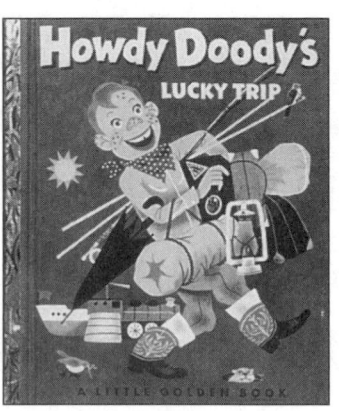

170

Best Of All!, A Story About The Farm, The
(Unstated 1st)
Illus.: Cauley, Lorinda Bryan
Author: Hogan, Cecily Rugh
1978   24 Pages
1st Edition $5.00

171

Howdy Doody's Lucky Trip
Illus.: Mc Naught, Harry
Author: Kean, Edward
1953   28 Pages
"A" Edition   **$25.00**

171

Whales
(Unstated 1st)
Illus.: Ruth, Rod
Author: Watson, Jane Werner
1978   24 Pages
1st Edition   **$7.00**

172

Howdy Doody In Funland
Illus.: Seiden, Art
Author: Kean, Edward
1953   28 Pages
"A" Edition   **$24.00**

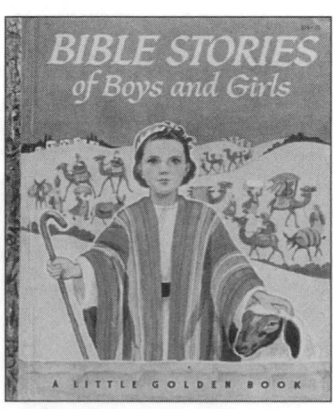

174
(1955)   24 Pages
"C" Edition   **$6.00**

173

Three Billy Goats Gruff, The
Illus.: Scarry, Richard
1953   28 Pages
"A" Edition $14.00

173

Rabbit Is Next, The
(Unstated 1st)
Illus.: Powell, Linda
Author: Leithauser, Gladys;
Betmeyer, Lois
1978   24 Pages
1st Edition $5.00

174

Bible Stories
Illus.: Dixon, Rachel Taft; Hartwell, Marjore
Author: Werner, Jane
1953   28 Pages
"A" Edition   **$8.00**

175

Uncle Mistletoe
Illus.: Malvern, Corinne
Author: Werner, Jane
1953   28 Pages
"A" Edition $27.00

175

Where Will All The Animals Go?
(Unstated 1st)
Illus.: Grant, Leigh
Author: Holaves, Sharon
1978   24 Pages
1st Edition $6.00

176

Little Golden Cut-Out Christmas Manger, The
Illus.: Lerch, Steffie
Author: Werner, Jane
1953   28 Pages
"A" Edition $18.00

176

ABC Around The House
(Unstated 1st)
Illus.: Irvin, Fred
Author: Holaves, Sharon
1978   24 Pages
1st Edition $6.00

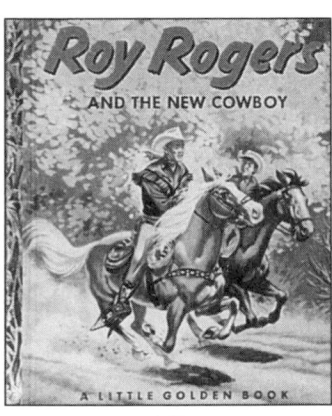

177

Roy Rogers
Illus.: Crawford, Mel
Author: Bedford, Annie North
1953   28 Pages
"A" Edition $22.00

178

Brave Little Tailor, The
Illus.: Miller, J.P.
Author: Bros. Grimm
1953   28 Pages
"A" Edition $10.00

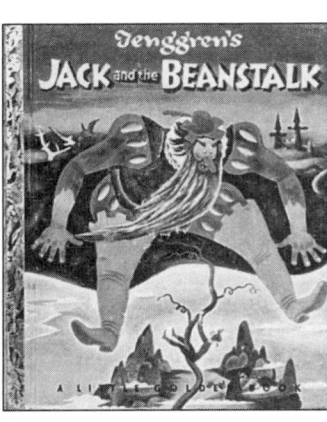

179

Jack And The Beanstalk
Illus.: Tenggren, Gustaf
Author: English Folk Tale
1953   28 Pages
"A" Edition $15.00

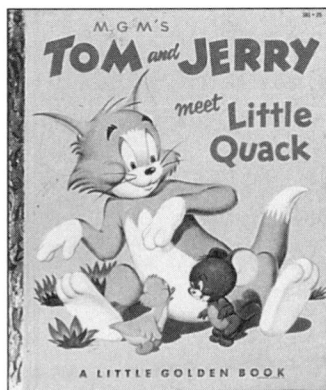

180

Airplanes
Illus.: Combes, Herbert & Lenora
Author: Lachman, Ruth Mabee
1953   28 Pages
"A" Edition $10.00

181

(1971)   24 Pages
3rd Edition $4.00

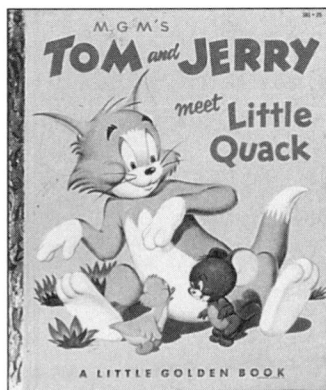

181

Tom And Jerry Meet Little Quack
Illus.: Maclaughlin, Don; Eisenberg, Harvey
Author: MGM
1953   28 Pages
"A" Edition $10.00

182

Gingerbread Man, The
(Unstated 1st)
Illus.: Elfrieda
1965   24 Pages
1st Edition $6.00

183

Bugs Bunny At The Easter Party
Illus.: Warner Bros.; Strobl, Tony; Kudo, Ben
Author: Hitte, Kathryn
1953   28 Pages
"A" Edition $14.00

183
(1963)   24 Pages
"C" Edition $7.00

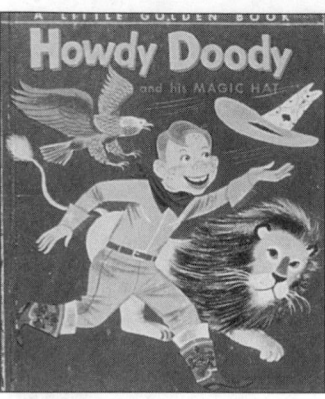

184
Howdy Doody And His Magic Hat
Illus.: Seiden, Art
Author: Kean, Edward
1954   28 Pages
"A" Edition $25.00

184
Birds
(Unstated 1st)
Illus.: Wilkin, Eloise
Author: Watson, Jane Werner
1973   24 Pages
1st Edition $7.00

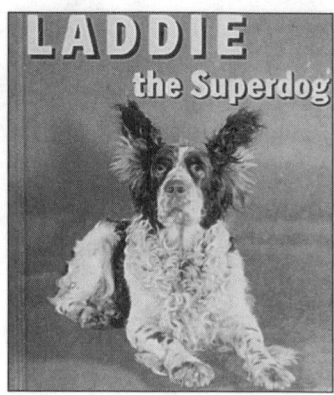

185
Laddie The Superdog
Illus.: Gottlieb, William P.
Author: Gottlieb, William P.
1954   28 Pages
"A" Edition $12.00

185
Let's Go, Trucks!
(Unstated 1st)
Illus.: Dugan, William
Author: Harrison, David L.
1973   24 Pages
1st Edition $6.00

186
Madeline
Illus.: Bemelmans, Ludwig
Author: Bemelmans, Ludwig
1954   28 Pages
"A" Edition $18.00

186
Petey And I, A Story About Being A Friend
(Unstated 1st)
Illus.: Irvin, Fred
Author: Conn, Martha Orr
1973   24 Pages
1st Edition $6.00

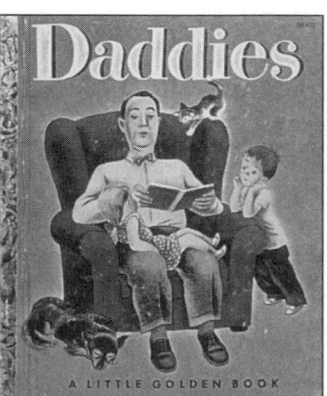

187
Daddies
Illus.: Gergely, Tibor
Author: Frank, Janet
1954   28 Pages
"A" Edition $20.00

188
Hi! Ho! Three In A Row
Illus.: Wilkin, Eloise
Author: Woodcock, Louise
1954   28 Pages
"A" Edition $27.00

189
Musicians Of Bremen, The
Illus.: Miller, J.P.
Author: Bros. Grimm
1954   28 Pages
"A" Edition $8.00

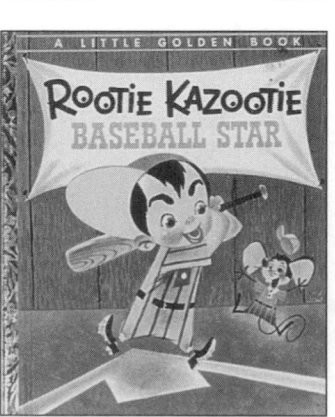

190
Rootie Kazootie Baseball Star
Illus.: Crawford, Mel
Author: Carlin, Steve
1954   28 Pages
"A" Edition $30.00

191
Party Pig, The
Illus.: Scarry, Richard
Author: Jackson, Kathryn & Byron
1954   28 Pages
"A" Edition $25.00

192

Heidi
Illus.: Malvern, Corinne
Author: Spyri, Johanna
1954   28 Pages
"A" Edition $8.00

193

Paper Doll Wedding, The
Illus.: Miloche, Hilda; Kane, Wilma
Author: Miloche, Hilda; Kane, Wilma
1954   28 Pages
"A" Edition $125.00
With cut-out clothes and dolls $35.00
Missing clothes and dolls $5.00

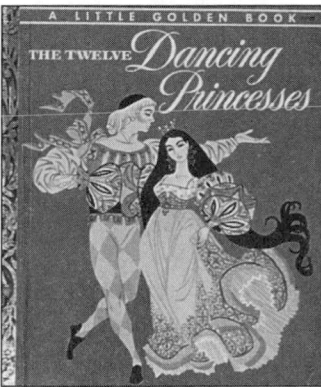

194

Twelve Dancing Princesses, The
Illus.: Beckett, Sheilah
Author: Bros. Grimm; Werner, Jane
1954   28 Pages
"A" Edition $25.00

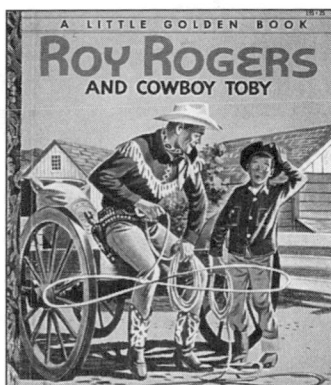

195

Roy Rogers And Cowboy Toby
Illus.: Crawford, Mel
Author: Beecher, Elizabeth
1954   28 Pages
"A" Edition $22.00

196

Georgie Finds A Grandpa
Illus.: Wilkin, Eloise
Author: Young, Miriam
1954   28 Pages
"A" Edition $25.00

197

Tom And Jerry's Merry Christmas
Illus.: MGM; Eisengerg, Harvey
Author: Archer, Peter
1954   28 Pages
"A" Edition $8.00

197

(1955)   24 Pages
"C" Edition $5.00

197

Christmas Spine
(1965)   24 Pages
"H" Edition $6.00

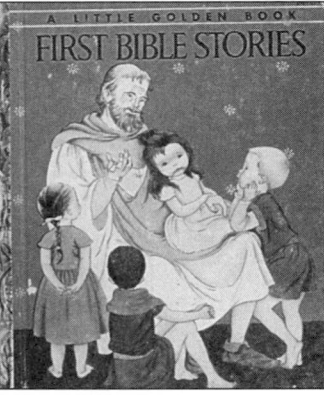

198

First Bible Stories
Illus.: Wilkin, Eloise
Author: Werner, Jane
1954   28 Pages
"A" Edition $20.00

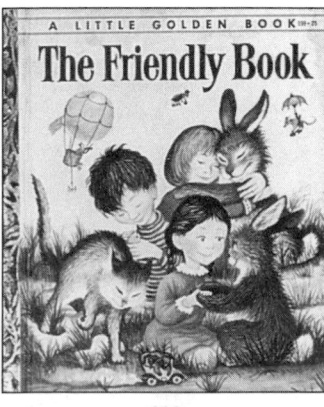

199

Friendly Book, The
Illus.: Williams, Garth
Author: Brown, Margaret Wise
1954   28 Pages
"A" Edition $15.00

200

Golden Goose, The
Illus.: Tenggren, Gustaf
Author: Folk Tale
1954   28 Pages
"A" Edition $12.00

201

From Then To Now
Illus.: Gergely, Tibor
Author: Leventhal, J.P.
1954   28 Pages
"A" Edition $10.00

202

Little Indian
Illus.: Scarry, Richard
Author: Brown, Margaret Wise
1954   28 Pages
"A" Edition $15.00

203

Little Lulu And Her Magic Tricks
Illus.: Buell, Marjorie Henderson
Author: Buell, Marjorie Henderson
1954   28 Pages
"A" Edition   **$60.00**
W/out Kleenex   **$25.00**
W/out table & Kleenex   **$10.00**

204

Three Bears, The
(Unstated 1st)
Illus.: Goldsborough, June
Author: Watts, Mabel
1965   28 Pages
1st Edition   **$6.00**

204

Howdy Doody And Mr. Bluster
Illus.: Marge, Elias
Author: Kean, Edward
1955   28 Pages
"A" Edition   **$25.00**

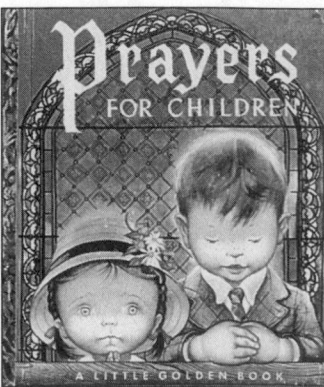

205

Prayers For Children
Illus.: Wilkin, Eloise
1952   28 Pages
"A" Edition   **$10.00**

205

(1955)   24 Pages
"F" Edition   **$5.00**

205

Christmas Spine
(1963)   24 Pages
"O" Edition   **$6.00**

205

Red cover background
(1968)   24 Pages
"S" Edition   **$4.00**

205

Red cover background
Ethnic children added
(1976)   24 Pages
35th Edition   **$4.00**

206

Little Gray Donkey
Illus.: Gergely, Tibor
Author: Lunt, Alice
1954   28 Pages
"A" Edition   **$12.00**

207

Open Up My Suitcase
Illus.: Malvern, Corinne
1954   28 Pages
"A" Edition   **$20.00**

208

Tiger's Adventure
Illus.: Gottlieb, William P.
Author: Gottlieb, William P.
1954   28 Pages
"A" Edition   **$11.00**

209

Little Red Hen, The
Illus.: Miller, J.P.
Author: Folk Tale
1954   28 Pages
"A" Edition   **$8.00**

210

Kitten Who Thought He Was A Mouse, The
Illus.: Williams, Garth
Author: Norton, Miriam
1954   28 Pages
"A" Edition   **$18.00**

211

Animals Of Farmer Jones, The
Illus.: Freund, Rudolf
1953   28 Pages
"A" Edition   **$8.00**

212

Pierre Bear
Illus.: Scarry, Richard
1954   28 Pages
"A" Edition   **$30.00**

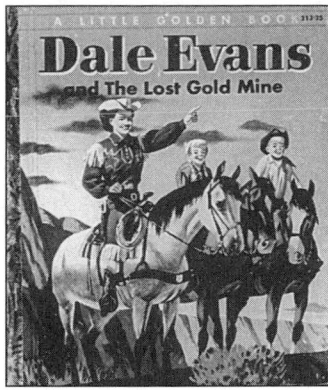

213

Dale Evans And The Lost Gold Mine
Illus.: Crawford, Mel
Author: Hill, Monica
1954   28 Pages
"A" Edition   **$20.00**

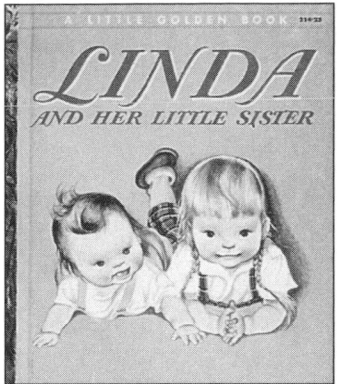

214

Linda And Her Little Sister
Illus.: Wilkin, Eloise
Author: Wilkin, Esther Burns
1954   28 Pages
"A" Edition   **$75.00**

215

(1973)   24 Pages
2nd Edition   **$4.00**

215

Bunny Book, The
Illus.: Scarry, Richard
Author: Scarry, Pat
1955   28 Pages
"A" Edition   **$8.00**

216

Happy Family, The
Illus.: Malvern, Corinne
Author: Nicole
1955   28 Pages
"A" Edition   **$16.00**

217

Hansel And Gretel
Illus.: Wilkin, Eloise
Author: Bros. Grimm
1954   28 Pages
"A" Edition   **$8.00**

218

House That Jack Built, The
Illus.: Miller, J.P.
Author: Mother Goose
1954   28 Pages
"A" Edition   **$11.00**

219

Giant With The Three Golden Hairs, The
Illus.: Tenggren, Gustaf
1955   28 Pages
"A" Edition   **$16.00**

220

Pony For Tony, A
Illus.: Gottlieb, William P.
Author: Gottlieb, William P.
1955   28 Pages
"A" Edition   **$12.00**

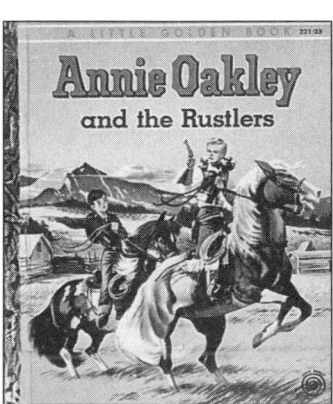

221

Annie Oakley
Illus.: Crawford, Mel
Author: Mcgovern, Ann
1955   28 Pages
"A" Edition   **$20.00**

222

Circus ABC, The
Illus.: Miller, J.P.
Author: Jackson, Kathryn & Byron
1955   28 Pages
"A" Edition   **$18.00**

223

It's Howdy Doody Time
Illus.: Seiden, Art
Author: Kean, Edward
1955   28 Pages
"A" Edition   **$25.00**

224

Smokey The Bear
Illus.: Scarry, Richard
Author: Werner, Jane
1955   28 Pages
"A" Edition   **$20.00**

225

Three Little Kittens
Four Color and Three Color
Illus.: Masha
1942 (1955) 28 Pages
"A" Edition   **$7.00**

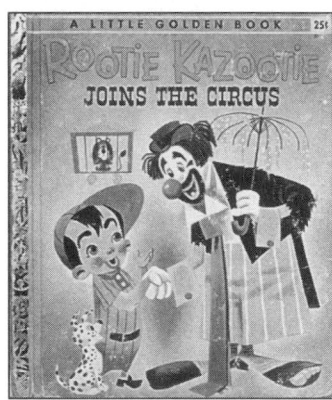

226

Rootie Kazootie Joins The Circus
Illus.: Crawford, Mel
Author: Carlin, Steve
1955   28 Pages
"A" Edition   **$25.00**

227

Twins, The
Illus.: Wilkin, Eloise
Author: Shane, Ruth & Harold
1955   28 Pages
"A" Edition   **$75.00**

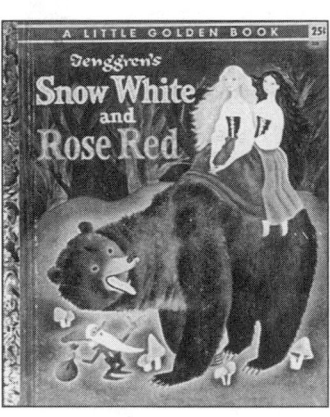

228

Snow White And Rose Red
Illus.: Tenggren, Gustaf
1955   28 Pages
"A" Edition   **$14.00**

229

Houses
Illus.: Gergely, Tibor
Author: Werner, Elsa Jane
1955   28 Pages
"A" Edition   **$10.00**

230

Gene Autry
Illus.: Crawford, Mel
Author: Fletcher, Steffie
1955   28 Pages
"A" Edition   **$22.00**

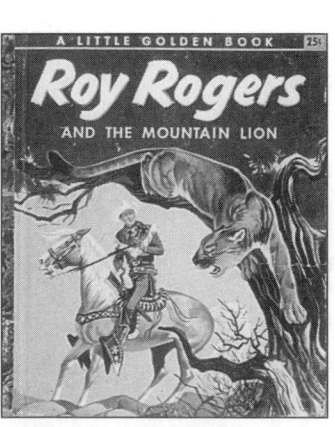

231

Roy Rogers And The Mountain Lion
Illus.: Crawford, Mel
Author: Mcgovern, Ann
1955   28 Pages
"A" Edition   **$22.00**

232

Skyscraper, The
(Never Printed)

232

Little Red Riding Hood
(Unstated 1st)
Illus.: Watts, Mable
Author: Grey, Les
1972   28 Pages
1st Edition   **$5.00**

235
(1973)   24 Pages
2nd Edition $4.00

233

My Puppy
Illus.: Wilkin, Eloise
Author: Scarry, Patsy
1955   28 Pages
"A" Edition   **$15.00**

234

J. Fred Muggs
Illus.: Schmidt, Edwin
Author: Shapiro, Irwin
1955   28 Pages
"A" Edition   **$17.00**

235

Tom And Jerry's Party
Illus.: MGM; Eisenberg, Harvey
Author: Fletcher, Steffi
1955   28 Pages
"A" Edition   **$7.00**

236
(1973)   24 Pages
2nd Edition   **$5.00**

236

Heroes Of The Bible
Illus.: Dixon, Rachel Taft
Author: Watson, Jane Werner
1955   28 Pages
"A" Edition   **$11.00**

237

Howdy Doody And Santa Claus
Illus.: Seiden, Art
Author: Kean, Edward
1955   28 Pages
"A" Edition   **$27.00**

238

5 Pennies To Spend
Illus.: Malvern, Corinne
Author: Young, Miriam
1955   28 Pages
"A" Edition   **$20.00**

239

Bedtime Stories
Illus.: Tenggren, Gustaf
Author: Misc. Authors
1942 (1955) 28 Pages
A Edition   **$7.00**

240

Mother Goose
Illus.: Elliott, Gertrude
Author: Mother Goose
1942 (1955) 28 Pages
A Edition   **$12.00**

241

Night Before Christmas, The
Illus.: Wilkin, Eloise
Author: Watson, Jane Werner
1955   28 Pages
"A" Edition   **$25.00**

242

Our World
Illus.: Sayeles, William
Author: Reed, Mary; Oswald, Edith
1955   28 Pages
"A" Edition   **$8.00**

243

Numbers
Illus.: La Mont, Violet
Author: Crampton, Gertrude
1955   28 Pages
"A" Edition   **$6.00**

244

Scuffy The Tugboat
Illus.: Gergely, Tibor
Author: Crampton, Gertrude
1955   28 Pages
"A" Edition   **$6.00**

245

Out Of My Window
Illus.: Jackson, Polly
Author: Low, Alice
1955   24 Pages
"A" Edition   **$15.00**

246

Rin Tin Tin And Rusty
Illus.: Crawford, Mel
Author: Hill, Monica
1955   28 Pages
"A" Edition   **$18.00**

246

(1955)   24 Pages
"B" Edition   **$15.00**

247

Happy Days
Illus.: Dart, Eleanor
Author: Frank, Janet
1955   24 Pages
"A" Edition   **$10.00**

248

Shy Little Kitten, The
Illus.: Tenggren, Gustaf
Author: Schurr, Cathleen
1956 (1956) 24 Pages
A Edition   **$7.00**

249

Animal Gym, The
Illus.: Gergely, Tibor
Author: Hoffman, Beth Greiner
1956   24 Pages
"A" Edition   **$14.00**

250

My Snuggly Bunny
Illus.: Wilkin, Eloise
Author: Scarry, Patsy
1956   24 Pages
"A" Edition   **$25.00**

251

Cars
Illus.: Dugan, William J.
Author: Jackson, Kathryn
1956   24 Pages
"A" Edition   **$8.00**

252

Howdy Doody's Animal Friends
Illus.: Seiden, Art
Author: Daly, Kathleen N.
1956   24 Pages
"A" Edition   **$25.00**

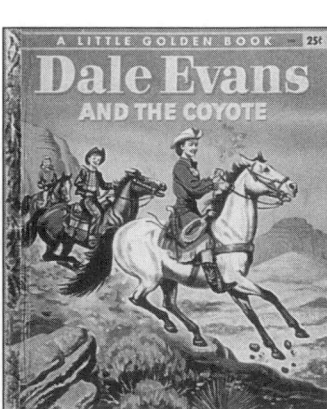

253

Dale Evans And The Coyote
Illus.: Dreany, E. Joseph
Author: Wyatt, Gladys
1956   24 Pages
"A" Edition   **$20.00**

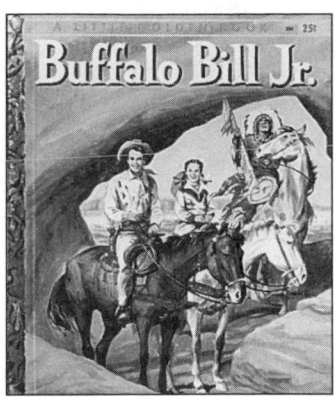

254

Buffalo Bill, Jr.
Illus.: Greene, Hamilton
Author: Wyatt, Gladys
1956   24 Pages
"A" Edition   **$20.00**

255

Lassie Shows The Way
Illus.: Ames, Lee
Author: Hill, Monica
1956   24 Pages
"A" Edition   **$14.00**

256

Daniel Boone
Illus.: Story, Miriam
Author: Shapiro, Irwin
1956   24 Pages
"A" Edition   **$12.00**

257

Counting Rhymes
Illus.: Malvern, Corinne
1947 (1956) 24 Pages
A Edition   **$7.00**

258

Heidi
Illus.: Malvern, Corinne
Author: Spyri, Johanna
1954 (1956) 24 Pages
A Edition   **$8.00**

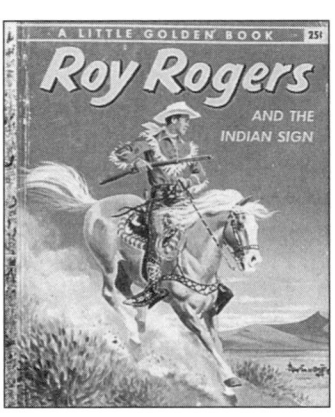

259

Roy Rogers And The Indian Sign
Illus.: Crawford, Mel
Author: Wyatt, Gladys
1956   24 Pages
"A" Edition   **$22.00**

260

Dogs
Illus.: Gergely, Tibor
Author: Jones, Nita
1952 (1956) 24 Pages
"A" Edition   **$8.00**

261

Captain Kangaroo
Illus.: Seiden, Art
Author: Daly, Kathleen N.
1956   24 Pages
"A" Edition   **$12.00**

262

Raggedy Ann And The Cookie Snatcher
(Unstated "A")
Illus.: Goldsborough, June
Author: Hazen, Barbara Shook
1972   24 Pages
"A" Edition   **$6.00**

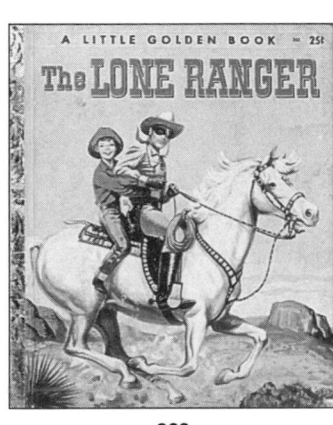

263

Lone Ranger, The
Illus.: Dreany, E. Joseph
Author: Fletcher, Steffi
1956   24 Pages
"A" Edition   **$22.00**

264

Just For Fun
(Unstated "A")
Illus.: Scarry, Richard
Author: Scarry, Patricia
1960   24 Pages
"A" Edition   **$6.00**

265

Pal And Peter
Illus.: Gottlieb, William P.
Author: Gottlieb, William P.
1956   24 Pages
"A" Edition   **$10.00**

266

Winky Dink
Illus.: Scarry, Richard
Author: Mcgovern, Ann
1956   24 Pages
"A" Edition   **$20.00**

267

Gene Autry And Champion
Illus.: Bolle, Frank
Author: Hill, Monica
1956   24 Pages
"A" Edition   **$22.00**

268

My Little Golden Book About God
Illus.: Wilkin, Eloise
Author: Watson, Jane Werner
1956   24 Pages
"A" Edition   **$8.00**

268

Ethnic children added
(1974)   24 Pages
10th Edition   **$4.00**

269

My Little Golden Book About Travel
Illus.: Gergely, Tibor
Author: Daly, Kathleen N.
1956   24 Pages
"A" Edition   **$7.00**

270

My Little Golden Book About The Sky
Illus.: Gergely, Tibor
Author: Wyler, Rose
1956   24 Pages
"A" Edition   **$8.00**

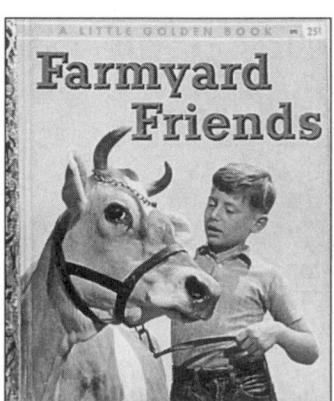

271

Poky Little Puppy, The
Illus.: Tenggren, Gustaf
Author: Lowrey, Janet Sebring
1942 (1956) 24 Pages
A Edition   **$7.00**

272

Farmyard Friends
Illus.: Gottlieb, William P.
Author: Gottlieb, William P.
1956   24 Pages
"A" Edition   **$7.00**

273

Romper Room Do Bees
Illus.: Dart, Eleanor
Author: Claster, Nancy
1956   24 Pages
"A" Edition   **$8.00**

274

Baby Animals
Illus.: Williams, Garth
Author: Williams, Garth
1957   24 Pages
"A" Edition   **$7.00**

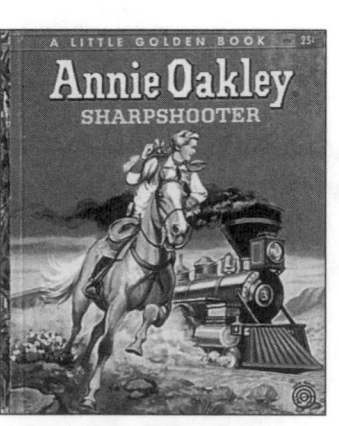

275

Annie Oakley Sharpshooter
Illus.: Dreany, E. Joseph
Author: Verral, Charles Spain
1956   24 Pages
"A" Edition   **$20.00**

276

Rin Tin Tin And The Last Indian
Illus.: Greene, Hamilton
Author: Hill, Monica
1956   24 Pages
"A" Edition   **$17.00**

277

Lassie And The Daring Rescue
Illus.: Dreany, E. Joseph
Author: Verral, Charles Spain
1956   24 Pages
"A" Edition $16.00

278

Captain Kangaroo And The Panda
Illus.: Schmidt, Edwin
Author: Daly, Kathleen N.
1951 (1957) 24 Pages
"A" Edition $13.00

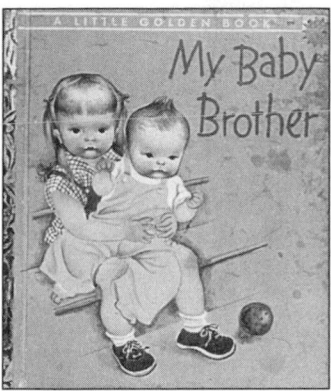

279

My Baby Brother
Illus.: Wilkin, Eloise
Author: Scarry, Patricia
1956   24 Pages
"A" Edition $25.00

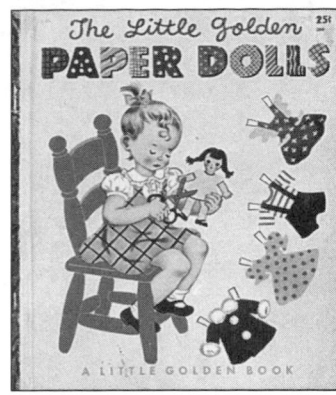

280

Little Golden Paper Dolls, The
Illus.: Miloche, Hilda; Kane, Wilma
Author: Miloche, Hilda; Kane, Wilma
1951 (1956) 24 Pages
"A" Edition $125.00
With cut-out clothes and dolls $35.00
Missing clothes and dolls $5.00

281

Jack And The Beanstalk
Illus.: Tenggren, Gustaf
Author: Folk Tale
1953 (1957) 24 Pages
A Edition $8.00

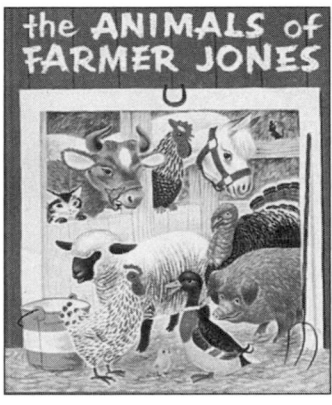

282

Animals Of Farmer Jones, The
Illus.: Scarry, Richard
Author: Gale, Leah
1953 (1957) 24 Pages
"A" Edition $10.00

283

The Little Golden Mother Goose
Illus.: Rojankovsky, Feodor
1957   24 Pages
"A" Edition $7.00

284

About the Seashore
Illus.: Gergely, Tibor
Author: Daly, Kathleen N.
1957   24 Pages
"A" Edition $7.00

285

How To Tell Time
(Gruen)
Illus.: Dart, Eleanor
Author: Watson, Jane Werner
1957   26 Pages
"A" Edition $20.00

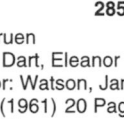

285

No Gruen
Illus.: Dart, Eleanor
Author: Watson, Jane Werner
1957 (1961) 20 Pages
"F" Edition $15.00

285

Soft Cover
Illus.: Dart, Eleanor
Author: Watson, Jane Werner
1957 (1962) 20 Pages
"H" Edition $5.00

286

Fury
Illus.: Crawford, Mel
Author: Irwin, Kathleen
1957   24 Pages
"A" Edition $16.00

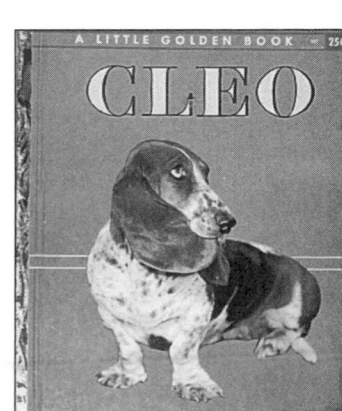

287

Cleo
Illus.: Graybill, Edward B.
Author: Shapiro, Irwin
1957   24 Pages
"A" Edition $14.00

288

Three Little Kittens
Four Color and Three Color
Illus.: Masha
1942 (1957) 24 Pages
"A" Edition   **$7.00**

289

Child's Garden Of Verses, A
Illus.: Wilkin, Eloise
Author: Stevenson, Robert Louis
1957   24 Pages
"A" Edition   **$10.00**

290

Circus Boy
Illus.: Anglund, Joan Walsh
Author: Shapiro, Irwin
1957   24 Pages
"A" Edition   **$25.00**

291

New Baby, The
Illus.: Wilkin, Eloise
Author: Shane, Ruth & Harold
1948 (1957) 24 Pages
"J" Edition   **$15.00**

291

New Baby, The
New pictures
Illus.: Wilkin, Eloise
Author: Shane, Ruth & Harold
1975   24 Pages
"A" Edition   **$14.00**

292

Our Puppy
Illus.: Rojankovsky, Feodor
Author: Nast, Ruth Elsa
1948 (1957) 24 Pages
"E" Edition   **$7.00**

293

Wonders Of Nature
Illus.: Wilkin, Eloise
Author: Watson, Jane Werner
1957   24 Pages
"A" Edition   **$14.00**

294

Brave Eagle
Illus.: Vanderlaan, Si
Author: Verral, Charles Spain
1957   24 Pages
"A" Edition   **$17.00**

295

Doctor Dan, The Bandage Man
Illus.: Malvern, Corinne
Author: Gaspard, Helen
1950 (1957) 24 Pages
"C" Edition   **$125.00**
W/out Band-Aids   **$15.00**

296

Little Red Hen, The
Cover by Rudolf Freund
Illus.: Miller, J. P.
Author: Folk Tale
1954 (1957) 24 Pages
"C" Edition   **$7.00**

297

Lone Ranger And Tonto, The
Illus.: Schmidt, Edwin
Author: Verral, Charles Spain
1957   24 Pages
"A" Edition   **$20.00**

298

My Christmas Book
Cover by Richard Scarry
Illus.: Beckett, Sheilah
Author: Traditional
1957   24 Pages
"A" Edition   **$17.00**

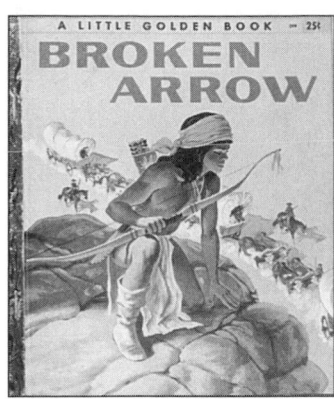

299

Broken Arrow
Illus.: Crawford, Mel
Author: Verral, Charles Spain
1957   24 Pages
"A" Edition $17.00

300

My Kitten
Illus.: Wilkin, Eloise
Author: Scarry, Patsy
1953 (1957) 24 Pages
"B" Edition $12.00

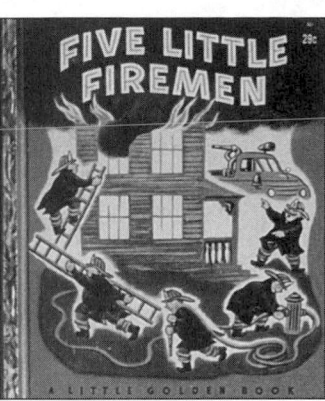

301

Five Little Firemen
Illus.: Gergely, Tibor
Author: Brown, Margaret Wise
1948 (1957) 24 Pages
"N" Edition $12.00

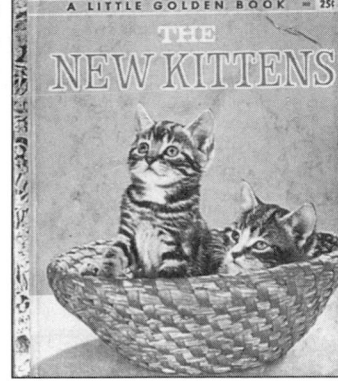

302

New Kittens, The
Illus.: Gottlieb, William P.
Author: Gottlieb, William P.
1957   24 Pages
"A" Edition $9.00

303

Baby's Mother Goose
Illus.: Battaglia, Aurelius
1948 (1957) 24 Pages
"A" Edition $8.00

304

Rin-Tin-Tin And The Outlaw
Illus.: Crawford, Mel
Author: Verral, Charles Spain
1957   24 Pages
"A" Edition $18.00

305

White Bunny And His Magic Nose, The
Illus.: Rojankovsky, Feodor
Author: Duplaix, Lily
1957   24 Pages
"A" Edition $12.00

305

Yellow background
(1965)   24 Pages
"B" Edition $6.00

305

Red-orange background
(1965)   24 Pages
"C" Edition $6.00

306

Red Little Golden Book Of Fairy Tales, The
Illus.: Dugan, William J.
Author: Bros. Grimm; Anderson, H.C.
1958   24 Pages
"A" Edition $13.00

307

Lassie And Her Day In The Sun
Illus.: Crawford, Mel
Author: Verral, Charles Spain
1958   24 Pages
"A" Edition $9.00

308

Jack's Adventure
Illus.: Miller, J.P.
Author: Hurd, Edith Thacher
1958   24 Pages
"A" Edition $10.00

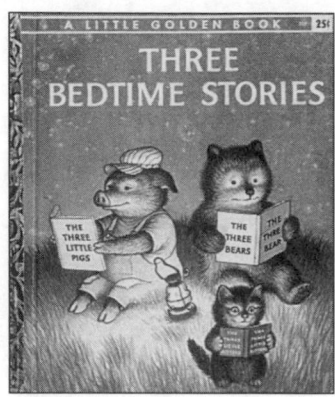

309

Three Bedtime Stories
Illus.: Williams, Garth
Author: Fairy Tales
1958   24 Pages
"A" Edition $8.00

310

Lone Ranger And The Talking Pony, The
Illus.: Bolle, Frank
Author: Brown, Emily
1958   24 Pages
"A" Edition $20.00

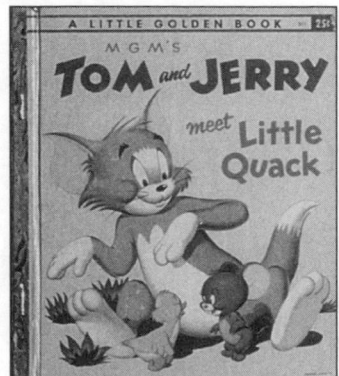

311

Tom And Jerry Meet Little Quack
Illus.: Eisenberg, Harvey; Maclaughlin, Don
Author: MGM
1953 (1958) 24 Pages
"B" Edition $7.00

312

Bugs Bunny
Illus.: Warner Bros.
Author: Warner Bros.
1949 (1958) 24 Pages
"I" Edition $8.00

313

Peter Rabbit
Illus.: Saviozzi, Adriana Mazza
Author: Potter, Beatrix
1958   24 Pages
"A" Edition $7.00

314

Pussy Willow
Illus.: Weisgard, Leonard
Author: Brown, Margaret Wise
1951   24 Pages
"A" Edition $10.00

314

White background
(1965)   24 Pages
"B" Edition $6.00

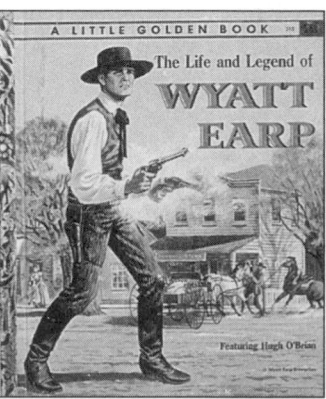

315

Life And Legend Of Wyatt Earp, The
Illus.: Crawford, Mel
Author: Hill, Monica
1958   24 Pages
"A" Edition $18.00

315

Sesame Street, The Together Book
(Unstated 1st)
Illus.: Bradfield, Roger
Author: Dwight, Revena
1971   24 Pages
1st Edition $4.00

316

Barker The Puppy
(Never Printed)

316

Monster At The End Of This Book, The
(Unstated 1st)
Illus.: Smollin, Mike
Author: Stone, Jon
1971   24 Pages

317

More Mother Goose Rhymes
Illus.: Rojankovsky, Feodor
Author: Mother Goose
1958   24 Pages
"A" Edition $6.00

319
Orange Spine
(1965)   24 Pages
"L" Edition $8.00

318
Cheyenne
Illus.: Schmidt, Al
Author: Verral, Charles Spain
1958   24 Pages
"A" Edition   **$20.00**

319
Little Red Caboose, The
Illus.: Gergely, Tibor
Author: Potter, Marion
1953 (1958) 24 Pages
"C" Edition   **$10.00**

320
Gunsmoke
Illus.: Dreany, E. Joseph
Author: Reit, Seymour
1958   24 Pages
"A" Edition   **$20.00**

321
Bert's Hall Of Great Inventions
(Unstated 1st)
Illus.: Bradfield, Roger
Author: Dwight, Revina
1972   24 Pages
1st Edition   **$4.00**

322
Four Little Kittens
Illus.: Saviozzi, Adriana Mazza
Author: Daly, Kathleen N.
1957   24 Pages
"A" Edition   **$6.00**

323
Ali Baba
Illus.: Hess, Lowell
Author: The Arabian Nights
1958   24 Pages
"A" Edition   **$12.00**

324
Day At The Zoo, A
Illus.: Gergely, Tibor
Author: Conger, Marion
1950 (1958) 24 Pages
"D" Edition   **$8.00**

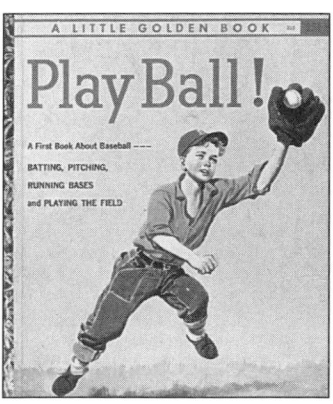

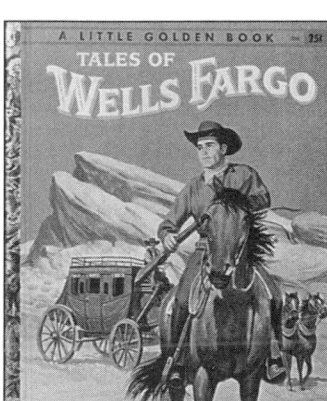

325
Play Ball!
Illus.: Mc Cann, Gerald
Author: Verral, Charles Spain
1958   24 Pages
"A" Edition   **$12.00**

326
Wagon Train
Illus.: Bolle, Frank
Author: Broun, Emily
1958   24 Pages
"A" Edition   **$18.00**

327
Good-bye, Tonsils
Illus.: Vaughn, Frank
Author: Cuy, Anne Welsh
1966   24 Pages
"A" Edition   **$7.00**

328
Tales Of Wells Fargo
Illus.: Leone, John
Author: Lazarus, Leon
1958   24 Pages
"A" Edition   **$20.00**

329
Animals' Merry Christmas, The
Illus.: Scarry, Richard
Author: Jackson, Kathryn
1958   24 Pages
"A" Edition $16.00

330
Woody Woodpecker
Illus.: Thompson, Riley
Author: Bedford, Annie North
1952 (1958) 24 Pages
"C" Edition $6.00

331
Rudolph The Red-Nosed Reindeer
Illus.: Scarry, Richard
Author: Hazen, Barbara Shook
1958   24 Pages
"A" Edition $12.00

331
Christmas Spine
(1963)   24 Pages
"G" Edition $8.00

331
Red Spine
(1968)   24 Pages
"L" Edition $6.00

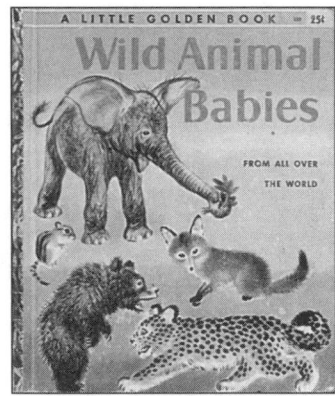

332
Wild Animal Babies
Illus.: Rojankovsky, Feodor
Author: Daly, Kathleen N.
1958   24 Pages
"A" Edition $6.00

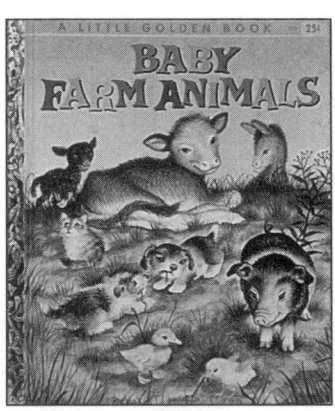

333
Baby Farm Animals
Illus.: Williams, Garth
Author: Williams, Garth
1958   24 Pages
"A" Edition $7.00

334
Animal Orchestra
Illus.: Gergely, Tibor
Author: Orleans, Ilo
1958   24 Pages
"A" Edition $8.00

335
Big Brown Bear, The
Illus.: Tenggren, Gustaf
Author: Duplaix, Georges
1947 (1958) 24 Pages
"D" Edition $8.00

335
Blue cover background
(1968)   24 Pages
"F" Edition $6.00

336
Fury Takes The Jump
Illus.: Crawford, Mel
Author: Reit, Seymour
1958   24 Pages
"A" Edition $15.00

336
Mother Goose In The City
(Unstated 1st)
Illus.: Leder, Dora
1974   24 Pages
1st Edition $4.00

337
Numbers
Illus.: La Mont, Violet
Author: Reed, Mary; Oswald, Edith
1955 (1958) 24 Pages
"B" Edition $5.00

337

Yellow cover background
(1968)   24 Pages
"L" Edition   **$3.00**

338

Deep Blue Sea, The
Illus.: Gergely, Tibor
Author: Parker, Bertha Morris
1958   24 Pages
"A" Edition   **$6.00**

339

Boats
Illus.: Combes, Lenora & Herbert
Author: Lachman, Ruth Mabee
1951   24 Pages
"A" Edition   **$6.00**

340

My Baby Sister
Illus.: Koester, Sharon
Author: Scarry, Patsy
1958   24 Pages
"A" Edition   **$18.00**

341

Captain Kangaroo's Surprise Party
Illus.: Schmidt, Edwin
Author: Lindsay, Barbara
1958   24 Pages
"A" Edition   **$12.00**

342

Exploring Space
Illus.: Gergely, Tibor
Author: Wyler, Rose
1958   24 Pages
"A" Edition   **$8.00**

343

Lassie And The Lost Explorer
Illus.: Bolle, Frank
Author: Lazarus, Leon
1958   24 Pages
"A" Edition   **$12.00**

344

Happy Golden ABC, The
Illus.: Allen, Joan
1972   24 Pages
"A" Edition   **$4.00**

345

Smokey The Bear Finds A Helper
Illus.: Anderson, Al
Author: Daly, Eileen
1972   24 Pages
"A" Edition   **$8.00**

346

Nurse Nancy
Illus.: Malvern, Corinne
Author: Jackson, Kathryn
1952 (1958) 24 Pages
"C" Edition   **$125.00**
W/out Band-Aids   **$40.00**

347

Leave It To Beaver
Illus.: Crawford, Mel
Author: Alson, Lawrence
1959   24 Pages
"A" Edition   **$25.00**

348

Nursery Songs
Illus.: Saviozzi, Adriana Mazza
Author: Gale, Leah
1959   24 Pages
"A" Edition   **$6.00**

349

Animal Alphabet
Illus.: Werber, Adele
Author: Hazen, Barbara Shook
1958   24 Pages
"A" Edition $10.00

350

Forest Hotel
Illus.: Benvenuti
Author: Davis, Barbara Steincrohn
1972   24 Pages
"A" Edition $5.00

351

Tiger's Adventure
Illus.: Gottlieb, William P.
Author: Gottlieb, William P.
1954(1958)   24 Pages
"B" Edition $6.00

352

We Help Mommy
Illus.: Wilkin, Eloise
Author: Cushman, Jean
1959   24 Pages
"A" Edition $15.00

352

Wallpaper design removed from cover
(1965)   24 Pages
"E" Edition $8.00

353

Tom Thumb
Illus.: Dugan, William J.
Author: Memling, Carl
1958   24 Pages
"A" Edition $8.00

354

Maverick
Illus.: Leone, John
Author: Memling, Carl
1959   24 Pages
"A" Edition $18.00

355

Dinosaurs
Illus.: Rutherford, William De
Author: Watson, Jane Werner
1959   24 Pages
"A" Edition $6.00

356

Steve Canyon
Illus.: Caniff, Milton
Author: Caniff, Milton
1959   24 Pages
"A" Edition $18.00

357

Helicopters
Illus.: Crawford, Mel
Author: Memling, Carl
1959   24 Pages
"A" Edition $9.00

358

Baby's First Book
Illus.: Williams, Garth
Author: Williams, Garth
1959   24 Pages
"A" Edition $7.00

359

Puss In Boots
Illus.: Miller, J.P.
Author: Jackson, Kathryn
1959   24 Pages
"A" Edition $6.00

360

Party In Shariland
Illus.: Henderson, Doris
Author: Mcgovern, Ann & Marion
1958   24 Pages
"A" Edition   **$17.00**

361

Counting Rhymes
Illus.: Kane, Sharon
1960   24 Pages
"A" Edition   **$6.00**

362

Pussycat Tiger, The
Illus.: Obligado, Lillian
Author: Bacon, Joan Chase
1972   24 Pages
"A" Edition   **$6.00**

363

Scuffy The Tugboat
Illus.: Gergely, Tibor
Author: Crampton, Certrude
1946 (1958) 24 Pages
"C" Edition   **$6.00**

364

Bedtime Stories
Illus.: Tenggren, Gustaf
1942 (1958) 24 Pages
"D" Edition   **$6.00**

365

Baby's Birthday
Illus.: Wilkin, Eloise
Author: Mowers, Patricia
1972   24 Pages
"A" Edition   **$10.00**

366

Cars And Trucks
Illus.: Scarry, Richard
Author: No Author
1959   24 Pages
"A" Edition   **$6.00**

367

Lion's Paw, The
Illus.: Tenggren, Gustaf
Author: Watson, Jane Werner
1959   24 Pages
"A" Edition   **$15.00**

367

"A Tale of African Animals" added to
cover title
(1970)   24 Pages
2nd Edition   **$12.00**

368

Baby's First Christmas
Illus.: Wilkin, Eloise
Author: Wilkin, Esther
1959   24 Pages
"A" Edition   **$12.00**

369

Little Golden Picture Dictionary
Illus.: Gergely, Tibor
Author: Hulick, Nancy
1959   24 Pages
"A" Edition   **$5.00**

370

New Puppy, The
Illus.: Obligado, Lillian
Author: Daly, Kathleen
1959   24 Pages
"A" Edition   **$7.00**

371

Aladdin
Illus.: Hess, Lowell
Author: Daly, Kathleen
1959   24 Pages
"A" Edition $13.00

372

Woody Woodpecker, Drawing Fun For Beginners
Illus.: Eisenberg, Harvey; Mccary, Norman
Author: Buettner, Carl
1959   24 Pages
"A" Edition $20.00

373

Airplanes
Illus.: Combes, Herbert & Lenora
Author: Lachman, Ruth Mabee
1953   24 Pages
"A" Edition $6.00

374

Blue Book Of Fairy Tales, The
Illus.: Laite, Gordon
1959   24 Pages
"A" Edition $15.00

375

Chipmunk's Merry Christmas, The
Illus.: Scarry, Richard
Author: Corwyn, David
1959   24 Pages
"A" Edition $10.00

376

Huckleberry Hound Builds A House
Illus.: Eisenberg, Harvey; White, Al
Author: Mcgovern, Ann
1959   24 Pages
"A" Edition $18.00

377

Naughty Bunny
Illus.: Scarry, Richard
Author: Scarry, Richard
1959   24 Pages
"A" Edition $27.00

378

Ruff And Reddy
Illus.: Eisenburg, Harvey; White, Al
Author: Mcgovern, Ann
1959   24 Pages
"A" Edition $10.00

379

Animal Dictionary
Illus.: Rojankovsky, Feodor
Author: Watson, Jane Werner
1960   24 Pages
"A" Edition $6.00

380

Birds Of All Kinds
Illus.: Ferguson, Walter
Author: Ferguson, Walter
1959   24 Pages
"A" Edition $6.00

381

Three Little Kittens
Illus.: Masha
1942 (1959) 24 Pages
"Z" Edition $6.00

382

Fire Engines
Illus.: Gergely, Tibor
Author: No Author
1959   24 Pages
"A" Edition $7.00

383
Baby Listens
Illus.: Wilkin, Eloise
Author: Wilkin, Esther
1960   24 Pages
"A" Edition $15.00

384
Happy Birthday
Illus.: Worcester, Retta
Author: Nast, Elsa Ruth
1960 (1960) 24 Pages
"B" Edition $15.00

385
Saggy Baggy Elephant, The
Illus.: Tenggren, Gustaf
Author: Jackson, Kathryn & Byron
1947 (1959) 24 Pages
"L" Edition $6.00

386
Dennis The Menace And Ruff
Illus.: Pratt, Hawley
Author: Memling, Carl
1959   24 Pages
"A" Edition $12.00

387
Smokey And His Animal Friends
Illus.: Crawford, Mel
Author: Verral, Charles Spain
1960   24 Pages
"A" Edition $16.00

388
Our Flag
Illus.: Cook, Steven
Author: Memling, Carl
1960   24 Pages
"A" Edition $6.00

388
Light-blue cover background
(1971)   24 Pages
2nd Edition $5.00

389
Cowboy ABC
Illus.: Smath, Jerry
Author: Saxon, Gladys R.
1960   24 Pages
"A" Edition $12.00

390
Little Golden Mother Goose, The
Illus.: Rojankovsky, Feodor
1957 (1960) 24 Pages
"D" Edition $6.00

391
Dogs
Illus.: Gergely, Tibor
Author: Jones, Nita
1952 (1960) 24 Pages
"E" Edition $6.00

392
Little Golden Book Of Hymns, The
Illus.: Malvern, Corinne
Author: Werner, Elsa Jane
1947 (1960) 24 Pages
"I" Edition $6.00

393
Happy Little Whale, The
Illus.: Gergely, Tibor
Author: Watson, Jane Werner
1960   24 Pages
"A" Edition $11.00

394

Wild Animals
Illus.: Rojankovsky, Feodor
Author: No Author
1961   24 Pages
"A" Edition   **$6.00**

395

Yogi Bear
Illus.: Kawaguchi, M.
Author: Hyatt, S. Quentin
1960   24 Pages
"A" Edition   **$18.00**

396

Animal Quiz
Illus.: Crawford, Mel
Author: Hulick, Nancy Fielding
1960   24 Pages
"A" Edition   **$6.00**

397

Bear In The Boat, The
Illus.: Vogel, Ilse-Margaret
Author: Vogel, Ilse-Margaret
1972   24 Pages
"A" Edition   **$5.00**

398

Quick Draw Mcgraw
Illus.: Pratt, Hawley
Author: Memling, Carl
1960   24 Pages
"A" Edition   **$18.00**

399

Doctor Dan At The Circus
Illus.: Sampson, Katherine
Author: Wilkins, Pauline
1960   24 Pages
"A" Edition   **$100.00**

399

W/out Band-Aids
            24 Pages
"A" Edition   **$15.00**

400

Old Macdonald Had A Farm
Illus.: Kennel, Moritz
1960   24 Pages
"A" Edition   **$6.00**

400

Cover background changed to bright
orange
(1972)   24 Pages
6th Edition   **$4.00**

401

**Raggedy Ann And Andy And The
Rainy Day Circus**
Illus.: Goldsborough, June
Author: Hazen, Barbara Shook
1973   24 Pages
"A" Edition   **$5.00**

402

Bravest Of All
Illus.: Anderson, Al
Author: Pogue, Katie Emery
1973   24 Pages
"A" Edition   **$10.00**

403

**Huckleberry Hound And The
Christmas Sleigh**
Illus.: Satterfield, Charles
Author: Cherr, Pat
1960   24 Pages
"A" Edition   **$18.00**

403

**Huckleberry Hounds And The
Christmas Sleigh**
(2nd Cover)
Yellow cover background
Christmas Spine
Illus.: Satterfield, Charles
Author: Cherr, Pat
1960 (1963) 24 Pages
"E" Edition $15.00

404

Baby Looks
Illus.: Wilkin, Eloise
Author: Wilkin, Eloise
1960   24 Pages
"A" Edition $17.00

405

Four Puppies
Illus.: Obligado, Lillian
Author: Heathers, Anne
1960   24 Pages
"A" Edition $6.00

406

**Huckleberry Hound And His
Friends**
Illus.: De Nunez, Ben; Totten, Bob
Author: Cherr, Pat
1960   24 Pages
"A" Edition $18.00

407

Day On The Farm, A
Illus.: Miller, J.P.
Author: Hulick, Nancy Fielding
1960   24 Pages
"A" Edition $6.00

408

Rocky And His Friends
Illus.: De Nunez, Ben; White, Al
Author: Mcgovern, Ann
1960   24 Pages
"A" Edition $20.00

408

Rocky And His Friends
(2nd Cover)
Illus.: De Nunez, Ben; White, Al
Author: Mcgovern, Ann
1960 (1973) 24 Pages
2nd Edition $13.00

409

Brownie Scouts
Illus.: Rumely, Louise
Author: Soskin, Lillian Gardner
1961   24 Pages
"A" Edition $17.00

410

New Pony, The
Illus.: Wilson, Dagmar
Author: Perin, Blanche Chenery
1961   24 Pages
"A" Edition $10.00

411

Sly Little Bear
Illus.: Pfloog, Jan
Author: Jackson, Kathryn
1960   24 Pages
"A" Edition $8.00

412

**Dennis The Menace A Quiet
Afternoon**
Illus.: Holley, Lee
Author: Memling, Carl
1960   24 Pages
"A" Edition $10.00

413

Chicken Little
Illus.: Scarry, Richard
Author: Benstead, Vivienne
1960   24 Pages
"A" Edition $7.00

413

Lime green cover background
(1968)   24 Pages
"F" Edition $5.00

413

Dark green cover background
(1963)   24 Pages
"D" Edition $6.00

414
Little Cottontail
Illus.: Obligado, Lillian
Author: Memling, Carl
1960   24 Pages
"A" Edition $6.00

415
Lassie Shows The Way
Illus.: Ames, Lee
Author: Hill, Monica
1956 (1960) 24 Pages
"D" Edition $7.00

416
Wacky Witch
Illus.: Alvarado, Peter; Spector, A.J;
Totten
Author: Lewis, Jean
1973   24 Pages
"A" Edition $10.00

417
Loopy De Loop Goes West
Illus.: Santos, George
Author: Hitte, Kathryn
1960   24 Pages
"A" Edition $18.00

418
My Dolly And Me
Illus.: Wilkin, Eloise
Author: Scarry, Patsy
1960   24 Pages
"A" Edition $40.00

419
Rupert The Rhinoceros
Illus.: Gergely, Tibor
Author: Memling, Carl
1960   24 Pages
"A" Edition $10.00

420
Jack And The Beanstalk
Illus.: Tenggren, Gustaf
1953 (1960) 24 Pages
"B" Edition $6.00

421
Captain Kangaroo And The Panda
Illus.: Schmidt, Edwin
Author: Daly, Kathleen N.
1957 (1960) 24 Pages
"D" Edition $7.00

422
Baby's Mother Goose
Illus.: Battaglia, Aurelius
Author: Folk Tale
1948 (1960) 24 Pages
"D" Edition $6.00

423
Smokey Bear And The Campers
Illus.: Crawford, Mel
Author: Hyatt, S. Quentin
1961   24 Pages
"A" Edition $10.00

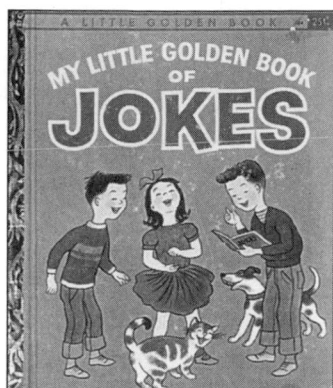

424

My Little Golden Book Of Jokes
Illus.: Gergely, Tibor
Author: George
1961   24 Pages
"A" Edition   **$6.00**

425

I'm An Indian Today
Illus.: Dugan, William J.
Author: Hitte, Kathryn
1961   24 Pages
"A" Edition   **$8.00**

426

Country Mouse And The City Mouse, The
Illus.: Scarry, Richard
Author: Scarry, Pat; Aesop Tales
1961   24 Pages
"A" Edition   **$7.00**

427

Captain Kangaroo And The Beaver
Illus.: Nonnast, Marie
Author: Memling, Carl
1961   24 Pages
"A" Edition   **$8.00**

428

Home For A Bunny
Illus.: Williams, Garth
Author: Brown, Margaret Wise
1961   24 Pages
"A" Edition   **$8.00**

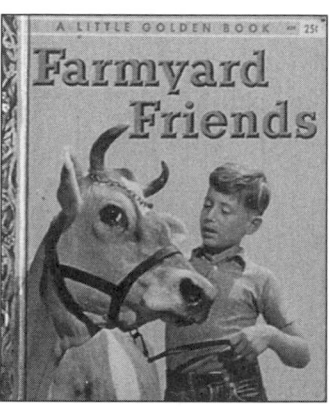

429

Farmyard Friends
Illus.: Gottlieb, William P.
Author: Gottlieb, William P.
1956 (1960) 24 Pages
"B" Edition   **$6.00**

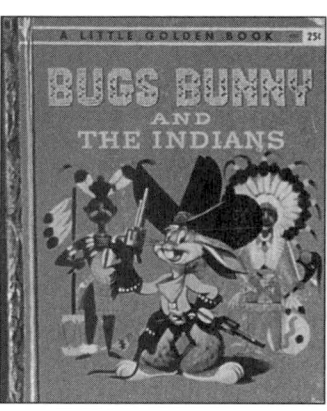

430

Bugs Bunny And The Indians
Illus.: Kelsey, Richmond I.; Mckimson, Tom
Author: Bedford, Annie North
1951 (1961) 24 Pages
"D" Edition   **$8.00**

431

National Velvet
Illus.: Crawford, Mel
Author: Hitte, Kathryn
1961   24 Pages
"A" Edition   **$14.00**

432

Dennis The Menace Waits For Santa Claus
Illus.: Wisman, Al
Author: Memling, Carl
1961   24 Pages
"A" Edition   **$17.00**

433

Yogi Bear, A Christmas Visit
Illus.: Mattinson, Sylvia & Burne
Author: Hyatt, S. Quentin
1961   24 Pages
"A" Edition   **$18.00**

433

Christmas Spine
(1962)   24 Pages
"C" Edition   **$16.00**

433

Blue cover background
Christmas Spine
(1963)   24 Pages
"E" Edition   **$15.00**

434

My First Counting Book
Illus.: Williams, Garth
Author: Moore, Lilian
1957 (1961) 24 Pages
"A" Edition $5.00

435

When You Were A Baby
Illus.: Malvern, Corinne
Author: Eng, Rita
1949 (1961) 24 Pages
"E" Edition $6.00

436

Color Kittens, The
Illus.: Provenson, Alice & Martin
Author: Brown, Margaret Wise
1949 (1961) 24 Pages
"C" Edition $10.00

437

Gingerbread Man, The
Illus.: Scarry, Richard
Author: Nolte, Nancy
1961   24 Pages
"A" Edition $8.00

437

Orange Spine
(1965)   24 Pages
"E" Edition $6.00

438

Little Red Hen, The
Illus.: Hauge, Carl & Mary
Author: Begley, Evelyn M.
1973   24 Pages
"A" Edition $6.00

439

Make Way For The Thruway
Illus.: Gergely, Tibor
Author: Emerson, Caroline
1961   24 Pages
"A" Edition $12.00

440

Bobby The Dog
Illus.: Probst, Pierre
Author: Probst, Pierre
1961   24 Pages
"A" Edition $20.00

441

Bunny's Magic Tricks
Illus.: Martin, Judy & Barry
Author: D'amato, Janet & Alex
1962   24 Pages
"A" Edition $14.00

441
Tricks cut/folded
              24 Pages
"A" Edition $6.00

442

Cindy Bear
Illus.: Eisenberg, Harvey
Author: Klinordlinger, Jean
1961   24 Pages
"A" Edition $18.00

442

Purple cover background
(1963)   24 Pages
"C" Edition $14.00

443
Puff The Blue Kitten
Illus.: Probst, Pierre
Author: Probst, Pierre
1961   24 Pages
"A" Edition   **$25.00**

444
Hokey Wolf And Ding-A-Ling
Illus.: Van Lamsweerde, Frans
Author: Hyatt, S. Quentin
1961   24 Pages
"A" Edition   **$18.00**

445
Woody Woodpecker Takes A Trip
Illus.: De Nunez, Ben; White, Al
Author: Mcgovern, Ann
1961   24 Pages
"A" Edition   **$7.00**

446
Bozo The Clown
Illus.: Satterfield, Charles
Author: Buettner, Carl
1961   24 Pages
"A" Edition   **$10.00**

447
Good Night, Little Bear
Illus.: Scarry, Richard
Author: Scarry, Patsy
1961   24 Pages
"A" Edition   **$10.00**

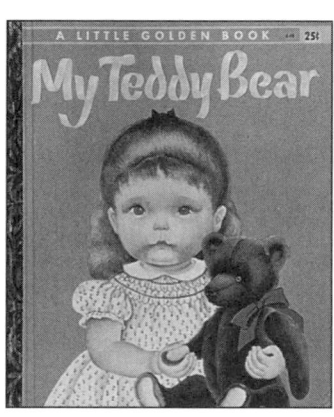

448
My Teddy Bear
Illus.: Wilkin, Eloise
Author: Scarry, Patricia
1953 (1961) 24 Pages
"I" Edition   **$20.00**

449
Yanky Doodle And Chopper
Illus.: White, Al
Author: Cherr, Pat
1962   24 Pages
"A" Edition   **$20.00**

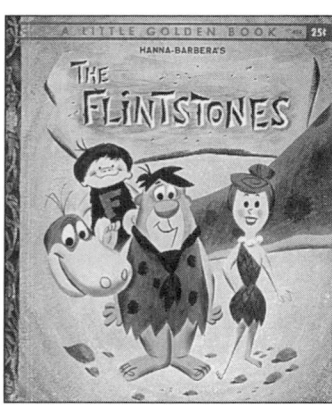

450
Flintstones, The
Illus.: Crawford, Mel
Author: Crawford, Mel
1961   24 Pages
"A" Edition   **$20.00**

451
Ten Little Animals
Illus.: Rojankovsky, Feodor
Author: Memling, Carl
1961   24 Pages
"A" Edition   **$6.00**

452
Busy Timmy
Illus.: Wilkin, Eloise
Author: Jackson, Kathryn & Byron
1948 (1961) 24 Pages
"G" Edition   **$13.00**

453
Top Cat
Illus.: Pratt, Hawley
Author: Memling, Carl
1962   24 Pages
"A" Edition   **$20.00**

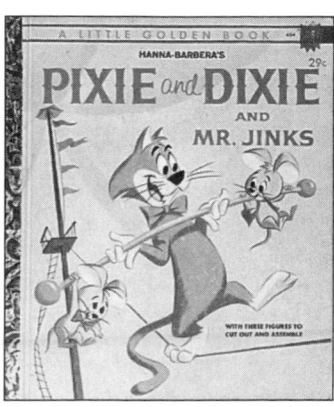

454
Pixi And Dixi And Mr. Jinks
Illus.: Mattinson, Sylvia & Burne
Author: Buettner, Carl
1961   24 Pages
"A" Edition   **$35.00**
W/out cut-out   **$12.00**

455

Machines
Illus.: Dugan, William J.
1961   24 Pages
"A" Edition   **$6.00**

456

Golden Egg Book, The
Illus.: Obligado, Lillian
Author: Brown, Margaret Wise
1962   24 Pages
"A" Edition   **$7.00**

456

Red cover background
(1963)   24 Pages
"B" Edition   **$5.00**

457

Littlest Raccoon, The
Illus.: Humbert, Claude
Author: Parish, Peggy
1961   24 Pages
"A" Edition   **$7.00**

458

Huckleberry Hound Safety Signs
Illus.: White, Al
Author: Mcgovern, Ann
1961   24 Pages
"A" Edition   **$18.00**

459

Horses
Illus.: Greene, Hamilton
Author: Perrin, Blanche Chenery
1962   24 Pages
"A" Edition   **$6.00**

460

My Little Golden Book Of Manners
Illus.: Scarry, Richard
Author: Parish, Peggy
1962   24 Pages
"A" Edition   **$6.00**

461

Pick Up Sticks
Illus.: Pfloog, Piet
Author: Wilkins, Pauline
1962   24 Pages
"A" Edition   **$10.00**

462

Bullwinkle
Illus.: Pratt, Hawley
Author: Corwyn, David
1962   24 Pages
"A" Edition   **$18.00**

463

Wait-For-Me-Kitten, The
Illus.: Obligado, Lillian
Author: Scarry, Patsy
1962   24 Pages
"A" Edition   **$8.00**

464

Baby Farm Animals
Illus.: Williams, Garth
Author: Williams, Garth
1962   24 Pages
"D" Edition   **$6.00**

465

My Little Golden Animal Book
Illus.: Kennel, Moritz
Author: Macpherson, Elizabeth
1962   24 Pages
"A" Edition   **$7.00**

466

Baby Dear
Illus.: Wilkin, Eloise
Author: Wilkin, Esther
1962   24 Pages
"A" Edition   **$18.00**

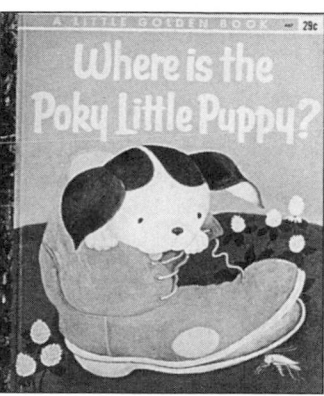

467

Where Is The Poky Little Puppy
Illus.: Tenggren, Gustaf
Author: Lowrey, Janet Sebring
1962   24 Pages
"A" Edition   **$8.00**

468

We Help Daddy
Illus.: Wilkin, Eloise
Author: Stein, Mini
1962   24 Pages
"A" Edition   **$12.00**

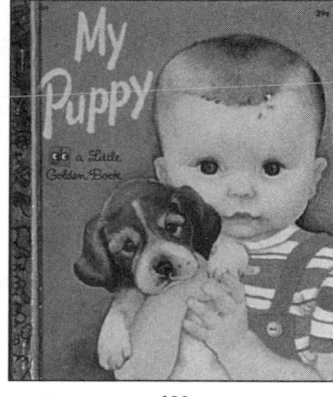

469

My Puppy
Illus.: Wilkin, Eloise
Author: Scarry, Patsy
1955 (1962) 24 Pages
"D" Edition   **$10.00**

470

Heidi
Illus.: Malvern, Corinne
Author: Spyri, Johanna
1954 (1962) 24 Pages
"G" Edition   **$6.00**

471

Tommy's Camping Adventure
Illus.: Crawford, Mel
Author: Saxon, Gladys
1962   24 Pages
"A" Edition   **$10.00**

472

Little Golden Mother Goose, The
Illus.: Rojankovsky, Feodor
1957 (1962) 24 Pages
"F" Edition   **$6.00**

473

Nurse Nancy
Illus.: Malvern, Corinne
Author: Jackson, Kathryn
1958 (1962) 24 Pages
"D" Edition   **$125.00**
W/out Band-Aids   **$40.00**

474

Touché Turtle
Illus.: White, Al; Mc Gary, Norm;
Lorencz
Author: Memling, Carl
1962   24 Pages
"A" Edition   **$20.00**

475

Bugs Bunny
Illus.: Warner Bros.
Author: Warner Bros.
1949 (1962) 24 Pages
"K" Edition   **$6.00**

476

Little Lulu
Illus.: Kimbrell, Woody; White, Al
Author: Weiner, Gina Ingoglia
1962   24 Pages
"A" Edition   **$15.00**

477

Ruff And Reddy
Illus.: Eisenburg, Harvey; White, Al
Author: Mcgovern, Ann
1959 (1962) 24 Pages
"C" Edition   **$10.00**

478

Christmas ABC, The
Illus.: Wilkin, Eloise
Author: Johnson, Florence
1962   24 Pages
"A" Edition $25.00

479

Rusty Goes To School
Illus.: Probst, Pierre
Author: Weingarden, Ann
1962   24 Pages
"A" Edition $15.00

480

Tommy Visits The Doctor
Illus.: Scarry, Richard
Author: Seligmann, Joan
1969   24 Pages
"A" Edition $6.00

481

Smokey The Bear
Illus.: Scarry, Richard
Author: Werner, Jane
1955 (1962) 24 Pages
"F" Edition $11.00

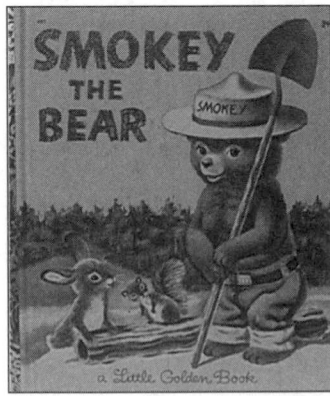

481

Yellow cover background
(1963)   24 Pages
"G" Edition $9.00

482

Big Little Book, The
Illus.: Kennel, Moritz
Author: Smith, Hall
1962   24 Pages
"A" Edition $7.00

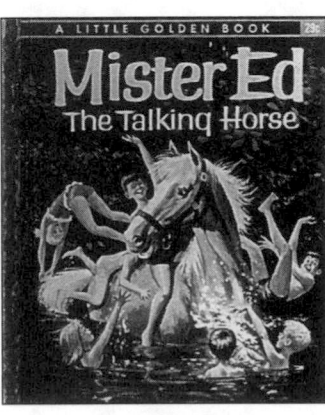

483

Mister Ed The Talking Horse
Illus.: Crawford, Mel
Author: Hazen, Barbara Shook
1962   24 Pages
"A" Edition $20.00

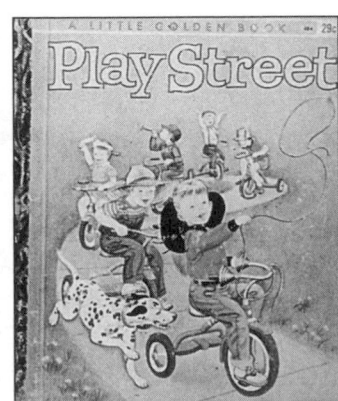

484

Play Street
Illus.: Esley, Joan
Author: Wilkin, Esther
1962   24 Pages
"A" Edition $17.00

485

Bozo Finds A Friend
Illus.: Pratt, Hawley
Author: Golberg, Tom
1962   24 Pages
"A" Edition $10.00

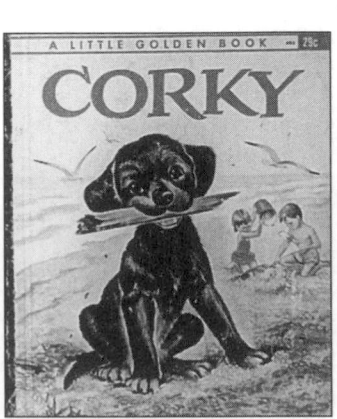

486

Corky
Illus.: Wilde, Irma
Author: Scarry, Patricia
1962   24 Pages
"A" Edition $12.00

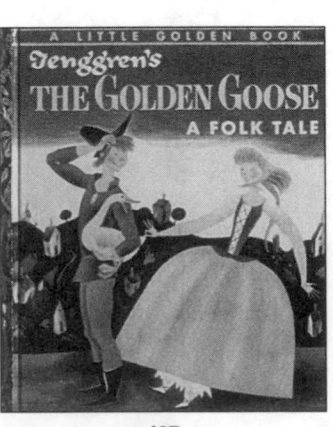

487

Golden Goose, The
Illus.: Tenggren, Gustaf
Author: Bros. Grimm
1954 (1962) 24 Pages
"B" Edition $6.00

488

Gay Purr-ee
Illus.: Pratt, Hawley
Author: Memling, Carl
1962   24 Pages
"A" Edition $22.00

489
Aren't You Glad
Illus.: Kurtz, Eliane
Author: Zolotow, Charlotte
1962   24 Pages
"A" Edition $6.00

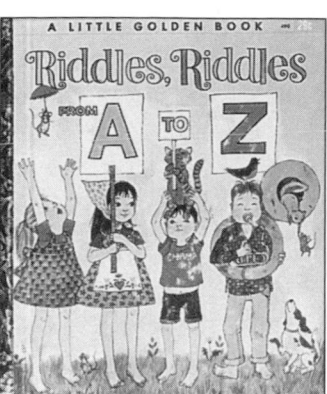

490
Riddles, Riddles From A To Z
Illus.: Schart, Trina
Author: Memling, Carl
1962   24 Pages
"A" Edition $6.00

491
Hansel And Gretel
Illus.: Wilkin, Eloise
Author: Bros. Grimm
1954 (1962) 24 Pages
"J" Edition $4.00

492
Supercar
Illus.: Crawford, Mel
Author: Sherman, George
1962   24 Pages
"A" Edition $25.00

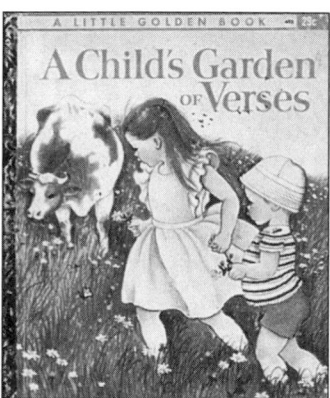

493
Child's Garden Of Verses, A
Illus.: Wilkin, Eloise
Author: Stevenson, Robert Louis
1957 (1962) 24 Pages
"B" Edition $15.00

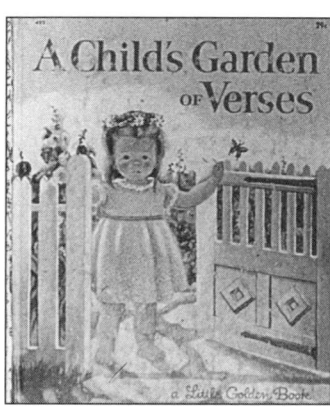

493
Child's Garden Of Verses, A
(2nd Cover)
Illus.: Wilkin, Eloise
Author: Stevenson, Robert Louis
1957 (1969) 24 Pages
"E" Edition $7.00

494
Shy Little Kitten, The
Illus.: Tenggren, Gustaf
Author: Schurr, Kathleen
1946 (1962) 24 Pages
"C" Edition $7.00

494
Shy Little Kitten, The
(2nd Cover)
Illus.: Tenggren, Gustaf
Author: Schurr, Kathleen
1946 (1972) 24 Pages
6th Edition $5.00

495
I Have A Secret
Illus.: Giordano, Joseph
Author: Memling, Carl
1962   24 Pages
"A" Edition $8.00

496
Colors Are Nice
Illus.: Shortall, Leonard
Author: Holl, Adelaide
1962   24 Pages
"A" Edition $6.00

497
Dick Tracy
Illus.: Pratt, Hawley
Author: Memling, Carl
1962   24 Pages
"A" Edition $22.00

498
**Rumpelstiltskin And The Princess
And The Pea**
Illus.: Dugan, William J.
Author: Bros. Grimm; Anderson, H.C.
1962   24 Pages
"A" Edition $8.00

499

Wild Animals
Illus.: Rojankovsky, Feodor
Author: No Author
1962   24 Pages
"B" Edition   **$5.00**

500

Jetsons, The
Illus.: Pratt, Hawley
Author: Memling, Carl
1962   24 Pages
"A" Edition   **$25.00**

500

Buck Rogers And The Children Of Hopetown
(Unstated 1st)
Illus.: Schaffenberger, Kurt
Author: Dwight, Revena
1971   24 Pages
1st Edition   **$5.00**

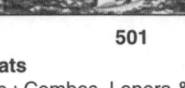

501

Boats
Illus.: Combes, Lenora & Herber
Author: Lachman, Ruth Mabee
1951 (1962) 24 Pages
"E" Edition   **$5.00**

501

Black Hole, The
(Unstated 1st)
Illus.: Walt Disney Studios
Author: Walt Disney Studios
1979   24 Pages
1st Edition   **$5.00**

502

Wally Gator
Illus.: Pratt, Hawley; Lorencz, Bill
Author: Goldberg, Tom
1963   24 Pages
"A" Edition   **$18.00**

503

Corky's Hiccups
Illus.: O'sullivan, Tom
Author: Stack, Nicolete Meredith
1973   24 Pages
"A" Edition   **$6.00**

504

Seven Little Postmen
Illus.: Gergely, Tibor
Author: Brown, Margaret Wise
1952 (1962) 24 Pages
"C" Edition   **$6.00**

505

Peter Rabbit
Illus.: Saviozzi, Adriana Mazza
Author: Potter, Beatrix
1958 (1962) 24 Pages
"B" Edition   **$7.00**

505

Yellow cover background
(1963)   24 Pages
"C" Edition   **$6.00**

505

Peter Rabbit
(2nd Cover)
Illus.: Saviozzi, Adriana Mazza
Author: Potter, Beatrix
1958 (1968) 24 Pages
"E" Edition   **$5.00**

505

Peter Rabbit
(3rd Cover)
Illus.: Saviozzi, Adriana Mazza
Author: Potter, Beatrix
1958 (1970) 24 Pages
"F" Edition   **$6.00**

506
Poky Little Puppy, The
Illus.: Tenggren, Gustaf
Author: Lowrey, Janet Sebring
1942 (1963) 24 Pages
"C" Edition $5.00

507
Who Needs A Cat?
Illus.: Johnson, Audean
Author: Cassidy, Clara
1963   24 Pages
"A" Edition $7.00

508
Lippy The Lion And Hardy Har Har
Illus.: Pratt, Hawley
Author: Weiner, Gina Ingoglia
1963   24 Pages
"A" Edition $18.00

509
What Am I?
Illus.: De Witt, Cornelius
Author: Ruth, Leon
1949 (1963) 24 Pages
"G" Edition $6.00

510
Large And Growly Bear, The
Illus.: Crawford, Mel
Author: Hazen, Barbara Shook
1961   24 Pages
"A" Edition $8.00

511
Visit To The Children's Zoo, A
Illus.: Crawford, Mel
Author: Hazen, Barbara Shook
1963   24 Pages
"A" Edition $7.00

511
Yellow cover background with green
lettering
(1968)   24 Pages
"D" Edition $5.00

511
Yellow cover background with red
lettering
(1972)   24 Pages
7th Edition $5.00

512
Chipmunk's ABC
Illus.: Scarry, Richard
Author: Miller, Roberta
1963   24 Pages
"A" Edition $7.00

512
Yellow Spine
(1965)   24 Pages
"B" Edition $6.00

512
"Richard Scarry's" added to cover
(1972)   24 Pages
5th Edition $4.00

513
My Baby Sister
(Never printed)

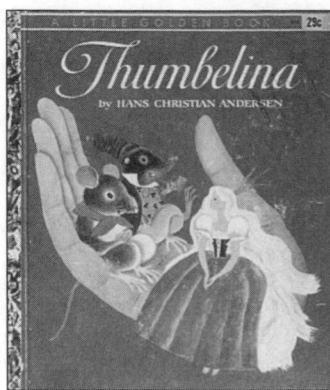

514

Thumbelina
Illus.: Tenggren, Gustaf
Author: Anderson, Hans Christian
1953 (1963) 24 Pages
"B" Edition   **$6.00**

515

Neatos And The Litterbugs, The
Illus.: Bracke, Charles
Author: Smaridge, Norah
1973   24 Pages
"A" Edition   **$6.00**

516

Cow Went Over The Mountain, The
Illus.: Rojankovsky, Feodor
Author: Krinsley, Jeanette
1963   24 Pages
"A" Edition   **$6.00**

517

Baby Animals
Illus.: Williams, Garth
Author: Williams, Garth
1957 (1963) 24 Pages
"H" Edition   **$6.00**

518

Lassie And Her Day In The Sun
Illus.: Crawford, Mel
Author: Verral, Charles Spain
1958 (1963) 24 Pages
"D" Edition   **$6.00**

519

Little Red Hen, The
Cover by Rudolf Freund
Illus.: Miller, J.P.
Author: Folk Tale
1954 (1963) 24 Pages
"H" Edition   **$7.00**

519

Little Red Hen, The
(2nd Cover)
Illus.: Miller, J.P.
Author: Folk Tale
1954 (1978) 24 Pages
17th Edition   **$7.00**

520

**Happy Man And His Dump Truck,
The**
Illus.: Gergely, Tibor
Author: Miryam
1950 (1963) 24 Pages
"D" Edition   **$7.00**

521

Fun For Hunkydory
Illus.: D'avegnon, Sue
Author: Justus, May
1963   24 Pages
"A" Edition   **$7.00**

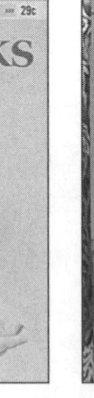

522

Jamie Looks
Illus.: Wilkin, Eloise
Author: Holl, Adelaide
1963   24 Pages
"A" Edition   **$18.00**

523

**Bow Wow! Meow!, A First Book Of
Sounds**
Illus.: Shart, Trina
Author: Bellah, Melanie
1963   24 Pages
"A" Edition   **$6.00**

523

Title lettering changed
(1968)   24 Pages
"C" Edition   **$4.00**

524

Chicken Little
Illus.: Goldsborough, June
Author: Nathan, Stella Williams
1973   24 Pages
"A" Edition $4.00

525

My Word Book
Illus.: Humbert, Claude
Author: Miller, Roberta
1963   24 Pages
"A" Edition $6.00

526

Twelve Days Of Christmas, The
Illus.: De Luna, Tony
1963   24 Pages
"A" Edition $8.00

527

Romper Room Exercise Book, The
Illus.: Leone, Sergio
Author: Claster, Nancy
1964   24 Pages
"A" Edition $8.00

528

My Kitten
Illus.: Wilkin, Eloise
Author: Scarry, Patsy
1953 (1963) 24 Pages
"D" Edition $10.00

529

Nursery Rhymes
Illus.: Malvern, Corinne
1947 (1963) 24 Pages
"A" Edition $6.00

530

Four Little Kittens
Illus.: Saviozzi, Adriana Mazza
Author: Daly, Kathleen N.
1957 (1963) 24 Pages
"D" Edition $6.00

531

Pebbles Flintstone
Illus.: Crawford, Mel
Author: Lewis, Jean
1963   24 Pages
"A" Edition $20.00

532

Dogs
Illus.: Gergely, Tibor
Author: Jones, Nita
1952 (1963) 24 Pages
"F" Edition $6.00

533

Animal Dictionary
Illus.: Rojankovsky, Feodor
Author: Watson, Jane Werner
1960 (1963) 24 Pages
"B" Edition $6.00

534

First Golden Geography, The
Illus.: Sayeles, William
Author: Watson, Jane Werner
1955 (1963) 24 Pages
"B" Edition $6.00

536

Little Boy And The Giant, The
Illus.: Rofry
Author: Harrison, David L.
1973   24 Pages
"A" Edition $6.00

537

Beany Goes To Sea
Illus.: Pratt, Hawley; Lorencz, Bill
Author: Hill, Monica
1963   24 Pages
"A" Edition   **$22.00**

538

Bedtime Stories
Illus.: Tenggren, Gustaf
1942 (1963) 24 Pages
"H" Edition   **$5.00**

538

Bedtime Stories
(2nd Cover)
Illus.: Tenggren, Gustaf
1942 (1965) 24 Pages
"J" Edition   **$5.00**

539

Cave Kids
Illus.: Crawford, Mel
Author: Carrick, Bruce R.
1963   24 Pages
"A" Edition   **$25.00**

540

Bamm-Bamm
Illus.: Pratt, Hawley
Author: Lewis, Jean
1963   24 Pages
"A" Edition   **$22.00**

541

New Baby, The
Illus.: Wilkin, Eloise
Author: Shane, Ruth & Harold
1948 (1963) 24 Pages
"O" Edition   **$8.00**

542

Hey There-It's Yogi Bear
Illus.: Pratt, Hawley
Author: Memling, Carl
1964   24 Pages
"A" Edition   **$18.00**

543

ABC Rhymes
Illus.: Rodegast, Roland; Clarke
Author: Memling, Carl
1964   24 Pages
"A" Edition   **$6.00**

543

ABC Rhymes
(2nd Cover)
Illus.: Rodegast, Roland; Clarke
Author: Memling, Carl
1964 (1972) 24 Pages
6th Edition   **$5.00**

544

Three Little Pigs, The
Illus.: R.O. Fry
Author: Ross, Elizabeth
1973   24 Pages
"A" Edition   **$5.00**

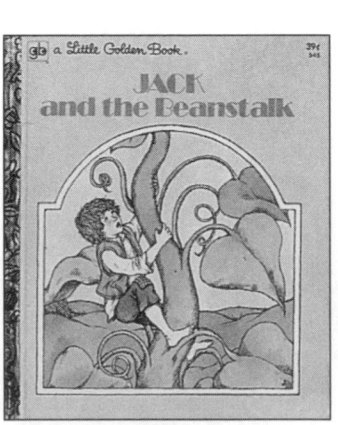

545

Jack And The Beanstalk
Illus.: Leder, Dora
Author: Nathan, Stella Williams
1973   24 Pages
"A" Edition   **$5.00**

546

Fireball XL5
Illus.: Pratt, Hawley
Author: Hazen, Barbara Shook
1964   24 Pages
"A" Edition   **$27.00**

547

Magilla Gorilla
Illus.: Pratt, Hawley
Author: Carrick, Bruce R.
1964   24 Pages
"A" Edition   **$18.00**

548

Little Engine That Could, The
Illus.: Hauman, George & Doris
Author: Piper, Wally
1954 (1964) 24 Pages
"A" Edition   **$10.00**

549

Tarzan
Illus.: Crawford, Mel
Author: Weiner, Gina Ingoglia
1964   24 Pages
"A" Edition   **$20.00**

550

Good Humor Man, The
Illus.: Gergely, Tibor
Author: Daly, Kathleen N.
1964   24 Pages
"A" Edition   **$75.00**

551

Lively Little Rabbit, The
Illus.: Tenggren, Gustaf
Author: Ariane
1943 (1964) 24 Pages
"P" Edition   **$6.00**

552

We Like Kindergarten
Illus.: Wilkin, Eloise
Author: Cassidy, Clara
1965   24 Pages
"A" Edition   **$6.00**

553

Jingle Bells
Illus.: Miller, J.P.
Author: Daly, Kathleen N.
1964   24 Pages
"A" Edition   **$7.00**

553

Jingle Bells
(2nd Cover)
Illus.: Miller, J.P.
Author: Daly, Kathleen N.
1964(1971) 24 Pages
"B" Edition   **$6.00**

554

Charmin' Chatty
Illus.: Wilson, Dagmar
Author: Hazen, Barbara Shook
1964   24 Pages
"A" Edition   **$20.00**

555

Pepper Plays Nurse
Illus.: Fernie, John
Author: Weiner, Gina Ingoglia
1964   24 Pages
"A" Edition   **$18.00**

556

Peter Potamus
Illus.: Pratt, Hawley
Author: Memling, Carl
1964   24 Pages
"A" Edition   **$18.00**

557

Fuzzy Duckling, The
Illus.: Provensen, Alice & Martin
Author: Werner, Jane
1949 (1964) 24 Pages
"F" Edition   **$6.00**

559
Missing dolls and clothes
24 Pages $6.00

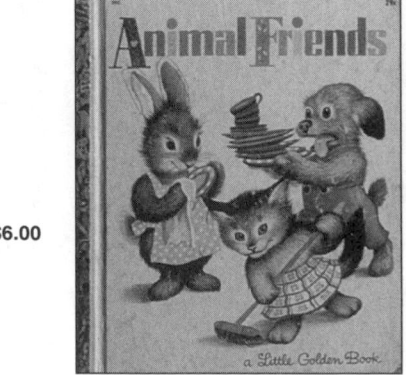

558
Hop, Little Kangaroo!
Illus.: Rojankovsky, Feodor
Author: Scarry, Patricia
1965   24 Pages
"A" Edition $6.00

559
Betsy McCall
Illus.: Hofmann, Ginnie
Author: Robinson, Selma
1965   24 Pages
"A" Edition $75.00

560
Animal Friends
Edition letter my not be visible
Last title listed is D115
Illus.: Williams, Garth
Author: Werner, Jane
1953 (1965) 24 Pages
"B" Edition $5.00

561
Tom And Jerry
Illus.: Eisenberg, Harvey; Maclaughlin, Don
Author: MGM
1951 (1965) 24 Pages
"E" Edition $6.00

562
Good Little Bad Little Girl
Illus.: Wilkin, Eloise
Author: Wilkin, Esther
1965   24 Pages
"A" Edition $35.00

563
Mr. Puffer Bill Train Engineer
Illus.: Gergely, Tibor
Author: Arland, Leonard
1965   24 Pages
"A" Edition $6.00

564
New Brother, New Sister
Illus.: Esley, Joan
Author: Fiedler, Jean
1966   24 Pages
"A" Edition $16.00

565
Dragon In A Wagon, A
Illus.: Gilbert, John Martin
Author: Rainwater, Jeanette
1966   24 Pages
"A" Edition $5.00

566
Cars
Illus.: Totten, Bob
Author: Dugan, William
1973   24 Pages
"A" Edition $4.00

567
Play With Me
Illus.: Wilkin, Eloise
Author: Wilkin, Esther
1967   24 Pages
"A" Edition $15.00

568
Where Is The Bear?
Illus.: Crawford, Mel
Author: Hubka, Betty
1967   24 Pages
"A" Edition $6.00

568

Where Is The Bear
(2nd Cover)
Illus.: Crawford, Mel
Author: Hubka, Betty
1967 (1978) 24 Pages
3rd Edition   **$6.00**

569

Little Mommy
Illus.: Kane, Sharon
Author: Kane, Sharon
1967   24 Pages
"A" Edition   **$75.00**

570

Things In My House
Illus.: Kaufman, Joe
Author: Kaufman, Joe
1968   24 Pages
"A" Edition   **$5.00**

571

My Little Dinosaur
Illus.: Vogel, Ilse-Margaret
Author: Vogel, Ilse-Margaret
1971   24 Pages
"A" Edition   **$6.00**

572

Lassie And The Big Clean-up Day
Illus.: Schaar, Bob
Author: Graham, Kennon
1971   24 Pages
"A" Edition   **$6.00**

573

Animals On The Farm
Illus.: Pfloog, Jan
Author: Pfloog, Jan
1968   24 Pages
"A" Edition   **$4.00**

574

So Big
"A" has Red Spine
Illus.: Wilkin, Eloise
Author: Wilkin, Eloise
1968   24 Pages
"A" Edition   **$14.00**

575

Who Comes To Your House
Illus.: O'sullivan, Tom
Author: Hillert, Margaret
1973   24 Pages
"A" Edition   **$5.00**

576

Animal Daddies And My Daddy
Illus.: Vogel, Ilse-Margaret
Author: Hazen, Barbara Shook
1968   24 Pages
"A" Edition   **$5.00**

577

Hush, Hush, It's Sleepytime
Illus.: Crawford, Mel
Author: Parish, Peggy
1968   24 Pages
"A" Edition   **$6.00**

578

When I Grow Up
Illus.: Vogel, Ilse-Margaret
Author: Vogel, Ilse-Margaret
1968   24 Pages
"A" Edition   **$5.00**

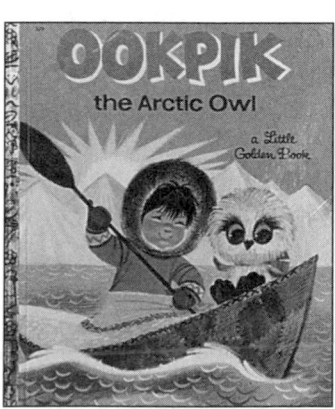

579

Ookpik The Arctic Owl
Illus.: Edwards, Beverly
Author: Hazen, Barbara Shook
1968   24 Pages
"A" Edition   **$20.00**

580

Sam The Firehouse Cat
(Unstated 1st)
Illus.: Parsons, Virginia
Author: Parsons, Virginia
1968   24 Pages
1st Edition $7.00

581

ChittyChitty BangBang
(Unstated 1st)
Illus.: Laite, Gordon
Author: Lewis, Jean
1968   24 Pages
1st Edition $10.00

582

Wonderful School, The
(Unstated 1st)
Illus.: Hoffman, Hilde
Author: Justus, May
1969   24 Pages
1st Edition $8.00

583

Little Book, The
(Unstated 1st)
Illus.: Wilkin, Eloise
Author: Horvath, Sherl
1969   24 Pages
1st Edition $10.00

584

Animal Counting Book
(Unstated 1st)
Illus.: Kennel, Moritz
Author: Old Nursery Poem
1969   24 Pages
1st Edition $5.00

585

Raggedy Ann And Fido
(Unstated 1st)
Illus.: Boonshaft, Rochelle
Author: Hazen, Barbara Shook
1969   24 Pages
1st Edition $6.00

586

Rags
Illus.: Miller, J.P.
Author: Scarry, Patsy
1970   24 Pages
"A" Edition $7.00

587

Charlie
Illus.: Obligado, Lillian
Author: Downs, Diane Fox
1970   24 Pages
"A" Edition $7.00

588

Boy With A Drum, The
Illus.: Wilkin, Eloise
Author: Harrison, David L.
1969   24 Pages
"A" Edition $15.00

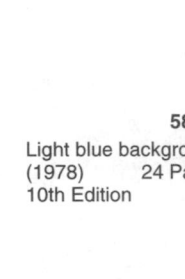

589

Light blue background
(1978)   24 Pages
10th Edition $3.00

589

Eloise Wilkin's Mother Goose
(Unstated 1st)
Light green background
Illus.: Wilkin, Eloise
Author: Wilkin, Eloise
1961 (1970) 24 Pages
1st Edition $5.00

590

Tiny, Tawny Kitten, The
Illus.: Pfloog, Jan
Author: Hazen, Barbara Shook
1969   24 Pages
"A" Edition $6.00

591
Old Mother Hubbard
(Unstated 1st)
Illus.: Battaglia, Aurelius
Author: Battaglia, Aurelius
1970   24 Pages
1st Edition   **$5.00**

592
Friendly Book, The
Illus.: Williams, Garth
Author: Brown, Margaret Wise
1954 (1969) 24 Pages
"B" Edition   **$5.00**

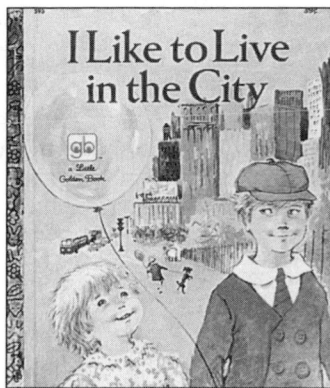

593
I Like To Live In The City
(Unstated 1st)
Illus.: Obligado, Lillian
Author: Hillart, Margaret
1970   24 Pages
1st Edition   **$7.00**

594
1, 2, 3, Juggle With Me!
(Unstated 1st)
Illus.: Vogel, Ilse-Margaret
Author: Vogel, Ilse-Margaret
1970   24 Pages
1st Edition   **$6.00**

595
Christmas Carols
Illus.: Malvern, Corinne
Author: Wyckoff, Marjorie
1946 (1968) 24 Pages
"Q" Edition   **$5.00**

595
Christmas Carols
(2nd Cover)
Illus.: Malvern, Corinne
Author: Wyckoff, Marjorie
1946 (1972) 24 Pages
18th Edition   **$4.00**

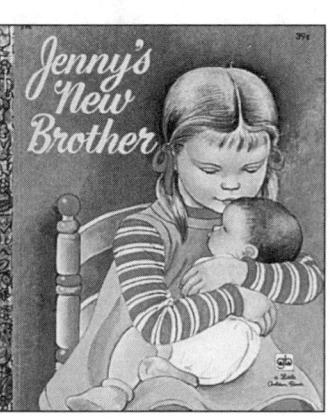

596
Jenny's New Brother
Illus.: Esley, Joan
Author: Evans, Elaine
1970   24 Pages
"A" Edition   **$17.00**

597
Fly High
(Unstated 1st)
Illus.: Parsons, Virginia
Author: Parsons, Virginia
1971   24 Pages
1st Edition   **$7.00**

598
**Bozo And The Hide 'n' Seek
Elephant**
Illus.: Hubbard, Allen; Jancar, M
Author: Johnson, William
1968   24 Pages
"A" Edition   **$8.00**

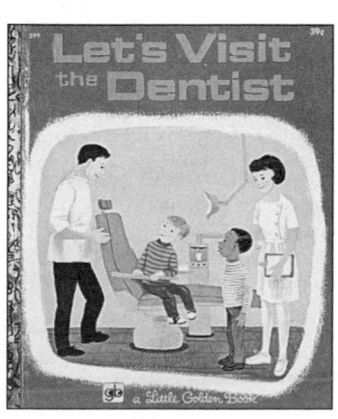

599
Let's Visit The Dentist
Illus.: Wilson, Dagmar
Author: Scarry, Patricia M.
1970   24 Pages
"A" Edition   **$6.00**

600
Susan In The Driver's Seat
(Unstated 1st)
Illus.: Ilke, Jane
Author: Gibeault, Kathi
1973   24 Pages
1st Edition   **$15.00**

Little Golden Books—New Numbering

Please note: Because the books in this section were not produced numerically, I have chosen to list them alphabetically. Under each title I have listed the numbers I'm aware of that have the same cover design. It is possible that you may have a title with a number not listed; if this is the case, match by cover design. If you find that I've omitted a number, please let me know so I can add it to a future guide. I have not shown covers that have only a logo change. The values in this section are for hard-cover versions only; some of the titles were produced in a soft-cover version.

201-2
123 Juggle With Me!
Illus.: Vogel, Ilse-Margaret
Author: Vogel, Ilse-Margaret
1981 $3.00

201-32
                                 $2.00

200-5
ABC Around The House
Illus.: Irvin, Fred
Author: Holaves, Sharon
1980
2nd Edition $4.00

454-1
ABC Is For Christmas
Illus.: Augistiny, Sally
Author: Watson, Jane Werner
1974 (1980)
6th Edition $2.00

454-31
                                 $2.00

454-32
(1988) $2.00

454-41
                                 $2.00

200-3
ABC Rhymes
Illus.:Rodegast, Roland; Clarke
Author: Memling, Carl
1970 $3.00

200-33
                                 $3.00

111-72
**Adventures Of Buster Hood, The
(Tiny Toon Adventures)**
Illus.: Costanza, John
Author: Korman, Justine
1991
"A" Edition $4.00

201-10
Adventures Of Goat, The
Illus.: Hammond, Lucille
Author: Eugenie
1984 (1986)
                                 $3.00

201-46
"A" Edition $5.00

200-67
All My Chickens
Illus.: Kraus, Robert
Author: Kraus, Robert
1993
"A" Edition $5.00

107-73
Alvin's Daydreams
Illus.: Prebenna, David
Author: Teitelbaum, Michael
1990
"A" Edition $5.00
107-82
(1991) $3.00

204-56
Amanda's First Day Of School
Illus.: Goodman, Joan Elizabeth
Author: Goodman, Joan Elizabeth
1985
"A" Edition   **$4.00**
204-63
(1991)   **$4.00**

108-5
Amazing Mumford Forgets The Magic Words!, The
Illus.: Chartier, Normand
Author: Thackray, Patricia
1979   **$2.00**
108-45
     $2.00

98805-00
Anastasia
Illus.: Yee, Josie
Author: James, Kari
1997
"A" Edition   **$2.00**

208-33
Animal Daddies And My Daddy
Illus.: Vogel, Ilse-Margaret
Author: Hazen, Barbara Shook
1968   **$3.00**
208-43
     $3.00
208-53
     $3.00

205-1
Animal Dictionary
Illus.: Rojankovsky, Feodor
Author: Watson, Jane Werner
1960 (1980)   **$3.00**
205-31
(1982)   **$3.00**

308-44
Animal Quiz Book
Illus.: Kunhardt, Edith T.
Author: Oechsi, Kelly
1983   **$2.00**
308-54
"F" Edition   **$2.00**
309-50
"G" Edition   **$2.00**

309-50
Animal Quiz Book
Blue Cover Background
Illus.: Kunhardt, Edith T.
Author: Oechsi, Kelly
1983   **$2.00**

202-65
Animals' ABC
Illus.: Williams, Garth
1957 (1993)   **$2.00**

456-1
Animals' Christmas Eve, The
Illus: Robison, Jim
Author: Wiersum, Gale
1977   **$2.00**

456-09
(1979)
3rd Edition   **$2.00**
456-13
(1991)   **$2.00**
456-41
     $2.00

200-42
Animals Of Farmer Jones, The
Illus.: Scarry, Richard
Author: Gale, Leah
1970   **$4.00**

200-52
     $4.00
200-87
     $4.00
200-92
     $4.00
303-23
     $4.00

203-3 $2.00

203-33 $2.00

205-55 $2.00

205-92

(1990) $2.00

200-41

Animals On The Farm
Illus.: Pfloog, Jan
Author: Pfloog, Jan
1968   **$2.00**

98842

Annabelle's Wish
Illus.: Allan Nowell & Associates
Author: Korman, Susan
1997
"A" Edition   **$2.00**

98769-01

Another Monster At The End Of This Book
Illus.: Smollin, Michael
Author: Stone, Jon
1996   **$3.00**

305-66

Arthur's Good Manners
Illus.: Mc Cue Karston, Lisa
Author: Calmenson, Stephanie
1987 (1991)   **$3.00**

305-58

Arthur's Good Manners
Illus.: Mc Cue Karston, Lisa
Author: Calmenson, Stephanie
1987 (1990)
"A" Edition   **$5.00**

204-2

Baby Animals
Illus.: Williams, Garth
Author: Williams, Garth
1952   **$2.00**

304-57   **$2.00**

304-57

Baby Animals
Orange title lettering
Illus.: Williams, Garth
Author: Williams, Garth
1952
"O" Edition   **$2.00**

304-64

Baby Brown Bear's Big Bellyache
Illus.: Nez, John
Author: Coco, Eugene Bradley
1989
"A" Edition   **$5.00**

306-42

Baby Dear
Illus.: Wilkin, Eloise
Author: Wilkin, Esther
1962   **$5.00**

306-52

(1986) $5.00

306-67

(1991) $5.00

309-34 $5.00

203-2

Baby Farm Animals
Illus.: Williams, Garth
Author: Williams, Garth
1958   **$2.00**

203-32   **$2.00**

309-46   **$2.00**

200-56
Baby Farm Animals
Pink Title Lettering
Illus.: Williams, Garth
Author: Williams, Garth
1958 (1988)   **$3.00**

200-66
Baby Farm Animals
Illus.: Williams, Garth
Author: Williams, Garth
1958 (1992)
"R" Edition   **$3.00**

111-89
Baby Fonzie Visits The Doctor
Illus.: Brannon, Tom
Author: Weiss, Ellen
1995
"A" Edition   **$3.00**

306-55
Baby Sister
Illus.: Friedman, Joy
Author: Sachs, Dorothea M.
1986
"A" Edition   **$5.00**

460-08
Baby's Christmas
Illus.: Wilkin, Eloise
Author: Wilkin, Esther
1959 (1988)
"B" Edition   **$4.00**
460-12
(1991)   **$3.00**

98785-01
Baby's Christmas
Illus.: Lanza, Barbara
Author: Muldrow, Diane
1996
"A" Edition   **$2.00**

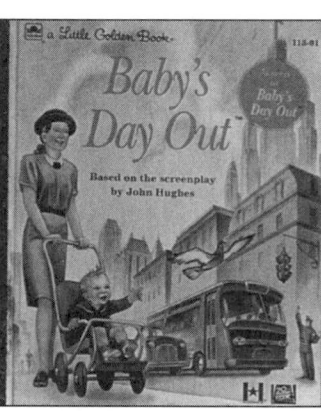

113-01
Baby's Day Out
Illus.: Hughes, John
1994
"A" Edition   **$5.00**

107-96
Barbie And The Scavenger Hunt
Illus.: S. I. Artists
Author: Packard, Mary
1996
"A" Edition   **$4.00**

107-70
Barbie A Picinic Surprise
Illus.: Ellis, Art & Kim
Author: Mc Guire, Leslie
1990
"A" Edition   **$5.00**
107-80
(1991)   **$2.00**

96000-00
Barbie Holiday Helpers
Author: Muldrow, Diane
1998
"A" Edition   **$2.00**

98862-00
Barbie In The Spotlight
Author: Morreale, Marie
1998
"A" Edition   **$2.00**

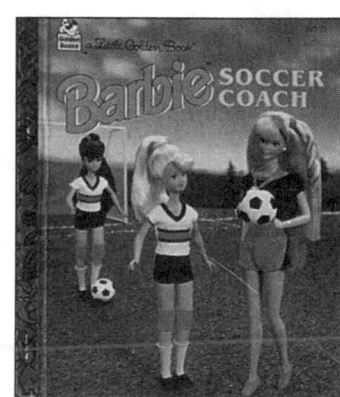

107-71
Barbie Soccor Coach
Illus.: Ruiz, Art; Stevenson, Nancy
Author: Slate, Barbara
1995
"A" Edition   **$3.00**

107-86

Barbie The Big Splash
Illus.: Tierney, Tom
Author: Slate, Barbara
1992
"A" Edition   **$4.00**

107-94

(1993)   **$3.00**

98864-00

Barbie The Jewel Thief
Illus.: Bazaldua, Barbara
Author: Bazaldua, Barbara
1998
"A" Edition   **$3.00**

98808-00

Barbie The Special Sleepover
Illus.: S. I. Artists
Author: Hughes, Francine
1997
"A" Edition   **$2.00**

98815

Barney The Best Christmas Eve!
Illus.: Baker, Darrell
Author: White, Stephen
1997
"A" Edition   **$2.00**

98807-00

Barney Catch That Hat!
Illus.: Langley, Bill A.
Author: Bernthal, Mark S.
1997
"A" Edition   **$2.00**

98790

Barney Sharing Is Caring
Illus.: Valentine, June
Author: Bernthal, Mark S.
1996
"A" Edition   **$3.00**

211-68

Batter Up!
Illus.: Friedman, Joy
Author: Gutelle, Andrew
1991
"A" Edition   **$5.00**

208-57

Beach Day
Illus.: Wilburn, Kathy
Author: Manushkin, Fran
1988
"A" Edition   **$4.00**

306-57

Bears' New Baby, The
Illus.: Goodman, Joan Elizabeth
Author: Goodman, Joan Elizabeth
1988
"A" Edition   **$5.00**

111-6

Benji Fastest Dog In The West
Illus.: Willis, Werner
Author: Ingoglia, Gina
1978 (1979)
2nd Edition   **$2.00**

111-36   **$2.00**

111-46   **$2.00**

109-23

Bert's Hall Of Great Inventions
Illus.: Bradfield, Roger
Author: Dwight, Revina
1972   **$2.00**

109-3   **$2.00**

208-68
Best Balloon Ride Ever!
Illus.: Scarry, Richard
Author: Scarry, Richard
1994
"A" Edition $3.00

209-46
Best Friends
Illus.: Di Salvoryan, Dyanne
Author: Kenworthy, Cathryn
1983
"A" Edition $5.00

312-01
Best Little Word Book Ever!
Illus.: Scarry, Richard
Author: Scarry, Richard
1992
"A" Edition $3.00
                312-13
(1993) $2.00

203-4
The Best Of All! A Story About The Farm
Illus.: Cauley, Lorinda Bryan
Author: Hogan, Cecily Rugh
1978 $3.00

211-69
Bettina The Ballerina
Illus.: Steadman, Barbara
Author: Nelson, Mary Alexander
1991
"A" Edition $60.00
Soft Cover Version $5.00

204-55
Bialosky's Special Picnic
Illus.: Joyner, Jerry
Author: Mcmguire, Leslie
1985
"A" Edition $5.00

409-1
Bible Stories From The Old Testament
Illus.: Robison, Jim
Author: Lee, Sing
1977 (1980)
3rd Edition $3.00
                409-2
(1980)   3rd Edition $3.00

404-1
Bible Stories Of Boys And Girls
Illus.: Dixon, Rachel Taft;Hartwell,Marjore
Author: Werner, Jane
1953 (1980)
20th Edition $1.00
                404-2
(1980)   20th Edition $1.00

108-57
Big Bird Brings Spring To Sesame Street
Illus.: Winborn, Marsha
Author: Swindler, Lauren
1985
"A" Edition $5.00
                108-63
(1991) $2.00

89914-01
Big Bird Meets Santa Claus
Illus.: Brannon, Tom
Author: Alexander, Liza
1997 $3.00

108-68
Big Bird Visits Navajo Country
Illus.: Swanson, Maggie
Author: Alexander, Liza
1992
"A" Edition $3.00

98865-00
Big Bird's Baby Book
Illus.: Brannon, Tom
Author: Muntean, Michaela
1998
"A" Edition $2.00

200-50
$2.00

109-58
(1990)
$2.00

109-65
(1991)
$2.00

109-68
(1993)
$2.00

107-61
Big Bird's Day On The Farm
Illus.: Swanson, Maggie
Author: Rosenbergturow, Cathi
1985 (1986)
"A" Edition $5.00

108-2
Big Bird's Red Book
Illus.: Smollin, Michael J.
Author: Cert, Rosanne & Jonathon
1977 $2.00

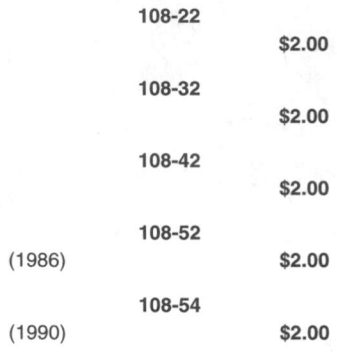

108-22
$2.00

108-32
$2.00

108-42
$2.00

108-52
(1986)
$2.00

108-54
(1990)
$2.00

108-55
Big Bird's Red Book
Blue Background
Illus.: Smollin, Michael J.
Author: Cert, Rosanne & Jonathon
1977 (1991) $3.00

98829-01
Big Bird's Ticklish Christmas
Illus.: Ewers, Joe
Author: Albee, Sarah
1997
"A" Edition $2.00

304-41
Big Brown Bear, The
Illus.: Tenggren, Gustaf
Author: Duplaix, Georges
1975 $5.00
304-51
$5.00

206-51
Big Elephant, The
Illus.: Rojankovsky, Feodor
Author: Jackson, Kathryn & Byron
1949 (1990)
"A" Edition $4.00

208-5
Big Enough Helper, The
Illus.: O'Sullivan, Tom
Author: Hall, Nancy
1978 $4.00
204-41
$4.00

459-8
Biggest, Most Beautiful Christmas Tree, The
Illus.: Rosenberg, Amye
Author: Rosenberg, Amye
1985
"A" Edition $3.00

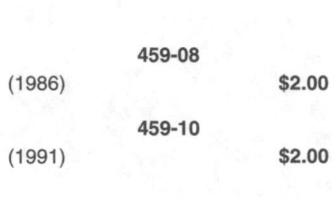

459-08
(1986)
$2.00

459-10
(1991)
$2.00

202-1
Birds
Illus.: Wilkin, Eloise
Author: Watson, Jane Werner
1958 (1979) $3.00

202-31

Birds

$3.00

309-55

$3.00

107-47

Bisketts In Double Trouble
Illus.: Kostanza, John
Author: Ingolia, Gina
1985 $3.00

111-49

"A" Edition $6.00

203-59

Blue Barry Bear Counts From 1 To 20
Illus.: Bollen, Roger
Author: Sadler, Marilyn
1991
"A" Edition $3.00

211-60

Blue Book Of Fairy Tales, The
Illus.: Laite, Gordon
1959 $4.00

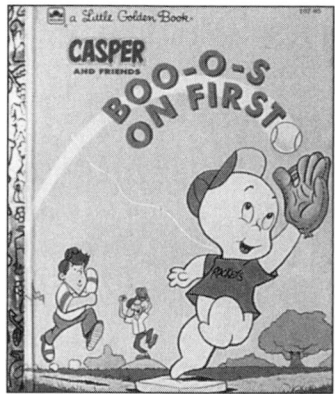

107-85

Boo-o-s On First (Casper And Friends)
Illus.: Wildman, George
Author: St. Pierre, Stephanie
1992 $3.00

207-33

Bow Wow! Meow! A First Book Of Sounds
Illus.: Shart, Trina
Author: Bellah, Melanie
1963 $2.00

211-41

Boy With A Drum, The
Illus.: Wilkin, Eloise
Author: Harrison, David L.
1969 $5.00

211-43

$5.00

211-53

$5.00

311-35

$5.00

311-5

$5.00

475-01

Bugs Bunny
Illus.: Warner Bros.
Author: Warner Bros.
1949 (1990) $2.00

475-02

(1991) $2.00

110-60

Bugs Bunny And The Health Hog
Illus.: Baker, Darrell
Author: Slater, Teddy
1986
"A" Edition $5.00

110-77

(1991) $2.00

110-63

Bugs Bunny And The Pink Flamingos
Illus.: Costanza, John
Author: Ingoglia, Gina
1987
"A" Edition $5.00

110-71

(1991) $2.00

111-70

Bugs Bunny Calling!
Illus.: Messerli, Joe
Author: West, Cindy
1988
"A" Edition $5.00

111-80

(1991) $2.00

110-55

Bugs Bunny Marooned!
Illus.: Messerli, Joe
Author: Korman, Justine
1985
"A" Edition $5.00

111-69

Bugs Bunny Party Pest
Illus.: Anderson, Al; Mc Kimson,
Thomas J
Author: Johnston, William
1976
"A" Edition $4.00

111-82
(1991) $2.00

110-33
                             $2.00

110-43
                             $2.00

110-53
                             $2.00

111-65
(1989) $2.00

111-77
(1991) $2.00

110-52

Bugs Bunny Pirate Island
Author: Korman, Justine
1991 (1993)
"R" Edition $4.00

110-66

Bugs Bunny Stowaway
Author: Korman, Justine
1991
"A" Edition $4.00

110-23

Bugs Bunny's Carrot Machine
Illus.: Totten, Bob
Author: Carlisle, Clark
1971 $2.00

110-4

Bugs Bunny, Pioneer
Illus.: Baker, Darrell
Author: Brown, Fern G.
1979
3rd Edition $2.00

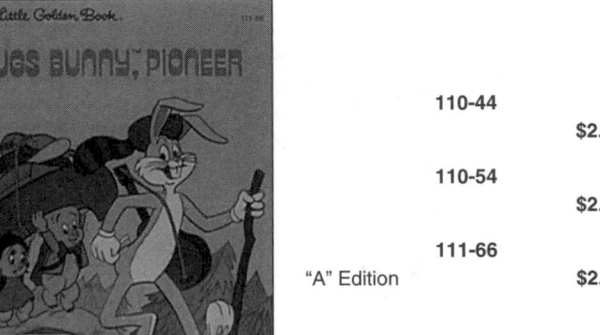

110-44
                             $2.00

110-54
                             $2.00

111-66
"A" Edition $2.00

110-1

Bugs Bunny, Too Many Carrots
Illus.: Alverado,Peter; Totten, Bob
Author: Lewis, Jean
1976 $2.00

110-31
                             $2.00

110-41
                             $2.00

110-41
                             $2.00

110-64
(1990)   "A" Edition $2.00

110-74
(1991) $2.00

202-56

Bunnies' ABC
Illus.: Wiliams, Garth
1985 (1987)
"A" Edition $3.00

202-62
(1991) $2.00

203-58

Bunnies' Counting Book, The
Illus.: Rodger, Elizabeth
Author: Rodger, Elizabeth
1991
"A" Edition $3.00

311-63

(1988) $2.00

473-1

                                $2.00

473-21

                                $2.00

311-43
Bunny Book, The
Illus.: Scarry, Richard
Author: Scarry, Pat
1955   **$2.00**

98791-01
Bunny Hop, The (Sesame Street)
Illus.: Swanson, Maggie
Author: Albee, Sarah
1997
"A" Edition   **$2.00**

204-64
Bunny's New Shoes
Illus.: Karsten, Lisa Mc Cue
Author: Calmenson, Stephanie
1987 (1991)   **$2.00**
                  204-60
"A" Edition   **$4.00**

208-66
Busiest Fire Fighters Ever!
Yellow lettering
Illus.: Scarry, Richard
Author: Scarry, Richard
1993
"A" Edition   **$3.00**

208-66
Busiest Fire Fighters Ever!
Red Lettering
Illus.: Scarry, Richard
Author: Scarry, Richard
1993   **$2.00**

111-76
**Buster Bunny And The Best,
Friends Ever**
Author: Aber, Linda
1991
"A" Edition   **$4.00**

302-57
Buster Cat Goes Out
Illus.: Berlin, Rose Mary
Author: Cole, Joanna
1989
"A" Edition   **$5.00**

206-58
But, You're A Duck
Illus.: Berlin, Rose Mary
Author: Teitelbaum, Michael
1990
"A" Edition   **$3.00**
                  206-64
(1991)   **$2.00**

98872
Butterfly Kisses
Illus.: Ewing, Carolyn
Author: Carlisle, Bob & Brooke
1997
"A" Edition   **$2.00**

210-43

                                $2.00

210-53

                                $2.00

190-02
Cars
Illus.: Totten, Bob
Author: Dugan, William
1973   **$2.00**

210-52 $2.00

210-88 $2.00

211-2 $2.00

210-42

Cars And Trucks
Illus.: Scarry, Richard
1976 $2.00

458-03

Cat That Climbed The Christmas Tree, The
Illus.: Santoro, Christopher
Author: Whayne, Susanne Santoro
1992
"A" Edition $3.00

309-54

Cats
Illus.: Crawford, Mel
Author: French, Laura
1976 $2.00

309-72

Cats
Illus.: Gay, Patti
Author: French, Laura
1976 (1994)
"R" Edition $3.00

302-44

Charlie
Illus.: Obligado, Lillian
Author: Downs, Diane Fox
1970
"D" Edition $5.00

98818-01

Chelli And The Great Sandbox Adventure
Illus.: Shiff, Andrew
Author: Albee, Sarah
1997
"A" Edition $2.00

98822-01

Chelli Tells The Truth
Illus.: O'Malia, Carol
Author: Albee, Sarah
1997
"A" Edition $2.00

201-56

Cheltenham's Party
Illus.: Mc Queen, Lucinda
Author: Wahl, Jan
1985
"A" Edition $5.00

300-9

Child's Garden Of Verses, A
Illus.: Wilkin, Eloise
Author: Stevenson, Robert Louis
1957 $3.00

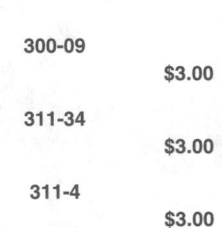

300-09 $3.00

311-34 $3.00

311-4 $3.00

312-06

Child's Year, A
Illus.: Anglund, Joan Walsh
Author: Anglund, Joan Walsh
1992
"A" Edition $5.00

312-56 $2.00

202-54

(1986) "Q" Edition $2.00

202-60

(1992) $2.00

202-44
Chipmunk's ABC
Illus.: Scarry, Richard
Author: Miller, Roberta
1963
"H" Edition $2.00

202-63
Chipmunk's ABC
Illus.: Scarry, Richard
Author: Miller, Roberta
1963 (1994)
"R" Edition $3.00

450-13
Christmas Bunny, The
Illus.: Ewing, Carolyn
Author: Rabin, Arnold
1994
"A" Edition $3.00

469
Christmas Carols
Illus.: Malvern, Corinne
Author: Wyckoff, Marjorie
1972 (1988)
"A" Edition $2.00

469-00

(1988) $2.00

460-9
Christmas Donkey, The
Blue sky
Illus.: Brooks, Andrea
Author: Taylor, William T.
1984
"A" Edition $3.00

460-09

$2.00

460-41
Christmas Donkey, The
Illus.: Brooks, Andrea
Author: Taylor, William T.
1984
"A" Edition $1.00

456-8
Christmas Story, The
Illus.: Wilkin, Eloise
Author: Werner, Jane
1952
"H" Edition $2.00

456-08

$1.00

456-11
Christmas Story, The
Illus.: Wilkin, Eloise
Author: Werner, Jane
1952 (1991) $2.00

456-42

"B" Edition $1.00

456-15
Christmas Story, The
Illus.: Wilkin, Eloise
Author: Werner, Jane
1952 (1992)
"R" Edition $2.00

461-31

$1.00

458-1
Christmas Tree That Grew, The
Illus.: Wilburn, Kathy
Author: Krasilousky, Phyllis
1987
"A" Edition $4.00

458-02

(1991) $2.00

201-4
Circus Is In Town, The
Illus.: Ross, Larry
Author: Harrison, David L.
1978 (1980)
3rd Edition $2.00

201-34
Circus Is In Town, The

$2.00

203-43

$2.00

203-53

$2.00

202-28
Color Kittens, The
Illus.: Provenson, Alice & Martin
Author: Brown, Margaret Wise
1977 (1980)
15th Edition $4.00

(1981)   **202-38**
                16th Edition $4.00

              205-41
"T" Edition $4.00

202-66
Color Kittens, The
Illus.: Ember, Kathi
Author: Brown, Margaret Wise
1994
"R" Edition $3.00

211-71
Colorful Mouse, The
Illus.: Durrell, Julie
Author: Durrell, Julie
1991
"A" Edition $4.00

207-1
Colors Are Nice
Illus.: Shortall, Leonard
Author: Holl, Adelaide
1981 $2.00

207-21

$2.00

207-31

$2.00

109-2
Cookie Monster And The Cookie Tree
Illus.: Mathieu, Joe
Author: Korr, David
1977 $2.00

109-32

$2.00

109-42

$2.00

109-52
Cookie Monster And The Cookie Tree
Name removed from tree.
Illus.: Mathieu, Joe
Author: Korr, David
1977
"A" Edition $3.00

(1991)   **109-53**

$2.00

              109-57

$2.00

203-56
Count All The Way To Sesame Street
Illus.: Brown, Richard
Author: Anastasio, Dina
1985
"A" Edition $4.00

203-57

Count All The Way To Sesame Street
Yellow Background
Illus.: Brown, Richard
Author: Anastasio, Dina
1985 (1990)
"K" Edition   **$3.00**
203-60
(1991)   **$2.00**

311-1

Counting Rhymes
Illus.: Kane, Sharon
1960   **$2.00**
            311-31
                                   $2.00

207-55

Country Mouse And The City Mouse, The
Illus.: Scarry, Richard
Author: Scarry, Pat; Aesop Tales
1961
"F" Edition   **$3.00**

(No number)

Country Mouse And The City Mouse, The
Special printing for Chick-fil-A
Illus.: Severn, Jeffery
Author: Benjamin, Alan
1987   (1997)   **$5.00**

304-48

Cow And The Elephant, The
Illus.: Whitilock, R.Z.
Author: Smith, Claude Clayton
1983   **$5.00**
            304-58
                                   $3.00

304-10

Cow Went Over The Mountain, The
Illus.: Rojankovsky, Feodor
Author: Krinsley, Jeanette
1963   **$2.00**
            304-45
"H "Edition   **$2.00**

206-57

Curious Little Kitten Around The House, The
Illus.: Swanson, Maggie
Author: Hayward, Linda
1986
"A" Edition   **$5.00**
        206-63
(1992)   **$5.00**

201-69

Daddies All About The Work They Do
Illus.: Meisel, Paul
Author: Lundell, Margo
1996
"A" Edition   **$2.00**

311-62

Daniel In The Lions' Den
Illus.: Lapadula, Tom
Author: Broughton, Pamela
1987
"A" Edition   **$5.00**

311-50

David And Goliath
Illus.: Lee, Robert J.
Author: Hazen, Barbara Shook
1974   **$2.00**
            401-1
                                   $2.00

309-56

Day In The Jungle, A
Illus.: Kassian, Olena
Author: Patterson, Pat
1985
"A" Edition   **$5.00**

203-1

Day On The Farm, A
Illus.: Miller, J.P.
Author: Hulick, Nancy Fielding
1960   **$2.00**

203-31
Day On The Farm, A
$2.00

304-56
$2.00

108-59
Day Snuffy Had The Sniffles, The
Illus.: Brannon, Tom
Author: Maifair, Linda Lee
1988
"A" Edition $5.00
108-65
(1991) $2.00

202-26
Dinosaurs
Illus.: Rutherford, William De
Author: Watson, Jane Werner
1959 $2.00

308-42
$2.00

308-52
$2.00

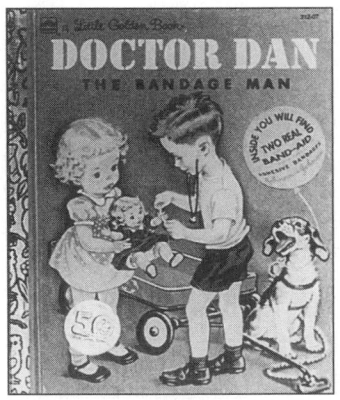

312-07
Doctor Dan, The Bandage Man
Illus.: Malvern, Corinne
Author: Gaspard, Helen
1950 (1992)
"R" Edition $5.00

202-33
Dogs
Illus.: Gergely, Tibor
Author: Daly, Kathleen N.
1980 $2.00

209-53
Dogs
Illus.: Maccombie, Turi
Author: Lewis, Jean
1980 $2.00

209-45
Duck And His Friends
Illus.: Scarry, Richard
Author: Jackson, Kathryn & Byron
1949 $2.00
475-1
$2.00

98846-00
Elmo Loves You
Illus.: Swanson, Maggie
Author: Albee, Sarah
1997   "A" Edition $2.00

98787-01
Elmo's 12 Days Of Christmas
Illus.: Swanson, Maggie
Author: Albee, Sarah
1996 $3.00

98897-00
Elmo's New Puppy
Illus.: Swanson, Maggie
Author: Samuel, Catherine
1998   "A" Edition $2.00

98871-00
Elmo's Tricky Tongue Twister
Illus.: Swanson, Maggie
Author: Albie, Sarah
1998   "A" Edition $2.00

300-2
Eloise Wilkin's Mother Goose
Illus.: Wilkin, Eloise
Author: Wilkin, Eloise
1961   **$2.00**

300-10	
	$2.00
300-22	
	$2.00
300-32	
	$2.00
300-43	
	$2.00
300-60	
(1990)	**$2.00**
307-67	
	$2.00

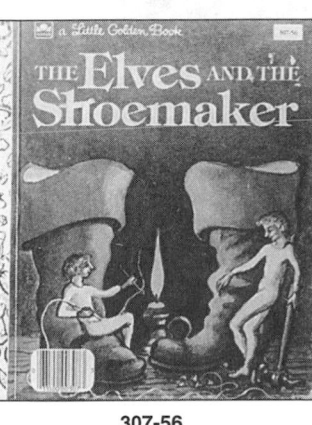

307-56
Elves And The Shoemaker, The
Illus.: Bloom, Lloyd
Author: Suben, Eric
1983   "D" Edition   **$2.00**

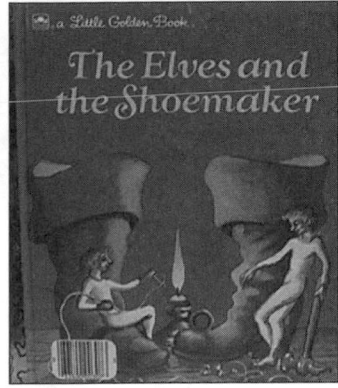

307-61
Elves And The Shoemaker, The
Blue Background
Illus.: Bloom, Lloyd
Author: Suben, Eric
1983   "A" Edition   **$3.00**

207-64
Elves And The Shoemaker, The
Illus.: Smath, Jerry
Author: Suben, Eric
1983 (1992) "A" Edition   **$3.00**

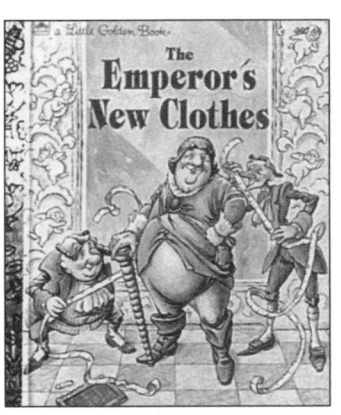

207-66
Emperor's New Clothes, The
Illus.: Walz, Richard
Author: Bonder, Rebecca
1993   "A" Edition   **$3.00**

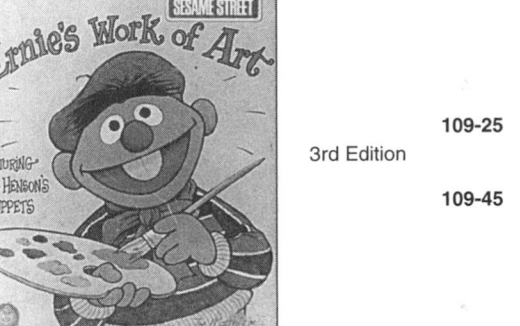

109-5
Ernie's Work Of Art
Illus.: Mathieu, Joe
Author: Mclenighan, Valjean
1979   "A" Edition   **$2.00**

109-25	
3rd Edition	**$4.00**
109-45	
	$2.00

111-48
Fairy Princess, The (Superstar Barbie)
Illus.: Robison, Jim; Irvin, Fred
Author: Foster, Anne
1977   **$5.00**
111-33
"B "Edition   **$5.00**

111-29
Family Circus Daddy's Surprise Day, The
Illus.: Keane, Bill
Author: Wiersum, Gale Charlotte
1980   **$25.00**

200-6
Feelings From A To Z
Illus.: Ruth, Rod
Author: Visser, Pat
1979   **$5.00**

210-2
Fire Engines
Illus.: Gergely, Tibor
1959   **$2.00**

210-32
(1981)   15th Edition   **$2.00**

310-56
"A" Edition $2.00

310-88
                              $2.00

310-46
Fire Engines
Yellow Cover Background
Illus.: Gergely, Tibor
1959 (1979)   **$2.00**

306-58
Fire Engines To The Rescue
Illus.: Courtney Studios
Author: Cambell, Janet
1991   "A" Edition   **$3.00**

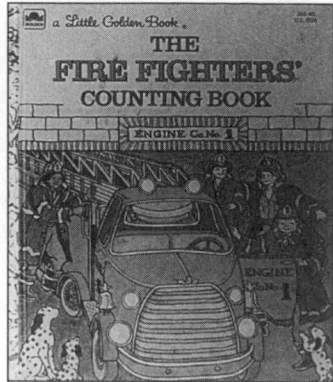

203-45
Fire Fighters' Counting Book, The
Illus.: Stewart, Pat
Author: Curren, Polly
1983   "A" Edition   **$5.00**

203-55
                              $4.00

310-57
First Airplane Ride, A
Illus.: Super, Terri
Author: North, Carol
1986   "F" Edition   **$3.00**

208-65
Floating Bananas
Illus.: Scarry, Richard
Author: Scarry, Richard
1993   "A" Edition   **$3.00**

309-51
Flying Dinosaurs
Illus.: Santro, Christopher
Author: Lindbolm, Steven
1990   "A" Edition   **$4.00**
309-52
                              $3.00

310-53
Flying Is Fun
Illus.: Super, Terri
Author: North, Carol
1986   "A" Edition   **$5.00**

201-35
Forest Hotel
Illus.: Benvenuti
Author: Davis,Barbara Steincrohn
1972 (1979)   **$2.00**

210-5
                   $2.00

203-21
Four Little Kittens
Illus.: Saviozzi, Adriana Mazza
Author: Daly, Kathleen N.
1957   **$2.00**

302-31
(1981)   14th Edition   **$2.00**

302-42
                              $2.00

302-52
                              $2.00

202-4
Four Puppies
Illus.: Obligado, Lillian
Author: Heathers, Anne
1960   **$2.00**

303-42

Four Puppies

$2.00

303-52

$2.00

108-24
Four Seasons, The
Unstated 1st Edition
Illus.: Cooke, Tom
Author: Geiss, Tony
1979   "A" Edition $2.00

108-4

$2.00

108-25

$2.00

108-26

$2.00

108-44

$2.00

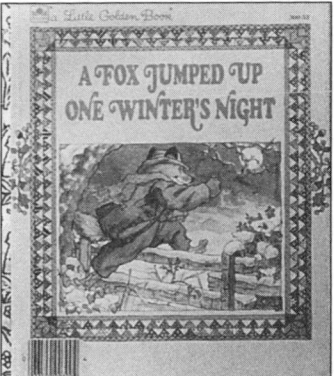

300-53
Fox Jumped Up One Winter's Night, A
Illus.: Barbaresi, Nina
Author: Barbaresi, Nina
1985   "A" Edition $5.00

98849-00
Fozzie's Fabulous Easter Parade
Illus.: Daste, Larry
Author: Gikow, Louise
1998   "A" Edition $2.00

111-87
Fozzie's Funnies
Author: Brannon, Tom
1993   "A" Edition $3.00

209-9
Friendly Book, The
Illus.: Williams, Garth
Author: Brown, Margaret Wise
1954 $2.00

206-34

$2.00

209-41

$2.00

209-61
Friendly Bunny, The
Formerly The Scarebunny
Illus.: Wilburn, Kathy
Author: Kunhardt, Dorothy
1985   "B" Edition $5.00

108-70
From Trash To Treasure
Illus.: Ewers, Joe
Author: Alexander, Liza
1993 $3.00

451-1
Frosty The Snowman
Illus.: Malvern, Corinne
Author: Bedford, Annie North
1972 $2.00

451-9

$2.00

451-09

(1979) $2.00

451-31

$2.00

451-34

$2.00

451-41

$2.00

451-11

Frosty The Snowman
Illus.: Super, Terri
Author: Bedford, Annie North
1989   "A" Edition   **$4.00**

451-12

$2.00

451-15

Frosty The Snowman
Illus.: Chandler, Jean
Author: Bedford, Annie North
1992   "A" Edition   **$3.00**

304-59

Funny Bunny
Illus.: Provensen, Alice & Martin
Author: Learnard, Rachel
1950   "A" Edition   **$3.00**

203-44

Fuzzy Duckling, The
Illus.: Provenson, Alice & Martin
Author: Werner, Jane
1949 (1982) 19th Edition   **$2.00**

482-1
(1979)   15th Edition   **$2.00**

482-2
(1980)   16th Edition   **$2.00**

482-3
(1981)   17th Edition   **$2.00**

(No number)

Fuzzy Duckling, The
Special printing for Chick-fil-A
Illus.: Provenson, Alice & Martin
Author: Werner, Jane
1949 (1997) 21st Edition   **$5.00**

110-61

Garfield The Cat Show
Illus.: Fentz, Mike
Author: Simone, Norma
1990   "A" Edition   **$4.00**
110-70

$2.00

107-65

Garfield And The Space Cat
Illus.: Davis, Jim
Author: Mc Guire, Leslie
1988   "A" Edition   **$4.00**

107-79

$2.00

207-4

Giant Who Wanted Company, The
Unstated 1st
Illus.: Hockerman, Dennis
Author: Priestly, Lee
1979   "A" Edition   **$5.00**

209-42

Giant Who Wanted Company, The
Illus.: Hockerman, Dennis
Author: Priestly, Lee
1979   "E" Edition   **$4.00**

209-52

$2.00

98802-01

Gift Of Christmas, The
(Precious Moments)
Illus.: Butcher, Sam
Author: Miller, Matt
1997   "A" Edition   **$2.00**

310-1

Gingerbread Man, The
Illus.: Elfrieda
1972   **$3.00**

310-21

$3.00

311-7
Ginghams, The Backward Picnic, The
Illus.: Koenig, Jo Anne E.
Author: Bowden, Joan Chase
1976 (1979) 2nd Edition   **$3.00**

304-11
Golden Egg Book, The
Illus.: Obligado, Lillian
Author: Brown, Margaret Wise
1962   **$2.00**

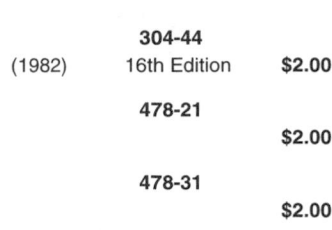

304-44		
(1982)	16th Edition	**$2.00**
478-21		
		$2.00
478-31		
		$2.00

307-69
Golden Egg Book, The
Illus.: Obligado, Lillian
Author: Brown, Margaret Wise
1962   "R" Edition   **$3.00**

208-44
Good Night, Aunt Lilly
Illus.: Dawson, Diane
Author: Madagan, Margaret
1983   "A" Edition   **$5.00**

208-54
$2.00

301-44
Good Night, Little Bear
Pink cover background
Illus.: Scarry, Richard
Author: Scarry, Patsy
1961   "D "Edition   **$3.00**

301-54	
"G" Edition	**$2.00**
301-60	
	$2.00

301-44
Good Night, Little Bear
Yellow cover background
Illus.: Scarry, Richard
Author: Scarry, Patsy
1961   **$3.00**

204-58
Good Old Days, The
Illus.: Borgo, Deborah
Author: Werner, Dave
1988   A" Edition   **$5.00**

209-57
Good-By Day, The
Illus.: Eugenie
Author: Anderson, Leone Castell
1984   "A" Edition   **$5.00**

305-55
Grandma And Grandpa Smith
Illus.: Super, Terri
Author: Kunhardt, Edith
1985   "A" Edition   **$5.00**

109-57
Grover Takes Care Of Baby
Illus.: Cooke, Tom
Author: Thompson, Emily
1987   "A" Edition   **$5.00**

109-64
$2.00

108-46 $2.00

108-56 $2.00

109-50 $2.00

109-66
Grover's Guide To Good Manners
Illus.: Prebenna, David
Author: Allen, Constance
1992   "A" Edition $3.00
98084-01
Grover's Guide To Good Manners
Illus.: Prebenna, David
Author: Allen, Constance
1992 (1991) $3.00

108-36
Grover's Own Alphabet
Illus.: Murdocca, Sal
1978 $5.00

98794-01
Growing Up Grouchy (Sesame Street)
Illus.: Prebenna, David
Author: Muntean, Michaela
1997   "A" Edition $2.00

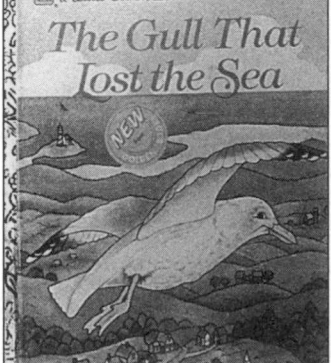

308-32 $3.00

207-41 $3.00

207-51 $3.00

206-45
Gull That Lost The Sea, The
Illus.: Mc Queen, Lucinda
Author: Claytonsmith, Claude
1984   "A" Edition $5.00
206-55 $4.00

313-01
Halloween ABC
Illus.: Meisel, Paul
Author: Albee, Sarah
1993   "A" Edition $3.00

308-2
Hansel And Gretel
Illus.: Wilkin, Eloise
Author: Bros. Grimm
1954 $3.00

111-67
Happy Birthday Babs' (Tiny Toon Adventures)
Illus.: Costanza, Johnaber
Author: Aber, Linda
1990   "A" Edition $4.00

111-78
(1991) $2.00

207-51
Hansel And Gretel
Blue cover background
Illus.: Bros. Grimm
Author: Bros. Grimm
1954 $3.00

207-65
Hansel And Gretel
Illus.: Bros. Grimm
Author: Bros. Grimm
1954   "R" Edition $4.00

108-67
Happy And Sad, Grouch And Glad (Sesame Street)
Illus.: Brannon, Tom
Author: Allen, Constance
1992   "A" Edition $3.00

200-54
Happy Farm Animals, The
Illus.: Gergely, Tibor
Author: Bedford, Annie North
1950   "A" Edition $3.00

200-32
Happy Golden ABC, The
Illus.: Allen, Joan
1972 $2.00

206-9
Heidi
Illus.: Malvern, Corinne
Author: Spyri, Johanna
1954 $2.00

	207-42	$2.00
	207-52	$2.00
	308-1	$2.00
(1981)	308-21 18th Edition	$2.00
(1981)	308-31 19th Edition	$2.00

406-1
Heroes Of The Bible
Illus.: Dixon, Rachel Taft
Author: Watson, Jane Werner
1955 $2.00

208-64
Hilda Needs Help!
Illus.: Scarry, Richard
Author: Scarry, Richard
1993   "A" Edition $3.00

204-43
Hiram's Red Shirt
Illus.: Battaglia, Aurelius
Author: Watts, Mabel
1981   "B" Edition $5.00

	204-51	$4.00
"A" Edition	207-36	$5.00

98817-00
Ho-Ho-Ho, Baby Fozzie!
Illus.: Attinello, Lauren
Author: Gilkow, Louise
1997   1st Edition $2.00

477-1
Home For A Bunny
Illus.: Williams, Garth
Author: Brown, Margaret Wise
1961 (1979) $2.00

(1980)	477-21 5th Edition	$2.00
	477-31	$2.00
	206-9	$2.00
	206-09	$2.00
(1993)	206-10	$2.00
	206-41	$2.00

304-63
House For A Mouse, A
Illus.: Miller, John P.
Author: Daly, Kathleen
1990   "A" Edition $4.00
(1991)   304-71 $2.00

308-55

How Does Your Garden Grow?
Illus.: Clark, Brenda; Perma, Debi
Author: Patterson, Pat
1985   "A" Edition   **$5.00**

308-57

How Things Grow
Illus.: Allert, Kathy
Author: Buss, Nancy
1986   "A" Edition   **$5.00**

98821-01

Hurry-Up, Halloween Costume, The (Big Bag)
Illus.: Linn, Laurent
Author: Albie, Sarah
1997   "A" Edition   **$2.00**

301-43

Hush, Hush, It's Sleepytime
Illus.: Pinchevsky, Leonid
Author: Parish, Peggy
1984   "A" Edition   **$5.00**

301-53
                              $2.00

312-12

I Can Fly
Illus.: Blair, Mary
Author: Krauss, Ruth
1979 (1992) "R" Edition   **$4.00**

312-32
                              $4.00

109-10
(1991)   **$3.00**

109-47
                              $5.00

456-10

I Can't Wait Until Christmas
Illus.: Ewers, Joe
Author: Maifair, Linda Lee
1989   "A" Edition   **$5.00**

456-12
(1991)   **$2.00**

205-40

If I Had A Dog
Illus.: Obligado, Lillian
Author: Obligado, Lillian
1984   **$5.00**

208-59

I Don't Want To Go
Illus.: Rosenberg, Amye
Author: Korman, Justine
1989   "A" Edition   **$5.00**

208-63
(1991)   **$2.00**

205-50
                              $3.00

303-46
                              $2.00

109-9

I Think That It Is Wonderful
Illus.: Delaney, A.
Author: Korr, David
1984   "A" Edition   **$3.00**

107-49

Inspector Gadget In Africa
Illus.: Baris, Sandra
Author: Baris, Sandra
1984   **$5.00**

107-59
                              $5.00

307-33
$2.00

207-4
$2.00

207-43
(1981)   "J" Edition $2.00

307-3
Jack And The Beanstalk
Illus.: Leder, Dora
Author: Nathan, Stella Williams
1973 (1979) 6th Edition $2.00

207-53
Jack And The Beanstalk
Illus.: Leder, Dora
Author: Nathan, Stella Williams
1973 $2.00

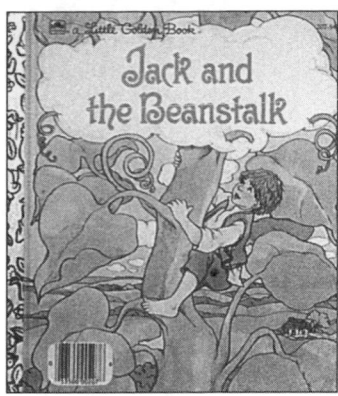

207-54
Jack And The Beanstalk
Illus.: Leder, Dora
Author: Nathan, Stella Williams
1990   "A" Edition $4.00

207-63
(1991) $1.00

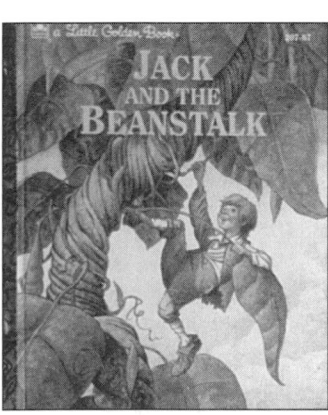

207-67
Jack And The Beanstalk
Illus.: Balducci, Rita
Author: Walz, Richard
1992 $3.00

204-39
Jenny's Surprise Summer
Illus.: Eugenie
Author: Eugenie
1981 $20.00

204-41
$12.00

458-1
Jingle Bells
Illus.: Miller, J. P.
Author: Daly, Kathleen N.
1964 (1979) 10th Edition $2.00
458-9
"U" Edition $2.00
458-09
"Y" Edition $2.00

458
$2.00

458-10
(1991) $2.00

458-31
(1981)   12th Edition $2.00

200-54
Jolly Barnyard, The
Illus.: Gergely, Tibor
Author: Bedford, Annie North
1950 $2.00

303-22
$2.00

98872-00
Just A Bad Day
Book #1
Illus.: Mayer, Gina & Mercer
Author: Mayer, Gina & Mercer
1998   "A" Edition $2.00

98875-00
Just A Little Different
Book #2
Illus.: Mayer, Gina & Mercer
Author: Mayer, Gina & Mercer
1998   "A" Edition $2.00

311-6
Just For Fun
Illus.: Scarry, Richard
Author: Scarry, Patricia
1960 (1979) 5th Edition $2.00

311-36
$2.00

211-52
$2.00

211-61

Just Imagine 'A Book Of Fairyland Rhymes'
Illus.: Gilchrists, Guy
Author: Gilchrists, Guy
1990   "A" Edition   **$4.00**

211-63

(1991)   **$3.00**

98876-00

Just Like Dad
Book #4
Illus.: Mayer, Gina & Mercer
Author: Mayer, Gina & Mercer
1998   "A" Edition   **$2.00**

96017-00

Just Say Please
Book #5
Illus.: Mayer, Gina & Mercer
Author: Mayer, Gina & Mercer
1998   "A" Edition   **$2.00**

111-84

Kermit, Save The Swamp!
Illus.: Leigh, Tom
Author: Chevat, Richard
1992   "A" Edition   **$3.00**

98810-01

King Midas And The Golden Touch
Illus.: Quintal Daily, Renee
Author: Lundell, Margo
1997   "A" Edition   **$2.00**

200-57

Kitty On The Farm
Formerly A Name For Kitty
Illus.: Rojankovsky, Feodor
Author: Mc Ginley
1948 (1989) "A" Edition   **$3.00**

210-63

Kitty's New Doll
Illus.: Mc Queen, Lucinda
Author: Kunhardt, Dorothy M.
1984 (1993)   **$5.00**

107-57

Lady Lovely Locks Silkypup Saves The Day
Illus.: Paris, Pat
Author: Brown, Kristin
1987   "A" Edition   **$5.00**

304-1

Large And Growly Bear, The
Pink Background
Illus.: Crawford, Mel
Author: Hazen, Barbara Shook
1961   **$3.00**

304-42

Large And Growly Bear, The
Yellow Background
Illus.: Crawford, Mel
Author: Hazen, Barbara Shook
1961   **$3.00**

301-3

Lassie And Her Day In The Sun
Illus.: Crawford, Mel
Author: Verral, Charles Spain
1958 (1979)   **$4.00**

301-33

$4.00

111-62

Let's Fly A Kite, Charlie Brown
Illus.: Schultz, Charles M.
Author: Verr, Harry Coe
1987   "A" Edition   **$5.00**

208-58
Let's Go Shopping!
Illus.: Allert, Kathy
Author: Lindbolm, Steven
1988 $5.00

211-1
Let's Go, Trucks!
Illus.: Dugan, William
Author: Harrison, David L.
1973 (1979) $2.00

211-31		
		$2.00
310-42		
"I" Edition		$2.00
310-52		
		$2.00

205-58
Lily Pig's Book Of Colors
Illus.: Rosenberg, Amye
Author: Rosenberg, Amye
1987 $5.00

205-65
(1990) $3.00

304-62
Lions Mixed-Up Friends
Illus.: Santoro, Christopher
Author: Hammond,Lucille
1987   "A" Edition $5.00

209-3
Little Book, The
Illus.: Wilkin, Eloise
Author: Horvath, Sherl
1969 (1979) $10.00

209-3
                        $10.00

304-60
Little Brown Bear
Illus.: Watson, Wendy
Author: Watson, Wendy
1985   "A" Edition $5.00

476-1
Little Cottontail
Illus.: Obligado, Lillian
Author: Memling, Carl
1960 (1979) $2.00

	476-21	
(1980)	15th Edition	$2.00
	304-9	
$2.00		
	304-43	
(1982)	16th Edition	$2.00

304-73
Little Cottontail
Illus.: Obligado, Lillian
Author: Memling, Carl
1960 (1994) "A" Edition $5.00

305-2
Little Engine That Could, The
Illus.: Hauman, George & Doris
Author: Piper, Wally
1954 (1979) $5.00

200-1
Little Golden Book ABC, The
Illus.: De Witt, Cornelius
1951 (1979) $2.00

202-53
                        $2.00

209-58

Little Golden Book Of Holidays, The
Illus.: Wilburn, Kathy
Author: Lewis, Jean
1985   "A" Edition   **$5.00**

211-44

Little Golden Book Of Hymns, The
Illus.: Malvern, Corinne
Author: Werner, Elsa Jane
1985   **$2.00**

211-57

Little Golden Book Of Hymns, The
Illus.: Mitchell, Frances Score
Author: Werner, Elsa, Ebsum,E.D.
1985   "A" Edition   **$5.00**

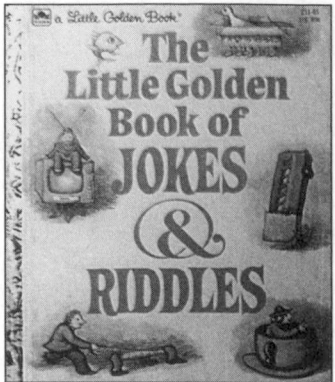

211-45

Little Golden Book Of Jokes & Riddles, The
Illus.: O'Brien, Ken
Author: Ebsun, E. D.
1983   "A" Edition   **$5.00**

211-55
$2.00

300-1

Little Golden Mother Goose, The
Illus.: Rojankovsky, Feodor
1957   **$2.00**
300-31
$2.00

205-2

Little Golden Picture Dictionary
Illus.: Gergely, Tibor
1981   **$2.00**

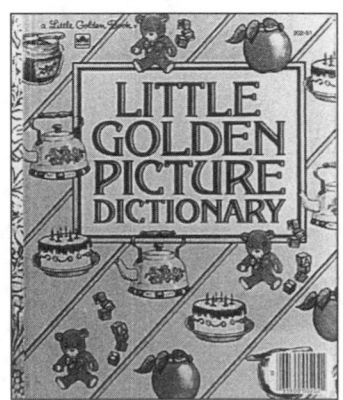

205-32

Little Golden Picture Dictionary
Illus.: De John, Marie
1981   "A" Edition   **$4.00**

202-41
$2.00

202-51
$2.00

202-55
(1991)   **$2.00**

202-67
(1994)   **$2.00**

302-56

Little Lost Kitten
Illus.: Rojankovsky, Feodor
Author: Nina
1979 (1987) "A" Edition   **$3.00**

211-74

Little Mouse's Book Of Colors
Illus.: Durrell, Julie
Author: Durrell, Julie
1991 (1993)   **$4.00**
211-71
"A" Edition   **$3.00**

302-51

Little Pussycat
Illus.: Weisgard, Leonard
Author: Brown, Margaret Wise
1979   **$5.00**

306-2

Little Red Caboose, The
Illus.: Gergely, Tibor
Author: Potter, Marion
1953 (1979)   **$3.00**

306-22
Little Red Caboose, The
$3.00

306-32
(1981)   27th Edition $1.00

210-56
$3.00

210-61
(1991) $3.00

210-86
$3.00

309-1
Little Red Riding Hood
Illus.: Watts, Mable
Author: Grey, Les
1972 (1979) $3.00

309-21
(1980) $3.00

309-31
(1981) $3.00

307-45
$3.00

307-55
$3.00

307-59
Little Red Riding Hood
Illus.: Winborn, Marsha
Author: Heller, Rebecca
1985 (1987) "A" Edition $5.00

307-66
(1991) $2.00

300-65
Little Red Riding Hood
Illus.: Ewers, Joe
Author: Watts, Mabel
1972
(1992)   "A" Edition $3.00

459-00
Littlest Christmas Elf, The
Illus.: Super, Terri
Author: Buss, Nancy
1987   "A" Edition $5.00

459-12
(1991) $2.00

201-44
Lively Little Rabbit, The
Illus.: Tenggren, Gustaf
Author: Ariane
1971 (1982) 28th Edition $1.00

481-31
$2.00

311-60
Lord Is My Shephard, The 'The Twenty-Third Psalm'
Illus.: Lapadula, Tom
1986   "A" Edition $5.00

111-68
Lost In The Funhouse (Tiny Toon Adventures)
Illus.: Costanza, John
Author: Harris, Jack
1990   "A" Edition $4.00

111-79
(1991) $2.00

310-55
Make Way For The Highway
Formerly Make Way For The Thruway
Illus.: Gergely, Tibor
Author: Emerson, Caroline
1961 (1982) "D" Edition $5.00

109-4
Many Faces Of Ernie, The
Illus.: Chartier, Normand
Author: Freuderg, Judy
1979   "A" Edition $5.00

109-34
$2.00

109-44
$2.00

109-54
$2.00

109-69

"Me Cookie!"
Illus.: Swanson, Maggie
Author: Jones, Emma
1994   "A" Edition   **$3.00**

98854-00

Miss Piggy Queen Of Hearts
Illus.: De Reuver, Stef
Author: Inches, Alison
1997   "A" Edition   **$2.00**

107-63

Missing Wedding Dress Featuring Barbie, The
Illus.: Westlake, Laura
Author: Krugman, Karen
1986
"A" Edition   **$6.00**

204-27

Mister Dog
Illus.: Williams, Garth
Author: Brown, Margaret Wise
1952   **$3.00**

303-41
          $3.00

303-51
          $3.00

98811-01

Mommies All About The Work The Do
Illus.: Meisel, Paul
Author: Lundell, Margo
1997   "A" Edition   **$2.00**

109-1

Monster At The End Of This Book, The
Illus.: Smollin, Mike
Author: Stone, Jon
1971 (1979)   **$2.00**

109-31
          $2.00

109-41
          $2.00

108-47
(1990)   "A" Edition   **$2.00**

108-48
(1991)   **$2.00**

108-53
          $2.00

109-59

Monsters' Picnic, The
Illus.: Ewers, Joe
Author: Alexander, Liza
1991   "A" Edition   **$3.00**

300-3

Mother Goose In The City
Illus.: Leder, Dora
1974 (1979)   **$2.00**

200-23
(1981)   7th Edition   **$2.00**

209-57

Moving Day
Formerly Goodbye Day
Illus.: Eugenie
Author: Anderson, Leone Castell
1984   **$5.00**

204-26
Mr. Bears Birthday
Illus.: Butrik, Lyn Mcclure
Author: Wilcox, Veva
1981 $5.00

210-34
Mr. Bell's Fixit Shop
Illus.: Battaglia, Aurelius
Author: Peltzman, Ronne
1981 "A" Edition $5.00

204-42
$4.00

204-52
$4.00

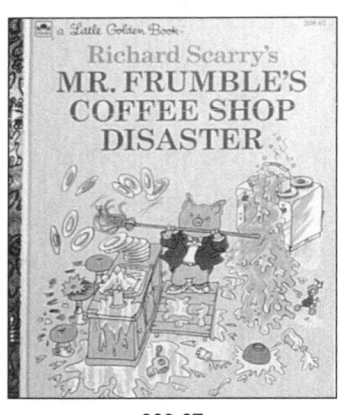

208-67
Mr. Fumble's Coffee Shop Disaster
Illus.: Scarry, Richard
Author: Scarry, Richard
1993 "A" Edition $3.00

110-38
Mrs. Brisby And The Magic Stone
Illus.: Nicklaus, Carol
Author: Ingoglia, Gina
1982 "A" Edition $6.00

111-88
Muppet Treasure Island
Illus.: Brannon, Tom
Author: Weiss, Ellen
1995 "A" Edition $3.00

307-47
Musicians Of Bremen, The
Illus.: Schweninger, Ann
Author: Cruise, Ben
1983 "A" Edition $5.00

307-57
$3.00

211-58
My Book Of Poems
Illus.: Solly, Gloria
Author: Cruise, Ben
1985 (1987) "A" Edition $4.00

455-1
My Christmas Treasury
Green Cover
(1st Cover)
Illus.: Wiersum, Gale
Author: Emrich, Sylvia
1976 (1979) 3rd Edition $2.00
455-31
(1981) $1.00

455
My Christmas Treasury
(2nd Cover)
Orange lettering & red cover
Illus.: Wiersum, Gale
Author: Emrich, Sylvia
1976 $2.00

455
My Christmas Treasury
(3rd Cover)
White Lettering & Red Cover
Illus.: Wiersum, Gale
Author: Emrich, Sylvia
1976 "A" Edition $5.00

308-56
My First Book Of The Planets
Illus.: Nez, John
Author: Winthrop, Elizabeth
1985 "A" Edition $5.00

203-41 $2.00

203-51 $3.00

205-54

My First Book Of Sounds
Formerly Bow Wow! Meow!
Illus.: Schart, Trina
Author: Bellah, Melanie
1963 (1989) "A" Edition $3.00

205-62
(1991) $2.00

201-31

My First Counting Book
Illus.: Williams, Garth
Author: Moore, Lilian
1956 $2.00

203-52

My First Counting Book
Blue Lettering
Illus.: Williams, Garth
Author: Moore, Lillian
1956 (1990) $3.00

206-31 $2.00

305-44 $2.00

305-54 $2.00

206-1

My Home
Illus.: Rofry
1976 $3.00

301-68

My Kindergarten Counting Book
Illus.: Mitter, Kathryn
Author: Lundell, Margo
1995   "A" Edition $3.00

304-2

My Little Dinosaur
Illus.: Vogel, Ilse-Margaret
Author: Vogel, Ilse-Margaret
1971 (1979)
6th Edition $2.00

304-32 $2.00

209-43 $2.00

209-53 $2.00

309-57

My Little Golden Book About Cats
Illus.: Leder, Dora
Author: Ryder, Joanne
1988   "A" Edition $5.00

309-69
(1991) $2.00

309-71

My Little Golden Book Of Dogs
Illus.: Mac Combie, Turi
Author: Lewis, Jean
1983 (1992) "R" Edition $5.00

407-1

My Little Golden Book About God
Illus.: Wilkin, Eloise
Author: Watson, Jane Werner
1956 (1978) $2.00

308-9
My Little Golden Book About God
$2.00

308-43
$2.00

311-52
$2.00

311-53
My Little Golden Book About God
Illus.: Wilkin, Eloise
Author: Watson, Jane Werner
1974 (1994)
"R" Edition $2.00

210-57
**My Little Golden Book Of Cars
And Trucks**
Illus.: Courtney, Richard & Trish
Author: Sue, Chari
1990
"A" Edition $5.00
210-62
(1992) $2.00

211-62
**My Little Golden Book Of Fairy
Tales**
Illus.: Laite, Gordon
1990
"A" Edition $3.00

205-57
My Little Golden Book Of Manners
Illus.: Scarry, Richard
Author: Parish, Peggy
1962 (1987)
"A" Edition $3.00

205-64
My Little Golden Book Of Manners
Illus.: Scarry, Richard
Author: Parish, Peggy
1962 (1991) $2.00

300-69
My Little Golden Mother Goose
Illus.: Brooks, Nan
Author: Cohen, Robin
1994   "A" Edition $3.00

305-53
My Little Golden Word Book
Illus.: Kaufman, Joe
1968 (1986) $3.00

208-56
My Own Grandpa
Illus.: Wilburn, Kathy
Author: Anderson, Leone Castell
1987   "A" Edition $5.00

312-11
My Puppy
Illus.: Wilkin, Eloise
Author: Scarry, Patsy
1955   "R" Edition $3.00

209-1
New Baby, The
Illus.: Wilkin, Eloise
Author: Shane, Ruth & Harold
1975 (1979) 6th Edition $3.00

306-43
(1982)   7th Edition $3.00

306-53
"I" Edition $3.00

306-68
New Baby, The
Formerly Baby Dear
Illus.: Wilkin, Eloise
Author: Wilkin, Esther
(1992)   "R" Edition   **$3.00**

98886-00
New Kid In School - Mc Kids
Illus.: Pederson, Alice
Author: Patrick, Ellen
1998   "A" Edition   **$2.00**

202-5
New Puppy, The
Illus.: Obligado, Lillian
Author: Daly, Kathleen
1969 (1979)
7th Edition   **$2.00**

203-55
                    $2.00

309-42
                    $2.00

303-55
                    $2.00

303-55
New Puppy, The
Illus.: Obligado, Lillian
Author: Daly, Kathleen
1969   **$2.00**

450-1
Night Before Christmas, The
Illus.: Malvern, Corinne
Author: Moore, Clement C.
1949 (1979) 35th Edition   **$1.00**

450
(1982)   40th Edition   **$1.00**

450- 9
                    $1.00

450-09
                    $1.00

450-31
                    $1.00

450-10
Night Before Christmas, The
Illus.: Wilburn, Kathy
Author: Moore, Clement C.
1987   "A" Edition   **$4.00**

450-11
(1991)   **$2.00**

400-1
Noah's Ark
Illus.: Gergely, Tibor
Author: Hazen, Barbara Shook
1969   **$2.00**

307-41
                    $2.00

307-51
                    $2.00

311-64
Noah's Ark
Illus.: La Padula, Tom
Author: Broughton, Pamela
1985 (1990) "A" Edition   **$5.00**

456-16
Noel
Illus.: Langley, Bill A.
Author: Muller, Romeo
1991 (1992) "A" Edition   **$3.00**

460-15
Nutcracker, The
Illus.: Lanza, Barbara
Author: Balducci, Rita
1991   "A" Edition   **$4.00**

460-16
(1992)   **$2.00**

304-50
Oh, Little Rabbit!
Illus.: Wilburn, Kathy
Author: Lexau, Joan M.
1989   "A" Edition   **$5.00**

303-21
Old MacDonald Had A Farm
Illus.: Kennel, Moritz
1960   **$2.00**

200-43   **$2.00**

200-53   **$2.00**

200-55
Old MacDonald Had A Farm
Illus.: Hauge, Carl & Mary
Author: Hauge, Carl & Mary
1975 (1987) "A" Edition   **$3.00**

200-62
(1991)   **$2.00**

200-65
Old MacDonald Had A Farm
Barn-siding background
Illus.: Hauge, Carl & Mary
Author: Hauge, Carl & Mary
1975 (1992) "R" Edition   **$4.00**

98806-01
Old MacDonald Had A Farm
Illus.: Ember, Kathi
1997   "A" Edition   **$2.00**

300-54
**Old Mother Goose And Other
Nursey Rhymes**
Illus.: Provensen, Alice & Martin
198   8"A" Edition   **$4.00**

300-42
Old Mother Hubbard
Illus.: Battaglia, Aurelius
Author: Battaglia, Aurelius
1970   **$2.00**

300-52
"N" Edition   **$2.00**

208-42
One Of The Family
Illus.: Sanderson, Ruth
Author: Archer, Peggy
1983   "A" Edition   **$5.00**

208-50   **$3.00**

208-52   **$3.00**

108-1
Oscar's Book
Illus.: Gross, Michael
Author: Moss, Jeffery
1975   **$2.00**

108-21   **$2.00**

108-41   **$2.00**

108-51   **$2.00**

109-67

Oscar's New Neighbor
Illus.: Attinello, Lauren
Author: Margulies, Teddy Slater
1992   "A" Edition   **$3.00**

109-70
(1994)   **$3.00**

307-10
        $2.00

307-42
(1982)   15th Edition   **$2.00**

311-46
        $2.00

479-21
        $2.00

479-31
        $2.00

300-41

Owl And The Pussy Cat
Illus.: Sanderson, Ruth
Author: Lear, Edward
1982   "A" Edition   **$5.00**

300-51
        $2.00

300-57

Pied Piper, The
Illus.: Walz, Richard
Author: Benjamin, Alan
1991   "A" Edition   **$3.00**

110-35
        $2.00

110-45
        $2.00

210-1

Pano The Train
Illus.: Giannini
Author: Holvaes, Sharon
1975 (1979)   **$4.00**

310-44
        $3.00

312-04

Pierrot's ABC Garden
Illus.: Lobel, Anita
Author: Lobel, Anita
1992   "A" Edition   **$4.00**

312-24
        $3.00

307-9

Peter Rabbit
Illus.: Saviozzi, Adriana Mazza
Author: Potter, Beatrix
1970   "A" Edition   **$3.00**

111-60

Pink Panther And Sons Fun At The Picnic
Illus.: Gantz, David
Author: Baris, Sandra
1985   "A" Edition   **$4.00**

110-5

Pink Panther In The Haunted House, The
Illus.: Baker, Darrell; Jason Studios
Author: Graham, Kennon
1975   **$2.00**

98812-01

Please And Thank You
Illus.: Smath, Jerry
Author: Hazen, Barbara Shook
1997   "R" Edition   **$3.00**

312-05

Pocketful Of Nonsense
Illus.: Marshall, James
Author: Marshall, James
1992   "A" Edition   **$4.00**

312-25
        $2.00

98781-01

Poky Little Puppy Comes To Sesame Street, The
Illus.: Brannon, Tom
Author: Dickson, Anna H.
1997   "A" Edition $2.00

301-1

Poky Little Puppy Follows His Nose Home, The
Illus.: Miclat, Alex
Author: Holl, Adelaide
1975 $3.00

301-31
                            $2.00

303-57

Poky Little Puppy's Naughty Day, The
Illus.: Chandler, Jean
Author: Chandler, Jean
1985   "A" Edition $4.00

301-2

Poky Little Puppy, The
Illus.: Tenggren, Gustaf
Author: Lowrey, Janet Sebring
1942 $2.00

301-32
                            $2.00

303-43
                            $2.00

303-53
"A" Edition $1.00

303-62
(1991) $2.00

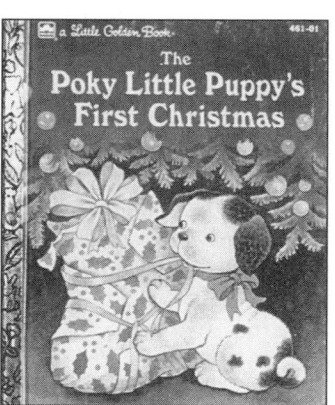

461-01

Poky Little Puppy's First Christmas, The
Illus.: Chandler, Jean
Author: Korman, Justine
1993   "A" Edition $4.00

302-55

Polly's Pet
Illus.: Rosenberg, Amye
Author: Hammond, Lucille
1984   "A" Edition $4.00

110-2

Porky Pig And Bugs Bunny Just Like Magic
Illus.: Totten, Bob
Author: Nathan, Stella Williams
1976 $2.00

110-22
(1980)   8th Edition $2.00

110-32
                            $2.00

110-42
                            $2.00

110-65
(1990) $2.00

110-75
(1991) $2.00

111-61

Pound Puppies 'Problem Puppies'
Illus.: Bouman, Carol
Author: Korman, Justine; Codor, Dick
1986   "A" Edition $4.00

110-59

Pound Puppies Pick Of The Litter
Illus.: Bouman, Carol; Cododr, Dick
Author: Slater, Teddy
1985   "A" Edition $4.00

301-09

Prayers For Children
Illus.: Wilkin, Eloise
1952 $2.00

301-9
Prayers For Children

$2.00

301-45

$1.00

405-32

$1.00

405-1

$1.00

301-93
Prayers For Children
Purple background
Illus.: Wilkin, Eloise
1952
$2.00

301-10
Prayers For Children
Illus.: Wilkin, Eloise
1952 (1993) "R" Edition $2.00

207-68
Princess And The Pea, The
Illus.: Brooks, Nan
Author: Lundell, Margo
1994 $3.00

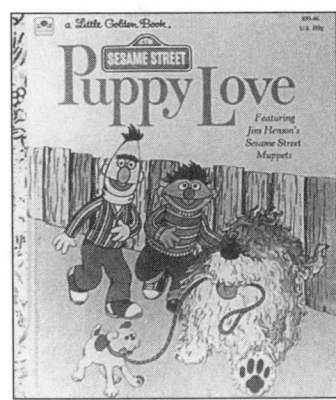

109-56

$2.00

109-63

$2.00

(1991)

109-46
Puppy Love
Illus.: Nicklaus, Carol
Author: Sunshine, Madeline
1983" A" Edition $5.00

304-52
Puppy On The Farm
Formerly Duffy On The Farm
Illus.: Mc Cue, Lisa
Author: Elson, Marilyn, Elson
1989   "A" Edition $4.00

300-58
Puss In Boots
Illus.: Mc Queen, Lucinda
Author: Perrault, Charles; Suben, Eric
1991   "A" Edition $3.00

302-34
Pussy Willow
Illus.: Weisgard, Leonard
1951   "C" Edition $3.00

302-41

"E" Edition $2.00

98809-01
Pussy Willow
Illus.: Bossen, Jo-Ellen C.
Author: Muldrow, Diane (Edited By)
1951 (1997) "R" Edition $3.00

107-84
Put On A Happy Face!
(Precious Moments)
Illus.: Butcher, Samuel J.
Author: Wiersma, Debbie
1992   "A" Edition $3.00

107-72
Quints 'The Cleanup'
Illus.: Di Ciccio, Sue
Author: Mc Guire, Leslie
1990 $3.00

107-81

"A" Edition $4.00

472-1

Rabbit And His Friends
Illus.: Scarry, Richard
Author: Scarry, Richard
1953   **$2.00**

209-44
           $2.00

474-21

Rabbit Is Next, The
Illus.: Powell, Linda
Author: Leithauser, Gladys; Betmeyer, Lois
1978 (1980) 2nd Edition   **$3.00**

471-31

Rabbit's Adventure, The
Illus.: Swanson, Maggie
Author: Wright, Betty Ren
1977   **$2.00**

107-2

Raggedy Ann And Andy And The Rainy Day Circus
Illus.: Goldsborough, June
Author: Hazen, Barbara Shook
1973   **$4.00**

107-42
           $4.00

457-1

Raggedy Ann And Andy Help Santa Claus
Illus.: Goldsborough, June
Author: Curren, Polly
1977   **$4.00**

457-31
           $4.00

107-4
"A" Edition   **$5.00**

107-44
"D" Edition   **$4.00**

107-21

Raggedy Ann And Andy The Little Gray Kitten
Illus.: Goldsborough, June
Author: Curren, Polly
1975   **$4.00**

107-31
"H" Edition   **$4.00**

107-41
10th Edition   **$4.00**

107-34

Raggedy Ann And Andy, Five Birthday Parties In A Row
Illus.: Mc Clain, Mary S.
Author: Daly, Eileen
1979   "B" Edition   **$4.00**

107-3

Raggedy Ann And The Cookie Snatcher
Illus.: Goldsborough, June
Author: Hazen, Barbara Shook
1972   **$4.00**

107-33
           $4.00

107-43
(1984)   12th Edition   **$4.00**

111-47
           $4.00

111-57
           $4.00

303-44

Rags
Illus.: Miller, John P.
Author: Scarry, Patricia
1970   "G" Edition   **$4.00**

107-48

Rainbow Brite And The Brook Meadow Deer
Illus.: Wilson, Roy
Author: Leslie, Sarah
1984   "A" Edition   **$5.00**

107-58

"B" Edition   **$4.00**

206-35

Rainy Day Play Book
Illus.: Ohlsson, Ib
Author: Young, Susan
1981   "A" Edition   **$5.00**

211-51

$2.00

207-57

Rapunzel
Illus.: Beckett, Sheilah
Author: Mayer, Marianna
1991   "A" Edition   **$4.00**

109-71

Ready, Set, Go! A Counting Book
Illus.: Cooke, Tom
Author: Jones, Emma
1995   "A" Edition   **$3.00**

308-68

Ready, Set, Grow!
Illus.: Clark, Brenda; Perma, Debi
Author: Patterson, Pat
(1991)   **$4.00**

200-9

Right's Animal Farm
Illus.: Goodman, Joan Elizabeth
Author: Goodman, Joan Elizabeth
1983   "A" Edition   **$5.00**

	111-25	
(1981)	8th Edition	**$1.00**
	111-35	
(1981)	9th Edition	**$1.00**
	111-45	
12th Edition		**$1.00**
	111-71	
(1990)	"A" Edition	**$1.00**
	111-83	
(1991)		**$1.00**

111-5

Road Runner, The 'A Very Scary Lesson'
Illus.: Delara, Phil; Totten, Bob
Author: Schroeder, Russel
1974   **$1.00**

110-57

Road Runner, The 'Mid-Mesa Marathon'
Illus.: Costanza, John
Author: Slater, Teddy
1985   "A" Edition   **$5.00**

110-58

Robotman And His Friends At School
Illus.: Kostanza, John
Author: Korman, Justine
1985   "A" Edition   **$5.00**

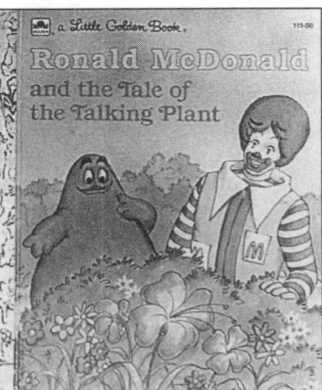

111-50

Ronald Mcdonald And The Tale Of The Talking Plant
Illus.: Kostanza, John
Author: Albano, John
1984   "A" Edition   **$15.00**

452-1

Rudolph The Red-Nosed Reindeer
Illus.: Scarry, Richard
Author: Hazen, Barbara Shook
1958   **$1.00**

452-9
Rudolph The Red-Nosed Reindeer
$1.00

452-09
$1.00

452-31
$1.00

452-41
$1.00

452-10
Rudolph The Red-Nosed Reindeer
Illus.: Scarry, Richard
Author: Hazen, Barbara Shook
1985 (1990) $2.00

452-11
(1991) $1.00

98829-00
Rudolph The Red-Nosed Reindeer
Illus.: Arkadia
Author: Bunsen, Rick
1998   "A" Edition $2.00

460-31
**Rudolph The Red-Nosed Reindeer
Shines Again**
Illus.: Baker, Darrell
Author: May, Robert L.
1982   "A" Edition $4.00

452-8
$2.00

452-42
"H" Edition $2.00

452-08
$2.00

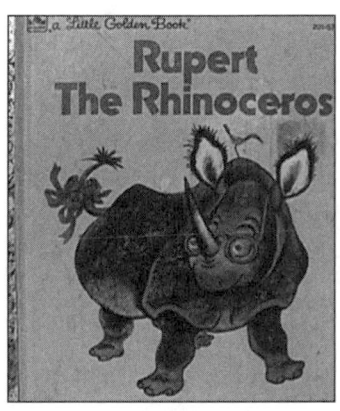

300-56
Rumpelstiltskin
Formerly Red Little Golden Book Of
Fairy Tale
Illus.: Dugun, William J.
Author: Bros. Grimm
1958 (1988) "A" Edition $5.00

201-57
Rupert The Rhinoceros
Illus.: Gergely, Tibor
Author: Memling, Carl
1960 $5.00

304-4
Saggy Baggy Elephant, The
Illus.: Tenggren, Gustaf
Author: Jackson, Kathryn & Byron
1947 $2.00

304-34
$2.00

201-42
$2.00

201-52
$2.00

201-54
$2.00

(1992)

201-88
$2.00

305-59
**Saggy Baggy Elephant No Place
For Me**
Illus.: Walz, Richard
Author: Ingoglia, Gina
1989 (1990) $4.00

312-08
Sailor Dog, The
Illus.: Williams, Garth
Author: Brown, Margaret Wise
1953 (1992) "R" Edition $3.00

459-1
Santa's Surprise Book
Illus.: Winship, Florence
Author: Elwart, Joan Rotter
1966 $2.00

459-31
(1988)   11th Edition $2.00

209-59
Scarebunny, The
Illus.: Wilburn, Kathy
Author: Kunhardt, Dorothy
1985   "A" Edition   **$5.00**

305-1
Scuffy The Tugboat
Illus.: Gergely, Tibor
Author: Crampton, Certrude
1946   **$1.00**

305-21	$1.00
305-31	$1.00
305-31	$1.00
310-41	$1.00
310-51	$1.00
310-54 (1991)	$1.00
310-87	$1.00

108-69
Sesame Street's Mother Goose Rhymes
Illus.: Swanson, Maggie
Author: Allen, Constance
1993   **$3.00**

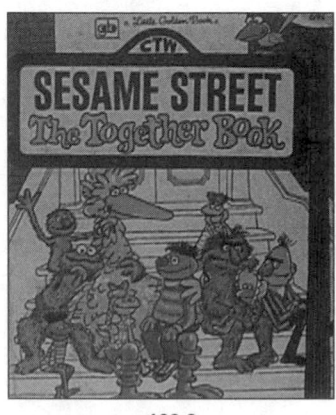

108-3
Sesame Street, The Together Book
Illus.: Bradfield, Roger
Author: Dwight, Revena
1971   **$2.00**

108-23 (1980)	16th Edition	$2.00
108-33		$2.00

96002-00
Shall We Dance (A Book About Opposites)
Illus.: Nicklaus, Carol
Author: Albee, Sarah
1998   "A" Edition   **$2.00**

110-36
Shazam! A Circus Adventure
Illus.: Shafenburger, Kurt
Author: Ottum, Bob
1977   **$3.00**

211-56
Shoelace Box, The
Illus.: Wilburn, Kathy
Author: Winthrop, Elizabeth
1984   "A" Edition   **$5.00**

302-2
Shy Little Kitten, The
Illus.: Tenggren, Gustaf
Author: Schurr, Kathleen
1946   **$1.00**

302-22	$1.00
302-32	$1.00
302-53	$1.00
302-87 (1987)	$1.00

312-10
Shy Little Kitten, The
Illus.: Tenggren, Gustaf
Author: Schurr, Kathleen
1946 (1992)"R" Edition   **$2.00**

302-58

Shy Little Kitten's Secret Place
Illus.: Jones, Keenan
Author: Lawrence, Jim
1989 (1990) $4.00

302-68

(1991) $3.00

204-59

Silly Sisters, The
Illus.: Mc Queen, Lucinda
Author: Werner, Dave
1989   "A" Edition $5.00

98856-00

Sing With Me My Name Is Ernie
Illus.: Swanson, Maggie
Author: Rabe, Tish
1997 $3.00

209-27

Sleepy Book, The
(Fomerly: The Golden Sleepy Book
Yellow cover background)
Illus.: Williams, Garth
Author: Brown, Margaret Wise
1975 $2.00

209-37

(1980)   "D" Edition $3.00

301-41

"E" Edition $3.00

301-51

Sleepy Book, The
Violet cover background
Illus.: Williams, Garth
Author: Brown, Margaret Wise
1948 $3.00

301-59

(1991) $2.00

301-62

Sleepy Book, The
Yellow squared cover background
Illus.: Williams, Garth
Author: Brown, Margaret Wise
1975 (1993) $2.00

202-57

Sleepytime ABC
Illus.: Chandler, Jean
Author: Campbell, Janet
1991   "A" Edition $3.00

208-55

Snoring Monster, The
Illus.: Walz, Richard
Author: Harrison, David L.
1985   "A" Edition $4.00

208-92

$2.00

208-69

Snowstorm Surprise, The
1994   "A" Edition $3.00

209-26

So Big
Illus.: Wilkin, Eloise
Author: Wilkin, Eloise
1968 $7.00

209-6

$8.00

98879-00

Star Wars - Adventure In Beggar's Canyon
Illus.: Ciccarelli, Gary
Author: Mason, Jane
1998   "A" Edition $2.00

98202-00

Star Wars - Meltdown On Hoth
Illus.: Trevas, Chris
Author: Mason, Jane
1998   "A" Edition   **$2.00**

204-54

Store-Bought Doll, The
Illus.: Sanderson, Ruth
Author: Meyer, Lois
1983   **$2.00**

204-44
"A" Edition   **$5.00**

402-1

Stories Of Jesus
Illus.: Forberg, Ari
Author: Richards, Jean H.
1974   **$2.00**

402-2
                                      $2.00

98902-00

Story Of Easter, The
Illus.: Pinkney-Davis, Debbie
Author: Miller, Jean
1999   "A" Edition   **$2.00**

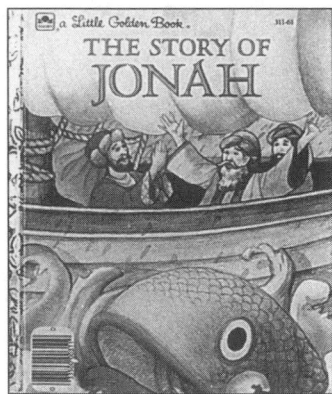

311-61

Story Of Jonah, The
Illus.: Collier, Roberta
Author: Broughton, Pamela
1986   "A" Edition   **$4.00**

206-56

Summer Vacation
Illus.: Allert, Kathy
Author: Kunhardt, Edith
1986   "A" Edition   **$4.00**

206-93
                                      $2.00

98880-00

Taking Care Of Mom
Book #2
Illus.: Mayer, Gina & Mercer
Author: Mayer, Gina & Mercer
1998   "A" Edition   **$2.00**

304-23		
(1981)	14th Edition	**$1.00**
304-33		
(1981)	15th Edition	**$1.00**
201-43		
18th Edition		**$1.00**
201-53		
"Z" Edition		**$1.00**
201-61		
(1991)		**$1.00**
201-87		
		$1.00

307-9

Tale Of Peter Rabbit, The
Illus.: Saviozzi, Adriana Mazza
Author: Potter, Beatrix
1958   **$2.00**

307-10
(1992)   **$2.00**

307-11

Tale Of Peter Rabbit, The
Illus.: Szekeres, Cindy
Author: Potter, Beatrix
1994   "A" Edition   **$3.00**

304-3

Tawny Scrawny Lion
Illus.: Tenggren, Gustaf
Author: Jackson, Kathryn
1952   **$1.00**

201-58

Tawny Scrawny Lion Saves The Day
Illus.: Ellis, Art & Kim
Author: Teitelbaum, Michael
1989 (1990)   **$4.00**

312-09

Taxi That Hurried, The
Illus.: Gergely, Tibor
Author: Mitchell, Lucy Sprague; Simonton
1946 (1992) "R" Edition   **$1.00**

312-29
(1992)   "R" Edition   **$1.00**

203-54

Ten Items Or Less
Illus.: Super, Terri
Author: Calmerson, Stephanie
1985   "A" Edition   **$5.00**

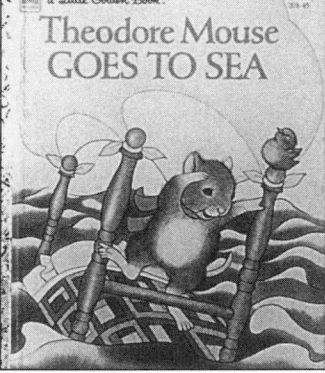

201-45

Theodore Mouse Goes To Sea
Illus.: Mc Queen, Lucinda
Author: Muntean, Michaela
1983   "A" Edition   **$5.00**

201-55
     $2.00

204-57

Theodore Mouse Up In The Air
Illus.: Mc Queen, Lucinda
Author: Muntean, Michaela
1986   "A" Edition   **$5.00**

209-64

There Are Tyrannosaurs Trying On Pants In My Bedroom
Illus.: Heartney, Jim
Author: Heartney, Jim
1991   "A" Edition   **$10.00**

209-9

Things I Like
Illus.: Williams, Garth
Author: Brown, Margaret Wise
1982   Red Edition   **$2.00**

206-2

Things In My House
Illus.: Kaufman, Joe
Author: Kaufman, Joe
1968   **$2.00**

206-32
     $2.00

205-53
     $2.00

305-53
(1986)   **$3.00**

96012-00

This Is My Body
Book #6
Illus.: Mayer, Gina & Mercer
Author: Mayer, Gina & Mercer
1998   "A" Edition   **$2.00**

312-02

This Is My Family
Illus.: Mayer, Gina & Mercer
Author: Mayer, Gina & Mercer
1992   "A" Edition   **$4.00**

312-15
(1993)   **$2.00**

307-2

Three Bears, The
Illus.: Goldsborough, June
Author: Watts, Mabel
1948   **$2.00**

307-22
     $2.00

307-32
     $2.00

307-1
     $2.00

307-21
     $2.00

301-5 $2.00

301-53 $2.00

(1991)

301-87 $2.00

311-58 $2.00

301-31
Three Bears, The
Illus.: Rojankovsky, Feodor
1948 (1981) 41st Edition   **$2.00**

311-23
Three Bedtime Stories
Illus.: Williams, Garth
Author: Fairy Tales
1958 $2.00

311-33 $2.00

302-3
Three Little Kittens
Illus.: Masha
1942 $2.00

302-33 $2.00

307-43 $2.00

309-22 $2.00

309-32 $2.00

300-50
Three Little Pigs, The
Illus.: R.O.Fry
Author: Ross, Elizabeth
1973   **$2.00**

300-55
Thumbelina
Blue cover background
Illus.: Palmer, Jan
Author: Anderson, Hans Christian
1953 (1988) "A" Edition   **$2.00**

300-66
Thumbelina
Illus.: Palmer, Jan
Author: Anderson, Hans Christian
1953 (1992) "R" Edition   **$5.00**

300-68
Thumbelina
Illus.: Palmer, Jan
Author: Anderson, Hans Christian
1993 (1993) "A" Edition   **$3.00**

308-51
Tickety-Tock, What Time Is It?
Illus.: Durrell, Julie
Author: Durrell, Julie
1990   "A" Edition   **$4.00**

308-53 $2.00

(1991)

98827-01
Tickle Me My Name Is Elmo
Illus.: Swanson, Maggie
Author: Allen, Constance
1997   "A" Edition   **$2.00**

301-55
Time For Bed
Illus.: Goodman, Joan Elizabeth
Author: Goodman, Joan Elizabeth
1989   "A" Edition   **$5.00**

98881-00
Timid Little Kitten, The
Formerly The Tiny Tawny Kitten
Illus.: Pfloog, Jan
Author: Hazen, Barbara
1998   "R" Edition $2.00

209-60
Timothy Tiger's Terrible Tooth-ache
Illus.: Mc Cue Karsten, Lisa
Author: Wahl, Jan
1988   "A" Edition $5.00

209-63
(1990) $3.00

308-58
Tiny Dinosaurs
Illus.: Gino, D'achille
Author: Lindblom, Steven
1988   "A" Edition $4.00

308-69
(1991) $2.00

306-21
                             $1.00

306-31
                             $1.00

210-44
(1980)   43rd Edition $1.00

210-54
                             $1.00

210-55
(1991) $1.00

210-87
                             $1.00

457-42
Tom And Jerry's Merry Christmas
Illus.: Eisenberg, Harvey; Arm-strong,Samuel
Author: Archer, Peter
1954   "J" Edition $3.00

211-59
Tommy Visits The Doctor
Illus.: Scarry, Richard
Author: Seligmann, Joan
1962 (1988)"C" Edition $2.00

306-1
Tootle
Illus.: Gergely, Tibor
Author: Crampton, Gertrude
1945 (1979) $1.00

207-56
Tortoise And The Hare, The
Illus.: Nez, John
Author: Lundell, Margo
1987   "A" Edition $5.00

210-41
Train To Timbuctoo, The
Illus.: Seiden, Art
Author: Brown, Margaret Wise
1951 $4.00

210-51
                             $4.00

211-34
                             $4.00

110-78
Tweety And Sylvester In 'Birds Of A Feather'
Illus.: Messerli, Joe
Author: Lewis, Jean
1992   "A" Edition $3.00

110-82
Tweety Global Patrol
Illus.: Messerli, Joseph
Author: Lewis, Jean
1993   "A" Edition $3.00

111-24
(1981)   5th Edition $2.00

111-34
6th Edition $2.00

111-54
    $1.00

111-4
Tweety Plays Catch The Puddy Tat
Illus.: Alverado, Peter; Lorencz, William
Author: Daly, Eileen
1975 $1.00

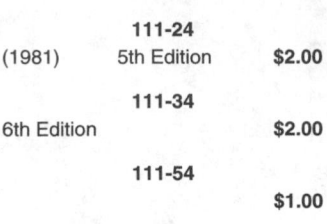

111-54
Tweety Plays Catch The Puddy Tat
Violet cover background
Illus.: Alverado, Peter; Lorencz, William
Author: Daly, Eileen
1975   "Z" Edition $1.00
111-51
(1990)   "Y" Edition $2.00

301-64
Twelve Dancing Princesses, The
Illus.: Marvin, Fred
Author: Muldrow, Diane
1995   "A" Edition $3.00

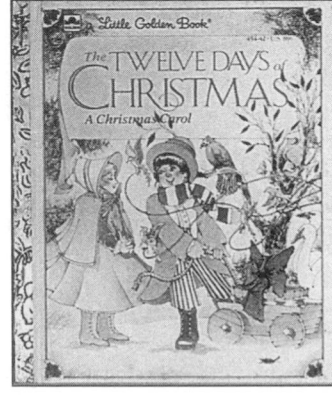

454-09
    $2.00

454-10
(1991) $2.00

454-42
    $5.00

454-9
Twelve Days Of Christmas, The
Illus.: Eagle, Mike
1983 $2.00

451-16
Twelve Days Of Christmas, The
Illus.: Beckett, Sheilah
1992   "A" Edition $4.00

308-59
Two Little Gardeners
Illus.: Elliott, Gertrude
Author: Brown, Margaret Wise
1951 (1988)"A" Edition $2.00

207-72
Ugly Duckling, The
Illus.: Mc Cue, Lisa
Author: Anderson, Hans Christian
1995   "A" Edition $3.00

307-68
Velveteen Rabbit, The
Illus.: Sutton, Judith
Author: Williams, Margery
1992   "A" Edition $4.00

304-25
Very Best Home For Me!, The
Illus.: Williams, Garth
Author: Watson, Jane Werner
1953 (1981) 2nd Edition $3.00

204-25
    $4.00

206-42
    $3.00

206-52
    $3.00

206-52

Very Best Home For Me!, The
Illus.: Williams, Garth
Author: Watson, Jane Werner
1953   "N" Edition   **$3.00**

107-90

Very Busy Barbie
Text missing at bottom of page 11
Illus.: Mortimer, Winslow
Author: Slate, Barbara
1993   "A" Edition   **$3.00**

204-31

Visit To The Children's Zoo, A
Illus.: Crawford, Mel
Author: Hazen, Barbara Shook
1963   **$3.00**

204-1

(1979)   **$3.00**

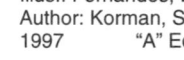

98848

Wake Up, Groundhog!
Illus.: Fernandes, Eugenie
Author: Korman, Susan
1997   "A" Edition   **$2.00**

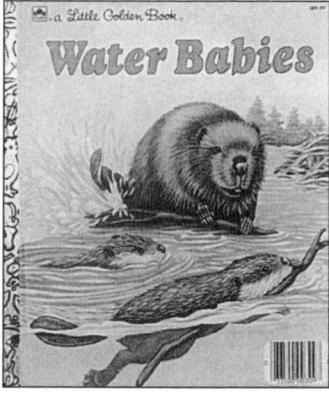

309-59

Water Babies
Illus.: Bonforte, Lisa
Author: Ingoglia, Gina
1990   "A" Edition   **$4.00**

309-70

(1991)   **$2.00**

208-1

We Help Daddy
Smoking Pipe Removed From Cover
Illus.: Wilkin, Eloise
Author: Stein, Mini
1979   8th Edition   **$3.00**

305-41

                                    $3.00

305-51

"P" Edition   **$3.00**

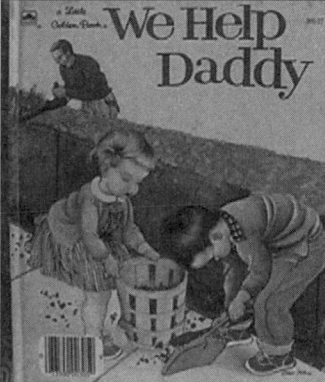

305-57

We Help Daddy
Smoking Pipe Removed From Story
Illus.: Wilkin, Eloise
Author: Stein, Mini
1962 (1989) "A" Edition   **$3.00**

305-42

We Help Mommy
Illus.: Wilkin, Eloise
Author: Cushman, Jean
1959   **$3.00**

305-52

                                    $3.00

305-64

(1991)   **$3.00**

305-67

(1992)   **$3.00**

305-87

                                    $3.00

205-43

We Like Kindergarten
Illus.: Wilkin, Eloise
Author: Cassidy, Clara
1965   **$2.00**

205-53

                                    $2.00

207-2

                                    $2.00

207-22

                                    $2.00

207-32

                                    $2.00

205-59

We Like Kindergarten
Light-blue cover background
Illus.: Wilkin, Eloise
Author: Cassidy,Clara
1965 (1990) "L" Edition   **$3.00**

205-66

(1991)   **$2.00**

98877-00

Wedding Is Beautiful, A
Illus.: Butcher, Samuel J.
Author: Mitter, Mat
1998   "A" Edition   **$2.00**

209-62

Welcome To Little Golden Book Land
Illus.: Mateu
Author: West, Cindy
1989   **$4.00**

204-4

Whales
Illus.: Ruth, Rod
Author: Watson, Jane Werner
1978   **$2.00**

308-41

$2.00

308-51

"I" Edition   **$2.00**

470-1

What Lily Goose Found
Illus.: Sumera, Anabelle
Author: Cawley, Lorinda Bryan
1977   **$3.00**

470-21

(1980)   4th Edition   **$2.00**

470-31

5th Edition   **$2.00**

204-42

What Will I Be?
Illus.: Conner, Eulala
Author: Cowles, Kathleen Krull
1979   **$3.00**

205-42

$2.00

206-3

$2.00

206-61

What's Next, Elephant?
Formerly The Big Elephant
Illus.: Rojankovsky, Feodor
Author: Jackson, Kathryn & Byron
1949 (1992)   **$4.00**

108-58

What's Up In The Attic?
Illus.: Cooke, Tom
Author: Alexander, Liza
1987   "A" Edition   **$4.00**

108-64

(1991)   **$2.00**

311-71
When Bunny Grows Up
Fomerly: The Bunny Book
Illus.: Scarry, Richard
Author: Scarry, Patsy
1955 (1992) $3.00

209-39
When You Were A Baby
Illus.: Malvern, Corinne
Author: Eng, Rita
1982   "A" Edition $3.00

306-41
          $3.00

306-51
          $3.00

306-56
(1987) $3.00

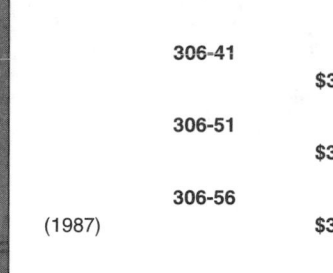

209-2
Where Did The Baby Go?
Illus.: Wilkin, Eloise
Author: Hayes, Sheila
1974 $3.00

306-44
          $3.00

306-54
          $3.00

204-3
Where Is The Bear?
Illus.: Crawford, Mel
Author: Hubka, Betty
1978 $2.00

204-33
          $2.00

206-44
          $2.00

408-2
Where Jesus Lived
Illus.: Le Hew, Ronald
Author: Watson, Jane Werner
1977 $2.00

204-5
Where Will All The Animals Go?
Illus.: Grant, Leigh
Author: Holaves, Sharon
1978   1st Edition $4.00

206-43
          $2.00

111-63
Where's Woodstock?
Illus.: Schultz, Charles M.;Ellis,Art &
Kim
Author: Lundell, Margo
1988   "A" Edition $4.00

98770-01
Which Witch Is Which?
Illus.: Brannon, Tom
Author: Muntean, Michaela
1996   "A" Edition $2.00

312-03
Whispering Rabbit, The
From The Sleepy Book
Illus.: Szekeres, Cindy
Author: Brown, Margaret Wise
1992   "A" Edition $3.00

309-58
Wild Animal Babies
Illus.: Rojankovsky, Feodor
Author: Daly, Kathleen N.
1958 **$2.00**

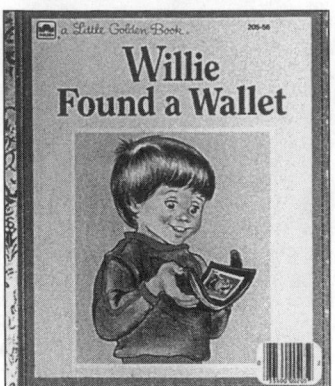

205-56
Willie Found A Wallet
Illus.: Obligado, Lilian
Author: Markham, Mary Beth
1984 "A" Edition **$5.00**

107-69
Wizard of Oz, The
Illus.: Turner, Don; Jason Studios
Author: Carey, Mary
1975 **$2.00**

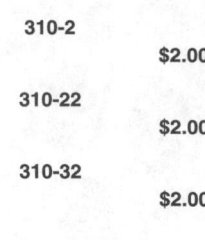

310-2
$2.00

310-22
$2.00

310-32
$2.00

98796-01
Wonder Of Easter, The
Illus.: Butcher, Sam
Author: Mitter, Matt
1997 "A" Edition **$2.00**

111-3
Woody Woodpecker At The Circus
Illus.: Mc Savage, Frank
Author: Nathan, Stella Williams
1976 **$2.00**

111-43
$2.00

111-2
Woody Woodpecker Takes A Trip
Illus.: De Nunez, Ben; White,Al
Author: Mcgovern, Ann
1961 **$2.00**

111-32
$2.00

111-42
$2.00

205-4
Words
Illus.: Cary, Louis
Author: Chambers, Lola
1948 **$2.00**

205-34
$2.00

202-42
$2.00

202-52
$2.00

202-52
Words
New Cover
Illus.: Cary, Louis
Author: Chambers, Lola
1948 **$2.00**

107-64
Xavier's Birthday Surprise!
(Cabbage Patch Kids)
Illus.: Hill, Ari
1987 **$5.00**

Disney—By Book Number

D1

Through The Picture Frame
Four Color and Black & White
Blue Spine w/ Dust
Jacket $50-$150
Illus: Walt Disney Studios
Author: Edmonds, Robert
1944   24 Pages
"A" Edition $45.00

D2

Cold-Blooded Penguin, The
Four Color and Black & White
Blue Spine w/ Dust
Jacket $50-$150
Illus: Walt Disney Studios
Author: Edmonds, Robert
1944   24 Pages
"A" Edition $45.00

D3

Dumbo
Four Color and Black & White
Blue Spine w/ Dust
Jacket $50-$200
Illus: Walt Disney Studios
Author: Walt Disney Studios
1947   42 Pages
"A" Edition $45.00

D3

Four Color and Three Color
Foil Spine
(1950)   42 Pages
"J" Edition $15.00

D3

Dumbo
(2nd Cover)
Four Color and Three Color
Foil Spine
Illus: Walt Disney Studios
Author: Walt Disney Studios
(1952)   28 Pages
"L" Edition $18.00

D3

Four Color and Three Color
Mickey Mouse Club Spine
(1955)   28 Pages
"P" Edition $10.00

D3

Four Color and Three Color
Foil Spine
(1957)   24 Pages
"W" Edition $5.00

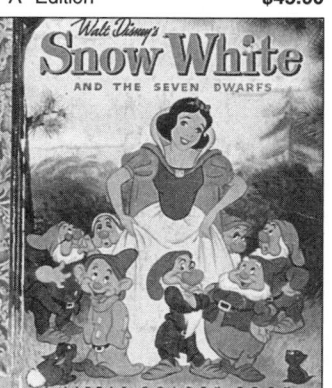

D4

Snow White And The Seven Dwarfs
Four Color and Black & White
Golden Paper Spine
Illus: O'brien, Ken
Author: Bros. Grimm
1948   42 Pages
"A" Edition $18.00

D4

Four Color and Black & White
Golden Paper Spine
Label on the back cover auto-
graphed by the stars of Snow White
at The Ice Capades
(1949)   42 Pages
"B" Edition $25.00

D4

Snow White And The Seven Dwarfs
(2nd Cover), White cover background
Four Color and Three Color, Foil Spine
Illus: O'Brien, Ken, Auth: Bros. Grimm
1948 (1951) 28 Pages
"K" Edition $12.00

D4

Four Color and Three Color
Mickey Mouse Club Spine
Light blue background
(1955)   28 Pages
"N" Edition

D5

Peter And The Wolf
Four Color and Black & White
Golden Paper Spine
Illus: Kelsey, Richard
Author: Bros. Grimm; Serge;
Prokofieff Musi
1947   42 Pages
"A" Edition $18.00

D5

Four Color and Three Color
Foil Spine
(1948)   42 Pages
"I" Edition $15.00

D5

Four Color and Three Color
Foil Spine
(1952)   28 Pages
"J" Edition $10.00

D6

Uncle Remus
Four Color and Black & White
Golden Paper Spine
Illus: Grant, Bob; Palmer, Marion
Author: Harris, Joel
1947   42 Pages
"A" Edition   **$25.00**

D6
Four color and B&W
Golden Paper Spine
Title lettering changed from black to red
(1948)   42 Pages
"C" Edition   **$22.00**

D6
Four Color and Three Color
Foil Spine
(1952)   42 Pages
"K" Edition   **$18.00**

D6
Four Color and Three Color
Mickey Mouse Club Spine
(1955)   28 Pages
"N" Edition   **$15.00**

D7

Bambi
Four Color and Black & White
Golden Paper Spine
Illus: Grant, Bob
Author: Salten, Felix
1948   42 Pages
"A" Edition   **$18.00**

D7
Four Color and Three Color
Golden Paper Spine
(1952)   28 Pages
"I" Edition   **$10.00**

D7
Four Color and Three Color
Mickey Mouse Club Spine
(1956)   24 Pages
"O" Edition   **$10.00**

D8

Pinocchio
Four Color and Black & White
Golden Paper Spine
Illus: Grant, Campbell
Author: Walt Disney Studios
1948   42 Pages
"A" Edition   **$18.00**

D8
Four Color and Three Color
Foil Spine
(1952)   28 Pages
"J" Edition   **$10.00**

D8
Foil Spine
(1952)   28 Pages
"L" Edition   **$8.00**

D8
Mickey Mouse Club Spine
(1956)   24 Pages
"O" Edition   **$10.00**

D8
Foil Spine
(1958)   24 Pages
"Q" Edition   **$5.00**

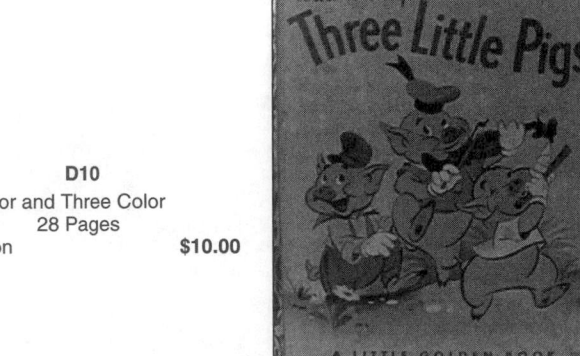

D9

Bongo
Four Color and Black & White
Golden Paper Spine
Illus: Grant, Campbell
Author: Lewis, Sinclair
1948   42 Pages
"A" Edition   **$18.00**

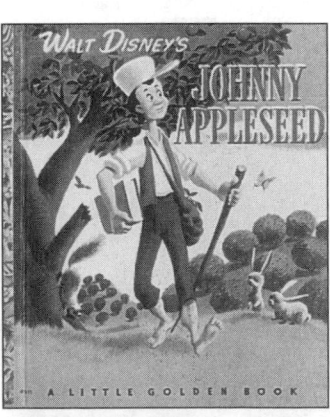

D10

Three Little Pigs
Four Color and Black & White
Golden Paper Spine
Illus: Banta, Milt; Dempster, Al
Author: Walt Disney Studios
1948   42 Pages
"A" Edition   **$18.00**

D10
Four Color and Three Color
(1952)   28 Pages
"L" Edition   **$10.00**

D10

Three Little Pigs
(2nd Cover)
Four Color and Three Color
Mickey Mouse Club Spine
Illus: Banta, Milt; Dempster, Al
Author: Walt Disney Studios
1948 (1955) 24 Pages
"P" Edition   **$12.00**

D10
Four Color and Three Color
Foil Spine
(1957)   24 Pages
"R" Edition

D11

Johnny Appleseed
Four Color and Black & White
Golden Paper Spine
Illus: Parmalee, Ted
Author: Walt Disney Studios
1949   42 Pages
"A" Edition   **$18.00**

D11
Johnny Appleseed
Four Color and Three Color
(1951)   42 Pages
"D" Edition   **$15.00**

D13
Foil Spine
Light blue cover background
(1954)28 Pages
"C" Edition   **$8.00**

D 12
Once Upon A Wintertime
Four Color and Three Color
Golden Paper Spine
Illus: Oreb, Tom
Author: Walt Disney Studios
1950   42 Pages
"A" Edition   **$20.00**

D13
Cinderella
Foil Spine
Illus: Grant, Campbell
Author: Walt Disney Studios
1950   28 Pages
"A" Edition   **$16.00**

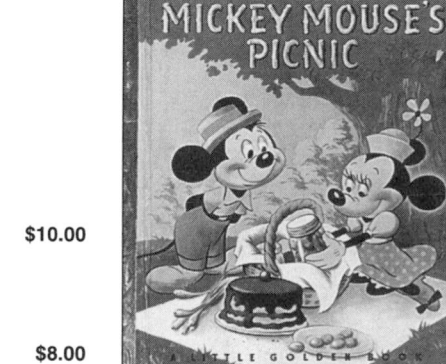

D14
Green cover lettering
(1955)   28 Pages
"E" Edition   **$10.00**

D14
Green cover lettering
(1960)   24 Pages
"G" Edition   **$8.00**

D15
(1956)   24 Pages
"E" Edition   **$6.00**

D15
Disneyland Contest in back
(1960)   24 Pages
"F" Edition   **$7.00**

D14
Donald Duck's Adventure
Illus: Grant, Campbell
Author: Bedford, Annie North
1950   28 Pages
"A" Edition   **$16.00**

D15
Mickey Mouse's Picnic
Foil Spine
Illus: Walt Disney Studios
Author: Werner, Jane
1950   28 Pages
"A" Edition   **$16.00**

D16
Mickey Mouse Club Spine
(1956)   24 Pages
"C" Edition   **$8.00**

D16
Christmas Spine
(1958)   24 Pages
"J" Edition   **$8.00**

D15
Mickey Mouse's Picnic
(2nd Cover)
Solid blue background
Illus: Walt Disney Studios
Author: Werner, Jane
1950 (1964) 24 Pages
"I" Edition   **$5.00**

D16
Santa's Toy Shop
Illus: Dempster, Al
Author: Walt Disney Studios
1950   28 Pages
"A" Edition   **$16.00**

D16
Santa's Toy Shop
(2nd Cover)
Yellow cover background
Red Spine
Illus: Dempster, Al
Author: Walt Disney Studios
1950 (1968) 24 Pages
"N" Edition   **$7.00**

D16
Santa's Toy Shop
Foil Spine
(1969)   24 Pages
15th Edition

D17
Cinderella's Friends
Illus: Dempster, Al
Author: Werner, Jane
1950   28 Pages
"A" Edition $16.00

D18
Donald Duck's Toy Train
Illus: Kelsey, Dick; Justice, Bill
Author: Werner, Jane
1950   28 Pages
"A" Edition $16.00

D18
Mickey Mouse Club Spine
(1955)   24 Pages
"F" Edition $8.00

D18
Foil Spine
Disneyland Contest in back
(1960)   24 Pages
"K" Edition $6.00

D19
Alice In Wonderland Meets The White Rabbit
Illus: Dempster, Al
Author: Werner, Jane
1951   28 Pages
"A" Edition $16.00

D20
Alice In Wonderland Finds The Garden Of Live Flowers
Illus: Grant, Cambell
Author: Werner, Jane
1951   28 Pages
"A" Edition $16.00

D21
Grandpa Bunny
Illus: Werner, Jane
Author: Walt Disney Studios
1951   28 Pages
"A" Edition $25.00

D22
Ugly Duckling, The
Illus: Maclaughlin, Don
Author: Bedford, Annie North
1952   28 Pages
"A" Edition $18.00

D23
Mad Hatter's Tea Party, The
Illus: Kelsey, Richmond I; Griffith, Don
Author: Werner, Jane
1952   28 Pages
"A" Edition $16.00

D24
Peter Pan And Wendy
Illus: Earle, Eyvind
Author: Bedford, Annie North
1952   28 Pages
"A" Edition $16.00

D24
Mickey Mouse Club Spine
(1956)   24 Pages
"C" Edition $12.00

D25
Peter Pan And The Pirates
Illus: Moore, Bob
Author: Barrie, Sir James
1952   28 Pages
"A" Edition $16.00

D26
Peter Pan And The Indians
Illus: Mack, Brice; Kinney, Dick
Author: Bedford, Annie North
1952   28 Pages
"A" Edition $16.00

D27
Donald Duck And Santa Claus
Illus: Dempster, Al
Author: Bedford, Annie North
1952   28 Pages
"A" Edition $16.00

D27
Mickey Mouse Club Spine
(1956)   24 Pages
"C" Edition $8.00

D27
Donald Duck And Santa Claus
(2nd Cover)
Yellow cover background
Illus: Dempster, Al
Author: Bedford, Annie North
1952 (1965) 28 Pages
"F" Edition $6.00

D28
Noah's Ark
Illus: Grant, Campbell
Author: Bedford, Annie North
1952   28 Pages
"A" Edition $16.00

D29
Mickey Mouse And His Space Ship
Illus: Banta, Milton; Ushler, John
Author: Werner, Jane
1952   28 Pages
"A" Edition $16.00

D30
Pluto Pup Goes To Sea
Illus: Gracey, Yale
Author: Bedford, Annie North
1952   28 Pages
"A" Edition $16.00

D30
Mickey Mouse Club Spine
(1956)   24 Pages
"C" Edition

D31
Hiawatha
Illus: Walt Disney Studios
Author: Walt Disney Studios
1953   28 Pages
"A" Edition $16.00

D32
Mickey Mouse And Pluto Pup
Illus: Grant, Campbell
Author: Beecher, Elizabeth
1953   28 Pages
"A" Edition $15.00

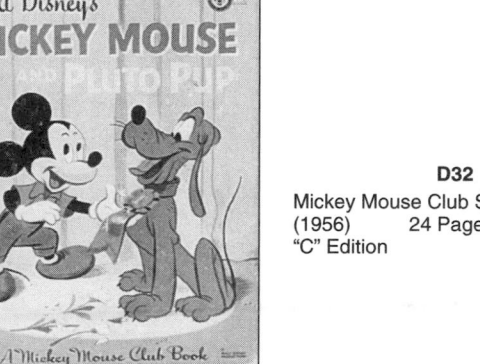

D32
Mickey Mouse And Pluto Pup
(2nd Cover)
Mickey Mouse Club Spine
Illus: Grant, Campbell
Author: Beecher, Elizabeth
1953 (1955) 28 Pages
"B" Edition $15.00

D32
Mickey Mouse Club Spine
(1956)   24 Pages
"C" Edition $8.00

D33
Mickey Mouse Goes Christmas Shopping
Illus: Moore, Bob; Atencio, Xavier
Author: Bedford, Annie North
1953   28 Pages
"A" Edition $15.00

D33
Mickey Mouse Goes Christmas Shopping
(2nd Cover)
Green cover background
Christmas Spine
Illus: Moore, Bob; Atencio, Xavier
Author: Bedford, Annie North
1953 (1963) 24 Pages
"G" Edition $6.00

D33
Red Spine
(1968)   24 Pages
"I" Edition

D34
Donald Duck And The Witch
Illus: Kelsey, Dick
Author: Bedford, Annie North
1953   28 Pages
"A" Edition $20.00

D35
Seven Dwarfs Find A House
Illus: Svendsen, Julius
Author: Bedford, Annie North
1952   28 Pages
"A" Edition $15.00

D35
Mickey Mouse Club Spine
(1950)   24 Pages
"C" Edition $10.00

D36
Mother Goose
Illus: Dempster, Al
Author: Walt Disney Studios
1952   28 Pages
"A" Edition $35.00

D37
Ben And Me
Illus: Grant, Campbell
Author: Lawson, Robert
1954   28 Pages
"A" Edition $16.00

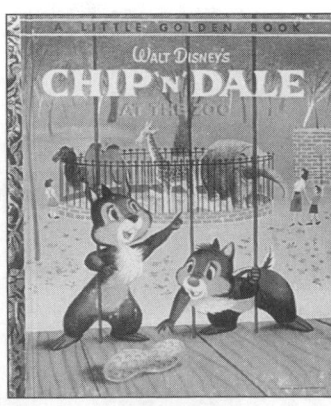

D38
Chip 'n' Dale At The Zoo
Illus: Bosche, Bill
Author: Bedford, Annie North
1954   28 Pages
"A" Edition $17.00

D39
Donald Duck's Christmas Tree
Illus: Moore, Bob
Author: Bedford, Annie North
1954   28 Pages
"A" Edition $16.00

D39
Mickey Mouse Club Spine
(1957)   24 Pages
"C" Edition $10.00

D40
Donald Duck's Toy Sailboat
Illus: Armstrong, Samuel
Author: Bedford, Annie North
1954   28 Pages
"A" Edition $16.00
D40
(1957)   24 Pages
"E" Edition $8.00

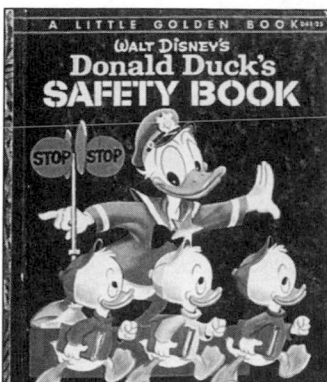

D41
Mickey Mouse Club Spine
(1955)   28 Pages
"B" Edition $18.00

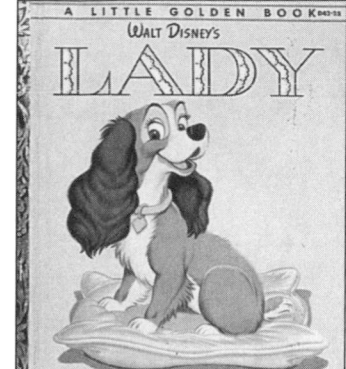

D40
Donald Duck's Toy Sailboat
(2nd Cover)
Blue cover background
Illus: Armstrong, Samuel
Author: Bedford, Annie North
1954 (1963) 24 Pages
"F" Edition $5.00

D41
Donald Duck's Safety Book
Illus: Gonzales, Manuel; Wheeler,
George
Author: Bedford, Annie North
1954   28 Pages
"A" Edition $20.00

D42
Lady
Illus: Greene, Ward
Author: Armstrong, Samuel
1954   28 Pages
"A" Edition $16.00

D43
Mickey Mouse Club Spine
(1956)   24 Pages
"B" Edition $10.00

D43
Disneyland On The Air
Illus: Armstrong, Samuel
Author: Bedford, Annie North
1955   28 Pages
"A" Edition $15.00

D43
Disneyland On The Air
Red cover background
Illus: Armstrong, Samuel
Author: Bedford, Annie North
1955 (1965) 24 Pages
"C" Edition $8.00

D44
Donald Duck In Disneyland
Illus: Walt Disney Studios
Author: Bedford, Annie North
1954   28 Pages
"A" Edition $16.00

D44
(1956)   24 Pages
"B" Edition $10.00

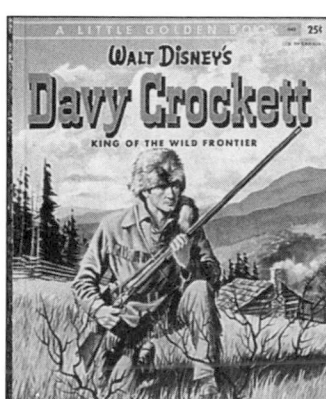

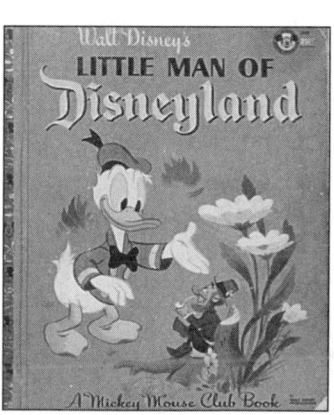

D45
**Davy Crockett 'King Of The Wild
Frontier'**
Illus: Crawford, Mel
Author: Shapiro, Irwin
1955   28 Pages
"A" Edition $16.00

D46
Little Man Of Disneyland
Mickey Mouse Club Spine
Illus: Kelsey, Dick
Author: Bedford, Annie North
1955   28 Pages
"A" Edition $16.00

D47
Davy Crockett's Keelboat Race
Mickey Mouse Club Spine
Illus: Shapiro, Irwin
1955   24 Pages
"A" Edition $18.00

D48

Robin Hood
Mickey Mouse Club Spine
Illus: Walt Disney Studios
Author: Bedford, Annie North
1955   24 Pages
"A" Edition   **$16.00**

D49

Donald Duck Prize Driver
Mickey Mouse Club Spine
Illus: Boyle, Neil
Author: Bedford, Annie North
1956   24 Pages
"A" Edition   **$18.00**

D49

Foil Spine
(1960)   24 Pages
"B" Edition   **$16.00**

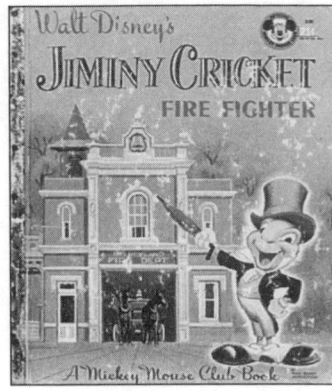

D50

Jiminy Cricket Fire Fighter
Mickey Mouse Club Spine
Illus: Armstrong, Samuel
Author: Bedford, Annie North
1956   24 Pages
"A" Edition   **$18.00**

D51

Mother Goose
Mickey Mouse Club Spine
Illus: Dempster, Al
1952 (1956) 24 Pages
"A" Edition   **$15.00**

D52

Goofy, Movie Star
Mickey Mouse Club Spine
Illus: Armstrong, Samuel
Author: Bedford, Annie North
1956   24 Pages
"A" Edition   **$18.00**

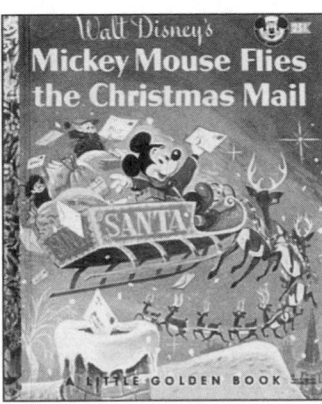

D53

Mickey Mouse Flies The Christmas Mail
Mickey Mouse Club Spine
Illus: Svendsen, Julius; Boyle, Niel
Author: Bedford, Annie North
1956   24 Pages
"A" Edition   **$16.00**

D53

Foil Spine
(1958)   24 Pages
"C" Edition   **$12.00**

D54

Perri And Her Friends
Mickey Mouse Club Spine
Illus: Walt Disney Studios
Author: Salten, Felix; Bedford, Annie
North
1956   24 Pages
"A" Edition   **$16.00**

D54

Foil Spine
(1957)   24 Pages
"B" Edition   **$14.00**

D55

Donald Duck And The Mouseketeers
Mickey Mouse Club Spine
Illus: Armstrong, Samuel
Author: Bedford, Annie North
1956   24 Pages
"A" Edition   **$16.00**

D56

Peter And The Wolf
1956 Mickey Mouse Club Spine
Illus: Kelsey, Richard
Author: Prokofieffl, Serge
1946 (1956) 24 Pages
"A" Edition   **$9.00**

D56

Foil Spine
Yellow title lettering
(1977)   24 Pages
3rd Edition

D57

Mickey Mouse And The Missing Mouseketeers
Mickey Mouse Club Spine
True "A" Edition
Illus: Svendsen, Juluis; Totten, Bob
Author: Bedford, Annie North
1956   24 Pages
"A" Edition   **$12.00**

D57

Foil Spine
(1958)   24 Pages
"A" Edition   **$10.00**

D 58

Cinderella's Friends
Mickey Mouse Club Spine
Illus: Dempster, Al
Author: Werner, Jane
1950 (1956) 24 Pages
"A" Edition   **$10.00**

D58

Foil Spine
(1959)   24 Pages
"E" Edition

D58

Mickey Mouse Club Stamp Book
Never printed as this number. See A10

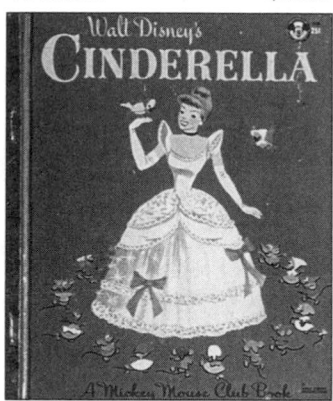

D59

Cinderella
Mickey Mouse Club Spine
Illus: Grant, Campbell
Author: Walt Disney Studios
1950 (1956) 24 Pages
"A" Edition   **$10.00**

D61

Sleeping Beauty
Foil spine but a few "A" Edition's
have been found w/ the Mickey
Mouse Club spine.
Illus: Svendsen, Julius; Armitage,
Frank
Author: Bedford, Annie North
1957   24 Pages
"A" Edition   **$15.00**

D62

Bongo
Mickey Mouse Club Spine
Illus: Grant, Campbell
Author: Lewis, Sinclair
1948 (1957) 24 Pages
"A" Edition   **$10.00**

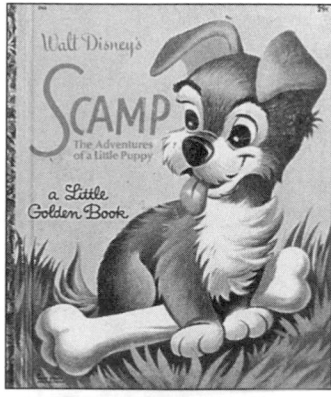

D63

Scamp
Illus: Rinaldi, Joe; Mcgary, Norm
Author: Bedford, Annie North
1957   24 Pages
"A" Edition   **$12.00**

D64

Paul Revere
Illus: Luhrs, Paul
Author: Shapiro, Irwin
1957   24 Pages
"A" Edition   **$12.00**

D64

Paul Rever in yellow lettering
(1975)   24 Pages
"B" Edition   **$6.00**

D65

Old Yeller
Illus: Schmidt, Edwin; Daly, E.J
Author: Shapiro, Irwin
1957   24 Pages
"A" Edition   **$15.00**

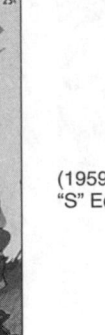

D65

Old Yeller
(2nd Cover)
Blue cover background
Illus: Schmidt, Edwin; Daly, E.J
Author: Shapiro, Irwin
1957 (1965) 24 Pages
"B" Edition   **$7.00**

D66

Snow White
Four Color and Three Color
Illus: O'brien, Ken; Dempster, Al
Author: Bros. Grimm
1948 (1958) 24 Pages
"P" Edition   **$8.00**

D66

(1959)   24 Pages
"S" Edition   **$7.00**

D67

Seven Dwarfs Find A House
Mickey Mouse Club Spine
Illus: Svendsen, Julius
Author: Bedford, Annie North
1948 (1957) 24 Pages
"D" Edition   **$9.00**

D67

Foil Spine
(1961)   24 Pages
"F" Edition

D68

Zorro
Illus: Steel, John
Author: Verrral, Charles Spain
1958   24 Pages
"A" Edition   **$18.00**

D68

Zorro
Yellow Cover
Illus: Steel, John
Author: Verrral, Charles Spain
1958 (1965) 24 Pages
"D" Edition   **$12.00**

D70

Scamp's Adventure
Illus: Rinaldi, Joe; Boyle, Neil
Author: Bedford, Annie North
1958   24 Pages
"A" Edition   **$12.00**

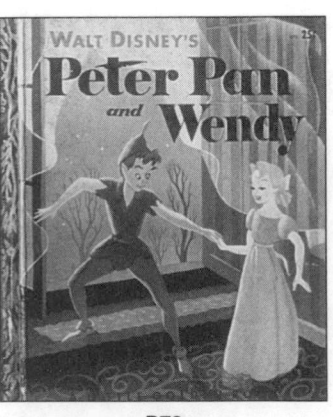

D71

Sleeping Beauty And The Good Fairies
Illus: Svendsen, Julius; Strobe, Dorothy
Author: Bedford, Annie North
1958   24 Pages
"A" Edition   **$12.00**

D72

Peter Pan And Wendy
Illus: Earle, Eyvind
Author: Bedford, Annie North
1952 (1958) 24 Pages
"D" Edition   **$9.00**

D73

Peter Pan And The Pirates
Illus: Moore, Bob
Author: Walt Disney Studios
1952 (1958) 24 Pages
"B" Edition   **$9.00**

D74

Peter Pan And The Indians
Illus: Mack, Brice; Kinney, Dick
Author: Bedford, Annie
1952 (1958) 24 Pages
"B" Edition   **$9.00**

D75
Manni The Donkey
Illus: Walt Disney Studios
Author: Salten, Felix
1959   24 Pages
"A" Edition $13.00

D76
Mickey Mouse And Pluto Pup
Illus: Grant, Campbell
Author: Beecher, Elizabeth
1953 (1959) 24 Pages
"E" Edition $8.00

D77
Zorro And The Secret Plan
Illus: Greene, Hamilton
Author: Verral, Charles Spain
1958   24 Pages
"A" Edition $18.00

D77
Red cover background
Illus: Greene, Hamilton
Author: Verral, Charles Spain
1958 (1964) 24 Pages
"B" Edition $12.00

D78
Three Little Pigs
Full color and three color
Illus: Banta, Milt; Dempster, Al
Author: Walt Disney Studios
1953 (1958) 24 Pages
"S" Edition $11.00

D78
Full color
(1960)   24 Pages
"V" Edition $5.00

D79
Mother Goose
Illus: Dempster, Al
Author: Walt Disney Studios
1952 (1959) 24 Pages
"E" Edition $8.00

D80
Tonka
Illus: Walt Disney Studios
Author: Beecher, Elizabeth
1959   24 Pages
"A" Edition $16.00

D81
Darby O'gill
Illus: Gantz, David
Author: Bedford, Annie North
1959   24 Pages
"A" Edition $16.00

D82
Shaggy Dog, The
Illus: Anderson, Rus
Author: Verral, Charles Spain
1959   24 Pages
"A" Edition $15.00

D83
Goliath II
Illus: Peet, Bill
Author: Peet, Bill
1959   24 Pages
"A" Edition $15.00

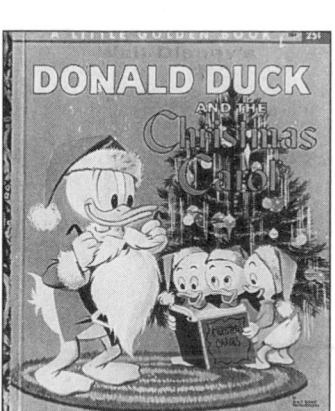

D84
Donald Duck And The Christmas Carol
Illus: Mc Gary, Norman
Author: Bedford, Annie
1960   24 Pages
"A" Edition $40.00

D85

Name "Walt Disney" on cover
changed to black
(1971)   24 Pages
22nd Edition

D84

**Donald Duck And The Christmas
Carol**
(2nd Cover)
Green cover background
Christmas Spine
Illus: Mc Gary, Norman
Author: Bedford, Annie
1960 (1963) 24 Pages
"B" Edition $25.00

D85

Uncle Remus
Illus: Harris, Joel Chandler
Author: Palmer, Marion
1947 (1959) 24 Pages
"Q" Edition $10.00

D86

Donald Duck, Lost And Found
Illus: Grant, Bob; Totten, Bob
Author: Buettner, Carl
1960   24 Pages
"A" Edition $15.00

D87

Toby Tyler
Illus: Mc Kim, Sam
Author: Memling, Carl
1960   24 Pages
"A" Edition $14.00

D88

Scamp's Adventure
Illus: Rinaldi, Joe
Author: Bedford, Annie North
1958 (1960) 24 Pages
"C" Edition $10.00

D89

Lucky Puppy, The
Illus: Hubbard, Allen; Bester, Don
Author: Watson, Jane Werner
1960   24 Pages
"A" Edition $13.00

D89

Lucky Puppy
(2nd Cover)
No window panes on cover
Illus: Hubbard, Allen; Bester, Don
Author: Watson, Jane Werner
1960 (1960) 24 Pages
"B" Edition $12.00

D89

"Hundred One Dalmatians" added to
title
1960 (1966) 24 Pages
"G" Edition

D89

Lucky Puppy
(3rd Cover)
Illus: Hubbard, Allen; Bester, Don
Author: Watson, Jane Werner
1960 (1965) 24 Pages
"F" Edition $8.00

D90

Bambi
Illus: Grant, Bob
Author: Salten, Felix
1948 (1960) 24 Pages
"T" Edition $8.00

D90

Bambi
(2nd Cover)
White cover background
Illus: Grant, Bob
Author: Salten, Felix
1948 (1965) 24 Pages
"X" Edition $4.00

D91
Pollyanna
Illus: Hedstrom, Karen
Author: Beecher, Elizabeth
1960   24 Pages
"A" Edition   **$20.00**

D92
Donald Duck In Disneyland
Illus: Campbell, Grant
Author: Bedford, Annie North
1960 (1960) 24 Pages
"D" Edition   **$12.00**

D93
Bedknobs & Broomsticks
Illus: Walt Disney Studios
Author: Walt Disney Studios
1971   24 Pages
"A" Edition   **$8.00**

D94
Donald Duck Private Eye
Illus: White, Al
Author: Buettner, Carl
1961   24 Pages
"A" Edition   **$16.00**

D95
Swiss Family Robinson
Illus: Granger, Paul
Author: Lewis, Jean
1961   24 Pages
"A" Edition   **$14.00**

D96
Flying Car, The
Illus: Irvin, Fred
Author: Verral, Charles Spain
1961   24 Pages
"A" Edition   **$15.00**

D97
Babes In Toyland
Green Background
Illus: Marshall, Earl & Carl
Author: Hazen, Barbara Shook
1961 (1961) 24 Pages
"B" Edition   **$12.00**

D97
Babes In Toyland
Blue Background
Illus: Marshall, Earl & Carl
Author: Hazen, Barbara Shook
1961   24 Pages
"A" Edition   **$13.00**

D98
Ludwig Von Drake
Illus: Pratt, Hawley
Author: Ingoglia, Gina; Sherman,
George
1961   24 Pages
"A" Edition   **$15.00**

D99
Toy Soldiers, The
Illus: Thompson, Robert
Author: Hazen, Barbara Shook
1961   24 Pages
"A" Edition   **$12.00**

D100
Pinocchio
Illus: Grant, Campbell
Author: Walt Disney Studios
1948 (1961) 24 Pages
"V" Edition   **$8.00**

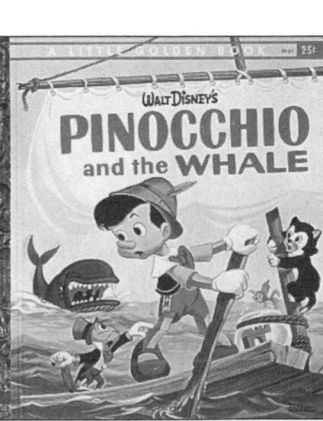

D101
Pinocchio And The Whale
Illus: White, Al
Author: Ingoglia, Gina
1961   24 Pages
"A" Edition   **$20.00**

D102

Big Red
Illus: Crawford, Mel
Author: Daly, Kathleen N.
1962   24 Pages
"A" Edition   **$12.00**

D103

Lady
Illus: Greene, Ward
Author: Armstrong, Samuel
1954 (1961) 24 Pages
"E" Edition   **$7.00**

D104

Savage Sam
Illus: Greene, Hamilton
Author: Memling, Carl
1963   24 Pages
"A" Edition   **$10.00**

D105

Surprise For Mickey Mouse
Illus: Walt Disney Studios
Author: Walt Disney Studios
1971   24 Pages
"A" Edition   **$5.00**

D106

Sword In The Stone, The
Illus: White, Al
Author: Mcgary, Norm
1963   24 Pages
"A" Edition   **$12.00**

D107

Wizards' Duel, The
Illus: White, Al
Author: Memling, Carl
1963   24 Pages
"A" Edition   **$15.00**

D108

Mickey Mouse And His Space Ship
Illus: Banta, Milton; Ushler, John
Author: Werner, Jane
1963 (1962) 24 Pages
"C" Edition   **$10.00**

D109

Donald Duck In Disneyland
Illus: Grant, Campbell
Author: Bedford, Annie North
1954 (1963) 24 Pages
"F" Edition   **$10.00**

D110

Peter Pan And Wendy
Illus: Earle, Eyvind
Author: Bedford, Annie North
1952 (1963) 24 Pages
"E" Edition   **$7.00**

D111

Bunny Book
Originally Grandpa Bunny #D21
Illus: Kelsey, Dick; Justice, Bill
Author: Werner, Jane
1951 (1964) 24 Pages
"C" Edition   **$15.00**

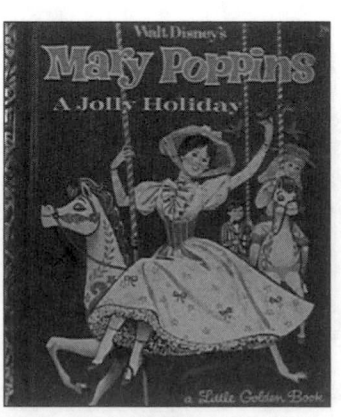

D112

Mary Poppins, A Jolly Holiday
Illus: Edwards, Beverly; Jason, Leon
Author: Bedford, Annie North
1964   24 Pages
"A" Edition   **$12.00**

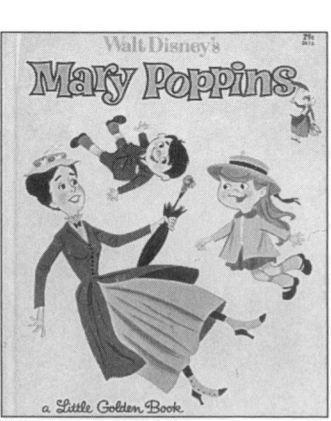

D113

Mary Poppins
Illus: White, Al
Author: Bedford, Annie North
1964   24 Pages
"A" Edition   **$12.00**

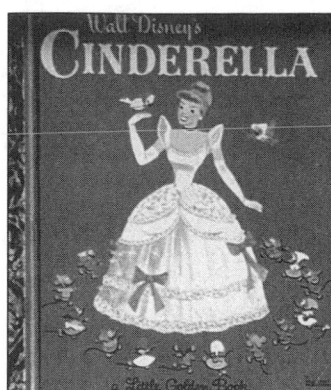

D114
Cinderella
Illus: Grant, Campbell
Author: Walt Disney Studios
1950 (1964) 24 Pages
"N" Edition $10.00

D115
Cinderella's Friends
Illus: Dempster, Al
Author: Werner, Jane
1950 (1964) 24 Pages
"F" Edition $7.00

D116
Winnie-The-Pooh The Honey Tree
Illus: Totten, Bob
Author: Milne, A.A.
1965 24 Pages
"A" Edition $8.00

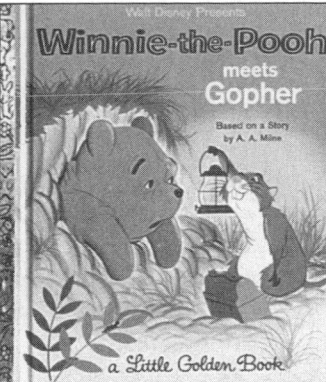

D117
Winnie-The-Pooh Meets Gopher
Illus: De Santis, George
Author: Milne, A.A.
1972 24 Pages
"A" Edition $7.00

D118
Ugly Dachshund, The
Illus: Crawford, Mel
Author: Memling, Carl
1966 24 Pages
"A" Edition $15.00

D119
Thumper
Illus: Walt Disney Studios
Author: Walt Disney Studios
1942 (1964) 24 Pages
"A" Edition $10.00

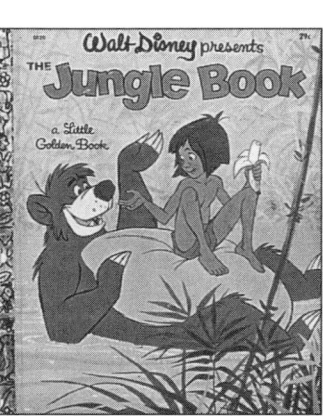

D120
Jungle Book, The
Illus: Crawford, Mel
Author: Bedford, Annie North
1967 24 Pages
"A" Edition $8.00

D121
Winnie-The-Pooh And Tigger
Illus: Walt Disney Studios
Author: Milne, A.A.
1968 24 Pages
"A" Edition $7.00

D122
Aristocats, The
Illus: Walt Disney Studios
1970 24 Pages
"A" Edition $15.00

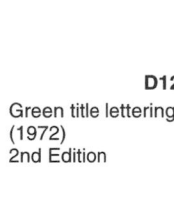

D123
Green title lettering
(1972) 24 Pages
2nd Edition $6.00

D123
Disneyland Parade
Blue title lettering
Illus: Walt Disney Studios
1971 24 Pages
"A" Edition $8.00

D124
Pluto And The Adventure Of The Golden Scepter
Illus: Walt Disney Studios
1972 24 Pages
"A" Edition $6.00

D125

Favorite Nursery Tales
Illus: Walt Disney Studios
1973   24 Pages
"A" Edition $6.00

D126

Robin Hood
Illus: Walt Disney Studios
1973   24 Pages
"A" Edition $8.00

D127

Donald Duck And The Witch Next Door
Illus: Walt Disney Studios
1974   24 Pages
"A" Edition $6.00

D128

Robin Hood And The Daring Mouse
Illus: Walt Disney Studios
1974   24 Pages
"A" Edition $10.00

D129

Mickey Mouse And The Great Lot Plot
Illus: Walt Disney Studios
1974   24 Pages
"A" Edition $6.00

D130

Love Bug, The
Illus: Walt Disney Studios
1974   24 Pages
"A" Edition $11.00

D131

Donald Duck In America On Parade
Illus: Walt Disney Studios
1975   24 Pages
"A" Edition $9.00

D132

Bambi Friends Of The Forest
Illus: Walt Disney Studios
1975   24 Pages
"A" Edition $6.00

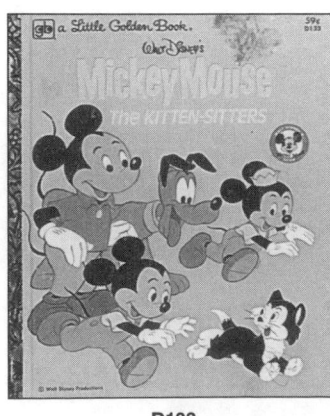

D133

Mickey Mouse The Kitten-Sitters
Illus: Walt Disney Studios
1976   24 Pages
"A" Edition $6.00

D134

Mickey Mouse And The Best-Neighbor Contest
Illus: Walt Disney Studios
1977   24 Pages
"A" Edition $6.00

D135

Mickey Mouse And The Mouseketeers Ghost Town Adventure
Illus: Walt Disney Studios
1977   24 Pages
"A" Edition $6.00

D136

Rescuers, The
Illus: Walt Disney Studios
1977   24 Pages
"A" Edition $7.00

D137

Pete's Dragon
Illus: Walt Disney Studios
1977   24 Pages
"A" Edition $7.00

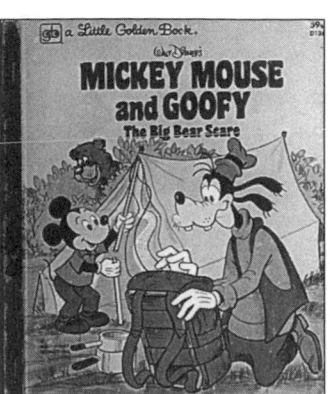

D138

Mickey Mouse And Goofy, The Big Bear Scare
Illus: Walt Disney Studios
1978   24 Pages
"A" Edition $6.00

D139

Donald Duck And The One Bear
Illus: Walt Disney Studios
1978   24 Pages
"A" Edition $6.00

D140

Donald Duck 'Instant Millionaire'
Illus: Walt Disney Studios
Author: Walt Disney Studios
1978   24 Pages
"A" Edition $7.00

Disney—New Numbering

105-65

101 Dalmatians
Illus.: Walt Disney Studios
Author: Walt Disney Studios
1985   **$4.00**

105-81

101 Dalmatians
Illus.: Langley, Bill; Dias, Ron
Author: Korman, Justine
1991 (1991)   **$3.00**

105-84

(1991)   **$3.00**

98069-01

101 Dalmatians
Illus.: Langley, Bill & Dias, Ron
Author: Korman, Justine
1991   **$2.00**

107-88

Aladdin
Illus.: Baker, Darrell
Author: Kreider, Karen
1992
"A" Edition   **$3.00**

107-92

Aladdin - The Magic Carpet Ride
Illus.: Thompkins, Kenny; Eggleston,
Gary
Author: Margulies, Teddy Slater
1993
"A" Edition   **$3.00**

105-77

Alice In Wonderland
Illus.: Mateu, Franc
Author: Slater, Teddy
1991
"A" Edition   **$3.00**

103-1

**Alice In Wonderland Meets The
White Rabbit**
Illus.: Dempster, Al
Author: Werner, Jane
1951 (1979)   **$1.00**

103-21	
	$1.00
103-31	
(1981)	
17th Edition	**$1.00**
103-41	
	$1.00
105-40	
	$1.00
105-50	**$1.00**

105-67

Aristocats, The
Illus.: Walt Disney Studios
Author: Walt Disney Studios
1970
"A" Edition   **$4.00**

105-9

Bambi
Illus.: Grant, Bob
Author: Salten, Felix
1948   **$1.00**

106-1

(1979)
46th Edition   **$1.00**

106-9

Bambi
Illus.: Dias, Ron
Author: Salten, Felix
1984   **$1.00**

106-21	
	$1.00
106-41	
"A" Edition	**$4.00**
106-60	
(1991)	**$1.00**
106-61	
	$1.00

98071-01
Bambi
Illus.: Dias, Ron
Author: Salten, Felix
1984   **$2.00**

106-22
Bambi - Friends Of The Forest
Illus.: Walt Disney Studios
1975   **$1.00**

106-42	$1.00
107-46	$1.00
107-56	$1.00
101-50	$1.00
101-59 (1991)	$2.00

101-62
Bambi - Friends Of The Forest
Illus.: Walt Disney Studios
1975 (1993)
"R" Edition   **$5.00**

104-65
Beauty And The Beast
Illus.: Dias, Ron; Gonzalez, Ric
Author: Slater, Teddy
1991
"A" Edition   **$3.00**

96009-00
Best Thanksgiving Day, The (Pooh)
Illus.: Arkadia
Author: Braybrooks, Ann
1998
"A" Edition   **$2.00**

105-54
Black Caldron Taran Finds A Friend, The
Illus.: Walt Disney Studios
Author: Walt Disney Studios
1985
"A" Edition   **$5.00**

107-52
Cave Monster, The (The Lion King)
Illus.: Williams, Don
Author: Korman, Justine
1996
"A" Edition   **$3.00**

105-78
Chip 'n Dale Rescue Rangers 'The Big Cheese Caper'
Illus.: Baker, Darrell
Author: Kovacs, Deborah
1991
"A" Edition   **$3.00**

103-3
Cinderella
Illus.: Grant, Campbell
Author: Walt Disney Studios
1950 (1979)   **$1.00**

103-23	$1.00
103-33	$1.00
103-43	$1.00
103-51	$1.00

103-57
Cinderella
Illus.: Dias, Ron
Author: Walt Disney Studios
1986 (1987)
"A" Edition   **$4.00**

103-65
(1991)   **$1.00**

103-68

Cinderella (Pink Title Lettering)
Illus.: Dias, Ron
Author: Walt Disney Studios
1986 (1993)   **$2.00**

100-63

Cowboy Mickey
Illus.: Guelle
Author: West, Cindy
1990
"A" Edition   **$3.00**

100-70

(1991)   **$1.00**

102-67

Darkwing Duck 'The Silly Canine Caper'
Unstated 1st
Illus.: Williams, Don
Author: Korman, Justine
1992   **$3.00**

100-58

Detective Mickey Mouse
Illus.: Walt Disney Studios
Author: Walt Disney Studios
1985
"A" Edition   **$5.00**

100-72

          $1.00

102-56

Donald Duck - Some Ducks Have All The Luck
Illus.: Walt Disney Studios
Author: Walt Disney Studios
1987   **$5.00**

102-63

(1993)   **$1.00**

102-68

(1991)   **$1.00**

102-55

Donald Duck And The Big Dog
Illus.: Walt Disney Studios
Author: Walt Disney Studios
1986 (1987)
"D" Edition   **$4.00**

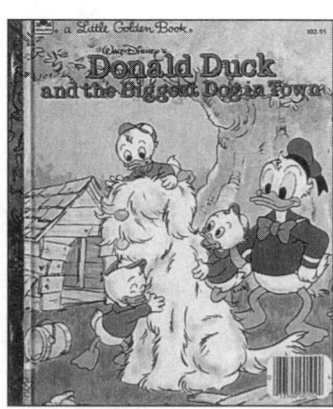

102-55

Donald Duck And The Biggest Dog In Town
Illus.: Walt Disney Studios
Author: Walt Disney Studios
1986
"A" Edition   **$5.00**

102-3

Donald Duck And The One Bear
Illus.: Walt Disney Studios
Author: Walt Disney Studios
1978 (1979)   **$2.00**

102-43

          $2.00

102-53

          $2.00

102-2

Donald Duck And The Witch Next Door
Illus.: Walt Disney Studios
Author: Walt Disney Studios
1974 (1979)   **$2.00**

102-32

          $2.00

102-42

          $2.00

102-24
Donald Duck Instant Millionaire
Illus.: Grant, Campbell
Author: Bedford, Annie North
1984 $2.00

102-44

$2.00

102-54

$2.00

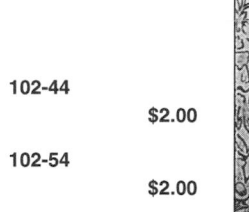

460-13
Donald Duck's Christmas Tree
Illus.: Moore, Bob
Author: Bedford, Annie North
1991
"A" Edition $2.00

102-1
Donald Duck's Toy Sailboat
Illus.: Armstrong, Samuel
Author: Bedford, Annie North
1954 (1979) $2.00

102-41

$2.00

102-51

$1.00

102-59
Donald Duck's Toy Sailboat
Illus.: Armstrong, Samuel
Author: Bedford, Annie North
1954 (1990)
"A" Edition $2.00
102-66
(1991) $1.00

102-58
Duck Tales 'The Hunt For The Giant Pearl'
Illus.: Walt Disney Studios
Author: Walt Disney Studios
1989
"A" Edition $4.00

102-65
(1991) $2.00

102-57
Duck Tales - The Secret City Under The Sea
Illus.: Langley, Bill; Guenther, Annie
Author: Newman, Paul S.
1988
"A" Edition $4.00

102-64
(1991) $2.00

104-3
Dumbo
Illus.: Walt Disney Studios
Author: Walt Disney Studios
1947 (1979) $1.00

104-33

$1.00

104-43

$1.00

104-53

$1.00

104-59
Dumbo
Illus.: Dias, Ron; Guenther, Annie
Author: Walt Disney Studios
1988
"A" Edition $4.00
104-67
(1990) $1.00

98765-01
Eeyore, You're The Best!
Illus.: Kurtz, John
Author: Braybrooks, Ann
1996 $2.00

89928-01
Enchanted Christmas, The (Beauty And The Beast)
Illus.: Nowell, Alan
Author: Muldrow, Diane
1997
"A" Edition $2.00

106-4
Favorite Nursery Tales
Illus.: Walt Disney Studios
1973 (1979) $1.00

106-34		
	$1.00	
106-44		
	$1.00	
106-54		
	$1.00	

104-62
Ghost Ship (Tale Spin)
Illus.: Di Cicco, Sue
Author: Helfer, Andrew
1991
"A" Edition $3.00

101-64
Grand And Wonderful Day, The
Illus.: Baker, Darrell
Author: Packard, Mary
1995
"A" Edition $2.00

107-87
Great Egg-Spectations (Goof Troop)
Illus.: Williams, Don
Author: Gilbert, Janet
1992
"A" Edition $6.00

98800-01
Hercules
Illus.: Emslie, Peter; William, Don
Author: Korman, Justine
1997
"A" Edition $2.00

98801-01
Hercules - A Race To The Rescue
Illus.: Cardona Studio
Author: Bazaldua, Barbara
1997
"A" Edition $2.00

105-26
Hide & Seek (The Fox And The Hound)
Unstated 1st
Illus.: Walt Disney Studios
Author: Walt Disney Studios
1981
                     $5.00

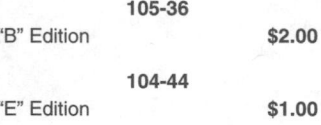

105-36	
"B" Edition	$2.00
104-44	
"E" Edition	$1.00

104-46
Hide & Seek (The Fox And The Hound)
Illus.: Walt Disney Studios
Author: Walt Disney Studios
1981
"R" Edition $2.00

107-35
Hunchback Of Notre Dame, The
Illus.: Williams, Don
Author: Korman, Justine
1996
"A" Edition $2.00

103-64
(1991) $2.00

104-45
"A" Edition $3.00

104-55
"C" Edition $2.00

103-56
Jungle Book, The
Illus.: Crawford, Mel
Author: Bedford, Annie North
1967 (1986)
"E" Edition $3.00

98820-00
King Of The Beasties (Pooh)
Illus.: Baker, Darrell
Author: Braybrooks, Ann
1998
"A" Edition $2.00

105-45
$2.00

105-55
(1986) $3.00

105-35
Lady
Illus.: Greene, Ward
Author: Armstrong, Samuel
1954 $2.00

105-55
Lady And The Tramp
Illus.: Walt Disney Studios
Author: Greene, Ward
1954 $2.00

105-72
Lady And The Tramp
Illus.: Dias, Ron; Langley, Bill
Author: Slater, Teddy
1991
"A" Edition $2.00

98804-01
Let's Go To The Vet
Illus.: Di Cico Digital Arts
Author: Lewis, Zoe
1997
"A" Edition $2.00

105-58
Lady And The Tramp
Illus.: Walt Disney Studios
Author: Greene, Ward
1954 (1990)
"A" Edition $2.00

98833-01
Let's Go To The Airport
Illus.: Di Cico Digital Arts
Author: Bazaldua, Barbara
1997
"A" Edition $2.00

98802-01
Let's Go To The Fire Station
Illus.: Di Cico Digital Arts
Author: Geist, Lucy
1997
"A" Edition $2.00

107-93

Lion King, The
Illus.: Williams, Don; Russell, H. R.
Author: Korman, Justine
1994
"A" Edition $3.00

105-68

Little Mermaid, The
Illus.: Dias, Ron
Author: Teitelbaum, Michael
1989
"A" Edition $4.00

105-68

Little Mermaid, The 'Ariel's Under-water Adventure'
Illus.: Dias, Ron
Author: Teitelbaum, Michael
1989
"E" Edition $4.00

105-82

(1991) $2.00

105-79

Little Mermaid, The
Pictures From Movie
Author: Teitelbaum, Michael
1991
"A" Edition $4.00

105-85

Little Mermaid, The
Whole Story
Illus.: Di Cicco, Sue
Author: Teitelbaum, Michael
1992 (1992)
"A" Edition $3.00

103-59

Mickey And The Beanstalk
Illus.: Ross, Sharon
Author: Anastasio, Dina
1988
"A" Edition $4.00

103-66

(1991) $2.00

103-69

Mickey And The Beanstalk
Illus.: Ross, Sharon
Author: Anastasio, Dina
1988 (1993)
"R" Edition $2.00

100-61

Mickey Mouse - Those Were The Days
Illus.: Mones
Author: Carey, Mary
1988
"A" Edition $4.00

100-76

(1991) $2.00

100-4

$1.00

100-44

"I" Edition $1.00

100-54

"A" Edition $2.00

100-73

(1991) $1.00

100-34

Mickey Mouse And Goofy, The Big Bear Scare
Illus.: Walt Disney Studios
1978 $1.00

100-3

Mickey Mouse And The Best-Neighbor Contest
Illus.: Walt Disney Studios
1974 (1979) $1.00

100-43

$1.00

100- 2

Mickey Mouse And The Great Lot Plot
Illus.: Walt Disney Studios
1974 (1979)
2nd Edition $1.00

100-32
Mickey Mouse And The Great Lot Plot
$1.00

100-42
$1.00

100-66
"A" Edition $1.00

100-74
(1991) $1.00

105-21
Mickey Mouse And The Missing Mouseketeers
Illus.: Svendsen, Juluis; Totten, Bob
Author: Bedford, Annie North
1956 $1.00

105-53
$1.00

105-2
Mickey Mouse And The Mouseketeers Ghost Town Adventure
Illus.: Walt Disney Studios
1977 (1979)
3rd Edition $1.00

105-21
$1.00

105-31
$1.00

105-42
$1.00

100-60
Mickey Mouse Heads For The Sky
Illus.: Walt Disney Studios
Author: Walt Disney Studios
1987
"A" Edition $4.00

100-68
(1991) $2.00

100-60
Mickey Mouse Heads For The Sky
Illus.: Walt Disney Studios
Author: Walt Disney Studios
1987 (1989)
"H" Edition $3.00

100- 5
Mickey Mouse's Picnic
Illus.: Walt Disney Studios
Author: Werner, Jane
1950 $1.00

100-55
$1.00

100-62
Mickey Mouse's Picnic
Illus.: Walt Disney Studios
Author: Werner, Jane
1950 (1989) $3.00

100-69
(1991) $2.00

100-21
Mickey Mouse, The Kitten-Sitters
Illus.: Walt Disney Studios
1976 $1.00

100-31
$1.00

100-41
$1.00

100-51
"P" Edition $1.00

100-52
(1990)
"A" Edition $1.00

459-42
Mickey's Christmas Carol
Illus.: Dias, Ron
Author: Walt Disney Studios
1983
"A" Edition $5.00

459-9
"B" Edition $2.00

459-09
"G" Edition $2.00

459-11
(1991) $2.00

98789-01
Mickey's Christmas Carol
Illus.: Dias, Ron
Author: Walt Disney Studios
1983 **$2.00**

98842-00
Mickey's Walt Disney World Adventure
Illus.: Tilley, Scott
Author: Hapka, Cathy
1997
"A" Edition **$5.00**

100-65
Minnie's Slumber Party
Author: West, Cindy
1990
"A" Edition **$3.00**

	100-78	
(1993)		$2.00
	100-71	
(1991)		$2.00

106-35
Mother Goose
Illus.: Dempster, Al
Author: Walt Disney Studios
1949 **$1.00**
106-45
$1.00

106-55
Mother Goose
Violet Background
Illus.: Dempster, Al
Author: Walt Disney Studios
1949 **$2.00**

106-61
Mother Goose
Illus.: Dempster, Al
Author: Walt Disney Studios
1949 (1991) **$2.00**
106-62
(1993) **$1.00**

98861-00
Mulan
Illus.: Cardona, Jost
Author: Ingoglia, Gina
1998
"A" Edition **$2.00**

107-97
No Worries (The Lion King)
Illus.: Williams, Don; Russell, H. R.
Author: Korman, Justine
1995
"A" Edition **$3.00**

105- 4
Pete's Dragon
Illus.: Walt Disney Studios
1977 (1979)
2nd Edition **$3.00**
105-44
$2.00

104-60
Peter Pan
Illus.: Dias, Ron
Author: Coco, Eugene Bradley
1989
"A" Edition **$4.00**
104-68
(1991) **$2.00**

104- 1
Peter Pan And Wendy
Illus.: Earle, Eyvind
Author: Bedford, Annie North
1952 **$2.00**

104-21
Peter Pan And Wendy $1.00

104-31 $1.00

104-41 $1.00

104-51 $1.00

104-2
Pinocchio
Illus.: Grant, Campbell
Author: Walt Disney Studios
1981 $1.00

104-22 $1.00

104-32 $1.00

104-42 $1.00

104-69 $1.00
(1991)

104-87 $1.00

104-52
Pinocchio
Illus.: Walt Disney Studios
Author: Walt Disney Studios
1948 $2.00

104-61
Pinocchio
Illus.: Dias, Ron
Author: Coco, Eugene Bradley
1990
"A" Edition $3.00

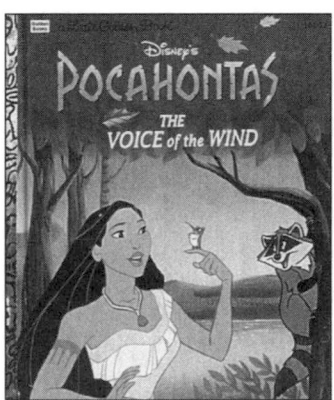

104-72
Pocahontas 'The Voice Of The Wind'
Illus.: Emslie, Peter; Williams, Don
Author: Korman, Justine
1995
"A" Edition $2.00

104-71
Pocahontas
1st Edition Unstated
Illus.: Williams, Don
Author: Korman, Justin
1995 $2.00

98798-01
Pooh And The Dragon
Illus.: Baker, Darrell
Author: Braybrooks, Ann
1997 $2.00

98841-00
Pooh's Grand Adventure
Illus.: Rigol
Author: Korman, Justine
1997
"A" Edition $2.00

105-71
Prince And The Pauper, The
Illus.: Schroeder, Russel; Williams, Don
Author: Manushkin, Fran
1990
"A" Edition $4.00

98797-01
Quasimodo The Hero
Illus.: Williams, Don
Author: Bazaldua, Barbara
1997
1st Edition $2.00

107-36
Quasimodo's New Friend
Illus.: Michaels, Serge; Gutierrez, Edward
Author: Korman, Justine
1996
"A" Edition $2.00

98858-00

Rainbow Puppies (101 Dalmatians)
Illus.: Smith, Len; Bothner, Cindi
Author: Bazaldua, Barbara
1998
"A" Edition   **$2.00**

98290

Rapunzel
Illus.: Smith, Len; Devaney, Adam
Author: Onish, Liane B.
1998
"A" Edition   **$2.00**

105-3

Rescuers, The
Illus.: Walt Disney Studios
1977 (1979)
"D" Edition   **$1.00**

105-43
                                               $1.00

105-69

Rescuers, The
Illus.: Walt Disney Studios
Author: Walt Disney Studios
1977
"A" Edition   **$3.00**

105-70

Rescuers Down Under, The
Illus.: Mateu, Franc
Author: Teitelbaum, Michael
1990
"A" Edition   **$4.00**

105-83

(1991)   **$2.00**

103-55

Return To Oz 'Dorothy Saves The Emerald City'
Illus.: Walt Disney Studios
Author: Walt Disney Studios
1985
"A" Edition   **$9.00**

105-56

Return To Oz 'Escape From The Witches Castle'
Illus.: Walt Disney Studios
Author: Walt Disney Studios
1985
"A" Edition   **$9.00**

453- 1

Santa's Toy Shop
Illus.: Walt Disney Studios
Author: Dempster, Al
1950 (1979)   **$1.00**

453-31
                                               $1.00

451-8

Santa's Toy Shop
White Background
Illus.: Walt Disney Studios
Author: Dempster, Al
1950   **$1.00**

451-08
                                               $2.00

451-08

Santa's Toy Shop
Green Background
Illus.: Walt Disney Studios
Author: Dempster, Al
1950
"L" Edition   **$2.00**

451-10
                                               $1.00

451-17

Santa's Toy Shop
Illus.: Walt Disney Studios
Author: Dempster, Al
1950
"R" Edition   **$2.00**

104-56

Sleeping Beauty
Illus.: Dias, Ron
Author: Walt Disney Studios
1986   **$5.00**

104-66

(1991)
"A" Edition   **$2.00**

98273-01
Sleeping Beauty
Illus.: Dias, Ron
Author: Teitelbaum, Michael
1997 **$2.00**

98786-01
Snow Puppies (101 Dalmatians)
Illus.: Williams, Don
Author: Bazaldua, Barbara
1996
"A" Edition **$2.00**

103- 2
Snow White And The Seven Dwarfs
Illus.: O'Brien, Ken
Author: Bros. Grimm
1948 (1979) **$1.00**

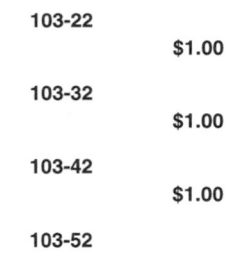

103-22
$1.00

103-32
$1.00

103-42
$1.00

103-52
$1.00

103-58
Snow White And The Seven Dwarfs
Illus.: Dias, Ron
Author: Walt Disney Studios
1984
"A" Edition **$5.00**

103-60
Snow White And The Seven Dwarfs
Illus.: Dias, Ron
Author: Walt Disney Studios
1984 (1990) **$1.00**

103-67
Snow White And The Seven Dwarfs
Illus.: Dias, Ron
Author: Walt Disney Studios
1984 (1991) **$1.00**

103-70
Snow White And The Seven Dwarfs
Illus.: Dias, Ron
Author: Walt Disney Studios
1984 (1994) **$1.00**

103-87
Snow White And The Seven Dwarfs
Illus.: O'Brien, Ken
Author: Bros. Grimm
1984 **$1.00**

100-79
Sorcerer's Apprentice
Illus.: Emslie, Peter
Author: Ferguson, Don
1994
"A" Edition **$3.00**

100-47
Sport Goofy And The Racing Robot
Illus.: Walt Disney Studios
Author: Walt Disney Studios
1984 **$2.00**

100-47
"A" Edition **$8.00**

105-57
1984 **$2.00**

104-70
Teapot's Tale, The (Beauty And The Beast)
Illus.: Emslie, Peter; Hunt, Darren
Author: Korman, Justine
1993
"A" Edition $2.00

100-6
Surprise For Mickey Mouse
Illus.: Walt Disney Studios
Author: Walt Disney Studios
1971 $2.00

98788-01
Sweetest Christmas, The (Pooh)
Illus.: Yee, Josie
Author: Braybrooks, Ann
1996
"A" Edition $2.00

106-3
Three Little Pigs
Illus.: Banta, Milt; Dempster, Al
Author: Walt Disney Studios
1948 $1.00

106-33 $1.00

106-43 $1.00

106-53 $1.00

106-59
Three Little Pigs
Illus.: Banta, Milt; Dempster, Al
Author: Walt Disney Studios
1948 (1992) $2.00

103-44
Toad Flies High
Illus.: Walt Disney Studios
Author: Grahame, Kenneth
1982
"A" Edition $5.00
103-54
                     $2.00

98838-01
Trick Or Treat (Pooh)
Illus.: Arkadia
Author: Braybrooks, Ann
1997
"A" Edition $2.00

105-66
Uncle Remus
Illus.: Walt Disney Studios
Author: Walt Disney Studios
1947 $2.00

98795-01
Very Best Easter Bunny, The (Pooh)
Illus.: Yee, Josie
Author: Braybrooks, Ann
1997
"A" Edition $2.00

100-77
Where's Fifi (Minnie 'n Me)
Illus.: Vaccaro Associates, Inc.
Author: Calder, Lyn
1992
"A" Edition $2.00

102-62
Winnie The Pooh 'Eeyore, Be Happy!'
Author: Ferguson, Don
1991
"A" Edition $3.00

	101-44	
(1986)		$1.00
	101-53	
		$1.00
	101-54	
		$1.00

101-26
Winnie-The-Pooh A Day To Remember
Unstated 1st
Illus.: Walt Disney Studios
Author: Walt Disney Studios
1980 $10.00

101- 4
Winnie-The-Pooh And The Honey Patch
Unstated 1st
Illus.: Walt Disney Studios
Author: Walt Disney Studios
1980 $5.00

101- 3
Winnie-The-Pooh And The Honey Tree
Illus.: Totten, Bob
Author: Milne, A.A.
1980 (1979) $2.00

	101-33	
(1981)		$2.00
	101-43	
		$2.00
	101-53	
		$2.00
	101-63	
(1994)		
"A" Edition		$2.00

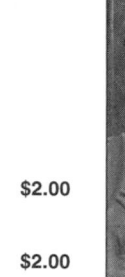

98267-01
Winnie The Pooh And The Honey Tree
Illus.: Hicks, Russell
Author: Pickard, Mary
(1996) $2.00

101-55
Winnie The Pooh And The Missing Bullhorn
Illus.: Schroeder, Russel; Williams, Don
Author: Teitelbaum, Michael
1990
"A" Edition $5.00
101-61
(1991) $2.00

101-25
Winnie-The-Pooh And The Special Morning
Unstated 1st
Illus.: Walt Disney Studios
Author: Walt Disney Studios
1980 $8.00
101-35
$3.00

	101-32	
		$2.00
	101-42	
		$2.00

101-21
Winnie-The-Pooh And Tigger
Illus.: Walt Disney Studios
Author: Milne, A.A.
1968 $2.00
101-41
$2.00

101- 2
Winnie-The-Pooh Meets Gopher
Illus.: De Santis, George
Author: Milne, A.A.
1965 (1979)
16th Edition $2.00

101-52
Winnie The Pooh Meets Gopher
Illus.: De Santis, George
Author: Milne, A.A.
1965 $2.00

Activity Books

A1

Words
(Wheel Book)
Illus.: Elliott, Gertrude
Author: Chambers, Selma Lola
1955   20 Pages
"A" Edition   **$35.00**
Without wheel
        20 Pages   **$6.00**

A2

Circus Time
(Wheel Book)
Illus.: Gergely, Tibor
Author: Conger, Marion
1955   20 Pages
"A" Edition   **$35.00**

Without wheel   **$6.00**

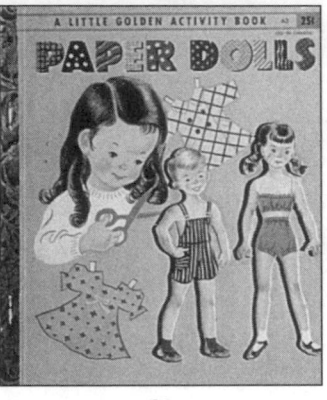

A3

Paper Dolls
Illus.: Miloche, Hilda; Kane, Wilma
Author: Miloche, Hilda; Kane, Wilma
1951   20 Pages
"A" Edition   **$125.00**

A3
With cut-out clothes and
dolls   **$35.00**
Missing clothes and
dolls   **$5.00**

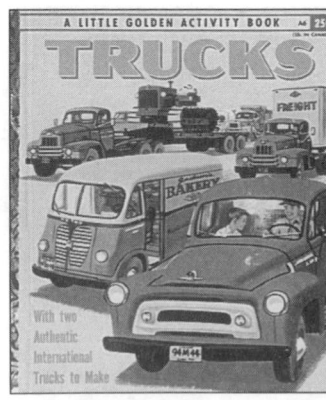

A4

Animal Paint Book
(3 Paints In Cover)
Illus.: Helweg, Hans
Author: Helweg, Hans
1955   20 Pages
"A" Edition   **$65.00**

A4
Painted   **$5.00**

A5

Clown Coloring Book
1955   20 Pages
"A" Edition   **$85.00**

A5
Without color crayons
(uncolored)   **$15.00**
Colored and missing
crayons   **$4.00**

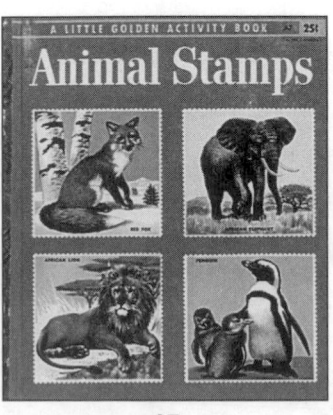

A6

Trucks
(2 Paper Model Trucks)
Illus.: Quigley, Ray
Author: Jackson, Kathryn
1955   24 Pages
"A" Edition   **$150.00**
Without trucks   **$15.00**

A7

Animal Stamps
Illus.: Irving, James Gordon; Dugan,
William
Author: Daly, Kathleen
1955   24 Pages
"A" Edition   **$45.00**
Stamps pasted in book **$8.00**

A8

Bird Stamps
Illus.: Irving, James Gordon
Author: Daly, Kathleen
1955   24 Pages
"A" Edition   **$45.00**
Stamps pasted in book **$8.00**

A9

Dog Stamps
Illus.: Megargee, Edwin
Author: Mcgovern, Ann
1955   24 Pages
"A" Edition   **$45.00**
Stamps pasted in book **$8.00**

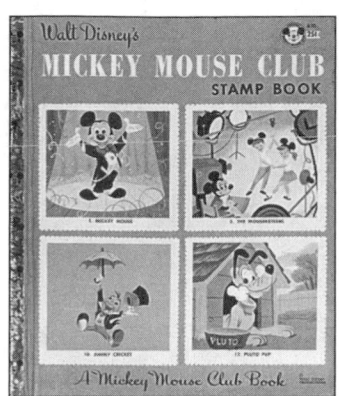

A10

Mickey Mouse Club Stamp Book
Illus.: Svendsen, Julius
Author: Daly, Kathleen
1956   24 Pages
"A" Edition   **$75.00**

Stamps pasted in book   **$8.00**

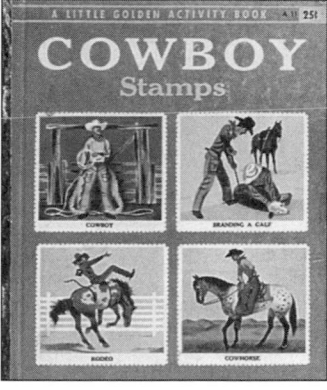

A11

Cowboy Stamps
Illus.: Scarry, Richard
Author: Shimek, John Lyle
1957   24 Pages
"A" Edition   **$45.00**

Stamps pasted in book   **$8.00**

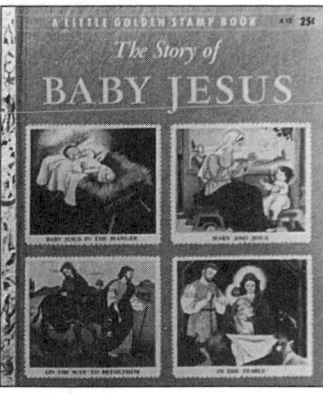

A12

The Story Of Baby Jesus
Illus.: Wilkin, Eloise
1957   24 Pages
"A" Edition   **$150.00**

Stamps pasted in book   **$25.00**

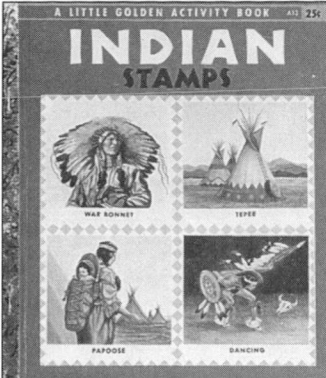

A13

Indian Stamps
Illus.: Schmidt, Edwin
Author: Huberman, Edward
1957   24 Pages
"A" Edition   **$45.00**

Stamps pasted in book   **$8.00**

A14

Ginger Paper Doll
Illus.: Saviozzi, Adriana Mazza
Author: Daly, Kathleen
1957   24 Pages
"A" Edition   **$90.00**
With cut-out clothes and
dolls   **$35.00**
Missing clothes and dolls   **$5.00**

A 15

Trim The Christmas Tree
Illus.: Henderson, Doris & Marion
Author: Nast, Elsa Ruth
1957   24 Pages
"A" Edition   **$45.00**

Activities cut out   **$3.00**

A16

Count To Ten
(Wheel Book)
Illus.: Krush, Bob
Author: Moore, Lilian
1957   24 Pages
"A" Edition   **$35.00**

Without wheel   **$6.00**

A17

Stop And Go
(Wheel Book)
Illus.: Anglund, Joan Walsh
Author: Higgins, Loyta
1957   24 Pages
"A" Edition   **$40.00**
Without wheel
              24 Pages
"A" Edition   **$8.00**

A18

ABC Around The House
(Wheel Book)
Illus.: La Mont, Violet
1957   24 Pages
"A" Edition   **$35.00**

Without wheel   **$6.00**

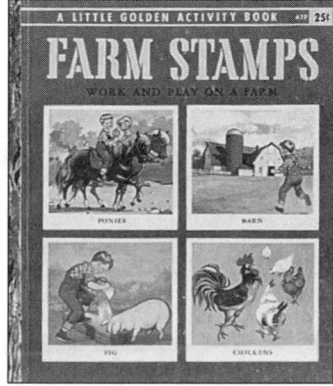

A19

Farm Stamps
Illus.: Saviozzi, Adriana Mazza
Author: Jackson, Kathryn
1957   24 Pages
"A" Edition   **$45.00**

Stamps pasted in   **$6.00**

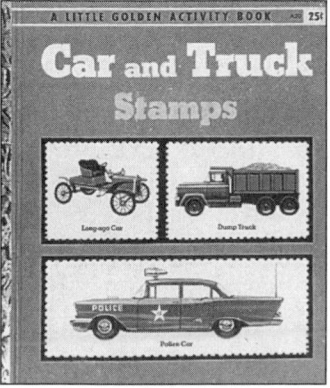

A20

Car And Truck Stamps
Illus.: Dreany, E. Joseph
Author: Daly, Kathleen
1957   24 Pages
"A" Edition   **$45.00**

Stamps pasted in book   **$6.00**

A21

Let's Save Money
(Wheel Book)
Illus.: La Mont, Violet
Author: Higgins, Loyta
1958   24 Pages
"A" Edition   **$30.00**
Without wheel   **$6.00**

A22
Paper Doll Wedding, The
Illus.: Miloche, Hilda; Kane, Wilma
Author: Miloche, Hilda; Kane, Wilma
1958   24 Pages
"B" Edition   **$125.00**
With cut-out clothes and
dolls   **$35.00**
Missing clothes and dolls   **$5.00**

A 24
Reading, Writing And Spelling
Illus.: Obligado, Lilian; La Mont, Vio-
let
Author: Kaufman, Carol
1959   24 Pages
"A" Edition   **$45.00**
Stamps pasted in book   **$6.00**

A25
Insect Stamps
Illus.: Zallenger, Jean
Author: Martin, Richard A.
1958   24 Pages
"A" Edition   **$45.00**

Stamps pasted in book   **$6.00**

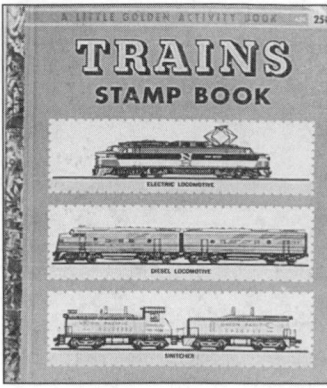

A26
Train Stamp Book
Illus.: Dreany, E. Joseph
Author: Daly, Kathleen N.
1958   24 Pages
"A" Edition   **$45.00**

Stamps pasted in book   **$8.00**

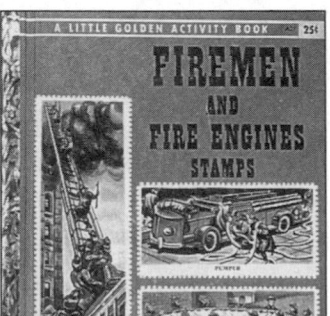

A27
Firemen And Fire Engines Stamps
Illus.: Scarry, Richard
Author: Goldsmith, Jane
1959   24 Pages
"A" Edition   **$45.00**

Stamps pasted in book   **$8.00**

A28
Colors
(Wheel Book)
Illus.: Scarry, Richard
Author: Daly, Kathleen N.
1959   24 Pages
"A" Edition   **$40.00**
Without wheel   **$6.00**

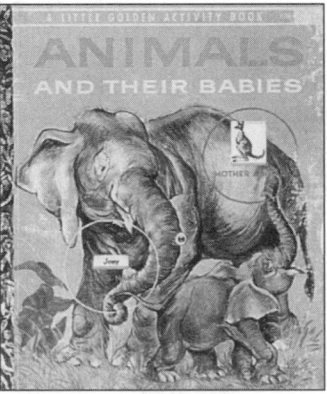

A29
Animals And Their Babies
(Wheel Book)
Illus.: Obligado, Lilian
Author: Hazen, Barbara Shook
1959   24 Pages
"A" Edition   **$35.00**
Without wheel   **$6.00**

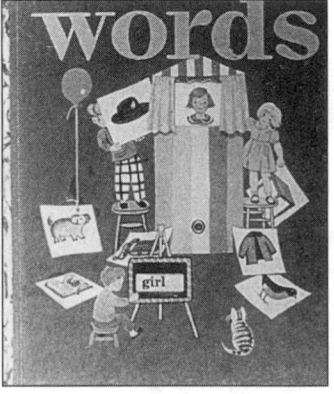

A30
Words
(Wheel Book)
Illus.: Elliott, Gertrude
Author: Chambers, Selma Lola
1955   24 Pages
"B" "Edition   **$30.00**
Without wheel   **$6.00**

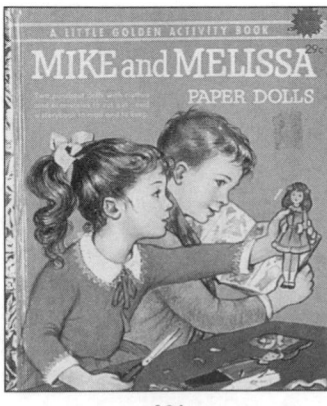

A31
Mike And Melissa
(Paper Dolls)
Illus.: Saviozzi, Adriana Mazza
Author: Watson, Jane
1959   24 Pages
"A" Edition   **$125.00**

A31
With cut-out clothes and
dolls   **$35.00**
Missing clothes and dolls   **$5.00**

A32
Ginger Paper Doll
Illus.: Saviozzi, Adriana Mazza
Author: Daly, Kathleen
1957   24 Pages
"C" Edition   **$85.00**
With cut-out clothes and
dolls   **$25.00**
Missing clothes and dolls   **$5.00**

A33
Sleeping Beauty
(Paper Dolls)
Illus.: Svendsen, Julius; Armitage,
Frank
Author: Walt Disney Studios
1959   24 Pages
"A" Edition   **$175.00**

A33

With cut-out clothes and
dolls   **$50.00**
Missing clothes and dolls   **$5.00**

A34

Little Red Riding Hood
(Paper Dolls)
1959   24 Pages
"A" Edition   **$175.00**

With cut-out clothes and
dolls   **$40.00**
Missing clothes and dolls   **$7.00**

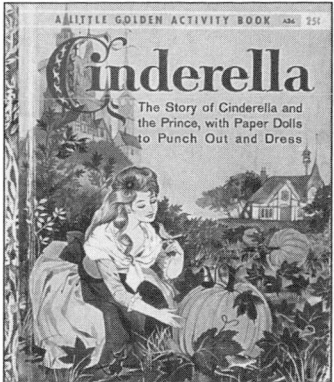

A36

Cinderella
(Paper Dolls)
Illus.: Laite, Gordon
1960   24 Pages
"A" Edition   **$175.00**

With cut-out clothes and
dolls   **$50.00**
Missing clothes and dolls   **$5.00**

A39

My Little Golden Calendar for 1961
Illus.: Scarry, Richard
1961   24 Pages
"A" Edition   **$90.00**

A41

Hansel & Gretel
(Paper Dolls)
Dolls Punch-out of book
Illus.: Martin, Judy & Barry
Author: Bros. Grimm
1961   24 Pages
"A" Edition   **$150.00**

A41

Dolls cut out of book
(1961)   24 Pages
"B" Edition   **$125.00**

With cut-out clothes and
dolls   **$35.00**
Missing clothes and dolls   **$5.00**

A43

Count To Ten
(Wheel Book)
Illus.: Krush, Beth
Author: Moore, Lillian
1957   24 Pages
"D" Edition   **$25.00**

A43

Without wheel
            24 Pages
"A" Edition   **$6.00**

A44

ABC Around The House
(Wheel Book)
Illus.: La Monte, Voilet
Author: Daly, Kathleen
1957   24 Pages
"A" Edition   **$30.00**
Without wheel   **$6.00**

A45

Words
(Wheel Book)
Illus.: Elliott, Gertrude
Author: Chambers, Selma Lola
1955   24 Pages
"C" Edition   **$30.00**
Without wheel   **$6.00**

A47

Paper Dolls
Illus.: Miloche, Hilde; Kane, Wilma
Author: Miloche, Hilde; Kane, Wilma
1951   24 Pages
"B" Edition   **$100.00**
With cut-out clothes and
dolls   **$30.00**
Missing clothes and dolls   **$5.00**

A48

Gordon's Jet Flight
(Paper Model Jet)
Illus.: Crawford, Mel
Author: Glasson, Naomi J.
1961   24 Pages
"A" Edition   **$150.00**
Without plane   **$15.00**

A49
Snow White And Rose Red
(Paper Doll)
(Never printed)

A50
Trim The Christmas Tree
Illus.: Henderson, Doris & Marion
Author: Nast, Elsa Ruth
1957   24 Pages
"B" Edition $30.00

Missing activities $3.00

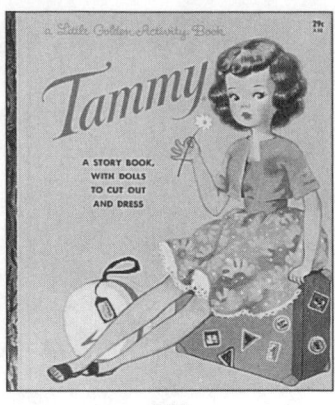

A52
Tammy
(Paper Doll)
Illus.: Salva, Ada
Author: Daly, Kathleen N.
1963   24 Pages
"A" Edition $65.00
With cut-out clothes and
dolls $15.00
Missing clothes and dolls $5.00

Ding Dong School Books

On November 24, 1952, *Ding Dong School* appeared on NBC Television. The show was hosted by Dr. Frances Horwich. One of Miss Frances' characters that appeared occasionally on the show was a puppet named Lucky Rabbit. Lucky later appeared in his own book under numbers 221 and DIN 7, which was later done as a Little Golden Book, *Lucky Rabbit*.

Rand McNally originally published the series A Ding Dong School Book around July 1953. These books were produced in the same format as Little Golden Books, with the exception of a silver foil spine. All of the titles produced by Rand McNally contained 28 pages. Books were numbered 200 to 225, with the printing run listed on the last page at bottom left.

The show was taken off the air in 1956 for lack of sponsors and because of its limited appeal.

Miss Frances was very upset with the quality of TV shows being produced for children, and in 1959 she was finally able to get *Ding Dong School* reproduced. The show ran for another 130 episodes before being taken off the air forever.

During the show's new release (1959–1960), Golden Press published A Ding Dong School Book. The numbers ran from DIN1 to DIN8 and contained 24 pages. First printings have an "A" on the last page at bottom right.

200
Your Friend, The Policeman
Illus.: Nebbe, William
Author: Horwich, Dr. Frances R.
1953   24 Pages $8.00

201
Debbie And Her Nap
Illus.: Wehr, Adele
Author: Horwich, Dr. Frances R.
1953   24 Pages $10.00

202
Suitcase With A Surprise, A
Illus.: Tellingen, Ruth Van
Author: Horwich, Dr. Frances R.
1953   24 Pages $8.00

203
Big Coal Truck, The
Illus.: Nebbe, William
Author: Horwich, Dr. Frances R.
1953   24 Pages $8.00

204
I Decided
Illus.: Opitz, Marge
Author: Horwich, Dr. Frances R.
1953   24 Pages $8.00

205
Day Downtown With Daddy, A
Illus.: Pickett, Helen
Author: Horwich, Dr. Frances R.
1953   24 Pages $8.00

206
Dressing Up
Illus.: Evans, Katherine
Author: Horwich, Dr. Frances R.
1953   24 Pages $8.00

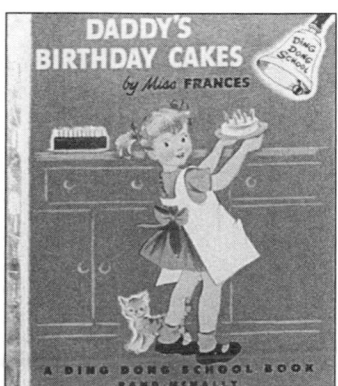

207
Daddy's Birthday Cakes
Illus.: Tellingen, Ruth Van
Author: Horwich, Dr. Frances R.
1953   24 Pages $8.00

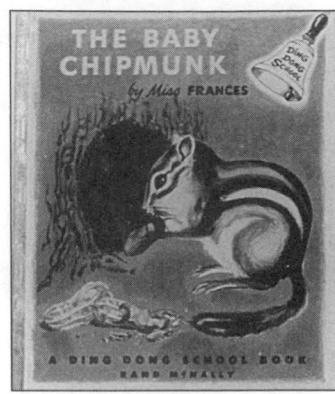

208
Baby Chipmunk, The
Illus.: Nebbe, William
Author: Horwich, Dr. Frances R.
1953   24 Pages   **$8.00**

209
Peek In
Illus.: Evans, Katherine
Author: Horwich, Dr. Frances R.
1954   24 Pages   **$8.00**

210
Growing Things
Illus.: Tellingen, Ruth Van
Author: Horwich, Dr. Frances R.
1954   24 Pages   **$8.00**

211
My Goldfish
Illus.: McLean, Mina Grow
Author: Horwich, Dr. Frances R.
1954   24 Pages   **$8.00**

212
In My House
Illus.: Friend, Esther
Author: Horwich, Dr. Frances R.
1954   24 Pages   **$8.00**

213
Dolls Of Other Lands
Illus.: Flory, Jane
Author: Horwich, Dr. Frances R.
1954   24 Pages   **$10.00**

214
My Big Brother
Illus.: McLean, Mina Grow
Author: Horwich, Dr. Frances R.
1954   24 Pages   **$8.00**

215
Robin Family, The
Illus.: Ozone, Lucy
Author: Horwich, Dr. Frances R.
1954   24 Pages   **$8.00**

216
Grandmother Is Coming
Illus.: Tellingen, Ruth Van
Author: Horwich, Dr. Frances R.
1954   24 Pages   **$8.00**

217
Looking Out The Window
Illus.: Shortall, Leonard
Author: Horwich, Dr. Frances R.
1954   24 Pages   **$8.00**

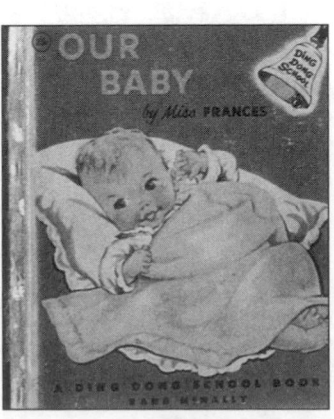

218
Our Baby
Illus.: Pointer, Priscilla
Author: Horwich, Dr. Frances R.
1955   24 Pages   **$18.00**

219
Jingle Bell Jack
Illus.: Evans, Katherine
Author: Horwich, Dr. Frances R.
1955   24 Pages   **$10.00**

220
Mr. Meyer's Cow
Illus.: Nebbe, William
Author: Horwich, Dr. Frances R.
1955   24 Pages   **$8.00**

221
Lucky Rabbit
Illus.: Bendel, Ruth
Author: Horwich, Dr. Frances R.
1955   24 Pages   **$10.00**

222
Magic Wagon, The
Illus.: Webbe, Elizabeth
Author: Horwich, Dr. Frances R.
1955   24 Pages   **$8.00**

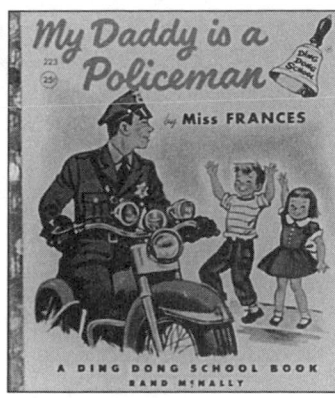

223
My Daddy Is A Policeman
Illus.: Pickett, Helen
Author: Horwich, Dr. Frances R.
1956   24 Pages   **$8.00**

224
Here Comes The Band
Illus.: Timmins, William
Author: Horwich, Dr. Frances R.
1956   24 Pages   **$8.00**

225
We Love Grandpa
Illus.: Grider, Dorothy
Author: Horwich, Dr. Frances R.
1956   24 Pages   **$8.00**

Ding Dong School Books by Golden Press

The following books were published in the Little Golden Book format. The authors, illustrators, and copyrights of these books are the same as the Rand McNally editions. The printing of these books appears to have been late 1959 or early 1960

DIN1

Jingle Bell Jack
Illus.: Evans, Katherine
Author: Horwich, Dr. Frances R.
1955   24 Pages   **$15.00**

DIN2

Mr. Meyer's Cow
Illus.: Nebbe, William
Author: Horwich, Dr. Frances R.
1955   24 Pages   **$10.00**

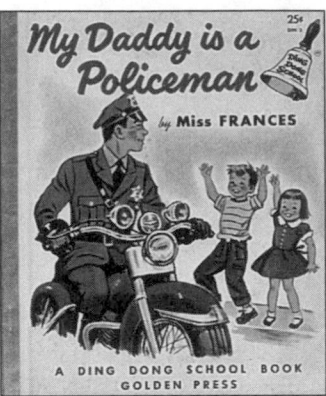

DIN3

My Daddy Is A Policeman
Illus.: Prickett, Helen
Author: Horwich, Dr. Frances R.
1956   24 Pages   **$12.00**

DIN4

We Love Grandpa
Illus.: Grider, Dorothy
Author: Horwich, Dr. Frances R.
1956   24 Pages   **10.00**

DIN5

Here Comes The Band
Illus.: Timmins, William
Author: Horwich, Dr. Frances R.
1956   24 Pages   **$10.00**

DIN6

Magic Wagon, The
Illus.: Webbe, Elizabeth
Author: Horwich, Dr. Frances R.
1955   24 Pages   **$10.00**

DIN7

Lucky Rabbit
Illus.: Bendel, Ruth
Author: Horwich, Dr. Frances R.
1955   24 Pages   **$12.00**

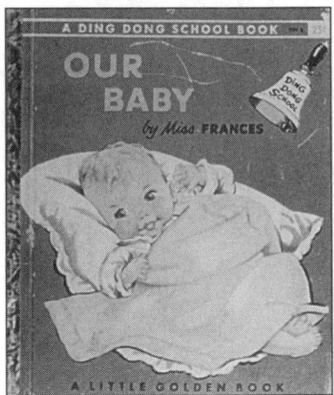

DIN8

Our Baby
Illus.: Pointer, Priscilla
Author: Horwich, Dr. Frances R.
1955   24 Pages   **$20.00**

My First Golden Learning Library

My First Golden Learning Library contained sixteen volumes with more than 1,500 full-color illustrations. Each book was identical in size to a Little Golden Book, with the foil spines being different solid colors. The books were written by Jane Werner Watson, with the consulting help of Berth Morris Parker, author of *The Golden Book Encyclopedia*, and the illustrations were done by William Dugan. Each book contained 24 pages, and they were released around August 1965. The books were sold in a boxed carrying case and may have been sold individually. (Value: Boxed Set **$90.00**)

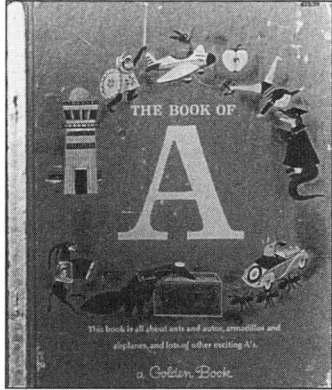

615
Book Of A, The
Illus.: Dugan, William J.
Author: Watson, Jane Werner
1965   24 Pages   **$5.00**

616
Book Of B, The
Illus.: Dugan, William
Author: Watson, Jane Werner
1965   24 Pages   **$5.00**

617
Book Of C, The
Illus.: Dugan, William
Author: Watson, Jane Werner
1965   24 Pages   **$5.00**

618
Book Of D E, The
Illus.: Dugan, William
Author: Watson, Jane Werner
1965   24 Pages   **$5.00**

619
Book Of F, The
Illus.: Dugan, William
Author: Watson, Jane Werner
1965   24 Pages   **$5.00**

620
Book Of G H, The
Illus.: Dugan, William
Author: Watson, Jane Werner
1965   24 Pages   **$5.00**

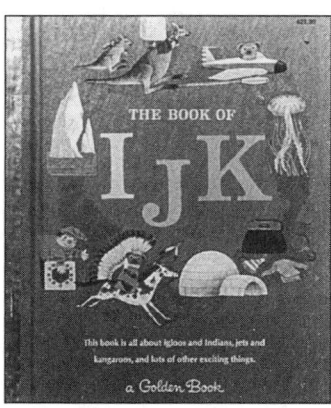

621
Book Of I J K, The
Illus.: Dugan, William
Author: Watson, Jane Werner
1965   24 Pages   **$5.00**

622
Book Of L, The
Illus.: Dugan, William
Author: Watson, Jane Werner
1965   24 Pages   **$5.00**

623
Book Of M, The
Illus.: Dugan, William
Author: Watson, Jane Werner
1965   24 Pages   **$5.00**

624
Book Of N O, The
Illus.: Dugan, William
Author: Watson, Jane Werner
1965   24 Pages   **$5.00**

625
Book Of P Q, The
Illus.: Dugan, William
Author: Watson, Jane Werner
1965   24 Pages   **$5.00**

626
Book Of R, The
Illus.: Dugan, William
Author: Watson, Jane Werner
1965   24 Pages   **$5.00**

628
First Book Of S, The
Illus.: Dugan, William
Author: Watson, Jane Werner
1965   24 Pages   **$5.00**

628
Second Book Of S, The
Illus.: Dugan, William
Author: Watson, Jane Werner
1965   24 Pages   **$5.00**

629
Book Of T U V, The
Illus.: Dugan, William
Author: Watson, Jane Werner
1965   24 Pages   **$5.00**

630
Book Of W X Y Z, The
Illus.: Dugan, William
Author: Watson, Jane Werner
1965   24 Pages   **$5.00**

My First Golden Learning Library
boxed carrying case.

Giant Little Golden Books

5001

My Little Golden Dictionary
Illus.: Scarry, Richard
Authors: Reed, Mary; Oswald, Edith
1957   56 Pages
"A" Edition   **$16.00**

5002

5 Bedtime Stories
Illus.: Tenggren, Gustaf
1957   56 Pages
"A" Edition   **$16.00**

5003

My Christmas Treasury
Illus.: Hess, Lowell
1957   72 Pages
"A" Edition   **$25.00**

5003

1958   56 Pages
"B" Edition   **$20.00**

5004

Walt Disney Favorite Stories
Illus.: Walt Disney Studios
Author: Walt Disney Studios
1957   56 Pages
"A" Edition   **$25.00**

5005

Donald Duck Treasury
Illus.: Walt Disney Studios
Author: Walt Disney Studios
1957   56 Pages
"A" Edition   **$25.00**

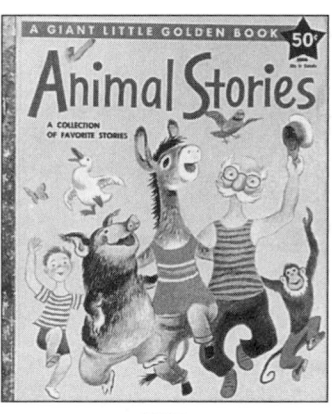

5006

Animal Stories
Illus.: Gergely, Tibor
Authors: Miryam; Hoffman, Beth; Du-
plaix, George
1957   56 Pages
"A" Edition   **$16.00**

5007

Mother Goose
Illus.: La Mont, Violet
Author: Folk Tales
1958   56 Pages
"A" Edition   **$18.00**

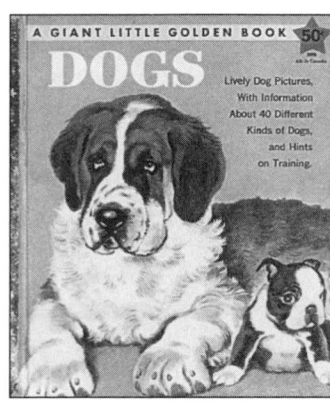

5008

Dogs
Illus.: Gergely, Tibor
Author: Daly, Kathleen N.
1957   56 Pages
"A" Edition   **$18.00**

5009

Nursery Tales
Illus.: Scarry, Richard
1958   72 Pages
"A" Edition   **$18.00**

5010

Wild Animals
Illus.: Suschitzky, W.
1958   72 Pages
"A" Edition   **$16.00**

5011

Birds
Illus.: Wilkin, Eloise
Author: Watson, Jane Werner
1958   56 Pages
"A" Edition   **$16.00**

5012
Adventures Of Lassie, The
Illus.: Crawford; Dreany, E. Joseph;
Ames, Lee
Authors: Verral, Charles Spain; Hill,
Monica
1958   56 Pages
"A" Edition   **$25.00**

5013
Kittens
Illus.: Masha; Tenggren, Gustaf;
Wilkin, Eloise
Authors: Schurr, Cathleen; Scarry,
Patricia
1958   56 Pages
"A" Edition   **$18.00**

5014
Walt Disney's Storytime Book
Illus.: Walt Disney Studios
Author: Walt Disney Studios
1958   56 Pages
"A" Edition   **$27.00**

5015
Off To School
Illus.: Malvern, Corrine; La Mont,
Violet
Author: Jackson, Kathleen
1958   56 Pages
"A" Edition   **$18.00**

5016
Mother Goose Rhymes
Illus.: Rojankovsky, Feodor
1958   56 Pages
"A" Edition   **$18.00**

5017
Plants And Animals
Illus.: Chaiko, Ted
Author: Watson, Jane Werner
1958   56 Pages
"A" Edition   **$16.00**

5018
Train Stories
Illus.: Gergely, Tibor; Seiden, Art
Authors: Potter, Mariam; Crampton;
Brown
1958   56 Pages
"A" Edition   **$18.00**

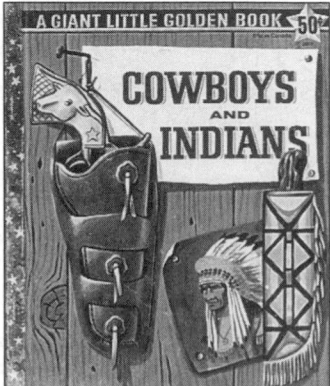

5019
Cowboys And Indians
Illus.: Scarry, Richard
Author: Lindquist, Willis
1958   72 Pages
"A" Edition   **$20.00**

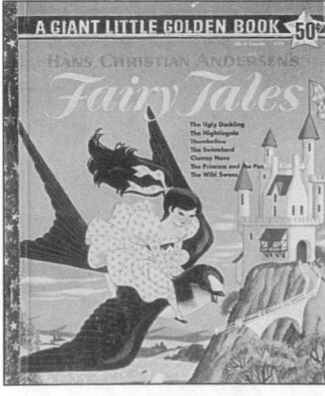

5020
Fairy Tales
Illus.: Hess, Lowell
Author: Anderson, Hans; H.C. White
1958   72 Pages
"A" Edition   **$18.00**

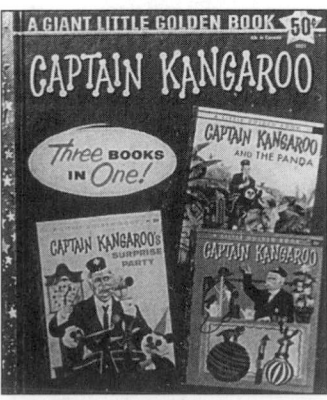

5021
Captain Kangaroo
Illus.: Seiden, Art; Schmidt, Edwin
Author: Daly, Kathleen N.; Lindsay,
Barb
1959   56 Pages
"A" Edition   **$20.00**

5022
Cub Scouts
Illus.: Crawford, Mel
Author: Brian, Bruce
1959   56 Pages
"A" Edition   **$25.00**

5023
Fish
Illus.: Jean Zallinger
Author: Herbert S. Zimm
1959   56 Pages
"A" Edition   **$16.00**

5024
Quiz Fun
Illus.: Gergely, Tibor
Authors: Elmo, Horace; Hullick, Nancy
Fielding
1959   56 Pages
"A" Edition   **$16.00**

5025
My Magic Slate Book
Illus.: Dugan, William
Author: Memling, Carl
1959   22 Pages
"A" Edition   **$30.00**

5026
This World Of Ours
Illus.: Wilkin, Eloise
Author: Watson, Jane Werner
1959   56 Pages
"A" Edition   **$25.00**

5027
My Pets
Illus.: Wilkin, Eloise
Author: Scarry, Patsy
1959   56 Pages
"A" Edition   **$40.00**

Eager Reader Series

These books were identical to Little Golden Books, but with a solid gold spine. Each book had large type and easy words for beginning readers. The books were sold individually with a 39-cent cover price, starting around 1974. A boxed set of eight titles sold for $3.95 when it was released around July 1975.

800

New Home For Snow Ball, A
Illus.: Pyk, Jan
Author: Bowden, Joan
1974   24 Pages   **$5.00**

801

Pet In The Jar, The
Illus.: Stang, Judy
Author: Stang, Judy
1974   24 Pages   **$5.00**

802

Hat For The Queen, A
Illus.: Giacomini, Olindo
Author: Bacon, Joan Chase
1974   24 Pages   **$5.00**

803

Boo And The Flying Flews
Illus.: Leake, Donald
Author: Bacon, Joan Chase
1974   24 Pages   **$5.00**

804

Little Black Puppy, The
Illus.: Obligado, Lilian
Author: Zolotow, Charlotte
1974   24 Pages   **$10.00**

805

Who Took The Top Hat Trick?
Illus.: Cummins, Jim
Author: Bowden, Joan
1974   24 Pages   **$5.00**

806

Cat Who Stamped His Feet, The
Illus.: O'sullivan, Tom
Author: Wright, Betty Ren
1974   24 Pages   **$5.00**

807

Elephant On Wheels
Illus.: Scott, Jerry
Author: Thacher, Alida McKay
1974   24 Pages   **$5.00**

808

Monster! Monster!
Illus.: Fry, Rosalind
Author: Harrison, David L.
1974   24 Pages   **$5.00**

809

Bear's Surprise Party
Illus.: Scott, Jerry
Author: Bowden, Joan
1974   24 Pages   **$5.00**

Little Golden Book Land Series

In 1989, a series of eight Little Golden Books—*Tootle, Poky Little Puppy, Shy Little Kitten, Saggy Baggy Elephant, Baby Brown Bear, Scuffy The Tugboat,* and *The Tawny Scrawny Lion*—were supposed to be released. Each character's story was to take place in the magical Little Golden Book Land. Two characters did not appear in their scheduled Little Golden Books (Scuffy and Baby Brown Bear), but they did appear in larger-sized editions.

Two different back covers were printed for these Little Golden Books, and both are marked as first editions. The original back cover has a full-color picture of the Little Golden Books gang taking a ride through the mountains on Tootle. The second back cover is the standard yellow one used on all Little Golden Books of the period.

Value: Mountain back cover $3.00; Regular back cover $2.00

GBL370
Welcome To Little Golden Book Land
Illus.: Mateu
Author: West, Cindy
1989   24 Pages $5.00

GBL371
Poky Little Puppy's Special Day
Illus.: Jones, Keenan
Author: West, Cindy
1989   24 Pages $5.00

GBL372
Shy Little Kitten's Secret Place
Illus.: Jones, Keenan
Author: Lawrence, Jim
1989   24 Pages $5.00

GBL373
Saggy Baggy Elephant No Place For Me
Illus.: Walz, Richard
Author: Ingoglia, Gina
1989   24 Pages   **$5.00**

GBL374
Tootle And Katy Caboose 'A Special Treasure'
Illus.: Mones, Isidre
Author: Ingoglia, Gina
1989   24 Pages   **$5.00**

GBL377
Tawny Scrawny Lion 'Saves The Day'
Illus.: Ellis, Art & Kim
Author: Teitelbaum, Michael
1989   24 Pages   **$5.00**

Original Little Golden Book Land cover

Other Series in the Little Golden Books Family

The following series of book titles can still being found regularly at garage sales and flea markets, and the values given may be higher then you'd pay in your local area. Use the same procedures for identifying editions you use for later Little Golden Books.

Big Little Golden Books
(1986–1988)

10250

Bugs Bunny And The Health Hog
Illus.: Baker, Darrell
Author: Slater, Teddy
1986 $5.00

10251

Never Printed

10252

Grab-Bag Party, The
Illus.: Maestro, Giulio
Author: Maestro, Betsy
1986 $3.00

10253

House That Had Enough, The
Illus.: O'Brien, Ken
Author: King, P. E.
1986 $3.00

10254

Little Raccoon Takes Charge
Illus.: Borgo, Deborah
Author: Moore, Lilian
1986 $3.00

10255

Little Raccoon's Nighttime Adventure
Illus.: Borgo, Deborah
Author: Moore, Lilian
1986 $3.00

10256

Little Sister
Illus.: Eugenie
Author: Daly, Kathleen
1986 $3.00

10257
Old Friends, New Friends
Illus.: Chambless-Rigie, Jane
Author: Ryder, Joanne
1986 **$3.00**

10258
Pandas Take A Vacation, The
Illus.: Maestro, Giulio
Author: Maestro, Betsy
1986 **$3.00**

10259
Peter Pan In Tinker Bell And The Pirates
Illus.: Walt Disney Studio
Author: Walt Disney Studios
1986 **$3.00**

10260
Secret Life Of Walter Kitty, The
Illus.: Goodman, Joan Elizabeth
Author: Goodman, Joan Elizabeth
1986 **$3.00**

10261
Sleep-Over Visit, The
Illus.: Tierney, Tom
Author: Dale, Jack
1986 **$3.00**

10262
Bialosky And The Big Parade Mystery
Illus.: Cooke, Tom
Author: Korman, Justine
1986 **$3.00**

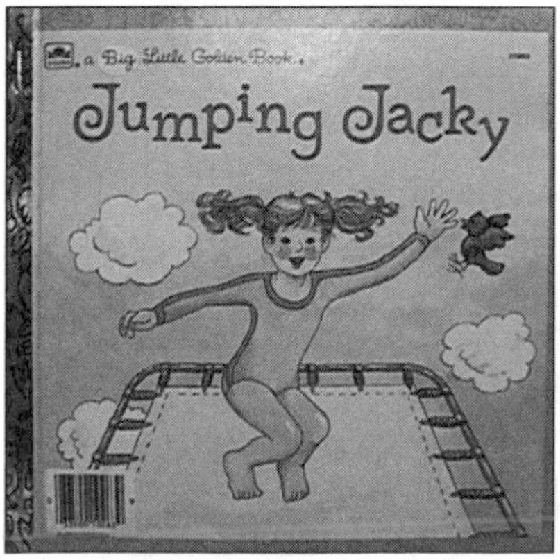

10263
Jumping Jacky
Illus.: Bracken, Carolyn
Author: Manushkin, Fran
1986 **$3.00**

10264
King Mitch Had An Itch
Illus.: Harston, Jerry
Author: Harston, Jerry
1987 **$3.00**

10265
Best Nickname, The
Illus.: Garcia, Thomas R.
Author: Anastasio, Dina
1986 **$3.00**

10266

Perfect Picnic, The
Illus.: Maestro, Giulio
Author: Maestro, Betsy
1986   **$3.00**

10267

Red Jacket Mix-Up, The
Illus.: Lemerise, Bruce
Author: Hill, Ari
1986   **$3.00**

10268

Right House For Rabbit, The
Illus.: Lee, Jody
Author: Saunders, Susan
1986   **$3.00**

10269

Ordinary Amos And The Amazing Fish
Illus.: Fernandes, Henry
Author: Fernandes, Eugenie & Henry
1986   **$3.00**

10270

Puppy Nobody Wanted, The (Pound Puppies)
Illus.: Paris, Pat
Author: Weinberg, Larry
1986   **$3.00**

10271

Animals In The Woods
Illus.: Bonforte, Lisa
Author: Ryder, Joanne
1987   **$3.00**

10272

Dinosaurs
Illus.: Nenzioni, Gabriele & Cutrona, Mauro
Author: Eltring, Mary
1987   **$3.00**

10273

How Come You're So Shy?
Illus.: Dolce, Ellen
Author: Anderson, Leone Castell
1987   **$3.00**

10274

Let's Go Fishing!
Illus.: Lemerise, Bruce
Author: Wahl, Jan
1987   **$3.00**

10275

**Big Little Golden Book Of Knock-Knocks
And Other Jokes, The**
Illus.: Harvey, Paul
Author: Hall, Nancy
1987 **$3.00**

10276

**Big Little Golden Book Of Funny Poems,
The**
Illus.: Lemerise, Bruce
Author: Feldman, Thea
1987 **$3.00**

10277

**Lady Lovely Locks Silkypup's Butterfly
Adventure**
Illus.: Paris, Pat
Author: Lewis, Jean
1987 **$3.00**

10278

Duck Tales: The Road To Riches
Illus.: Walt Disney Studios
Author: Walt Disney Studios
1987 **$3.00**

10279

Big Little Golden Book Of Planets, The
Illus.: La Padula, Tom
Author: Bell, Robert A.
1987 **$3.00**

10280

Snoopy, The World's Greatest Author
Illus.: Schultz, Charles M.
Author: Korman, Justine
1988 **$3.00**

10281

It's How You Play The Game (Snoopy)
Illus.: Schultz, Charles M.
Author: Korman, Justine
1988 **$3.00**

10282

Garfield The Fussy Cat
Illus.: Davis, Bill
Author: Simone, Norma
1988 **$3.00**

10283

Dinosaur Discoveries
Illus.: Barrett, Peter
Author: Bell, Robert
1988 **$3.00**

10284

No Stage Fright For Me!
Illus.: Berlin, Rose Mary
Author: Calmenson, Stephanie
1988   **$3.00**

10285

Be Kind To Animals!
Illus.: Lattimer, Evans
Author: Duffy, James
1988   **$3.00**

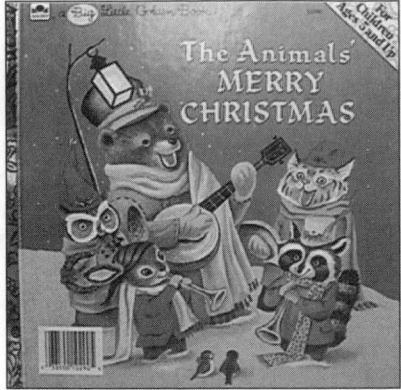

10290

Animals' Merry Christmas, The
Illus.: Scarry, Richard
Author: Jackson, Kathryn B.
1958   **$3.00**

10291

My Christmas Tree
Illus.: Schweninger, Ann
Author: Schweninger, Ann
1987   **$3.00**

Little Little Golden Books

(1988–present)
Value: 25¢-$3.00 for individual books
The first 12 titles on their original two-pack cards, listing only 12 titles. $5.00-$10.00
The original released numbers in a two-pack were:

1-12	1 & 2, 3 & 4, 5 & 6, 7 & 8, 9 & 10, 11 & 12
13-24	13 & 24, 14 & 23, 15 & 22, 16 & 21, 17 & 20, 18 & 19
25-40	25 & 26, 27 & 28, 29 & 30, 31 & 32, 33 & 34, 35 & 36, 37 & 38, 39 & 40
41-46	41 & 43, 42 & 44, 45 & 46, 47 & 48
49-60	49 & 50, 51 & 52, 53 & 54, 55 & 56, 57 & 58, 59 & 60
61-71	61 & 62, 63 & 64, 65 & 66, 67 & 68, 69 & 70

You may find the two-packs with random numbers. These are normally not first releases of packs.

1
Poky Little Puppy, The

2
Fire Engines

3
Little Red Hen, The

4
Saggy Baggy Elephant, The

5
Scuffy The Tugboat

6
Theodore Mouse Goes To Sea

7
Curious Little Kitten Around The House, The

8
Tootle

9
Fuzzy Duckling, The

10
Sleepy Book, The

11
We Help Mommy

12
Baby Farm Animals

13
Animals Of Farmer Jones, The

14
We Help Daddy

15
Four Little Kittens

16
Three Little Pigs, The

17
Very Best Home For Me!, The

18
Little Red Riding Hood

19
Four Puppies

20
Tawny Scrawny Lion

21
Walt Disney's Pinocchio

22
Three Bears, The

23
Walt Disney's Snow White And The Seven Dwarfs

24
Jack And The Beanstalk

25
I Can Dress Myself

26
Big Bird's Busy Day

27
We Like Kindergarten

28
My First Book Of Sounds

29
Walt Disney's Peter Pan

30
Walt Disney's Dumbo

31
Welcome To Little Golden Book Land

32
Poky Little Puppy's Special Day

33
Walt Disney's Mickey's Christmas Carol

34
Walt Disney's Santa's Toy Shop

35
Baby's Christmas

36
Christmas Story, The

37
Rudolph The Red-Nosed Reindeer

38
Littlest Christmas Elf, The

39
Baby Animals

40
Bunnies' ABC

41 Walt Disney's Bambi	**42** Little Mermaid, The	**43** Walt Disney's Alice In Wonderland	**44** Walt Disney's Cinderella	**45** Nutcracker, The
46 Christmas Pageant, The	**47** Colorful Mouse, The	**48** Blue Barry Bear Counts From 1 To 20	**49** Frosty The Snowman	**50** Twelve Days Of Christmas, The
51 Christmas Mice	**52** Curious Little Kitten's First Christmas, The	**53** Aladdin	**54** Beauty And The Beast	**55** Prince And The Pauper, The
56 101 Dalmatians	**57** Tale Of Peter Rabbit, The	**58** When Bunny Grows Up	**59** Velveteen Rabbit, The	**60** Bunny's New Shoes

61
Natasha's Daddy
62
Grover's Mommy
63
Count To Ten
64
Shake A Leg

65
Grover's Own Alphabet
66
First Times
67
Monsters Come In Many Colors
68
Grover's Guide To Manners

69
Night Before Christmas, The

70
101 Dalmatians 'Bark If You Love Santa'

71
Pooh 'The Merry Christmas Mystery'

First Little Golden Books

(1981–present)
Value 50¢-$2.00

Alice's First Words
Illus.: Gayler, Anne
Author: Dickson, Anna H.
1989

Animal Fair
Illus.: Wilburn, Kathy
Author: Wilburn, Kathy
1990

Animal Homes
Illus.: Goldsborough, June
Author: Davis, E. K.
1982

Baby Animals On The Farm
Illus.: Tien
Author: Heller, Rebecca
1981

Baby Animals On The Farm
Illus.: Dolce, J. Ellen
Author: Shooter, James C.
1990

Baby Mickey Plays Follow-The-Leader
Illus.: Chow, Tad Zar Austen
Author: Namm, Diane
1991

Baby Mickey's Book Of Opposites
1987

Baby Mickey's Book Of Shapes
1986

Baby Mickey's Book Of Sounds
1988

Baby's First Book
Illus.: Williams, Garth
Author: Williams, Garth
1959

Bambi & The Butterfly
1982

Bananas in Pajamas

Barney's Sand Castle
Illus.: Beckett, Sheila
Author: Calmenson, Stephanie
1983

Be Nice!

Beauty And The Beast 'The Tale Of Chip The Teapot'
Illus.: Gutierrez, Edward R. & Mones
Author: Birney, Betty
1992

Big Bird's Busy Day
Illus.: Appleby, Ellen
Author: Smith, Jessie
1987

Busy Timmy
Illus.: Goldsborough, June
Author: Jackson, Kathryn & Byron
1982

Chip 'N' Dale's Book Of Seasons
Illus.: Edwards, Paul
Author: West, Cindy
1989

Christmas Mice
Illus.: Scarry, Richard
Author: Scarry, Richard
1965

Christmas Mice
(2nd Cover)

Christmas Pageant, The
Illus.: Wilburn, Kathy
Author: Winthrop, Elizabeth
1984

Come Play At Home!
Illus.: Güell, Frenando
Author: Breen, Susan
1998

Come Play At The Park!
Illus.: Güell, Fernando
Author: Breen, Susan
1998

Count To Ten (Sesame Street)
Illus.: Nez, John
Author: Thompson, Emily
1986

Count's Poems, The (Sesame Street)

Creation Story, The

Country Mouse And The City Mouse, The
Illus.: Severn, Jeffrey
Author: Benjamin, Alan
1987

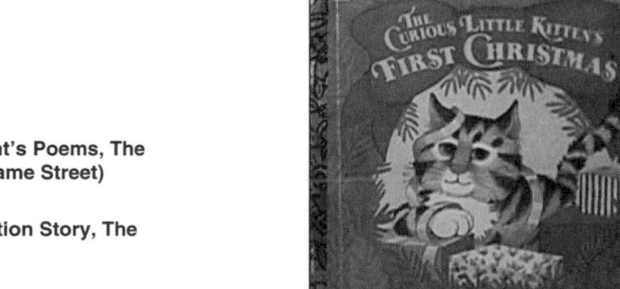

Curious Little Kitten's First Christmas, The
Illus.: Swanson, Maggie
Author: Hayward, Linda
1984

Day In The Park, A
Illus.: Eugenie
Author: Peltzman, Ronne
1985

Day With My Dad, A
Illus.: Allert, Kathy
Author: Arno, Hiskey
1989

Disney Babies Merry Christmas

Dog Goes To Nursery School
Illus.: Eugenie
Author: Hammond, Lucille
1982

Dumbo's Book Of Colors
1988

Elmo Says...
Illus.: Leigh, Tom
Author: Allen, Constance
1998

Five Little Bunnies
Illus.: Sanderson, Ruth
Author: Hayward, Linda
1985

Flounder to the Rescue

Friendly Beasts, The
Illus.: Sanderson, Ruth
1983

Fuzzy Duckling, The
Illus.: Provenson, Alice & Martin
Author: Werner, Jane

Gingerbread Man, The
Illus.: Scarry, Richard
1975

Good Morning, Muffin Mouse
Illus.: DiFiori, Lawrence
Author: DiFiori, Lawrence
1989

**Good Night, Magellan (Eureeka's
Castle)**
Illus.: Brannon, Tom
Author: Calder, Lyn
1991

Grover's Mommy
Illus.: Prebenna, David
Author: Alexander, Liza
1994

Happy Easter, Mother Duck
Illus.: Hearn, Diane Dawson
Author: Winthrop, Elizabeth
1985

Happy Halloween

**Happy Man And His Dump Truck,
The**
Illus.: Gergely, Tibor
Author: Miryam

Henry And Theresa's Race
Illus.: Nez, John
Author: Peltzman, Ronne
1984

How Big Are You?
Illus.: Lanza, Barbara
Author: Malvern, Corrine
1993

I Can Do It

I Can Dress Myself (Sesame Street)
Illus.: Nicklaus, Carol
Author: Dickson, Anna H.
1983

I Can Fly
Illus.: Brett, Jan
Author: Krauss, Ruth
1981

I Like To Help My Mommy
Illus.: Baer, Mary Alice
Author: Kenworthy, Catherine
1981

I Love You More

I'll Share With You
Illus.: Wilburn, Kathy
Author: Apolzon, Linda
1986

It's Bedtime
Illus.: Rao, Anthony
Author: Ford, B. G.
1981

It's Christmas
Illus.: Cooke, Tom
Author: Alexander, Liza
1992

Jungle Book, The 'Mowgli and the Jungle Animals'
Illus.: Mateu, Franc
Author: West, Cindy
1990

Just Joking
Illus.: Prebenna, David
Author: Muntean, Michaela
1995

Katie The Kitten
Illus.: Morrill, Leslie
Author: Jackson, Kathryn & Byron
1982

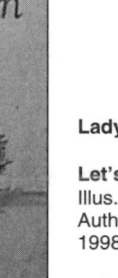

Lady and the Tramp 'The Lost Tag'

Let's Count Our Blessings
Illus.: Pfeiffer, Judith
Author: Benjamin, Alan
1998

Let's Go All Around The Neighborhood
Illus.: Rao, Anthony
Author: Thomas, Patty
1982

Let's Play Peek-A-Boo!
Illus.: Mulkey, Kim
Author: Webb, Joan
1981

Let's Play Peek-A-Boo!
Illus.: Prebenna, David
Author: Worth, Bonnie
1996

Little Calf That Couldn't Moo, The
Illus.: Lanza, Barbara
Author: Hiskey, Iris
1992

Little Christmas Treasury, A

Little Duck And The New Baby
Illus.: Cruickshank, Kathy
Author: Calmenson, Stephanie
1988

Little Duck's Moving Day
Illus.: Cruickshank, Cathy
Author: Calmenson, Stephanie
1986

Little Quack And Baby Ducky
Illus.: Cooke, Tom
Author: Smith, Ward
1991

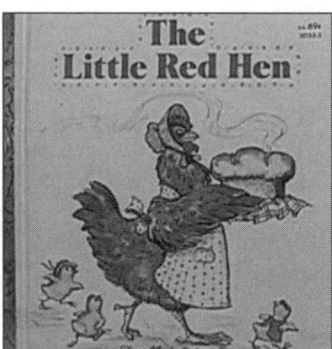

Little Red Hen, The
Illus.: Obligado, Lilian
1981

Little Squirt The Fire Engine
Illus.: Barbaresi, Nina
Author: Kenworthy, Catherine
1983

Love Letters

Martha's House
Author: Kunhardt, Edith
1982

Max Helps Out
Illus.: Stott, Dorothy M.
Author: Neison, Linda Apolzon
1983

Meet My Buddy
Illus.: Wilson, Roy
Author: Hill, Ari
1986

Mickey Mouse's Book of Cars and Trucks
Illus.: Baker, Darrell
Author: Campbell, Janet
1993

Muffin Mouse On The Go
Illus.: DiFiori
Author: DiFiori
1989

My Alphabet
Illus.: Stewart, Pat
Author: Davis, E. K.
1981

My Book Of The Seasons
Illus.: Eugenie
Author: Calmenson, Stephanie
1982

My Book Of Words
Illus.: Stillerman, Robbie
Author: Heller, Rebecca
1982

My First Book Of Animal Sounds
Illus.: Mc Cue, Lisa
Author: Corsello, Marguerite Muntean
1982

My First Book Of Sounds
Illus.: Wilburn, Kathy
Author: Bellah
1991

My First Little Mother Goose
Illus.: McQueen, Lucinda
1996

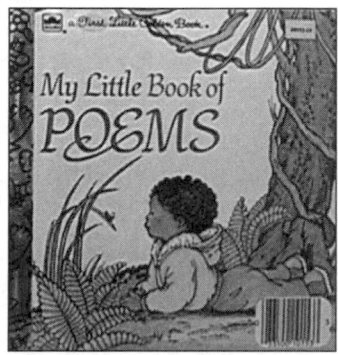

My Little Book Of Poems
Illus.: Mitchell, Frances Score
Author: Heller, Rebecca
1983

My Little Book Of Prayers
Illus.: Allert, Kathy
1982

My Little Book Of Words
Illus.: Lanza, Barbara
Author: Horvath, Sherl
1969

My Little Mother Goose
Illus.: Rosenberg, Amy
1981

Natasha's Daddy
Illus.: Attinello, Lauren
Author: Allen, Constance
1993

Ned's Number Book
Illus.: Eugenie
Author: Hunhardt, Edith
1981

No Nap Today!

Over In The Meadow
Illus.: Obligado, Lilian
1983

Over in the Meadow
Illus.: Banta, Susan
1996

Panda Bear's Paintbox
Illus.: Santoro, Christopher
Author: Muntean, Michaela
1981

Panda Bear's Secret
Illus.: Santoro, Christopher
Author: Muntean, Michaela

Perfect Lunch, The (Eureeka's Castle)
Illus.: Stevenson, Nancy
Author: Burr, Daniella
1992

Pinky's First Spring Day
Illus.: Rosenberg, Amye
Author: Rosenberg, Amye
1985

Pinocchio
Illus.: Grant, Campbell
Author: Walt Disney Studios
1992

Poky Little Puppy's Wonderful Winter Day, The
Illus.: Chandler, Jean
Author: Chandler, Jean
1982

Polite Elephant
Illus.: Scarry, Richard
Author: Scarry, Richard
1963

Puppy Roundup! (101 Dalmatians)

Saggy Baggy Elephant's Birthday
Illus.: Jones, Keenan
Author: Ingoglia, Gina
1990

Shake A Leg! (Sesame Street)
Illus.: Cooke, Tom
Author: Allen, Constance
1991

Shut the Door!
Illus.: Lopshire, Robert
Author: Lopshire, Robert
1993

Simon Visits The Doctor
Illus.: Schories, Patricia
Author: Koenigsberg, Lakin
1984

Sleepy Story, A
Illus.: Brown, Richard
Author: Burrowes, Elisabeth
1982

Stable In Bethlehem, A
Illus.: Dolce, J. Ellen
Author: Julme, Joy N.
1989

Stevie's Tricycle
Illus.: Tomai, Lorna
Author: Moed-Kass, Pnina
1982

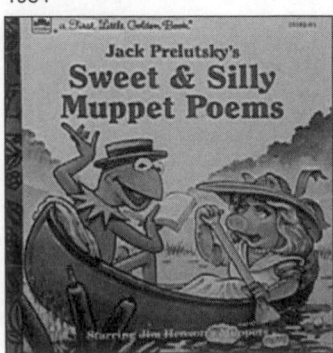

Sweet & Silly Muppet Poems
Illus.: Ewers, Joe
Author: Prelutsky, Jack
1992

Sweetie Book Of ABC, The (Tiny Toons)
Illus.: Costanza, John & Valdivia, Rochelle
Author: Calder, Lyn & Hover, M.
1991

Thank You, Pooh
1996

Three Bears, The
Illus.: McCue, Lisa
Author: North, Carol
1983

Three Billy Goats Gruffs , The
Illus.: Obligado, Lilian
Author: Rudin, Ellen
1982

Three Little Kittens, The
Illus.: Masha
1942

Three Little Pigs, The
Illus.: Obligado, Lilian
Author: Benjamin, Alan
1988

To Grandmother's House We Go
Illus.: DiFiori, Lawrence
Author: DiFiori, Lawrence
1986

Tommy's New Bed
Illus.: MacCombie, Turio
Author: Moed-Kass, Pnina
1984

Truck That Drove All Night, The
Illus.: Boyd, Patti
Author: Offerman, Lynn
1986

Tweety Trap!, The
Illus.: Messerli, Joe
Author: Lewis, Jean
1992

Very Best Picnic, The
Illus.: Eugenie
Author: Eugenie

Visit From Grandma And Grandpa, A
Illus.: Allert, Kathy
Author: Kenworthy, Catherine
1982

Way To Go, Simba!

We Like To Do Things
Illus.: Bracken, Carolyn
Author: Mason, Walter M.
1977

What Am I?
Illus.: De Witt, Cornelius
Author: Leon, Ruth

What Kind Of Truck?
Illus.: Battaglia, Aurelius
Author: Hover, Margo
1983

Wheels On The Bus, The
Illus.: Alley, R. W.
1992

When Dog Grows Up
Illus.: Eugenie
Author: Hammond, Lucille
1987

When Dog Was Little
Illus.: Eugenie
Author: Hammond, Lucille
1983

Where's Goldie?
Illus.: DiFiori, Lawrence
Author: DiFiori, Lawrence
1983

Who Says That?
Illus.: McCue, Lisa
Author: Corsello, Marguerite Muntean
1982

Winnie-The-Pooh And The Pebble Hunt
1982

Wolf And The Seven Kids, The
Illus.: Scarry, Richard

Yes, I Love You
Illus.: Aitken, Amy
Author: Havill, Juanita
1990

Zip! Pop! Hop! And Other Fun Words To Say
Illus.: Prebenna, David
Author: Muntean, Michaela
1996

Promotional and Special Little Golden Books

Burger King
Value: $3.00

Sometime in the late 1980s, Burger King gave away *The Train To Timbuctoo* during its TRAK-PAK CLASSIC TRAIN BOOKS promotion. Three other stories, *The Circus Train*, *Roundabout Train*, and *My Little Book Of Trains*, all previous Tell-A-Tales, were also given away.

Chick-fil-A
Meal bag value: $4.00-$8.00
Books value: $3.00-$4.00

In 1995, Chick-fil-A, a fast-food chain specializing in the original, boneless breast of chicken sandwich, gave eight Little Golden Book titles away in its children's meal. The meal was served in a bag decorated with Little Golden Book characters, puzzles, and games. Of the 620 family-owned stores in the chain, most are located in the Southeast and Midwest.

The back cover has the chain's logo and lists the following books: *Poky Little Puppy*, *Tawny Scrawny Lion*, *Saggy Baggy Elephant*, *Sailor Dog*, *Little Red Caboose*, *Velveteen Rabbit*, *Little Red Riding Hood*, and *The Elves and the Shoemaker*.

Hardee's
Value: Box with book: $14.00
Book only: $3.00

Hardee's gave away a Little Little Golden Book with its children's meal in the late 1980s and early 1990s. Each meal box was printed with characters from the book that was enclosed. There were three series of four books each.

Series One
Poky Little Puppy, The
Little Red Riding Hood (Illustrated by Watts)
Little Red Hen, The
Three Little Pigs, The

Series Two
Three Little Kittens
Little Red Caboose,
The Three Bears, The
Old MacDonald Had A Farm

Series Three (Pound Puppies & Pound Purries)
Pick Of The Litter
Puppy Nobody Wanted, The
Problem Puppies
Kitten Companions

KIMBIES
Value: $3.00-$5.00

KIMBIES disposable diapers were packaged with soft-cover Little Golden Books around 1976. The books' covers and insides were identical to regular Little Golden Books except they have a black and white photo of a box of KIMBIES diapers in either the left or right bottom corner. The back covers had full-page ads for KIMBIES. No numbers or prices were noted on the covers.

The following are some of the titles given away, and there may have been others:

The Lively Little Rabbit
The Poky Little Puppy
The Shy Little Kitten
The Saggy Baggy Elephant
The Little Red Caboose
Scuffy the Tugboat
Tootle

Wienerschnitzel Hot Dogs
Value: $3.00

Wienerschnitzel hot dog shops gave out regular hardcover Little Golden Books, with its logo in the bottom left corner, sometime around 1987–1988. I know of only the following two titles, but there may have been more:

The Poky Little Puppy's Naughty Day
When You Were A Baby

Crispy Critters® Special Edition Little Golden Books

Value: Crispy's Bedtime Book: $15.00
Others: $5.00

These books were packaged on the backs of Crispy Critters cereal boxes. The two titles were *Crispy In The Birthday Band* and *Crispy In No Place Like Home*. A third title, *Crispy's Bedtime Book*, was also available, but only through the mail. The stories used character animal shapes found in the cereal. Each book was published in

1987 and contained 36 pages. The books were all written by Justine Korman, illustrated by Dave Yaegle, and painted by Mike Favata.

Cleo Storybook Greetings

Value: $3.00

Three Little Golden Book titles were printed in this series of four holiday stories. They were manufactured and distributed by Cleo, Inc., a Gibson Greeting Company, in 1991. These soft cover Little Golden Books came with an envelope to be mailed like a Christmas card. Measuring 6 inches by 7-3/4 inches, these books were a little smaller than a Little Golden Book, with the same 24 pages. They originally sold for around $2.00.

Mickey's Christmas Carol
Frosty The Snowman (illustrated By Terri Super)
Rudolph The Red-Nosed Reindeer

Non-LGB Title
The Night Before Christmas
Author: Moore, Clement
Illus.: Szekeres, Cyndy

A Little Golden Book Special Edition

Value: $8.00

Six titles were done in 1985 with dust jackets. These books, measuring 7 inches by 8-1/4 inches, were a little larger than the normal Little Golden Book. These titles were also released as normal Little Golden Books with copyrights of 1985.

11630   Cheltenham's Party
11631   A Fox Jumped Up One Winter's Day
11632   Little Brown Bear
11633   Little Red Riding Hood
          Marsha Winborn illustrated edition
11634   My Book Of Poems
11635   The Scarebunny

Soft-cover Little Golden Books

Value: $2.00

I'm not giving much space to soft-cover editions because there is no way of telling how many titles have been printed over the years. They have been in print since the 1950s and were sold through the same outlets as their hard-cover counterparts, with many also being sold through elementary school book clubs.

Special Bound-in-Cloth Little Golden Books

Value: Same as regular Little Golden Books

In 1948, seven Little Golden Book titles were released in special cloth-bound editions. Each book has the familiar golden wheat spine design of the 1930s. Along the opposite sides, in a 1/4-inch white border, are the words, "Special bound in cloth." These words are repeated around the border. The regular Little Golden Book covers (front and back) were reproduced on these books. The books were the same width as a regular Little Golden Books but 1/4 inch taller.

Known titles are:
Fix It, Please
Animal Babies
Shy Little Kitten
Saggy Baggy Elephant
Taxi That Hurried
New House In The Forest
Noises And Mr. Flibberty-Jib

Follett Duro-Tuff Editions

Value: Same or a little less than a regular LGB

These editions were produced in a solid-color cloth cover with two-color artwork around 1950. The books are the same size as regular Little Golden Books, but with very dull cover art. Follett Duro-Tuff bindings were supposed to be washable and vermin proof.

Soft Cover and Goldencraft Editions

Value: Same as regular Little Golden Books

These books were bound in a cloth fabric for heavy handling in schools and libraries. There have been different cover style variations since they were first produced in the early 1950s. All hard-cover editions were 1/4 inch taller than regular Little Golden Books.

The first covers had a solid-colored background with a basket-weave pattern. The cover art consisted of a 4-1/4- x 5-1/2-inch full-color picture. This picture is different from the "regular" cover art on every copy I've seen.

The next style change came around 1955—a solid background with a continuing leaf pattern. The Little Golden Book cover pictures were the same as the first style, but this time the pictures were done in only three colors, with more of a line-drawn effect, and placed more to the upper right portion the cover.

The cover style changed again in the late 1950s, when the leaf pattern was changed to a solid dot and asterisk pattern. The three-color art was not centered on the cover.

Sometime in the early 1960s, the covers were changed to copy the original Little Golden Books cover. The artwork filled the entire cover except for a 1/4-inch colored border that matched the spine and back of the book.

Some soft-cover editions were also done by Goldencraft. These had stiff cardboard covers with a fabric spine. The covers had the weave pattern with a full-color cover picture.

Products Marketed Using Licensed Little Golden Book Characters

Aladdin Plastic lunchbox 1989

Value: $10.00

Little Golden Book Land

Applause Inc.

Miniature plastic figures with soft cover Little Golden Book
1991–present
Value: $5.00 each

Poky Little Puppy and book
Saggy Baggy Elephant and book
Scuffy The Tugboat and book
Tawny Scrawny Lion and book
Curious Little Kitten and book
Tootle and book
Babs and Lost in the Funhouse book
Buster Bunny and Lost in the Funhouse book
Porky Pig and Just Like Magic book
Bugs Bunny and Just Like Magic book
Minnie Mouse and Mickey Mouse's Picnic book
Mickey Mouse and Mickey Mouse's Picnic book
Patch and 101 Dalmatians book
Belle and Beauty and the Beast book

Plastic bookmark 1992
Value: $4.00 each

Poky Little Puppy
Shy Little Kitten
Tootle

Stuffed animals 6 inches 1991
Value: $8.00

Poky Little Puppy
Tawny Scrawny Lion

Collegeville costumes in the 1970s
Value: $25.00 each

904	Shy Little Kitten
902	Saggy Baggy Elephant
907	Lively Little Rabbit
914	Little Bear
905	Tawny Scrawny Lion
	Poky Little Puppy

Beach products 1987–1992
Values: $1.00-$10.00

Plates, invitations, napkins, tablecloths, and wrapping paper

Collegeville Costumes

Lively Little Rabbit #907
Poky Little Puppy #
Shy Little Kitten #904
Saggy Baggy Elephant #902
Little Bear #914
Tawny Scrawny Lion #905

Dolly Toy Co., The 1972

Wall plaques
Value: $25.00 each

349	Poky Little Puppy
350	Shy Little Kitten
351	Tawny Scrawny Lion

Nursery lamp and shade
Value: $35.00 each

Shy Little Kitten
Poky Little Puppy

Enesco Corporation 1989

Gift bags
Value: $2.00-$4.00

225274	Little Golden Book Land medium
225266	Little Golden Book Land mid-size
225258	Little Golden Book Land large

Bookends (wooden)
Value: $25.00

408360	Tootle the Train and Katy Caboose

Baby's sipper cup
Value: $8.00

860417	Little Golden Book Land

Child's cup and toothbrush
Value: $8.00

860409	Little Golden Book Land

Ceramic nightlights
Value: $25.00 each

415138	Saggy Baggy Elephant
408999	Scuffy The Tugboat

Ceramic musical figurine
Value: $25.00

415154	Scuffy the Tugboat

Picnic basket tin with coloring book
Value: $15.00

569518	Little Golden Book Land

Ceramic figures
Value: $10.00 each

409022	Poky Little Puppy sitting
409022	Poky Little Puppy lying
409022	Shy Little Kitten sitting
409022	Shy Little Kitten standing

Ceramic train set

409014	Tootle The Train (musical)	$25.00
410365	Tawny Scrawny Lion	$10.00
410357	Baby Brown Bear	$10.00
410373	Poky Little Puppy	$10.00

| 410349 | Katy Caboose | $15.00 |

Bank
Value: $15.00

| 414662 | Tootle the Train |

Melamine child's dinner set (six-piece)
Value: $25.00

860396   Little Golden Book Land (plate, bowl, mug, bib, spoon, fork, and *Welcome To Little Golden Book Land* book)

English candy tins 1950s
Value: $50.00

Three Little Kittens

Gund Mfg. Co. 1970s

Puppets
Value: $5.00

Saggy Baggy Elephant

Stuffed animals
Value: $15.00 each

Tawny Scrawny Lion
Poky Little Puppy

Handkerchief 1950s
Value: $10.00 each

Saggy Baggy Elephant	Gustaf Tenggren
Lively Little Rabbit	Gustaf Tenggren
Poky Little Puppy	Gustaf Tenggren
Old Mother Hubbard	Alice and Martin Provensen
Cat And The Fiddle	Alice and Martin Provensen

Kleenex 1954

Value: $20.00

Yellow wrapper advertising *Little Lulu And Her Magic Tricks*. Wrapper went around three boxes of Kleenex. The wrapper also had instructions for making Mr. Scarecrow.

Larami Corp. 1978

Hard plastic toys

1950-5	Tootle Wind-Up Train-Set	$40.00
1900-0	Poky Little Puppy Wind-Up Rocker	$15.00
1900-0	Saggy Baggy Elephant Wind-Up Rocker	$15.00

Ideal Toy Company 1955 Talking Toys
Value: With box $200.00 each
Value: Without box $100.00 each

4302	Scuffy The Tugboat
4303	Tootle The Train
4304	Poky Little Puppy
4305	Saggy Baggy Elephant

Miscellaneous

Plastic cup (yellow) 1982
Value: $8.00 each

Saggy Baggy Elephant
Tawny Scrawny Lion
The Curious Little Kitten
Poky Little Puppy

Sheets and pillowcase 1970s
From the World of Little Golden Books
Sheets $20.00
Pillowcase $10.00

Miscellaneous giveaways

A Billion Golden Memories 1987
Medallion $10.00
Book mark (metal) $15.00
Lucite cube paperweight (soft-cover miniature *Poky Little Puppy* book inside) $25.00

50th Anniversary 1992
Mug (Share The Golden Moments 50 Year Golden Books blue with gold lettering coffee cup) $10.00

Play Pal Plastics Inc. 1972

Plastic bank and nightlight
The same figures were produced in both formats by removing the bottom plug out of the bank and inserting in the light base.
Value: $12.00 each

Poky Little Puppy
Shy Little Kitten

Playskool 1989

Stuffed animals
Value: $30.00 each

263/264	Poky Little Puppy
266/264	Tawny Scrawny Lion
267/264	Saggy Baggy Elephant
268/264	Shy Little Kitten (smaller quantity produced)

Plastic figures
Value: $7.00

Playskool Plastic Figures

272/271 Poky Little Puppy
273/271 Tawny Scrawny Lion
274/271 Saggy Baggy Elephant
275/271 Shy Little Kitten
276/271 Baby Brown Bear
277/271 Little Red Hen

Rosewall Inc. 1989

Little Golden Book Land growth chart and
   character set $20.00
Little Golden Book Land peel and place
   stickers $25.00
Wallpaper rolls $25.00
Wallpaper border rolls $20.00
Wallpaper Book, An Adventure In Little
   Golden Book Land $50.00

Simon & Schuster 1951

Forty-two pieces of stationery consisting of 12 single and six double sheets, 12 postcards, and envelopes. Each piece is decorated with characters from The Poky Little Puppy, The Saggy Baggy Elephant, Tootle, The Lively Little Rabbit, The Golden Sleepy Book, I Can Fly, Color Kittens, Little Black Sambo, Big Brown Bear, and The Fuzzy Duckling. Box originally sold for 50 cents.

350   My Little Golden Writing Paper
           (rabbit and dog on box cover) $75.00
351   My Little Golden Writing Paper
           (little boy lying down writing on
           box cover) $70.00

Stevan-Silbro jewelry pins 1950s

Value: $20.00 each

Lively Little Rabbit
Poky Little Puppy
Saggy Baggy Elephant
Scuffy The Tugboat
Shy Little Kitten
Tootle

The Wormser Co. 1988

Story Time pajamas and book
   Produced in both pajamas and nightshirts
Value: $17.00 each

Poky Little Puppy
Tootle

Worcester Toy Co. 1970s

Value: $35.00

7034   Saggy Baggy Elephant plastic tea set

Foreign Little Golden Books

Argentina (Spanish)

UN LIBRITO DE ORO

Distributed by Liberia Hachette S.A. and printed by Pablo Paoppi e Hijos, both of Buenos Aires. I have found no edition markings, but some editions do contain the date of printing.

Australia

The first books were printed by Geo. Gibbons Ltd., Leicester, England. These books had spines identical to the American gold-paper spines of the 1940s. The second spines were black with coppery-golden leaves and flowers. These were printed by Colourtone Pty. Ltd, Australia. Spines are either a gold paper similar to early American Little Golden Books, with black and gold flaked look or black with gold leaves on spine. If the spines are black with silvery leaves and flowers, they were printed in Singapore by the Toppan Printing Company, Ltd. The books are now published by Golden Press PTY. Ltd., Sydney.

Titles with an * were only published as a Little Golden Book in Australia.

369	Three Bears
370	We Help Daddy
371	Hansel And Gretel
372	My Teddy Bear
373	New Puppy, The
374	Daddies
375	Baby's Mother Goose
376	Play Street
377	My Teddy Bear
378	Animal Daddies and My Daddy
*379	Skippy The Bush Kangaroo

*380	Skippy To The Rescue

381	Chittychitty Bangbang
382	Sam The Firehouse Cat
383	Good Night Little Bear
384	Little Fat Policeman
385	Indian, Indian
386	Kitten's Surprise
387	Wonderful School, The
388	Little Book, The
389	Animal Counting Book
390	Raggedy Ann And Fido
391	Boy With A Drum, The
392	Tiny, Tawny Kitten

*395	Skippy And The Intruder

*396	Woobinda 'Animal Doctor'

397	Eloise Wilkin's Mother Goose
398	Old Mother Hubbard
399	Prayers For Children
400	Visit To Children's Zoo
401	Bozo And The Hide 'N' Seek Elephant
402	Let's Visit The Dentist
403	Rags
404	Goodbye Tonsils
404	Peter Rabbit
405	Captain Kangaroo
406	Charlie
407	Jenny's New Brother
408	Wiggles
409	Bullwinkle
410	Saggy Baggy Elephant, The
411	Shy Little Kitten, The
412	Little Cottontale
413	Country Mouse And The City Mouse, The
414	Lion's Paw, The
415	Birds
416	Never Pat A Bear
417	I Like To Live In The City
419	Bug Bunny's Carrot Machine
420	So Big
421	Dinosaurs
422	123! Juggle With Me!
423	Smokey The Bear & The Campers
424	Lassie And The Big Clean Up Day
425	Monster At The End Of The Book
426	My Little Dinosaur

427	Captain Kangaroo & The Beaver
428	Little Golden Mother Goose
429	Raggedy Ann & The Cookie Snatcher
430	Just For Fun
431	Bert's Hall Of Great Inventions
432	Pussy Cat Tiger
434	Santa's Surprise Book
435	Baby's Birthday
436	Wacky Witch & The Mystery Of Kings Gold
437	Forest Hotel
438	Happy Golden ABC
439	Chipmunk's ABC
440	Smokey The Bear Finds A Friend
441	My Home
442	Bear In The Boat
443	Bravest Of All
444	Corky's Hiccups
445	Little Boy & The Giant
446	Large And Growly Bear
447	Three Little Pigs
448	Gingerbread Man
450	Little Engine That Could
*451	Little Binjy
*452	Legend Of Three Sisters

*453	Aboriginal Tales

D78	Mary Poppins
D79	Cinderella's Friends
D80	Mad Hatter's Tea Party
D81	Chip 'n Dale At The Zoo
D82	Donald Duck Prize Driver
D83	Three Little Pigs
D85	Winnie The Pooh & The Honey Tree
D86	Winnie The Pooh Meets Gopher
D87	Mickey Mouse & His Space Ship
D88	Peter Pan & The Indians
D89	Uncle Remus
D90	Mother Goose
D91	Ugly Dachshund
D92	Thumper
D93	Mickey Mouse & The Mouseketeers
D94	Hiawatha
D95	Donald Duck And The Mouseketeers
D96	Ugly Duckling, The
D97	Mickey Mouse And Pluto Pup
D98	Bunny Book
D99	Peter And The Wolf
D100	Disneyland On The Air
D101	Jungle Book, The
D102	Little Man Of Disneyland
D103	Paul Revere
D104	Donald Duck And The Witch
D105	Donald Duck In Disneyland
D106	Dumbo
D107	Perri And Her Friends
D108	Jiminy Cricket Fire Fighter
D109	Donald Duck's Toy Sailboat
D110	Winnie The Pooh And Tigger
*D111	Story Of Black Beauty, The

*D112	How The Camel Got His Hump
*D113	Acting Out The ABC
*D114	Seven Dwarfs And Their Diamond Mine
*D115	Goldilocks And The Three Bears
*D116	Mickey Mouse Brave Little Tailor

*D117	Grasshopper And The Ants, The

*D118	Story Of Rapunzel
*D119	Bremen Town Musicians
D120	Aristocats, The
D121	Disneyland Parade
*D122	Mickey And The Beanstalk

*D123	Wizard Of Oz, The
D124	Surprise For Mickey Mouse
D126	Pluto & The Adventure Of The Golden Scepter
*D127	More Jungle Book
*D128	It's A Small World
*D129	Little House, The
*D131	Susie The Little Blue Coupe
*D132	Lampert The Sheepish Lion
*D133	Thumper's Race

*D135	Emperor's New Clothes
D136	Story Of The Ugly Duckling
D143	Robin Hood
D144	Robin Hood & The Daring Mouse
*LLP322	Story Of Heidi, The
*LLP350	Pecos Bill

*LLP364 Johnny Fedora And Alice Bluebonnet

Croatia

Denmark

FREMADS GULDBOGER

Copyrighted by Forlaget Fremad, Copenhagen.

England

In the 1950s, Little Golden Books were distributed throughout Great Britain by Frederick Muller Limited, London. In the 1960s, the Happy Time Series was produced by Golden Pleasure Books, Ltd. London.

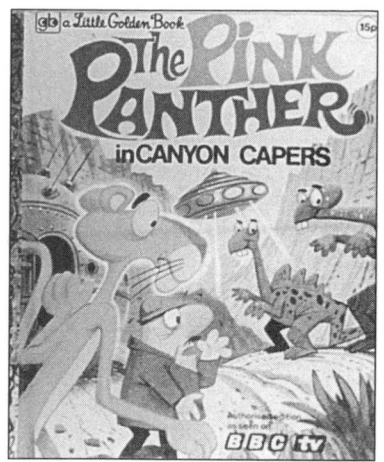

Each book was a soft cover with 24 pages. All of the more than 65 titles were previously done as Little Golden Books. In the 1970s, the books were printed in the Netherlands or Singapore and distributed by World Distributors (Manchester) Limited. These editions contained only 16 pages. The only non-American titles I know of were No. 19, *The Road Runner 'Tumbleweed Trouble,'* and No. 25, *The Pink Panther in Canyon Caper.* Soft-cover, 24-page Little Golden Books called A Golden TV Book were done in the 1970s. One title from this series was *Tom and Jerry 'Kangaroo Wrangle'.* Today, the books are printed and published by Western Publishing Company, Inc., in the United States.

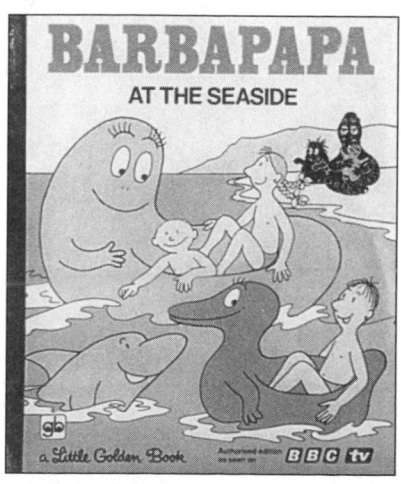

Finland

TAMMEN KULTAISET KIRJAT

In the 1980s, these books were published by Arvi A. Karisto Oy, kirjapaino, Hameenlinna. The spines were similar in design to the 1950s American design, but with brown-outlined flowers and animals on the gold.

France

UN PETIT LIVRE D'OR

Originally published by Cocorico and printed by M. Dechaux, both of Paris. Later Deux d'Or became the publisher with printing by Cite-Press-Paris. With both of these publishers, the spines remained a solid gold foil. Titles did appear in this series that were not printed in an American edition.

LES ALBUMS ROSES

This series contained Little Golden Book stories along with others and were printed by Imprimeries d Bobigny or Gilbert-Clarey. The spines were of a yellow ribbon material.

UN PETIT LIVRE D'ARGENT

These soft-cover editions were the American "Little Silver Books." The printings were done by the same publishers as the UN PETIT LIVRE D'OR series. More than 120 titles were printed, but the titles did not have the same numbering as the previous series.

Germany

EIN GOLDENES KINDERBUCH

Holland

EEN GOUDEN BOEKJE

Distributed by Annie M.G. Schmidt and Han G. Hoekstra, Holland. The spines were originally gold with a black design similar to a half star. Later spines had a solid silvery-gold.

Israel

The books had a gold foil spine and were published by Steimatsky's Agency Ltd., Tel-Aviv, Israel. The books are hinged on the right side.

Mexico

UN PEQUEN LIBRO DE ORO

Published by: Editorial Novaro,

Mexico, S.A. Editorial Novaro had offices in Mexico City, Mexico; Barcelona, Spain; Bogota, Columbia; Lima, Peru; and Santiago, Chili. Some editions published by Editorial Novaro will tell you how many copies were printed along with the day, month, and year of printing. This information will be found on either the copyright page or the last page. Soft-cover editions have been printed since the 1960s.

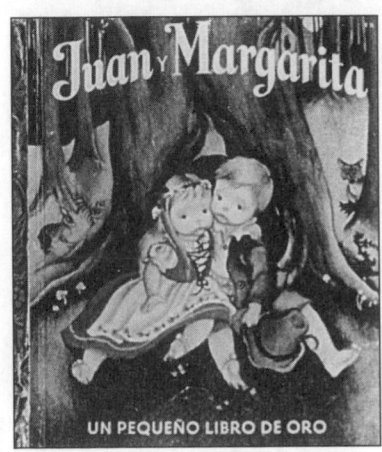

Norway

TIDENS GULL BOKE

Some of the later printing was done by Tiden Norsk Forlag of Finland. Spines were a golden ribbon with brownish leaves.

Philippines

This special edition of My Little Golden Dictionary lists hundreds of familiar words in both English and the Philippino language of Tagalog.

Sweden

FIB:S GYLLENE BOK

Published by Folket i Bilds Forlag, Stockholm.

Dating Little Golden Books by Spine Design

1942–47 Solid blue spine: Blue-bound books had dust jackets

1947–49 Gold paper spine: Pattern of leaves, flowers, and animals

1949–69 Antique gold spine: Various patterns of leaves, flowers, and plants

1955–59 Christmas spine: Christmas design used on Christmas stories

1954–56 Mickey Mouse Club spine: Only used on Mickey Mouse Club Edition, red spine with portraits

1969–present gold spine: Design of chickens, crickets, and elephants

Back Cover Designs Through the Years

One can date Little Golden Books by the design on the back cover. Use the following pages as a guide—the date provided should give you the date of issue of your book, plus or minus six months.

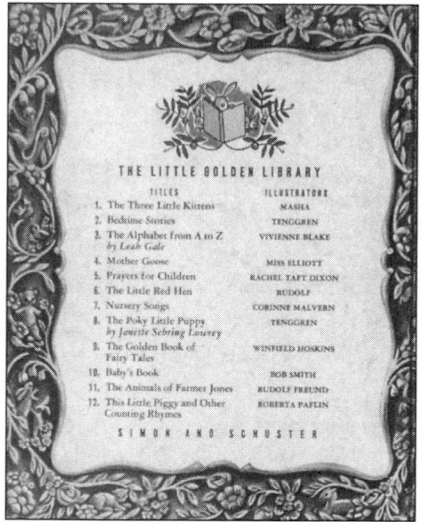

Last title listed is #12   1942-1943

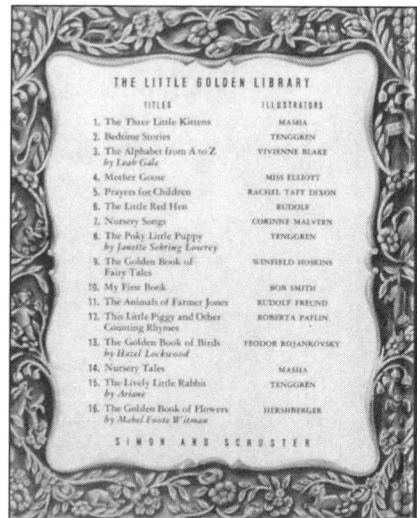

Last title listed is #16	1943-1945
Last title listed is #19	1945-1946
Last title listed is #20	1946-1947
Last title listed is #27	1947-1948
Last title listed is #34	1948
Last title listed is #D6	1948
Last title listed is #D8	1948
Last title listed is #53/#D10	1948-1949
Last title listed is #59	1949
Last title listed is #64	1949
Last title listed is #78	1949-1950
Last title listed is #D11	1950
Last title listed is #D12	1950

Last title listed is #97	1950
Last title listed is #99	1950-1951
Last title listed is #114	1951
Last title listed is #119	1951-1952
Last title listed is #143	1952
Last title listed is #D23	1952
Last title listed is #D30	1952-1953
Last title listed is #D31	1953
Last title listed is #D32	1953-1954
Last title listed is #D38	1954
Last title listed is #D44	1954-1955
Last title listed is #D45	1955
Last title listed is #A6	1955-1956
Last title listed is #D9	1956

300,000,000 Message
1954-1955

1954-1955

Last title listed is D48   ©*1955*
Last title listed is D52   ©*1955–1956*
Last title listed is D58   ©*1955–1956*

1957–1958

1958

1959

1959-1960

1959-1960

1959-1960

1960

1960-1961

1960-1962

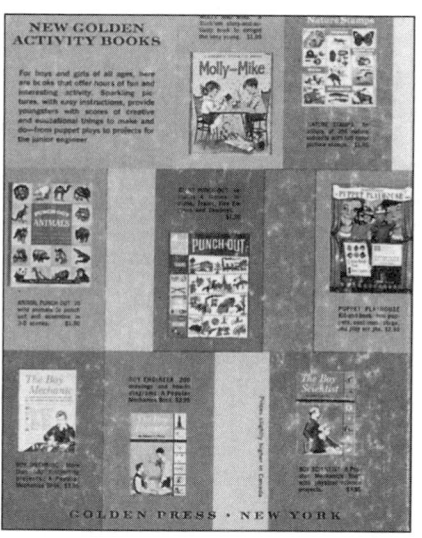

1960-1962

1960-1962

1960-1962

1960-1962

1960-1962

1961

Back Cover Designs Through the Years   211

1961–1962

1962

1962

1962

1962

1963

1963

1963

1963

1963

1963

1963

1963

1963

1964–1970

1970–1971

1970–1973

1973–1976

1976–1983

1972

1983–1986

1986–1996

1996-1999

1955–1956

2000

New Titles for 2000

99500
Big, Terrible Trouble? (The Powerpuff Girls)
Illus: McCracken, Craig & Romano, Lou
Author: McCracken, Craig
1999   16 Pages $2.00

98915
Great Riddle Contest, The (Pooh)
Illus: DRi Artworks
Author: Braybrooks, Ann\
2000   24 Pages $2.00

99504
Haunted Carnival, The (Scooby-Doo)
Illus: Vaccaro Associates, Inc and Binder, Eric
Author: Kidd, Ronald
1999   16 Pages $2.00

99505
Peter Cottontail And The Great Mitten Hunt
Illus: Karl, Linda & Nowell, Christopher
Author: Norton, Laura
2000   16 Pages $2.00

99506
Peter Cottontail Is On His Way
Illus: Karl, Linda & Nowell, Christopher
Author: Posner, Andrea
2000   16 Pages $2.00

98795
Very Best Easter Bunny, The (Pooh)
New Cover
Illus: Yee, Josi & DRi Artworks
Author: Braybrooks, Ann
2000   24 Pages $2.00

98796
Wonder Of Easter, The (Precious Moments)
New Cover
Illus: Butcher, Sam
Author: Mitter, Matt
1997   (2000)24 Pages $2.00

Little Golden Books Index

If the Little Golden Book title you are looking for has a dash (-) in the number, go to the **Little Golden Books—New Numbering** section on page if it is a non-Disney title. If it's a **Disney—New Numbering**, go to page. Titles listed in the New Numbering sections are listed alphabetically because these numbers represent book codes and are not numerical. I treat the 90000 numbers as New Numbering titles. The asterisk (*) represents the second title of a number.

Little Golden Records

Little Golden Records were the idea of Leon Shimkin. Originally distributed by Simon and Schuster, Western Printing and Lithographing printed the recored covers. The records were prcied at 25 cents. Many of the orchastrations on the records were conducted by Mitch Miller and featured the The Sandpiper singers, including Ireene Wick, the Singing Lady, Anne Lloyd, Gilbert Mack, Dick Byron, Betty Clooney, Ralph Nyland, and Bob Miller. Some of these singers were given credit as the lead singer, while other times they were part of The Sandpipers. Many popular singers and actors of the period also recorded Little Golden Records, like Roy Rogers, Dale Evans, and the Sons of the Pioneers, Bing Crosby, Danny Kaye, Hoagy Carmichael, Jimmy Durante, Howdy Doody, and Buffalo Bob. With the popularity of the Wonderful World of Disney and the Mickey Mouse Club, there are also recordings by Jimmy Dodd and the Mouseketeers, along with the voices of the Walt Disney Characters.

The early numbered records had both a regular title series and a Disney series. Because there isn't a way to tell a first edition, below there is some information to help you date them. The sleeves for records 1 to 12 were originally printed 6-3/4 inches by 8 inches tall and opened to show a brief description of the story/song, artist, and a yellow 78 rpm record in a slot on the inside right. The covers of these first 12 titles showed about three-quarters of a yellow circle that contained information about the record and performers. These were released in 1948.

In 1949, the sleeve format was changed to 7-1/2 inches by 6-3/4 inches tall, with an opening for the record at the top. The records were still yellow 78s. The yellow circle mentioned above was still present on the sleeve cover, but lines were added to make it look more like a record. The graphics on these 1949 picture sleeves were not very picturesque; they normally had a solid background with a couple of pictures of either a Disney character or a picture from a Little Golden Book. The regular titles had just a number, while the Disney titles were prefixed by a "D" as in "D1."

Between 1949 and 1950, the picture sleeves were changed to a nice graphic that covered most of the sleeve. The regular series started to see the addition of a prefix of "R" and Disney an "RD" between 1950 and 1951. The 78s were still yellow. Around 1952, the large yellow Golden Record logo on the sleeves was replaced with a 3-inch diameter logo and in 1954 with one about the size of a quarter.

Extended Play records, released in 1956, contained three Little Golden Records on one record. Their prefix was "EP." The first EP title produced, Golden Mother Goose, is number EP317. The first EPs were yellow 45 rpm and were quickly changed to the standard black 45. It was also in 1956 that the Little Golden Records were sold as yellow 78 rpm and black 45s. The artwork was the same on both formats, with the 45s normally having a banner down the right side stating that it was a 45 record. The 78s were 6-inch records, and the 45s were 7-inch.

Number prefixes were no longer used after 1959, except for the EP records. It appears that the prefixes started being dropped around record 471 and were completely gone by 490.

The last of the original numbered Little Golden Records was #777 Row, Row Row Your Boat, starring Captain Kangaroo, in 1964. Golden Records were produced after this but were no longer called Little Golden Records.

To help you date records, the following listing of numbers and release dates may be useful. If your record has a number lower than the last number of the record listed on the back of the sleeve, you can look up the last number to get an approximate selling date.

#	Date
1	1948
25	1949
50	1950
100	1952
150	1954
200	1955
250	1955
300	1956
350	1957
400	1957
450	1958
500	1959
550	1959
600	1959
650	1960
675	1961
700	1962
750	1964

Little Golden Book Records

1

Scuffy The Tugboat
Side 1: Scuffy The Tugboat
Side 2: Good Morning

$15.00

D1

From Walt Disney's Snow White
Side 1: Hi-Ho Hi-Ho
Side 2: Seven Dwarfs

$6.00

RD1

From Walt Disney's Snow White
Side 1: Hi-Ho Hi-Ho
Side 2: Seven Dwarfs, The

$10.00

2

Lively Little Rabbit, The
Side 1: Lively Little Rabbit, The
Side 2: Bizet's Farandole

$15.00

D2

From Walt Disney's Snow White
Side 1: Whistle While You Work
Side 2: Snow White In The Cottage

$6.00

RD2

From Walt Disney's Snow White
Side 1: Whistle While You Work
Side 2: Snow White In The Cottage

$10.00

3

Shy Little Kitten, The
Side 1: Shy Little Kitten, The
Side 2: Tschaikowsky's Humoresque

$15.00

RD3

From Walt Disney's Pinocchio
Side 1: Give A Little Whistle
Side 2: Pinocchio And Jiminy Cricket

$8.00

4

Tootle
Side 1: Tootle
Side 2: Grieg's Norwegian Dance

$15.00

RD4

From Walt Disney's Pinocchio
Side 1: I've Got No Strings
Side 2: Pinocchio, The Little Puppet

$8.00

5
Poky Little Puppy, The
Side 1: Poky Little Puppy The
Side 2: Naughty Duck, The
$15.00

D5
From Walt Disney's Mickey Mouse
Side 1: Mickey Mouse And His Friends
Side 2: Pluto And His Phonograph
$6.00

6
Circus Time
Side 1: Circus Time (Bigtop)
Side 2: Circus Time (Sideshow)
$15.00

RD6
From Walt Disney's Donald Duck
Side 1: Donald Singing Lesson
Side 2: Pluto The Pup
$6.00

7
Tall Giraffe, The
Side 1: Tall Giraffe, The
Side 2: Funny Little Mouse, The
$15.00

RD7
Walt Disney's Mickey's New Car
Side 1: Mickey Mouse' New Car
Side 2: Donald Duck At The Opera
$8.00

RD7
Walt Disney's Mr. Mickey Mouse
Side 1: Mickey's New Car
Side 2: Mr. Mickey Mouse
$9.00

8
Wynken Blynken And Nod
Side 1: Wynken Blynken And Nod
Side 2: Storm In The Bathtub
$15.00

RD8
Walt Disney's Donald Duck
Side 1: Donald Duck Baby Sitter
Side 2: Mickey Mouse And The Farmer Rush Rush
$10.00

9

Little Pee Wee
Side 1: Little Pee Wee
Side 2: Mozart's Turkish March

$15.00

RD9

Walt Disney's Cinderella
Side 1: Bibbidi-Bobbidi-Boo
Side 2: Bibbidi-Bobbidi-Boo March

$8.00

10

Golden Egg, The
Side 1: Golden Egg, The
Side 2: Beethoven's Country Dance

$15.00

RD10

Walt Disney's Cinderella
Side 1: Cinderella Work Song
Side 2: Work Song

$7.00

11

Big Brown Bear, The
Side 1: Big Brown Bear, The
Side 2: Schubert's Merry Music

$15.00

RD11

Walt Disney's Cinderella
Side 1: A Dream Is A Wish Your Heart Makes
Side 2: A Dream Is A Wish
(Sung By The Mice)

$10.00

12

Out Of My Window
Side 1: Out Of My Window
Side 2: Busy Elevator, The

$15.00

RD12

Walt Disney's Happy Birthday
Side 1: Happy Birthday To You (Snow White, Dwarfs, Pluto & Pinocchio)
Side 2: Happy Birthday To You (Mickey, Donald, Cinderella)

$8.00

RD12

Walt Disney's Happy Birthday
(Without cake)
Side 1: Happy Birthday To You (Snow White, Dwarfs, Pluto & Pinocchio)
Side 2: Happy Birthday To You (Mickey, Donald, Cinderella)

$7.00

13
Animals Of Farmer Jones
Side 1: Animals Of Farmer Jones
Side 2: Happy Farmer, The
$7.00

RD13
Walt Disney's Donald Duck
Side 1: Donald Duck Cowboy
Side 2: Donald Duck Cowboy
$15.00

14
Five Little Firemen
Side 1: Five Little Firemen
Side 2: Bach's Flute Dance
$7.00

14
Five Little Firemen
Side 1: Five Little Firemen
Side 2: Bach's Flute Dance
$10.00

RD14
Walt Disney's Santa's Toy Shop
Side 1: Santa's Toyshop
Side 2: Santa's Toyshop Song
$10.00

15
Taxi That Hurried, The
Side 1: Taxi That Hurried, The
Side 2: Children's Dance (From Hansel & Gretel)
$7.00

RD15
From Walt Disney's Three Little Pigs
Side 1: Who's Afraid Of The Big Bad
Wolf? (Part 1)
Side 2: Who's Afraid Of The Big Bad
Wolf? (Part 2)
$10.00

16
Favorite Songs From Mother Goose
Side 1: Three Little Kittens
Side 2: Pop Goes The Weasel; Rain Rain Go Away
$5.00

16
Mitch Miller's Three Little Kittens
Side 1: Three Little Kittens
Side 2: Pop Goes The Weasel; Rain
Rain Go Away
$8.00

RD16

From Walt Disney's Ferdinand The Bull
Side 1: Ferdinand
Side 2: Ferdinand

$12.00

17

Folk Songs
Side 1: Turkey In The Straw
Side 2: Oh, Susanna

$5.00

17

Turkey In The Straw
Side 1: Turkey In The Straw
Side 2: Oh, Susanna

$6.00

RD17

Walt Disney's Funny Little Bunnies
Side 1: Funny Little Bunnies
Side 2: Bouncy-Bouncy-Bally

$8.00

18

Favorite Songs From Mother Goose
Side 1: Farmer In The Dell, The
Side 2: Ten Little Indians; Sing A Song Of Sixpence

$5.00

18

Farmer In The Dell, The
Side 1: Farmer In The Dell, The
Side 2: Sing A Song Of Sixpence, Ten
Little Indians

$6.00

RD18

Walt Disney's Alice In Wonderland
Side 1: Alice In Wonderland
Side 2: In A World Of My Own

$12.00

19

Yankee Doodle And Dixie
Side 1: Yankee Doodle
Side 2: Dixie

$5.00

19

Yankee Doodle
Side 1: Yankee Doodle
Side 2: Dixie

$7.00

RD19

From Walt Disney's Alice In Wonderland
Side 1: I'm Late
Side 2: Alice In The White Rabbit's House
$12.00

20

Muffin Man, The
Side 1: Muffin Man, The; Hot Cross Buns
Side 2: A Tisket A Tasket; Pussycat Pussycat
$6.00

RD20

From Walt Disney's Alice In Wonderland
Side 1: Very Good Advice
Side 2: Caucus Race, The
$12.00

21

Folk Songs
Side 1: De Camptown Races
Side 2: Clementine
$5.00

21

Clementine And De Camptown Races
Side 1: De Camptown Races
Side 2: Clementine
$6.00

RD21

From Walt Disney's Alice In Wonderland
Side 1: Walrus And The Carpenter With Tweedle-
Dum And Tweedle-Dee
Side 2: Walrus And The Carpenter
$15.00

R22

London Bridge
Side 1: London Bridge
Side 2: Did You Ever See A Lassie?;
Baa Baa Black Sheep
$5.00

RD22

From Walt Disney's Alice In Wonderland
Side 1: All In A Golden Afternoon
Side 2: Alice In The Garden Of Live Flowers
$12.00

R23

Mother Goose And Other Favorites
Side 1: Humpty Dumpty, Jack And Jill
Side 2: Skip To My Lou, Cockadoodle Doo
$5.00

R23

Humpty Dumpty
Side 1: Humpty Dumpty, Jack And Jill
Side 2: Skip To My Lou Cockadoodle Doo
$6.00

R23

Humpty Dumpty
Side 1: Humpty Dumpty, Jack And Jill
Side 2: Skip To My Lou Cockadoodle Doo
$6.00

45 RPM Variation

RD23

Walt Disney's Alice In Wonderland
Side 1: Alice Meets The Caterpillar 'twas Brillig
Side 2: How D'ye Do And Shake Hands
$12.00

R24

Old Mac Donald Had A Farm
Side 1: Old King Cole, Ring Around A Rosy
Side 2: Little Miss Muffet, Pat-A-Cake
$5.00

R24

Old King Cole
Side 1: Old King Cole, Ring Around A Rosy
Side 2: Little Miss Muffet, Pat-A-Cake
$5.00

Old King Cole
Side 1: Old King Cole, Ring Around A
Rosy
Side 2: Little Miss Muffet, Pat-A-Cake
$6.00

Old King Cole
Side 1: Old King Cole, Ring Around A Rosy
Side 2: Little Miss Muffet, Pat-A-Cake
$6.00

RD24

From Walt Disney's Alice In Wonderland
Side 1: A Very Merry Unbirthday
Side 2: Mad Tea Party, The
$15.00

R25

Old Mac Donald Had A Farm
Side 1: Old Mac Donald Had A Farm
Side 2: Owl And The Pussycat, The
$5.00

R25

Mitch Miller's Old Macdonald Had A Farm
Side 1: Old Mac Donald Had A Farm
Side 2: Owl And The Pussycat, The
$6.00

RD25

From Walt Disney's Alice In Wonderland
Side 1: Painting The Roses Red
Side 2: March Of The Cards, The
$8.00

R26

Three Blind Mice
Side 1: Three Blind Mice
Side 2: Little Bo Peep, Little Jack Horner
$6.00

RD26

Walt Disney's Bongo
Side 1: Bongo (Song)
Side 2: Bongo (Story)
$10.00

R27

Barnyard And Round And Round The Village, The
Side 1: Barnyard, The
Side 2: Round And Round The Village
$5.00

RD27

From Walt Disney's Song Of The South Zip-A-Dee Doo-Dah
Side 1: Zip-A-Dee Doo-Dah
Side 2: Laughing Place
$15.00

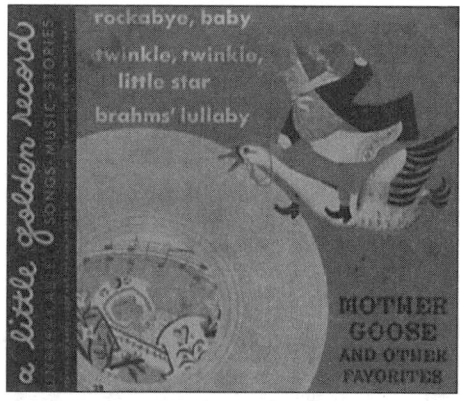

R28

Mother Goose And Other Favorites
Side 1: Brahms' Lullaby
Side 2: Twinkle Twinkle Little Star, Rockabye Baby
$5.00

RD28

From Walt Disney's Melody Time
Side 1: Little Toot (Part 1)
Side 2: Little Toot (Part 2)
$12.00

R29

Favorite Songs From Mother Goose
Side 1: Frog He Would A Wooing Go
Side 2: Baby Shaftoe, Hickory Dickory Dock
$5.00

RD29

Walt Disney's Snow White And The Seven Dwarfs
Side 1: Yodel Song, The
Side 2: Doin' The Dopey Dance
$8.00

RD30

Bluddle-Uddle-Um-Dum
Side 1: Bluddle-Uddle-Um-Dum
$7.00

R31

Folk Songs
Side 1: Bluetail Fly, The
Side 2: Rock Candy Mountain
$5.00

R31

Blue Tail Fly And Rock Candy Mountain
Side 1: Bluetail Fly, The
Side 2: Rock Candy Mountain
$9.00

R31

Blue Tail Fly And Rock Candy Mountain
Side 1: Bluetail Fly, The
Side 2: Rock Candy Mountain

$6.00

R32
R33

Night Before Christmas, The
Side 1: Night Before Christmas, The (Part 1)
Side 2: Night Before Christmas, The (Part 2)

$8.00

R33

Night Before Christmas, The
Side 1: Night Before Christmas, The (Part 1)
Side 2: Night Before Christmas, The (Part 2)

$5.00

R34

Favorite Christmas Carols
Side 1: Silent Night
Side 2: It Came Upon A Midnight Clear

$5.00

R34

Silent Night
Side 1: Silent Night
Side 2: It Came Upon A Midnight Clear

$6.00

R34

Silent Night
Side 1: Silent Night
Side 2: It Came Upon A Midnight Clear

$5.00

R35

Favorite Christmas Songs
Side 1: Jingle Bells
Side 2: Deck The Halls; Up On The House Top

$5.00

R35

Jingle Bells
Side 1: Jingle Bells
Side 2: Deck The Halls; Up On The House Top

$7.00

R35

Jingle Bells
Side 1: Jingle Bells
Side 2: Deck The Halls; Up On The House Top

$7.00

RD35

From Walt Disney's Peter Pan
Side 1: Peter Pan Theme Song
Side 2: You Can Fly

$10.00

R36

Favorite Christmas Songs
Side 1: God Rest Ye Merry Gentlemen
Side 2: Hark! The Herald Angles Sing

$5.00

RD36

From Walt Disney's Peter Pan
Side 1: Second Star To The Right
Side 2: March Of The Lost Boys

$10.00

R37

Side 1: O Little Town Of Bethlehem
Side 2: O Christmas Tree; Joy To The World

$5.00

RD37

From Walt Disney's Peter Pan
Side 1: What Made The Red Man Red
Side 2: Your Mother And Mine

$12.00

R38

Side 1: O Come All Ye Faithful
Side 2: Away In A Manger

$5.00

RD38

From Walt Disney's Peter Pan
Side 1: A Pirates Life
Side 2: Elegant Captain Hook, The

$12.00

RD39

Two Walt Disney Songs
Side 1: Lambert The Sheepish Lion
Side 2: Trick Or Treat

$15.00

R40

Side 1: A Little Golden Sleepy Record
Side 2: Close Your Eyes Sleeping Child

$7.00

RD40

From Walt Disney's Peter Pan
Side 1: Never Smile At A Crocodile
Side 2: Peter Pan's Song

$12.00

R41

White Bunny And His Magic Nose, The
Side 1: White Bunny And His Magic Nose, The
Side 2: Bunny Hop

$8.00

RD41

Walt Disney's Donald Duck Fire Chief
Side 1: Donald Duck Song
Side 2: Donald Duck Firechief

$8.00

R42

Saggy Baggy Elephant, The
Side 1: Saggy Baggy Elephant
Side 2: Elephant Walk

$10.00

RD42

From Walt Disney's Pinocchio
Side 1: When You Wish Upon A Star

$9.00

R43

Seven Sneezes, The
Side 1: Seven Sneezes, The
Side 2: My Tooth Brush Song

RD43

Pinocchio
Side 1: Hi Diddle Dee Dee

$8.00

R44

Magic Golden Record, The
Side 1: Magic Record, The
Side 2: Dancing Record, The

$7.00

RD44

From Walt Disney's Adventures In Music "Melody"
Side 1: Bird And The Cricket And The Willow Tree, The
Side 2: Melody

$8.00

R45

Little Fat Policeman, The
Side 1: Little Fat Policeman, The
Side 2: Safety Song

$12.00

R46

Brave Cowboy Bill
Side 1: Brave Cowboy Bill (Part 1)
Side 2: Brave Cowboy Bill (Part 2)

$15.00

RD46

Walt Disney's Mr. Chip'n Mr. Dale And Goofy's Song
Side 1: Mr. Chip'n Mr. Dale
Side 2: Goofy's Song

$8.00

R47

Santa Claus Is Comin' To Town
Side 1: Santa Claus Is Coming To Town
Side 2: Christmas Song

$6.00

R47

Santa Claus Is Comin' To Town
Side 1: Santa Claus Is Coming To Town
Side 2: Christmas Song

$6.00

R48

Pirates And Sailors Songs
Side 1: Sea Chanty
Side 2: Sailing, Sailing ; Sailor's Hornpipe

$10.00

R49

Wizard Of Oz, The
Side 1: Over The Rainbow
Side 2: Explosion Polka (By Johann Strauss)

$18.00

R50

Wizard Of Oz, The
Side 1: We're Off To See The Wizard
Side 2: Swan's Dance (Tschaikowsky)

$18.00

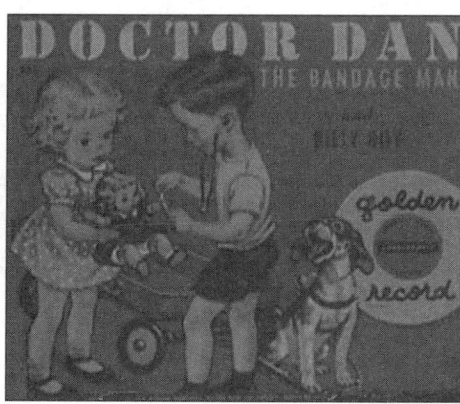

R51

Doctor Dan, The Bandage Man
Side 1: Doctor Dan, The Bandage Man
Side 2: Billy Boy

$15.00

R52

Busy Timmy
Side 1: Timmy Is A Big Boy Now
Side 2: Three Bears, The

$15.00

R53

Poor Mr. Flibberty-Jib
Side 1: Poor Mr. Fliberty-Jib
Side 2: Noise Song, The

$15.00

R53

Back Cover

R54

Happy Man And His Dump Truck, The
Side 1: Happy Man And His Dump Truck, The
Side 2: Happy Man's Dance, The (Hayden)

$15.00

R55

Scuffy The Tugboat
Side 1: Scuffy The Tugboat
Side 2: My Bonnie Lies Over The Ocean

$15.00

R56

Tootle Stay On The Right Track
Side 1: Tootle
Side 2: Choo-Choo Train, The

$15.00

R57

Peter Cottontail
(Purple background)
Side 1: Peter Cottontail (Easter Version)
Side 2: Peter Cottontail (Year Round Version)

$6.00

R57

Peter Cottontail
(Blue background)
Side 1: Peter Cottontail (Easter Version)
Side 2: Peter Cottontail (Year Round Version)

$6.00

R58

Woody Woodpecker Song, The
Side 1: Woody Woodpecker Song
Side 2: Woodpecker's Dance

$10.00

R59

Marge's Little Lulu
Side 1: Little Lulu
Side 2: Lavender's Blue

$15.00

R60

Popeye The Sailor Man
Side 1: I'm Popeye The Sailor Man
Side 2: Blow The Man Down

$12.00

RD60

Walt Disney's Mickey Mouse's Birthday Party
Side 1: Mickey Mouse's Birthday Party
Side 2: Mickey Mouse's Birthday March

$9.00

R61

Casper The Friendly Ghost
Side 1: Casper The Friendly Ghost
Side 2: Little Ghost Dance, The (Bartok)

$15.00

D61
Walt Disney's School Days
Side 1: School Days (Part 1)
Side 2: School Days (Part 1)

$8.00

R62
Winnie-The-Pooh
Side 1: Winnie-The-Pooh
Side 2: Sing-Ho Cottleston Pie

$12.00

RD62
Walt Disney's Mickey Mouse's Christmas Party
Side 1: Jingle Bells
Side 2: Christmas Symphony

$10.00

R63
S64
Rodgers And Hammersteins's Songs For Children From Oklahoma And Carousel
Side 1: Oh! What A Beautiful Morning
Side 2: June Is Bustin'out All Over

$6.00

D65
March From Peter And The Wolf
Side 1: March For Peter And The Wolf (Serge Prokofieff)
Side 2: Jing-A-Ling Jing-A-Ling (From Beaver Valley)

$10.00

D65
Back Cover

R66
Icka-Backa-Soda-Cracker
Side 1: Icka-Backa-Soda-Cracker
Side 2: Come To Barn Dance

$7.00

R66
Back Cover

R67
Edgar Rice Burroughs' Tarzan Song
Side 1: Tarzan Song
Side 2: Jungle Dance
(Tschaikowsky)

$15.00

R68
Rudolph The Red-Nosed Reindeer
Side 1: Rudolph The Red-Nosed Reindeer
Side 2: Reindeers' Dance, The

$6.00

R68

Rudolph The Red-Nosed Reindeer
Side 1: Rudolph The Red-Nosed Reindeer
Side 2: Reindeers' Dance, The

$6.00

R69

Frosty The Snowman
Side 1: Frosty The Snowman (Part 1)
Side 2: Frosty The Snowman (Part 2)

$6.00

R70

Side 1: Little Audrey Says
Side 2: Let's Go Shopping

$15.00

R71

Parade Of The Wooden Solders
Side 1: Parade Of The Wooden Solders
Side 2: Sparrow In The Tree Top

$7.00

R71

Back Cover

R72

Irving Berlin's Alexander's Ragtime Band
Side 1: Alexander's Ragtime Band
Side 2: Alexander's Ragtime Band

$7.00

SD73

Disney's Friends

$10.00

R74

Chocolate Cowboy, The
Side 1: Chocolate Cowboy
Side 2: Daddy's Whistle

$7.00

R75

Irving Berlin's Easter Parade
Side 1: Easter Parade
Side 2: Irving Berlins Easter Parade By Peter Hanley

$6.00

R76

Ukelele And Her New Doll
Side 1: Ukelele (Part 1)
Side 2: Ukelele (Part 2)

$15.00

R77

Tawny Scrawny Lion
Side 1: Tawny Scrawny Lion (Part 1)
Side 2: Tawny Scrawny Lion (Part 2)

$15.00

SD78

Walt Disney's Little Friends
Side 1: Lil' Bad Wolf, The, Tinker Bell
Side 2: Huey, Louie, Dewey, Dopey's Whistle

$12.00

R79

Star Spangled Banner, The
Side 1: My Country ' Tis Of Thee
Side 2: Star Spangled Banner

$8.00

R80

Egbert The Easter Egg
Side 1: Egbert The Easter Egg
Side 2: Bunny Bunny Bunny

$5.00

R80

Egbert The Easter Egg
Side 1: Egbert The Easter Egg
Side 2: Bunny Bunny Bunny

$3.00

S81

Songs About The Woodwind
Side 1: Antoinette, The Clarinet; Bobo, The Oboe
Side 2: Knute, The Flute; Muldon, The Old
Bassoon

$6.00

S82

Jimmy Durante Sings
Side 1: Rudolph The Red-Nosed Reindeer
Side 2: Santa Claus Is Comin' To Town

$15.00

S82

Back Cover

S83

Oh! How I Hate To Get Up In The Morning
Side 1: Oh! How I Hate To Get Up In The Morning

$8.00

R84

Irving Berlin's God Bless America
Side 1: God Bless America
Side 2: God Bless America

$6.00

R85

Mr. Shortsleeves' Supermarket
Side 1: Mr. Shortsleeves' Supermarket
Side 2: Stop Look And Listen

$12.00

R85

Back Cover

R86

Willie The Whistling Giraffe And The Poky Little Puppy
Side 1: Poky Puppy
Side 2: Willie The Whistling Giraffe

$15.00

R87

Little Train Who Said "Ah Choo", The
Side 1: Little Train Who Said "Ah Choo!"
Side 2: Down By The Station

$6.00

R88

When Santa Gets Your Letter
Side 1: When Santa Gets Your Letter - I
Side 2: When Santa Gets Your Letter - Ii

$12.00

R89

Tom Corbett Space Cadet Song And March
Side 1: Tom Corbett Space Academy Song
Side 2: Tom Corbett Space Cadet March

$18.00

R89

Back Cover

R90

Fuzzy Wuzzy
Side 1: Fuzzy Wuzzy
Side 2: Riddle Song

$6.00

R91

Dennis The Menace
Side 1: Dennis The Menace (Part 1)
Side 2: Dennis The Menace (Part 2)

$12.00

R91

Back Cover

R92

From Gilbert And Sullivan's H.M.S. Pinafore
Side 1: I'm Called A Buttercup
Side 2: We Sail The Ocean Blue

$7.00

R93

Smoky The Bear
Side 1: Smoky The Bear
Side 2: Smoky The Bear March

$15.00

R94

Bert Parks Sings
Side 1: You're a Grand Old Flag
Side 2: I'm a Yankee Doodle Dandy

$6.00

R95

Gandy Dancers' Ball, The
Side 1: Gandy Dancer's Ball
Side 2: Hambone

$6.00

R95

Back Cover

R96

Shrimp Boats And On Top Of Old Smoky
Side 1: Shrimp Boats
Side 2: On Top Of Old Smoky

$6.00

R96

Back Cover

R97

Pull Together And Santa's Other Reindeer
Side 1: Pull Together
Side 2: Santa's Other Reindeer

$6.00

R98

Rootie Kazootie And Polka Dottie Polka
Side 1: Rootie Kazootie And Polka Dottie Polka
Side 2: Polka Dottie Polka, The

$15.00

R99

Jimmy Durante Sings Yankee Doodle Dandy
Side 1: Yankee Doodle Dandy
Side 2: I Like People

$5.00

S100

Rogers And Hammerstein's Songs For Children From The King And I
Side 1: I Whistle A Happy Tune
Side 2: Getting To Know You

$8.00

R101

On The Good Ship Lollipop
Side 1: Good Ship Lollipop
Side 2: Riddle Song, The

$8.00

R102

I'm Gonna Get Well Today And Bumble Bee Bumble Bee
Side 1: Bumble Bee Bumble Bee
Side 2: I'm Gonna Get Well Today

$8.00

R103

Irving Berlin's White Christmas
Side 1: White Christmas
Side 2: White Christmas

$8.00

R103

Irving Berlin's White Christmas
Side 1: White Christmas
Side 2: White Christmas

$5.00

R104

When The Red Red Robin Comes Bob Bob Bobbin Along
Side 1: When The Red Red Robin Comes Bob Bob Bobbin Along
Side 2: Walkin' To Missouri

$5.00

R105

Paper Doll And The Paper Family
Side 1: Paper Doll
Side 2: Paper Family, The

$15.00

R105

Back Cover

S106

Songs From South Pacific
Side 1: Happy Talk
Side 2: Dites-Mo!

$8.00

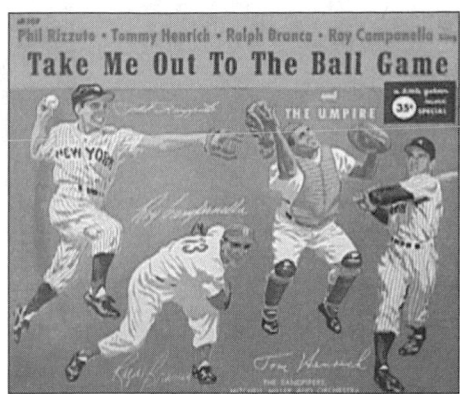

S107

Take Me Out To The Ball Game
Side 1: Take Me Out To The Ball Game Sung By Phil Rizzuto
Side 2: Umpire, The

$45.00

S108

Bert Parks Sings Me And My Shadow
Side 1: Me And My Shadow
Side 2: Ski-Da-Me-Rink-A-Doo

$7.00

R109

Rootie Kazootie In Polka Dottie's Garden
Side 1: Polka Dottie's Garden

$15.00

R110

I Saw Mommy Kissing Santa Claus
Side 1: I Saw Mommy Kissing Santa Claus
Side 2: Christmas Chopsticks

$7.00

S111

Songs About The Army, Airforce, Navy, Marines
Side 1: Anchors Aweigh, Halls Of Montezuma
Side 2: Caissons Go Rolling Along, Army Air Corps Song

$6.00

R112

Night Before Christmas
Side 1: Night Before Christmas Song
Side 2: Crackerjack Christmas

$7.00

R113

Me And My Teddy Bear
Side 1: Me And My Teddy Bear
Side 2: Teddy Bears On Parade

$8.00

R114

No Title Info.

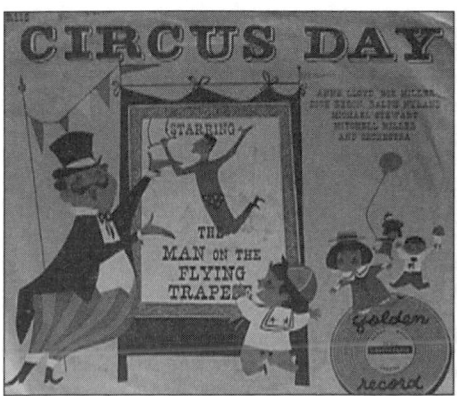

R115

Circus Day
Side 1: Man On The Flying Trapeze, The (Part 1)
Side 2: Man On The Flying Trapeze, The (Part 2)

$6.00

R116

Tweet And Toot
Side 1: Tweet And Toot (Part 1)
Side 2: Tweet And Toot (Part 2)

$6.00

R117

Ta-Ra-Ra-Boom-Der-E And Pony Boy
Side 1: Ta-Ra-Ra-Boom-De-Re
Side 2: Pony Boy

$6.00

R118

Mac Namera's Band
Side 1: Mac Namera's Band
Side 2: Mac Namera's Band (Orchestration)
$6.00

R119

Singin' In The Rain And Let's All Sing Like The Birdies Sing
Side 1: Singin' In The Rain
Side 2: Let's All Sing Like The Birdies Sing
$6.00

R120

There's A Rainbow 'Round My Shoulder
Side 1: There's A Rainbow 'Round My Shoulder
Side 2: Inky Dinky Bob-O-Linki
$6.00

D121

Disney's The World Owes Me A Living
$8.00

R122

R123

R124

Little Rag Doll
Side 1: Little Rag Doll With Shoe Button Eyes
Side 2: Lollipop Tree, The
$8.00

R125

Sleigh Ride
Side 1: Sleigh Ride
Side 2: I Just Can't Wait Till Christmas
$7.00

R126

Syncopated Clock, The
Side 1: Syncopated Clock
Side 2: Clock Symphony
$6.00

R127

Hop Scotch Polka And Music, Music, Music
Side 1: Hop Scotch Polka
Side 2: Music Music Music
$7.00

S128

Songs About The Brass
Side 1: Monsieur Forlorn, The French Horn; Crumpet The Trumpet
Side 2: Mcmalone, The Slide Trombone; Poohbah, The Tuba
$6.00

R129

R130

From Samuel Goldwyn's Production Hans Christian Andersen
Side 1: Thumbelina
Side 2: Wonderful Copenhagen
$6.00

R131
Rootie Kazootie And Mr. Deetle Dootle
Side 1: Mister Deetle Dootle Song
Side 2: Rootie Kazootie And Mr. Deetle Dootle
$15.00

R132
Playmates "Come Out And Play With Me"
Side 1: Playmates
Side 2: Tattle Tale Duck, The
$7.00

R133
Music Goes 'Round And Around', The
Side 1: Three Little Fishes
Side 2: Music Goes 'round And Around
$7.00

R134
Daddy's Report Card
Side 1: Daddy's Report Card
Side 2: Daddies
$7.00

R135
Pig Polka And Crazy Quilt Farm
Side 1: Pig Polka
Side 2: Crazy Quilt Farm
$8.00

R136

R137
My Bunny And My Sister Sue
Side 1: My Bunny And My Sister Sue
Side 2: Polly-Wolly-Doodle
$5.00

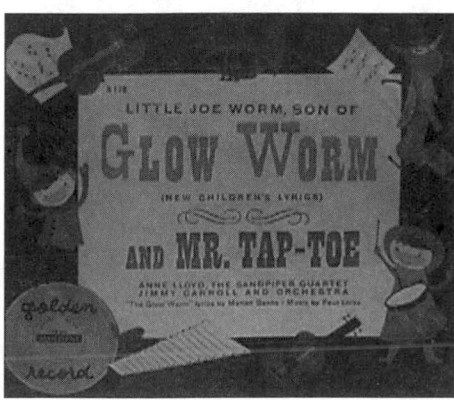

R138
Little Joe Worm, Son Of Glow Worm And Mr. Tap-Toe
Side 1: Little Joe Worm, Son Of Glow Worm
Side 2: Mr. Tap-Toe
$5.00

R139
Animal Play Time With Uncle Win Stracke
Side 1: Bling Blang Build A House For Baby, Pick It Up
Side 2: Mailman, Don't You Push Me Down
$6.00

R140

S141
Side 1: Jesus Wants Me For A Sunbeam; Jesus Loves Me
Side 2: Now The Day Is Over; Onward Christian Soldiers
$6.00

R142
Mary Rogers' Songs For Children
$6.00

S143

Jelly On My Head
Side 1: Jelly On My Head, I Wish I Wuz A Whisker
Side 2: Flippity Floppity Bunny, The Bunny With
The Big Blue Eyes

$6.00

R144

Little Engine That Could, The
Side 1: Little Engine That Could, The (Part 1)
Side 2: Little Engine That Could, The (Part 2)

$6.00

R145

How Much Is That Doggie In The Window?
Side 1: That Doggie In The Window
Side 2: Three Little Puppies

$7.00

R146

Eustis The Useless Rabbit
Side 1: Eustis The Useless Rabbit
Side 2: Animal Dance, The

$6.00

R147

Arfy The Doggie In The Window
Side 1: Arfy, The Doggie In The Window
Side 2: Mairzy Doats

$7.00

R147

Back Cover

R149

Rootie Kazootie And Gala Poochie Pup
Side 1: Rootie Kazootie And Gala Poochie Pup
Side 2: Rootie Kazootie's Gala Poochie March

$15.00

D150

Walt Disney's The Tortoise And The Hare
Side 1: Tortoise And The Hare, The (Part 1)
Side 2: Tortoise And The Hare, The (Part 2)

$10.00

D151

From Walt Disney's Goofy The Toreador
Side 1: Goofy The Toreador
Side 2: Goofy The Toreador

$15.00

R152

Gaston And Josephine
Side 1: Gaston And Josephine
Side 2: Cobbler On Cobblestone Road, The
$12.00

R152

Back Cover

S154

God Bless Us All
Side 1: God Bless Us All
Side 2: Now I Lay Me Down To Sleep
$12.00

R155

I Want A Hippopotamus For Christmas
Side 1: I Want A Hippopotamus For Christmas
Side 2: I Dreamt That I Was Santa Claus
$10.00

R155

Back Cover

R156

Tootle
Side 1: Tootle
Side 2: Choo Choo Rain, The
$12.00

S157

Songs About The Strings
Side 1: Lucy Lynn The Violin, Mello Fello The Cello
Side 2: Nola The Viola, Lovelace The Bass
$6.00

R159

Tweetie Pie
Side 1: I Taut I Saw A Puddytat (Part 1)
Side 2: I Taut I Saw A Puddytat (Part 2)
$8.00

S160

Little White Duck And Little Sir Echo, The
Side 1: Little White Duck
Side 2: Little Sir Echo
$6.00

S161

Marge's Little Lulu And Her Magic Trick
Side 1: Little Lulu And Her Magic Trick (Part 1)
Side 2: Little Lulu And Her Magic Trick (Part 2)
$18.00

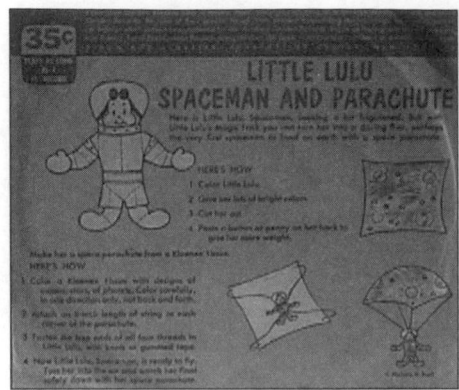

S161

Back Cover

R161

Marge's Little Lulu And Her Magic Trick
Side 1: Little Lulu And Her Magic Trick (Part 1)
Side 2: Little Lulu And Her Magic Trick (Part 2)
$15.00

R161

Back Cover

R162

Walt Disney's Adventures In Music Series
Side 1: Toot And A Whistle A Plunk And A Boom A
Side 2: Toot And A Whistle A Plunk And A Boom A
$12.00

S163

Big Bell Little Bell
Side 1: Big Bell Little Bell
$6.00

D164

Songs From Walt Disney's Bambi
Side 1: Thumper Song
Side 2: Little April Shower
$9.00

R166

Where did My Snowman Go..?
Side 1: Where did My Snowman Go..?
Side 2: Little Fir Tree
$8.00

R167

That's What I Want For Christmas
Side 1: That's What I Want For Christmas
Side 2: Little Stowaway On Santa's Sleigh
$7.00

D168

From Walt Disney's Melody Time Johnny Appleseed
Side 1: Pioneer Song
Side 2: Apple Song
$8.00

D169

Songs From Walt Disney's Dumbo
Side 1: When I See And Elephant Fly
Side 2: It's Circus Day Again
$10.00

SD172

From Walt Disney's Melody Time Pecos Bill
Side 1: Pecos Bill (Part 1)
Side 2: Pecos Bill (Part 2)

$10.0

D174

20,000 Leagues Under The Sea Whale Of A Tale
Side 1: 20,000 Leagues Under The Sea Whale Of A Tale
Side 2: Snoopy The Seal

$10.00

SD175

Walt Disney's The Reluctant Dragon
Side 1: Reluctant Dragon, The (Part 1)
Side 2: Reluctant Dragon, The (Part 2)

$10.00

R176

Roy Rogers And Dale Evans Sing Happy Trails To You
Side 1: Happy Trails To You
Side 2: A Cowboy Needs A Horse

$18.00

R176

Roy Rogers And Dale Evans Sing Happy Trails To You
(2nd cover)
Side 1: Happy Trails To You
Side 2: A Cowboy Needs A Horse

$15.00

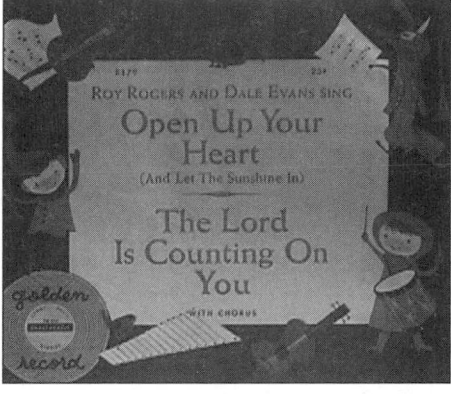

R179

Roy Rogers And Dale Evans Sing
Side 1: Open Up Your Heart
Side 2: Lord Is Counting On You, The

$6.00

R179

Roy Rogers And Dale Evans Sing
(2nd cover)
Side 1: Open Up Your Heart
Side 2: Lord Is Counting On You, The

$6.00

R180

Bugs Bunny "What's Up Doc?"
Side 1: Bugs Bunny (Part 1)
Side 2: Bugs Bunny (Part 2)

$8.00

R183

Roy Rogers And Dale Evans Sing The Night Before
Side 1: Night Before Christmas, The (Part 1)
Side 2: Night Before Christmas, The (Part 2)

$15.00

R184

Annie Oakley Sings
Side 1: Annie Oakley Song, The
Side 2: Bright Eyed And Bushy Tailed

$16.00

R185

Roy Rogers Sings
Side 1: Swedish Rhapsody
Side 2: Bamboo Boat

$16.00

R186

Daffy Duck Song, The
Side 1: Daffy Duck (Part 1)
Side 2: Daffy Duck (Part 2)

$15.00

R187

Roy Rogers An Dale Evans Sing
Side 1: Daniel The Cocker Spaniel
Side 2: Chicki Wicki Choctaw

$16.00

R188

From Walt Disney's At The Country Fair
Side 1: Donald Duck On The Ferris Wheel, Goofy
In The Fun House
Side 2: Chip 'n' Dale On The Roller Coaster, Pinoc-
chio On The Merry-Go-Round

$8.00

R189

Warner Bros. Elmer Fudd
Side 1: Elmer Fudd (Part 1)
Side 2: Elmer Fudd (Part 2)

$12.00

D190

Songs From Walt Disney's Lady And The Tramp
Side 1: Lady
Side 2: He's A Tramp

$12.00

R191

**Warner Bros. Bugs Bunny Easter Song And Mr.
Easter Rabbit**
Side 1: Bugs Bunny Easter Song
Side 2: Mr. Easter Rabbit

$8.00

R192

Roy Rogers And Dale Evans Sing
Side 1: Easter Is A Loving Time
Side 2: Candy Cane Cake Walk

$16.00

D194

Disneyland Theme Song
Side 1: Disneyland
Side 2: When You Wish Upon a Star

$16.00

R195
Songs From Walt Disney's Lady And The Tramp
Side 1: Siamese Cat Song
Side 2: What Is A Baby? La, La, Lu
$10.00

R196
Roy Rogers And Dale Evans Sing
(Red cover)
Side 1: Little Shoemaker, The
Side 2: Happy Wanderer, The
$8.00

R196
Roy Rogers And Dale Evans Sing
(White cover)
Side 1: Little Shoemaker, The
Side 2: Happy Wanderer, The
$8.00

D197
Walt Disney's The Ballad Of Davy Crockett
Side 1: Ballad Of Davy Crockett, The (Part 1)
Side 2: Ballad Of Davy Crockett, The (Part 2)
$10.00

R198
Roy Rogers And Dale Evans Sing
Side 1: Little Boy That Couldn't Find Christmas
Side 2: Story Of Christmas, The
$14.00

R199
Pat Brady Sings "Roy Rogers Had A Ranch"
Side 1: Roy Rogers Had A Ranch
Side 2: Chuck Wagon Song, The
$18.00

R200
Mister Sandman And The Mama Doll Song
Side 1: Mister Sandman
Side 2: Mama Doll Song, The
$5.00

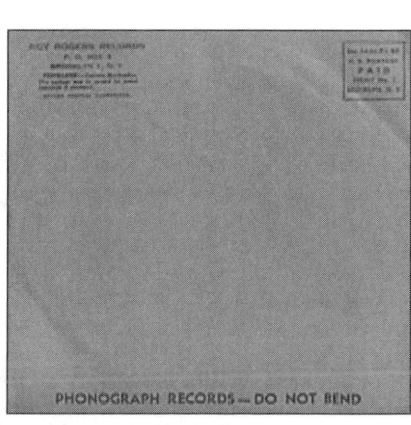

Roy Rogers Special Record Offer
(2 record set in white mailer)
BB202 Side 1: A Good Night Prayer
Side 2: Keep In Touch
BB203 Side 1: Come And Get It
Side 2: Hoofbeat Serenade
$25.00

R202
I Saw Mommy Do The Mambo
Side 1: I Saw Mommy Do The Mambo
Side 2: Don't Let The Kiddygedin
$6.00

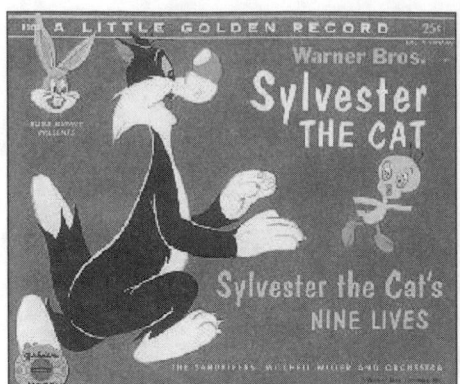

R203

Warner Bros. Sylvester The Cat
Side 1: Sylvester The Cat
Side 2: Sylvester The Cat's Nine Lives

$10.00

R204

Tweedle Dee And Ko Ko Mo
Side 1: Tweedle Dee
Side 2: I Got A Rag Doll

$5.00

R205

Roy Rogers And Dale Evans Sing
Side 1: Goodnight Prayer

$15.00

R206

Porky Pig
Side 1: Porky Pig (Part 1)
Side 2: Porky Pig (Part 2)

$10.00

R209

Warner Bros. Foghorn Leghorn And Henery Hawk
Side 1: Foghorn Leghorn
Side 2: Henery Hawk

$15.00

R210

Cinderella
Side 1: Cinderella

$7.00

R211

Happy Birthday
Side 1: Happy Birthday

$7.00

R212

A Howdy Doody Record
Side 1: Lean One Lean One Long One Lickpot Thumbo
Side 2: Look For The Bright Side

$15.00

D213

From Walt Disney's Davy Crockett Davy's Song Message To Everyone
Side 1: Be Sure Your Right
Side 2: Old Betsy

$18.00

D213

Back Cover

D214

Bella Note From Walt Disney's Lady And The Tramp
Side 1: Siamese Cat Song, The
Side 2: Bella Note

$12.00

D214

Back Cover

R217

From Paul Terry's Barker Bill TV Show
Side 1: Farmer Al Falfa
Side 2: Mighty Mouse

$15.00

R217

Back Cover

R218

From Paul Terry's Barker Bill TV Show
Side 1: Barker Bill
Side 2: Step Right Up

$10.00

R219

A Howdy Doody Record
Side 1: Look! Look!
Side 2: Will My Dog Be Proud Of Me?

$17.00

R220

A Howdy Doody Record
Side 1: Laughing Song, The
Side 2: John J. Fedoozle

$17.00

R221

A Howdy Doody Record
Side 1: Cowabonga

$17.00

D222

Songs From Walt Disney's Mickey Mouse Club
Side 1: Official Mickey Mouse Club Song
Side 2: Official Mickey Mouse Club Song

$6.00

D223

Songs From Walt Disney's Mickey Mouse Club
Side 1: Official Mickey Mouse Club Pledge
Side 2: Sho-Jo-Ji (A Japanese Play Dong)

$6.00

D224

Songs From Walt Disney's Mickey Mouse Club
Side 1: You, The Human Animal
Side 2: Mickey Mouse Club Book Song, The
$7.00

D225

Songs From Walt Disney's Mickey Mouse Club
Side 1: Picture House Song, The
Side 2: When I Grow Up
$6.00

R226

Champion The Wonder Horse
Side 1: Champion The Wonder Horse
Side 2: Bridle And Saddle
$15.00

R227

Annie Oakley Sings
Side 1: Ten Gallon Hat
Side 2: I Gotta Crow
$17.00

R231

Buffalo Bill Jr.
Side 1: Buffalo Bill Jr. (Part 1)
Side 2: Buffalo Bill Jr. (Part 2)
$17.00

D232

Songs From Walt Disney's Mickey Mouse Club
Side 1: I'm No Fool
Side 2: Frere Jacques
$6.00

D232

Songs From Walt Disney's Mickey Mouse Club
(2nd cover)
Side 1: I'm No Fool
Side 2: Frere Jacques
$6.00

D233

Songs From Walt Disney's Mickey Mouse Club
Side 1: Animals And Clowns' Song
Side 2: Who Am I?
$6.00

D234

Songs From Walt Disney's Mickey Mouse Club
Side 1: Mickey Mouse Newsreel Music, The
Side 2: Anyone for Exploring
$15.00

D235

Mickey Mouse Club, The Merry Mouseketeers
Side 1: Talent Roundup
Side 2: Merry Mouseketeers, The
$10.00

D238

From Disneyland Walt Disney's Davy Crockett And The River Pirates
Side 1: King Of The River
Side 2: Yaller, Yaller Gold
$12.00

R239

Rogers And Hammerstein's Oklahoma!
Side 1: Oklahoma! (Part 1)
Side 2: Oklahoma! (Part 2)
$7.00

R240

Roy Rogers And Dale Evans Sing
Side 1: Lords Prayer, The
Side 2: Ave Maria
$16.00

R240

Back Cover

R241

Roy Rogers And Dale Evans Sing
Side 1: Bible Tells Me So, The
Side 2: Have You Read The Bible Today
$16.00

R242

Yellow Rose Of Texas
Side 1: Yellow Rose Of Texas
Side 2: Piddily Patter Patter
$7.00

R243

My First Alphabet Song
Side 1: Alphabet Song
Side 2: Counting Song
$7.00

R243

Back Cover

R244

From Rodgers And Hammerstein's Oklahoma!
Side 1: Surrey With The Fringe On Top, The (Vocal)
Side 2: Surrey With The Fringe On Top, The (Instrumental)
$8.00

R246

Roy Rogers And Dale Evans Sing
Side 1: Jesus Loves The Little Children
Side 2: Lord Is Going To Take Good Care Of You, The
$15.00

D247

From Disneyland Songs From Walt Disney's Robin Hood
Side 1: Robin Hood Ballad
Side 2: Riddle-De-Diddle-De-Day
$16.00

R248

Annie Oakley Safety Songs
Side 1: Traffic Light Song, The
Side 2: I Like To Ride My Bike
$15.00

R248

Back Cover

R249

Warner Bros. Bugs Bunny Railroad Engineer And Yosemite Sam Hold-Up Man
Side 1: Bugs Bunny Railroad Engineer
Side 2: Yosemite Sam Hold-Up Man
$15.00

R250

Cowboy Daffy Duck
Side 1: Cowboy Daffy Duck
Side 2: Kangaroo Hop
$15.00

R251

Walt Disney Presents Quack, Quack, Quack Donald Duck
Side 1: Quack Quack Quack!
Side 2: Donald Duck (Donald Sings Around The World)
$10.00

D253

Mickey Mouse Club, The Merry Mouseketeers
Side 1: Hi To You
Side 2: Do-Me-So
$10.00

D254

Mickey Mouse Club, The Merry Mouseketeers
Side 1: Mickey Mouse Mambo; Pussycat Polka
Side 2: Mousekedance; Mouseketap
$12.00

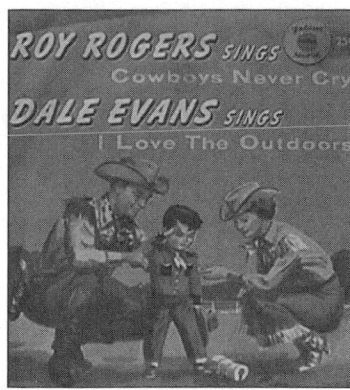

D255

Roy Rogers Sings/Dale Evans Sings
Side 1: Cowboys Never Cry
Side 2: I Love the Outdoors
$17.00

R261

A Howdy Doody Record
Side 1: Charles Dickens' A Christmas
Carol (Part 1)
Side 2: Charles Dickens' A Christmas
Carol (Part 2)
$17.00

R261

Back Cover

R262

16 Tons And Bonnie Blue Gal
Side 1: 16 Tons
Side 2: Bonnie Blue Gal
$6.00

R263

Welcome To Romper Room
$5.00

R264

Romper Room The Do Bee Song
$5.00

R265

Romper Room Singing Games
$5.00

R266

Romper Room Nursery Songs
$5.00

R267

**Romper Room Learn About The
Farm Songs**
$5.00

R268

Romper Room Sing-A-Long Songs
Side 1: Sing-A-Long Songs (Part 1)
Side 2: Sing-A-Long Songs (Part 2)
$5.00

R269

Hansel And Gretel Song And Story
$5.00

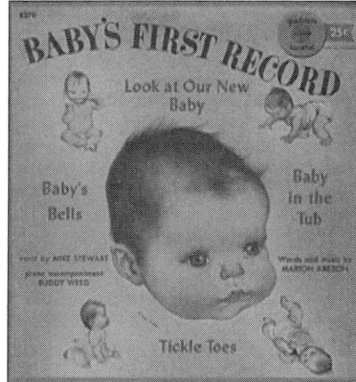

R270

Baby's First Record
Side 1: Look At Our New Baby; Baby's
Bells
Side 2: Baby In The Tub; Tickle Toes
$12.00

R271

R272

Lullaby Time
Side 1: Twinkle, Twinkle Little Star;
Rock A Bye, Baby
Side 2: Now I Lay Me Down To Sleep
$6.00

R273

Nursery Songs
$6.00

R274

Three Bears, The
Side 1: Three Bears, The (Part 1)
Side 2: Three Bears, The (Part 2)
$7.00

R274

Three Bears, The
Side 1: Three Bears, The (Part 1)
Side 2: Three Bears, The (Part 2)
$6.00

R275

R276

**Get Well
(A Little Golden Record Greeting)**
Side 1: I'm Gonna Get Well Today
Side 2: Dr. Sniffleswiper
$12.00

R277

On Top Of Old Smoky
Side 1: On Top Of Old Smoky
Side 2: Pony Boy
$6.00

R278

D279
School Days
Side 1: School Days (Part 1)
Side 2: School Days (Part 2)
$6.00

D280
From Walt Disney's Cinderella
Side 1: Bibbidi Bobiddi Boo (Part 1)
Side 2: Bibbidi Bobiddi Boo (Part 2)
$10.00

D281
From Walt Disney's Cinderella
Side 1: Work Song, The
Side 2: Work Song, The
$10.00

D282
From Walt Disney's Cinderella
Side 1: A Dream Is A Wish
Side 2: A Dream Is A Wish
$10.00

D282
Back Cover

R283

GL284
From Prokofieff's Peter And The Wolf
Side 1: March From Peter And The Wolf
Side 2: Story Of Peter And The Wolf, The
$6.00

R285
Happy Birthday (A Little Golden Record Greeting)
Side 1: Happy Birthday To You (Part 1)
Side 2: Happy Birthday To You (Part 2)
$15.00

R286
Tommy And Jimmy Dorsey Play For Children
Side 1: Dungaree Doll (Not by the Dorsey's)
Side 2: My Friend The Ghost (by the Dorsey's)
$15.00

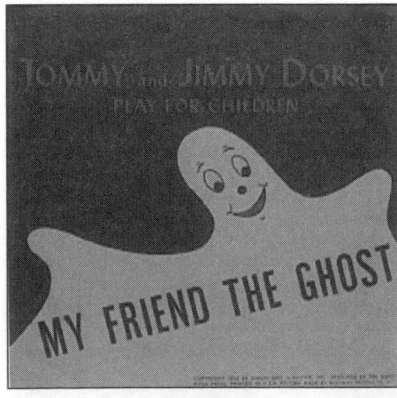

R286
Back Cover

R287
Happy Whistler, The
Side 1: Most Happy Fella, The
Side 2: Happy Whistler, The
$6.00

R288
Little Child
Side 1: Little Child
Side 2: Will You Come For A Walk
$6.00

R289

R290
I'm Gettin' Nuttin' For Christmas
Side 1: I'm Gettin' Nuttin' For Christmas
Side 2: Wishy Washy Wish
$6.00

R291
Huckleberry Finn And Tom Sawyer Painting Aunt Polly's Fence
Side 1: Huckleberry Finn And Tom Sawyer
Side 2: Painting Aunt Polly's Fence
$15.00

R292

Walt Disney's Good Night Little Wrangler
Side 1: Good Night Little Wrangler
Side 2: Triple R

$12.00

R293

Songs From Walt Disney's The Great Locomotive Chase
Side 1: Railroadin' Man
Side 2: Sons Of Old Aunt Dinah

$8.00

R294

Hooray For Cowboys
Side 1: Hooray For Cowboys
Side 2: Cowardly Cowboy

$8.00

R295

Circus Boy Theme Song
Side 1: Circus Boy (Part 1)
Side 2: Circus Boy (Part 2)

$15.00

R296

R295

Back Cover (Micky Dolenz)

R297

From The NBC Producer's Showcase Production Of Jack And The Beanstalk
Side 1: Jack And The Beanstalk
Side 2: March Of The Ill Assorted Guards

$6.00

R298

Train Songs
Side 1: Down By The Station
Side 2: I've Been Working On The Railroad

$6.00

R299

D300

Walt Disney's Song Of Fantasyland
Side 1: Fantasyland Song (Part 1)
Side 2: Fantasyland Song (Part 2)

$20.00

D301

Walt Disney's Song Of Frontierland
Side 1: Frontierland (Part 1)
Side 2: Frontierland (Part 2)

$20.00

R302

Walt Disney's Song Of Tomorrowland
Side 1: Tomorrowland (Part 1)
Side 2: Tomorrowland (Part 2)

$20.00

D303
Walt Disney's Song Of Adventureland
Side 1: Adventureland (Part 1)
Side 2: Adventureland (Part 2)
$20.00

R304
Story Of The Magi, The
(A Little Golden Record Greeting)
Side 1: Story Of The Magi, The
Side 2: Gift Of The Magi, The
$15.00

R305
A Merry, Merry, Merry Christmas
(A Little Golden Record Greeting)
Side 1: A Merry, Merry, Merry Christmas
Side 2: A Happy Little New Year
$15.00

R305
A Merry, Merry, Merry Christmas
Side 1: A Merry, Merry, Merry Christmas
Side 2: A Happy Little New Year
$6.00

R306
Drum Song, The
Side 1: Play A Polka
Side 2: Drum Song, The
$12.00

R306
Back Cover

R307
Four Hymns
Side 1: Now The Day Is Over, Onward
Christian Soldiers
Side 2: Jesus Wants Me For A Sunbeam,
Jesus Loves Me
$6.00

D308
From Walt Disney's Westward Ho, The Wagons!
Side 1: Westward Ho, The Wagons (Part 1)
Side 2: Westward Ho, The Wagons (Part 2)
$12.00

R309
O Come All Ye Faithful
Side 1: O Christmas Tree, Joy To The
World
Side 2: O Come All Yee Faithful
$6.00

D310
Songs From Walt Disney's Westward Ho, The Wagons!
Side 1: Wringle Wrangle
Side 2: Green Grow The Lilacs
$12.00

D310
Back Cover

R311
Ballad of John Coulter, The
Side 1: Ballad of John Coulter, The
Side 2: Pioneer's Prayer

$15.00

R312
Roy Rogers And Dale Evans Sing
Side 1: Let There Be Pease On Earth
Side 2: Sing Thank You God

$16.00

R312
Back Cover

R314
Warner Bros. Looney Tunes Merrie Melodies
Side 1: Merrie Melodies (Part 1)
Side 2: Merrie Melodies (Part 2)

$10.00

R316
Rock Island Line
Side 1: Hot Diggity
Side 2: Rock Island Line

$6.00

EP317
Golden Mother Goose

$6.00

EP318
Train Songs

$8.00

EP319
Songs About Animals
Side 1: Tawny Scrawny Lon, The Poky Little Puppy
Side 2: Willie The Whistling Giraffe, Saggy Baggy Elephant, Elephant Walk

$15.00

EP320
Golden Toy Parade
Side 1: Fuzzy Wuzzy, Parade Of The Wooden Soldiers, Me And My Teddy Bear
Side 2: Paper Doll, Paper Family, Teddy Bear's Parade

$8.00

EP321
TV Wild West Favorites
Side 1: Annie Oakley Song, Bright Eyed And Bush Tailed, Champion The Wonder Horse
Side 2: Bridle And Saddle, Buffalo Bill Jr.

$18.00

EP322
Golden Christmas Favorites
Side 1: Jingle Bells, Deck The Halls, Up
On The Housetop, Reindeer's Dance
Side 2: Rudolph, The Red Nosed Rein-
deer, Frosty The Snowman
$10.00

EP323
Looney Tunes
Side 1: Bugs Bunny, I Taut I Taw A
Puddy-Tat
Side 2: I Taut I Taw A Puddy-Tat, Porky Pig
$15.00

EP324
Roy Rogers' Cowboy Songs
Side 1: Happy Trails To You, A Cowboy
Needs A Horse, Roy Rogers Had A Ranch
Side 2: Chuck Wagon Song, The ,Cow-
boys Never Cry, Hoofbeat Serenade
$18.00

EP325
Dale Evans' Songs Of Faith
Side 1: Ave Maria, Happy Birthday Gen-
tile Saviour, The Lord Is Gonna Take
Good Care Of Me
Side 2: Have You Read The Bible To-
day, The Bible Tell Me So, Jesus Loves
The Little Children
$18.00

EP326
Golden Songs About America
$7.00

EP327
Howdy Doody And Buffalo Bob
Side 1: Little One, Lean One; Big Chief
Cowabonga; John J. Fedoozle
Side 2: Look! Look!, Laughing Song,
Will My Dog Be Proud Of Me?
$18.00

EP328
Golden Nursery Songs
$7.00

D335
Mickey Mouse Club Hardy Boys
Side 1: Gold Doubloon And Pieces Of
Eight
$15.00

R337
Rin Tin Tin
Side 1: I Wish I Had A Dog Like Rin-Tin-Tin
Side 2: I Love Dogs
$12.00
R338

R339
**From Bing Crosby's Ali Baba And The
40 Thieves**
Side 1: Ali Baba And The 40 Thieves
Side 2: All Lived Happily Ever After, The
$8.00

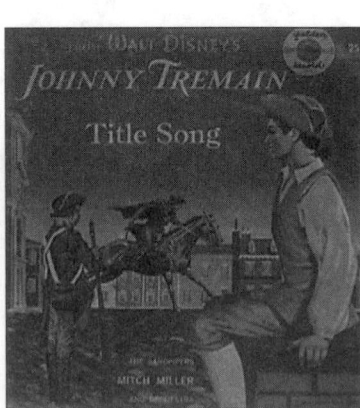

D340
From Walt Disney's Johnny Tremain
Side 1: Johnny Tremain (Part 1)
Side 2: Johnny Tremain (Part 2)
$10.00

D340

Back Cover

R341

Little Dog
Side 1: Little Dog
Side 2: A Dog Is A Mans Best Friend
$6.00

R342

Someday My Prince Will Come
Side 1: Someday My Prince Will Come
(Part 1)
Side 2: Someday My Prince Will Come
(Part 2)
$6.00

D344

From Walt Disney's Johnny Tremain
Side 1: Liberty Tree, The (Part 1)
Side 2: Liberty Tree, The (Part 2)
$10.00

D344

Back Cover

D345

Songs From Walt Disney's Mickey Mouse Club
Side 1: Proverbs
Side 2: Do What The Good Book Says
$8.00

D345

Back Cover

R346

I'm Popeye The Sailor Man
Side 1: I'm Popeye The Sailor Man
Side 2: Scuffy The Tugboat
$10.00

R346

Back Cover

D347

Walt Disney's Perri
Side 1: Perri Title Song
Side 2: Break Of Day
$10.00

D348
Songs From Walt Disney's Mickey Mouse Club
Side 1: A Mousekethought
Side 2: Smile and Face the Music
$8.00

R349

R350
Bing Crosby Sings Dan'l Boones Song-Story
Side 1: Indian Adventure (Part 1)
Side 2: Indian Adventure (Part 2)
$7.00

EP351
Rin Tin Tin Songs
Side 1: I Wish I Had A Dog Like Rin Tin Tin, A Dogs Best Friend, Cold Nose Warm Heart
Side 2: Rinny, Rusty, And Rip,101st Calvery Gallop, Rough Around The Edges
$15.00

EP352
Cowboy Songs
Side 1: Brave Cowboy Bill (Parts 1 & 2),Cowardly Cowboy
Side 2: Hooray For Cowboys, Chocolate Cowboy, Cowboy's Prayer
$15.00

EP353
Golden Folk Songs
$7.00

EP354
Let's Dance Songs
$7.00

R355
Bing Crosby's Emperor's New Clothes
Side 1: Emperor's New Clothes
Side 2: Never Be Afraid
$10.00

EP356
Navy Log
Side 1: Mighty Navy Wings, Navy Blue And Gold
Side 2: Anchors Aweigh, The Navy Hymn
$10.00

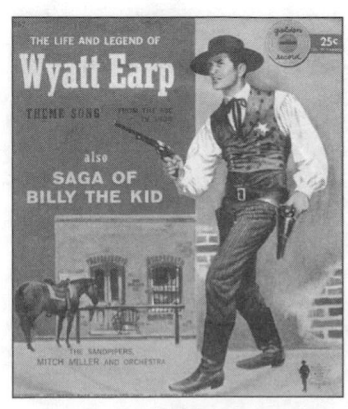

R357
Wyatt Earp
Side 1: Wyatt Earp
Side 2: Saga Of Billy The Kid
$15.00

R358

R359

R360

EP361
Play Songs
Side 1: Play Songs
$6.00

R362
Cindy, Oh! Cindy
Side 1: Cindy Oh! Cindy
Side 2: Mama From The Train
$7.00

R363

London Bridge
Side 1: London Bridge
Side 2: 3 Blind Mice

$6.00

R364

Bing Crosby Sings Mother Goose
Side 1: Humpty Dumpty
Side 2: Mistress Mary

$6.00

R365

When The Red Red Robin
Side 1: When The Red Red Robin
Side 2: Little White Duck

$6.00

R365

Back Cover

R370

Rin Tin Tin Songs
Side 1: A Dog's Best Friend
Side 2: Cold Nose, Warm Heart

$15.00

R371

Bing Crosby Sings A New Christmas Song
Side 1: How Lovely Is Christmas
Side 2: How Lovely Is Christmas

$6.00

R372

Moses Little Moses
Side 1: Moses Little Moses
Side 2: Moses And His People

$8.00

R372

Back Cover

R374

Happy Birthday
Side 1: Happy Birthday (Part 1)
Side 2: Happy Birthday (Part 2)

$6.00

R375

Banana Boat Song, The
Side 1: Just Walking In The Rain
Side 2: Banana Boat Song, The

$7.00

R376

Marianne And Jamaica Farewell
Side 1: Marianne
Side 2: Jamaica Farewell

$8.00

R377

Round And Round And The Music Goes 'Round And 'Round
Side 1: Round And Round
Side 2: Music Goes 'Round And 'Round", The

$6.00

EP378

Westward Ho The Wagons
Side 1: Wringle Wrangle/Westward Ho The Wagons
Side 2: Ballad Of John Colter

$10.00

EP379

From Walt Disney's Cinderella
Side 1: Bibidi-Bobbidi-Boo, Cinderella's Work Song (Part 1)
Side 2: A Dream, Cinderella's Work Song (Part 2),

$8.00

R380

Roy Rogers And Dale Evans
Side 1: Chilsom Trail, The
Side 2: Red River Valley, The

$16.00

R380

Back Cover

R381

Roy Rogers Had A Ranch
Side 1: Roy Rogers Had A Ranch
Side 2: Home On The Range

$6.00

R382

O Little Town Of Bethlehem
Side 1: O Little Town Of Bethlehem
Side 2: Hark! The Herald Angles Sing

$6.00

EP383

Calypso!
Side 1: Marianne, Goombay Drum, Let's
Go To De Market Place
Side 2: Banana Boat Song, The , De Best
I Like, Donkey Small

$8.00

EP384

**Songs From Walt Disney's Snow
White And The Seven Dwarfs**
Side 1: Snow White In The Cottage,
Whistle While You Work, Bluddle Uddle
Um Dum
Side 2: Hi, Ho; Whistle While You Work,
Someday My Prince Will Come

$8.00

R385

Captain Kangaroo
Side 1: Captain Kangaroo Theme Song
Side 2: Little Kangaroo Dance

$8.00

R386

Bing Crosby Sings
Side 1: Boy At The Window
Side 2: An Axe an Apple And Buckskin
Jacket

$6.00

D390

Walt Disney's Old Yeller
Side 1: Old Yeller (Part 1)
Side 2: Old Yeller (Part 2)

$10.00

R391

Play Songs From Mother Goose
Side 1: Sing A Song Of Sixpence
Side 2: Little Bo Peep, Humpty Dumpty

$6.00

EP392

4 Songs From My Fair Lady
Side 1: On The Street Where You Live,
Get Me To The Church On Time
Side 2: I Could Have Danced All Night,
Wouldn't It Be Lovely?

$7.00

D394

From Walt Disney's Perri
Side 1: Together Time
Side 2: Now To Sleep

$8.00

R395

Bing Crosby Sings
Side 1: Old King Cole
Side 2: Sing A Song Of Sixpence

$7.00

R396

Bing Crosby Sings
Side 1: Star Light, Star Bright
Side 2: Little Boy Blue

$6.00

R397

Songs We Sing In Nursery School
Side 1: All Work Together To Pick It Up,
Put Your Finger In The Air
Side 2: Dance Around Pretty And Shiny,
Little Seed

$5.00

EP400

Dog Songs

$8.00

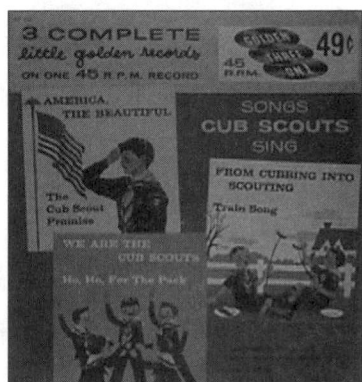

EP401

Favorite Lullabies
Side 1: Goodnight Prayer, My Very
Good Friend The Sandman, Close
Your Eyes
Side 2: Now I Lay Me Down To Sleep,
Sleepy Time Is A Happy Time and
Sleeping Child

$7.00

EP402

Christmas Songs
Side 1: I'm Dreaming Of A White Christ-
mas, Silent Night
Side 2: Santa Claus Is Coming To Town,
Crackerjack Christmas, Deck The Halls

$7.00

EP403

Silly Songs

$6.00

EP404

School Days

$6.00

EP405

Bear Songs
Side 1: Me And My Teddy Bear, Smoky
The Bear (Part 1)
Side 2: Teddy Bears On Parade, The
Three Bears, Smoky The Bear (Part 2)

$15.00

EP406

Songs Cub Scouts Sing
Side 1: America The Beautiful, Cub
Scout Promise, We Are The Cub Scouts
Side 2: Ho, Ho, For The Pack, Train
Song, From Cubbing Into Scouting

$15.00

EP407

**Bing Crosby Sings New Christmas
Songs**
Side 1: How Lovely Is Christmas
Side 2: Boy At A Window

$7.00

EP408

Bing Crosby Sings Mother Goose

$6.00

R438

Paul Terry's Heckle And Jeckle
Side 1: Heckle & Jeckle (Part 1)
Side 2: Heckle & Jeckle (Part 2)

$8.00

R439

Brahms' Lullaby
Side 1: Brahms' Lullaby
Side 2: Rockabye Baby; Twinkle Twinkle
Little Star

$7.00

R440

Fury
Side 1: Fury Theme Song
Side 2: What Did You Do Before You
Had TV?

$12.00

R441

Clementine And De Camptown Races
Side 1: De Camptown Race
Side 2: Clementine
$6.00

EP442
Side 1: Popeye Mighty Mouse Bugs Bunny
$12.00

EP445

Sailor Songs
Side 1: Shrimp Boats ; Blow The Man
Down; Sailing Sailing; Anchors Away
Side 2: Pirate Song The; John Silver
$8.00

EP446

Mother Goose And Nursery Songs
$6.00

FF449

**From Walt Disney's The Saga Of Andy
Burnett**
Side 1: Saga Of Andy Burnett, The (Part 1)
Side 2: Saga Of Andy Burnett, The (Part 2)
$13.00

EP443

Let's All Sing Like The Birdies Sing
Side 1: Let's All Sing...,Ballad Of The Un-
hatched Chick, Sparrow In The Treetop
Side 2: Dance Of The Little Swan's,
Red, Red Tobin, Peter's Friend
$6.00

EP447

Easter Parade
Side 1: Easter Parade, The Horse With
The Easter Bonnet, Peter Cottontail
Side 2: Easter Is A Loving Time, Egbert
The Easter Egg, Yankee Doodle Bunny
$7.00

R450

From TV's Adventures Of Lassie
Side 1: Lassie Them Song
Side 2: Lassie, My Four Footed Friend
$12.00

D452

From Walt Disney's Snow White
Side 1: Snow White
Side 2: Someday My Prince Will Come
$12.00

EP444

Ali Baba And The 40 Thieves 40
Side 1: 40 Thieves 40,Open Sesame
(Thief), Open Sesame (Baba)
Side 2: One Rick Brother (Kasim), One Of
Us Is A Thief, One Rich Brother (Baba)
$10.00

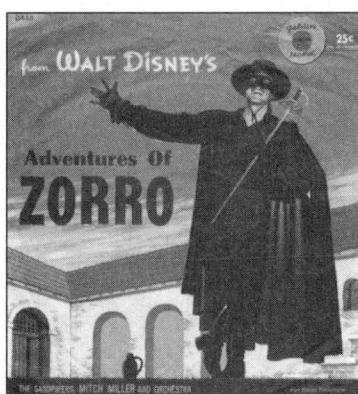

FF448

**From Walt Disney's Adventures Of
Zorro**
Side 1: Zorro
$15.00

FF454

**From Walt Disney's Adventures Of
Zorro**
Side 1: Adventures Of Zorro (Part 1)
Side 2: Adventures Of Zorro (Part 2)
$15.00

EP460

Walt Disney's Pinocchio & Peter Pan Songs

$8.00

EP461

Rocket To Mars!

$12.00

EP462

Captain Kangaroo's Best Loved Songs

$8.00

R463

Two Golden Song Hits
Side 1: Around The World
Side 2: Teddy Bear

$8.00

EP464

Bing Crosby Sings About 3 Western Heroes
Side 1: Daniel Boone
Side 2: Johnny Appleseed; Paul Bunyan

$8.00

EP466

Wagon Train, Wells Fargo, Restless Gun
Side 1: Square Dance, Restless Gun
Side 2: Lonely Rider

$12.00

EP467

TV Favorites
Side 1: Wyatt Earp Theme Song; Lassie Theme Song
Side 2: Jim Bowie Theme Song

$12.00

EP468

6 Best Loved Christmas Carols
Side 1: Joy To The World, O Little Town of Bethlehem, It Came Upon a Midnight Clear
Side 2: Come All Ye Faithful, Hark! The Herald Angels Sing, God Rest e Merry Gentlemen

$6.00

EP469

6 Popular Songs

$6.00

R470

Songs About Lassie
Side 1: I Love Lassie
Side 2: Lassie Is My Best Friend

$15.00

471

Captain Kangaroo Bob Keeshan
Side 1: March Of The Toys
Side 2: Toyland

$7.00

473

Captain Kangaroo Bob Keeshan
Side 1: I Love A Parade
Side 2: I Went To The Animal Fair

$7.00

EP474
TV Favorites
Side 1: Lassie
Side 2: Ruff And Reddy
$10.00

EP475
American Folk Songs
$6.00

EP476
Child's Introduction To The Orchestra
$6.00

EP478
Kittens And Cats
$8.00

FF479
From Walt Disney's Sleeping Beauty
Side 1: I Wonder (Part 1)
Side 2: I Wonder (Part 2)
$9.00

D480
From Walt Disney's Sleeping Beauty
Side 1: Once Upon A Dream (Part 1)
Side 2: Once Upon A Dream (Part 2)
$9.00

D481
From Walt Disney's Sleeping Beauty
Side 1: Hail Princess Aurora
$9.00

D482
From Walt Disney's Sleeping Beauty
Side 1: Sing A Smiling Song (Part 1)
Side 2: Sing A Smiling Song (Part 1)
$9.00

FF483
From Walt Disney's Sleeping Beauty
Side 1: Skumps (Part 1)
Side 2: Skumps (Part 2)
$9.00

EP484
Songs For Parties
$6.00

EP485
Disney Heroes
Side 1: Zorro, Andy Burnett
Side 2: Old Yeller
$16.00

FF486
From Walt Disney's Sleeping Beauty
Side 1: Sleeping Beauty (Story)
Side 2: Sleeping Beauty (Song)
$9.00

EP487
Treasury Of 6 Favorite American Folk Songs
Side 1: Casey Jones, Drill Ye Tarriers, Pick A Bale Of Cotton
Side 2: Old Dan Tucker, Buffalo Gals, Aunt Rhody
$7.00

EP488

Six Donald Duck Dongs

$10.00

EP489

Six Souza Songs & Marches

$7.00

EP490

3 Little Pigs, Fishes & Kittens

$6.00

EP491

Five Fairy Tales

$6.00

EP492

More TV Favorites
Side 1: Maverick Woody Woodpecker
Side 2: Leave It To Beaver

$7.00

493

Woody Woodpecker Song, The
Side 1: Woody Woodpecker Song, The
Side 2: Woodpecker's Dance

$8.00

494

Volare!
Side 1: Volare!
Side 2: Little Star

$6.00

495

Wagon Train
Side 1: Wagon Train
Side 2: Square Dance

$12.00

FF496

Walt Disney's John Slaughter
Side 1: Johnny Slaughter (Part 1)
Side 2: Johnny Slaughter (Part 2)

$12.00

497

Smokey The Bear
Side 1: Smokey The Bear (Part 1)
Side 2: Smokey The Bear (Part 2)

$15.00

498

Maverick
Side 1: Maverick (Part 1)
Side 2: Maverick (Part 2)

$12.00

499

Casey Jones
Side 1: Casey Jones
Side 2: John Henry

$7.00

500
Captain Kangaroo And Mr. Green Jeans
Side 1: Button Up Your Overcoat
Side 2: Bear Went Over The Mountain
$8.00

501
Hoagy Carmichael Sings Two Of His Greatest Hits
Side 1: Lazy Bones
Side 2: Small Fry!
$8.00

502
Lone Ranger Introduces, The
Side 1: I Ride On Old Paint
Side 2: Railroad Corral
$15.00

D503
Nine Lives Of Elfego Baca, The
Side 1: Elfego Baca (Part 1)
Side 2: Elfego Baca (Part 2)
$12.00

509
Tales Of Wells Fargo
Side 1: Tales Of Wells Fargo
Side 2: Lonely Rider
$12.00

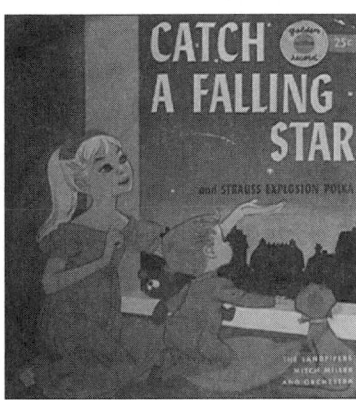

516
Catch A Falling Star
Side 1: Catch A Falling Star
Side 2: Strauss Explosion Polka
$6.00

518
Leave It To Beaver
Side 1: Toy Parade (Part 1)
Side 2: Toy Parade (Part 2)
$15.00

RR519
Mighty Mouse Theme Song
$7.00

EP520
Captain Kangaroo & Mr. Greenjeans
Side 1: Johnnyone-Note, In The Good Old Summertime
Side 2: Erie Canal, The, The Green Grass Grew, All Around
$7.00

521

Hi-Yo Silver! The Lone Ranger
Side 1: Lone Ranger Theme, The
Side 2: Hi Yo Silver!

$15.00

EP522

Lone Ranger!, The
Side 1: Hi-Yo Silver, I Ride An Old Paint
Side 2: Railroad Corral, Bridle And Saddle, Hi Yo Silver!

$15.00

EP523

Six Songs From Walt Disney's Peter Pan

$15.00

EP524

6 Songs America Sings
Side 1: John Henry, Kemo Kimo, Sourwood Mountain
Side 2: Paddy Works On The Railroad, Shenandoah, The E-R-I-E

$6.00

EP525

Mickey Mouse Club Favorites

$12.00

526

Lollipop
Side 1: Lollipop
Side 2: Dance Of The Clowns

$7.00

EP527

Walt Disney's Themes
Side 1: Sleeping Beauty, Mickey Mouse Club
Side 2: Mickey Mouse Club, Disneyland Theme, When You Wish Upon A Star

$7.00

EP528

Walt Disney Western Favorites
Side 1: John Slaughter
Side 2: Elfego Baca, Pecos Bill

$12.00

EP529

6 Great Golden Book Song Stories

$7.00

EP530

Walt Disney's Heroines
Side 1: Sleeping Beauty
Side 2: Cinderella, Snow White & The Seven Dwarfs

$8.00

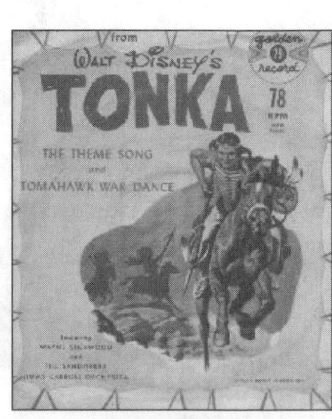

531

Walt Disney's Tonka
Side 1: Tonka (Part 1)
Side 2: Tonka (Part 2)

$12.00

532

From MGM Picture Tom Thumb
Side 1: Tom Thumb's Tune
Side 2: Story Of Tom Thumb, The
$7.00

EP537

Nursery School Play Songs
Side 1: I Pick It Up, Pretty And Shiny-O,
All Work Together
Side 2: Put Your Finger In The Air,
Dance Around, Cleavo, Little Seed
$5.00

EP541

**Art Carney Tell Me A Story Of The
Wizard Of Oz**
$8.00

547

From Walt Disney's Darby O'Gill
Side 1: Leprechaun's Dance (Part 1)
Side 2: Leprechaun's Dance (Part 2)
$12.00

533

Captain Kangaroo Sings
Side 1: April Showers
Side 2: In The Good Old Summertime
$7.00

534

**Hank Ketcham's Dennis The Men-
ace Songs**
Side 1: Dennis The Menace (Part 1)
Side 2: Dennis The Menace (Part 2)
$8.00

545

**From The 20th Century Fox Pro-
duction "The Inn Of The Sixth
Happiness"**
Side 1: Children's Marching Song,
The (Part 1)
Side 2: Children's Marching Song,
The (Part 2)
$7.00

548

From Walt Disney's Shaggy Dog
Side 1: Shaggy Dog (Part 1)
Side 2: Shaggy Dog (Part 2)
$12.00

535

Golden Bed-Time Songs
Side 1: Now I Lay Me Down To Sleep
Side 2: Cuddle Down
$7.00

536

Farmer Jones
Side 1: Farmer Jones
$7.00

546

Little Space Girl
Side 1: Little Space Girl
Side 2: Rolly-Polly Man In The Moon,
The
$20.00

549

**Walt Disney's Original Chipmunks
Chip And Dale With Clarice**
Side 1: Kris Kringle (Part 1)
Side 2: Kris Kringle (Part 2)
$12.00

550

Huckleberry Hound And Yogi Bear
Side 1: Huckleberry Hound Theme
Song
Side 2: Yogi Bear Theme Song
$15.00

551

**Atchenson Topeka And The Santa
Fe, The**
Side 1: Atchenson Topeka And Santa
Fe
Side 2: I Like The Sound Of A Train
$7.00

552

Animal Crackers In My Soup
Side 1: Animal Crackers In My Soup
Side 2: Lovely Bunch Of Coconuts
$6.00

553

**Captain Kangaroo And Mr. Green
Jeans Sing**
Side 1: Johnny One-Note
Side 2: Waltzing Matilda
$7.00

554

**Swanee River And My Old Kentucky
Home**
Side 1: Swanee River
Side 2: Old Kentucky Home
$7.00

555

**Shari Lewis Sings Aren't You Glad
You're You?**
Side 1: Aren't You Glad You're You?
Side 2: Tiki-Tiki-Timbo
$7.00

556

Where Has Dog Gone?
Side 1: Where Has Dog Gone?
$6.00

557

Shari Lewis Sings Hi-Lili, Hi-Lo
Side 1: Hi-Lili,Hi-Lo
Side 2: Swingin'on A Star
$8.00

558

**Ruff And Reddy And Professor
Gizmo**
Side 1: Ruff And Reddy
Side 2: Professor Gizmo
$15.00

559

**3 Stooges Sing All I Want For Christ-
mas Is My Two Front Teeth, The**
Side 1: All I Want For Christmas Is My
Two Front Teeth
Side 2: I Gotta Cold For Christmas
$20.00

560
Captain Kangaroo And Mr. Green Jeans Sing Sleigh Ride
Side 1: Sleigh Ride
Side 2: When Santa Claus Get's Your Letter
$10.00

EP561
Three Stooges Sing 6 Happy Yuletide Songs, The
$15.00

EP562
Rocket To The Moon!
$14.00

EP563
All Sing Together
$6.00

EP564
Away We Go!
$6.00

EP565
Popeye And His Friends
Side 1: I'm Popeye The Sailor Man, Never Pick A Fight With Popeye, Help! Help!
Side 2: Blow The Man Down, I Had A Hamburger Today, Sailing ,Sailing
$8.00

EP566
6 Great TV Adventures
Side 1: Superman, Ramar of the Jungle, The count of Monte Cristo
Side 2: Hawkeye, Yancy Derringer, Lawman
$15.00

EP568
Hi Kids! Starring Shari Lewis
Side 1: Waitin' For The Robert E. Lee
Side 2: Back In Your Own Backyard, Let a Smile Be Your Umbrella
$10.00

EP569
Three Stooges Starring Moe, Larry And Curly-Joe, The
Side 1: We're Coming To Your House, Give A Concert, At The Baseball Game
Side 2: At The Circus, At The Toy Store, Auld Lang Syne
$20.00

EP570
Huckleberry Hound
$15.00

EP571
Ruff And Reddy And Their Friends
Side 1: Ruff And Reddy, Professor Gizmo, Ubble And Ubble
Side 2: Killer And Diller, Capt, Greedy & Salt-Water Daffy, Harry Safari
$15.00

572

Mitch Miller's Me And My Teddy Bear
Side 1: Me And My Teddy Bear
Side 2: Parade Of The Wooden Soldiers

$15.00

573

Mitch Millers Playmates
Side 1: Put Your Finger In The Air
Side 2: Playmates

$8.00

574

Little Fat Policeman
Side 1: Little Fat Policeman

$12.00

EP575

Captain Kangaroo

$12.00

EP576

77 Sunset Strip and Peter Gunn
Side 1: 77 Sunset Strip
Side 2: Peter Gunn

$12.00

577

La Plume De Ma Tante Et Frere Jacques
Side 1: La Plume De Ma Tante
Side 2: Frere Jacques

$8.00

578

Captain Kangaroo
Side 1: Horse In Striped Pajamas
Side 2: Happy Hands

$8.00

580

77 Sunset Strip
Side 1: 77 Sunset Strip Theme Song
(Part 1)
Side 2: 77 Sunset Strip Theme Song
(Part 2)

$8.00

581

Scarlet Ribbons (For Her Hair)
Side 1: Scarlet Ribbons
Side 2: Billy Boy

$6.00

583

Deep In The Heart Of Texas
Side 1: Deep In The Heart Of Texas

$6.00

584

Walt Disney's Song For Toby Tyler
Side 1: Biddle-Dee-Dee (Part 1)
Side 2: Biddle-Dee-Dee (Part 2)

$12.00

585

Walt Disney's Swamp Fox
Side 1: Swamp Fox

$12.00

586

3 Stooges Come To Your House To Make A Record, The
Side 1: On Top Of Old Smoky
Side 2: We're Cutting A Record
$20.00

587

Never Pick A Fight With Popeye
Side 1: Never Pick A Fight With Popeye
Side 2: Help! Help!
$8.00

588

Mitch Miller's Little Sir Echo
Side 1: Little Sir Echo
Side 2: Bobby Shaftoe, Hickory Dickory Dock
$7.00

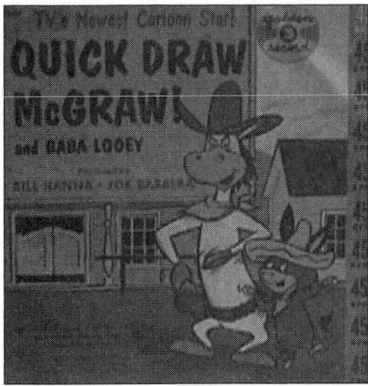

589

Quick Draw McGraw And Baba Looey
Side 1: That's Quick Draw McGraw
Side 2: Baba Looey
$15.00

591

Huckleberry Hound Present's Mr. Jinx And Boo Boo Bear
Side 1: Boo Boo Bear
Side 2: Mr. Jinks
$15.00

592

Yogi Bear Introduces Bill Hanna And Joe Barbera's Loopy De Loop
Side 1: Yogi Bear Introduces Loopy De Loop
Side 2: Let's Have A Song, Yogi Bear!
$15.00

593

Quick Draw McGraw As El Kabong!
Side 1: El Kabong!
Side 2: Ooch, Ooch, Ouch!
$15.00

EP594

A Child's Introduction to French
Side 1: Parler Francais, Common Saying, France is a Country
Side 2: Come to a Party, Quelle Heure Est-il?, Bonne Nuit, Cheri
$8.00

EP599

Walt Disney's Snow White
Side 1: Walt Disney's Snow White
Side 2: Pinocchio; Three Little Pigs
$8.00

600

High Hopes
Side 1: High Hopes
Side 2: Eatin' Goober Peas
$6.00

EP601

Quick Draw McGraw
Side 1: That's Quick Draw McGraw, Baba Looey, Ooch Ooch Ouch!
Side 2: Super Snooper, Blabber Mouse, Augie Doggie & Doggie Daddy

$15.00

EP602

6 Songs From Shirley Temple Movies
Side 1: On The Good Ship Lollipop, Early Bird, Animal Crackers In My Soup
Side 2: When I Grow Up, At The Codfish Ball, Polly Wolly Doodle

$12.00

603

Hank Ketcham's Dennis The Menace Songs
Side 1: Dennis The Menace Theme, The
Side 2: Ka Pow! Ka-Pow! Ka-Pow!

$8.00

EP604

Miss Frances Presents Ding Dong School
Side 1: Come With Me, Halls Of Montezuma, Lavender's Blue
Side 2: Turkey In The Straw, Skip To My Lou, Mozart's Turkish March

$7.00

605

Walt Disney's Donald Duck Sings Around The World
Side 1: Walt Disney's Donald Duck Sings Around The World
Side 2: Donald Duck Theme Song

$10.00

606

Songs Form Shirley Temple Movies
Side 1: On The Good Ship Lollipop
Side 2: Early Bird

$12.00

607

Polly Wolly Doodle And The Happy Wanderer
Side 1: Polly Wolly Doodle
Side 2: Happy Wanderer, The

$6.00

608

Ding Dong School Singing Games
Side 1: Ding Dong School Singing Games

$6.00

609

Walt Disney's Pollyanna
Side 1: Pollyanna Song, The
Side 2: America The Beautiful

$15.00

610

Huckleberry Hound Present's Pixie And Dixie And Iddy Biddy Buddy
Side 1: Pixie & Dixie
Side 2: Iddy Biddy Buddy

$15.00

612

From The Rogers And Hammerstein Hit Show, The Sound Of Music
Side 1: Do Re Me
Side 2: Alouette

$6.00

613

Battle Hymn Of The Republic And When Johnny Comes Marching Home
Side 1: Battle Hymn Of The Republic
Side 2: When Johnny Comes Marching Home

$6.00

614

Walt Disney's Zip-A-Dee-Doo-Dah
Side 1: Zip-A-Dee-Doo-Dah
Side 2: Laughin' Place

$16.00

615

I'm A Little Tea Pot And Polly Put The Kettle On
Side 1: I'm A Little Tea Pot
Side 2: Polly Put The Kettle On

$7.00

616

Winter Wonderland And Mr. Snow
Side 1: Winter Wonderland
Side 2: Mr. Snow

$6.00

617

Little Drummer Boy And Children's Christmas Carol
Side 1: Little Drummer Boy
Side 2: Children's Christmas Carol

$6.00

618

Twelve Days Of Christmas, The
Side 1: 12 Days Of Christmas, The (Part 1)
Side 2: 12 Days Of Christmas, The (Part 2)

$6.00

EP620

Woody Woodpecker
Side 1: Woody Woodpecker Song
Side 2: Andy Panda; Chilly Willie

$7.00

EP621

Twelve Days Of Christmas
Side 1: Twelve Days Of Christmas, Winter Wonderland
Side 2: Little Drummer Boy, Mr. Snow

$6.00

622

3 Stooges Sing Wreck The Halls With Boughs Of Holly, The
Side 1: Wreck The Halls With Boughs Of Holly
Side 2: Jingle Bells

$20.00

625

Quick Draw McGraw Snuffles And Augie Doggie

$15.00

626

Hank Ketcham's Dennis The Menace Songs
Side 1: I'm Home
Side 2: I Hate Spelling

$8.00

627

Walt Disney's 101 Dalmatians
Side 1: Cruella De Ville (Part 1)
Side 2: Cruella De Ville (Part 2)

$15.00

628

Cinderella A Bedtime Story-Song
Side 1: Cinderella (Part 1)
Side 2: Cinderella (Part 2)

$6.00

629

Danny Kaye Tells The Story Of The Big Oven By Leo Tolstoy
Side 1: Big Oven, The (Part 1)
Side 2: Big Oven, The (Part 2)

$6.00

630

Romper Room Do Bee Songs
Side 1: Do Bee Songs (Part 1)
Side 2: Do Bee Songs (Part 2)

$5.00

631

Romper Room Sing-A-Long Songs
Side 1: Will You Come And Play, Clapping And Stamping
Side 2: See Me Jump, Tippy Tip Toe, Hop Up, Hop Down, Marching To My Drum

$5.00

632

King Leonardo And His Short Subjects
Side 1: King Leonardo Theme Song
Side 2: Odie-O Colognie

$15.00

633

Oh, Susanna
Side 1: Oh, Susanna
Side 2: Turkey In The Straw

$6.00

634
Little Red Riding Hood
Side 1: Little Red Riding Hood (Part 1)
Side 2: Little Red Riding Hood (Part 2)
$8.00

635
Our Gang Mischief Makers
Side 1: Our Gang Mischief Makers
Side 2: Hip Hip Hooray!; Here We
Are Together
$12.00

636
Ballad Of The Alamo
Side 1: Ballad Of The Alamo (Part 1)
Side 2: Ballad Of The Alamo (Part 2)
$15.00

EP638
Happy Birthday
Side 1: Happy Birthday
$6.00

EP640
**Maurice Evans' Introduction To
Shakespeare**
Side 1: Julius Caesar
Side 2: Tempest, The
$7.00

EP642
Golden Funny Songs
$6.00

643
**Yogi Bear Present's Cindy Bear
And Snooper & Blabber**
Side 1: Cindy Bear
Side 2: Snooper And Blabber
$12.00

644
**Walt Disney's Swiss Family
Robinson**
Side 1: My Heart Is An Island (Part 1)
Side 2: My Heart Is An Island (Part 2)
$6.00

645
Pepe
Side 1: Pepe (Part 1)
Side 2: Pepe (Part 1)
$12.00

646
**Quick Draw's A-Comin' (And
Baba Looey, Too) To Clean Up
Your Town**
Side 1: Part 1
Side 2: Part 2

647

Yogi Bear And Cindy Bear
Side 1: Yogi Bear, Casanova Of The
Cave Set
Side 2: Cindy Bear, The Cutie Of The
Cave Set

$14.00

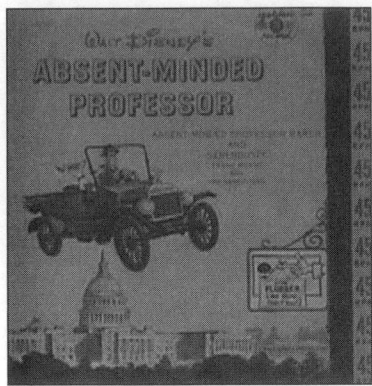

648

Walt Disney's Absent-Minded Professor
Side 1: Serendipityabsent-Minded Pro-
fessor March
Side 2: Absent-Minded Professor March

$10.00

649

**Merry Christmas From Hank Ket-
cham's Dennis The Menace**
Side 1: When Christmas Comes Around
Each Year
Side 2: That's What I Want For Xmas

$8.00

650

**A Hap-Hap-Happy Christmas From
Yogi Bear**
Side 1: Have Hap-Hap-Happy
Christmas
Side 2: Give A Goody For Christmas

$10.00

EP651

A Christmas Sing-A-Long
Side 1: Jingle Bells, We Wish You A
Merry Christmas, Sleigh Ride
Side 2: God Rest Ye Merry Gentlemen,
Hark The Herald Angels Sing

$6.00

EP654

Yogi Bear's Friends
Side 1: Like A Duck Takes to Water,
Little Feller, Fibber Fox Song
Side 2: Major Minor Song, Snaggle-
puss, Exit Stage Right

$15.00

EP653

Songs Of The Flintstones

$15.00

EP655

Songs Of Dennis The Menace
Side 1: Mommy And Daddy
Side 2: Margaret; I Hate Liver

$8.00

656

I Saw A Ship A Sailing
Side 1: I Saw A Ship A Sailing
Side 2: Rub-A-Dub-Dub Three Men In A
Tub

$6.00

657

Twinkles And His Pals
Side 1: Hide And Seek Game, The
Side 2: Parade, The

$16.00

658
Bugs Bunny "What's Up Doc?"
Side 1: What's Up Doc? (Part 1)
Side 2: What's Up Doc? (Part 2)
$8.00

659
Rocky And His Friends
Side 1: I'm Rocky's Pal
Side 2: I Was Born To Be Airborne
$15.00

660
Huckleberry Hound Presents Hokey Wolf And Ding-A-Ling
Side 1: Hokey Wolf And Ding-A-Ling
Side 2: A Wolf Work Is Never Done
$15.00

661
Walt Disney's Babes In Toyland
Side 1: Babes In Toyland March
Side 2: I Can Do The Sum
$8.00

662
Walt Disney's Babes In Toyland
Side 1: March Of The Toys
Side 2: Workshop Song
$8.00

663
Yogi Bear TV Theme
$15.00

664
Popeye Songs Of Health
Side 1: Lonely Tooth
Side 2: Ah-Choo
$8.00

665
Quick Draw McGraw's Pal's
Side 1: Super Snooper
Side 2: Blabber Mouse
$15.00

666
Fox And The Grapes, The
Side 1: Fox And The Grapes, The (Part 1)
Side 2: Fox And The Grapes, The (Part 2)
$5.00

EP667
Twinkles
Side 1: Twinkles
Side 2: King Leonardo
$16.00

668
Walt Disney's Ludwig Von Drake
Side 1: Here's Ludwig Von Drake (Part 1)
Side 2: Here's Ludwig Von Drake (Part 2)
$10.00

EP669
Pinocchio- Songs And Stories
$7.00

670
Walt Disney's Pinocchio
Side 1: I've Got No Strings
Side 2: Pinocchio The Puppet
$6.00

671
Walt Disney's Pinocchio
Side 1: Hi Diddle Dee Dee
$6.00

673
Mother Goose Songs
Side 1: Little Tommy Tucker, Pease
Porridge Hot
Side 2: Queen Of Hearts
$6.00

674
Huck, Yogi & Quick Draw's Safety Song
Side 1: We Three Believe In Safety
(Part 1)
Side 2: We Three Believe In Safety
(Part 2)
$12.00

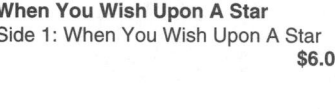

675
When You Wish Upon A Star
Side 1: When You Wish Upon A Star
$6.00

EP677
Rimpelstiltskin, The Nightingale, Pied Piper Of Hamelin
Side 1: Rimpelstiltskin, The Nightingale
Side 2: Nightingale, Pied Piper Of
Hamelin, The
$5.00

678
4 Mother Goose Songs
Side 1: Peter, Peter, Pumpkin Eater;
Solomon Grundy
Side 2: Deedle, Deedle, Dumpling
Little Robin Red Breast
$5.00

679
Two Songs Form Winnie-The-Pooh
Side 1: Sing Ho For The Life Of A Bear
Side 2: Cottleston Pie
$15.00

680

Songs Of The Flintstones
Side 1: Meet The Flintstones
Side 2: Rise And Shine

$18.00

681

Larry Harmon's TV Bozo The World's Most Famous Clown
Side 1: Bozo The Clown Like People
Side 2: Wowee!

$10.00

682

Little Engine That Could, The
Side 1: Little Engine That Could, The (Part 1)
Side 2: Little Engine That Could, The (Part 2)

$7.00

687

Popeye Songs Of Safety
Side 1: Red And Green
Side 2: Never Play With Matches

$15.00

EP688

New Songs Of Larry Harmon's TV Bozo
Side 1: Magic Whistle, Ding Dong, Dandy Time
Side 2: Good Guy Always Wins, I Like People,, The

$13.00

689

Top Cat
Side 1: Top Cat (Part 1)
Side 2: Top Cat (Part 1)

$16.00

692

Best Of Hanna-Barbera, The
Side 1: Top Cat, Wally Gator
Side 2: Dum Dum, Touché Turtle, Lippy The Lion And Hardy Har Har

$15.00

EP694

Bugs Bunny
Side 1: I Taut I Saw A Puddy Tat, Porky And Petunia, Porky Pig
Side 2: Merrily We Roll Along, Bugs Bunny Way Out West

$12.00

697

Hans Christian Andersen's The Ugly Duckling
Side 1: Ugly Duckling, The (Part 1)
Side 2: Ugly Duckling, The (Part 2)

$6.00

698

Larry Harmon's TV Bozo And His Magic Whistle
Side 1: Bozo And His Magic Whistle
Side 2: Belinda's Rainy Day
$10.00

699

Walter Lantz Woody Woodpecker March
Side 1: Woody Woodpecker March
Side 2: Andy Panda Polka
$10.00

700

Theme Songs Of Touché Turtle And Dum Dum
Side 1: Touché Turtle
Side 2: Dum Dum
$16.00

701

Wally Gator
Side 1: Wally Gator
Side 2: Lippy And Hardy Har Har
$16.00

702

Poky Little Puppy, The
Side 1: Poky Little Puppy
Side 2: Lambert The Sheepish Lion
$10.00

703

Songs About Words
Side 1: Alpha-Beetle
Side 2: Rattlesnake
$6.00

704

Casper The Friendly Ghost
Side 1: Casper, The Friendly Ghost
Side 2: Little Audry Says
$12.00

706

Songs About Counting
Side 1: 99 Eyes
Side 2: 1 Happy Family
$5.00

707

Saggy Baggy Elephant
Side 1: Saggy Baggy Elephant
Side 2: Mixed-Up Zoo, The
$7.00

EP708

Mister Ed The Talking Horse
Side 1: Mr. Ed Theme Song
Side 2: Pretty Little Filly
$15.00

EP709
Mister Ed The Talking Horse
Side 1: Mister Ed The Talking Horse,
The Chicken Or The Egg, A Million Kind
Of Animals
Side 2: Historic Force The Horse, The, It
Takes Five Senses, Out In Outer Space
$15.00

EP710
Nine Nursery Songs
$6.00

712
**Hans Christian Andersen's The
Princess And The Pea Told By
Danny Kaye**
Side 1: Princess And The Pea, The
(Part 1)
Side 2: Princess And The Pea, The
(Part 2)
$7.00

713
Paper Doll And The Paper Family
Side 1: Paper Doll
Side 2: Paper Family, The
$8.00

713
Back Cover

714
Little Train That Said Ahchoo
Side 1: Little Train That Said Ahchoo
$6.00

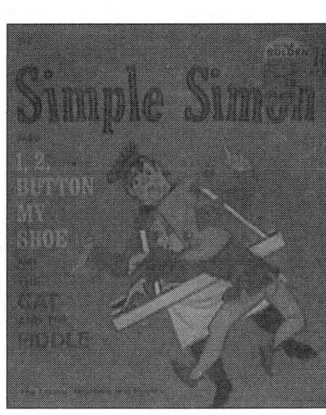

715
Simple Simon
Side 1: Cat And The Fiddle, The ;
One, Two Buckle My Shoe
Side 2: Simple Simon
$6.00

716
5 Songs Of Mother Goose
Side 1: Doctor Fell, Goosey Goosey
Gander, Dickery Dickery Dare
Side 2: See Saw Margery Da, Ride A
Cock Horse
$6.00

717
From The Movie The Music Man
Side 1: 76 Trombones (Part 1)
Side 2: 76 Trombones (Part 2)
$6.00

EP719
Grimm's Fairy Tales By Danny Kaye
Side 1: Grimm's Fairy Tales By Danny
Kaye
Side 2: Water Nixie, The Fox And The
Geese
$6.00

720
Jetsons Theme Song, The
Side 1: Jetsons, The
Side 2: Eep Opp Ork

$18.00

722
A Little Golden Sing-A-Long
Side 1: Loch Lomond
Side 2: Funiculi, Funicula

$5.00

723
Tarzan Song And Superman Song
Side 1: Tarzan Song
Side 2: Superman Song

$16.00

723

Back Cover

724
Billy Rose's Jumbo
Side 1: Circus Is On Parade (Part 1)
Side 2: Circus Is On Parade (Part 2)

$15.00

725
Romper Room Physical Fitness
Side 1: Posture Basket Song
Side 2: Bend And Stretch

$6.00

726
Little Drops Of Rain Song From The Movie Gay Purr-Ee
Side 1: Little Drops Of Rain
Side 2: My Bonnie Lies Over The Ocean

$16.00

727
Songs From The Wizard Of Oz Movie
Side 1: Over The Rainbow
Side 2: We're Off To The See The Wizard

$16.00

728
Fuzzy Wuzzy (Wuz A Bear)
Side 1: Fuzzy Wuzzy (Wuz A Bear)
Side 2: Teddy Bear's Parade

$7.00

729

Thumbelina
Side 1: Thumbelina
Side 2: Tom Thumb

$6.00

730

Hansel And Gretel
Side 1: Hansel And Gretel (Part 1)
Side 2: Hansel And Gretel (Part 2)
$6.00

731

A Christmas Song
Side 1: Chestnuts Roasting On A Open Fire
Side 2: We Wish You A Merry Christmas
$6.00

732

Here We Go Round The Mulberry Bush
Side 1: Here We Go Round The Mulberry Bush
Side 2: Here We Go Loop-De-Loop
$5.00

733

Blow The Man Down
Side 1: Blow The Man Down
Side 2: Sailing Sailing Over The Bounding Main
$5.00

734

On Top Of Old Smoky
Side 1: On Top Of Old Smoky
Side 2: Old Dan Tucker
$5.00

735

Songs Of Bozo
$8.00

736

Golden Funny Songs
Side 1: John Jacob Jingleheimer Schmidt; 1000 Legged Worm, Grasshopper Song
Side 2: A Peanut Sat On A Railroad Track, I Love You, Be Kind To Your Webfooted Friends
$5.00

737

Instruments Of The Orchestra
Side 1: Antoinette The Clarinet, Lucy Lynn The Violin
Side 2: Crumpet The Trumpet, Peter Percussion
$6.00

738

My Pony Macaroni
Side 1: My Pony Macaroni (Part 1)
Side 2: My Pony Macaroni (Part 2)
$5.00

739

Flintstones Dino The Dino, The
Side 1: Dino The Dino (Part 1)
Side 2: Dino The Dino (Part 2)
$15.00

740

Flintstones Lullaby Of Pebbles, The
Side 1: Pebbles' Lullaby (Part 1)
Side 2: Pebbles' Lullaby (Part 2)
$15.00

EP741

Songs Of Winnie-The-Pooh
$15.00

EP742

Jetsons, The
Side 1: Typical Family, Never Fear While Rosey's Here
Side 2: Astro, The Good Old Days
$15.00

EP745

Songs Of Rin Tin Tin
Side 1: I Wish I Had A Dog Like Rin Tin Tin, A Dog's Best Friend, Cold Nose Warm Heart
Side 2: Rinny Rusty And Rip,101 Calvery Gallop, Rough Around The Edges
$15.00

747

Lavender's Blue And Polly-Wolly-Doodle
Side 1: Lavender's Blue
Side 2: Polly-Wolly-Doodle
$6.00

EP749

Meet The Flintstones
Side 1: Meet The Flintstones
Side 2: Pebbles Lullaby; Dum Tot Song
$15.00

752

This Little Piggy
Side 1: This Little Piggy,30 Days
Hath September, As I Was Going To
St. Ives
Side 2: 2 Cats Of Kilkenny; There
Was A Maid, The Little Bird
$6.00

753

Puff The Magic Dragon
Side 1: Puff The Magic Dragon
Side 2: Reluctant Dragon, The
$6.00

755

Songs Of The Jetsons
Side 1: Push Bottom Blues
Side 2: Rama Rama Zoom
$15.00

756

Bugs Bunny
Side 1: Merrily We Roll Along
Side 2: I Taut I Taw A Puddy Tat
$8.00

EP759

**Song From The Walt Disney Movie
The Sword In The Stone**
Side 1: That's What Makes The
World For 'round
Side 2: How To Be A King
$7.00

760

**Songs From The Walt Disney Movie
The Sword In The Stone**
Side 1: Legend Of The Sword In The
Stone, The
Side 2: Higitus Figitus, What Did Merlin
Ever Do?
$8.00

EP761

My Bunny Rabbit Songs
Side 1: White Bunny And His Magic
Nose, Bunny Bunny Bunny, Lively Little
Rabbit
Side 2: Eustace, The Useless Rabbit,
My Bunny & Sister Sue, Pee Wee The
Bunny
$5.00

763

Elephant Record, The
Side 1: Here Come The Elephants
Side 2: Elephant Hop, The
$8.00

764

My Favorite Martian Starring Ray Walston
Side 1: Martian Theme Song
Side 2: When I Was A Boy On Mars
$18.00

765

Songs Of The Singing Nun
Side 1: Dominique
Side 2: I Go My Merry Way
$8.00

766

Voice Of President John F. Kennedy
Side 1: Nomination Acceptance Speech, Oath Of Office
Side 2: Highlight Of The Inaugural Address
$12.00

767

Brahms' Lullaby
Side 1: Rockabye Baby
Side 2: Twinkle Twinkle Little Star
$6.00

768

Campaign Songs Of Yogi Bear And Magilla Gorilla
Side 1: Magilla For President
Side 2: Yogi For President
$15.00

772

A Merry Merry Merry Merry Christmas
Side 1: Merry Merry Christmas
Side 2: Happy Little New Year
$6.00

773

How To Tell Time
Side 1: How To Tell Time
$6.00

774

Official Romper Room Do Bee Dance
Side 1: 10 Little Men
Side 2: Official Romper Room Do Bee Dance
$5.00

775

Songs From My Fair Lady
Side 1: I Could Of Danced All Night
Side 2: With A Little Bit Of Luck
$6.00

776

Astro Boy
Side 1: Astro Boy
Side 2: Whistle And March
$35.00

777

Row, Row, Row ,Your Boat Starring Captain Kangaroo
Side 1: Row, Row, Row ,Your Boat
Side 2: Erie Canal, The
$7.00

Little Golden Record Songs Index

This index contains songs only on regular Little Golden Records.

Other Little Golden Records

My Little Golden Record Tune Tote

Produced in yellow and red vinyl with black handles. The tote had seven paper record sleeves.

Yellow $30.00
Red $40.00

Little Golden Records LGR Series

These record sets came in with two or four yellow Little Golden a paper cover picture album. Produced from 1951–1952.

LGR1   A Little Golden Christmas Album (4 Records) $25.00

Side 1: Santa Claus Is Comin' To Town
Side 2: Christmas Song
Side 3: Frosty The Snowman (Part 1)
Side 4: Frosty The Snowman (Part 2)
Side 5: Jingle Bells

Side 6: Silent Night
Side 7: Night Before Christmas, The (Part 1)
Side 8: Night Before Christmas, The (Part 2)

LGR1   A Little Golden Christmas Album (4 Records) $25.00

Side 1: Santa Claus Is Comin'to Town
Side 2: Christmas Song
Side 3: Frosty The Snowman (Part 1)
Side 4: Frosty The Snowman (Part 2)
Side 5: Jingle Bells
Side 6: Silent Night
Side 7: Night Before Christmas, The (Part 1)
Side 8: Night Before Christmas, The (Part 2)

LGR2   Rudolph The Red-Nosed Reindeer
(2 Records)   **$20.00**
Side 1: Rudolph The Red-Nosed Reindeer
Side 2: Reindeer Dance, The
Side 3: Pull Together
Side 4: Santa's Other Reindeer

LGR3   Rudolph The Red-Nosed Reindeer
(4 Records)   **$25.00**
Side 1: Rudolph The Red-Nosed Reindeer
Side 2: Reindeer Dance, The
Side 3: O Come, All Ye Faithful
Side 4: O Little Christmas Tree, Joy To The World
Side 5: Santa's Other Reindeer
Side 6: Pull Together
Side 7: Hark The Herald Angels Sing
Side 8: God Rest Ye Merry, Gentlemen

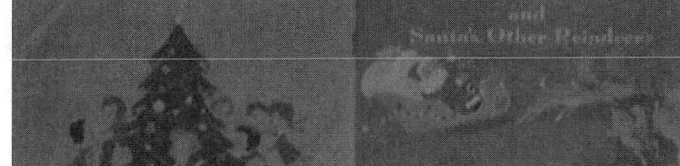

LGR4   Walt Disney's Mickey Mouse's Christmas
Party (4 Records)   **$50.00**
Side 1: Jingle Bells
Side 2: Hark the Herald Angels Sing
Side 3: Deck the Halls
Side 4: Santa's Toy Shop Song
Side 5: O Christmas Tree
Side 6: Unknown
Side 7: Jing-A-Ling
Side 8: Christmas Symphony

LGR5   Silent Night (4 records)   **$25.00**

Side 1: Silent Night
Side 2: It Came Upon A Midnight Clear
Side 3: O Little Town of Bethlehem
Side 4: O Christmas Tree, Joy To The World
Side 5: O Come, All Ye Faithful
Side 6: Away In A Manger
Side 7: Sleigh Ride
Side 8: I Just Can't Wait Till Christmas

LGR8   Roy Roger's Favorites (4 Records)   **$45.00**

Side 1: Happy Trails To You
Side 2: Bible Tells Me So, The
Side 3: Cowboy Needs A Horse, A
Side 4: Chuck Wagon Song, The
Side 5: Good Night Prayer A
Side 6: Hoofbeat Serenade
Side 7: Open Up Your Heart
Side 8: Friends And Neighbors

The Audio Library for Children

These were colored binders that held 7" black or yellow records. Each set contained a 24-page soft cover pamphlet about the set subject. The composer's pamphlet contained brief biographies while the orchestra was about the instruments. Produced in 1955 the record sets had the same records as its corresponding Golden Record Chest.

Great Composers (red cover) **$25.00**
The Orchestra (yellow cover) **$25.00**
Hymns $35.00

The Golden Record Chest Series

The Golden Record Chest contained 8 yellow Little Golden Records and were first released in 1955. Except for the Micky Mouse Club # LGRC1 and The Roy Rogers and Dale Evans Song Wagon # LGR8 which only came in 78 rpm the others could be purchased in 78's or 45's sets and originally sold for $3.95.

LGRC1 Songs From Walt Disney's Mickey Mouse Club $125.00

GRC1 A Child's Introduction To The Orchestra $50.00

1-A	Antoineet The Clarinet
1-B	Knute The Flute
2-A	Bobo The Oboe
2-B	Muldoon The Bassoon
3-A	Curmpet The Trumpet
3-B	Poobah The Tuba
4-A	Monsieur Forlorn The French Horn
4-B	Mike Malone The Slide Trombone
5-A	Lucy Lynn The Violin
5-B	Mello Fellow The Cello
6-A	Nola The Viola
6-B	Lovelace The Bass
7-A	Peter Percussion And Max Saxophone
7-B	Mort The Pianoforte And Lady Harp
8-A	The Orchestra
8-B	The Orchestra

GRC2 Walt Disney's Song Parade $100.00

1-A	When You Wish Upon A Star/Give A Little Whistle
1-B	I've Got No Strings/Hi Diddle Dee Dee
2-A	Hi-Ho/Whistle While You Work
2-B	Who's Afraid Of The Big Bad Wolf
3-A	Thumper's Song/When I See And Elephant Fly
3-B	Zip-A-Dee-Doo-Dah/Ev'rybody Has A Laughing Place

4-A Cinderella Work Song/A Dream Is A Wish Your Heart Makes

4-B Bibbidi-Bobbidi-Boo

5-A Peter Pan Theme/You Can Fly

5-B The Second Star To The Right/March Of The Lost Boys

6-A Alice In Wonderland Them/I'm Late

6-B A Very Merry Unbirthday/How D'ye Do And Shake Hands

7-A Ferdinand The Bull/The Reluctant Dragon

7-B Pecos Bill/Johnny Appleseed Song

8-A Mister Mickey Mouse/Donald Duck

8-B Goofy's Song/When You Wish Upon A Star

GRC3 The Golden Treasury of Hymns $50.00

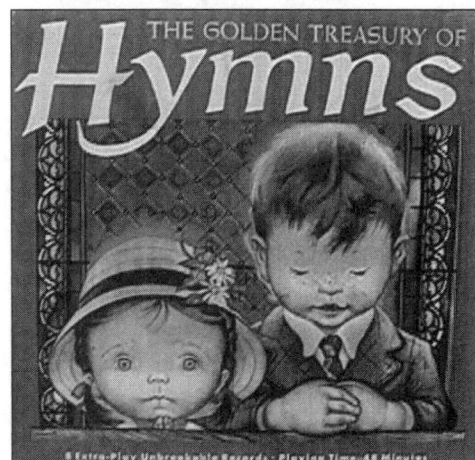

1-A Come , Ye Thankful People/Come We Gather Together To Ask The Lord's Blessing

1-B Praise God From Whom All Blessing Flow/Father, We Thank Thee For The Night

2-A Holy, Holy, Holy! Lord God Almighty!/O Worship The King

2-B My Faith Looks Up To Thee/Glorious Things Of Thee Are Spoken

3-A When Morning Gilds The Skies/Still, Still With Thee

3-B O Day Of Rest And Gladness/The Church's One Foundation

4-A Onward, Christian Soldiers/A Mighty Fortress Is Our God

4-B The Battle Hymn Of The Republic/America

5-A I Love To Tell The Story/Fling Out The Banner!

5-B From Greenland's Icy Mountains/O Zion, Haste, They Mission High Fulfilling

6-A Stand Up, Stand Up For Jesus/Jesus Calls Us, O'er The Tumult

6-B Lead On, O King Eternal/Come, Thou Almighty King

7-A When I Survey The Wondrous Cross/Rock Of Ages, Cleft For Me

7-B Saviour, Again To They Dear Name/O Jesus, I Have Promised

8-A Jesus Loves Me/Jesus Wants Me For Sunbeam

8-B Abide With Me/Now The Day Is Over

GRC4 A Child's Introduction To The Great Composers $50.00

1-A Bach-Gavotte/Handle-Bourrée From Water Music

1-B Gluck-Ballet Music From Iphigenia In Aulis/Haydn-Finale For Symphony No.88

2-A Mozart-Turkish Rondo From Piano Sonata In A Major/Bethoven-Contra-Dance No. 1

2-B Schubert-Incidental Music From Rosamunde/Rossini-Ballet Music From William Tell

3-A Mendelssohn-Dance Of The Clowns From A Midsummer Night's Dream/Berlioz-Dance Of The Sylphs From The Damnation Of Faust

3-B Chopin-The Minute Waltz/Schumann-The Happy Farmer From Album For The Young

4-A Wagner-Pilgrim's Chorus From Tannhauser/Liszt-Liebestraum

4-B Verdi-Anvil Chorus From Il Trovatore/Gounod-Funeral March Of A Marionette

5-A Franck-Second Movement From Symphony In D Minor/Strauss-Explosion Polka

5-B Borodin-Polovtsian Dance From Prince Igor/Brahms-Hungarian Dance No.5

6-A Moussorgsky-Ballet Of The Unhatched Chick From Pictures From An Exhibition/Bizet-Farandole From L'arlesienne Suite No.2

6-B Saint-Saëns-The Swan From Carnival Of The Animals/Tchaikovsky-Dance Of The Little Swans From Swan Lake

7-A Rimsky-Korsakov-Dance Of The Clowns From The Snow Maiden/Grieg-Norwegian Dance

7-B Dvorak-Largo From The New World Symphony/Humperdink-Children's Dances From Hansel And Gretel

8-A Debussy-Golliwog's Cake Walk From The Children's Corner/Ravel-Bolero

8-B Prokofieff-March From Peter And The Wolf/Bartok-Rumanian Dance

GRC5 No Chest Produced

**GRC6 Roy Rogers and Dale Evans' Song
Wagon** $150.00

1-A	Song Wagon
1-B	I Ride An Old Paint
2-A	Whoopee Ti Yi Yo
2-B	Home On The Range
3-A	The Old Chisholm Trail
3-B	Colorado Trail
4-A	The Railroad Corral
4-B	Tumbling Tumble Weeds
5-A	Cool Water
5-B	The Street Of Laredo
6-A	The Night Herding Song
6-B	Red River Valley
7-A	Doney Gal
7-B	Good-Bye, Old Paint
8-A	Bury Me Out On The Lone Prairie
8-B	The Cowman's Prayer

**GRC7 Rodgers and Hammerstein's Saturday
Matinee** $85.00

1-A	Oh! What A Beautiful Mornin'-Oklahoma
1-B	Oklahoma!-Oklahoma
2-A	The Surrey With The Fringe On Top-Oklahoma!
2-B	You'll Never Walk Alone-Carousel
3-A	June Is Bustin' Out All Over-Carousel

3-B	Carousel Waltz-Carousel
4-A	A Real Nice Clambake-Carousel
4-B	Blow High, Blow Low-Carousel
5-A	Dites-Moi And Bali-Hái-South Pacific
5-B	Happy Talk-South Pacific
6-A	One Foot, Other Foot-Allegro
6-B	Getting To Know You-The King And I
7-A	I Whistle A Happy Tune-The King And I7-BThe

March Of The Siamese Children-The King
     And I

8-A	On A Lop-Sided Bus-Pipe Dream
8-B	All I Owe Ioway —State Fair

**LGRC1 Songs From Walt Disney's Mickey Mouse
Club** $125.00

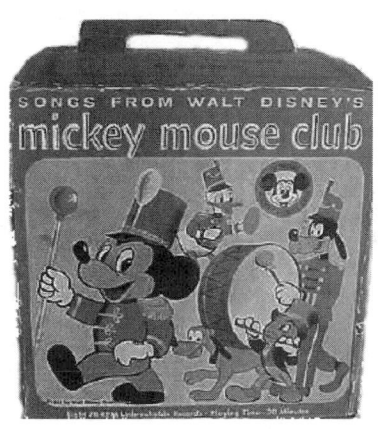

Golden Story Book and Record Album (1966)

Each boxed set contained one 12-inch 33-1/3 long-playing record and six soft cover books. The book covers were each a different solid colored background with a circled number at the bottom left corner and a picture of the Little Golden Book in the upper right corner. The record had three stories on each side. Produced by A. A. Records of New York.

Book cover example.

GST-1 $25.00

1. The Three Bears
2. Thumbelina
3. Smokey the Bear
4. Hansel and Gretel
5. Wizard of Oz
6. Peter Rabbit

GST-2 $25.00

1. Little Red Riding Hood
2. Old MacDonald Had A Farm
3. Bozo
4. Heidi
5. Peter and the Wolf
6. Puss 'n Boots

GST-3 $25.00

1. Jack and the Beanstalk
2. The Gingerbread Man
3. Snow White and Rose Red
4. The Saggy Baggy Elephant
5. The Little Red Caboose
6. A Country Mouse and A City Mouse

GST-4 $25.00

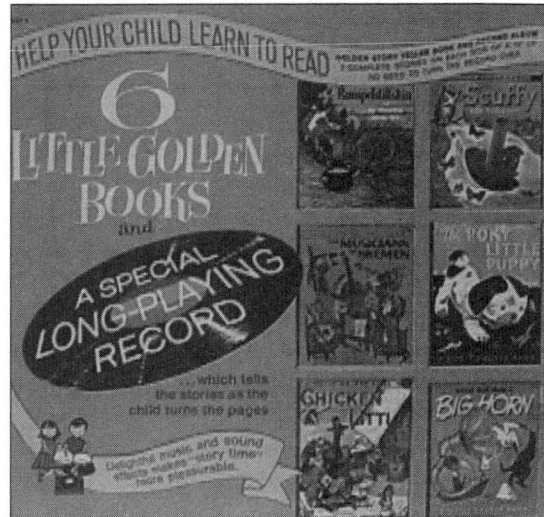

1. Rumpelstiltskin
2. Scuffy the Tugboat
3. The Musicians of Bremen
4. The Poky Little Puppy
5. Chicken Little
6. Little Boy with a Big Horn

GST-5, GST-6, GST-7 were probably never released
GST-8 $30.00

1. How Lovely is Christmas
2. Jingle Bells
3. The Night Before Christmas
4. Rudolph the Red-Nosed Reindeer
5. The Twelve Days of Christmas
6. Frosty the Snowman

Book and Record Sets (Hard cover)

There are four different packagings for the regular hard cover Little Golden Book and record sets. I'm listing the titles listed on the back of the packaging. It is possible that some of the title were not released under their series and were moved into the next.

The first series sets sold for 79 cents and were cardboard envelopes that opened at the top. This set had a banner at the top of the sleeve that read "Little Golden Books that read themselves." These sets were produced around 1956/1957 with 78 rpm records.

C-329   The Night Before Christmas $20.00

C-330   Hansel and Gretel $20.00
C-331   Heidi $20.00
C-332   The Saggy Baggy Elephant $20.00

C-333   Roy Rogers and Cowboy Toby $35.00

C-334   Walt Disney's Little Man of Disneyland $30.00

The second series sets sold for 79 cents. The titles from the first series carried over and new ones were added. The covers had a leaf-like pattern at the top and also opened at the top. These sets were produced around 1957 with 78 rpm records.

C-329   The Night Before Christmas $20.00
C-330   Hansel and Gretel $20.00
C-331   Heidi$20.00
C-332   The Saggy Baggy Elephant $20.00
C-333   Roy Rogers and Cowboy Toby $35.00
C-334   Walt Disney's Little Man of Disneyland $30.00
C-428   The Poky Little Puppy $20.00

C-429   Walt Disney's Seven Dwarfs Find a
        House $25.00

C-430   The Three Bears $20.00

C-431   Little Red Riding Hood $20.00
C-432   Jack and the Beanstalk $20.00
C-433   Walt Disney's Bambi $20.00

The third series was called "Read and Hear." The hard cover book and record where in a cardboard fold-over envelope that opened at the bottom. The sets sold for 69 cents and were released around 1963 with 45rpm records.

00151	Hansel & Gretel	$15.00
00152	Heidi	$15.00
00153	The Saggy Baggy Elephant	$15.00
00154	The Poky Little Puppy	$15.00
00155	The Three Bears	$15.00
00156	Little Red Riding Hood	$15.00

00157	Three Bedtime Stories	$15.00
00158	Baby's Mother Goose	$15.00
00159	The Little Red Caboose	$15.00
00160	How To Tell Time	$15.00
00161	Nursery Songs	$15.00
00162	Chicken Little	$15.00

The fourth series had the familiar boy and girl holding a book and a record. This set was a cardboard envelope that opened at the top. These sets were produced around 1963/1964 with rpm records.

00151	Hansel & Gretel	$15.00
00152	Heidi	$15.00
00153	The Saggy Baggy Elephant	$15.00
00154	The Poky Little Puppy	$15.00
00155	The Three Bears	$15.00
00156	Little Red Riding Hood	$15.00
00157	Three Bedtime Stories	$15.00
00158	Baby's Mother Goose	$15.00
00159	The Little Red Caboose	$15.00
00160	How To Tell Time	$15.00
00161	Nursery Songs	$15.00
00162	Chicken Little	$15.00
00163	Jack and the Beanstalk	$15.00

00164	The Gingerbread Man	$15.00
00165	Rumpelstiltskin	$15.00
00166	The Little Red Hen	$15.00
00167	Numbers	$15.00
00168	The Night Before Christmas	$15.00

Read and Hear Little Golden Book & Record Sets (Soft cover)

Numbers 151 to around 206 were originally produced by A.A. Records. Later, the Golden Record Division produced the sets through 264. Some titles can also be found with cassettes.

151
Hansel And Gretel
$5.00

152
Heidi
$5.00

153
Saggy Baggy Elephant
$5.00

154
Poky Little Puppy, The
$5.00

155
Three Bears, The
$5.00

156
Little Red Riding Hood
$6.00

157
Three Bedtime Stories
$5.00

158
Baby's Mother Goose
$5.00

159
Little Red Caboose, The
$6.00

160
How To Tell Time
$6.00

162
Chicken Little
$5.00

163
Jack And The Beanstalk
$5.00

161
Nursery Songs
$5.00

164
Gingerbread Man, The
$6.00

165
Rumpelstiltskin And The Princess And The Pea
$5.00

166
Little Red Hen, The
$5.00

167
Numbers
$5.00

168
Night Before Christmas, The
$6.00

169
Bozo Finds A Friend
$6.00

170
Smokey The Bear
$10.00

171
Happy Birthday Party
$15.00

172
Cinderella
$75.00

173
Peter Rabbit
$5.00

174
A Country Mouse And A City Mouse
$5.00

175
Puss In Boots
$5.00

176
Snow White And Rose Red
$6.00

177
Musicians Of Bremen, The
$5.00

178
Rudolph The Red-Nosed Reindeer
$6.00

179
Frosty The Snowman
$6.00

180
Wizard Of Oz, The
$6.00

181
Scuffy The Tugboat
$5.00

182
Old Macdonald Had A Farm
$5.00

183
Little Boy With A Big Horn
$6.00

184
Thumbelina
$5.00

185
Peter And The Wolf

$5.00

186
Jingle Bells

$5.00

187
Silly Sidney

$10.00

188
Bingity Bangity School Bus

$6.00

193
Romper Room Laughing Book, The

$5.00

194
Tuggy The Tugboat

$5.00

205
Peter Cottontail

$5.00

206
Puff The Magic Dragon

$5.00

207
Twelve Days Of Christmas, The

$5.00

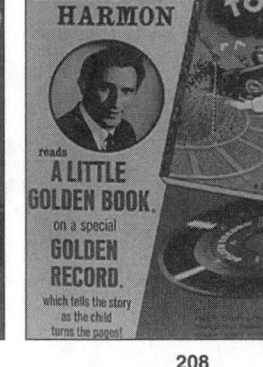

208
Tootle

$5.00

209
Three Little Pigs, The

$5.00

210
Pinocchio

$5.00

211
Ugly Duckling (Danny Kaye), The

$5.00

212
Bozo The Clown

$6.00

213
Three Little Kittens

$5.00

214
Seven Little Postmen

$5.00

215
How Lovely Is Christmas
$6.00

216
Little Engine That Could, The
$6.00

217
White Bunny And His Magic Nose, The
$5.00

218
Animals Of Farmer Jones, The
$5.00

219
Happy Man And His Dump Truck, The
$5.00

220
Big Brown Bear, The
$6.00

221
Three Billy Goats Gruff, The
$6.00

222
Romper Room Book Of Finger Plays And Action Rhymes, The
$5.00

223
Romper Room What Time Is It?
$5.00

224
Romper Room Book Of Happy Animals, The
$5.00

225
Romper Room Safety Book, The
$5.00

226
Snow White And The Seven Dwarfs
$5.00

227
Peter Pan
$5.00

228
Sleeping Beauty
$5.00

229
Black Beauty
$5.00

230
Jungle Book, The Story Of Mowgli
$6.00
231
Jungle Book, The Rikkitikki Tavi
$6.00

233
ABC Rhymes

$5.00

234
Riddles From A To Z

$5.00

235
Day On The Farm, A

$5.00

232
Visit To The Children's Zoo, A

$5.00

237
Counting Rhymes

238
Chitty Chitty Bang Bang

$6.00

$9.00

239
Circus Time

$7.00

240
Taxi That Hurried, The

$5.00

236
Child's Garden Of Verses, A

$6.00

241
Five Little Firemen

$7.00

242
Shy Little Kitten, The

$5.00

243
Lively Little Rabbit, The

$5.00

244
When I Grow Up

$5.00

246
Fat Little Policeman, The

$5.00

247
Tawny Scrawny Lion, The

$5.00

248
Wonderful School, The

$6.00

249
Ukelele And Her New Doll

$10.00

251
Naughty Bunny

$15.00

252
Happy Days

$5.00

253
Tiger's Adventure

$5.00

245
Ali Baba

$6.00

250
Mister Dog

$8.00

254
Boy With A Drum, The
$6.00

255
Little Indian
$6.00

256
Fuzzy Duckling, The
$5.00

257
Cinderella
$5.00

258
Nonsense Alphabet, The
$5.00

260
Bravest Of All
$10.00

261
Wacky Witch
$10.00

262
Corky's Hiccups
$5.00

263
Who Comes To Your House
$5.00

264
Susan In The Driver's Seat
$7.00

259
Pussycat Tiger, The
$6.00

A Little Golden Book and Record
(Soft cover)

Produced by Disneyland Vista Records, this series started with 201 in 1975. Numbers 201 through 255 were regular Little Golden Book titles, while numbers 301 through 384 were primarily Disney titles with a few from other studios.

201

Saggy Baggy Elephant, The

$5.00

202

Tawny Scrawny Lion

$5.00

203

Poky Little Puppy, The

$5.00

204

Rumpelstiltskin

$5.00

205

Scuffy The Tugboat

$5.00

206

Thumbelina

$6.00

204

Rumpelstiltskin

$5.00

205

Scuffy The Tugboat

$5.00

206

Thumbelina

$6.00

207

Little Boy With A Big Horn

$6.00

208

Puss In Boots

$5.00

209

Chicken Little

$5.00

210

Large And Growly Bear, The

$5.00

211

Tootle

$5.00

212

Color Kittens, The

$6.00

213

Happy Man And His Dump Truck

$5.00

214

Taxi That Hurried, The

$5.00

215

Smokey The Bear

$10.00

216

Little Engine That Could, The

$6.00

217

Pussycat Tiger, The

$5.00

A Little Golden Book and Record (Soft cover)   319

218

David And Goliath

$5.00

219

Noah's Ark

$5.00

220

Lively Little Rabbit, The

$5.00

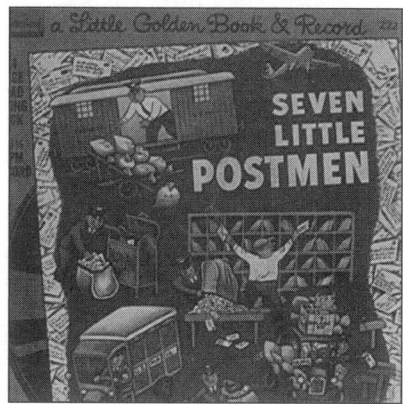

221

Circus Time

$6.00

222

Seven Little Postmen

$5.00

223

There's No Such Thing As A Dragon

$6.00

224

Little Fat Policeman, The

$5.00

252

Rudolph The Red-Nosed Reindeer

$5.00

253

Frosty The Snowman

$5.00

254

Twelve Days Of Christmas, The

$5.00

255

Jingle Bells

$5.00

301

Sleeping Beauty

$5.00

302

Mary Poppins

$5.00

303

Three Little Pigs

$5.00

304

Peter Pan

$5.00

305

101 Dalmatians

$5.00

306

Alice In Wonderland

$5.00

307

Lady And The Tramp

$5.00

307

Lady And The Tramp
2nd Cover

$5.00

308

Cinderella

$5.00

309

Bambi

$5.00

A Little Golden Book and Record (Soft cover)

309

Bambi

$5.00

310

Snow White

$5.00

Pinocchio

311

Pinocchio

$5.00

312

Mother Goose Rhymes

$5.00

313

Winnie The Pooh And The Honey Tree

$5.00

314

Seven Dwarfs And Their Diamond Mine, The

$5.00

315

Goldilocks And The Three Bears

$5.00

316

Gnome-Mobile, The

$12.00

317

Hansel And Gretel

$5.00

318

Black Beauty

$5.00

319

Jungle Book, The

$5.00

320

Happiest Millionaire, The

$12.00

321

Peter And The Wolf

$5.00

322

Heidi

$5.00

323

It's A Small World

$6.00

324

Dumbo

$5.00

325

How The Camel Got His Hump

$8.00

326

Acting Out The ABCs

$5.00

327

Winnie The Pooh And The Blustery Day

$7.00

328

Little Red Riding Hood

$5.00

329

Babes In Toyland

$5.00

330

Little Hiawatha

$6.00

331

Grasshopper And The Ants, The

$6.00

332

Little Red Hen, The

$5.00

333

Winnie The Pooh And Tigger

$7.00

334

Mickey Mouse, Brave Little Tailor

$5.00

335

Johnny Appleseed

$5.00

336

Pirates Of The Caribbean

$20.00

337

Gingerbread Man, The

$5.00

338

More Jungle Book

$5.00

339

Haunted Mansion, The

$20.00

340

Ugly Duckling, The

$5.00

341

Emperor's New Clothes, The

$5.00

342

Robin Hood

$5.00

343

Thumper's Race

$5.00

344

Night Before Christmas, The

$5.00

345

Bremen Town Musicians

$5.00

346

Rapunzel

$5.00

347

Wizard Of Oz, The

$6.00

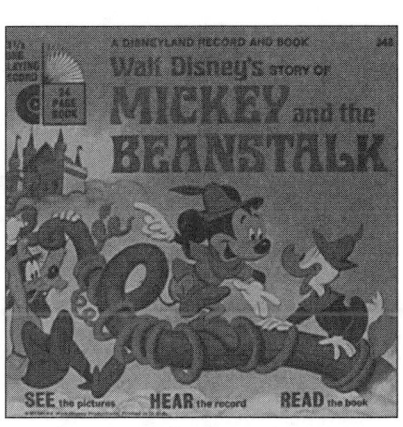

348

Mickey And The Beanstalk

$5.00

349

Aristocats, The

$6.00

A Little Golden Book and Record (Soft cover)   325

350

Pecos Bill

$6.00

351

Lambert, The Sheepish Lion

$6.00

352

Susie, The Little Blue Coup

$6.00

353

Little House, The

$6.00

354

Johnny Fedora And Alice Blue Bonnet

$6.00

355

The Whale Who Wanted To Sing At The Met

$10.00

356

Aladdin And His Lamp

$5.00

357

Swiss Family Robinson, The

$5.00

358

20,000 Leagues Under The Sea

$7.00

359

Sinbad The Sailor

$5.00

360

Davy Crockett

$5.00

361

Treasure Island

$5.00

362

More Mother Goose

$5.00

363

Brer Rabbit And The Tar Baby

$5.00

364

Bedknobs And Broomsticks

$7.00

365

Robin Hood

$5.00

366

Winnie The Pooh And Tigger Too

$7.00

367

Rescuers, The

$6.00

368

Hobbit, The

$6.00

369

Pete's Dragon

$5.00

381
Black Hole, The
$5.00

382
Return Of The King
$6.00

383
Fox And The Hound, The
$5.00

384
Dragonslayer, The
$6.00

Read-Along Collection
(Soft cover)

Produced in 1977 by Disneyland Vista Records, this boxed set contained 20 Little Golden Books and records. The set does not bring as much as the individual book and records, which may be because collectors may have most the sets prior to finding the boxed set. Value: $20.00-$40.00

Read-Along Collection boxed set.

A Brief History of Rand McNally

In 1856, William Rand, a young printer from Boston, arrived in Chicago and opened his own print shop. While Rand was starting up his company, another young man was getting ready to leave his homeland in search of his fortune in the United States. Andrew McNally, having finished his seven years as a printer's apprentice, was preparing to leave the county of Armagh in Ireland.

McNally arrived in Chicago and, while looking for work, came upon Rand's business. In just a few years the two men were able to purchase the Chicago Tribune's job printing shop and formed Rand McNally & Company. While looking for new ventures, they started printing passenger tickets, timetables, and guides for railroads. Later they started printing the Railroad Guide, a route map for a single railroad.

By the early 1900s, the automobile started allowing people to move outside of their neighborhoods and see the country. To help people in their travels, the company started producing road maps. In 1907, Andrew McNally II and his wife drove from Chicago to New York, taking pictures of every turn they made on their trip. This was later published as the Chicago-to-New York Auto Guide.

As more and more roads crossed the country, Rand McNally, not the government, created the numbering of highways. The first road map to list major roads with numbers was for the state of Illinois. Road maps of the 48 states were available by 1922. The Rand McNally Road Atlas that is in print today was first printed in 1924.

The company had been printing children's books since around 1913. In 1949, the company acquired the W.B. Conkey Company and started printing books on a much larger scale. With the proven success of Little Golden Books, the company released the first four titles of its own 6-5/8-inch x 8-3/4-inch books, A Rand McNally Elf Book, around September 1947. Later titles were not released until around the summer or fall of 1948.

The primary construction difference between Elf Books and Little Golden Books is that Elf Books are not flush-cut. A Little Golden Book is put together and then the sides are trimmed, making the pages flush to the cover, but most Elf Books had the cover made separately from the book (although some were done flush-cut between 1954 and 1957). The front and back cover are one piece, which is glued to the cover cardboard. The pages are stitched together and are then glued to the cover by the first and last page. With this method, the cover extends past the pages by about 1/4 inch. Because the covers on Elf Books did not hold up to use as well as Little Golden Books did, they are a lot harder to find in nice condition.

From 1947 until around 1954, the books were called a Rand McNally Book/Elf Book and had a picture of an elf in a 3/4-inch x 7/8-inch box in the upper left corner; in 1954 the picture of the elf grew to 1/2-inch x 1-1/4 inches. In 1955, the books were called A Rand McNally Elf Book. Tip-Top Elf Books, which were first printed around 1959, have a little elf standing on a globe. Start-Right Elf Books were started around 1966. These have an elf sitting down reading a book in the upper left corner and "Rand McNally Publisher" appears at the bottom of the cover. Rand McNally also printed Ding Dong School Books between July 1953 and June 1956 before they were done as Golden Books.

When trying to date a Rand McNally Elf Book prior to February 1963, look on the last page. You will see a number preceded by CS. The first number preceding the dash stands for the month, while the next number is the year of printing. For example, CS6-54 means the book was printed in June 1954, and CS12-52 stands for December 1952. There is no way of telling for sure if a book is first edition on most books after February 1963.

You will also see two numbers on the last page separated by a dash (-). These two numbers denote the recommended reading age for that particular book. The first number is the recommended beginning age, while the second is the ending age, divided by 10. For example, a book with "50-90" would be for children 5 to 9 years of age.

Elf books were originally printed with 36 pages, but books below number 600 could have had 28, 30, or 32 pages. Books numbered higher than 3000 typically had 20 pages, although some had 28.

Quite a few of the books were printed in different numbered series over the years. The first series ran from 425 to as high as 620, but some numbers had no titles before the 8300 period. The second series was from 3800 to around 8460. The fourth series was the Tip-Top Elf Book series which originally went from 1001 to 1038, before it was changed to 8600 and continued to around 8743. The fifth series, the Start-Right Elf Book, began with 8500.

Rand McNally sold its low-end children's line to MacMillan Publishing in 1986. Checkerboard Press was formed and became a subsidiary from 1986 to 1990. In 1990, Checkerboard Press became a private company. The name of the company comes from the very popular *Rand McNally Reads Mother Goose*, first printed in 1916. This book has a checkerboard background on the front cover.

Rand McNally Elf Books

424

Mother Goose
Illus.: Friend, Esther
1947   **$15.00**

424

Mother Goose
(2nd Cover)
Illus.: Friend, Esther
1947   **$7.00**

425

Peppy, The Lonely Little Puppy
Illus.: Blake, Vivienne
Author: Friedman, Frieda
1947   **$15.00**

426

Twilight Tales
Illus.: Bryant, Dean
Author: Potter, Miriam Clark
1947   **$15.00**

427

Wonderful Train Ride, The
Illus.: Mastri, Fiore & Jackie
Author: Weir, R. C.
1947   **$7.00**

427

Wonderful Train Ride, The
(2nd Cover)
Illus.: Mastri, Fiore & Jackie
Author: Weir, R. C.
1947   **$7.00**

428
Can't Verify Title

429

Teddy Bear Of Bumpkin Hollow
Illus.: Bryant, Dean
Author: Boucher, Sharon
1948   **$25.00**

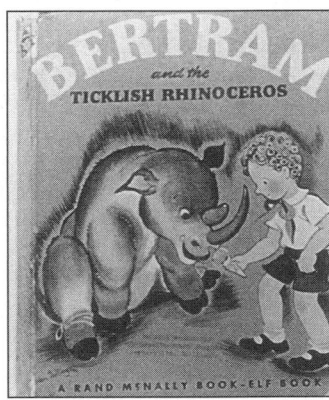

430

Bertram And The Ticklish Rhinoceros
Illus.: Thompson Van Tellingen, Ruth
Author: Gilbert, Paul
1948   **$25.00**

431

My Truck Book
Illus.: Grider, Dorothy
Author: Reichert, E. C.
1948   **$15.00**

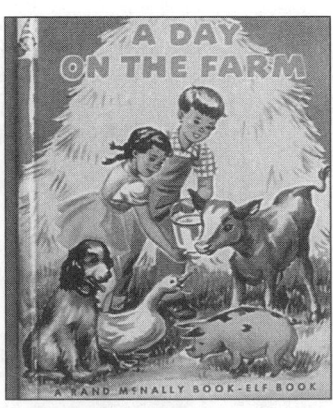

432

Day On The Farm, A
Illus.: Grider, Dorothy
Author: Evers, Alf
1948   **$15.00**

432

Day On The Farm, A
(2nd Cover)
Illus.: Grider, Dorothy
Author: Evers, Alf
1948   **$7.00**

433

Wonderful Plane Ride, The
Illus.: Mastri, Fiore & Jackie
1947   **$15.00**

434

Penny And Pete's Surprise
Illus.: Mc Kinley, Clare
1949   **$15.00**

435

Forest Babies
Illus.: Webbe, Elizabeth
1949   **$15.00**

436

Kerry, The Fire-Engine Dog
Illus.: Grider, Dorothy
Author: Lewis, Frank; Corchia, Alfred J.
1949   **$15.00**

437

Cowboy Eddie
Illus.: Grider, Dorothy
Author: Glasscock, Joyce
1950   **$12.00**

438

One, Two, Cock-A-Doodle-Doo
Illus.: Wosmek, Frances
Author: Pease, Josephine Van
Dolzen
1950   **$12.00**

439

Johnny And The Birds
Illus.: Webbe, Elizabeth
Author: Munn, Ian
1950   **$12.00**

440

Little Kittens' Nursery Rhymes, The
Illus.: Frees, Harry Whittier
1941   **$12.00**

441

Smart Little Mouse, The
Illus.: Phillips, Katherine L.
Author: Sherwan, Earl
1950   **$12.00**

442

Hiawatha
Illus.: Wilde, Irma
Author: Gridley, Marion E.
1950   **$12.00**

443

Three Little Bunnies
Illus.: Rooks, Dale & Sally
Author: Dixon, Ruth
1950   **$12.00**

444

Number 9 The Little Fire Engine
Illus.: Corwin, Eleanor
Author: Wadsworth, Wallace
1950   **$12.00**

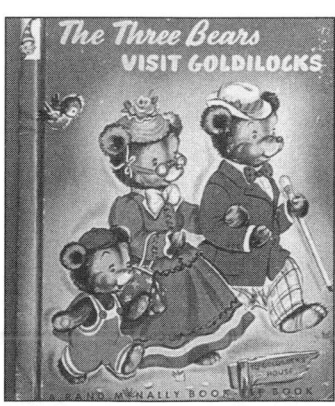

445

Three Bears Visit Goldilocks, The
Illus.: Mc Kinley, Clare
1950   **$12.00**

446

Amos Learns To Talk: The Story Of A Little Duck
Illus.: Mc Kinley, Clare
Author: Bradbury, Bianca
1950 **$12.00**

447

Three Little Puppies
Illus.: Rooks, Dale & Sally
Author: Dixon, Ruth
1951 **$12.00**

448

Farm For Andy, A
Illus.: Gayer, Marguerite
1951 **$12.00**

449

Mr. Punnymoon's Train
Illus.: Phillips, Katherine L.
Author: Hadsell, Alice
1951 **$12.00**

450

My Happy Day: A Word Book
Illus.: Bruce, Suzanne
Author: Shaw, Thelma
1963 **$10.00**

451

Alice In Wonderland
Illus.: Holland, Janice
Author: Carroll, Lewis
1951 **$18.00**

452

Chester, The Little Pony
Illus.: Mc Kinley, Clare
Author: Gunder, Eman
1951 **$10.00**

453

Children That Lived In A Shoe, The
Illus.: Webbe, Elizabeth
Author: Pease, Josephine Van Dolzen
1951 **$10.00**

454

Wild Animals
Illus.: Vlasaty, J.L.
Author: Ratzesberger, Anna
1951 **$10.00**

455

Little Friends: Kittens, Puppies, Bunnies
Illus.: Gaddis, Rie
Author: Dixon, Ruth
1951 **$10.00**

456

Buddy, The Little Taxi
Illus.: Corwin, Elizabeth
Author: Grider, Dorothy
1951 **$10.00**

457

Our Auto Trip
Illus.: Grider, Dorothy
Author: Edsall, Marian
1952 **$10.00**

458

Little Mailman Of Bayberry Lane, The
Illus.: Webbe, Elizabeth
Author: Munn, Ian
1952 **$20.00**

459

Busy Bulldozer, The
Illus.: Grider, Dorothy
Author: Browning, James
1952 **$8.00**

460

To The Store We Go
Illus.: Walker, O
1952 **$8.00**

461

Noah's Ark
Illus.: Webbe, Elizabeth
Author: Briggs, Dorothy Bell
1952 **$8.00**

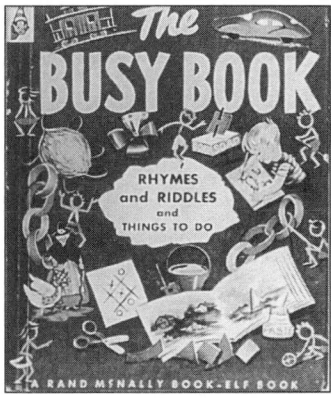

462

Busy Book, The (Rhymes & Riddles & Things To Do)
Illus.: Szepelak, Helen
Author: Bartlett, Floy; Pease, Josephine
1952 **$8.00**

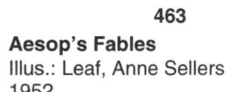

463

Aesop's Fables
Illus.: Leaf, Anne Sellers
1952 **$8.00**

464

Old Woman And Her Pig, The
Illus.: Friend, Esther
Author: Wadsworth, Wallace
1952 **$8.00**

465

Lucinda, The Little Donkey
Illus.: Wilde, George
Author: Wilde, Irma
1952 **$8.00**

466

Hide-Away Puppy
Illus.: Dottie
Author: Broderick, Jessica Potter
1952 **$8.00**

467

Farm Animals
Illus.: Gayer, Marguerite
Author: Ratzesberger, Anna
1952 **$8.00**

468

Popcorn Party
Illus.: Szepelak, Helen
Author: Boyles, Trudy; Macmartin, Louise
1952 **$8.00**

469

Goat That Went To School, The
Illus.: Tamburine, Jean
Author: Francis, Sally R.
1952 **$8.00**

470

Goody: A Mother Cat Story
Illus.: Leaf, Anne Sellers
Author: Bertail, Inez
1957   **$8.00**

471

Bartholomew The Beaver
Illus.: Pierce, Alice
Author: Dixon, Ruth
1952   **$8.00**

472

Little Bobo And His Blue Jacket
Illus.: Brice, Tony
Author: Evers, Alf
1953   **$10.00**

473

Space Ship To The Moon
Illus.: Bilder, A.K.
Author: Reichert, E.C.
1952   **$16.00**

474

**Superliner United States, The:
World's Fastest Liner**
Illus.: Bilder, A.K.
1953   **$16.00**

475

Mr. Bear's House
Illus.: Mc Kinley, Clare
Author: Rothe, Fenella
1953   **$10.00**

476

Squiffy The Skunk
Illus.: Neff, George; Brett, Grace Neff
Author: Brett, Grace Neff
1953   **$10.00**

477

Scalawag The Monkey
Illus.: Gaddis, Rie
Author: Dixon, Ruth
1953   **$10.00**

478

Funland Party
Illus.: Szepelak, Helen
Author: Devine, Louise Lawrence
1953   **$8.00**

479

Outdoor Fun
Illus.: Tamburine, Jean
Author: Shaw, Thelma & Ralph
1953   **$8.00**

480

Find The Way Home
Illus.: Wilson, Beth
Author: Broderick, Jessica Potter
1953   **$8.00**

481

Can't Verify Title

482

Happy Holidays
Illus.: Bruce, Suzanne
Author: Reichert, E.C.
1953   **$8.00**

483

Little Lost Angel
Illus.: Scott, Janet Laura
Author: Heath, Janet Field
1953 **$12.00**

484

Stories Of The Christ Child
Illus.: Corwin, Eleanor
Author: Jones, Mary Alice
1953 **$8.00**

485

Choo-Choo, The Little Switch Engine
Illus.: Chase, Mary Jane
Author: Wadsworth, Wallace
1954 **$8.00**

486

Pets
Illus.: Webbe, Elizabeth
Author: Ratzesberger, Anna
1954 **$8.00**

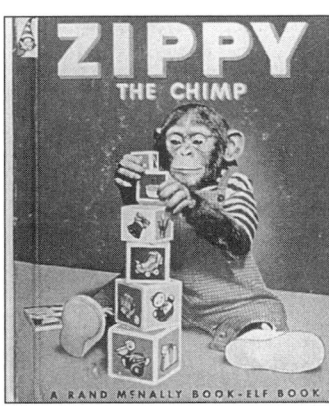

487

Zippy The Chimp
Illus.: Mitchell, Benn
Author: Ecuyer, Lee
1953 **$10.00**

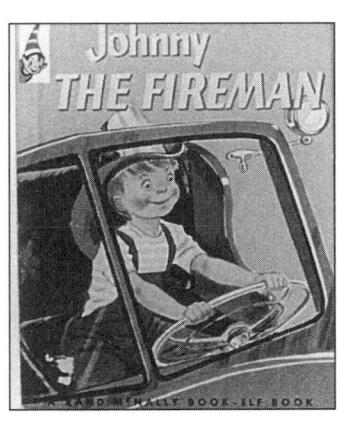

488

Johnny The Fireman
Illus.: Wood, Ruth
Author: Sprinkle, Rebecca K.
1954 **$10.00**

489

Zippy Goes To School
Illus.: Westelin, Albert G.; Ecuyer, Lee
Author: Ecuyer, Lee
1954 **$10.00**

490

Parakeet Peter
Illus.: Grider, Dorothy
Author: Sprinkle, Rebecca K.
1954 **$8.00**

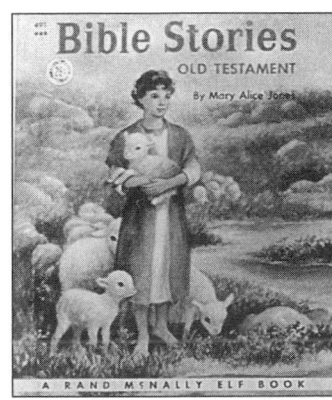

491

Bible Stories: Old Testament
Illus.: Webbe, Elizabeth
Author: Jones, Mary Alice
1954 **$8.00**

493

Campbell Kids At Home, The
Illus.: Schlining Studios, G
Author: Lack, Alma S.
1954 **$22.00**

494

Campbell Kids Have A Party, The
Illus.: Schlining Studios, G
1954 **$22.00**

495

Sparky The Fire Dog
Illus.: Chase, Mary Jane
Author: Browning, James
1954 **$15.00**

492

Can't Verify Title

496

**Wild Bill Hickok And Deputy
Marshal Joey**
Illus.: Timmons, William
1954 **$20.00**

497

Sailing On A Very Fine Day
Illus.: Myers, Lou
Author: Ives, Burl
1954 **$8.00**

498

Five Little Bears
Illus.: Tamburine, Jean
1955 **$8.00**

499

Bedtime Stories
Illus.: Clyne, Barbara
Author: Watts, Mabel
1955 **$7.00**

500

Sergeant Preston And Yukon King
Illus.: Neebe, William
Author: Comfort, Mildred H.
1955 **$16.00**

501

Playtime Poodles
Illus.: Westelin, Albert; Schmidling,
Jack
Author: Wing, Helen
1955 **$10.00**

502

**Prayers And Graces For A Small
Child**
Illus.: Webbe, Elizabeth
Author: Webbe, Elizabeth
1955 **$7.00**

503

Super Circus
Illus.: Timmins, William
Author: Wing, Helen
1955 **$16.00**

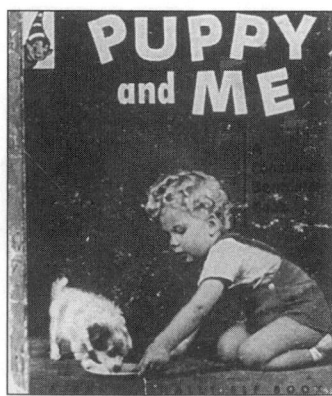

504

Puppy And Me
Illus.: Bannister, Constance
Author: Ratzesberger, Anna
1955 **$7.00**

505

Daniel The Cocker Spaniel
Illus.: Grider, Dorothy
Author: Watts, Mabel
1955 **$10.00**

506

Zippy's Birthday Party
Illus.: Photographs
1955 **$10.00**

507

Puss-In-Boots
Illus.: Myers, Bernice & Lou
1955 **$7.00**

508

Elephant's Child, The: A "Just So" Story
Illus.: Weihs, Erika
1955 $8.00

509

Snoopy, The Nosey Little Puppy
Illus.: Neebe, William
Author: Lieberthal, Jules M.
1955 $10.00

510

Wild Animals
Illus.: Vlasaty, J.L.
Author: Ratzesberger, Anna
1951 $6.00

511

Mr. Bear's House
Illus.: Mc Kinley, Clare
Author: Rothe, Fenella
1953 $8.00

512

One, Two, Cock-A-Doodle-Doo
Illus.: Wosmek, Frances
Author: Pease, Josephine Van Dolzen
1950 $6.00

513

Puss-In-Boots
Illus.: Myers, Bernice & Lou
1955 $6.00

514

Farm Animals
Illus.: Photographs
Author: Hunter, Virginia
1956 $6.00

515

Can't Verify Title

516

Can't Verify Title

517

Can't Verify Title

518

Can't Verify Title

519

Can't Verify Title

520

Can't Verify Title

521

Can't Verify Title

522

Can't Verify Title

523

Davy Crockett: American Hero
Illus.: Timmons, William
1955 $8.00

524

Can't Verify Title

525

Can't Verify Title

526

Can't Verify Title

527

Can't Verify Title

528

Can't Verify Title

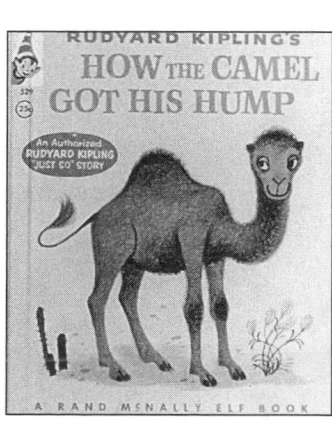

529

How The Camel Got His Hump: "Just So" Story
Illus.: Weihs, Erika
Author: Kipling, Rudyard
1955 $8.00

530

Fussbunny
Illus.: Evers, Helen & Alf
Author: Evers, Helen & Alf
1955 $6.00

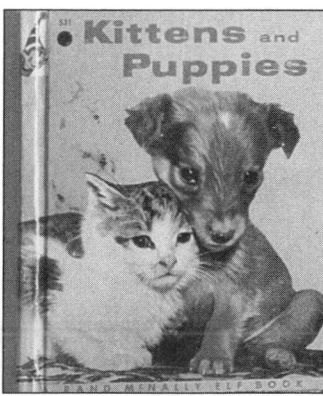

531

Kittens And Puppies
Illus.: Photographs
Author: Burrows, Peggy
1955 $8.00

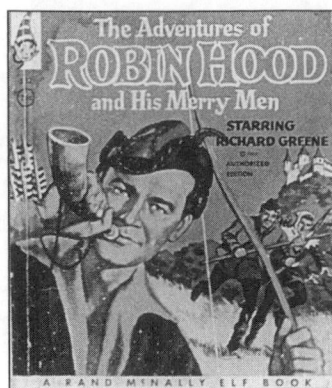

532

Adventures Of Robin Hood And His Merry Men, The
Illus.: Timmins, William
Author: Grant, Bruce Starring Richard Green
1955 $16.00

533

Davy's Little Horse
Illus.: Dennis, Wesley
Author: Devine, Louise Lawrence
1956 $6.00

534

Freight Train
Illus.: Pollard, G.
1956 $8.00

535

Hey, Diddle, Diddle And Other Nonsense Rhymes
Illus.: Botts, Davi
1956 $6.00

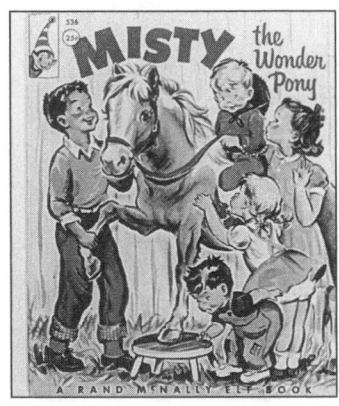

536

Misty The Wonder Pony
Illus.: Mc Kinley, Clare
1956 $8.00

537

Muggsy, The Make-Believe Puppy
Illus.: Webbe, Elizabeth
1956 $10.00

538

Billy Whiskers' Twins
Illus.: Tamburine, Jean
1956 $7.00

539

Farm Babies
Illus.: Photographs
Author: Hunter, Virginia
1956 $6.00

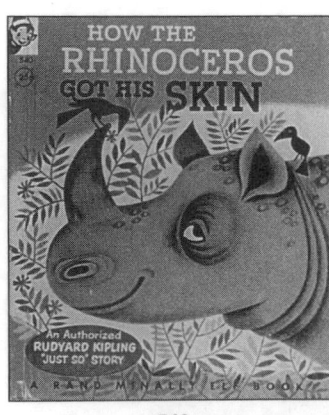

540

How The Rhinoceros Got His Skin: "Just So" Story
Illus.: Weihs, Erika
Author: Kipling, Rudyard
1956 $7.00

541

Dennis The Menace
Illus.: Paplo, Bob
Author: Toole, Fred
1956 $10.00

542

Plump Pig
Illus.: Evers, Helen & Alf
Author: Evers, Helen & Alf
1956 $7.00

543

Ten Commandments For Children, The
Illus.: Bonfils, Robert
Author: Jones, Mary Alice
1956 $6.00

544

Little Lost Kitten: A Story Of Williamsburg
Illus.: Lee, Manning De V
Author: Comfort, Mildred
1956   **$7.00**

545

Goody: A Mother Cat Story
Illus.: Leaf, Anne Sellers
Author: Bertail, Inez
1957   **$6.00**

546

Forest Babies
Illus.: Webbe, Elizabeth
1956   **$6.00**

547

Crybaby Calf
Illus.: Evers, Helen & Alf
1954   **$8.00**

548

Seven Wonderful Cats, The
Illus.: Neebe, William
1956   **$6.00**

549

This Is The World
Illus.: Wood, Ruth
Author: Pease, Josephine
1957   **$5.00**

550

Nonsense ABC's
Illus.: Lear, Edward
1956   **$6.00**

551

Cinderella
Illus.: Endred, Helen; Nebbe, William
Author: Bates, Katherine Lee
1956   **$7.00**

552

Pillowtime Tales
Illus.: Tamburine, Jean
Author: De Groot, Marion K.
1956   **$6.00**

553

Peppy, The Lonely Little Puppy
Illus.: Blake, Vivienne
Author: Friedman, Frieda
1957   **$8.00**

554

Pony Express
Illus.: Timmins, William
Author: Grant, Bruce
1956   **$6.00**

555

Little Boy Blue And Other Nursery Rhymes
Illus.: Leaf, Anne Sellers
1956   **$6.00**

556

Little Miss Muffet And Other Nursery Rhymes
Illus.: Chase, Mary Jane
1956 $6.00

557

Mr. Punnymoon's Train
Illus.: Phillips, Katherine L.
Author: Hadsell, Alice
1951 $15.00

558

Teddy The Terrier
Illus.: Latimer, Constance; Love, Mary
Author: Hunter, Virginia
1956 $9.00

559

Mr. Wizard's Junior Science Show
Illus.: Bonfils, Robert
Author: Thayer, Ruth Hubley
1957 $8.00

560

Growing Up
Illus.: Webbe, Elizabeth
Author: Fritz, Webbe
1956 $5.00

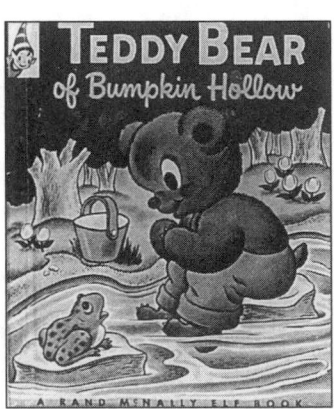

561

Teddy Bear Of Bumpkin Hollow
Illus.: Bryant, Dean
Author: Boucher, Sharon
1948 $10.00

562

Surprise!
Illus.: Ozone, Lucy
Author: Ozone, Lucy
1956 $6.00

563

Our Animal Friends
Illus.: Photographs
Author: Hunter, Virginia
1956 $6.00

564

Buddy, The Little Taxi
Illus.: Corwin, Elizabeth
Author: Grider, Dorothy
1951 $8.00

565

Hiawatha
Illus.: Wilde, Irma
Author: Gridley, Marion E.
1950 $10.00

566

Four Little Kittens
Illus.: Frees, Harry Whittier
Author: Dixon, Ruth
1957 $6.00

567

Busy Bulldozer, The
Illus.: Grider, Dorothy
Author: Browning, James
1952 $6.00

568
Santa's Rocket Sleigh
Illus.: Webbe, Elizabeth
Author: Storch, Florence
1957 **$10.00**

569
Sergeant Preston And Rex
Illus.: Neebe, William
1956 **$16.00**

570
Wild Bill Hickok And The Indians
Illus.: Timmons, William
Author: Stone, Ethel B.
1956 **$18.00**

571
Wynken, Blynken And Nod And Other Nursery Rhymes
Illus.: Mc Kinley, Clare
1956 **$6.00**

572
Goody Naughty Book
Illus.: Prickett, Helen
Author: Watts, Mabel
1956 **$6.00**

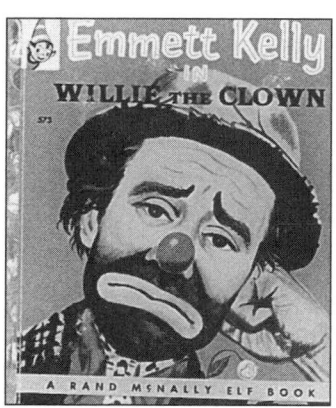

573
Emmett Kelly In Willie The Clown
Illus.: Timmins, William
Author: Wing, Helen
1957 **$18.00**

574
Bunny Tales
Illus.: Endred, Helen; Nebbe, William
Author: Burroes, Peggy
1956 **$7.00**

575
Pocahontas, A Little Indian Girl Of Jamestown
Illus.: Lee, Manning De V
Author: Cavanah, Frances
1957 **$7.00**

576
Amos Learns To Talk: The Story Of A Little Duck
Illus.: Mc Kinley, Clare
Author: Bradbury, Bianca
1958 **$10.00**

577
Enchanted Egg, The
Illus.: Webbe, Elizabeth
Author: Burrows, Peggy
1956 **$7.00**

578
Four Little Puppies
Illus.: Frees, Harry Whittier
Author: Dixon, Ruth
1957 **$6.00**

579
Kerry, The Fire-Engine Dog
Illus.: Grider, Dorothy
Author: Lewis, Frank; Corchia, Alfred J.
1949 **$10.00**

580
Little Lost Angel
Illus.: Scott, Janet Laura
Author: Heath, Janet Field
1953 **$10.00**

581

Chester, The Little Pony
Illus.: Mc Kinley, Clare
Author: Gunder. Eman
1951   **$8.00**

582

Slowpoke, The Lazy Little Puppy
Illus.: Neebe, William
Author: Lieberthal
1957   **$6.00**

583

Three Billy Goats Gruff, The
Illus.: Neebe, William
Author: O'Grady, Alice; Throop,
Frances
1957   **$6.00**

584

Copy-Kitten
Illus.: Evers, Helen & Alf
1954   **$7.00**

585

Number 9 The Little Fire Engine
Illus.: Corwin, Eleanor
Author: Wadsworth, Wallace
1950   **$10.00**

586

Day On The Farm, A
Illus.: Grider, Dorothy
Author: Evers, Alf
1948   **$6.00**

587

Hide-Away Puppy
Illus.: Dottie
Author: Broderick, Jessica Potter
1952   **$6.00**

588

Moving Day
Illus.: Grider, Dorothy
Author: Conmfort, Mildred
1958   **$6.00**

589

Three Little Bunnies
Illus.: Rooks, Dale & Sally
Author: Dixon, Ruth
1950   **$6.00**

590

**Little Mailman Of Bayberry Lane,
The**
Illus.: Webbe, Elizabeth
Author: Munn, Ian
1952   **$15.00**

591

Parakeet Peter
Illus.: Grider, Dorothy
Author: Sprinkle, Rebecca K.
1954   **$6.00**

592

Lucinda, The Little Donkey
Illus.: Wilde, George
Author: Wilde, Irma
1952   **$6.00**

593

**Little Friends: Kittens, Puppies,
Bunnies**
Illus.: Gaddis, Rie
Author: Dixon, Ruth
1951   **$8.00**

594
Goat That Went To School, The
Illus.: Tamburine, Jean
Author: Francis, Sally R.
1952 $6.00

595
Bedtime Stories
Illus.: Clyne, Barbara
Author: Watts, Mabel
1955 $6.00

596
Farm For Andy, A
Illus.: Gayer, Marguerite
1951 $6.00
597
Bartholomew The Beaver
Illus.: Pierce, Alice
Author: Dixon, Ruth
1952 $6.00

598
Three Little Puppies
Illus.: Rooks, Dale & Sally
Author: Dixon, Ruth
1951 $6.00

599
Cowboy Eddie
Illus.: Grider, Dorothy
Author: Glasscock, Joyce
1950 $10.00

1001
Jack And Jill
Illus.: Leaf, Anne Sellers
1958 $7.00

1002
Dennis The Menace Camps Out
Illus.: Ketchum, Hank
1958 $9.00

1003
Little Ballerina
Illus.: Grider, Dorothy
Author: Grider, Dorothy
1958 $6.00

1004
Cowboys
Illus.: Timmins, William
1958 $5.00

1005
Snuggles
Illus.: Frees, Harry Whittier
Author: Dixon, Ruth
1958 $6.00

1006
What Happened To George?
Illus.: Opitz, Marge
Author: Engebretson, Betty
1958 $6.00

1007
Old Mother Hubbard
Illus.: Leaf, Anne Sellers
1958 $7.00

1008
Johnny And The Birds
Illus.: Webbe, Elizabeth
Author: Munn, Ian
1950 $5.00

1009
Can't Verify Title

1010
Can't Verify Title

1011
Can't Verify Title

1012
Can't Verify Title

1013
Can't Verify Title

1014
Kitten Twins, The
Illus.: Webbe, Elizabeth
Author: Wing, Helen
1960 $5.00

1015
Can't Verify Title

1016
Can't Verify Title

1017
Can't Verify Title

1018
Can't Verify Title

1019
Aesop's Fables
Illus.: Leaf, Anne Sellers
1958 $6.00

1020
Noah's Ark
Illus.: Webbe, Elizabeth
Author: Briggs, Dorothy Bell
1952 $5.00

1021
Moonymouse
Illus.: Evers, Helen & Alf
1958 $8.00

1022
Yip And Yap
Illus.: Frees, Harry Whittier
Author: Dixon, Ruth
1958 $5.00

1023
Penny And Pete's Surprise
Illus.: Mc Kinley, Clare
1949 $6.00

1024
Children That Lived In A Shoe, The
Illus.: Webbe, Elizabeth
Author: Pease, Josephine Van
Dolzen
1951 $5.00

1025
Pets
Illus.: Webbe, Elizabeth
Author: Ratzesberger, Anna
1954 $3.00

1026
Little Bobo And His Blue Jacket
Illus.: Brice, Tony
Author: Evers, Alf
1953 $6.00

1027
Bugle, A Puppy In Old Yorktown
Illus.: Lee, Manning De V
Author: Andrews, Mary
1958 $4.00

1028
Mother Goose
Illus.: Friend, Esther
194 $5.00

1029
Storybook For Little Tots
Illus.: Devine, Louise Lawrence
Author: Hunter, Virginia
1958 $4.00

1030
Can't Verify Title

1031
Three Bears Visit Goldilocks, The
Illus.: Mc Kinley, Clare
Author: Rarick, Carrie
1950 $10.00

1032
ABC Book
Illus.: Bryant, Dean
1958 $4.00

1033
Can't Verify Title

1034
Choo-Choo, The Little Switch Engine
Illus.: Chase, Mary Jane
Author: Wadsworth, Wallace
1954 $5.00

1035
Old Woman And Her Pig, The
Illus.: Friend, Esther
Author: Wadsworth, Wallace
1952 $4.00

1036
So Long
Illus.: Evers, Helen & Alf
1958 $5.00

1037
Little Red Riding-Hood
Illus.: Leaf, Anne Sellers
1958 $7.00

1038
Busy Book, The (Rhymes & Riddles & Things To Do)
Illus.: Szepelak, Helen
Author: Bartlett, Floy; Pease, Josephine
1952 $5.00

1039
Smart Little Mouse, The
Illus.: Phillips, Katherine L.
Author: Sherwan, Earl
1950 $5.00

8300
Mother Goose
Illus.: Friend, Esther
1947 $5.00

8300
Mother Goose
(2nd Cover)
Illus.: Friend, Esther
1947 $5.00

8301
Kittens And Puppies
Illus.: Photographs
Author: Burrows, Peggy
1955 $6.00

8302
Little Miss Muffet And Other Nursery Rhymes
Illus.: Chase, Mary Jane
1956 $5.00

8302

Little Miss Muffet And Other Nursery Rhymes
(2nd Cover)
Illus.: Chase, Mary Jane
1956 $5.00

8303

Popcorn Party
Illus.: Szepelak, Helen
Author: Boyles, Trudy; Macmartin, Louise
1952 $8.00

8303

Popcorn Party
(2nd Cover)
Illus.: Szepelak, Helen
Author: Boyles, Trudy; Macmartin, Louise
1952 $6.00

8304

Hey, Diddle, Diddle And Other Nonsense Rhymes
Illus.: Botts, Davi
1956 $5.00

8305

Peppy, The Lonely Little Puppy
Illus.: Blake, Vivienne
Author: Friedman, Frieda
195                    $6.00

8306

Zippy The Chimp
Illus.: Mitchell, Benn
Author: Ecuyer, Lee
1953 $7.00

8306

Zippy The Chimp
(2nd Cover)
Illus.: Mitchell, Benn
Author: Ecuyer, Lee
1953 $7.00

8307

Hiawatha
Illus.: Wilde, Irma
Author: Gridley, Marion E.
1950 $6.00

8308

Teddy The Terrier
Illus.: Latimer, Constance; Love, Mary
Author: Hunter, Virginia
1956 $5.00

8309

Plump Pig
Illus.: Evers, Helen & Alf
Author: Evers, Helen & Alf
1956 $7.00

8310

Goody: A Mother Cat Story
Illus.: Leaf, Anne Sellers
Author: Bertail, Inez
1957 $5.00

8311

Little Kittens' Nursery Rhymes, The
Illus.: Frees, Harry Whittier
1941 $5.00

8312

House That Jack Built, The
Illus.: Leaf, Anne Sellers
1959 $6.00

8313
Three Bears, The
Illus.: Webbe, Elizabeth
1959 $5.00

8314
Funny Hat, The
Illus.: Grider, Dorothy
Author: Barrows, Marjorie
1959 $5.00

8315
Elves And The Shoemaker, The
Illus.: Lee, Manning De V
1959 $5.00

8316
Helpful Henrietta
Illus.: Caraway, James
Author: Watts, Mabel
1959 $5.00

8317
Mommy Cat And Her Kittens
Illus.: Rockwell, Eve
Author: Devine, Louise Lawrence
1959 $7.00

8318
Rumpelstiltskin
Illus.: Webbe, Elizabeth
1959 $5.00

8319
Fraidy Cat
Illus.: Tamburine, Jean
Author: Barrows, Marjorie
1959 $5.00

8320
Sleeping Beauty
Illus.: Webbe, Elizabeth
1959 $5.00

8321
Tubby Turtle
Illus.: Adler, Helen
Author: Wing, Helen
1959 $5.00

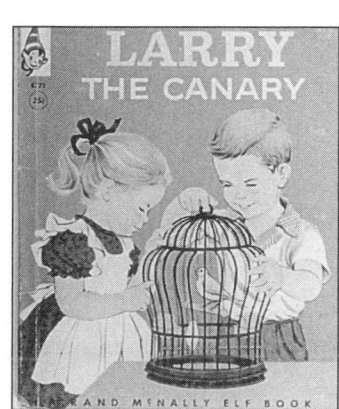

8322
Larry The Canary
Illus.: Koester, Sharon
Author: Wilkie, Ellen
1959 $5.00

8323
Tom Thumb
Illus.: Wallace, Lucille
1959 $5.00

8324
Timothy Tiger
Illus.: Wilde, Irma
1959 $5.00

8325

Trucks
Illus.: Wilde, George
Author: Reichert, E.C.
1959 **$5.00**

8326

Scamper
Illus.: Tamburine, Jean
1959 **$5.00**

8327

Ugly Duckling, The
Illus.: Opitz, Marge
1959 **$5.00**

8328

Forest Babies
Illus.: Webbe, Elizabeth
1956 **$5.00**

8329

Farm Friends
Illus.: Photographs
Author: Hunter, Virginia
1956 **$5.00**

8330

Playtime Poodles
Illus.: Westelin, Albert; Schmidling,
Jack
Author: Wing, Helen
1955 **$7.00**

8331

Daniel The Cocker Spaniel
Illus.: Grider, Dorothy
Author: Watts, Mabel
1955 **$8.00**

8332

My Happy Day: A Word Book
Illus.: Bruce, Suzanne
Author: Shaw, Thelma
1963 **$5.00**

8333

Billy Whiskers' Twins
Illus.: Tamburine, Jean
1956 **$5.00**

8334

Teddy Bear Of Bumpkin Hollow
Illus.: Bryant, Dean
Author: Boucher, Sharon
1948 **$8.00**

8335

Four Little Puppies
Illus.: Frees, Harry Whittier
Author: Dixon, Ruth
1957 **$5.00**

8335

Four Little Puppies
(2nd Cover)
Illus.: Frees, Harry Whittier
Author: Dixon, Ruth
1957 **$5.00**

8336
Four Little Kittens
Illus.: Frees, Harry Whittier
Author: Dixon, Ruth
1957 **$5.00**

8337
Farm Animals
Illus.: Photographs
Author: Hunter, Virginia
1956 **$5.00**

8338
Pillowtime Tales
Illus.: Tamburine, Jean
Author: De Groot, Marion K.
1956 **$5.00**

8339
Our Auto Trip
Illus.: Grider, Dorothy
Author: Edsall, Marian
1952 **$5.00**

8340
Snuggles
Illus.: Frees, Harry Whittier
Author: Dixon, Ruth
1958 **$5.00**

8341
Cowboys
Illus.: Timmins, William
1958 **$5.00**

8342
So Long
Illus.: Evers, Helen & Alf
1958 **$5.00**

8343
Happy Holidays
Illus.: Bruce, Suzanne
Author: Reichert, E.C.
1953 **$5.00**

8344
Pony Express
Illus.: Timmons, William
Author: Grant, Bruce
1956 **$5.00**

8345
Animal ABC Book
Illus.: Kane, Herbert
1964 **$0.00**

8346
Sleepy-Time Rhymes
Illus.: Szepelak, Helen
Author: Smith, Goldie Capers
1964 **$5.00**

8347
Little Horseman
Illus.: Grider, Dorothy
1961 **$4.00**

8348
Wild Animals
Illus.: Vlasaty, J.L.
Author: Ratzesberger, Anna
1951 **$5.00**

8348
Wild Animals
(2nd Cover)
Illus.: Vlasaty, J.L.
Author: Ratzesberger, Anna
1951 **$5.00**

8349

Mr. Bear's House
Illus.: Mc Kinley, Clare
Author: Rothe, Fenella
1953   **$6.00**

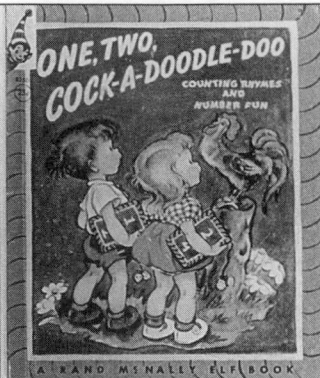

8350

One, Two, Cock-A-Doodle-Doo
Illus.: Wosmek, Frances
Author: Pease, Josephine Van Dolzen
1950   **$5.00**

8351

Buddy, The Little Taxi
Illus.: Corwin, Elizabeth
Author: Grider, Dorothy
1951   **$6.00**

8352

Amos Learns To Talk: The Story Of A Little Duck
Illus.: Mc Kinley, Clare
Author: Bradbury, Bianca
1950   **$5.00**

8352

Amos Learns To Talk: The Story Of A Little Duck
(2nd Cover)
Illus.: Mc Kinley, Clare
Author: Bradbury, Bianca
1950   **$5.00**

8353

Kerry, The Fire-Engine Dog
Illus.: Grider, Dorothy
Author: Lewis, Frank; Corchia, Alfred J.
1949   **$8.00**

8354

Chester, The Little Pony
Illus.: Mc Kinley, Clare
Author: Gunder. Eman
1951   **$6.00**

8354

Chester, The Little Pony
(2nd Cover)
Illus.: Mc Kinley, Clare
Author: Gunder. Eman
1951   **$5.00**

8355

Bedtime Stories
Illus.: Clyne, Barbara
Author: Watts, Mabel
1955   **$5.00**

8356

Puss-In-Boots
Illus.: Myers, Bernice & Lou
1955   **$5.00**

8357

Hide-Away Puppy
Illus.: Dottie
Author: Broderick, Jessica Potter
1952   **$5.00**

8358

Farm For Andy, A
Illus.: Gayer, Marguerite
1951   **$5.00**

8359

Can't Verify Title

8360

Day On The Farm, A
Illus.: Grider, Dorothy
Author: Evers, Alf
1948   **$5.00**

8361

Little Mailman Of Bayberry Lane, The
Illus.: Webbe, Elizabeth
Author: Munn, Ian
1952   **$10.00**

8362
Lucinda, The Little Donkey
Illus.: Wilde, George
Author: Wilde, Irma
1952 $5.00

8362
Lucinda, The Little Donkey
Illus.: Wilde, George
Author: Wilde, Irma
1952 $5.00

8363
Three Little Puppies
Illus.: Rooks, Dale & Sally
Author: Dixon, Ruth
1951 $5.00

8364
ABC Book
Illus.: Bryant, Dean
1958 $5.00

8365
Hansel And Gretel
Illus.: Smith, Kay Lovelace
1960 $4.00

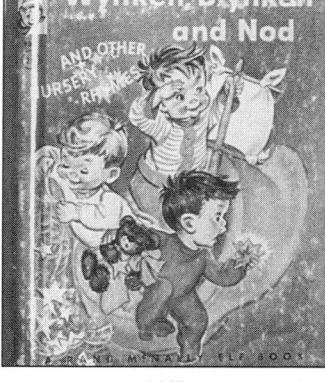

8366
Little Boy Blue And Other Nursery Rhymes
Illus.: Leaf, Anne Sellers
1956 $5.00

8367
Wynken, Blynken And Nod And Other Nursery Rhymes
Illus.: Mc Kinley, Clare
1956 $5.00

8368
Three Billy Goats Gruff, The
Illus: Neebe, William
Author: O'Grady, Alice; Throop, Frances
1957 $5.00

8369
Number 9 The Little Fire Engine
Illus.: Corwin, Eleanor
Author: Wadsworth, Wallace
1950 $6.00

8370
Copy-Kitten
Illus.: Evers, Helen & Alf
1957 $5.00

8371
Where From?
Illus.: Smith, E
1961 $5.00

8372
Jack And The Beanstalk
Illus.: Leaf, Anne Sellers
1961 $6.00

8373
Angel Child
Illus.: Doane, Pelagie
Author: Teal, Val
1946 $6.00

8374

Parakeet Peter
Illus.: Grider, Dorothy
Author: Sprinkle, Rebecca K.
1954 $4.00

8375

Busy Bulldozer, The
Illus.: Grider, Dorothy
Author: Browning, James
1952 $4.00

8376

Little Lost Angel
Illus.: Scott, Janet Laura
Author: Heath, Janet Field
1953 $8.00

8377

Johnny And The Birds
Illus.: Webbe, Elizabeth
Author: Munn, Ian
1950 $4.00

8378

Little Bobo And His Blue Jacket
Illus.: Brice, Tony
Author: Evers, Alf
1953 $5.00

8379

Old Woman And Her Pig, The
Illus.: Friend, Esther
Author: Wadsworth, Wallace
1952 $5.00

8380

Yip And Yap
Illus.: Frees, Harry Whittier
Author: Dixon, Ruth
1958 $4.00

8381

Squirrel Twins, The
Illus.: Webbe, Elizabeth
Author: Wing, Helen
1961 $4.00

8382

My Flower Book
Illus.: Webbe, Elizabeth
Author: Landis, Dorothy Thompson
1961 $5.00

8383

Rip Van Winkle
Illus.: Leaf, Anne Sellers
Author: Briggs, Dorothy Bell
1961 $6.00

8384

Surprise!
Illus.: Ozone, Lucy
Author: Ozone, Lucy
1956 $4.00

8385

Goody Naughty Book
Illus.: Prickett, Helen
Author: Watts, Mabel
1956 $4.00

8386
Goat That Went To School, The
Illus.: Tamburine, Jean
Author: Francis, Sally R.
1952 **$4.00**

8387
Davy's Little Horse
Illus.: Dennis, Wesley
Author: Devine, Louise Lawrence
1956 **$4.00**

8388
Three Little Bunnies
Illus.: Rooks, Dale & Sally
Author: Dixon, Ruth
1950 **$4.00**

8389
Little Skater
Illus.: Grider, Dorothy
Author: Sherman, Diane
1959 **$6.00**

8390
Little Ballerina
Illus.: Grider, Dorothy
Author: Grider, Dorothy
1958 **$6.00**

8391
Children That Lived In A Shoe, The
Illus.: Webbe, Elizabeth
Author: Pease, Josephine Van Dolzen
1951 **$4.00**

8392
Pets
Illus.: Webbe, Elizabeth
Author: Ratzesberger, Anna
1954 **$4.00**

8393
Storybook For Little Tots
Illus.: Chase, Mary Jane
Author: Hunter, Virginia
1958 **$4.00**

8394
Choo-Choo, The Little Switch Engine
Illus.: Chase, Mary Jane
Author: Wadsworth, Wallace
1954 **$4.00**

8395
Jack And Jill
Illus.: Leaf, Anne Sellers
1958 **$6.00**

8396
Penny And Pete's Surprise
Illus.: Mc Kinley, Clare
1949 **$4.00**

8397
Growing Up
Illus.: Webbe, Elizabeth
Author: Fritz, Webbe
1956 **$4.00**

8398
Story Of Our Flag, The
Illus.: Wilde, Irma
1955 $4.00

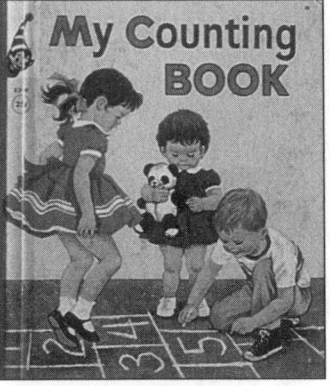

8399
My Counting Book
Illus.: Koester, Sharon
Author: Sherman, Diane
1960 $4.00

8400
Moonymouse
Illus.: Evers, Helen & Alf
1958 $6.00

8401
Three Bears Visit Goldilocks, The
Illus.: Mc Kinley, Clare
Author: Rarick, Carrie
1950 $6.00

8402
Busy Book, The (Rhymes & Riddles & Things To Do)
Illus.: Szepelak, Helen
Author: Bartlett, Floy; Pease, Josephine
1952 $4.00

8403
Our Animal Friends
Illus.: Photographs
Author: Hunter, Virginia
1956 $4.00

8404
Five Busy Bears, The
Illus.: Tamburine, Jean
Author: North, Sterling
1955 $4.00

8405
Fussbunny
Illus.: Evers, Helen & Alf
Author: Evers, Helen & Alf
1955 $4.00

8406
Bunny Tales
Illus.: Endred, Helen; Nebbe, William
Author: Burroes, Peggy
1956 $4.00

8407
Enchanted Egg, The
Illus.: Webbe, Elizabeth
Author: Burrows. Peggy
1956 $5.00

8408
Little Friends: Kittens, Puppies, Bunnies
Illus.: Gaddis, Rie
Author: Dixon, Ruth
1951 $5.00

8409
What Happened To George?
Illus.: Opitz, Marge
Author: Engebretson, Betty
1958 $6.00

8410
Little Majorette
Illus.: Grider, Dorothy
Author: Grider, Dorothy
1959 $4.00

8411

Seven Wonderful Cats, The
Illus.: Neebe, William
1956   **$4.00**

8412

Johnny The Fireman
Illus.: Wood, Ruth
Author: Sprinkle, Rebecca K.
1954   **$8.00**

8413

Old Mother Hubbard
Illus.: Leaf, Anne Sellers
1958   **$6.00**

8414

Freight Train
Illus.: Pollard, G.
1956   **$6.00**

8415

Mr. Punnymoon's Train
Illus.: Phillips, Katherine L.
Author: Hadsell, Alice
1951   **$6.00**

8416

Little Swimmers
Illus.: Grider, Dorothy
Author: Grider, Dorothy
1960   **$6.00**

8417

Cinderella
Illus.: Endred, Helen; Neebe, William
Author: Bates, Katherine Lee
1956   **$4.00**

8418

Cowboy Eddie
Illus.: Grider, Dorothy
Author: Glasscock, Joyce
1950   **$6.00**

8419

Little Red Riding-Hood
Illus.: Leaf, Anne Sellers
1958   **$6.00**

8420

Puppy Twins, The
Illus.: Bendel, Ruth
Author: Wing, Helen
1959   **$4.00**

8421

Smart Little Mouse, The
Illus.: Phillips, Katherine L.
Author: Sherwan, Earl
1950   **$4.00**

8422

Kitten Twins, The
Illus.: Webbe, Elizabeth
Author: Wing, Helen
1960   **$4.00**

8423

Bartholomew The Beaver
Illus.: Pierce, Alice
Author: Dixon, Ruth
1952 $4.00

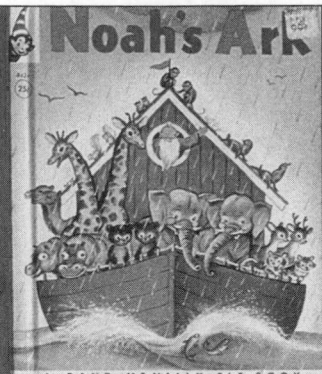

8424

Noah's Ark
Illus.: Webbe, Elizabeth
Author: Briggs, Dorothy Bell
1952 $4.00

8425

Present For The Princess, A
Illus.: Webbe, Elizabeth
Author: Paschall, Janie Lowe
1959 $8.00

8426

Crybaby Calf
Illus.: Evers, Helen & Alf
1954 $6.00

8427

Twilight Tales
Illus.: Bryant, Dean
Author: Potter, Miriam Clark
1947 $4.00

8428

Bunny Twins, The
Illus.: Cooper, Marjorie
Author: Wing, Helen
1964 $4.00

8429

Pony Twins, The
Illus.: Cooper, Marjorie
Author: Wing, Helen
1964 $4.00

8430

Three Pigs, The
Illus.: Storytoon Express
1962 $8.00

8431

Tortoise And The Hare, The
Illus.: Storytoon Express
1962 $8.00

8432

Sugarplum Tree, The
Illus.: Storytoon Express
1962 $8.00

8433

Magic Pot, The
Illus.: Storytoon Express
1962 $8.00

8434

Silly Joe
Illus.: Storytoon Express
Author: Storytoon Express
1962 $8.00

8435

Lazy Jack
Illus.: Storytoon Express
Author: Storytoon Express
1962 $8.00

8436

Early One Morning
Illus.: Cooper, Marjorie
Author: Graland, Valerie
1963 $5.00

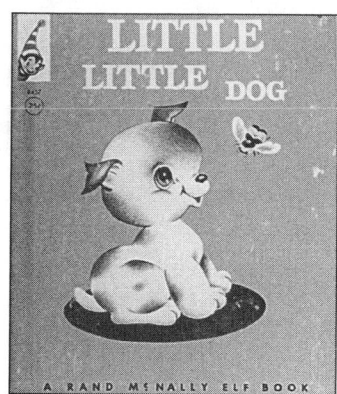

8437
Little Little Dog
Illus.: Adler, Helen
Author: Brailsford, Frances
1963 **$4.00**

8438
Garden Is Good, A
Illus.: Cooper, Marjorie
Author: Chaffin, Lillie D.
1963 **$4.00**

8439
Little Campers
Illus.: Grider, Dorothy
Author: Watts, Mabel
1963 **$4.00**

8440
Aesop's Fables
Illus.: Leaf, Anne Sellers
1952 **$5.00**

8441
Pudgy The Little Bear
Illus.: Tamburine, Jean
Author: Barrows, Marjorie
1964 **$4.00**

8442
Crosspatch
Illus.: Evers, Helen & Alf
Author: Evers, Helen & Alf
1964 **$4.00**

8443
Baby Sister
Illus.: Cooper, Marjorie
Author: Grayland, Valerie
1964 **$5.00**

8444
Muggins Mouse
Illus.: Leaf, Anne Sellers
Author: Barrows, Marjorie
1964 **$7.00**

8445
Little Cub Scout
Illus.: Timmins, William
Author: Watts, Mabel
1964 **$6.00**
8446
Can't Verify Title

8447
Muggins' Big Balloon
Illus.: Leaf, Anne Sellers
Author: Barrow, Marjorie
1964 **$7.00**
8448
Muggins Becomes A Hero
Illus.: Leaf, Anne Sellers
1965 **$7.00**

8449
Volksy: The Little Yellow Car
Illus.: Chase, Mary Jane
Author: Wing, Helen
1965 **$9.00**

8450
Jo Jo
Illus.: Wallace, Ivy L.
Author: Barrows, Marjorie
1964 **$4.00**

8451

Pokey Bear
Illus.: Evers, Helen & Alf
Author: Evers, Helen & Alf
1965   **$5.00**

8452

**Pink Lemonade
(And Other Peter Patter Rhymes)**
Illus.: Grider, Dorothy
Author: Jackson, Leroy F.
1965   **$4.00**

8453

Teddy Bear Twins, The
Illus.: Cooper, Marjorie
Author: Wing, Helen
1965   **$7.00**

8455

Princess And The Pea, The
    $6.00

8454

Can't Verify Title

8456

Jeepers, The Little Frog
Illus.: Cooper, Marjorie
Author: Cooper, Marjorie
1965   **$4.00**

8457

Gingerbread Man, The
Illus.: Leaf, Anne Sellers
1965   **$7.00**

8458

Rocket For A Cow, A
Illus.: Wilde, Irma
Author: Devine, Louise Lawerence
1965   **$6.00**

8459

Animal Show, The
Illus.: Grider, Dorothy
Author: Jackson, Leroy F.
1965   **$4.00**

8460

Happy Twins, The
Illus.: Cooper, Marjorie
Author: Wing, Helen
1956   **$4.00**

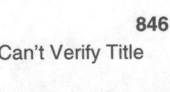

8461

Can't Verify Title

8462

Three Little Kittens
Illus.: Cooper, Marjorie
1966   **$4.00**

8549

People Who Work At Night
Illus.: Sherman, Diane
Author: Doremus, Robert
1973   **$4.00**

8550

From Tadpoles To Frogs
1973   **$4.00**

8551

Busy Ants, The
Illus.: Street, T.
1973   **$4.00**

8552
Building A Skyscraper
Illus.: Frame, Paul
Author: Kozak, Louis Lawrence
1973 $4.00

8553
Alphabet Walks
Illus.: Stahlman, Catherine
Author: Petie, Haris
1973 $4.00

8554
Homes In The City
Illus.: Frame, Paul
Author: Bartkowski, Renee
1973 $4.00

8555
My First Book Of Jesus
      $4.00

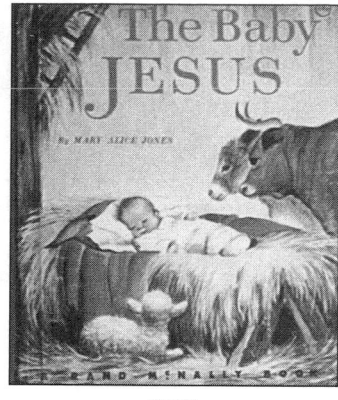

8556
Baby Jesus, The
Illus.: Webbe, Elizabeth
Author: Jones, Mary Alice
1961 $4.00

8557
Prayers For Little Children
Illus.: Bruce, Suzanne
Author: Jones, Mary Alice
1959 $4.00

8558
Look For A Rainbow
Illus.: Cooper, Marjorie
1972 $4.00

8559
Honeybee, The
Illus.: Street, Theodore
Author: Farley, Karin Clafford
1972 $4.00

8560
Billy's Treasure
Illus.: Grider, Dorothy
Author: Snow, Dorothea J.
1972 $4.00

8561
Turtles Turn Up On Tuesday
Illus.: Frame, Paul
Author: Shaw, Thelma
1972 $4.00

8562
Time For Everything
Illus.: Kane, Sharon
1972 $4.00

8563
Who Wants A Pop Can Park?
Illus.: Leaf, Anne Sellers
Author: Bartkowski, Renee
1972 $8.00

8564
Can't Verify Title

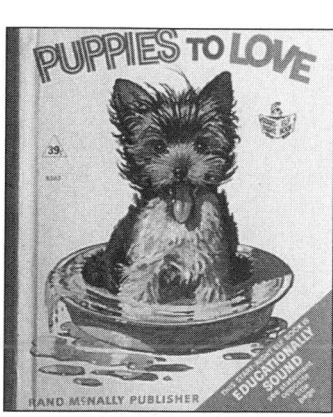

8565
Puppies To Love
Illus.: Lougheed, Robert
Author: Wing, Helen
1971 $4.00

8566

Trip In Space, A
Illus.: Fleishman, Seymour
Author: Grant, Bruce
1968   **$6.00**

8567

Emperor's New Clothes, The
Illus.: Leaf, Anne Sellers
1968   **$7.00**

8568

Looking In And Other Poems
Illus.: Grider, Dorothy
Author: Aldis, Dorothy
1968   **$4.00**

8569

Lion And The Mouse, The
Illus.: Blake, Vivienne
Author: Duff, Emma Lorne
1968   **$4.00**

8570

One, Two, Cock-A-Doodle-Doo
Illus.: Wosmek, Frances
Author: Pease, Josephine Van
Dolzen
1950   **$4.00**

8571

Let's Grow Things
Illus.: Wilde, Irma
Author: Comfort, Iris Tracy
1967   **$4.00**

8572

Hop-Away Joey
Illus.: Fleishman, Seymour
Author: Broderick, Jessica Potter
1967   **$5.00**

8573

Puss-In-Boots
Illus.: Myers, Bernice & Lou
1955   **$4.00**

8574

Read Me Some Poems
Illus.: Cooper, Marjorie
1968   **$4.00**

8575

Bronto The Dinosaur
Illus.: Wilde, George
Author: Landis, Dorothy Thompson
1967   **$4.00**

8576

Chatterduck
Illus.: Evers, Helen & Alf
Author: Evers, Helen & Alf
1967   **$5.00**

8577

Our World Of Color And Sound
Illus.: Cooper, Marjorie
Author: Bartkowski, Renee
1967   **$4.00**

8578
Farmer In The Dell, The
Illus.: Kane, Sharon
1967   **$7.00**

8579
Cap That Mother Made, The
Illus.: Friend, Esther
Author: O'grady, Alice; Throop, Frances
1967   **$4.00**

8580
Snow-White And Rose-Red
Illus.: Cooper, Marjorie
1967   **$4.00**

8581
Can't Verify Title

8582
Three Little Kittens
Illus.: Cooper, Marjorie
1966   **$4.00**

8583
Surprise!
Illus.: Ozone, Lucy
Author: Ozone, Lucy
1956   **$4.00**

8584
Lucinda, The Little Donkey
Illus.: Wilde, George
Author: Wilde, Irma
1952   **$4.00**

8585
Can't Verify Title

8586
Day On The Farm, A
Illus.: Grider, Dorothy
Author: Evers, Alf
1948   **$4.00**

8587
Hide-Away Puppy
Illus.: Dottie
Author: Broderick, Jessica Potter
1952   **$4.00**

8588
Billy Whiskers' Twins
Illus.: Tamburine, Jean
1956   **$0.00**

8589
Daniel The Cocker Spaniel
Illus.: Grider, Dorothy
Author: Watts, Mabel
1955   **$5.00**

8590
Ugly Duckling, The
Illus.: Opitz, Marge
1959   **$4.00**

8591
Can't Verify Title

8592
Plump Pig
Illus.: Evers, Helen & Alf
Author: Evers, Helen & Alf
1956   **$4.00**

8593
Goody Naughty Book
Illus.: Prickett, Helen
Author: Watts, Mabel
1956   **$4.00**

8594

Goat That Went To School, The
Illus.: Tamburine, Jean
Author: Francis, Sally R.
1952 $4.00

8595

Bedtime Stories
Illus.: Clyne, Barbara
Author: Watts, Mabel
1955 $4.00

8596

Happy Holidays
Illus.: Bruce, Suzanne
Author: Reichert, E.C.
1953 $5.00

8597

Four Little Puppies
Illus.: Frees, Harry Whittier
Author: Dixon, Ruth
1957 $3.00

8598

Peaky Beaky
Illus.: Oeshsli, Kelly
1967 $5.00

8599

Gingerbread Man, The
Illus.: Leaf, Anne Sellers
1965 $6.00

8600

Little Lost Kitten: A Story Of Williamsburg
Illus.: Lee, Manning De V
Author: Comfort, Mildred
1956 $4.00

8601

Pocahontas, A Little Indian Girl Of Jamestown
Illus.: Lee, Manning De V
Author: Cavanah, Frances
1957 $4.00

8602

Present For The Princess, A
Illus.: Webbe, Elizabeth
Author: Paschall, Janie Lowe
1959 $5.00

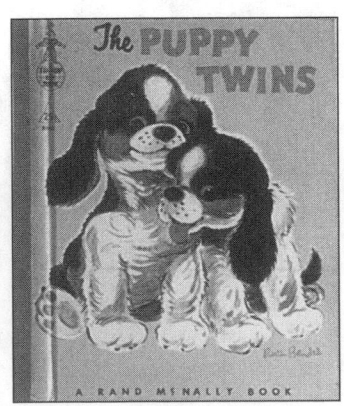

8603

Puppy Twins, The
Illus.: Bendel, Ruth
Author: Wing, Helen
1959 $4.00

8604

Ten Commandments For Children, The
Illus.: Bonfils, Robert
Author: Jones, Mary Alice
1956 $4.00

8604

Ten Commandments For Children, The
(2nd Cover)
Illus.: Bonfils, Robert
Author: Jones, Mary Alice
1956 $4.00

8605

Little Majorette
Illus.: Grider, Dorothy
Author: Grider, Dorothy
1959   **$4.00**

8606

Crybaby Calf
Illus.: Evers, Helen & Alf
1954   **$5.00**

8607

Seven Wonderful Cats, The
Illus.: Neebe, William
1956   **$4.00**

8608

Twilight Tales
Illus.: Bryant, Dean
Author: Potter, Miriam Clark
1947   **$4.00**

8608

Twilight Tales
(2nd Cover)
Illus.: Bryant, Dean
Author: Potter, Miriam Clark
1947   **$4.00**

8609

Prayers And Graces For A Small Child
Illus.: Webbe, Elizabeth
Author: Webbe, Elizabeth
1955   **$4.00**

8610

Little Skater
Illus.: Grider, Dorothy
Author: Sherman, Diane
1959   **$4.00**

8611

Johnny The Fireman
Illus.: Wood, Ruth
Author: Sprinkle, Rebecca K.
1954   **$6.00**

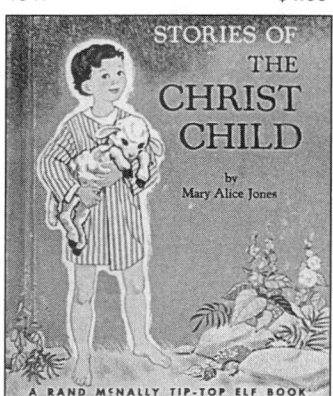

8612

Stories Of The Christ Child
Illus.: Corwin, Eleanor
Author: Jones, Mary Alice
1953   **$4.00**

8612

Stories Of The Christ Child
(2nd Cover)
Illus.: Corwin, Eleanor
Author: Jones, Mary Alice
1953   **$4.00**

8613

Bible Stories: Old Testament
Illus.: Webbe, Elizabeth
Author: Jones, Mary Alice
1954   **$4.00**

8614

Little Ballerina
Illus.: Grider, Dorothy
Author: Grider, Dorothy
1958   **$4.00**

8615

Aesop's Fables
Illus.: Leaf, Anne Sellers
1952   **$5.00**

8616

Children That Lived In A Shoe, The
Illus.: Webbe, Elizabeth
Author: Pease, Josephine Van
Dolzen
1951   **$4.00**

8617

Pets
Illus.: Webbe, Elizabeth
Author: Ratzesberger, Anna
1954   **$4.00**

8617

Pets
(2nd Cover)
Illus.: Webbe, Elizabeth
Author: Ratzesberger, Anna
1954   **$4.00**

8618

Bugle, A Puppy In Old Yorktown
Illus.: Lee, Manning De V
Author: Andrews, Mary
1958   **$4.00**

8619

Storybook For Little Tots
Illus.: Chase, Mary Jane
Author: Hunter, Virginia
1958   **$4.00**

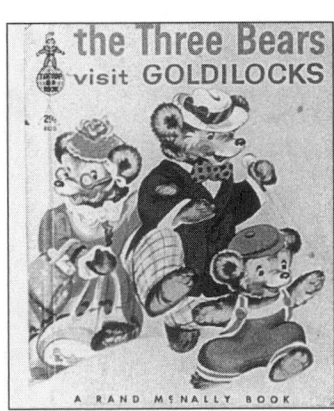

8620

Three Bears Visit Goldilocks, The
Illus.: Mc Kinley, Clare
Author: Rarick, Carrie
1950   **$4.00**

8621

Choo-Choo, The Little Switch Engine
Illus.: Chase, Mary Jane
Author: Wadsworth, Wallace
1954   **$4.00**

8622

So Long
Illus.: Evers, Helen & Alf
1958   **$4.00**

8623

Busy Book, The (Rhymes & Riddles & Things To Do)
Illus.: Szepelak, Helen
Author: Bartlett, Floy; Pease, Josephine
1952   **$4.00**

8624

Old Mother Hubbard
Illus.: Leaf, Anne Sellers
1958   **$5.00**

8625

Jack And Jill
Illus.: Leaf, Anne Sellers
1958   **$5.00**

8626

Smart Little Mouse, The
Illus.: Phillips, Katherine L.
Author: Sherwan, Earl
1950   **$4.00**

8627

Penny And Pete's Surprise
Illus.: Mc Kinley, Clare
1949   **$4.00**

8628
Misty The Wonder Pony
Illus.: Mc Kinley, Clare
1956 $4.00

8629
Five Busy Bears, The
Illus.: Tamburine, Jean
Author: North, Sterling
1955 $4.00

8630
Our Animal Friends
Illus.: Photographs
Author: Hunter, Virginia
1956 $4.00

8631
Freight Train
Illus.: Pollard, G
1956 $4.00

8632
Mr. Punnymoon's Train
Illus.: Phillips, Katherine L.
Author: Hadsell, Alice
1951 $6.00

8632
Mr. Punnymoon's Train
(2nd Cover)
Illus.: Phillips, Katherine L.
Author: Hadsell, Alice
1951 $6.00

8633
Little Swimmers
Illus.: Grider, Dorothy
Author: Grider, Dorothy
1960 $4.00

8634
Growing Up
Illus.: Webbe, Elizabeth
Author: Fritz, Webbe
1956 $4.00

8635
Story Of Our Flag, The
Illus.: Wilde, Irma
1955 $4.00

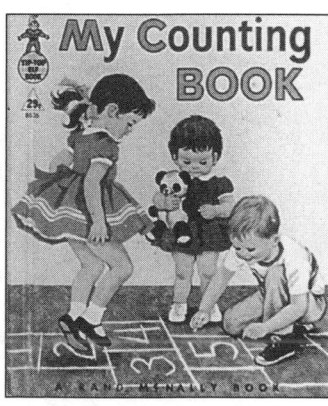

8636
My Counting Book
Illus.: Koester, Sharon
Author: Sherman, Diane
1960 $4.00

8637
Kitten Twins, The
Illus.: Webbe, Elizabeth
Author: Wing, Helen
1960 $4.00

8637
Teddy Bear Twins, The
Illus.: Cooper, Marjorie
Author: Wing, Helen
1965 $6.00

8638
Hansel And Gretel
Illus.: Smith, Kay Lovelace
1960 $4.00

8639

Moonymouse
Illus.: Evers, Helen & Alf
1958   **$5.00**

8640

Enchanted Egg, The
Illus.: Webbe, Elizabeth
Author: Burrows, Peggy
1956   **$4.00**

8641

Bunny Tales
Illus.: Endred, Helen; Nebbe, William
Author: Burroes, Peggy
1956   **$4.00**

8642

Fussbunny
Illus.: Evers, Helen & Alf
Author: Evers, Helen & Alf
1955   **$4.00**

8643

Bartholomew The Beaver
Illus.: Pierce, Alice
Author: Dixon, Ruth
1952   **$4.00**

8643

Bartholomew The Beaver
(2nd Cover)
Illus.: Pierce, Alice
Author: Dixon, Ruth
1952   **$4.00**

8644

Cinderella
Illus.: Endred, Helen; Nebbe, William
Author: Bates, Katherine Lee
1956   **$4.00**

8645

Cowboy Eddie
Illus.: Grider, Dorothy
Author: Glasscock, Joyce
1950   **$4.00**

8645

Cowboy Eddie
(2nd Cover)
Illus.: Grider, Dorothy
Author: Glasscock, Joyce
1950   **$4.00**

8646

Little Red Riding-Hood
Illus.: Leaf, Anne Sellers
1958   **$5.00**

8647

Mother Goose
Illus.: Friend, Esther
1947   **$4.00**

8648

Noah's Ark
Illus.: Webbe, Elizabeth
Author: Briggs, Dorothy Bell
1952   **$4.00**

8649
Little Horseman
Illus.: Grider, Dorothy
1961   **$4.00**

8650
Snuggles
Illus.: Frees, Harry Whittier
Author: Dixon, Ruth
1958   **$4.00**

8651
Child's Thought Of God, A
Illus.: Grider, Dorothy
1957   **$4.00**

8652
I Think About Jesus
Illus.: Friend, Esther
1958   **$4.00**

8653
ABC Book
Illus.: Bryant, Dean
1958   **$4.00**

8654
Little Bobo And His Blue Jacket
Illus.: Brice, Tony
Author: Evers, Alf
1953   **$4.00**

8655
Misty Makes A Movie
Illus.: Photographs
1961   **$6.00**

8656
Early One Morning
Illus.: Cooper, Marjorie
Author: Grayland, Valerie
1963   **$4.00**

8657
Garden Is Good, A
Illus.: Cooper, Marjorie
1963   **$4.00**

8658
Animal ABC Book
Illus.: Kane, Herbert
1964   **$4.00**

8659
Pony Twins, The
Illus.: Cooper, Marjorie
Author: Wing, Helen
1964   **$4.00**

8660
Little Campers
Illus.: Grider, Dorothy
1963   **$4.00**

8661

Little Little Dog
Illus.: Adler, Helen
Author: Brailsford, Frances
1963 $4.00

8662

Fraidy Cat
Illus.: Tamburine, Jean
Author: Barrows, Marjorie
1959 $5.00

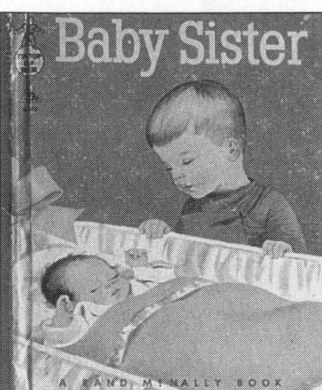

8663

Baby Sister
Illus.: Cooper, Marjorie
Author: Grayland, Valerie
1964 $4.00

8664

Sleepy-Time Rhymes
Illus.: Szepelak, Helen
Author: Smith, Goldie Capers
1964 $4.00

8665

Little Cub Scout
Illus.: Timmins, William
Author: Watts, Mabel
1964 $6.00

8666

Cowboys
Illus.: Timmins, William
1958 $4.00

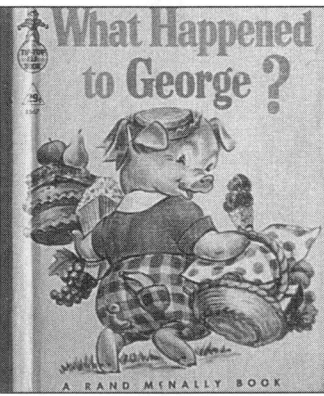

8667

What Happened To George?
Illus.: Opitz, Marge
Author: Engebretson, Betty
1958 $6.00

8668

Jack And The Beanstalk
Illus.: Leaf, Anne Sellers
1961 $5.00

8669

Rumpelstiltskin
Illus.: Webbe, Elizabeth
1959 $4.00

8670

Squirrel Twins, The
Illus.: Webbe, Elizabeth
Author: Wing, Helen
1961 $4.00

8671

Rip Van Winkle
Illus.: Leaf, Anne Sellers
Author: Briggs, Dorothy Bell
1961 $4.00

8672

Timothy Tiger
Illus.: Wilde, Irma
1959 $4.00

8673

Muggins Mouse
Illus.: Leaf, Anne Sellers
1964 $5.00

8674

Pudgy The Little Bear
Illus.: Tamburine, Jean
Author: Barrows, Marjorie
1964 $4.00

8675

Crosspatch
Illus.: Evers, Helen & Alf
Author: Evers, Helen & Alf
1964 $4.00

8676

Bunny Twins, The
Illus.: Cooper, Marjorie
Author: Wing, Helen
1964 $5.00

8677

Funny Hat, The
Illus.: Grider, Dorothy
Author: Barrows, Marjorie
1959 $5.00

8678

Mommy Cat And Her Kittens
Illus.: Rockwell, Eve
Author: Devine, Louise Lawrence
1959 $5.00

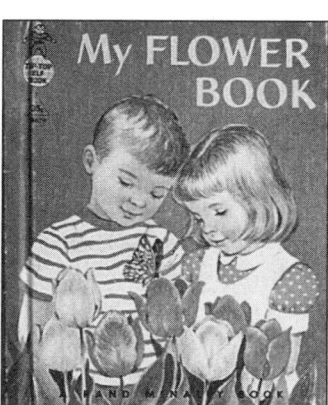

8679

My Flower Book
Illus.: Webbe, Elizabeth
Author: Landis, Dorothy Thompson
1961 $4.00

8680

Little Lost Angel
Illus.: Scott, Janet Laura
Author: Heath, Janet Field
1953 $7.00

8680

Little Lost Angel
(2nd Cover)
Illus.: Scott, Janet Laura
Author: Heath, Janet Field
1953 $5.00

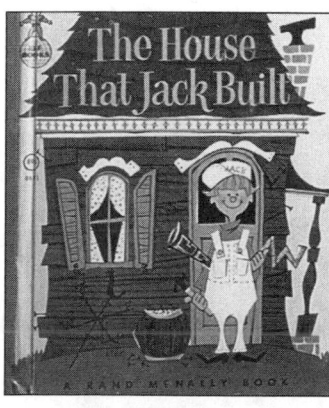

8681

House That Jack Built, The
Illus.: Leaf, Anne Sellers
1959 $7.00

8682

Elves And The Shoemaker, The
Illus.: Lee, Manning De V
1959 $4.00

8683

Sleeping Beauty
Illus.: Webbe, Elizabeth
1959 $4.00

8684

Tom Thumb
Illus.: Wallace, Lucille
1959 $4.00

8684

Tom Thumb
(2nd Cover)
Illus.: Wallace, Lucille
1959   **$4.00**

8685

Larry The Canary
Illus.: Koester, Sharon
Author: Wilkie, Ellen
1959   **$4.00**

8686

Hiawatha
Illus.: Wilde, Irma
Author: Gridley, Marion E.
1961   **$4.00**

8687

Trucks
Illus.: Wilde, George
Author: Reichert, E.C.
1959   **$4.00**

8688

Parakeet Peter
Illus.: Grider, Dorothy
Author: Sprinkle, Rebecca K.
1954   **$4.00**

8689

Copy-Kitten
Illus.: Evers, Helen & Alf
Author: Evers, Helen & Alf
1957   **$4.00**

8690

Yip And Yap
Illus.: Frees, Harry Whittier
Author: Dixon, Ruth
1958   **$4.00**

8691

Kittens And Puppies
Illus.: Photographs
Author: Burrows, Peggy
1955   **$5.00**

8692

Tubby Turtle
Illus.: Adler, Helen
Author: Wing, Helen
1959   **$5.00**

8693

Goody Naughty Book
Illus.: Prockett, Helen
Author: Watts, Mabel
1956   **$4.00**

8694

**Amos Learns To Talk: The Story
Of A Little Duck**
Illus.: Mc Kinley, Clare
Author: Bradbury, Bianca
1950   **$5.00**

8695

Volksy: The Little Yellow Car
Illus.: Chase, Mary Jane
Author: Wing, Helen
1965   **$9.00**

8696

My Bible Book
Illus.: Bryant, Dean
Author: Walker, Janie
1946   **$4.00**

8697

My Prayer Book
Illus.: Friend, Esther
Author: Clemens, Margaret
1947   **$4.00**

8698

Twenty-Third Psalm, The
Illus.: Lee, Manning De V
1964   **$4.00**

8699

When God Imagined A World
Illus.: Richards, Jean H.
Author: Goldsborough, June
1964   **$4.00**

8700

Muggins Takes Off
Illus.: Leaf, Anne Sellers
Author: Barrows, Marjorie
1964   **$7.00**

8701

Muggins' Big Balloon
Illus.: Leaf, Anne Sellers
1964   **$5.00**

8702

Muggins Becomes A Hero
Illus.: Leaf, Anne Sellers
Author: Barrow, Marjorie
1965   **$5.00**

8703

Jo Jo
Illus.: Wallace, Ivy L.
Author: Barrows, Marjorie
1964   **$4.00**

8704

Johnny And The Birds
Illus.: Webbe, Elizabeth
Author: Munn, Ian
1950   **$4.00**

8705

Zippy The Chimp
Illus.: Mitchell, Benn
Author: Ecuyer, Lee
1953   **$4.00**

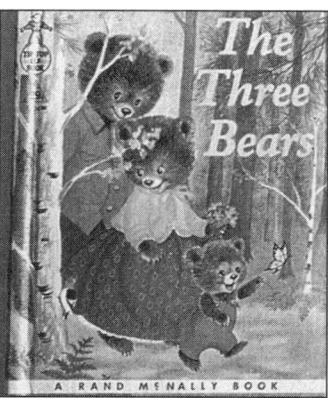

8706

Three Bears, The
Illus.: Webbe, Elizabeth
1959   **$4.00**

8707

Mr. Bear's House
Illus.: Mc Kinley, Clare
Author: Rothe, Fenella
1953   **$4.00**

8708

Number 9 The Little Fire Engine
Illus.: Corwin, Eleanor
Author: Wadsworth, Wallace
1950   **$5.00**

8709

**Little Miss Muffet And Other
Nursery Rhymes**
Illus.: Chase, Mary Jane
1956   **$4.00**

8710

Kerry, The Fire-Engine Dog
Illus.: Grider, Dorothy
Author: Lewis, Frank; Corchia, Alfred J.
1949   **$6.00**

8711

Little Boy Blue And Other Nursery Rhymes
Illus.: Leaf, Anne Sellers
1956 $5.00

8711

Little Boy Blue And Other Nursery Rhymes
(2nd Cover)
Illus.: Leaf, Anne Sellers
1956 $5.00

8712

Three Billy Goats Gruff, The
Illus.: Neebe, William
Author: O'Grady, Alice; Throop, Frances
1957 $5.00

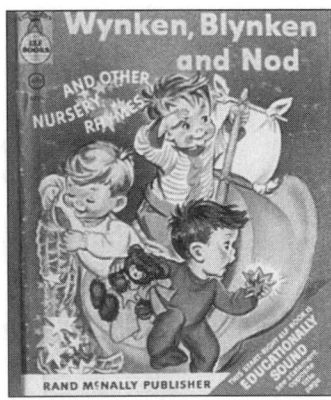

8713

Where From?
Illus.: Smith, Eunice Young
Author: Smith, Eunice Young
1961 $4.00

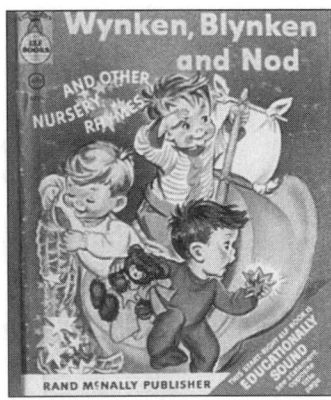

8714

Wynken, Blynken And Nod And Other Nursery Rhymes
Illus.: Mc Kinley, Clare
1956 $4.00

8715

Angel Child
Illus.: Doane, Pelagie
Author: Teal, Val
1946 $5.00

8716

Scamper
Illus.: Tamburine, Jean
1959 $4.00

8717
Can't Verify Title

8718

Four Little Kittens
Illus.: Frees, Harry Whittier
Author: Barrows, Marjorie
1957 $4.00

8719

Farm Friends
Illus.: Photographs
Author: Hunter, Virginia
1956 $5.00

8720

Pokey Bear
Illus.: Evers, Helen & Alf
Author: Evers, Helen & Alf
1965 $4.00

8721
Can't Verify Title

8722

Kitten Twins, The
Illus.: Webbe, Elizabeth
Author: Wing, Helen
1960 $7.00

8722

Teddy Bear Twins, The
Illus.: Cooper, Marjorie
Author: Wing, Helen
1965 $6.00

8723

Mother Goose
Illus.: Friend, Esther
1947 **$4.00**

8724

Story Of Joseph, The
Illus.: Lee, Manning De V
1965 **$4.00**

8725

Story Of David, The
Illus.: Lee, Manning De V
1965 **$4.00**

8726

Nancy Plays Nurse
Illus.: Grider, Dorothy
Author: Sherman, Diane
1965 **$4.00**

8727

Princess And The Pea, The
Illus.: Leaf, Anne Sellers
1965 **$7.00**

8728

Hey, Diddle, Diddle And Other Nonsense Rhymes
Illus.: Botts, Davi
1956 **$4.00**

8729

Little Mailman Of Bayberry Lane, The
Illus.: Webbe, Elizabeth
Author: Munn, Ian
1952 **$8.00**

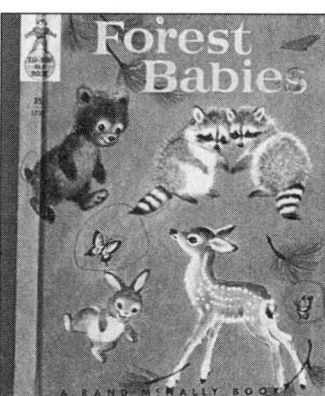

8730

Forest Babies
Illus.: Webbe, Elizabeth
Author: Parrish, Jean J.
1949 **$4.00**

8731

Chester, The Little Pony
Illus.: Mc Kinley, Clare
Author: Gunder. Eman
1951 **$5.00**

8732

Busy Bulldozer, The
Illus.: Grider, Dorothy
Author: Grider, Dorothy
1952 **$4.00**

8733

Jeepers The Little Frog
Illus.: Cooper, Marjorie
Author: Cooper, Marjorie
1965 **$4.00**

8734

Goody: A Mother Cat Story
Illus.: Leaf, Anne Sellers
Author: Bertail, Inez
1957 **$4.00**

8735

Farm Animals
Illus.: Gayer, Marguerite
Author: Ratzesberger, Anna
1952 $4.00

8736

Buddy, The Little Taxi
Illus.: Corwin, Elizabeth
Author: Grider, Dorothy
1951 $5.00

8737

Little Friends: Kittens, Puppies, Bunnies
Illus.: Gaddis, Rie
Author: Dixon, Ruth
1951 $5.00

8738

Can't Verify Title

8739

Little Kittens' Nursery Rhymes, The
Illus.: Frees, Harry Whittier
1941 $5.00

8740

Pillowtime Tales
Illus.: Tamburine, Jean
Author: De Groot, Marion K.
1956 $4.00

8741

Farm For Andy, A
Illus.: Gayer, Marguerite
1951 $5.00

8742

Three Little Bunnies
Illus.: Rooks, Dale & Sally
Author: Dixon, Ruth
1950 $4.00

8743

Popcorn Party
Illus.: Szepelak, Helen
Author: Boyles, Trudy; Macmartin, Louise
1952 $4.00

8744

Can't Verify Title

8745

Three Little Puppies
Illus.: Rooks, Dale & Sally
Author: Dixon, Ruth
1951 $4.00

8746

Peppy, The Lonely Little Puppy
Illus.: Blake, Vivienne
Author: Friedman, Frieda
1957 $5.00

8747

Rocket For A Cow, A
Illus.: Wilde, Irma
Author: Devine, Louise Lawerence
1965 $6.00

8748

Animal Show, The
Illus.: Grider, Dorothy
Author: Jackson, Leroy F.
1965 $4.00

8749

Happy Twins, The
Illus.: Cooper, Marjorie
Author: Wing, Helen
1956 $4.00

Hanna-Barbera Character Series

HANNA01
Devlin
Illus.: Carleton, Jim
Author: Daly, Kathleen
1975 $8.00

HANNA02
Dynomutt And The Pie In The Sky
Caper
1977 $8.00

HANNA03
Great Grape Ape At The Circus
1976 $8.00

HANNA04
Hong Kong Phooey And The Bird
Nest Snatchers
Illus.: Ostapczuk, Phil
Author: Lewis, Jean
1976 $8.00

HANNA05
Hong Kong Phooey And The Fire
Engine Mystery
1977 $8.00

HANNA06
Hong Kong Phooey And The
Fortune Cookie Caper
1975 $8.00

HANNA07
Jabberjaw Out West
1977 $8.00

HANNA08
Josie And The Pussycats/The Bag
Factory Detour
Illus.: Franzen, Jim
Author: Russell, Solveig Paulson
1976 $8.00

HANNA09
Mumbly To The Rescue
1977 $8.00

HANNA10
Scooby-Doo And The Case Of The
Counterfeit Money
Illus.: Lowe, Richard
Author: Brown, Fern G.
1976 $8 .00

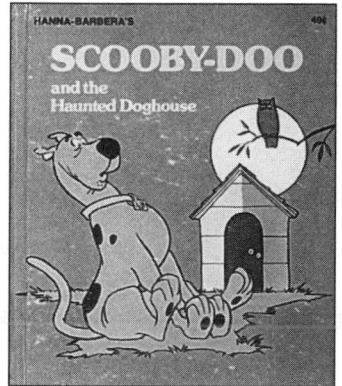

HANNA11
Scooby-Doo And The Haunted
Doghouse
1975 $8.00

HANNA12
Scooby-Doo And The Headless
Horseman
1976 $8.00

HANNA13
Scooby-Doo And The Mystery
Monster
1975 $8.00

HANNA14
Scooby-Doo And The Old Ship
Mystery
1977 $8.00

HANNA15

Speed Buggy And The Secret Message

Illus.: Anderson, Bill & Judie
Author: Warren, Mary Phraner
1976   **$8.00**

HANNA16

Valley Of The Dinosaurs

1975   **$8.00**

HANNA17

Wheelie And The Chopper Bunch

1975   **$8.00**

HANNA18

Clue Club The Case Of The Missing Racehorse

Illus.: Franzen, Jim
Author: Brown, Fern G.
1972   **$8.00**

Rand McNally Elf Books Index

A Brief History of Wonder Books

Around 1898, two men, Alexander Grosset and George T. Dunlap, with combined capital of $1,350, formed the partnership of Grosset & Dunlap. The company was created to sell and distribute books.

While using the works of authors like Rudyard Kipling, the company moved into the business of rebinding paperbacks with hard covers. This method was used for a few years before the company started producing its own reprints of books. The company's reprints sold for around 50 cents at this time.

The year 1908 saw Grosset & Dunlap publishing its own line of children's books after the purchase of the Chatterton & Peck Company, which was already successful with The Rover Boys and The Bobbsey Twins. Around 1910, the company was publishing the adventures of Tom Swift, and by the 1920s, it was producing popular book series like Zane Grey and The Hardy Boys. With the success of The Hardy Boys, the company gave girls their own sleuth, Nancy Drew, in the 1930s.

A paper shortage during WWII, similar the one during WWI, pushed the selling cost of reprinted books up to around $1.00, but when the war ended, the price went back to 50 cents.

In 1944, the Book-of-the-Month Club, Harper, Little, Brown, Scribners, and Random House purchased Grosset & Dunlap. A year later Bantam Books was formed—the Curtis Company owned 30 percent. Bantam was to eventually become one of the largest paperback publishers.

Wonder Books, Inc. was formed in 1947 with a joint Curtis-Grosset distribution. The first Wonder Books were distributed by Random House, then Grosset & Dunlap, and by the early 1950s, by Wonder Books, Inc. In 1952 Treasure Books was formed (see page 420). Treasure Books were the same size as Wonder Books, but their bindings were in red tape and the books were side stapled like Little Golden Books.

The first Wonder Books measured 7-1/2 inches x 9-3/4 inches and contained 46 pages, with 20 in full color. This size was around for only a short while and was changed to the 6-1/2-inch x 8-1/8-inch size around 1948.

Of the first fifteen titles, most were carried over to this new size except for the following:

#508 How The Rabbit Fooled The Whale And The Elephant And Other Stories
Illus.: Sari

#511 Animal Stories
Illus.: Robinson

#515 How The Baby Hippo Found A Home
Illus.: Ruth Ganneet
Author: Dorothy Thomas

These three numbers were eventually replaced with different titles. Bound in dirt-resistant "Durasheen," Wonder Books became known as the books with the washable covers. Even though their covers were washable, their spines did not hold up very well. With a paper cover that went from front to back, the more the book was opened, the more chances there were of the spine falling off or tearing.

Filmways purchased Grosset & Dunlap in 1974. In turn, Grosset & Dunlap purchased Platt & Munk in 1977. The Putnam Publishing Group purchased Grosset & Dunlap in 1982. Price Stern Sloan now owns the rights to Wonder Books. Because of the frequent changes in ownership through the years, it is difficult to pinpoint accurate historical Wonder Books information.

How To Tell Wonder Book Editions

There are no markings on Wonder Books that will tell you exactly what edition you own, but you should be able to narrow down the time period of publication by using a little deductive reasoning.

I do not give page numbers for first edition Wonder Books because it would get too confusing. With Little Golden Books, when the books were cut to 28 pages, all subsequent printings of 42-page books would have 28 pages. This was not always the case with Wonder Books; you could have 42- and 34-page books being printed during the same time period.

In the back of the earlier books there is a page with titles in print. You can use this list to approximate the time of a book's printing. For example, you own #557, *Billy And His Steam Roller*, with a copyright of 1951. The last title listed is #742, *Whose Hat Is That*. When you look up #742, you find that it has a copyright of 1960, so your copy of #557 must have been published around 1960. If the last title number had been #560 instead of #742, the book probably would be a first edition. Unfortunately, this method of dating Wonder Books cannot guarantee that you have a first edition. Once the company stopped listing the books in print, one is only able to approximate the date of printing by using the cover price. Prices stayed steady for years at a time, so this method will only give you a period of printing.

Wonder Books, like most Elf Books, had a one-piece wrap around cover. This makes it very difficult to find nice early copies with their spines intact. Some titles, like those by certain illustrators and books based on cartoon and TV characters, will continue to increase in value.

Note: The first 15 titles were published in the larger 7-1/2-inch x 9-3/4-inch size.

Wonder Books—By Book Number

501
Mother Goose
Illus.: Hirsch, Joseph
1946 **$40.00**

503
Favorite Nursery Tales
Illus.: Dixon, Rachel Taft
Author: Graham, Eleanor
1946 **$30.00**

505
Famous Fairy Tales
Illus.: Jules, Mervin
Author: Graham, Eleanor
1946 **$30.00**

508
How the Rabbit Fooled the Whale and the Elephant
Illus.: Sari
Author: Williams, Louise B.
1946 **$30.00**

509
Randolph: The Bear Who Said "No"
Illus.: Walker, Nedda
Author: Nelson, Faith
1946 **$35.00**

511
Animal Stories
Illus.: Robinson
Author: Scott, Therese
1947 **$30.00**

515
How the Baby Hippo Found a Home
Illus.: Gannett, Ruth
Author: Thomas, Dorothy
1949 **$40.00**

The preceding 7 titles were published in the larger 7-1/2" x 9-3/4" size.

501
Mother Goose
Illus.: Hirsch, Joseph
1946 **$15.00**

501
Mother Goose
Illus.: Hirsch, Joseph
1946 **$5.00**

502
Cozy Little Farm, The
Illus.: Angela
Author: Bonino, Louise
1946 **$15.00**

503
Three Little Kittens And Other Nursery Tales
Illus.: Dixon, Rachel Taft
Author: Graham, Eleanor
1946 **$15.00**

504

Little Dog Who Forgot How To Bark, The
Illus.: Hopkins, Hildegard
Author: Bailey, Carolyn S.
1946   **$15.00**

505

Famous Fairy Tales
Illus.: Jules, Mervin
Author: Graham, Eleanor
1946   **$15.00**

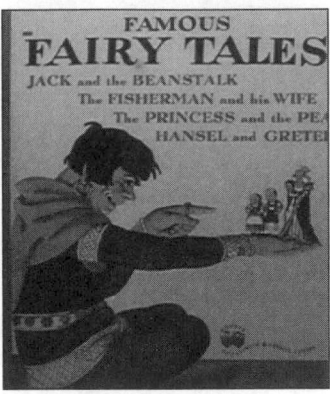

505

Famous Fairy Tales
(2nd Cover)
Illus.: Jules, Mervin
Author: Graham, Eleanor
1946   **$10.00**

506

ABC And Counting Book
Illus.: Sarkin, Jack
Author: Fraser, Phyllis
1946   **$15.00**

507

Bedtime Stories
Illus.: Masha
Author: Graham, Eleanor
1946   **$15.00**

507

Bedtime Stories
(2nd Cover)
Illus.: Masha
Author: Graham, Eleanor
1946   **$10.00**

507

Bedtime Stories
(3rd Cover)
Illus.: Masha
Author: Graham, Eleanor
1946   **$6.00**

507

Bedtime Stories
(4th Cover)
Illus.: Masha
Author: Graham, Eleanor
1946   **$4.00**

508

Why The Bear Has A Short Tail
Illus.: Sari
Author: Williams, Louise B.
1946   **$15.00**

509

Randolph: The Bear Who Said "No"
Illus.: Walker, Nedda
Author: Nelson, Faith
1946   **$25.00**

510

Race Between The Monkey And The Duck, The
Illus.: Hurd, Clement
Author: Hurd, Clement
1940   **$20.00**

511

Shy Little Horse, The
Illus.: Robinson
Author: Scott, Therese
1947   **$15.00**

512

Little Train That Won A Medal, The
Illus.: Loeb, Anton
Author: Geis, Darlene
1947   **$15.00**

513

Peter Rabbit And Other Stories
Illus.: Erickson, Phoebe
Author: Potter, Beatrix
1947   **$15.00**

514

Storytime Favorites
Illus.: Leob, Anton
Author: Scott, Theresa Ann
1947   **$15.00**

514

Storytime Favorites
(2nd Cover)
Illus.: Leob, Anton
Author: Scott, Theresa Ann
1947   **$10.00**

514

Storytime Favorites
(3rd Cover)
Illus.: Leob, Anton
Author: Scott, Theresa Ann
1947   **$5.00**

515

Little Puppy Who Would Not Mind His Mother, The
Illus.: Hopkins, Hildegarde
Author: Misc.
1949   **$12.00**

516

Magic Bus, The
Illus.: Gergely, Tibor
Author: Dolbier, Maurice
1948   **$25.00**

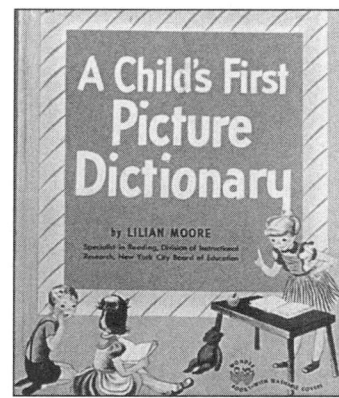

517

Childs First Picture Dictionary, A
Illus.: Weber, Nettie & Clement, Charles
Author: Moore, Lilian
1948   **$10.00**

518

Who Lives On The Farm?
Illus.: Jackson, Pauline
Author: Elting, Mary
1949   **$10.00**

519

Surprise Doll, The
Illus.: Lerch, Steffie
Author: Gipson, Morrell
1949   **$40.00**

520

Make-Believe Parade, The
Illus.: Wilkin, Eloise
Author: Margo, Jan
1949   **$20.00**

521

Monkey See, Monkey Do
Illus.: Moyers, William
Author: Tooze, Ruth
1949   **$12.00**

522

Five Little Finger Playmates
Illus.: Steiner, Charlotte
1949   **$10.00**

523

Mr. Bear Squash-You-All-Flat
Illus.: Angela
Author: Gipson, Morrell
1950   **$150.00**

524

Wheels And Noises
Illus.: Dauber, Elizabeth
Author: Elting, Mary
1950   **$8.00**

525

Who Does Baby Look Like?
Illus.: Rowand, Phyllis
Author: Rowand, Phyllis
1950   **$10.00**

526

Too Little Fire Engine, The
Illus.: Flory, Jane
Author: Flory, Jane
1950   **$10.00**

527

Kitten's Secret, The
Illus.: Barton, Mary
Author: Gossett, Margaret
1950   **$12.00**

528

Little Lost Puppy, The
Illus.: Spicer, Jesse
Author: Otto, Margaret G.
1950   **$10.00**

529

**Kittens Who Hid From Their
Mother, The**
Illus.: Werber, Adele; Laslo, Doris
Author: Woodcock, Louise
1950   **$10.00**

530

**Four Puppies Who Wanted A
Home, The**
Illus.: Frankel, Simon
Author: Bryan, Dorothy & Marguerite
1950   **$10.00**

530

**Four Puppies Who Wanted A
Home, The**
(2nd Cover)
Illus.: Frankel, Simon
Author: Bryan, Dorothy & Marguerite
1950   **$8.00**

531

Hungry Little Bunny, The
Illus.: Wilde, Irma
Author: Wilde, Irma
1950   **$8.00**

532

Heidi: Child Of The Mountains
Illus.: Lerch, Steffie
Author: Spyri, Johanna
1950   **$8.00**

532
Heidi: Child Of The Mountains
(2nd Cover)
Illus.: Lerch, Steffie
Author: Spyri, Johanna
1950 **$3.00**

533
Three Mice And A Cat
Illus.: Seiden, Art
Author: Berg, Jean Horton
1950 **$25.00**

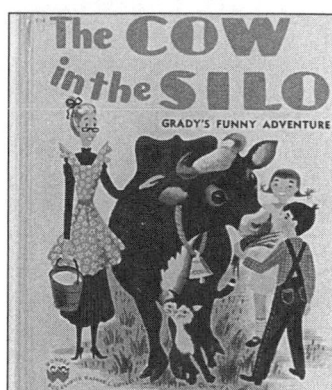

534
Cow In The Silo, The
Illus.: Cunningham, Dellwyn
Author: Goodell, Patricia
1950 **$20.00**

535
Puppy Who Chased The Sun, The
Illus.: Grand, Le
Author: Grand, Le
1950 **$10.00**

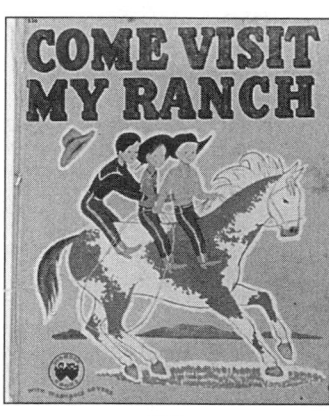

536
Come Visit My Ranch
Illus.: Hawes, Baldwin
Author: Hawes, Baldwin
1950 **$10.00**

536
Calling All Cowboys
(2nd Title)
Illus.: Hawes, Baldwin
Author: Hawes, Baldwin
1950 **$6.00**

537
Jolly Jumping Man, The
Illus.: Frankel, Simon
Author: Berg, Jean Horton
1950 **$10.00**

538
Let's Play Indian
Illus.: Chastain, Madye Lee
Author: Chastain, Madye Lee
1950 **$10.00**

539
Noisy Clock Shop, The
Illus.: Seiden, Art
Author: Berg, Jean Horton
1950 **$10.00**

540
It's A Secret
Illus.: Myers, Bernice
Author: Brewster, Benjamin
1950 **$10.00**

540
It's A Secret
(2nd Cover)
Illus.: Myers, Bernice
Author: Brewster, Benjamin
1950 **$4.00**

541
Baby Elephant, The
Illus.: Burchard, Peter
Author: Brewster, Benamine
1950 **$10.00**

542

Fraidy Cat Kitten, The
Illus.: Wilde, Irma
Author: Wilde, Irma
1950   **$10.00**

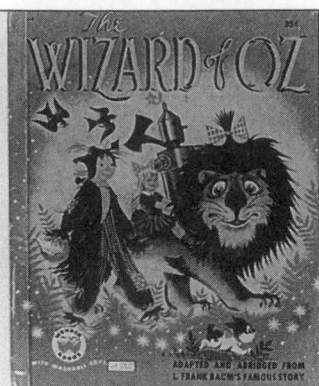

543

Wizard Of Oz, The
Illus.: Sinnickson, Tom
Author: Baum, Frank L.
1951   **$15.00**

544

Bambi's Children
Illus.: Bartlett, William
Author: Salten, Felix
1951   **$10.00**

545

Copycat Colt, The
Illus.: Steiner, Charlotte
Author: Steiner, Charlotte; Hoff, Virginia
1951   **$8.00**

546

Baby Susan's Chicken
Illus.: Cummings, Alison
Author: Berg, Jean Horton
1951   **$8.00**

547

Churkendoose, The
Illus.: Cunningham, Dellwyn
Author: Berenberg, Ben Ross
1946   **$25.00**

548

Baby Bunny, The
Illus.: Stone, Dick
Author: Evers, Alf
1951   **$8.00**

549

Roly-Poly Puppy, The
Illus.: Berthold
Author: Bates, Barbara S.
1950   **$8.00**

550

Bingity-Bangity School Bus, The
Illus.: Wood, Ruth
Author: Conkling, Fleur
1950   **$25.00**

550

Bingity-Bangity School Bus, The
(2nd Cover)
Illus.: Wood, Ruth
Author: Conkling, Fleur
1950   **$5.00**

551

Giraffe Who Went To School, The
Illus.: Wilde, Irma
Author: Wilde, Irma
1951   **$8.00**

552

Five Jolly Brothers, The
Illus.: Sinnickson, Tom
Author: Chaffee, Tish
                       $8.00

553

Boy Who Wanted To Be A Fish, The
Illus.: Le Grand
Author: Le Grand
1951 $8.00

554

Blowaway Hat, The
Illus.: Cunningham, Dellwyn
Author: Adelson, Leone
1946 $8.00

555

Brave Little Steam Shovel, The
Illus.: Myers, Bernice
Author: Bertail, Inez
1951 $8.00

555

Brave Little Steam Shovel, The
(2nd Cover)
Illus.: Myers, Bernice
Author: Bertail, Inez
1951 $4.00

556

Cats Who Stayed For Dinner, The
Illus.: Burchard, Peter
Author: Rowand, Phyllis
1951 $12.00

557

Billy And His Steam Roller
Illus.: Myers, Bernice
Author: Bertail, Inez
1951 $8.00

558

Little John Little
Illus.: Steiner, Charlotte
Author: Steiner, Charlotte
1951 $8.00

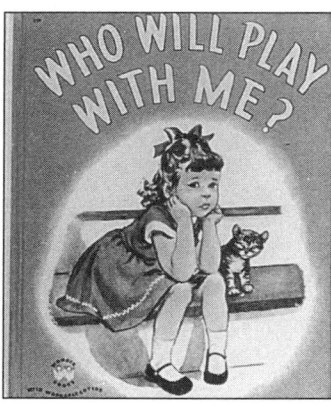

559

Who Will Play With Me?
Illus.: Dillon, Corinne
Author: Sutton, Margaret
1951 $8.00

560

Playtime For Nancy
Illus.: Stolberg, Doris
Author: Hyde, Margaret O.
1951 $10.00

561

Puppy Who Found A Boy, The
Illus.: Wilde, George & Irma
Author: Wilde, George & Irma
1951 $8.00

562

Playful Little Dog, The
Illus.: Robertson, Maurice
Author: Berg, Jean Horton
1951 $8.00

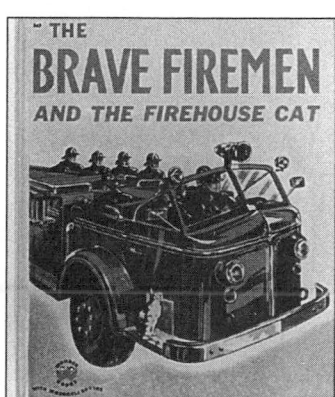

563

Brave Firemen, The
Illus.: Medvey, Steven
Author: Bradbury, Bianca
1951 $8.00

564

Happy Birthday Present, The
Illus.: Scott, Marguerite
Author: Bates, Barbara S.
1951   **$8.00**

565

Are Dogs Better Than Cats?
Illus.: Le Grand
Author: Le Grand
1953   **$8.00**

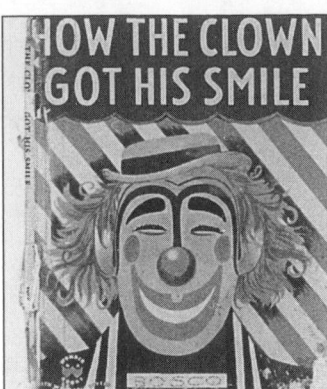

566

How The Clown Got His Smile
Illus.: Hull, John
Author: Martin, Marcia
1951   **$8.00**

567

Goose Who Played The Piano, The
Illus.: Cunningham, Dellwyn
Author: Evers, Alf
1951   **$10.00**

568

Hide And Seek Duck, The
Illus.: Wilde, Irma
Author: Wilde, Irma
1952   **$8.00**

569

Wonder Book Of Trains, The
Illus.: Sinnickson, Tom
Author: Peters, Lisa
1952   **$10.00**

570

Little Cowboy's Christmas, A
Illus.: Dart, Eleanor
Author: Martin, Marcia
1951   **$19.00**

570

Little Cowboy's Christmas, A
(2nd Cover)
Illus.: Dart, Eleanor
Author: Martin, Marcia
1951   **$10.00**

571

**Little Train That Saved The Day,
The**
Illus.: Steiner, Charlotte
Author: Steiner, Charlotte
1952   **$8.00**

571

**Little Train That Saved The Day,
The**
(2nd Cover)
Illus.: Steiner, Charlotte
Author: Steiner, Charlotte
1952   **$6.00**

572

**Snowman's Christmas Present,
The**
Illus.: Wilde, Irma
Author: Wilde, Irma
1951   **$13.00**

572

**Snowman's Christmas Present,
The**
(2nd Cover)
Illus.: Wilde, Irma
Author: Wilde, Irma
1951   **$10.00**

573

Little Car That Wanted A Garage, The
Illus.: Meshekoff, Edward
Author: Woolley, Catherine
1952 **$10.00**

573

Little Car That Wanted A Garage, The
(2nd Cover)
Illus.: Meshekoff, Edward
Author: Woolley, Catherine
1952 **$6.00**

574

Alice In Wonderland
Illus.: Matulay, Laszlo
Author: Martin, Marcia
1951 **$15.00**

575

Wonder Book Of Christmas, The
Illus.: Myers, Lou
1951 **$10.00**

575

Wonder Book Of Christmas, The
(2nd Cover)
Illus.: Myers, Lou
1951 **$6.00**

576

Wonder Book Of Fun, The
Illus.: Cunningham, Dellwyn
Author: Orleans, Ilo
1951 **$8.00**

576

Wonder Book Of Fun, The
(2nd Cover)
Illus.: Cunningham, Dellwyn
Author: Orleans, Ilo
1951 **$4.00**

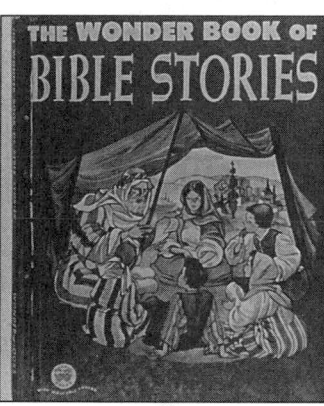

577

Wonder Book Of Bible Stories, The
Illus.: Frost, Bruno
Author: Juergens, Mary
1951 **$8.00**

578

Magic Word, The
Illus.: Dart, Eleanor
Author: Zolotow, Charlotte
1952 **$8.00**

579

Hoppy, The Curious Kangaroo
Illus.: Fraydas, Stan
Author: Fraydas, Stan
1952 **$8.00**

579

Hoppy, The Curious Kangaroo
(2nd Cover)
Illus.: Fraydas, Stan
Author: Fraydas, Stan
1952 **$4.00**

580

Wonder Book Of Boats, The
Illus.: Hurst, Earl Oliver
Author: Hurst, Earl Oliver
1953 **$8.00**

581

Wonderful Tar-Baby, The
Illus.: Cunningham, Dellwyn
Author: Harris, Joel Chandler
1952 **$18.00**

582

Happy Surprise, The
Illus.: Wood, Ruth
Author: Klein, Leonore
1952 **$8.00**

583

Good Morning, Good Night
Illus.: Derwinski, Beatrice
Author: Luther, Frank
1953 **$8.00**

584

Mr. Wishing Went Fishing
Illus.: Wilde, George
Author: Wilde, Irma
1952 **$10.00**

585

Christmas Puppy, The
Illus.: Wilde, Irma
Author: Wilde, Irma
1953 **$15.00**

586

Christmas In Song And Story
Illus.: Scholz, Catherine
Author: Berg, Jean Horton
1953 **$12.00**

586

Christmas In Songs And Stories
(2nd Cover)
Illus.: Scholz, Catherine
Author: Berg, Jean Horton
1953 **$6.00**

587

Story Of The Christ Child, The
Illus.: Lap, Pranas
Author: Edwards, Annette
1953 **$8.00**

588

**Raggedy Ann And Marcella's First
Day At School**
Illus.: Sinnickson, Tom
Author: Gruelle, Johnny
1952 **$22.00**

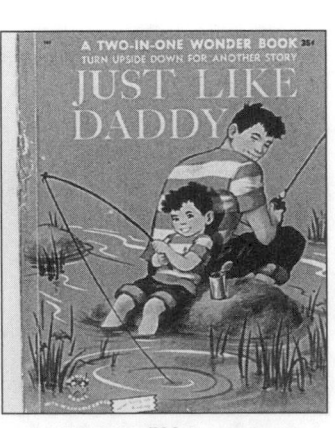

589

Just Like Mommy, Just Like Daddy
Illus.: Cummings, Alison
Author: Simon, Patty
1952 **$8.00**

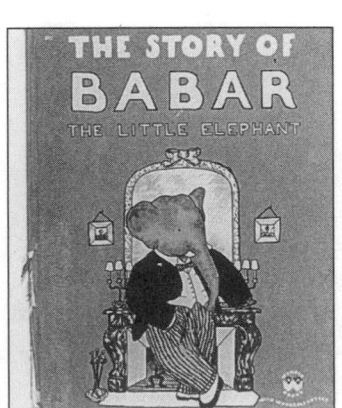

590

Story Of Babar, The
Illus.: Brunhoff, Jean De
Author: Brunhoff, Jean De
1952 **$18.00**

591

Sonny The Bunny
Illus.: Seiden, Art
Author: Martin, Marcia
1952 **$8.00**

592

Babar And Father Christmas
Illus.: Hass, Merle S.
Author: De Brunoff, Jean
1940 **$20.00**

593

Christmas Is Coming
Illus.: Cummings, Alison
Author: Martin, Marcia
1952 **$10.00**

594

Raggedy Ann's Merriest Christmas
Illus.: Sinnickson, Tom
Author: Gruelee, Johnny
1952 **$22.00**

595

Black Beauty
Illus.: Santos, George
Author: Martin, Marcia
1952 **$8.00**

595

Black Beauty
(2nd Title)
Illus.: Santos, George
Author: Martin, Marcia
1952 **$3.00**

595

Black Beauty
(3rd Title)
Illus.: Santos, George
Author: Martin, Marcia
1952 **$3.00**

596

Traveling Twins, The
Illus.: Smalley, Janet
Author: Berg, Jean Horton
1953 **$10.00**

597

Peter Pan
Illus.: Derwinski, Beatrice
Author: Martin, Marcia
1952 **$8.00**

598

Who Likes Dinner?
Illus.: Cunningham, Dellwyn
Author: Beyer, Evelyn
1953 **$8.00**

599

Hans Christian Andersen's Fairy Tales
Illus.: Caraway, James
Author: Andersen, Hans Christian
1952 **$8.00**

600

Peter Goes To School
Illus.: Doremus, Hal W.
Author: House, Wanda Rogers
1953 **$7.00**

600

Peter Goes To School
(2nd Cover)
Illus.: Doremus, Hal W.
Author: House, Wanda Rogers
1953 **$3.00**

601

Surprise For Mrs. Bunny, A
Illus.: Steiner, Charlotte
Author: Steiner, Charlotte
1953 $8.00

601

Surprise For Mrs. Bunny, A
(2nd Cover)
Illus.: Steiner, Charlotte
Author: Steiner, Charlotte
1953 $5.00

602

Babar The King
Illus.: Brunhoff, Jean De
Author: Brunhoff, Jean De
1953 $18.00

603

Tom Corbett's Wonder Book Of Space
Illus.: Vaughn, Frank
Author: Martin, Marcia
1953 $20.00

604

Raggedy Andy's Surprise
Illus.: Sinnickson, Tom
Author: Gruelle, Johnny
1953 $18.00

605

Guess What?
Illus.: Wood, Ruth
Author: Klein, Leonore
1953 $7.00

606

Baby's First Book
Illus.: Schad, Helen
Author: Edwards, Annette
1953 $7.00

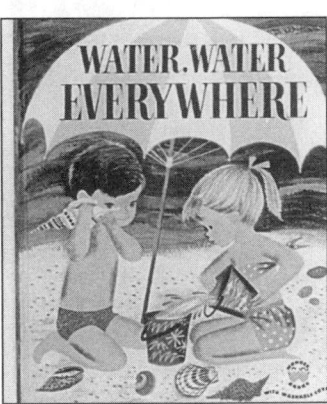

607

Water, Water Everywhere
Illus.: Seiden, Art
Author: Raphael, Ralph B.
1953 $7.00

608

Baby Animal Friends
Illus.: Erickson, Phoebe
Author: Erickson, Phoebe
1954 $7.00

609

Three Little Pigs, Little Red Riding Hood
Illus.: Peller, Jackie; Tamburine, Jean
1954 $7.00

610

My ABC Book
Illus.: Seiden, Art
1953 $7.00

610

My ABC Book
(2nd Cover)
Illus.: Seiden, Art
1953 $3.00

611
Peter Rabbit And Reddy Fox
Illus.: Hauge, Carl & Mary
Author: Burgess, Thorton W.
1954 $8.00

611
Peter Rabbit And Reddy Fox
(2nd Cover)
Illus.: Hauge, Carl & Mary
Author: Burgess, Thorton W.
1954 $6.00

612
Sleepy-Time For Everyone
Illus.: Castagnoli, Martha
Author: Castagnoli, Martha
1954 $7.00

613
Picnic At The Zoo, The
Illus.: Myers, Bernice & Lou
Author: Libbey, Ruth Everding
1954 $7.00

614
Bunny Hopwell's First Spring
Illus.: Dixon, Rachel
Author: Fritz, Jean
1954 $7.00

615
Pinocchio
Illus.: Seiden, Art
Author: Andreas, Evelyn
1954 $7.00

615
Pinocchio
Illus.: Seiden, Art
Author: Andreas, Evelyn
1954 $3.00

616
Wonder Book Of Trucks, The
Illus.: Schusker, James
Author: Peters, Lisa
1954 $7.00

616
Wonder Book Of Trucks, The
(2nd Cover)
Illus.: Schusker, James
Author: Peters, Lisa
1954 $3.00

617
Puppy On Parade, The
Illus.: Hoecker, Hazel
Author: Grilley, Virginia
1956 $7.00

617
Puppy On Parade, The
(2nd Cover)
Illus.: Hoecker, Hazel
Author: Grilley, Virginia
1956 $4.00

618
Johnny Grows Up
Illus.: Cummings, Alison
Author: Martin, Marcia
1954 $7.00

619

Wonder Book Of Nursery Songs, The
Illus.: Schlesinger, Alice
Author: Cummins, Dorothy Berliner
1954 **$7.00**

620

Surprise Party, The
Illus.: Newell, Crosby
Author: Newell, Crosby
1955 **$7.00**

621

My Poetry Book
Illus.: Smith, Flora
Author: Pierce, June
1954 **$7.00**

622

Nine Friendly Dogs, The
Illus.: Goldsborough, June
Author: Sutton, Felix
1954 **$7.00**

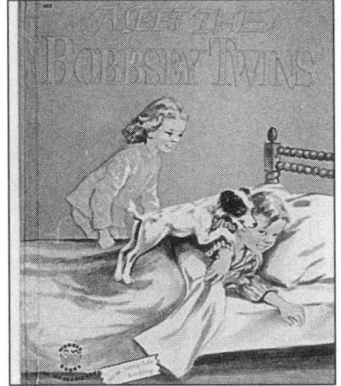

623

Meet The Bobbsey Twins
Illus.: Dillon, Corinne
Author: Hope, Laura Lee
1954 **$10.00**

624

Raggedy Ann's Tea Party
Illus.: Wilde, George & Irma
Author: Gruelle, Johnny
1954 **$18.00**

625

Littlest Christmas Tree, The
Illus.: Hauge, Carl & Mary
Author: Burgess, Thornton W.
1954 **$15.00**

625

Littlest Christmas Tree, The
(2nd Cover)
Illus.: Hauge, Carl & Mary
Author: Burgess, Thornton W.
1954 **$5.00**

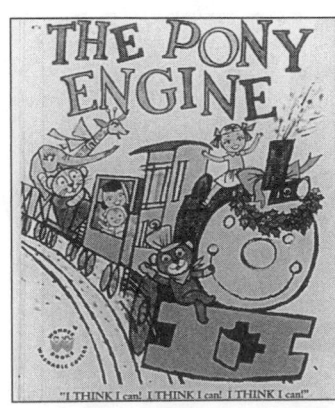

626

Pony Engine, The
Illus.: Prestopino, Grgorio
Author: Garn, Doris
1957 **$7.00**

627

Romper Room Book Of Finger Plays And Action Rhymes, The
Illus.: Wood, Ruth
Author: Pierce, June
1955 **$7.00**

628

Big Joke, The
Illus.: Newell, Crosby
Author: Bonsall, George
1955 **$7.00**

629

What Happened To Piggy?
Illus.: Hauge, Carl & Mary
Author: Potter, Miriam Clark
$7.00

630

See How It Grows
Illus.: Smith, Flora
Author: Walters, Marguerite
1954   **$7.00**

631

Helpful Friends, The
Illus.: Bonsall, George; Newell, Crosby
Author: Bonsall, George; Newell,
Crosby
1955   **$7.00**

632

It's A Lovely Day
Illus.: Smith, Flora
Author: Walters, Marguerite
1956   **$7.00**

633

Mrs. Goose's Green Trailer
Illus.: Weisgard, Leonard
Author: Potter, Miriam Clark
1956   **$7.00**

634

Make-Believe Book, The
Illus.: Newell, Crosby
Author: Newell, Crosby
1959   **$7.00**

635

Sleeping Beauty
Illus.: Ives, Ruth
Author: Andreas, Evelyn
1956   **$7.00**

635

Sleeping Beauty
(2nd Cover)
Illus.: Ives, Ruth
Author: Andreas, Evelyn
1956   **$2.00**

636

**Little Duck Said Quack, Quack,
Quack, The**
Illus.: Kendrick, Alcy
Author: Barnett, Grace & Olive
1955   **$7.00**

637

**Wonder Book Of Firemen And Fire
Engines, The**
Illus.: Weisner, William
Author: Peters, Lisa
1956   **$10.00**

637

**Wonder Book Of Firemen And Fire
Engines, The**
(2nd Cover)
Illus.: Weisner, William
Author: Peters, Lisa
1956   **$5.00**

638

Wonder Book Of Clowns, The
Illus.: Schucker, James
Author: Weigle, Oscar
1955   **$8.00**

639

Lassie Come-Home
Illus.: Drutzu, Anne Marie
Author: Knight, Eric
1956   **$8.00**

640

Wonder Book Of Cowboys, The
Illus.: Vaughn, Frank
Author: Peters, Lisa
1956   **$7.00**

641

Little Peter Cottontail
Illus.: Erickson, Phoebe
Author: Burgess, Thornton W.
1956   **$7.00**

642

Cowardly Lion, The
Illus.: Wood, Ruth
Author: Baum, Frank L.
1956   **$22.00**

643

Bible Treasures
Illus.: Raw, J. G.
Author: Ryder, Lillian
1961   **$7.00**

644

My Book About God
Illus.: Varga, Judith
1956   **$7.00**

645

Lonely Pony, The
Illus.: Oogjen, Barbara & Thomas
Author: Christopher, John
1956   **$7.00**

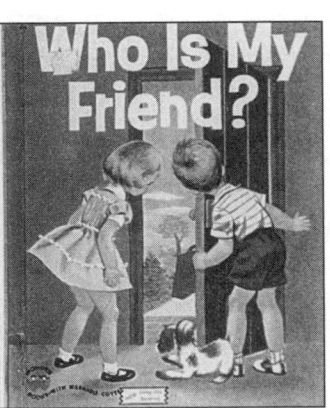

646

Who Is My Friend?
Illus.: Mc Laughlin, Birdice
Author: Corum, Louise
1959   **$7.00**

647C

Lord's Prayer, The (Catholic)
Illus.: Brulé, Al
1956   **$7.00**

647P

Lord's Prayer, The (Protestant)
Illus.: Brulé, Al
1956   **$7.00**

648

10 Rabbits
Illus.: Dixon, Rachel Taft
Author: Potter, Miriam Clark
1957   **$7.00**

649

Wild Bill Hickok
Illus.: Nielsen, Jon
Author: Sutton, Felix
1956   **$20.00**

650

Silver Chief
Illus.: Hauge, Carl & Mary
Author: Weigle, Oscar
1956   **$18.00**

651

Twelve Days Of Christmas, The
Illus.: Mars, W. T.
1956 **$8.00**

652

Kewtee Bear-Santa's Helper
Illus.: Dixon, Rachel Taft
Author: Reed, Alan; Stout, Bert;
Quigley, Truman
1956 **$15.00**

653

**Most Beautiful Tree In The World,
The**
Illus.: Weisgard, Leonard
Author: Weisgard, Leonard
1956 **$10.00**

654

Quiet Book, The
Illus.: Kendrick, Alcy
Author: Flynn, Helen M.
1958 **$7.00**

655

Rattle-Rattle Train, The
Illus.: Bobertz, Carl
Author: Geis, Darlene
1957 **$7.00**

656

Rattle-Rattle Dump Truck, The
Illus.: Bobertz, Carl
Author: Geis, Darlene
1958 **$7.00**

657

I Love You
Illus.: Bonsall, George; Newell,
Crosby
Author: Bonsall, George; Newell,
Crosby
1956 **$7.00**

658

Can't Verify Title

659

Snow White And The Seven Dwarfs
Illus.: Seiden, Art
1955 **$7.00**

659

Snow White And The Seven Dwarfs
(2nd Cover)
Illus.: Seiden, Art
1955 **$3.00**

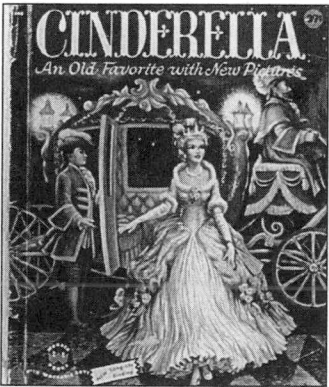

660

Cinderella
Illus.: Ives, Ruth
Author: Andreas, Evelyn
1954 **$7.00**

660

Cinderella
(2nd Cover)
Illus.: Ives, Ruth
Author: Andreas, Evelyn
1954 **$4.00**

661

My First Book Of Prayers
Illus.: Ives, Ruth
Author: Juergens, Mary
1953 **$7.00**

662

Mighty Mouse-Santa's Helper
Illus.: Chad
Author: Sutton, Felix
1955 $20.00

663

Baby's Day
Illus.: Pointer, Priscilla
Author: Edwards, Annette
1953 $7.00

664

Henry In Lollipop Land
Illus.: Anderson, Carl
Author: Anderson, Carl
1953 $16.00

665

Felix The Cat
Illus.: Sullivan, Pat
Author: Sullivan, Pat
1953 $18.00

665

Felix The Cat
(2nd Cover)
Illus.: Sullivan, Pat
Author: Sullivan, Pat
1953 $10.00

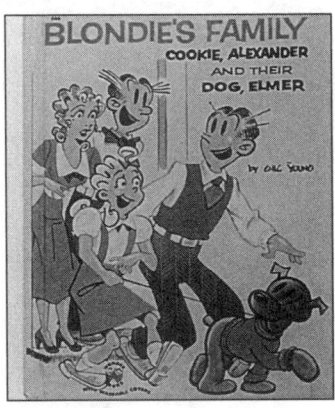

666

Blondie's Family Cookie, Alexander, And Their Dog, Elmer
Illus.: Young, Chic
Author: Young, Chic
1954 $18.00

667

Popeye
Illus.: Sagendorf, Bud
Author: Sagendorf, Bud
1955 $16.00

668

How Peter Cottontail Got His Name
Illus.: Jackson, Pauline
Author: Burgess, Thornton W.
1957 $7.00

669

Who Lives Here?
Illus.: Varga, Judith
Author: Varga, Judith
1958 $7.00

670
Can't Verify Title

671
Can't Verify Title

672
Just Like Me
Illus.: Weisgard, Leonard
Author: Weisgard, Leonard
1954 $6.00

673
Let's Take A Ride
Illus.: Dillon, Corrine
Author: Hope, Laura Lee
1954 $6.00

674

Lassie's Long Trip
Illus.: Hoecker, Hazel
Author: Knight, Jere
1957 $8.00

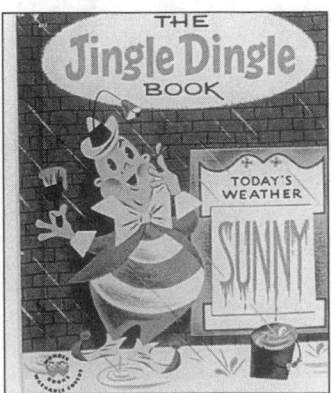

675

Jingle Dingle Book, The
Illus.: Ruhman, Ruth
Author: Jason, Leon
1957 $8.00

676

I Can I Can I Can
Illus.: Schad, Helen G.
Author: Schad, Helen G.
1958 **$6.00**

677

Mighty Mouse-Dinky Learns To Fly
Illus.: Chad
Author: Sutton, Felix
1953 **$16.00**

678

Mighty Mouse And The Scarecrow
Illus.: Chad
Author: Sutton, Felix
1954 **$16.00**

679

Puppy Who Would Not Mind His Mother, The
Illus.: Hopkins, Hildegarde
Author: Fyleman, Rose
1949 **$6.00**

680

Let's Pretend
Illus.: Clarke, Joan
Author: Clarke, Frances
1959 **$6.00**

681

Camping Trip With The Range Rider, A
Illus.: Nielsen, Jon
Author: Sutton, Felix
1957 **$6.00**

682

Wonder Book Of Counting Rhymes, The
Illus.: Parsons, Virginia
Author: Pierce, June
1957 **$6.00**

682

Wonder Book Of Counting Rhymes, The
(2nd Cover)
Illus.: Parsons, Virginia
Author: Pierce, June
1957 **$4.00**

683

Puzzle For Raggedy Ann And Andy, A
Illus.: Dixon, Rachel Taft
Author: Gruelee, Johnny
1957 **$16.00**

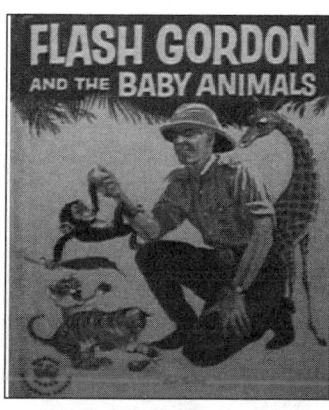

684

Flash Gordon And The Baby Animals
Illus.: Berger, Alex
Author: King Features Syndicate
1956 **$15.00**

685

Henny-Penny
Illus.: Ponter, James
1954 **$6.00**

686

Let's Play Nurse And Doctor
Illus.: Stang, Judy
Author: Stang, Judy
1953 **$6.00**

687

Wonder Book Of Happy Animals, The
Illus.: Jones, Robert
Author: Weigle, Oscar
1957 **$6.00**

688

Dress-Up Parade, The
Illus.: Wilde, George
Author: Wilde, Irma
1953 $7.00

689

What Time Is It?
(A Romper Room Book)
Illus.: Zabinski, Joseph
Author: Peter, John
1954 $6.00

689

What Time Is It?
(2nd Cover)
Illus.: Zabinski, Joseph
Author: Peter, John
1954 $3.00

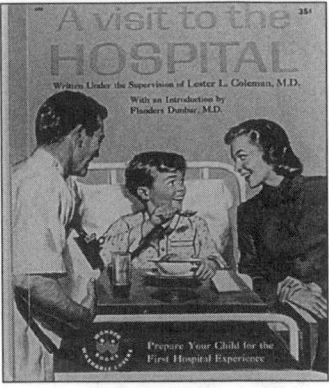

690

Visit To The Hospital, A
Illus.: Rossi, Ken
Author: Chase, Francine
1958 $6.00

690

Visit To The Hospital, A
(2nd Cover)
Illus.: Rossi, Ken
Author: Chase, Francine
1958 $3.00

691

Let's Go To School
Illus.: Hoecker, Hazel
Author: Edwards, Annette
1954 $6.00

691

Let's Go To School
(2nd Cover)
Illus.: Hoecker, Hazel
Author: Edwards, Annette
1954 $3.00

692

Counting Book, The
Illus.: Riley, Bob
Author: Peter, John
1957 $6.00

693

Let's Go Shopping
Illus.: Meyerhoff, Nancy
Author: Brooke, Guyon
1958 $6.00

694

Heckle And Jeckle
Illus.: Jason, Leon
Author: Jason, Leon
1957 $14.00

695

Gandy Goose
Illus.: Ruhman, Ruth
Author: Jason, Leon
1957 $18.00

696

Tuggy The Tugboat
Illus.: Hauge, Carl & Mary
Author: Berg, Jean Horton
1958 $6.00

697

Popeye Goes On A Picnic
Illus.: Sagendorf, Bud
Author: Newell, Crosby
1958   **$6.00**

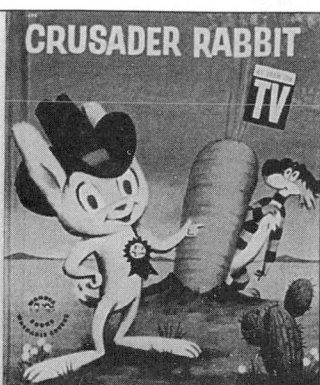

698

Crusader Rabbit
Illus.: Krusz, Arthur
Author: Weigle, Oscar
1958   **$20.00**

699

Frisky, The Black Colt
Illus.: Steiner, Charlotte
Author: Steiner, Charlotte; Hoff,
Virginia
1951   **$6.00**

700

Once Upon A Time
(The Cow In The Silo)
Illus.: Cunningham, Dellwyn
Author: Goudell, Patricia
1950   **$8.00**

701

Can You Guess? (Guess What)
Illus.: Wood, Ruth
Author: Klein, Leonore
1953   **$6.00**

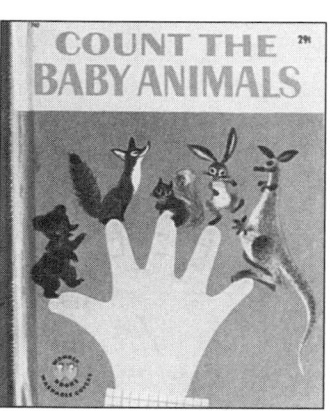

702

Count The Baby Animals
Illus.: Plummer, Virginia
Author: Walters, Marguerite
1958   **$6.00**

703

Tom Terrific With Mighty Manfred
The Wonder Dog
Illus.: Bartsch, Arthur
Author: Newell, Crosby
1958   **$16.00**

704

Child's Garden Of Versus, A
Illus.: Wood, Ruth
Author: Stevenson, Robert Louis
1958   **$6.00**

705

Dick Whittington And His Cat
Illus.: Cunningham, Dellwyn
Author: Weigle, Oscar
1958   **$6.00**

705

Dick Whittington And His Cat
(2nd Cover)
Illus.: Cunningham, Dellwyn
Author: Weigle, Oscar
1958   **$3.00**

706

Aesop's Fables
Illus.: Seiden, Art
1958   **$6.00**

707

Brave Little Tailor, The
Illus: Meyers, Bernice
Author: Weigle, Oscar
1958   **$6.00**

707

Magilla Gorilla And The Super Kite
Illus.: Hanna-Barbera Productions,
Inc.
Author: Elias, Horace J.
1976   **$10.00**

708

Mister Magoo
Illus.: Nofziger, Ed
Author: Newell, Crosby
1958 $16.00

709

Quiet Little Indian, The
Illus.: Wood, Ruth
Author: Geis, Darlene
1958 $6.00

710

Little Schoolhouse
Illus.: Elgin, Kathleen
Author: Newell, Crosby
1958 $6.00

710

Little Schoolhouse
(2nd Cover)
Illus.: Elgin, Kathleen
Author: Newell, Crosby
1958 $3.00

711

Terrytoon Space Train, The
Illus.: Gershen, Irv
Author: Waring, Barbara
1958 $18.00

712

Heckle And Jeckle Visit The Farm
Illus.: Gershen, Irv
Author: Waring, Barbara
1958 $16.00

713

Tom Corbett: A Trip To The Moon
Illus.: Vaughn, Frank
Author: Martin, Marcia
1953 $18.00

714

Ten Little Fingers
Illus.: Pointer, Priscilla
Author: Pointer, Priscilla
1954 $6.00

714

Ten Little Fingers
(2nd Cover)
Illus.: Pointer, Priscilla
Author: Pointer, Priscilla
1954 $2.00

715

Little Red Caboose That Ran Away, The
Illus.: Burchard, Peter
Author: Curren, Polly
1952 $6.00

716

Felix On Television
Illus.: Oriolo, Joe
Author: Shapiro, Irwin
1956 $14.00

717

Mighty Mouse To The Rescue
Illus.: Gershen, Irv
Author: Waring, Barbara
1958 $17.00

718
Choo Choo Train, The
Illus.: Kessler, Leonard
Author: Pennington, Lillian Boyer
$6.00

719
There Was Once A Little Boy
Illus.: Cook, Sunny B.
Author: Budney, Blossom
1959 $6.00

720
Littlest Snowman, The
Illus.: De Santis, George
Author: Tazewell, Charles
1958 $12.00

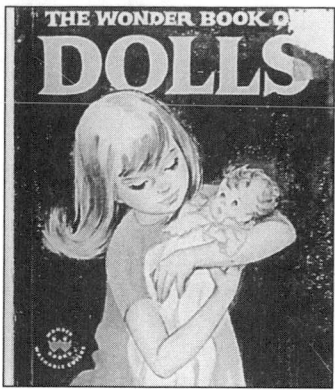

721
Wonder Book of Dolls, The
Illus.: Wohlberg, Meg
Author: Hamilton, Antoinette
1959 $10.00

722
Stacks Of Caps
(Monkey See Monkey Do)
Illus.: Moyers, William
Author: Tooze, Ruth
1949 $6.00

723
This Magic World
Illus.: Koehler, Cynthia Iliff
Author: Koehler, Cynthia Iliff
1959 $6.00

723
This Magic World
(2nd Cover)
Illus.: Koehler, Cynthia Iliff
Author: Koehler, Cynthia Iliff
1959 $2.00

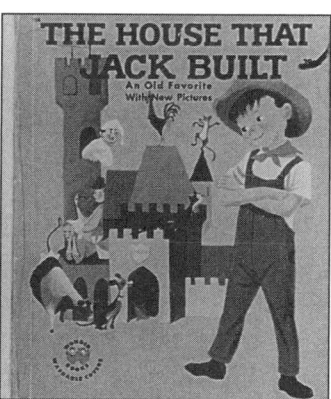

724
House That Jack Built, The
Illus.: Wilson, Dagmar
1959 $6.00

725
Nonsense Alphabet, The
Illus.: Seiden, Art
Author: Lear, Edward
1959 $6.00

726
Good Night Fairy Tales
Illus.: Weber, Adele; Heins, Doris
Author: Weigle, Oscar
1959 $6.00

727
Raggedy Ann's Secret
Illus.: Wood, Ruth
Author: Gruelle, Johnny
1959 $15.00

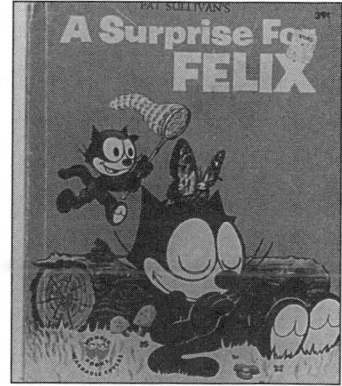

728
Surprise For Felix, A
Illus.: Oriolo, Joe
Author: Sullivan's. Pat
1959 $10.00

729

Little Engine That Laughed, The
Illus.: Seiden, Art
Author: Evers, Alf
1950   **$6.00**

730

Wonder Book Of Favorite Nursery Tales, The
Illus.: Peller, Jackie; Tamburine, Jean
1953   **$6.00**

731

Big-Little Dinosaur, The
Illus.: Jones, Bob
Author: Geis, Darlene
1959   **$6.00**

731

Big-Little Dinosaur, The
(2nd Cover)
Illus.: Jones, Bob
Author: Geis, Darlene
1959   **$3.00**

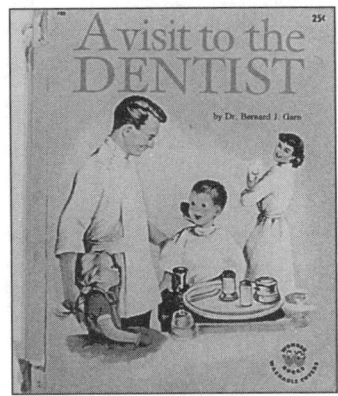

732

Visit To The Dentist, A
Illus.: Wallace, Lucille
Author: Garn, Dr. Bernard J.
1959   **$5.00**

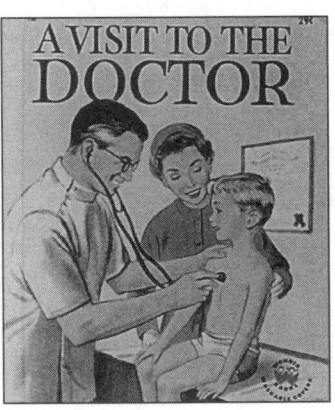

733

Visit To The Doctor, A
Illus.: Dowd, Vic
Author: Berger, Knute; Tidwell & Haseltine
1960   **$6.00**

734

Funny Mixed-Up Story, The
Illus.: Wilson, Dagmar
Author: Mcnulty, Faith
1959   **$6.00**

735

Tom Terrific's Greatest Adventure
Illus.: Newell, Crosby
Author: Newell, Crosby
1959   **$15.00**

736

Joke On Farmer Al Falfa, A
Illus.: Gershen, Irv
Author: Newell, Crosby
1959   **$18.00**

737

Busy Baby Lion, The
Illus.: Rik, Jottier
Author: Lucienne, Erville
1959   **$7.00**

738

Baby's First Christmas
Illus.: Dart, Eleanor
1959   **$8.00**

739

Summer Friends
Illus.: Wood, Ruth
Author: Krinsky, Jeanette
1960   **$6.00**

740

Blow, Wind, Blow
Illus.: D'amato, Janet & Alex
Author: D'amato, Janet & Alex
1960 $6.00

741

Bootsy
Illus.: Lear, Mirian
Author: Erville, Lucienne
1959 $6.00

742

Whose Hat Is That?
Illus.: Kessler, Leonard
Author: Kessler, Leonard
1960 $6.00

743

Come And See The Rainbow
Illus.: Scholz, Catherine
Author: Walters, Marguerite
1960 $6.00

744

Little Garage Man, The
Illus.: Binst, Claire
Author: Delahaye, Gilgert; Smith, George
1960 $6.00

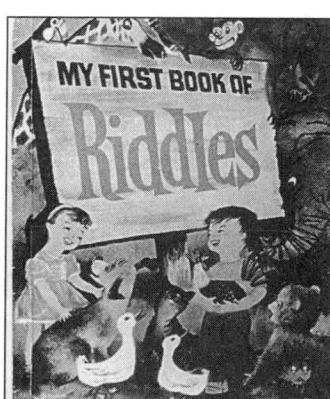

745

My First Book Of Riddles
Illus.: D'amato, Janet & Alex
Author: D'amato, Janet & Alex
1960 $6.00

745

My First Book Of Riddles
(2nd Cover)
Illus.: D'amato, Janet & Alex
Author: D'amato, Janet & Alex
1960 $2.00

746

I See The Sky
Illus.: Cook, Sunny B.
Author: Peters, Ann
1960 $6.00

747

Insects We Know
Illus.: Koehler, Cynthia Iliff
Author: Rood, Ronald N.
1960 $6.00

748

Runaway Baby Bird, The
Illus.: Mazza, Adriana
Author: Walters, Marguerite
1960 $6.00

749

Cozy Little Farm, The
Illus.: Angela
Author: Bonino, Louise
1946 $5.00

749

Cozy Little Farm, The
(2nd Cover)
Illus.: Angela
Author: Bonino, Louise
1946 $5.00

750

House That Popeye Built, The
Illus.: Sagendorf, Bud
Author: Newell, Crosby
1960 **$7.00**

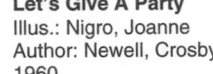

751

Hoppy The Puppy (The Roly-Poly Puppy)
Illus.: Berthold
Author: Bates, Barbara S.
1950 **$6.00**

752

Let's Give A Party
Illus.: Nigro, Joanne
Author: Newell, Crosby
1960 **$5.00**

753

Songs To Sing And Play
Illus.: Wood, Ruth
Author: Weigle, Oscar
1960 **$6.00**

754

Horse For Johnny, A
Illus.: Moyers, William
Author: Bookman, Charlotte
1952 **$6.00**

755

Littlest Angel, The
Illus.: Evans, Katherine
Author: Tazewell, Charles
1960 **$10.00**

755

Littlest Angel, The
(2nd Cover)
Illus.: Evans, Katherine
Author: Tazewell, Charles
1960 **$5.00**

756

Fixit Man, The
Illus.: Wilde, George
Author: Wilde, Irma
1952 **$6.00**

757

Wonder Book Of Birds, The
Illus.: Koehler, Alvin
Author: Koehler, Cynthia Iliff
1961 **$6.00**

758

Minute-And-A-Half-Man, The
Illus.: Kirkel, Stephen
Author: Newell, Crosby
1960 **$18.00**

759

Little Audrey And The Moon Lady
Illus.: Harvey Cartoon Studios
Author: Harvey Cartoon Studios
1960 **$18.00**

759

Little Audrey And The Moon Lady
(2nd Cover)
Illus.: Harvey Cartoon Studios
Author: Harvey Cartoon Studios
1960 **$10.00**

760

Deputy Dog
Illus.: Bezada, Herb; Trombetta,
Mario
Author: Newell, Crosby
1960 **$20.00**

761

Casper, The Friendly Ghost
Illus.: Harvey Cartoon Studios
Author: Harvey Cartoon Studios
1960 **$15.00**

762

Rolling Wheels
Illus.: Dauber, Elizabeth
Author: Elting, Mary
1950 **$6.00**

763

**Romper Room Do Bee Book Of
Manners, The**
Illus.: Seiden, Art
Author: Claster, Nancy
1960 **$6.00**

764

Let's Go Fishing
Illus.: Newell, Crosby
Author: Bonsall, George
1955 **$6.00**

765

Uncle Wiggily's Adventures
Illus.: Leone, Sergio
Author: Garis, Howard R.
1961 **$16.00**

766

Uncle Wiggily And His Friends
Illus.: Leone, Sergio
Author: Garis, Howard R.
1961 **$16.00**

767

Pecos Bill
Illus.: Canizares, Stephenie
Author: Walsh, Henry
1961 **$10.00**

768

I See The Sea
Illus.: Wood, Ruth
Author: Mcgovern, Ann
1961 **$6.00**

769

**Hector Crosses The River....With
George Washington**
Illus.: Crapanzano, Joe; Bezada Jr.,
Herbert
Author: Newell, Crosby
1961 **$18.00**

770

Deputy Dawg's Big Catch
Illus.: Bezada, Herb; Crapanzano,
Joseph
Author: Newell, Crosby
1961 **$20.00**

771

**Donkey Who Wanted To Be Wise,
The**
Illus.: Marsia, Robert
Author: Delahaye, Gilbert
1961 **$6.00**

772

Peter Hatches An Egg
Illus.: Marlier, Marcel
Author: Brialmont, Louise Bienvenu-Brialmont
1962 **$6.00**

772

Peter Hatches An Egg
Illus.: Marlier, Marcel
Author: Brialmont, Louise Bienvenu-Brialmont
1962 **$4.00**

773

Deputy Dawg And The Space Man
Illus.: Bezada, Herb; Crapanzano, Joseph
Author: Sand, Helen
1961 **$18.00**

774

Bunny Sitter, The
Illus.: Meyerhoff, Nancy
Author: Grilley, Virginia
1963 **$6.00**

775

To Market To Market
Illus.: Seiden, Art
Author: Potter, Miriam Clark
1961 **$6.00**

776

December Is For Christmas
Illus.: Kendrick, Alcy
Author: Scott, Ann
1961 **$6.00**

777

Brave Little Duck, The
Illus.: Gayer, Marguerite
Author: Conkling, Fluer
1953 **$6.00**

778

Henry Goes To A Party
Illus.: Anderson, Carl
Author: Anderson, Carl
1955 **$15.00**

779

Who Goes There?
Illus.: D'amato, Janet & Alex
Author: D'amato, Janet & Alex
1961 **$6.00**

780

Fluffy Little Lamb
Illus.: Baudoin, Simonne
Author: Delahaye, Gilbert
1962 **$6.00**

781

Sheri Lewis Wonder Book, The
Illus.: Wood, Ruth
Author: Newell, Crosby
1961 **$13.00**

782

Wonder Book Of Fish, The
Illus.: Koehler, Cynthia Iliff & Alvin
Author: Koehler, Cynthia Iliff & Alvin
1961 **$6.00**

783

Dondi
Illus.: Deson, Gus; Hasen, Erwin
Author: Deson, Gus; Hasen, Erwin
1961 **$15.00**

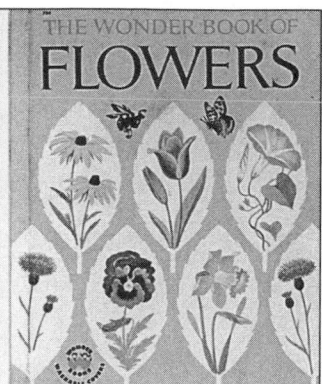

784

Wonder Book Of Flowers, The
Illus.: Koehler, Cynthia Iliff
Author: Koehler, Cynthia Iliff
1961 **$5.00**

785

Wonder Book Of The Seashore, The
Illus.: Koehler, Alvin
Author: Koehler, Cynthia Iliff
1962 **$5.00**

786

Wonder Book Of Kittens, The
Illus.: Koehler, Cynthia Iliff
Author: Waring, Barbara
1963 **$6.00**

787

Baby Huey
Illus.: Harvey Cartoon Studios
Author: Harvey Cartoon Studios
1961 **$20.00**

788

Herman And Katnip
Illus.: Harvey Cartoon Studios
Author: Harvey Cartoon Studios
1961 **$17.00**

789

What Is That?
Illus.: Hampson, Denman
Author: Hampson, Denman
1961 **$6.00**

790

Animals' Party, The
Illus.: Brozowska, Elisabeth
Author: Brozowska, Elisabeth
1962 **$10.00**

790

Jetsons The Great Pizza Hunt, The
Illus.: Hanna-Barbera Productions, Inc.
Author: Elias, Horace J.
1976 **$10.00**

791

Popeye's Big Surprise
Illus.: Sagendorf, Bud
Author: Waring, Barbara
1962 **$8.00**

792

What Are You Looking At?
Illus.: Bonsall, George; Newell, Crosby
Author: Bonsall, George; Newell, Crosby
1954 **$6.00**

793

Really Truly Treasure Hunt, The
Illus.: Newell, Crosby
Author: Bonsall, George
1954 **$6.00**

794

Moppets' Surprise Party, The
Illus.: Newell, Crosby
Author: Newell, Crosby
1955 **$6.00**

795

Morning Noises
Illus.: Gree, Alain
Author: Gree, Alain
1962 **$6.00**

796

Over In The Meadow
Illus.: Wood, Ruth
Author: Wadsworth, Olive A.
1962 **$6.00**

797

Baby Raccoon
Illus.: Baudoin, Simonne
Author: Berg, Jean Horton
1963 **$6.00**

798

Petey Parakeet
Illus.: Cook, Sunny B.
Author: Bonsall, George; Newell,
Crosby
1963 **$6.00**

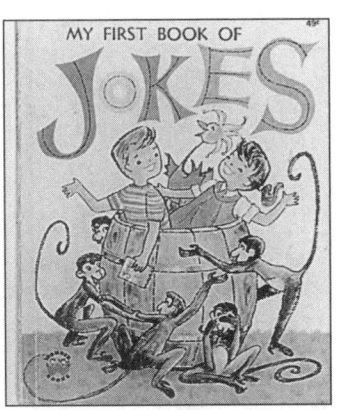

799

My First Book Of Jokes
Illus.: D'amato, Janet & Alex
Author: D'amato, Janet & Alex
1962 **$6.00**

800

Costume Party, The
Illus.: D'amato, Janet & Alex
Author: Morel, Eve
1962 **$6.00**

801

Who Has My Shoes?
Illus.: Kessler, Leonard
Author: Kessler, Leonard
1963 **$6.00**

802

Doll Family, The
Illus.: Harris, Martin
Author: Wilson, Dorothy
1962 **$8.00**

803

Pelle's New Suit
Illus.: Wilde, George
Author: Beskow, Elsa
1962 **$6.00**

804

Wonder Book Of Puppies, The
Illus.: Koehler, Cynthia Iliff & Alvin
Author: Koehler, Cynthia Iliff & Alvin
1963 **$6.00**

805

Casper And Wendy
Illus.: Harvey Cartoon Studios
Author: Harvey Cartoon Studios
1963 **$8.00**

806

Can't Verify Title

807
All In A Day's Work
Illus.: Leone, Sergio
Author: Emerson, Caroline D.
1964 **$6.00**

808
Romper Room Laughing Book, The
Illus.: Nankivel, Claudine
Author: Claster, Nancy
1963 **$6.00**
809
Can't Verify Title

810
City Boy, Country Boy
Illus.: Weigel, Susi
Author: Lobe, Mira
1963 **$6.00**

811
Rabbits Give A Party, The
Illus.: Baudoin, Simonne
Author: Dermine, Lucie
1963 **$5.00**

811
Rabbits Give A Party, The
(2nd Cover)
Illus.: Baudoin, Simonne
Author: Dermine, Lucie
1963 **$4.00**

812
Peter Rabbit
Illus.: Phoebe, Erickson
Author: Potter, Beatrix
1947 **$6.00**
813
Can't Verify Title
814
Can't Verify Title

815
Boy Who Wouldn't Eat His Breakfast, The
Illus.: Brozowska, Elizabeth
Author: Brozowska, Elizabeth
1963 **$6.00**

816
Freddy And The Indians
Illus.: Binst, Claire
Author: Delahaye, Gilbert
1963 **$6.00**

817
Animals Build A House, The
Illus.: Marsia, Robert
Author: Marsia, Robert, Delahaye, Gilbert
1963 **$6.00**

818
Merry Christmas Mr. Snowman!
Illus.: Wilde, Irma
Author: Wilde, Irma
1951 **$8.00**

818
Merry Christmas Mr. Snowman
(2nd Cover)
Illus.: Wilde, Irma
Author: Wilde, Irma
1951 **$6.00**

819
Polly's' Christmas Present
Illus.: Wilde, Irma
Author: Wilde, Irma
1953 **$6.00**

820

Merry Christmas Book, The
Illus.: Scholz, Catherine
Author: Berg, Jean Horton
1953 **$6.00**

821

Buzzy The Funny Crow
Illus.: Harvey Cartoon Studios
Author: Harvey Cartoon Studios
1963 **$7.00**

822

I Can Do Anything ... Almost
Illus.: Murtagh, Betty
Author: Hartman, Virginia
1963 **$5.00**

822

I Can Do Anything ... Almost
(2nd Cover)
Illus.: Murtagh, Betty
Author: Hartman, Virginia
1963 **$5.00**

823

ABC and Counting Rhymes
Illus.: Horton, Mary
1963 **$6.00**

824

Alvin's Lost Voice
Illus.: Kurtz, Bob
Author: Kurtz, Bob
1963 **$16.00**

825

Animals' Playground, The
Illus.: Seiden, Art
Author: Marshall, Virginia Stone
1964 **$6.00**

826

Around The World Cutout Book
Illus.: Galst, Annie
Author: Galst, Annie
1964 **$6.00**

827

Wonder Book Of Trees, The
Illus.: Koehler, Alvin
Author: Koehler, Cynthia Iliff
1964 **$6.00**

827

Wonder Book Of Trees, The
(2nd Cover)
Illus.: Koehler, Alvin
Author: Koehler, Cynthia Iliff
1964 **$4.00**

828

Muskie And His Friends
Illus.: Kirkel, Stephen; Bezada, Herb
Author: Bethell, Jean
1963 **$18.00**

829

Ollie Bakes A Cake
Illus.: Meyerhoff, Nancy
Author: Bethell, Jean
1964 **$20.00**

830

Trick On Deputy Dog, A
Illus.: Kirkel, Stephen; Bezada, Herb
Author: Bethell, Jean
1964 $20.00

831

Luno The Soaring Stallion
Illus.: Kirkel, Stephen; Bezada, Herb
Author: Bethell, Jean
1964 $14.00

832

Churkendoose, The
Illus.: Cunningham, Dellwyn
Author: Berenberg, Ben Ross
1946 $10.00

832

Churkendoose, The
(2nd Cover)
Illus.: Cunningham, Dellwyn
Author: Berenberg, Ben Ross
1946 $10.00

832

What Am I?
(Formerly The Churkendoose)
Illus.: Cunningham, Dellwyn
Author: Berenberg, Ben Ross
1946 $10.00

833

What Can We Do With Blocks?
Illus.: Herric, Pru
Author: Shaine, Frances
1964 $6.00

834

Look Who's Here!
Illus.: Gaulke, Gloria
Author: Walters, Marguerite
1964 $5.00

834

Look Who's Here!
(2nd Cover)
Illus.: Gaulke, Gloria
Author: Walters, Marguerite
1964 $5.00

835

Diz And Liz
Illus.: Allen, Colin
Author: Key, Ted
1965 $13.00

836

Tutu The Little Fawn
Illus.: Morel, Eve
Author: Simon, Romain
1964 $6.00

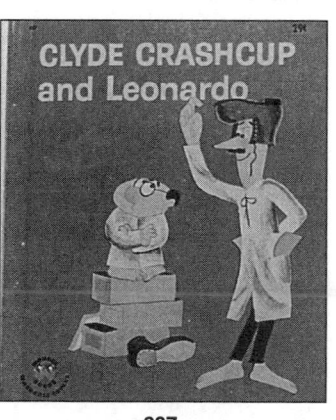

837

Clyde Crashcup And Leonardo
Illus.: Kurtz, Bob
Author: Kurtz, Bob
1965 $18.00

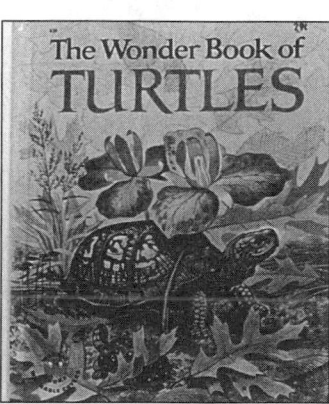

838

Wonder Book Of Turtles, The
Illus.: Koehlerm Cynthia & Alvin
Author: Morel, Eve
1964 $4.00

839

Animals' Vacation, The
Illus.: Haber, Shel & Jan
Author: Haber, Shel & Jan
1964   **$4.00**

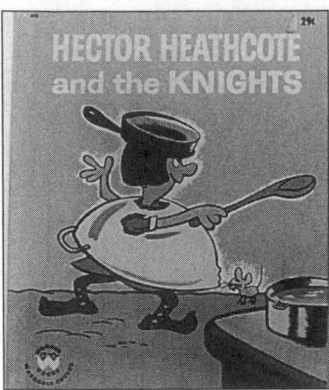

840

Hector Heathcote And The Knights
Illus.: Zaffo, George
Author: Bethell, Jean
1965   **$18.00**

841

Silly Sidney
Illus.: Cummings, Art
Author: Bethell, Jean
1965   **$18.00**

842

Once There Was A House
Illus.: Wood, Ruth
Author: Wynnw, Milton
1965   **$5.00**

843

Peter Cottontail And Reddy Fox
Illus.: Hauge, Carl & Mary
Author: Burgess, Thornton W.
1954   **$5.00**

843

Peter Cottontail And Reddy Fox
(2nd Cover)
Illus.: Hauge, Carl & Mary
Author: Burgess, Thornton W.
1954   **$4.00**

844

So This Is Spring!
Illus.: Dixon, Rachel
Author: Fritz, Jean
1954   **$5.00**

844

So This Is Spring!
(2nd Cover)
Illus.: Dixon, Rachel
Author: Fritz, Jean
1954   **$4.00**

845

Nine Rabbits And Another
Illus.: Dixon, Rachel Taft
Author: Potter, Miriam Clark
1957   **$5.00**

846

What's For Breakfast?
Illus.: Wilde, Irma
Author: Wilde, Irma
1950   **$5.00**

847

Hungry Baby Bunny, The
(Red Cover)
Illus.: Seiden, Bea Rabin
Author: Evers, Alf
1951   **$5.00**

847

Hungry Baby Bunny, The
(Yellow Cover) (2nd Cover)
Illus.: Seiden, Bea Rabin
Author: Evers, Alf
1951   **$4.00**

848
Sonny The Luck Bunny
Illus.: Seiden, Art
Author: Martin, Marcia
1952   **$5.00**

848
Sonny The Luck Bunny
(2nd Cover)
Illus.: Seiden, Art
Author: Martin, Marcia
1952   **$4.00**

849
Barbie - The Baby Sitter
Illus.: Nankivel, Claudine
Author: Bethell, Jean
1964   **$15.00**

850
Casper The Friendly Ghost In Ghostland
Illus.: Harvey Cartoon Studios
Author: Harvey Cartoon Studios
1965   **$8.00**

851
Puff The Magic Dragon
Illus.: Tallarico, Tony
Author: Newman, Paul
1965   **$7.00**

852
Wonder Book Of Cottontails And Other Rabbits, The
Illus.: Koehler, Alvin
Author: Koehler, Cynthia Iliff
1965   **$4.00**

853
Astronut And The Flying Bus
Illus.: Tallarico, Tony
Author: Lenhart, Ellen
1965   **$16.00**

854
Romper Room Safety Book, The
Illus.: Seiden, Art
Author: Claster, Nancy
1965   **$6.00**

855
Casper And Wendy Adventures
Illus.: Harvey Cartoon Studios
Author: Harvey Cartoon Studios
1969   **$12.00**
856
Can't Verify Title

857
Wonder Book Of Horses, The
Illus.: Koehler, Alvin
Author: Koehler, Cynthia Iliff
1965   **$4.00**

858
Night Before Christmas, The
Illus.: Leone, Sergio
Author: Moore, Clement C.
1965   **$6.00**

858
Night Before Christmas, The
(2nd Cover)
Illus.: Leone, Sergio
Author: Moore, Clement C.
1965   **$4.00**

860

Soupy Sales And The Talking Turtle
Illus.: Tallarico, Tony
Author: Bethell, Jean
1965   **$8.00**

861
Can't Verify Title

862
Can't Verify Title

863
Can't Verify Title

864
Can't Verify Title

865

Waiting For Santa Claus
Illus.: Cummings, Alison
Author: Martin, Marcia
1952   **$7.00**

866

How The Rabbit Found Christmas
Illus.: Kendrick, Alcy
Author: Scott, Ann
1961   **$6.00**

867

Kewtee Bear's Christmas
Illus.: Dixon, Rachel Taft
Author: Reed, Alan; Stout, Bert;
Quigley, Truman
1956   **$10.00**

868

Raggedy Ann's Christmas Surprise
Illus.: Sinnickson, Tom
Author: Gruelle, Johnny
1952   **$16.00**

869

Christmas Favorites (The Wonder Christmas Book)
Illus.: Myers, Lou
1951   **$5.00**

869

Christmas Favorites (The Wonder Christmas Book)
Illus.: Myers, Lou
1951   **$4.00**

876

Baby's First Christmas
Illus.: Dart, Eleanor
1959   **$6.00**

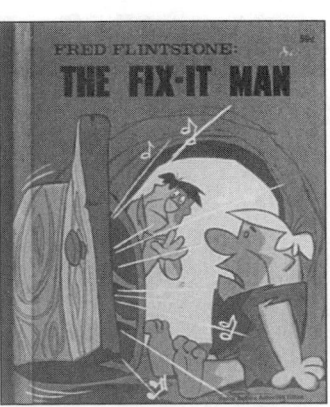

917

Fix-It Man, The
Illus.: Hanna-Barbera Productions, Inc.
Author: Elias, Horace J.
1976   **$8.00**

919

Pebbles And Bamm-Bamm Find Things To Do
Illus.: Hanna-Barbera Productions, Inc.
Author: Elias, Horace J.
1976   **$10.00**

921

Yogi Bear And The Baby Skunk
Illus.: Hanna-Barbera Productions, Inc.
Author: Elias, Horace J.
1976   **$8.00**

924
Yogi Bear Mosquito Flying Days
Illus.: Hanna-Barbera Productions,
Inc
Author: Elias, Horace J.
1976 $8.00

926
**Yogi Bear Playtime In Jellystone
Park**
Illus.: Hanna-Barbera Productions,
Inc.
Author: Elias, Horace J.
1976 $8.00

927
Flintstones, The: Everyone's Egg
Illus.: Hanna-Barbera Productions,
Inc.
Author: Elias, Horace J.
1976 $8.00

944
**Huckleberry Hound The Big
Blooming Rosebush**
Illus.: Hanna-Barbera Productions,
Inc.
Author: Elias, Horace J.
1976 $8.00

Wonder Books Index

A Brief History of Treasure Books

Treasure Books was a subsidiary of Grosset & Dunlap, the same company that printed Wonder Books. They were printed from 1952 to 1956. You may notice that some Treasure Book titles later appeared as Wonder Books (around 1957).

The books measured 6-5/8 inches x 7-7/8 inches and contained 28 full-color pages. Treasure Books were similar to Little Golden Books: the front and back covers were stapled together and covered with a paper spine. The spines changed four times over the books' short life: light tan (1952), very pale red (1953), vey dark red (late 1953), and yellow with thin colored stripes (around 1954).

How to Tell Treasure Book Editions

There are no markings to distinguish a first edition from a reprint, but you can use the last titles on the back of the book to approximate dates. Numbers 850 to 853 only listed four titles. If the last number listed on the back cover is close to the number of the book, you probably have a first edition. The back covers ended in the following numbers: 853, 857, 861, 863, 865, 869, 873, 878, 882, 887, 893, 899, 902, 903, and 906.

Treasure Books—By Book Number

850

City Boy And The Country Horse, The
Illus.: Woyers, William
Author: Bookman, Charlotte
1952 **$15.00**

851

Fixit Man, The
Illus.: Wilde, George
Author: Wilde, Irma
1952 **$12.00**

852

Little Red Caboose That Ran Away, The
Illus.: Burchard, Peter
Author: Curren, Polly
1952 **$12.00**

853

Wonderful Treasure Hunt, The
Illus.: Wilde, George
Author: Wilde, Irma
1952 **$12.00**

854

Brave Little Duck, The
Illus.: Gayer, Marguerite
Author: Conkling, Fleur
1953 **$12.00**

855

Treasure Book Of Riddles, The
Illus.: Wood, Ruth
Author: North, Robert
1950 **$12.00**

856

Treasure Book Of Favorite Nursery Tales, The
Illus.: Peller, Jackie; Tamburine, Jean
1953 **$12.00**

857

Little Engine That Laughed, The
Illus.: Seiden, Art
Author: Evers, Alf
1950 **$12.00**

858

My First Book Of Farm Animals
Illus.: Wilde, Irma
Author: Edward, Annette
1953 **$12.00**

859

Baby's Day
Illus.: Pointer, Priscilla
Author: Edwards, Annette
1953 **$12.00**

860

Mighty Mouse
Illus.: Chad
Author: Sutton, Felix
1953 **$18.00**

861

Dress-Up Parade, The
Illus.: Wilde, George
Author: Wilde, Irma
1953 **$18.00**

862

Let's Take A Ride
Illus.: Wilde, George
Author: Martin, Marcia
1953   **$12.00**

863

Let's Play Nurse And Doctor
Illus.: Stang, Judy
Author: Stang, Judy
1953   **$12.00**

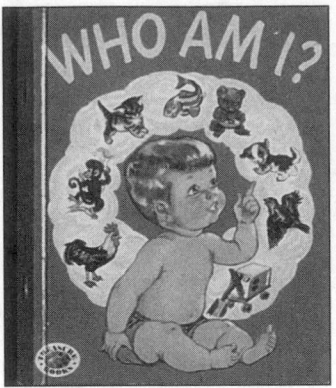

864

Who Am I?
Illus.: Schad, Helen G.
Author: Schad, Helen
1953   **$12.00**

865

Merry Mailman, The
Illus.: Wood, Ruth
Author: Martin, Marcia
1953   **$12.00**

866

Mighty Mouse: Dinky Learns To Fly
Illus.: Chad
Author: Sutton, Felix
1953   **$18.00**

867

Things To Make And Do For Christmas
Illus.: Shelly, Duke
Author: Shelly, Duke
1953   **$20.00**

868

My First Book Of Prayers
Illus.: Ives, Ruth
Author: Juergens, Mary
1953   **$10.00**

869

Wonderful Animal Band, The
Illus.: Burchard, Peter
Author: Luther, Frank
1953   **$10.00**

870

Let's Play Train
Illus.: Weisgard, Leonard
Author: Weisgard, Leonard
1953   **$25.00**

871

Henry In Lollipop Land
Illus.: Anderson, Carl
Author: Anderson, Carl
1953   **$18.00**

872

Felix The Cat
Illus.: Sullivan, Pat
Author: Sullivan, Pat
1953   **$18.00**

873

Tubby The Tuba
Illus.: Chad
Author: Tripp, Paul
1954   **$16.00**

874
Prince Valiant
Illus.: Foster, Hal
Author: Foster, Hal
1954   **$20.00**

875
Ten Little Fingers
Illus.: Pointer, Priscilla
Author: Pointer, Pricella
1954   **$10.00**

876
Magic Clown, The
Illus.: Schucker, James
Author: Sutton, Felix
1954   **$16.00**

877
Little Puppy Who Would Not Mind His Mother, The
Illus.: Hopkins, Hildegarde
1949   **$12.00**

878
Cozy Little Farm, The
Illus.: Angela
Author: Bonino, Louise
1946   **$10.00**

879
Cinderella
Illus.: Ives, Ruth
Author: Andreas, Evelyn
1954   **$10.00**

880
Shy Little Horse, The
Illus.: Robinson
Author: Scott, Therese
1947   **$10.00**

881
Just Like Me
Illus.: Weisgard, Leonard
Author: Weisgard, Leonard
1954   **$12.00**

882
Henny-Penny
Illus.: Ponter, James
1954   **$10.00**

883
Big And Little
Illus.: Hull, John
Author: Hull, John
1954   **$10.00**

884
Mighty Mouse And The Scared Scarecrow
Illus.: Chad
Author: Sutton, Felix
1954   **$18.00**

885
My Own Book Of Fun And Play
Illus.: Riley, Bob
Author: John, Peter
1954   **$10.00**

886
Help Mr. Willy Nilly
Illus.: Tamburine, Jean
Author: Fritz, Jean
1954   **$13.00**

887

Blondie's Family
Illus.: Young, Chic
Author: Young, Chic
1954   **$16.00**

888

Popeye
Illus.: Sagendorf, Bud
1955   **$16.00**

889

What Time Is It?
Illus.: Zabinski, Joseph
Author: Peter, John
1954   **$10.00**

890

Let's Take A Trip In Our Car
Illus.: Schucker, James
Author: Sutton, Felix
1954   **$25.00**

891

Really Truly Treasure Hunt, The
Illus.: Newell, Crosby
Author: Bonsall, George
1954   **$13.00**

892

Merry Mailman Around The World, The
Illus.: Wood, Ruth
Author: Martin, Marcia
1955   **$20.00**

893

Let's Go To School
Illus.: Hoecker, Hazel
Author: Edwards, Annette
1954   **$16.00**

894

Title Unknown

895

What Are You Looking At?
Illus.: Bonsall, George; Newell, Crosby
Authors: Bonsall, George; Newell, Crosby
1954   **$16.00**

896

Mighty Mouse-Santa's Helper
Illus.: Chad
Author: Sutton, Felix
1955   **$18.00**

897

Henry Goes To A Party
Illus.: Anderson, Carl
Author: Anderson, Carl
1955   **$18.00**

898

Snow White
Illus.: Seiden, Art
1955   **$12.00**

899

It's Fun To Peek
     $10.00

900

Title Unknown

901
Land Of Peek-A-Boo, The
Illus.: Newell, Crosby
Author: Bonsall, George
1955 **$15.00**

902
Sparkie-No School Today
Illus.: Jason, Leon
Author: Jason, Leon
1955 **$16.00**

903
Terry Bears Win The Cub Scout Badge, The
Illus.: Moore, Robert J.
Author: Sutton, Felix
1955 **$18.00**

904
Felix On Television
Illus.: Oriolo, Joe
Author: Shapiro, Irwin
1956 **$18.00**

905
Flash Gordon
Illus.: Berger, Alex
1956 **$18.00**

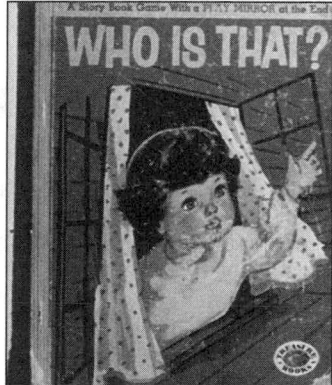

906
Who Is That?
Illus.: Schad, Helen G.
Author: Schad, Helen G.
1956 **$16.00**

Treasure Books Index

A Brief History of Tell-A-Tale Books

The Tell-A-Tale series was published by Whitman Publishing Company, a subsidiary of Western Publishing Company, Inc., from 1945 to 1984. Since 1985, the series has been published as A Golden Tell-A-Tale® Book. You will find some Tell-A-Tale titles from the A Golden Tell-A-Tale® Book series listed, but I primarily cover the Whitman series.

Whitman first started printing Tell-A-Tale books with number 850, Poor Kitty, in 1945. Some, if not all, of the titles printed in 1945 had dust jackets. When the numbers reached 899, somebody at Whitman questioned why the books had started with 850 and not 800. So around 1952, the company went back to 800 and numbered until 848.

Because the company used up all of the 800 numbers, it numbered the books 900 to 966 from 1953 through 1954. Books numbered 2500 through 2600 were published into the 1970s. Books published since 1955 can have more than one title for the same book number. Books with dashes were printed in the A Golden Tell-A-Tale® Book series.

Tell-A-Tale books measure 5-5/8 inches x 6-5/8 inches. The early editions contained 40 pages, including pastedowns, and sold for 15 cents. The exception to this page count was that Authorized titles (books approved by a show or actor) had 32 pages and Flocked titles (books with a "fuzziness" on the cover and some of the inside pages) had 20 pages. The books were later printed with 29 pages.

How to Tell Tell-A-Tale Editions

There is no way to tell a first edition, but you can look at the titles on the back of the book. If you see a TV character listed, you can date the book accordingly.

Tell-A-Tales—Alphabetical Listing

2407-2
1 Is Red
Illus.: Eugenie
Author: Daly, Eileen
1974 $2.00

2471-47
1 To 10 Again
Illus.: Baker, Darrell
1987 $3.00

896
ABC
Illus.: Flory, Jane
1949 $15.00

896
ABC
Illus.: Flory, Jane
1949 $12.00

808
ABC
Illus.: Vartanian, Raymond
1952 $15.00
2552
ABC
Illus.: Nugent, Alys
1956 $15.00

2658
ABC A Tale Of A Sale
Illus.: Heckler, William
Author: Hovelsrud, Joyce
1963 $4.00

2569
Alonzo Purr The Seagoing Cat
Illus.: Hafner, Marylin
Author: Carey, Mary
1966 $6.00

2430
Alphabet Rhymes (Previously ABC)
Illus.: Nugent, Alys
1956 $2.00

2512
Amy's Long Night
Illus.: Wheeling, Lynn
Author: Carber, Nancy
1970 $7.00

2462-46
And So To Bed
Illus.: Orville, Oliver
Author: Orville, Oliver
1989 $3.00

2543
Andy
Illus.: Hoecker, Hazel
Author: Michelson, Florence
1966 $5.00

906
Andy And Betsy At The Circus
Illus.: Friedel, Violet & Fred
Author: Friedel, Violet & Fred
1953 $15.00

887
Animal ABC
Illus.: Harriett
1949 $15.00

837
Animal Crackers
Illus.: Peller, Jackie
Author: Georgiana
1949 $20.00

837
Animal Jingles
Illus.: Peller, Jackie
Author: Georgiana
1951 $20.00

2556
Animal Train
Illus.: Williams, Ben D
Author: Roberts, Elizabeth
1969 $7.00

2474
Animals In Mother Goose
Illus.: Goldsborough, June
1956 $4.00

2516
Aristocats, The - A Counting Book
Illus.: Walt Disney Studio
Author: Walt Disney Studios
1970 $8.00

2493
Baby Goes Around The Block
Illus.: Merkling, Erica
Author: Horn, Gladys M.
1973 $3.00

917
Baby Moses
Illus.: Frost, Bruno
Author: Trent, Robbie
1952 $15.00

2422
Baby's First Book
Illus.: Allen, Joan
Author: Swetnam, Evelyn
1952 $2.00

2548
Bambi
Illus.: Walt Disney Studio
Author: Walt Disney Studios
1955 $6.00

2489
Barbie And Skipper Go Camping
Author: Daly, Eileen
1974 $8.00

2489
Barbie And Skipper Go Camping
(2nd Cover)
Author: Daly, Eileen
1974 $8.00

2450-01
Barbie On Skates
Illus.: Tierney, Tom
Author: Balducci, Rita
1992   **$3.00**

2551
Beany And Cecil Captured For The Zoo
Illus.: Bradbury, Jack; Wolfe, Gene
Author: Hammer, Barbara
1954   **$25.00**

904
Beany And His Magic Set
Illus.: Armstrong, Samuel; Eisenber, Harvey
Author: Clampett, Bob
1953   **$25.00**

2554
Bear Country
Illus.: Godwin, Edward & Stephani
Author: Wright, Betty Ren
1954   **$12.00**

2612
Bear County
(2nd Cover)
Illus.: Godwin, Edward & Stephani
Author: Wright, Betty Ren
1954   **$7.00**

2455-59
Beauty And The Beast
Illus.: Kicks, Russell
Author: Korman, Justine
1993   **$4.00**

2553
Beaver Valley
Illus.: Hartwell, Marjorie
Author: Wright, Betty Ren
1954   **$12.00**

2612
Beaver Valley
(2nd Cover)
Illus.: Hartwell, Marjorie
Author: Wright, Betty Ren
1954   **$7.00**

2541
Bedknobs And Broomsticks - A Visit To Naboombu
Illus.: Walt Disney Studio
Author: Walt Disney Studios
1971   **$5.00**

2475-32
Bedtime Book, The
Illus.: Winship, Florence Sarah
Author: Watts, Mabel
1963   **$3.00**

825
Beloved Son, The
Illus.: Frost, Bruno
Author: Wagstaff, Blanche Shoemaker
1951   **$15.00**

2518
Beloved Son,The
Illus.: Winship, Florence Sarah
Author: Watts, Mabel
1963   **$12.00**

2518
Beloved Son, The
(2nd Cover)
Illus.: Winship, Florence Sarah
Author: Watts, Mabel
1963   **$10.00**

2516

Benjamin Brownie and the Talking Doll
Illus.: Stang, Judy
Author: Ross, Geraldine
1962   **$18.00**

2640

Benji The Detective
Illus.: Willis, Werner
Author: Lewis, Jean
1970   **$4.00**

846

Benny The Bus
Illus.: Vaughan, Eillen Fox
Author: Horn, Gladys M.
1950   **$15.00**

2521

Best Surprise Of All, The
Illus.: D'amato, Alex
Author: Pape, Donna Lugg
196   **$15.00**

2508

Best Surprise of All, The
(2nd Cover)
Illus.: D'amato, Alex
Author: Pape, Donna Lugg
1961   **$4.00**

2553

Beware Of The Dog
Illus.: Nagel, Stina
Author: Woyke, Christine
1968   **$4.00**

2533

Big Albert Moves In
Illus.: Walt Disney Studio
Author: Walt Disney Studios
1971   **$8.00**

2474-33

Big And Little Are Not The Same
Illus.: Buckett, George
Author: Ottum, Bob
1972   **$2.00**

2510

Big Bark, The
Illus.: Nagel, Stina
Author: Woyke, Christine
1968   **$4.00**

2452-4

Big Bird Follows The Signs
Illus.: Delaney, A
Author: Kingsley, Emily Perl
1980   **$2.00**

869

Big Game Hunter, The
Illus.: Read, Isobel
Author: Alexander, Florence Bibo
1947   **$17.00**

2507

Big Game Hunter, The
(2nd Cover)
Illus.: Read, Isobel
Author: Alexander, Florence Bibo
1947   **$13.00**

942

Big Little Kitty
Illus.: Biggers, Jan D
Author: Biggers, Jan D
1953   **$15.00**

2525

Big Little Kitty
(2nd Cover)
Illus.: Biggers, Jan D
Author: Biggers, Jan D
1953 $12.00

840

Big Red Pajama Wagon, The
Illus.: Anderson, Betty
Author: Elting, Mary
1949 $15.00

2522

Big Whistle, The
Illus.: Myers, Louise
Author: Tompert, Ann
1968 $4.00

966

Bill's Birthday Surprise
Illus.: Hoecker, Hazel
Author: Blair, Irene
1954 $8.00

888

Billy Bunnyscoot - The Lost Bunny
Illus.: Tedder, Elizabeth
Author: Smith, Georgia Tucker
1948 $16.00

2560

Bingo
Illus.: Garris, Norma & Dan
Author: Hogstrom, Daphne
1966 $5.00

2576

Bingo
(2nd Cover)
Illus.: Garris, Norma & Dan
Author: Hogstrom, Daphne
1966 $4.00

2510

Box Of Important Things, The
Illus.: Bradfield, Roger
Author: Hellie, Anne
1968 $4.00

916

Boy's Friend, A
Illus.: Weiniger, Egon
Author: Trent, Robbie
1952 $10.00

2552

Bozo The Clown: King Of The Ring
Illus.: White, Al
1960 $15.00

870

Breezy -The Air Minded Pigeon
Illus.: Grider, Dorothy
Author: Grider, Dorothy
1947 $15.00

2610

Bremen-Town Musicians, The
Illus.: Mikolaycak, Charles
Author: Zens, Patricia Martin
1964 $7.00

2560

Brown Puppy And A Falling Star, A
Illus.: Winship, Florence Sarah
Author: Ross, Elizabeth
1956   **$6.00**

2526

Buffy And The New Girl
Illus.: Mode, Nathalee
Author: Bond, Gladys Baker
1969   **$12.00**

2453-48

Bugs Bunny Calling!
Illus.: Messerli, Joe
Author: Manuchkin, Fran
1988   **$2.00**

2410

Bugs Bunny Hangs Around
Illus.: Abranz, Alfred; Mcgary, Norm
Author: Hoag, Nancy
1957   **$8.00**

2543

Bugs Bunny In Something Fishy
Illus.: Abranz, Alfred; Mcgary, Norm
Author: Warner Bros Cartoons, Inc
1956   **$8.00**

2572

Bugs Bunny Keeps A Promise
Illus.: Heimdahl, Ralph; Dempster, Al
1951   **$8.00**

2607

Bugs Bunny Party Pest
Illus.: Anderson, Al; Mekimson, Thomas J.
Author: Johnston, William
1976   **$2.00**

2472-35

Bugs Bunny Rides Again
Illus.: Messerli, Joe
1986   **$2.00**

928

Bugs Bunny's Big Invention
Illus.: Heimdahl, Ralph
Author: Warner Brothers Cartoons
1969   **$8.00**

2421

Bugs Bunny's Birthday Surprise
Illus.: Abranza, Alfred & Thomas, Richard
Author: Theresa
1951   **$8.00**

2594

Bullwinkle's Masterpiece
Illus.: Jason, Leon
Author: Lewis, Jean
1976   **$12.00**

923

Bunny Button
Illus.: Myers, Bernice
Author: Revena
1953   **$7.00**

2526
Bunny Button
(2nd Cover)
Illus.: Myers, Bernice
Author: Revena
1953 **$4.00**

834
Buster Bulldozer
Illus.: Stoddard, Maru Alice
Author: Danner, Catherine
1952 **$10.00**

2615
Buster Bulldozer
(2nd Cover)
Illus.: Stoddard, Maru Alice
Author: Danner, Catherine
1952 **$5.00**

2585
Busy Body Book 'A First Book About You', The
Illus.: Beylon, Catherine
Author: Harrison, David L.
1975 **$6.00**

2473-42
Busy Machines
Illus.: Walz, Richard
Author: Harrison, David
1985 **$2.00**

2474-42
Busy Saturday Word Book, The
Illus.: Dolce, Ellen
1985 **$2.00**

2559
Butterfly! 'A Story Of Magic'
Illus.: Winship, Florence Sarah
Author: Daly, Eileen
1969 **$4.00**

2675
Buzzy Beaver
Illus.: Hart, Dick
Author: Sankey, Alice
1951 **$15.00**

2610
Captain Kangaroo And The Too-Small House
Illus.: Crawford, Mel
Author: Haas, Dorothy
1958 **$15.00**

2610
Captain Kangaroo Tick Tock Trouble
Illus.: Frost, Bruno
Author: Jones, Mary Voell
1961 **$12.00**

2547
Captain Kangaroo's Picnic
Illus.: Crawford, Mel
Author: Jones, Mary Voell
1959 **$4.00**

2450
Chicken Little
Illus.: Hartwell, Marjorie
1964 **$4.00**

2519
Child's Friend, A
(Also - A Boy's Friend)
Illus.: Weiniger, Egen
Author: Trent, Robbie
1953 **$5.00**

2519

Child's Friend, A
(2nd Cover)
Illus.: Weiniger, Egen
Author: Trent, Robbie
1953 $4.00

2624

Child's Ten Commandments, A
Illus.: Murray, Marjorie
Author: Regan, Jo B
1959 $6.00

2497

Childs Garden Of Verses, A
Illus.: Ruhman, Ruth
Author: Stevenson, Robert Louis
1964 $6.00

889

Chitter Chatter
Illus.: Read, Isobel
Author: Read, Isobel
1948 $15.00

2487-1

Christmas Sled, The
Illus.: Super, Terri
Author: North, Carol
1984 $2.00

2601

Christopher's "Hoppy" Day
Illus.: Winship, Florence Sarah
Author: Elliot, Edith F.
1967 $6.00

2672

Christopher John's Fuzzy Blanket
(Fuzzy)
Illus.: Winship, Florence Sarah
Author: Haas, Dorothy
1959 $15.00

964

Cinderella
Illus.: Wheeler, George
Author: Walt Disney Studios
1954 $12.00

2604

Cinderella
(2nd Cover)
Illus.: Wheeler, George
Author: Walt Disney Studios
1954 $6.00

2427-2

Cinderella
(3rd Cover)
Illus.: Wheeler, George
Author: Walt Disney Studios
1972 $5.00

2456-32

Cinderella
(4th Cover)
Illus.: Wheeler, George
Author: Walt Disney Studios
1972 $2.00

2674

Cinnamon Bear, The
(Fuzzy)
Illus.: Bakacs, George
Author: Hanson, Alice
1961 $15.00

2505
Circus Alphabet ABC
Illus.: Hudson, Patric
1959   **$6.00**

2563
Circus Alphabet
Illus.: Hudson, Patric
1954   **$4.00**

2608
Circus Boy And Captain Jack
Illus.: Boyle, Neil
Author: Snow, Dorothea J
1957   **$18.00**

2466-40
Circus Mouse
Illus.: Horne, Daniel R.
Author: Mc Guire, Leslie
1987   **$3.00**

890
Circus Train, The
Illus.: Dorcas
Author: Knittle, Jessie M.
1948   **$16.00**

2492
Clip Clop
Illus.: Winship, Florence Sarah
Author: Hoag, Nancy
1958   **$10.00**

826
Columbus, The Exploring Burro
Illus.: Koering, Ursula
Author: Brewster, Benjamin
1951   **$6.00**

2402-8
Cookie Monster's Book Of Cookie Shapes
Illus.: Brown, Richard
1979   **$2.00**

2506
Corey Baker Of Julia And His Show And Tell
Illus.: Harris, Larry
Author: Bond, Gladys Baker
1970   **$8.00**

2402
Count's Poem, The (Sesame Street)
Illus.: Cooke, Tom
Author: Sipherd, Ray
1978   **$2.00**

2530
Cousin Matilda And The Foolish Wolf
Illus.: Osborn, Richard
Author: Cole, Joanna
1970   **$4.00**

894
Cradle Rhymes
Illus.: Rachel
Author: Horn, Gladys M.
1949   **$18.00**

2621

Daffy Duck Space Creature
Illus.: Baker, Darrell
Author: Ingoglia, Gina
1977   **$4.00**

2506

Daktari Judy And The Kitten
Illus.: Harris, Larry
Author: Fiedler, Jean
1965   **$7.00**

2570

Dale Evans And Buttermilk
Illus.: Wegner, Helmuth G.
Author: Welden, Rose
1956   **$25.00**

802

Dally
Illus.: Clement, Charles
Author: Julian, Lee
1951   **$13.00**

2433

Daniel's New Friend
Illus.: Wilde, Irma
Author: Bach, Hilda
1968   **$3.00**

2512

Davy Plays Football
Illus.: Wilde, Carol
Author: Peake, Sylvia
1968   **$5.00**

2513

Davy's Wiggly Tooth
Illus.: Winship, Florence Sarah
Author: Borden, Marion
1964   **$4.00**

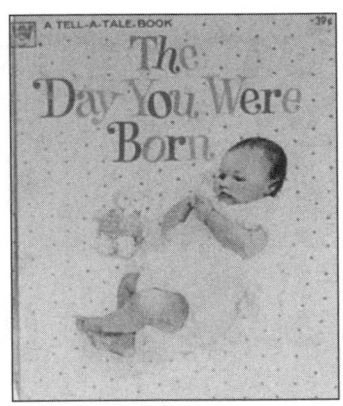

2524

Day You Were Born, The
Illus.: Wood, Muriel
Author: Swetnam, Evelyn
1972   **$2.00**

2451-4

Dennis The Menace Takes The Cake
Illus.: Matchette, Karen
Author: Namm, Diane
1955   **$4.00**

2538

Diddle Daddle Duckling
Illus.: Goldsborough, June
Author: Bennett, Grace Irene
1971   **$3.00**

908

Digger Dan
Illus.: Frankel, Simon
Author: Lynn, Patricia
1953   **$20.00**

2615

Digger Dan
(2nd Cover)
Illus.: Frankel, Simon
Author: Lynn, Patricia
1953   **$15.00**

2544

Digger Dan
(3rd Cover)
Illus.: Frankel, Simon
Author: Lynn, Patricia
1953 **$6.00**

882

Dipsy Donkey
Illus.: Laurence, Johnny
Author: Laurence, Johnny
1948 **$15.00**

891

Dodo The Little Wild Duck
Illus.: Grider, Dorothy
Author: Scheinert, Carlton A.
1948 **$15.00**

945

Donald Duck And Chip'n'Dale
Illus.: Walsh, Stan & Wolfe, Gene
Author: Walt Disney Studios
1965 **$8.00**

2516

Donald Duck And The New Bird-house
Illus.: Moores, Dick & Mcgary, Norm
Author: Walt Disney Studios
1955 **$8.00**

2425-6

Donald Duck And The Super-Sticky Secret
Illus.: Kohn, Arnie
Author: Watts, Mabel
1979 **$3.00**

900

Donald Duck Full Speed Ahead
Illus.: Banta, Milt; Mac Laughlin, Don
1953 **$10.00**

2609

Donald Duck Goes Camping
Illus.: Walt Disney Studios
Author: Walt Disney Studios
1977 **$4.00**

2559

Donald Duck Goes To Disneyland
Illus.: Banta, Milt ; Boyle, Neil
Author: Walt Disney Studios
1967 **$15.00**

2520

Donald Duck In Frontierland
Illus.: Boyle, Neil
Author: Walt Disney Studios
1969 **$10.00**

2409

Donald Duck On Tom Sawyer's Island
Illus.: Strobl, Tony & The Mattinsons
Author: Snow, Dorothea J
1978 **$8.00**

827

Donald Duck's Lucky Day
Illus.: Walt Disney Studios
Author: Walt Disney Studios
1971 **$7.00**

2635

Donnie And Marie The State Fair Mystery
Illus.: Giacomini, Olinda
Author: Daly, Eileen
1977   **$5.00**

841

Dr. Goat
Illus.: Clement, Charles
Author: Georgiana
1950   **$100.00**

841

Dr. Goat
Illus.: Clement, Charles
Author: Georgiana
1950   **$50.00**

2463

Dr. Hilda Makes House Calls
Illus.: Petruccio, Steven
Author: Watts, Mabel
1988   **$3.00**

2454

Duck Tales Silver Dollars For Uncle Scrooge
Illus.: Ito, Willy
Author: Weiner, Gina
1988   **$3.00**

2454

Eloise And The Old Blue Truck
Illus.: Winship, Florence Sarah
Author: Graham, Kennon
1971   **$7.00**

2496

Elves And The Shoemaker, The
Illus.: Miloche, Hilda
1598   **$6.00**

2561

Elves And The Shoemaker, The
Illus.: Robison, Jim
1973   **$3.00**

2604

Ernie The Cave King And Sherlock The Smart Person
Illus.: Children's Television Workshop
Author: Wilcox, Daniel
1975   **$2.00**

2452-34

Ernie's Telephone Call
Illus.: Duga, Irra
Author: Sipherd, Ray
1978   **$2.00**

2527

Especially From Thomas
Illus.: Ker, Edith M. Photos By Duesseldorf
Author: Haas, Dorothy
1965   **$6.00**

2543

Especially From Thomas
(2nd Cover)
Illus.: Ker, Edith M. Photos By Duesseldorf
Author: Haas, Dorothy
1965   **$6.00**

2462-43

Evening Walk, The
Illus.: Durrell, Julie
Author: Ryder, Joanne
1985   **$2.00**

862

Fanny Forgot
Illus.: Flory, Jane
Author: Flory, Jane
1946   **$15.00**

2468

Farm ABC
Illus.: Michell, Gladys Turlry
Author: Lynn, Patricia
1978   **$3.00**

2464-50

Farm Animals
Illus.: Krupp, Marion
Author: Relf, Patricia
1992   **$1.00**

838

Farmer John
Illus.: Flory, Jane
Author: Flory, Jane
1950   **$15.00**

2598

**Fat Albert And The Cosby Kids
Getting It Together**
Illus.: Hazelton, Herbert & Willoughby,
Jim
Author: French, Laura
1975   **$16.00**

2412

Fire Dog
Illus.: Clement, Charles
Author: Julian, Lee
1960   **$8.00**

2552

Flinstones At The Circus, The
Illus.: Mc Savage, Frank; Heiner,
Robert
Author: Lewis, Jean
1963   **$15.00**

872

**Fluffy And Tuffy The Twin
Ducklings**
Illus.: Mc Kean, Emma C
Author: Mc Kean, Emma C
1947   **$15.00**

820

Flying Sunbeam, The
Illus.: Anderson, Betty
Author: Fairbairn, D. N.
1950   **$16.00**

820

Franky, The Fuzzy Goat
Illus.: Suzanne
Author: Horn, Gladys M.
1951   **$15.00**

2660

Frisker
Illus.: Shortall, Leonard
Author: Nowak, Mary Lauer
1956   **$6.00**

2567
Funny Company, The
Illus.: Fletcher, James
Author: Patrick, Lenore
1965   **$16.00**

2647
Funny Friends In Mother Goose Land
Illus.: Ford, Pam
1978   **$2.00**

2611
Fury
Illus.: Bartram, Bob
Author: Haas, Dorothy
1958   **$15.00**

821
Fuzzy Dan
Illus.: Biers, Clarence
Author: Whitehead, Jane
1951   **$16.00**

912
Fuzzy Duckling
Illus.: Banigan, Sharon
1952   **$15.00**

914
Fuzzy Friends In Mother Goose Land
Illus.: Cunningham, Dellwyn
1952   **$15.00**

954
Fuzzy Joe Bear
Illus.: Berry, Anne
Author: Horn, Gladys M.
1954   **$15.00**

823
Fuzzy Mittens For Three Little Kittens
Illus.: Laqueur, Alys
1951   **$15.00**

2671
Fuzzy Pet, A
Illus.: Hartwell, Marjorie
Author: Hanson, Alice
1960   **$15.00**

915
Fuzzy Wuzzy Puppy, The
Illus.: Suzanne
Author: Winship, Florence Sarah
1954   **$15.00**

800
Gene Autry 'Makes A New Friend'
Illus.: Case, Richard
Author: Beecher, Elizabeth
1952   **$2.00**

932
Gene Autry And The Lost Dogie
Illus.: Armstrong, Samuel
1953   **$22.00**

2566

Gene Autry Goes To The Circus
Illus.: Ushler, John
1950   **$22.00**

2552

Gentle Ben And The Pesky Puppy
Illus.: Harris, Larry
Author: Fiedler, Jean
1969   **$7.00**

2530

Getting Ready For Roddy
Illus.: Helwig, Hans
Author: Lynn, Patricia
1955   **$8.00**

939

Gingerbread Man, The
Illus.: Lesko, Zillah
1953   **$12.00**

2596

Gingerbread Man, The
Illus.: Sari
1958   **$8.00**

2596

Gingerbread Man, The
Illus.: Mars, W.T.
Author: Zens, Patricia Martin
1963   **$6.00**

2580

Gingerbread Man, The
Illus.: Giacomini, Olindo
Author: Sukus, Jan
1969   **$5.00**

2619

Ginghams, The, The Ice-Cream Parade
Illus.: Land, Kate
Author: Bowden, Joan Chase
1976   **$3.00**

2595

Goby Goat And The Birthday Gift
Illus.: Rutherford, Bonnie & Bill
Author: Russell, Solveig Paulson
1975   **$2.00**

955

Good Night 'A Flocked Book'
Illus.: Paflín, Roberta
Author: Burrowes, Elizabeth
1954   **$15.00**

2487

Good Night Book, The
Illus.: Karch, Pat & Paul
Author: Well, Lynn & Mandy
1969   **$5.00**

2477

Goofy And His Wonderful Cornet
Illus.: Alvarado, Peter; Lorencz, William
Author: Brightman, Homer
1973   **$4.00**

2552

Goofy And The Tiger Hunt
Illus.: Moores, Dick And Armstrong, Samuel
Author: Walt Disney Studios
1954   **$7.00**

2670

Grandpa's House
Illus.: Stang, Judy
Author: Wright, Betty Ren
1969   **$15.00**

2665

Grandpa's Policemen Friends
Illus.: Winship, Florence Sarah
Author: Frankel, Bernice
1967   **$4.00**

2564

Great Fort, The
Illus.: Oechsli, Kelly
Author: Garber, Nancy
1970   **$3.00**

2402-6

Grover's Own Alphabet
Illus.: Murdocca, Sal
1978   **$2.00**

2552

Gumby And Gumby's Pal Pokey To The Rescue
Illus.: De Santis, George
Author: Lewis, Jean
1969   **$15.00**

2506

Gumby And Gumby's Pal Pokey
Illus.: De Santis, George
Author: Biesterveld, Betty
1968   **$15.00**

2624

H.R. Pufnstuf
Illus.: Moore, Sparky; Totten, Bob
Author: Lewis, Jean
1970   **$12.00**

919

Handy Andy
Illus.: Dreany, E. Joseph
Author: Lynn, Patricia
1953   **$8.00**

Number Unknown

Handy Andy
(2nd Cover)
Illus.: Dreany, E. Joseph
Author: Lynn, Patricia
1953   **$6.00**

2516

Happiest Christmas, The
Illus.: Wilde, Richard
Author: Fairweather, Jessie Home
1950   **$15.00**

2482

Happiest Christmas, The
(2nd Cover)
Illus.: Wilde, Richard
Author: Fairweather, Jessie Home
1950   **$10.00**

2631

Happy
Illus.: Garris, Norma & Dan
Author: Bordon, Marion
1964　　　　**$4.00**

2610

Happy Book, The
Illus.: Poehlmann, Jo Anna
Author: Zens, Patricia Martin
1965　　　　**$3.00**

2535

Have You Seen A Giraffe Hat?
Illus.: Storms, Robert
Author: Joyce, Irma
1969　　　　**$4.00**

2510

Hello, Joe
Illus.: Corrigan, Barbara
Author: Stempel, Ruth
1961　　　　**$6.00**

2616

Hello, Rock
Illus.: Bradfield, Roger
Author: Bradfield, Roger
1965　　　　**$6.00**

2472-42

Henrietta And The Hat
Illus.: Schweninger, Ann
Author: Watts, Mabel
1985　　　　**$2.00**

855

Henry The Helicopter (Previously Little Henry)
Illus.: Williams, Ben D
Author: Graham, Eleanor
1945　　　　**$15.00**

2602

Hey There-It's Yogi Bear!
Illus.: Mc Savage, Frank & Young, Harland
Author: Daly, Eileen
1964　　　　**$17.00**

847

Hi! Cowboy
Illus.: Williams, Ben
Author: Horn, Gladys M.
1950　　　　**$15.00**

938

Hide-Away Henry
Illus.: Biers, Clarence
Author: Sankey, Alice
1953　　　　**$8.00**

2553

Hiding Place, The
Illus.: O'Sullivan, Tom
Author: Meek, Pauline Palmer
1971　　　　**$4.00**

924

Hippety Hop Around The Block
Illus.: Dorcas
Author: Horn, Gladys M.
1953　　　　**$8.00**

2543
Ho-Hum
Illus.: Myers, Jack & Louise
Author: Lynn, Patricia
1957   **$12.00**

2510
Ho-Hum
(2nd Cover)
Illus.: Myers, Jack & Louise
Author: Lynn, Patricia
1957   **$5.00**

2466-46
Honey Bear Finds A Friend
Illus.: Orville, Oliver
Author: Pepper, Alice
1990   **$2.00**

2503
Hooray For Lassie!
Illus.: Marshall, Carol
Author: Borden, Marion
1964   **$6.00**

866
Hop, Skippy And Jump
Illus.: Vivienne
Author: Vivienne
1947   **$15.00**

2552
Hoppity Hooper Vs Skippity Snooper
Illus.: De Santis, George
Author: Lewis, Jean
1966   **$12.00**

2411-1
Horse For Charlie, A
Illus.: Elfrieda
Author: Tompert, Ann
1970   **$3.00**

2530
House My Grandpa Built, The
Illus.: Rutherford, Bonnie & Bill
Author: Gohn, Geraldine Everett
1971   **$3.00**

2480
House That Jack Built, The
Illus.: Suzanne
1961   **$4.00**

2601
How Big Is A Baby?
Illus.: Garris, Norma & Dan
Author: Holmgren, Virginia C.
1966   **$4.00**

2555
How Big Is A Baby?
(2nd Cover)
Illus.: Garris, Norma & Dan
Author: Holmgren, Virginia C.
1966   **$**

2660
How Can We Get To The Zoo?
Illus.: Rutherford, Bonnie & Bill
Author: Joyce, Irma
1966   **$2.00**

2521

How Does My Garden Grow?
Illus.: Goldsborough, June
Author: Benton, William & Elizabeth
1969   **$4.00**

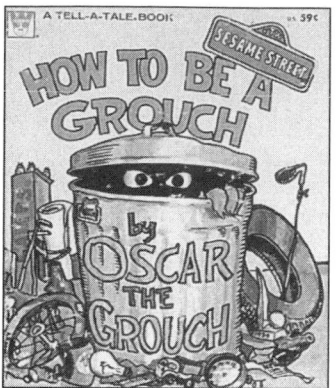

2618

How To Be A Grouch (Sesame Street)
Illus.: Bathman, Ed
Author: Spinney, Carol
1976   **$2.00**

944

Howdy Doody And The Magic Lamp
Illus.: Crawford, Mel
Author: Coppersmith, Jerry
1954   **$22.00**

902

Howdy Doody And The Monkey Tale
1953   **$22.00**

934

Howdy Doody's Clarabell And Pesky Peanut
Illus.: Kagran, Corporation
Author: Kagran Corporation
1953   **$20.00**

2558

Howdy Doody's Clarabell Clown And The Merry-Go-Round
Illus.: Crawford, Mel
Author: Barron, John
1955   **$20.00**

2611

Huckleberry Hound The Rainmaker
Illus.: Daly, Eileen
Author: Fletcher, Jim
1963   **$18.00**

2421-2

Huffin Puff Express, The
Illus.: Seiden, Art
Author: Harrison, David, L
1974   **$7.00**

815

Hullabaloo
Illus.: Weber, Nettie
Author: Georgiana
1951   **$12.00**

2610

Humpty Dumpty And Other Nursery Rhymes
Illus.: Ruth, Rod
197   **$3.00**

2659

Hungry Lion, The
Illus.: Stang, Judy
Author: Fletcher, Steffi
1960   **$7.00**

2616

Hurry, Scurry
Illus.: Tomes, Jackie
Author: Putnam, Nina; Williams, Gretchen
1963   **$3.00**

2527
I Know What A Farm Is
Illus.: Crawford, Mel
Author: Fiedler, Jean
1969   **$3.00**

2522
I Like The Farm
Illus.: Depper, Hertha
Author: Wolf, Nancy Hoag
1961   **$3.00**

2615
I Like To Be Little
Illus.: Mill, Eleanor
Author: Matthews, Ann
1976   **$2.00**

2443
I Like To See A Book About The Five Senses
Illus.: Goldsborough, June
Author: Tymms, Jean
1973   **$2.00**

2554
I Live In The City ABC
Illus.: O'Sullivan, Tom
Author: Moore, Lou
1969   **$3.00**

2671
I Love My Grandma
Illus.: Wilson, Dagmar
Author: Hoag, Florence Jenkins
1960   **$12.00**

2510
I Play In The Snow
Illus.: Rutherford, Bonnie & Bill
Author: Pape, Donna Lugg
1967   **$4.00**

2616
I Walk To The Park
Illus.: Nagel, Stina
Author: Schwalj, Marjory
1966   **$4.00**

2462-42
I'm Not Sleepy
Illus.: Beylon, Cathy
Author: Ryder, Joanne
1986   **$2.00**

2415
In Baby's House
Illus.: Sherwood, Stewart
Author: Swetnam, Evelyn
1974   **$3.00**

2666
In, On, Under, And Through
Illus.: Nagel, Stina
Author: Elwart, Joan Potter
1965   **$4.00**

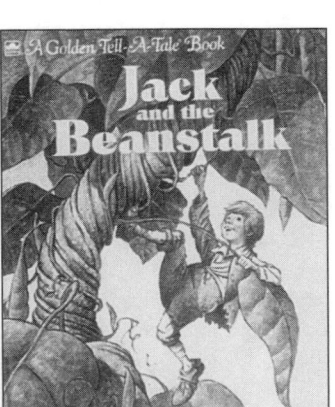

2461-51
Jack And The Beanstalk
Illus.: Walz, Richard
Author: Balducci ,Rita
1992   **$2.00**

898

Jasper Giraffe
Illus.: Myers, Louise W
Author: Ferrell, Polly
1949   **$18.00**

898

Jasper Giraffe
(2nd Cover)
Illus.: Myers, Louise W
Author: Ferrell, Polly
1949   **$15.00**

2508

Jean Ellen Learns To Swim
Illus.: Wilde, Carol
Author: Swetnam, Evelyn
1970   **$3.00**

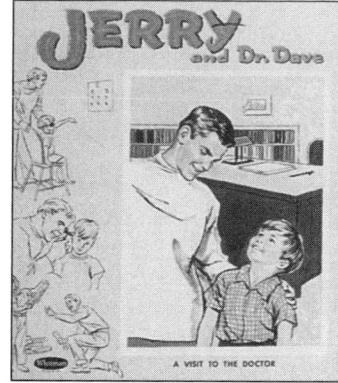

2601

Jerry And Dr. Dave
Illus.: Nankivel, Claudine
Author: Bordon, Marion
1964   **$4.00**

2527

Jim Jump
Illus.: Banigan, Sharon
Author: Wright, Betty Ren
1954   **$10.00**

2679

Johnny Appleseed
Illus.: Elfreda
Author: Russell, Solveig Paulson
1967   **$4.00**

2525

Johnny Go Round
Illus.: Walz, Richard
Author: Wright, Betty Ren
1960   **$12.00**

899

Jolly Jingles
Illus.: Williams, Ben
Author: Alexander, Florence Bibo
1959   **$14.00**

2488

**Jumpy, Humpy, Fuzzy, Buzzy,
Animal Book, The**
Illus.: Stone, David K.
Author: Davis, Douglas
1974   **$4.00**

2607

Jungle Book, The
Illus.: Walt Disney Studios
Author: Adapted From; Kipling,
Rudyard
1967   **$6.00**

2512

**Katy's First Day (Originally Katy
Did)**
Illus.: Aliki
Author: Soule, Jean Conder
1972   **$3.00**

2521

Kobo The Koala Bear
Illus.: Sampson, Katherine
Author: Schwalje, Marjory
1968   **$5.00**

2456-3

Lady
Illus.: Hubbard, Allan & Wolfe, Gene
Author: Walt Disney Studios
1954 $8.00

2617

Lambikin, The
Illus.: Myers, Jack & Louise
Author: Hansen, Helen S.
1962 $16.00

2607

Land Of The Lost The Dinosaur Adventure
Illus.: Purtle, John
Author: Godfry, Jane
1975 $5.00

2503

Lassie And The Cub Scout
Illus.: Anderson, Al
Author: Michelson, Florence
1966 $8.00

2462

Lassie And The Fire Fighters
Illus.: Harris, Larry
Author: Michelson, Florence
1968 $6.00

2503

Lassie And The Kittens
Illus.: Grant, Ena Klenetti
1956 $8.00

2406

Lassie Finds A Friend
Illus.: Anderson, Al
Author: Thresa
1960 $6.00

2571

Lassie's Brave Adventure
Illus.: Bartram, Bob
1958 $10.00

2484

Lassie: The Busy Morning
Illus.: Harris, Larry
Author: Lewis, Jean
1973 $4.00

2485

Lazy Fox And Red Hen
Illus.: Suzanne
1957 $5.00

2603

Lazy Fox And Red Hen
Illus.: Hauge, Carl & Mary
Author: Dwyer, Jane
1969 $2.00

2555

Learning To Count With Twelve Elves
Illus.: Giordano, Joe
Author: Wylie, Joanne
1972 $2.00

2615

Let Me See
Illus.: Stang, Judy
Author: Hilt, Mary L.
1963 **$5.00**

2407-4

Let's Count All The Animals!
Illus.: Wickart, Terry
Author: Lulas, Jim E.
1979 **$2.00**

907

Let's Play
Illus.: Gavy
Author: Georgiana
1952 **$10.00**

2601

Let's Play
(2nd Cover)
Illus.: Gavy
Author: Georgiana
1952 **$6.00**

876

Let's Visit The Farm
Illus.: Keyser, Evelyn
Author: Cunningham, Virginia
1948 **$15.00**

2567

Linus A Smile For Grouse
Illus.: Carleton, James F
Author: Patrick, Lenore
1966 **$15.00**

2519

Lion's Haircut, The
Illus.: Eugenie
Author: Giddings, Jennifer
1969 **$5.00**

2548

Little Bear And The Beautiful Kite
Illus.: Depper, Hertha
Author: Udry, Janice
1955 **$6.00**

2559

Little Bear And The Beautiful Kite
(2nd Cover)
Illus.: Depper, Hertha
Author: Udry, Janice
1955 **$6.00**

935

Little Beaver
Author: Beecher, Elizabeth
1954 **$15.00**

875

Little Bitty Raindrop
Illus.: Hanson, Marguerite
Author: Usher, Peggy
1948 **$17.00**

875

Little Bitty Raindrop
(2nd Cover)
Illus.: Hanson, Marguerite
Author: Usher, Peggy
1948 **$15.00**

2661

Little Black Sambo
Illus.: Suzanne
1950 **$50.00**

812

Little Black Sambo
Illus.: Michell, Gladys Turley
1953 **$42.00**

2661

Little Black Sambo
Illus.: Lamont, Violet
1959 **$35.00**

2661

Little Black Sambo
(2nd Cover)
Illus.: Lamont, Violet
1959 **$35.00**

2553

Little Boy In The Forest, The
Illus.: Osborne, Richard N
Author: Harrison, David
1969 **$4.00**

817

Little Caboose, The
Illus.: Flory, Jane
Author: O'Hearn, Nila
1951 **$15.00**

843

Little Chuff Chuff And Big Streamliner
Illus.: Barr, Catherine
Author: Barr Jr., Robert
1950 **$15.00**

863

Little Folks In Mother Goose
Illus.: Rachel
1946 **$15.00**

2651

Little Gray Rabbit
Illus.: Cauley, Lorinda Bryan
Author: Bowden, Joan Chase
1979 **$2.00**

883

Little Hank
Illus.: Williams, Ben
Author: Sankey, Alice
1948 **$15.00**

2604

Little Henry To The Rescue
Illus.: Williams, Ben D
Author: Graham, Eleanor
1945 **$15.00**

2560

Little Joe's Puppy
Illus.: Winship, Florence Sarah
Author: Haas, Dorothy
1957 **$12.00**

2622
Little Lulu Has An Art Show
Illus.: Buell, Marjorie Henderson
Author: Buell, Marjorie Henderson
1964 $10.00

2532
Little Lulu Has An Art Show
(2nd Cover)
Illus.: Buell, Marjorie Henderson
Author: Buell, Marjorie Henderson
1964 $8.00

2502
Little Lulu And The Birthday Mystery
Illus.: Baker, Darrell; Jason Studios
Author: Drake, Arnold
1974 $8.00

2437
Little Lulu Lucky Landlady!
1960 $8.00

2552
Little Lulu Uses Her Head
Illus.: Buell, Marjorie Henderson
Author: Buell, Marjorie Henderson
1955 $17.00

2483
Little Miss Muffet And Other Nursery Rhymes
Illus.: Wallace, Lucille
1958 $3.00

806
Little Pony, The
Illus.: Hartwell, Marjorie
Author: Hawley, Mary Alice
1952 $5.00

922
Little Red Bicycle, The
Illus.: King, Dorothy Urfer
Author: King, Dorothy Urfer
1953 $6.00

2543
Little Red Bicycle, The
(2nd Cover)
Illus.: King, Dorothy Urfer
Author: King, Dorothy Urfer
1953 $5.00

2508
Little Red Bicycle, The
(3rd Cover)
Illus.: King, Dorothy Urfer
Author: King, Dorothy Urfer
1953 $4.00

2603
Little Red Hen
Illus.: Wilson, Beth
1953 $6.00

937
Little Red Riding Hood
Illus.: Stella
1953 $8.00

2606
Little Red Riding Hood
Illus.: Lesko, Zillah
1957   **$10.00**

2651
Little Red Riding Hood
Illus.: Depper, Hertha
1959   **$4.00**

2670
Little Red Riding Hood
(A Fuzzy Wuzzy Book)
Illus.: Carroll, Nancy
1960   **$15.00**

2651
Little Red Riding Hood
Illus.: Goldsborough, June
1964   **$3.00**

2507
Little Red Riding Hood
Illus.: Dettmer, Mary Lou
1971   **$2.00**

2461-44
Little Red Riding Hood
Illus.: Dolce, Ellen J.
1989   **$2.00**

814
Little Tweet
Illus.: Gehr, Mary
Author: Holloway, Charles W
1951   **$15.00**

2561
Lone Ranger And The Ghost Horse, The
Illus.: Totten, Bob
Author: Sankey, Alice
1955   **$20.00**

2622
Lone Ranger Desert Storm, The
Illus.: Wenzel, Paul
Author: Revena
1957   **$18.00**

2418-1
Longest Birthday, The
Illus.: Leiner, Alan
Author: Garber, Nancy
1975   **$2.00**

2473-46
Look For Boats
Illus.: Nez, John
Author: Bell, Sally
1991   **$2.00**

2473-25
Look For Trucks!
Illus.: La Padu La, Thomas
Author: Weiner, Gina (Ingoglia)
1989   **$2.00**

2611
Loopy De Loop Odd Jobber
Illus.: Frost, Bruno
Author: Hagen, Patrick
1964 $16.00

893
Lucky Four Leaf Clover
Illus.: Peller, Jackie
Author: Antonie, Rosalind Lane
1949 $12.00

2476-39
Maggie To The Rescue
Illus.: Hunt, Judith
Author: Hill, Ari
1986 $2.00

2544
Magic Clothes Basket, The
Illus.: Rutherford, Bonnie And Bill
Author: Thomas, Sharon
1969 $4.00

2565
Magic Zoo, The - Or How To Tell Time
Illus.: Wylie, Joanne
Author: Mowers, Patricia
1972 $3.00

2552
Magilla Gorilla Takes A Banana Holiday
Illus.: Jason Studios
Author: Johnston, William
1965 $16.00

2521
Manuel's Cat
Illus.: Stone, David K.
Author: Fein, Dorothy A.
1971 $6.00

2632
Marvelous Monster, The
Illus.: Ruth, Rod
Author: Joyce, Carolyn
1977 $3.00

2606
Mary Poppins
Illus.: Neely, Jan
Author: Brightman, Homer
1964 $8.00

836
Matilda, Mac Elroy, And Mary
Illus.: Robison, I. E.
Author: Fairweather, Jessie Home
1950 $15.00

2616
Me Too!
Illus.: Zemsky, Jessica
Author: Nathan, Stella Williams
1962 $6.00

2633
Merton And His Moving Van
Illus.: Seiden, Art
Author: Watts, Mabel
1970 $2.00

2454-45

Mickey Mouse And The Lucky Goose Chase
Illus.: Wilson, Roy; William, Arthur; Mc Guire
Author: Scooter, M. J.
1986   **$3.00**

2631

Mickey Mouse And The Mouseke-teers - The Animal Guessing-Game Book
Illus.: Walt Disney Studios
Author: Walt Disney Studios
1977   **$3.00**

2454-2

Mickey Mouse And The Pet Show
Illus.: Walt Disney Studios
Author: Walt Disney Studios
1976   **$3.00**

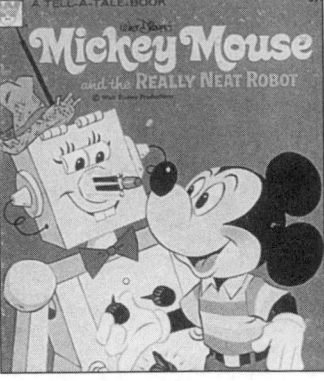

2475

Mickey Mouse And The Really Neat Robot
Illus.: Walt Disney Studios
Author: Walt Disney Studios
1970   **$3.00**

2418

Mickey Mouse And The Second Wish
Illus.: Walt Disney Studios
Author: Walt Disney Studios
1973   **$3.00**

2424-2

Mickey Mouse And The World's Friendliest Monster
Illus.: Walt Disney Studios
Author: Walt Disney Studios
1976   **$3.00**

2467

Mimi The Merry-Go-Round Cat
Illus.: Winship, Florence Sarah
Author: Haas, Dorothy
1958   **$7.00**

2599

Mister Rogers' Neighborhood Everyone Is Special
Illus.: Jason Art Studio
Author: Rogers, Fred M.
1975   **$4.00**

2452-39

Monsters Come In Many Colors! (Sesame Street)
Illus.: Mc Lean, Sammis
Author: Stevenson, Joyce
1980   **$3.00**

2523

More The Merrier, The
Illus.: Magagna, Anna Marie
Author: Michelson, Florence
1964   **$4.00**

925

Mother Goose
Illus.: Vaughan, Eillen Fox
1950   **$15.00**

2572

Mother Goose
Illus.: Clement, Charles
1955   **$12.00**

2511

Mother Goose
Illus.: Wallace, Lucille
1958   **$8.00**

2417

Mother Goose
Illus.: Scott, Marguerite K.
1960   **$6.00**

2511

Mother Goose
Illus.: Lesko, Zillah
1961   **$6.00**

2587

Mother Goose On The Farm
Illus.: Goldsborough, June
1975   **$3.00**

2464-44

Mother Goose On The Farm
Illus.: Aitken, Amy
1989   **$3.00**

2464-36

Mother Goose Rhymes
Illus.: Nez, John
1985   **$3.00**

2649

Mouseketeers Tryout Time, The
Illus.: Satterfield, Charles
Author: Revena
1956   **$5.00**

816

Mr. Grabbit
Illus.: Charlie
Author: Hoff, Virginia
1952   **$20.00**

2526

Mr. Grabbit
(2nd Cover)
Illus.: Charlie
Author: Hoff, Virginia
1952   **$16.00**

868

Mr. Jolly
Illus.: Spicer, Jesse
Author: Mathison, Jane
1948   **$15.00**

958

Mr. Mogg's Dogs
(Fuzzy)
Illus.: Frankel, Si
Author: Revena
1954   **$15.00**

2552

**Mushmouse And Punkin Puss
The Country Cousins**
Illus.: Alvarado, Peter; Jacobs,
Raymond
Author: Freman, Jay
1964   **$18.00**

2536

My Little ABC
Illus.: Ericksen, Barbara
Author: Vogels, Mary Prescott
1971   **$2.00**

2578

My Little Book About Our Flag
Illus.: Karch, Pat & Paul
Author: Mrowski, Jan
1975   **$2.00**

2466-4

My Little Book Of Big Animals
Illus.: Burridge, Marge Opitz
Author: Kulas, Jim E.
1978   **$2.00**

2589

My Little Book Of Big Machines
Illus.: Anderson, Al
Author: Ottum, Bob
1975   **$3.00**

2490

My Little Book Of Birds
Illus.: Dunnington, Tom
Author: Ray, Ora
1973   **$2.00**

2475-50

My Little Book Of Birds
Illus.: Solomon, Rosiland
Author: Ingoglia, Gina
1991   **$2.00**

247332

My Little Book Of Boats
Illus.: Dunnington, Tom
Author: Hanrahan, Mariellen
1974   **$2.00**

24750

My Little Book Of Bugs
Illus.: Solomon, Rosiland
Author: Silverman, Maida
1993   **$2.00**

2473

My Little Book Of Cars And Trucks
Illus.: Korta, Bob
Author: Graham, Kennon
1974   **$2.00**

2626

My Little Book Of Cats
Illus.: Ruth, Rod
Author: Greiner, N. Gretchen
1976   **$2.00**

2482

My Little Book Of Dinosaurs
Illus.: Ruth, Rod
Author: Daly, Eileen
1972   **$2.00**

2476-93

My Little Book Of Dogs
Illus.: Stone, David K.
Author: Draper, Delores
1976   **$2.00**

2559

My Little Book Of Farm Animals
Illus.: Hauge, Carl & Mary
Author: Hogstrom, Daphne
1972   **$3.00**

2414-4

My Little Book About Flying
Illus.: Irvin, Fred
Author: Graham, Kennon
1978   **$2.00**

2466-3
My Little Book Of Horses
Illus.: Dunnington, Tom
Author: Walrath, Jane Dwyer
1974   **$2.00**

2401
My Little Book Of Pets
Illus.: Hauge, Carl & Mary
Author: Sukus, Jan
1972   **$2.00**

2602
My Little Book Of Sea Life
Illus.: Ruth, Rod
Author: Michener, Lucille
19   **$2.00**

2643
My Little Book Of Trains
Illus.: Seward, James
Author: Manrahan, Mariellen
1978   **$2.00**

2407-3
My Little Counting Book
Illus.: Ruhman, Ruth
Author: Yerian, Margaret
1967   **$2.00**

2525
Nancy And Sluggo The Big Surprise
Illus.: Nofziger, Edward; Totten,
Robert
Author: Lewis, Jean
1974   **$8.00**

2538
Nibbler
Illus.: Winship, Florence Sarah
Author: Watts, Mabel
1973   **$5.00**

839
Night Before Christmas
Illus.: Newton, Ruth E
Author: Moore, Clement C.
1937   **$18.00**

839
Night Before Christmas
Illus.: Lesko, Zillah
Author: Moore, Clement C.
1953   **$16.00**

2517
Night Before Christmas, The
(2nd Cover)
Illus.: Lesko, Zillah
Author: Moore, Clement C.
1953   **$10.00**

2517
Night Before Christmas, The
Illus.: Munshi, Carol
Author: Moore, Clement C.
1963   **$10.00**

2517
Night Before Christmas, The
Illus.: Winship, Florence Sarah
Author: Moore, Clement C.
1969   **$6.00**

No Sit-Ups for Porky Pig
Illus.: Messerli, Joe
Author: Ingolia, Gina
1985   **$2.00**

2558
Noah And The Ark
Illus.: Gray, Leslie
Author: Ramsay, Devere
1967   **$5.00**

920
Nobody's Puppy
Illus.: Winship, Florence Sarah
Author: Lynn, Patricia
1953   **$6.00**

962
Not Quite Three
Illus.: Castagnoli, Martha
Author: Wolf, Helen
1954   **$7.00**

857
Nursery Rhymes
Illus.: Altson, Louise
1945   **$8.00**

2672
Oh, Look!
Illus.: Myers, Jack & Louise
Author: Haas, Dorothy
1961   **$10.00**

2589
Old Mac Donald Had A Farm
Illus.: Hauge, Carl & Mary
1975   **$3.00**

2610
Old Woman And Her Pig, The
Illus.: Mars, W. T.
1964   **$4.00**

2512
Once I Had A Monster
Illus.: Rutherford, Bonnie & Bill
Author: Hellie, Anne
1969   **$4.00**

865
Once Upon A Windy Day
Illus.: Flory, Jane
Author: Flory, Jane
1947   **$15.00**

2622
One Hundred And One Dalmatians
Illus.: Fletcher, James
Author: Walt Disney Studios
1960   **$7.00**

807
One Two Buckle My Shoe
Illus.: Kaula, Edna M.
1951   **$12.00**

926
One Two Three
Illus.: Charlie
Author: Charlie
1953 $8.00

2616
One Two Three
(2nd Cover)
Illus.: Charlie
Author: Charlie
1953 $5.00

2440
One Two Three
(3rd Cover)
Illus.: Charlie
Author: Charlie
1953 $2.00

2546
Outside With Baby
Illus.: Skibinski, Ray
Author: Swetnam, Evelyn
1974 $3.00

2544
Pals
Illus.: O'Sullivan, Tom
Author: Funk, Melissa Don
1966 $4.00

2424
Pamela Jane's Week 'A Story About Days Of The Week'
Illus.: Ike, Jane
Author: Robinson, Alberta
1973 $2.00

2562
Parade For Chatty Baby, A
Illus.: Mode, Nathalee
Author: Schwalj, Marjory
1965 $15.00

2475-4
Patsy The Pussycat
Illus.: Super, Terri
Author: Watts, Mabel
1986 $2.00

2622
Pebbles Flintstone ABC's
Illus.: Lorencz, Bill; Strobl, Anthony
Author: Daly, Eileen
1966 $18.00

2657
Pebbles Flintstone 'Daddy's Little Helper'
Illus.: Storms, Robert
Author: Hagen, Patrick
1964 $18.00

848
Peppermint
Illus.: Grider, Dorothy
Author: Grider, Dorothy
1950 $20.00

2502
Peppermint
Illus.: Burns, Raymond
Author: Grider, Dorothy
1966 $10.00

2405

Peppermint
(2nd Cover)
Illus.: Burns, Raymond
Author: Grider, Dorothy
1966   **$10.00**

2637

Pete's Dragon - The Best Of Friends
Illus.: Walt Disney Studio
Author: Walt Disney Studios
1977   **$6.00**

2616

Peter Pan And The Tiger
Illus.: Mc Natt Jr., Rich; Totten, Bob
Author: Carey, Mary
1976   **$8.00**

2506

Peter Potamus Meets The Black Knight
Illus.: Strobl, Anthony ; Jancar, Milli
Author: Freeman, Jane
1965   **$15.00**

929

Peter Rabbit
Illus.: Wilson, Beth
1953   **$8.00**

2515

Peter Rabbit
Illus.: Winship, Florence Sarah
1955   **$6.00**

2539

Peter Rabbit
Illus.: Myers, Jack & Louise
1959   **$5.00**

884

Peter The Lonesome Hermit
Illus.: Snow, Dorethea J.
Author: Snow, Dorethea J.
1948   **$18.00**

927

Peter's Pencil
Illus.: Butler, Paula Hurley
Author: Butler, Paula Hurley
1953   **$12.00**

2463-38

Peter's Welcome
Illus.: Schweninger, Ann
1985   **$2.00**

885

Petunia
Illus.: Williams, Ben
Author: Sankey, Alice
1948   **$16.00**

2475-48

Pig And The Witch, The
Illus.: Severn, Jeffery
Author: Goldsmith, Howard
1990   **$2.00**

2628

Pink Panther Rides Again, The
Illus.: Jason Art Studios
Author: Graham, Kennon
1976   **$3.00**

2428-2
Pinocchio
Illus.: Mc Savage, Frank & Fisher,
Frank
Author: Hass, Dorothy
1961 $6.00

2614
**Pippi Longstocking And The
South Sea Pirates**
Illus.: Baker, Darrell
Author: Carey, Mary
1976 $8.00

2641
Pitty Pat
(Fuzzy)
Illus.: Winship, Florence Sarah
Author: Horn, Gladys M.
1954 $15.00

2471-46
Play School ABC
Illus.: Stellerman, Robbie
1985 $2.00

803
Playmate For Peter
Illus.: Myers, Louise W
Author: Maritano, Adela Kay
1951 $8.00

2509
Pluto
Illus.: Strobl, Tony & Boyle, Neil
Author: Revena
1957 $10.00

2504
Pockets
Illus.: Ozone, Lucy
Author: Ozone, Lucy
1955 $8.00

2616
Pockets
(2nd Cover)
Illus.: Ozone, Lucy
Author: Ozone, Lucy
1955 $5.00

864
Polka Dot Tots
Illus.: Tedder, Elizabeth
Author: Lieberman, Nina Belle
1946 $16.00

2527
Pony
Illus.: Crawford, Mel; Photo's Haas,
Arthur
Author: Merow, Erva Loomis
1965 $5.00

2543
Pony Who Couldn't Say Neigh, The
Illus.: Thomas, Stephen
Author: Schwalje, Marjory
1964 $5.00

850
Poor Kitty
Illus.: Tedder, Elizabeth
Author: Tedder, Elizabeth
1945 $16.00

844

Pop-O The Clown
Illus.: Cummings, Alison
Author: Whitteberry, Caroline
1950 **$15.00**

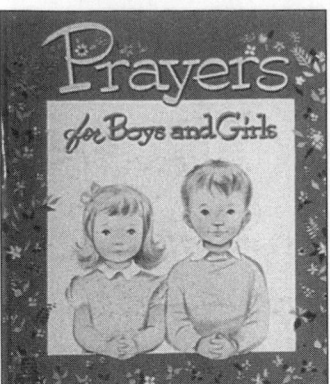

918

Prayers For Boys And Girls
Illus.: Cummings, Alison
1953 **$7.00**

2636

Prayers For Boys And Girls
Illus.: None Credited
1957 **$6.00**

2523

Prayers For Boys And Girls
(2nd Cover)
Illus.: Cummings, Alison
1972 **$3.00**

2520

Prayers For Boys And Girls
(3rd Cover)
Illus.: Cummings, Alison
1972 **$2.00**

2508

Prickly Tale, A
Illus.: Hauge, Carl & Mary
Author: Begley, Evelyn M
1965 **$5.00**

2519

Prickly Tale, A
(2nd Cover)
Illus.: Hauge, Carl & Mary
Author: Begley, Evelyn M
1965 **$4.00**

2610

Princess And The Pea
Illus.: Herric, Pru
1961 **$7.00**

2610

Princess Who Never Laughed, The
Illus.: Grunwald, Marcia
1961 **$7.00**

819

Puffy The Puppy
Illus.: Porter, Genevieve
Author: Georgiana
1952 **$8.00**

2476-45

Puppies On Parade
Illus.: Eubank, Mary Grace
Author: Helfand, Karen
1989 **$2.00**

2641

Purrrt
(Fuzzy Wuzzy Book)
Illus.: Hartwell, Marjorie
Author: Hartwell, Marjorie
1952 **$15.00**

895
Pussy Cat's Secret
Illus.: Spicer, Jessie
Author: Elting, Mary
1949 **$15.00**

873
Pussy-Willow
Illus.: Mac Kean, Emma C
Author: Mac Kean, Emma C
1948 **$15.00**

2615
Quiet Quincy And The Delivery Truck
Illus.: Steigerwald, Beverly
Author: Kemp, Polly G.
1961 **$6.00**

2541
Quiet Quincy And The Delivery Truck
(2nd Cover)
Illus.: Steigerwald, Beverly
Author: Kemp, Polly G.
1961 **$5.00**

893
Rackety-Boom
Illus.: Florian
Author: Wright, Betty Ren
1953 **$20.00**

2557
Rackety-Boom
(2nd Cover)
Illus.: Florian
Author: Wright, Betty Ren
1953 **$15.00**

2641
Raggedy Andy And The Jump-Up Contest
Illus.: Goldsborough, June
Author: Schwalj , Marjory
1978 **$6.00**

2417-2
Raggedy Andy's Treasure Hunt
Illus.: Goldsborough, June
Author: Schwalje, Marjory
1973 **$5.00**

2596
Raggedy Ann And Andy On The Farm
Illus.: Goldsborough, June
Author: Daly, Eileen
1958 **$5.00**

2417-1
Raggedy Ann And The Tagalong Present
Illus.: Krehbiel, Becky
Author: Schwalje, Marjory
1978 **$5.00**

2498
Raggedy Ann's Cooking School
Illus.: Goldsborough, June
Author: Schwalj, Marjory
1974 **$5.00**

2451-4
Rainbow Brite And The Magic Belt
Illus.: Costanza, John
Author: Grunewalt, Pine
1985 **$4.00**

2474-44

Rainbow Circus Comes To Town, The
Illus.: Steadman, Barbara
Author: Ryder, Joann C.
1986 $3.00

858

Rainy Day Story On The Farm
Illus.: Matson, Elizabeth
Author: Little, Irene
1944 $15.00

2429-3

Rescuers ABC, The
Illus.: Walt Disney Studios
Author: Walt Disney Studios
1977 $6.00

2622

Ricochet Rabbit Showdown At Gopher Gulch Bakery
Illus.: Anderson, Al & Alvaradom, Peter
Author: Hagen, Patrick
1964 $18.00

2571

Rinty And Pals For Rusty
Illus.: Bartram, Bob
Author: Francis, Dee
1957 $12.00

2408

Road Runner And The Bird Watchers, The
Illus.: De Lara, Phil
Author: Lewis, Jean
1968 $4.00

2466

Road Runner, The 'Tumbleweed Trouble'
Illus.: Leon Jason Studio
Author: Woolgar, Jack
1971 $3.00

2441

Robin Hood And Skippy's Best Birthday
Illus.: Walt Disney Studios
Author: Walt Disney Studios
1973 $5.00

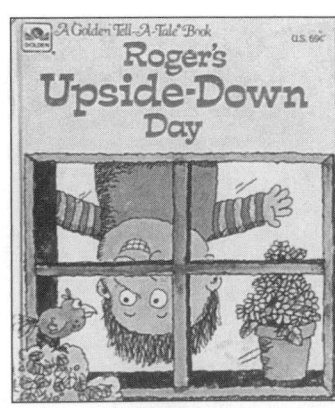

2463-4

Roger's Upside-Down Day
Illus.: Lee, Jared D
Author: Wright, Betty Ren
1979 $3.00

936

Rootie Kazootie And The Pineapple Pies
Illus.: Crawford, Mel
Author: Barrow, John
1953 $25.00

2436

Roundabout Train
Illus.: Clement, Charles
Author: Wright, Betty Ren
1953 $5.00

861

Rowdy
Illus.: Scott, Janet Laura
Author: Wyatt, Jane
1946 $15.00

811
Roy Rogers And The Lane Ranch
Illus.: La Grotta, J. M.
1950   **$25.00**

801
Roy Rogers And The Sure'Nough Cowpoke
Illus.: Steffen, Randy
Author: Beecher, Elizabeth
1952   **$22.00**

943
Roy Rogers' Surprise For Donnie
Illus.: Steel, John
Author: Sankey, Alice
1954   **$17.00**

2567
Roy Rogers' Bullet Leads The Way
Illus.: Doe, Bart
Author: Wood, Frances
1953   **$20.00**

2622
Rubbles And Bamm-Bamm, The 'Problem Present'
Illus.: Storms, Robert
Author: Carey, Mary
1965   **$18.00**

2517-2
Rudolph The Red-Nosed Reindeer
Illus.: Miyake, Yoshi
Author: Daly, Eileen
1980   **$4.00**

2483-02
Rudolph The Red-Nosed Reindeer
Illus.: Ortiz, Phil & Cuddy, Robbin
Author: Cohen, Robin
1993   **$2.00**

2567
Ruff And Reddy Go To A Party
Illus.: Eisenberg, Harvey; Boyle, Neil
1958   **$20.00**

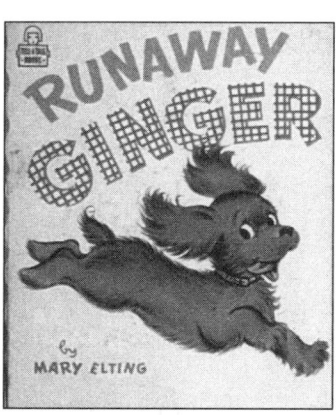

897
Runaway Ginger
Illus.: Lesko, Zillah
Author: Elting, Mary
1949   **$15.00**

2537
Runaway Ginger
(2nd Cover)
Illus.: Lesko, Zillah
Author: Elting, Mary
1949   **$10.00**

2465
Runaway Pancake, The
Illus.: Williams, Ben
1956   **$20.00**

842
Sailboat That Ran Away, The
Illus.: Chastain, Madye Lee
Author: Chastain, Madye Lee
1950   **$15.00**

2570
Scooby Doo At The Zoo
Illus.: Szwejkowski, Adam & Totten, Bob
Author: Nathan, Williams
1974   **$6.00**

805

See-It Goes!
Illus.: Wilde, George & Wilma
Author: Wilde, George & Wilma
1953 $8.00

2557

See-It Goes!
(2nd Cover)
Illus.: Wilde, George & Wilma
Author: Wilde, George & Wilma
1953 $5.00

2471-43

Sesame Street ABC
Illus.: Nez, John
Author: Calmenson, Stephanie
1987 $2.00

2465-43

Sesame Streets First Times
Illus.: Delaney, Toni
Author: Calmenson, Stephanie
1987 $2.00

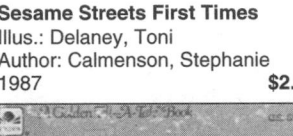

2606

Seven Wishes, The
Illus.: Miyake, Yoshi
Author: Cowles, Kathleen
1976 $3.00

2564

**Sherlock Hemlock And The Great
Twiddlebug Mystery**
Illus.: Children's Television Workshop
Author: Children's Television
Workshop
1972 $2.00

2649

Sleeping Beauty
Author: Mc Gary, Norm
1959 $10.00

2462

Sleepy Puppy, The
Illus.: Winship, Florence Sarah
Author: Chamberlin, Mary Jo
1961 $4.00

2457

Slowpoke At The Circus
Illus.: Ruhman, Ruth
Author: Richardson, Kay
1973 $3.00

2463

Smokey Bear Saves The Forest
Illus.: Gantz, David
Author: Graham, Kennon
1971 $8.00

867

Smoky The Baby Goat
Illus.: Reed, Veronica
Author: Elting, Mary
1947 $15.00

854

Sneezer
Illus.: Williams, Ben D.
Author: Upson, Estelle Mc Innes
1945 $15.00

851

Snooty
Illus.: Flory, Jane
Author: Flory, Jane
1944 $15.00

853
Snoozey
Illus.: Mc Kean, Emma C
Author: Mc Kean, Emma C
1944 **$15.00**

2358
Snoozey
(2nd Cover)
Illus.: Mc Kean, Emma C
Author: Mc Kean, Emma C
1944 **$12.00**

2578
Snow White And The Seven Dwarfs
Illus.: Wegner, Helmuth G
Author: Walt Disney Studios
1957 **$12.00**

2427
Snow White And The Seven Dwarfs
(2nd Cover)
Illus.: Wegner, Helmuth G
Author: Walt Disney Studios
1957 **$3.00**

2670
Snowball
(Fuzzy)
Illus.: Winship, Florence Sarah
Author: Wright, Betty Ren
1952 **$15.00**

886
Socks
Illus.: Winship, Florence Sarah
Author: Ryan, Betty Molgard
1949 **$15.00**

963
Somebody Forgot
Illus.: Stang, Judy
Author: Horn, Gladys M.
1954 **$8.00**

2659
Someplace For Sparky
Illus.: Walters, Audry
Author: Beatie, Bernadine
1965 **$4.00**

2521
Special Pet, A
Illus.: Giacomini, Olindo
Author: Schwalje, Marjory
1968 **$2.00**

874
Speckles And The Triplets
Illus.: Stevens, Mary
Author: Elting, Mary
1949 **$18.00**

2526
Splish Splash, And Splush
Illus.: Wilde, Irma
Author: Pape, Donna Lugg
1962 **$7.00**

2472-41
Spoon Necklace, The
Illus.: De Moth, Vivienne
Author: Young, Opal Dean
1986 **$3.00**

2560

Spotted Little Puppy, The
Illus.: Seiden, Art
Author: Fletcher, Steffi
1961 **$4.00**

2615

Stubby
Illus.: Seiden, Art
Author: Borden, Marion
1963 **$4.00**

2463-44

Stuck In The Tub
Illus.: Orville, Oliver
Author: Hylst, Marguerite Van
1988 **$2.00**

824

Sunny, Honey, And Funny
(Fuzzy)
Illus.: Lesko, Zillah
Author: Horn, Gladys M.
1951 **$15.00**

2573

Surprise For Howdy Doody
Illus.: Kean, Edward
1951 **$20.00**

2543

Surprise In The Barn
Illus.: Flory, Jane
Author: Flory, Jane
1955 **$6.00**

2543

Surprise In The Barn
(2nd Cover)
Illus.: Flory, Jane
Author: Flory, Jane
1955 **$5.00**

879

Susan And The Rain
Illus.: Chastain, Madye Lee
Author: Chastain, Madye Lee
1947 **$16.00**

879

Susan And The Rain
(2nd Cover)
Illus.: Chastain, Madye Lee
Author: Chastain, Madye Lee
1947 **$10.00**

2509

Swiss Family Duck
Illus.: Strobl, Anthony; Irvin, Fred
Author: Hagen, Patrick
1964 **$10.00**

2476-44

Tabitha Tabby's Fantastic Flavor
Illus.: Peltier, Phyllis A.
Author:
1988 **$2.00**

2601

Tag-Along Shadow
Illus.: Macpherson, Ruth Rosamond
Author: Macpherson, Ruth Rosamond
1959 **$8.00**

2488-02
Tale Of Peter Rabbit, The
Illus.: Schweninger, Ann
1992   **$2.00**

2534
Tall Tree Small Tree
Illus.: Winship, Florence Sarah
Author: Watts, Mabel
1970   **$3.00**

809
Teddy's Surprise
Illus.: Suzanne
Author: Georgiana
809   **$15.00**

2423
Teena And The Magic Pot
Illus.: Myers, Louise And Jack
1961   **$4.00**

2513
Teeny-Tiny Tale
Illus.: Williams, Ben D
1955   **$10.00**

2558
Teeny-Tiny Tale
(2nd Cover)
Illus.: Rose, Terry
Author: Sukus, Jan
1969   **$5.00**

2502
That Donkey
Illus.: Grider, Dorothy
Author: Georgiana
1954   **$8.00**

2675
That Puppy
Illus.: Zemsky, Jessica
Author: Haas, Dorothy
1961   **$10.00**

2534
That's Where You Live!
Illus.: Lewis, Jean
19882Fraser, Betty
Author: Vogels, Mary Prescott
1970   **$4.00**

2530
That's Where You Live!
(2nd Cover)
Illus.: Fraser, Betty
Author: Vogels, Mary Prescott
1970   **$2.00**

2691
Thin Arnold
Illus.: Heckler, Bill
Author: Bacon, Joan Chase
1970   **$6.00**

2643
This Room Is Mine
Illus.: Stang, Judy
Author: Wright, Betty Ren
1977   **$3.00**

877
This Way To The Zoo
Illus.: Weber, Nettie
Author: Cunningham, Virginia
1948   **$12.00**

2536
This Way To The Zoo
(2nd Cover)
Illus.: Weber, Nettie
Author: Cunningham, Virginia
1948   **$8.00**

859
Three Bears, The
Illus.: Yeakey, Carol
1945   **$15.00**
859
Three Bears, The
Illus.: Yeakey, Carol
1945   **$10.00**

2512
Three Bears, The
Illus.: Rowland, Helen
1952   **$5.00**

2512
Three Bears, The
Illus.: Suzanne
1955   **$7.00**
2512
Three Bears, The
Illus.: Sari
1960   **$6.00**

2462-35
Three Bears, The
Illus.: Gordon, Louise
Author: Russell, Solveig Paulson
1968   **$3.00**

2515
Three Billy Goats Gruff
Illus.: Ames, Lee J.
1954   **$5.00**

836
Three Little Mice (See Matilda Mac Elroy And Mary)
Illus.: Robison, I. E.
Author: Fairweather, Jessie Home
1950   **$10.00**

860
Three Little Pigs, The
Illus.: Irwin, Josephine
1944   **$15.00**

2547
Three Little Pigs, The
Illus.: Myers, Louise W
1953   **$8.00**

2542
Three Little Pigs, The
Illus.: Miloche, Hilda
1956   **$6.00**

2501
Three Little Pigs, The
Illus.: Bracke, Charles
Author: Wood, Jo Anne
1969   **$5.00**

2547
Three Little Pigs, The
Illus.: Williams, Ben
1959 **$4.00**

2522
Timothy Tinker The Wonderful Oilcan
Illus.: Stang, Judy
Author: Watts, Mabel
1968 **$4.00**

856
Timothy's Shoes
Illus.: Schad, Helen G.
1946 **$15.00**

856
Timothy's Shoes
(2nd Cover)
Illus.: Schad, Helen G.
1946 **$13.00**

2615
Tiny Tots 1 2 3
Illus.: Murray, Marjorie
1958 **$6.00**

2435
Tiny Tots 123
(2nd Cover)
Illus.: Murray, Marjorie
1958 **$3.00**

2555
Tip-Top Tree House, The
Illus.: Wilde, Carol
Author: Tucker, Daisy
1969 **$4.00**

2465-44
Toby Bunny's Secret Hiding Place
Illus.: Spence, James
Author: Werner, Dave
1988 **$1.00**

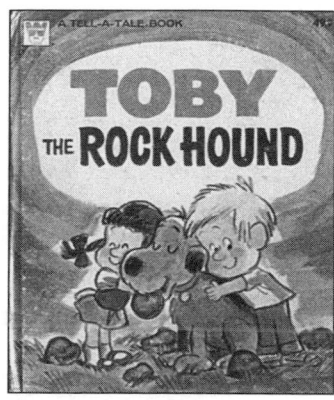

2408-6
Toby The Rock Hound
Illus.: Bradfield, Roger
Author: Walrath, Jane Dwyer
1979 **$3.00**

2505
Toby Zebra And The Lost Zoo
Illus.: Garris, Norma & Dan
Author: Pape, Donna Lugg
1963 **$4.00**

2509
Tom And Jerry And The Toy Circus
Illus.: Armstrong, Samuel; Ray, Tom
1953 **$8.00**

2509
Tom And Jerry In Model Mice
Illus.: Eisenberg, Harvey; Dempster, Al
Author: M-G-M Cartoons
1951 **$10.00**

2611

Tom And Jerry In Tom's Happy Birthday
Illus.: Eisenberg, Harvey And Wolfe, Gene
Author: M-G-M Cartoons, Inc
1955   **$8.00**

2451-38

Tom And Jerry's Big Movie
Illus.: Messerli, Joe
Author: Lewis, Jean
1985   **$2.00**

822

Tommy And Timmy
(Black Fuzzy)
Illus.: Berry, Anne Scheu
Author: Sankey, Alice
1951   **$15.00**

2644

Tommy And Timmy
(Yellow Fuzzy)
(2nd Cover)
Illus.: Berry, Anne Scheu
Author: Sankey, Alice
1951   **$15.00**

2557

Tommy On The Farm
Illus.: Elfrieda
Author: Russell, Solveig Paulson
1968   **$3.00**

881

Tommy Tractor
Illus.: Buehrig, Rosemary
Author: Mcpherson, Ge
1947   **$12.00**

2525

Too Many Kittens
Illus.: Suzanne
Author: Watts, Mabel
1963   **$8.00**

2614

Too Many Names
Illus.: Eugenie
Author: Peterson, Jeri
1970   **$3.00**

2561

Town Mouse And The Country Mouse, The
Illus.: Stang, Judy
Author: Horn, Gladys M.
1954   **$7.00**

878

Toy Party, The
Illus.: Wysse
Author: Christopher, Til B.
1948   **$15.00**

2518

Toy That Flew, The
Illus.: Depper, Hertha
Author: Smaridge, Nora
1974   **$5.00**

2556

Train Coming!
Illus.: Florian
Author: Wright, Betty Ren
1954   **$6.00**

813
Truck That Stopped At Village Small, The
Illus.: Dorcas
Author: Knittle, Jessie M.
1951   **$8.00**

931
Trumpet
Illus.: Myers, Bernice
Author: Lynn, Patricia
1953   **$6.00**

2460
Try Again, Sally!
Illus.: Tsambon, Athena
Author: Laughlin, Florence
1969   **$3.00**

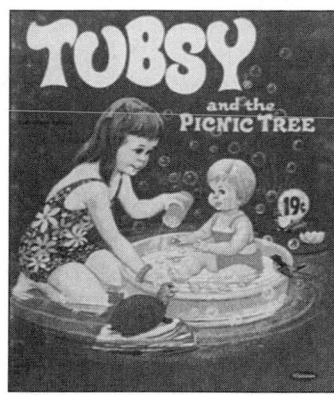

2552
Tubsy And The Picnic Tree
(Ideal Doll)
Illus.: Sampson, Katherine
Author: Daly, Eileen
1968   **$12.00**

2672
Tuffer (Fuzzy)
Illus.: Rutherford, Bonnie & Bill
Author: Wright, Betty Ren
1959   **$13.00**

880
Tuffy The Tugboat
Illus.: Williams, Ben
Author: Sankey, Alice
1947   **$15.00**

901
Tweety
Illus.: Abranz, Fred & Maclaughlin
Author: Warner Bros, Inc
1953   **$10.00**

2453-35
Tweety And Sylvester At The Farm
Illus.: Barto, Renzo
Author: Hogan, Cecily Ruth
1978   **$4.00**

2453-47
Tweety And Sylvester A Visit To The Vet
Illus.: Messerli, Joe
Author: Lewis, Jean
1988   **$2.00**

2448
Tweety And Sylvester Picnic Problems
Illus.: Leon Jason Studio
Author: Biesterveld, Betty
1970   **$3.00**

2525
Two Kittens
Illus.: Zfa-Duesseldorf
Author: Tiffany, Virginia
1966   **$4.00**

2526
Two Stories About Chap And Chirpy
Illus.: Wilde, Irma
Author: Bond, Gladys Baker
1965   **$4.00**

2510
Two Stories About Kate And Kitty
Illus.: Schlesinger, Alice
Author: Priestly, Lee
1968 $4.00

2683
Two Stories About Lollipop
Illus.: Eugenie
Author: Bell, Luann Stull
1969 $4.00

2601
Two Stories About Ricky
Illus.: Goldsborough, June
Author: Frankel, Bernice
1966 $4.00

2560
Two Stories About Wags
Illus.: Garris, Norma & Dan
Author: Biesterveld, Betty
1966 $4.00

2659
Two Stories About Wendy
Illus.: Nagel, Stina
Author: Schwalj, Marjory
1965 $4.00

2543
Two To Twins, The
Illus.: Goldsborough, June
Author: Priestly, Lee
1966 $5.00

2552
Uncle Scrooge, The Winner
Illus.: Strobl, Anthony; Andersen, Al
Author: Carter, Katherine
1964 $15.00

903
Uncle Wiggily And The Alligator
Illus.: Weaver, William
Author: Turner, Gill; Garis, Howard
1953 $7.00

2611
Under Dog
Illus.: Jason Art Studios
Author: Johnston, William
1966 $10.00

2543
Under The Saskatoon Tree
Illus.: Rutherford, Bonnie & Bill
Author: Russell, Solveig Paulson
1966 $4.00

2402-7
**Up And Down Book Staring Ernie
And Bert, The**
Illus.: Swanson, Maggie
1979 $2.00

2559
Very Best Of Friends, The
Illus.: Hauge, Carl & Mary
Author: Fletcher, Steffi
1963 $3.00

2546

Wacky Witch: The Royal Birthday
Illus.: Arens, Michael; Toten, Bob
Author: Lewis, Jean
1971   **$6.00**

2688

Waldo, The Jumping Dragon
Illus.: Oechsli, Kelly
Author: Detiege, Dave
1964   **$5.00**

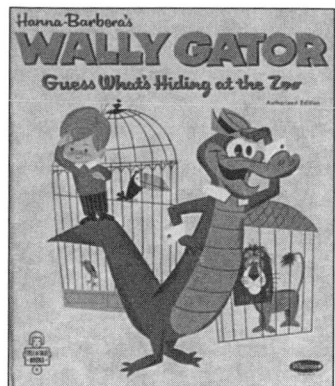

2506

Wally Gator Guess What's Hiding At The Zoo
Illus.: Crawford, Mel
Author: Daly, Eileen
1963   **$8.00**

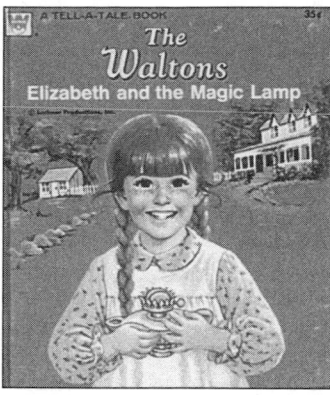

2579

Waltons, The: Elizabeth And The Magic Lamp
Illus.: Neely, Jan
Author: Graham, Charlotte
1975   **$4.00**

2564

Water Birds
Illus.: Hartwell, Marjorie
Author: Wright, Betty Ren; Hanson, Alice
1955   **$10.00**

2404-3

We Talk With God
Illus.: Mc Elwain, Diane
Author: Burdick, Faith Oliver
1979   **$3.00**

2541-41

We're Busy, Charlie Brown!
Illus.: Schulz, Charles; Ellis, Art
Author: Namm, Diane
1987   **$3.00**

2425

What Makes My Cat Purr?
Illus.: Elfrieda
Author: Tompert, Ann
1965   **$4.00**

2563

What Shall I Put In The Hole That I Dig?
Illus.: Aliki
Author: Thompson, Eleanor
1972   **$4.00**

2542

When I Go To Bed
Illus.: Ruhman, Ruth
Author: Yerian, Margaret
1967   **$12.00**

2469

Where Is The Keeper?
Illus.: Seiden, Art
Author: Watts, Mabel
1966   **$4.00**

2505

Where Timothy Lives
Illus.: Frost, Bruno
Author: Wright, Betty Ren
1958   **$6.00**

2505

Where Timothy Lives
(2nd Cover)
Illus.: Frost, Bruno
Author: Wright, Betty Ren
1958 $4.00

2546

Where's Harry?
Illus.: Stirnweis, Shannon
Author: Meek, Pauline Palmer
1969 $4.00

2521

Who Are You?
Illus.: Fitch, Winnie
Author: Bradfield, Joan & Rogers
1966 $4.00

2557

Whoa, Joey!
Illus.: Bracke, Charles
Author: Hogstrom, Daphne
1968 $4.00

884

Whoop-Ee, Hunkydory!
Illus.: Vaughan, Eillen Fox
Author: Justus, May
1952 $7.00

2553

Whose Baby Is That?
Illus.: Nagel, Stina
Author: Jones, Clair
1969 $4.00

2428

Why Do You Love Me?
Illus.: Sampson, Katherine
Author: Watts, Mabel
1970 $5.00

892

Why Roosty Sang
Illus.: Winship, Florence Sarah
Author: Page, Marguerita
1948 $15.00

892

Why Roosty Sang
(2nd Cover)
Illus.: Winship, Florence Sarah
Author: Page, Marguerita
1948 $12.00

852

Wiggletail
Illus.: Charlie
Author: Charlie
1944 $15.00

2475-3

Wild Animal Babies
Illus.: Hauge, Carl & Mary
1973 $2.00

2625

Wild Kingdom A Trip To A Game Park
Illus.: Seward, James/Creative Studios
Author: Dinneen, Betty
1976 $3.00

818
Willy Woo-Oo-Oo
Illus.: Winship, Florence Sarah
Author: Wright, Betty Ren
1951 **$15.00**

2444
Willy Woo-Oo-Oo
(2nd Cover)
Illus.: Winship, Florence Sarah
Author: Wright, Betty Ren
1951 **$10.00**

2627
Wilmer The Watchdog
Illus.: Giacomini, Olinda
Author: Kittke, Lael
1970 **$5.00**

2577
Winnie-The-Pooh 'The Blustery Day'
Illus.: Walt Disney Studios
Author: Milne, A.A.
1975 **$5.00**

2620
Winnie-The-Pooh And Eeyore's House
Illus.: Walt Disney Studios
Author: Milne, A.A.
1976 **$5.00**

2526
Winnie-The-Pooh And The Un-bouncing Of Tigger
Illus.: Walt Disney Studios
Author: Milne, A.A.
1974 **$5.00**

2561
Wolf And The Seven Kids, The
Illus.: Sondern, Ferdinand A.
Author: Hansen, Gretchen
1696 **$4.00**

871
Wonderful Tony
Illus.: Berry, Anne Scheu
Author: Page, Marguerita
1947 **$15.00**

2439
Woody Woodpecker Shoots The Works
Illus.: Mc Savage, Fran & Armstrong, Samuel
Author: Walter Lantz Studios
1955 **$7.00**

2562
Woody Woodpecker's Pogo Stick Adventures
Illus.: Abranz, Alfred; Knight, John
Author: Walter Lantz Studios
1954 **$8.00**

831
Woody Woodpecker's Peck Of Trouble
Illus.: Thompson, Riley & Armstrong, Sam
Author: Watts, Mabel
1951 **$10.00**

2523
Wrong-Way Howie Learns To Slide
Illus.: Wilde, Carol
Author: Peake, Sylvia
1969 **$4.00**

911

Yellow Cat, The
(Fuzzy)
Illus.: Sari
Author: Wright, Betty Ren
1952   **$15.00**

940

Yippie Kiyi
Illus.: Munson, Floyd
Author: Rose, Florella
1953   **$18.00**

2514

Yippie Kiyi And Whoa Boy
Illus.: Sari
Author: Rose, Florella
1955   **$15.00**

2642

Yogi Bear And The Super Scooper
Illus.: Hooper, L.; Thomas, R.
Author: Hoag, Nancy
1961   **$16.00**

2608

Yogi Bear's Secret
Illus.: Jason, Leon
Author: Jones, Mary Voell
1963   **$18.00**

2423

Zoo Friends Are At Our School Today!
Illus.: Brewer, Sally King
Author: Watts, Mabel
1979   **$3.00**

Knott's Berry Farm Burro In Ghost Town
(Knott's Berry Farm Promotion)
Illus.: Alvarado, Peter
Author: Klinordlinger, Jean
1955   **$15.00**

Search for Santa Claus, A
(Santa's Village Promotion)
Illus.: Boyle, Neil
Author: Nast, Elsa Ruth
1958   **$12.00**

Tell-A-Tale Books Index (Numerical)

For those of you who collect books numerically, the following list is for you. Because the early editions had only three digits, they are easy to recognize. After three digits, the books were done with four, and most of these had multiple titles through the years. Tell-A-Tales with dashes have no numerical significance. It is possible you may have a title with a different four-digit number than is listed here.

Company Products and Corporate Characters Index

Book Codes

Elf—Elf   Little Golden Book—LGB   Tell-A-Tale—TAT   Treasure—T   Wonder—W

Title	Type	No.
LGB L ABC, The	LGB	101
Little Red Riding Hood	LGB	42
Pets For Peter	LGB	82
Ukulele And Her New Doll	LGB	102
When I Grow Up	LGB	96

Raggedy Ann

Title	Type	No.
Puzzle For Raggedy Ann And Andy A	W	683
Raggedy Andy's Surprise	W	604
Raggedy Andy's Treasure Hunt	TAT	2417
Raggedy Ann And The Jump-Up Contest	TAT	2641
Raggedy Ann's Christmas Surprise	W	868
Raggedy Ann's Cooking School	TAT	2498
Raggedy Ann's Merriest Christmas	W	594
Raggedy Ann's Secret	W	727
Raggedy Ann's Tea Party	W	624
Raggedy Ann And Andy And The Rainy Day Circus	LGB	401
Raggedy Ann And Andy Five Birthdays In A Row	LGB	107- 4
Raggedy Ann And Andy Help Santa Claus	LGB	156
Raggedy Ann And Andy On The Farm	TAT	2596
Raggedy Ann And Andy The Grey Kitten	LGB	139
Raggedy Ann And Marcella's First Day At School	W	588
Raggedy Ann And The Cookie Snatcher	LGB	262
Raggedy Ann And The Tagalong Present	TAT	2417-1

Religious Titles

Title	Type	No.
Angel Child	Elf	8373
Angel Child	Elf	8715
Baby Jesus Stamps	LGB	A 12
Baby Jesus The	Elf	8556
Baby Moses	TAT	917
Beloved Son, The	TAT	825
Bible Stories	LGB	174
Bible Stories From The Old Testament	LGB	153*
Bible Stories: Old Testament	Elf	491
Bible Stories: Old Testament	Elf	8613
Bible Treasures	W	643
Book Of God's Gifts A	LGB	112
Child's Friend A	TAT	2519
Child's Ten Commandments A	TAT	2624
Daniel In The Lions' Den	LGB	311-62
David And Goliath	LGB	110*
First Book Of Bible Stories	LGB	198
Heroes Of The Bible	LGB	236
I Think About Jesus	Elf	8652
Little Lost Angel	Elf	580
Little Lost Angel	Elf	483
Little Lost Angel	Elf	8376
Little Lost Angel	Elf	8680
Littlest Angel, The	W	755
Lord's Prayer, The	W	647
Lord Is My Shepherd, The 'The twenty-third Psalm'	LGB	311-60
My Bible Book	Elf	8696
My Book About God	W	644
My First Book Of Bible Stories	LGB	19
My First Book Of Prayers	T	868
My Prayer Book	Elf	8697
Noah's Ark	LGB	109
Noah's Ark	LGB	311-64
Noah's Ark	LGB	D 28
Noah's Ark	Elf	461
Noah's Ark	Elf	1020
Noah's Ark	Elf	8424
Noah's Ark	Elf	8648
Noah And The Ark	TAT	2558
Prayers And Graces For A Small Child	Elf	502
Prayers And Graces For A Small Child	Elf	8609
Prayers For Boys And Girls	TAT	918
Prayers For Boys And Girls	TAT	2523
Prayers For Children	LGB	205
Prayers For Children	LGB	301-10
Prayers For Little Children	Elf	8557
Stories Of The Christ Child	Elf	484
Stories Of The Christ Child	Elf	8612
Story Of David The	Elf	8725
Story Of Jesus, The	LGB	27
Story Of Jonah, The	LGB	311-61
Story Of Joseph The	Elf	8724
Story Of The Christ Child, The	W	587
Ten Commandments For Children, The	Elf	543
Ten Commandments For Children, The	Elf	8604
twenty-third Psalm, The	Elf	8698
We Talk With God	TAT	2404-3
Where Jesus Lived	LGB	147
W Book Of Bible Stories, The	W	577

Romper Room

Title	Type	No.
Romper Room Do Bee Book Of Manners, The	W	763
Romper Room Do Bees	LGB	273
Romper Room Exercise Book, The	LGB	527
Romper Room Laughing Book	W	808
Romper Room Safety Book, The	W	854

Rootie Kazootie

Title	Type	No.
Rootie Kazootie	LGB	150
Rootie Kazootie Baseball Star	LGB	190
Rootie Kazootie Joins The Circus	LGB	226
Rootie Kazootie And The Pineapple Pies	TAT	936

Scouting Books

Title	Type	No.
Brownie Scouts	LGB	409
Cub Scouts	LGB	5022
Little Cub Scout	Elf	8665

Sesame Street/Muppets

Title	Type	No.
Amazing Mumford Forgets The Magic Word	LGB	108- 5
Bert's Hall Of Great Inventions	LGB	321*
Big Bird's Day On The Farm	LGB	107-61
Big Bird's Red Book	LGB	157*
Big Bird Brings Spring To Sesame Street	LGB	108-57
Big Bird Follows The Signs	TAT	2452-4
Big Bird Visits Navajo Country	LGB	108-68
Cookie Monster And The Cookie Tree	LGB	159
Cookie Monster And The Cookie Tree	LGB	109-52
Count's Poem, The	TAT	2402
Count All The Way To Sesame Street	LGB	203-56
Day Snuffy Had The Sniffles, The	LGB	108-59
Ernie's Telephone Call	TAT	2452-34
Ernie's Work Of Art	LGB	109- 5
Four Seasons, The	LGB	108- 4
Fozzie's Funnies	LGB	111-87
From Trash To Treasure	LGB	108-70
Grover's Guide To Good Manners	LGB	109-66
Grover's Own Alphabet	LGB	108-46
Grover's Own Alphabet	TAT	2402-6
Grover Takes Care Of Baby	LGB	109-57
Happy And Sad Grouch And Glad	LGB	108-67
How To Be A Grouch	TAT	2618
I Think That It Is Wful	LGB	109-47
Kermit Saves The Swamp!	LGB	111-84
Many Faces Of Ernie The	LGB	109- 4
"Me Cookie"	LGB	109-69
Monster At The End Of This Book, The	LGB	316*
Monsters' Picnic, The	LGB	109-59
Muppet -Treasure Island	LGB	111-88
Oscar's Book	LGB	120*
Oscar's New Neighbor	LGB	109-67
Puppy Love	LGB	109-46
Ready Set Go! A Counting Book	LGB	109-71
Sesame Street 'Mother Goose Rhymes'	LGB	108-69
Sesame Street 'The Together Book'	LGB	315*
Sesame Street ABC	TAT	2471-43
Sesame Streets Cookie Monster's Book Of Cookie Shapes	TAT	2402-8
Sesame Streets First Times	TAT	2465-43
Sherlock Hemlock And The Great Twiddlebug Mystery	TAT	2564
What's Up In The Attic?	LGB	108-58
Which Witch Is Which?	LGB	98770-01

Shari Lewis

Title	Type	No.
Party In Shariland	LGB	360
Shari Lewis W Book, The	W	781

Smokey The Bear

Title	Type	No.
Smokey And His Animal Friends	LGB	387
Smokey Bear 'Saves The Forest'	TAT	2463
Smokey Bear And The Campers	LGB	423
Smokey The Bear	LGB	224
Smokey The Bear	LGB	481
Smokey The Bear Finds A Helper	LGB	345

TV Shows (Misc.)

Title	Type	No.
Adventures Of Robin Hood And His Merry Men	Elf	532
Barney 'Sharing Is Caring'	LGB	98790
Benji 'Fastest Dog In The West'	LGB	165*
Benji 'The Detective'	TAT	2640
Buck Rogers And The Children Of Hopetown	LGB	500*
Bully And The New Girl	TAT	2526
Circus Boy	LGB	290
Circus Boy And Captain Jack	TAT	260
Cleo	LGB	287
Corey Baker Of Julia And His Show And Tell	TAT	2506
Daktari 'Judi And The Kitten'	TAT	2506
Donnie And Marie The Top Secret Project	LGB	160*
Donnie And Marie The State Fair Mystery	TAT	2635
Emmett Kelly In Willie The Clown	Elf	573
Gentle Ben And The Pesky Puppy	TAT	2552
H.R. Pufnstuf	TAT	2624
J. Fred Muggs	LGB	234
Land Of The Lost The Dinosaur Adventure	TAT	2607
Land Of The Lost The Surprise	LGB	136*
Leave It To Beaver	LGB	347
Little Beaver	TAT	2611

Illustrator Index

Abranz, Alfred
Bugs Bunny Hangs Around	TAT	2410
Bugs Bunny In Something Fishy	TAT	2543
Bugs Bunny's Birthday Surprise	TAT	2421
Woody Woodpecker's 'Pogo Stick Adventures'	TAT	2562

Abranz, Fred
Tweety	TAT	901

Adler, Helen
Little Little Dog	Elf	8437
Little Little Dog	Elf	8661
Tubby Turtle	Elf	8321

Aitken, Amy
Mother Goose On The Farm	TAT	2464-44

Aldrich, Andy
Little Crow	G	113*

Aliki
Katy's First Day	TAT	2512
What Shall I Put In The Hole That I Dig?	TAT	2563

Allen, Colin
Diz And Liz	W	835

Allen, Joan
Baby's First Book	TAT	2422
Happy Golden ABC, The	G	344

Allert, Kathy
How Things Grow	G	308-57
Let's Go Shopping!	G	208-58
Summer Vacation	G	206-56

Aloisel, Frank
Just Watch Me	G	104*

Altson, Louise
Nursery Rhymes	TAT	857

Alvarado, Peter
Bugs Bunny, Too Many Carrots	G	145*
Mushmouse And Punkin Puss 'The Country Cousins'	TAT	2552
New Friends For The Saggy Baggy Elephant	G	131*
Ricochet Rabbit 'Showdown At Gopher GulchBakery'	TAT	2622
Tweety Plays Catch The Puddy Cat	G	141*
Wacky Witch	G	416

Ames, Lee
Adventures Of Lassie:	G	5012
Lassie Shows The Way	G	255
Lassie Shows The Way	G	415
Three Billy Goats Gruff	TAT	2515

Anderson, Al
Bravest Of All	G	402
Bugs Bunny 'Party Pest'	G	111-69
Bugs Bunny Party Pest	TAT	2607
Lassie And The Cub Scout	TAT	2503
Lassie Finds A Friend	TAT	2406
My Big Book Of Big Machines	TAT	2414-3
My Little Book Of Big Machines	TAT	2589
Ricochet Rabbit 'Showdown At Gopher Gulch Bakery'	TAT	2622
Smokey The Bear Finds A Helper	G	345
Tom And Jerry Photo Finish	G	124*
Uncle Scrooge 'The Winner'	TAT	2552

Anderson, Betty
Big Red Pajama Wagon, The	TAT	840
Flying Sunbeam, The	TAT	820

Anderson, Bill & Judie
Speed Buggy And The Secret Message	Elf	

Anderson, Carl
Henry Goes To A Party	W	778
Henry Goes To A Party	T	897
Henry In Lollipop Land	T	871
Henry In Lollipop Land	W	664

Anderson, Rus
Shaggy Dog	G	D 82

Angela
Cozy Little Farm, The	W	502
Cozy Little Farm, The	W	749
Cozy Little Farm, The	T	878
Mr. Bear Squash-You-All-Flat	W	523

Anglund, Joan Walsh
Child's Year, A	G	312-06
Circus Boy	G	290
Stop And Go (Wheel Book)	G	A 17

Arens, Michael
Scooby Doo And The Pirate Treasure	G	126*
Wacky Witch: The Royal Birthday	TAT	2546

Armstrong, Samuel
Beany And His Magic Set	TAT	904
Disneyland On The Air	G	D 43
Donald Duck And The Mouseketeers	G	D 55
Donald Duck's Toy Sailboat	G	D 40
Gene Autry And The Lost Doggie	TAT	932
Goofy, Movie Star	G	D 52
Jiminy Cricket Fire Fighter	G	D 50
Tom And Jerry And The Toy Circus	TAT	2509
Tom And Jerry's Merry Christmas	G	457-42
Woody Woodpecker 'Shoots The Works'	TAT	2439
Woody Woodpecker's 'Peck Of Trouble'	TAT	831

Atencio, Xavier
Mickey Mouse Goes Christmas Shopping	G	D 33

Attinello, Lauren
Oscar's New Neighbor	G	109-67

Augistiny, Sally
ABC Is For Christmas	G	108*

Fritzie Goes Home	G	103*

Bakacs, George
Cinnamon Bear, The	TAT	2674

Baker, Darrell
Aladdin	G	107-88
Bugs Bunny And The Health Hog	G	110-60
Bugs Bunny, Pioneer	G	161*
Chip 'n Dale Rescue Rangers 'The Big Cheese Caper'	G	105-78
Daffy Duck Space Creature	TAT	2621
Grand And Wful Day, The	G	98737-01
Little Lulu And The Birthday Mystery	TAT	2502
Pink Panther In The Haunted House, The	G	140*
Pippi Longstocking And The South Sea Pirates	TAT	2614
Rudolph The Red-Nosed Reindeer Shines Again	G	452- 8
Walt Disney Babies 1 To 10 Again	TAT	2471-47

Banigan, Sharon
Fuzzy Duckling	TAT	912
Jim Jump	TAT	2527

Bannister, Constance
Puppy And Me	Elf	504

Banta, Milton
Donald Duck Full Speed Ahead	TAT	900
Donald Duck Goes To Disneyland	TAT	2559
Mickey Mouse And His Space Ship	G	D 29
Mickey Mouse And His Space Ship	G	D108
Three Little Pigs	G	D 10
Three Little Pigs	G	D 78

Barbaresi, Nina
Fox Jumped Up One Winters Night, A	G	300-53

Bartlett, William
Bambi's Children	W	544

Barto, Renzo
Tweety And Sylvester At The Farm	TAT	2453-35

Barton, Mary
Kitten's Secret, The	W	527

Bartram, Bob
Fury	TAT	2611
Lassie's Brave Adventure	TAT	2571
Rinty And Pals For Rusty	TAT	2571

Bartsch, Arthur
Tom Terrific With Mighty Manfred The Wonder Dog	W	703

Bathman, Ed
How To Be A Grouch	TAT	2618

Book Codes

Elf—Elf	Little Golden Book—LGB	Tell-A-Tale—TAT	Treasure—T	Wonder—W

Battaglia, Aurelius

Baby's Mother Goose	G	303
Baby's Mother Goose	G	422
Hiram's Red Shirt	G	204-43
Little Boy With A Big Horn	G	100
Mr. Bell's Fixit Shop	G	204-42
Old Mother Hubbard	G	591
Pat-A-Cake	G	54
Pets For Peter	G	82
Pets For Peter (Puzzle Edition)	G	82

Baudoin, Simonne

Baby Raccoon	W	797
Fluffy Little Lamb	W	780
Rabbits Give A Party, The	W	811

Beckett, Sheilah

My Christmas Book	G	298
Rapunzel	G	207-57
Twelve Dancing Princesses, The	G	194
Twelve Days Of Christmas, The	G	451-16

Beecher, Elizabeth

Bugs Bunny At The County Fair	G	164

Bemelmans, Ludwig

Madeline	G	186

Bendel, Ruth

Lucky Rabbit	D	221
Lucky Rabbit	D	DIN 7
Puppy Twins, The	Elf	8420
Puppy Twins, The	Elf	8603

Benvenuti

Forest Hotel	G	350

Berger, Alex

Flash Gordon	T	905
Flash Gordon And The Baby Animals	W	684

Berlin, Rose Mary

Buster Cat Goes Out	G	302-57
But, You're A Duck	G	206-58

Berry, Anne Scheu

Fuzzy Joe Bear	TAT	954
Tommy And Timmy	TAT	822
Tommy And Timmy	TAT	2644
Wful Tony	TAT	871

Berthold

Hoppy The Puppy	W	751
Roly-Poly Puppy, The	W	549

Bester, Don

Lucky Puppy, The	G	D 89

Beylon, Catherine

Busy Body Book 'A First Book About You', The	TAT	2585
I'm Not Sleepy	TAT	2462-42

Bezada, Herb

Deputy Dawg And The Space Man	W	773
Deputy Dawg's Big Catch	W	770
Deputy Dog	W	760
Hector Crosses The River.... With George Washington	W	769
Luno The Soaring Stallion	W	831
Muskie And His Friends	W	828
Trick On Deputy Dog	W	830

Biers, Clarence

Fuzzy Dan	TAT	821
Hide-Away Henry	TAT	938

Biesterveld, Betty

Barbie	G	125*

Biggers, Jan D.

Big Little Kitty	TAT	942

Bilder, A.K.

Space Ship To The Moon	Elf	473
Superliner United States, The: World's Fastest Liner	Elf	474

Binst, Claire

Freddy And The Indian	W	816
Little Garage Man, The	W	744

Blair, Mary

Baby's House	G	80
Baby's House (Puzzle Edition)	G	80
I Can Fly	G	92

Blake, Vivienne Leah

Alphabet A-Z, The	G	3
Lion And The Mouse, The	Elf	8569
Peppy, The Lonely Little Puppy	Elf	425
Peppy, The Lonely Little Puppy	Elf	553
Peppy, The Lonely Little Puppy	Elf	8305

Bloom, Lloyd

Elves And The Shoemaker, The	G	307-61

Bobertz, Carl

Rattle-Rattle Dump Truck, The	W	656
Rattle-Rattle Train, The	W	655

Bolle, Frank

Gene Autry And Champion	G	267
Lassie And The Lost Explorer	G	343
Lone Ranger And The Talking Pony, The	G	310
Wagon Train	G	326

Bollen, Roger

Blue Barry Bear Counts From 1 To 20	G	203-59

Bonfils, Robert

Mr. Wizard's Junior Science Show	Elf	559
Ten Commandments For Children, The	Elf	543
Ten Commandments For Children, The	Elf	8604

Bonforte, Lisa

Water Babies	G	309-59

Bonsall, George

Helpful Friends, The	W	631
I Love You	W	657
What Are You Looking At?	W	792
What Are You Looking At?	T	895

Boonshaft, Rochelle

Raggedy Ann And Fido	G	585

Borgo, Deborah

Good Old Days, The	G	204-58

Bosche, Bill

Chip 'n Dale At The Zoo	G	D 38

Botts, Davi

Hey, Diddle, Diddle And Other Nonsense Rhymes	Elf	535
Hey, Diddle, Diddle And Other Nonsense Rhymes	Elf	8304

Bouman, Carol

Pound Puppies 'Problem Puppies'	G	111-61
Pound Puppies In Pick Of The Litter	G	110-59

Boyle, Neil

Circus Boy And Captain Jack	TAT	2608
Donald Duck Goes To Disneyland	TAT	2559
Donald Duck In Frontierland	TAT	2520
Donald Duck Prize Driver	G	D 49

(continued)

Mickey Mouse Flies The Christmas Mail	G	D 53
Pluto	TAT	2509
Ruff And Reddy Go To A Party	TAT	2567

Bracke, Charles

Neatos And The Litterbugs, The	G	515
Three Little Pigs, The	TAT	2501
Whoa, Joey!	TAT	2557

Bradbury, Jack

Beany And Cecil Captured For The Zoo	TAT	2551

Bradfield, Roger

Bert's Hall Of Great Inventions	G	321*
Best Balloon Ride Ever	G	208-64
Box Of Important Things, The	TAT	2510
Hello, Rock	TAT	2616
Sesame Street 'The Together Book'	G	315*
Toby The Rock Hound	TAT	2408-6

Brannon, Tom

Baby Fozzie Visits The Doctor	G	111-89
Day Snuffy Had The Sniffles, The	G	108-59
Fozzie's Funnies	G	111-87
Happy And Sad, Grouch And Glad	G	108-67
Muppet -Treasure Island	G	111-88
Which Witch Is Which?	G	98770-01

Brewer, Sally King

Zoo Friends Are At Our School Today!	TAT	2423

Brice, Tony

Little Bobo And His Blue Jacket	Elf	472
Little Bobo And His Blue Jacket	Elf	1026
Little Bobo And His Blue Jacket	Elf	8378
Little Bobo And His Blue Jacket	Elf	8654

Brooks, Andrea

Christmas Donkey, The	G	460- 9

Brooks, Nan

My Little Golden Mother Goose	G	300-69
Princess And The Pea, The	G	207-68

Brown, Richard

Count All The Way To Sesame Street	G	203-56
Sesame Streets Cookie Monster's Book Of Cookie Shapes	TAT	2402-8

Brozowska, Elizabeth

Animals Party, The	W	790
Boy Who Wouldn't Eat His Breakfast, The	W	815

Bruce, Suzanne

Happy Holidays	Elf	482
Happy Holidays	Elf	8343
My Happy Day: A Word Book	Elf	450
My Happy Day: A Word Book	Elf	8332
Prayers For Little Children	Elf	8557

Brul, Al

Lord's Prayer, The	W	647

Brunhoff, Jean De

Babar The King	W	602
Story Of Babar, The	W	590

Bryant, Dean

ABC Book	Elf	1032
ABC Book	Elf	8364
ABC Book	Elf	8653
My Bible Book	Elf	8696
Teddy Bear Of Bumpkin Hollow	Elf	429

Teddy Bear Of Bumpkin Hollow	Elf	561
Teddy Bear Of Bumpkin Hollow	Elf	8334
Twilight Tales	Elf	426
Twilight Tales	Elf	8427
Twilight Tales	Elf	8608

Buckett, George

Big And Little Are Not The Same	TAT	2474-33

Buehrig, Rosemary

Tommy Tractor	TAT	881

Buell, Marjorie Henderson

Little Lulu 'Has An Art Show'	TAT	2622
Little Lulu And Her Magic Tricks	G	203
Little Lulu Uses Her Head	TAT	2552

Bunky

Runaway Squash, The	G	143*

Burchard, Peter

Baby Elephant, The	W	541
Cat's Who Stayed For Dinner, The	W	556
Little Red Caboose That Ran Away, The	W	715
Little Red Caboose That Ran Away, The	T	852
Wful Animal Band, The	T	869

Burns, Raymond

Peppermint, The Story Of A Kitten	TAT	2502
Peppermint, The Story Of A Kitten	TAT	2405

Burridge, Marge Opitz

My Little Book Of Big Animals	TAT	2466-4

Butcher, Samuel J.

Precious Moments 'Put On A Happy Face'	G	107-84

Butler, Paula Hurley

Peter's Pencil	TAT	927

Butrik, Lyn McClure

Mr. Bears Birthday	G	204-26

Campbell, Grant

Donald Duck In Disneyland	G	D 92

Canaday, Ralph

Scooby-Doo And The Mystery Monster	Elf	

Caniff, Milton

Steve Canyon	G	356

Canizares, Stephenie

Pecos Bill	W	767

Caraway, James

Hans Christian Andersen's Fairy Tales	W	599
Helpful Henrietta	Elf	8316

Carbe, Nino

Chip, Chip	G	28

Carleton, James F.

Devlin	Elf	
Linus 'A Smile For Grouse'	TAT	2567

Carroll, Nancy

Little Red Riding Hood	TAT	2670

Case, Richard

Gene Autry 'Makes A New Friend'	TAT	800

Cassan, Christine

I Think About God Two Stories About My Day	G	111*

Castagnoli, Martha

Not Quite Three	TAT	962

Sleepytime For Everyone	W	612

Cauley, Lorinda Bryan

Best Of All, A Story About The Farm	G	170*
Little Gray Rabbit	TAT	2651

Chad

Mighty Mouse	T	860
Mighty Mouse And The Scarecrow	W	678
Mighty Mouse And The Scared Scarecrow	T	884
Mighty Mouse-Dinky Learns To Fly	W	677
Mighty Mouse-Santa's Helper	T	896
Mighty Mouse-Santa's Helper	W	662
Mighty Mouse: Dinky Learns To Fly	T	866
Tubby The Tuba	T	873

Chaiko, Ted

Plants And Animals	G	5017

Chandler, Jean

Frosty The Snowman	G	451-15
Poky Little Puppy's First Christmas, The	G	461-01
Poky Little Puppy's Naughty Day, The	G	203-57
Sleepytime ABC	G	202-57

Charlie

Mr. Grabbit	TAT	816
Mr. Grabbit	TAT	2526
One Two Three	TAT	926
One Two Three	TAT	2616
One Two Three	TAT	2440
Wiggletail	TAT	852

Chartier, Normand

Amazing Mumford Forgets The Magic Word	G	108- 5
Many Faces Of Ernie, The	G	109- 4

Chase, Mary Jane

Choo-Choo, The Little Switch Engine	Elf	485
Choo-Choo, The Little Switch Engine	Elf	1034
Choo-Choo, The Little Switch Engine	Elf	8394
Choo-Choo, The Little Switch Engine	Elf	8621
Little Miss Muffet And Other Nursery Rhymes	Elf	556
Little Miss Muffet And Other Nursery Rhymes	Elf	8302
Little Miss Muffet And Other Nursery Rhymes	Elf	8709
Sparky The Fire Dog	Elf	495
Storybook For Little Tots	Elf	8393
Storybook For Little Tots	Elf	8619
Volksy: The Little Yellow Car	Elf	8695

Chastain, Madye Lee

Let's Play Indians	W	538
Sailboat That Ran Away	TAT	842
Susan And The Rain	TAT	879

Children's Television Workshop

Ernie The Cave King And Sherlock The Smart Person	TAT	2604
Sherlock Hemlock And The Great Twiddlebug Mystery	TAT	2564

Clare

Mr. Bear's House	Elf	475

Clark, Brenda

How Does Your Garden Grow ?	G	308-55

Clarke, Joan

Let's Pretend	W	680

Clement, Charles

Child's First Picture Dictionary,A	W	517
Dally	TAT	802
Dr. Goat	TAT	841
Dr. Goat (Second Cover)	TAT	841
Fire Dog	TAT	2412
Mother Goose	TAT	2511
Roundabout Train	TAT	2436

Clyne, Barbara

Bedtime Stories	Elf	499
Bedtime Stories	Elf	595
Bedtime Stories	Elf	8355

Collier, Roberta

Story Of Jonah, The	G	311-61

Combes, Herbert & Lenora

Airplanes	G	180
Airplanes	G	373

Combes, Lenora

Let's Go Shopping!	G	33

Combes, Lenora & Herbert

Boats	G	125
Boats	G	339
Boats	G	501

Conner, Eulala

What Will I Be?	G	204-42

Cook, Steven

Our Flag	G	388

Cook, Sunny B.

I See The Sky	W	746
Petey Parakeet	W	798
There Was Once A Little Boy	W	719

Cooke, Tom

Count's Poem, The	TAT	2402
Grover Takes Care Of Baby	G	109-57
Ready, Set, Go! A Counting Book	G	109-71
What's Up In The Attic?	G	108-58

Cooper, Marjorie

Baby Sister	Elf	8663
Bunny Book, The	Elf	8428
Bunny Twins, The	Elf	8676
Early One Morning	Elf	8436
Early One Morning	Elf	8656
Garden Is Good, A	Elf	8438
Garden Is Good, A	Elf	8657
Happy Twins, The	Elf	8460
Jeepers, The Little Frog	Elf	8456
Jeepers, The Little Frog	Elf	8733
Look For A Rainbow	Elf	8558
Our World Of Color And Sound	Elf	8577
Pony Twins, The	Elf	8429
Pony Twins, The	Elf	8659
Read Me Some Poems	Elf	8574
Snow White And Rose Red	Elf	8580
Teddy Bear Twins, The	Elf	8453
Teddy Bear Twins, The	Elf	8722
Three Little Kittens	Elf	8462
Three Little Kittens	Elf	8582

Corrigan, Barbara

Hello Joe	TAT	2510

Corwin, Eleanor

Number 9 The Little Fire Engine	Elf	444
Number 9 The Little Fire Engine	Elf	585
Number 9 The Little Fire Engine	Elf	8369
Number 9 The Little Fire Engine	Elf	8708
Stories Of The Christ Child	Elf	484
Stories Of The Christ Child	Elf	8612

Title	Pub	No.
Little Red Riding Hood	TAT	2651
Toy That Flew, The	TAT	2518

Derwinski, Beatrice

Title	Pub	No.
Good Morning, Good Night	W	583
Peter Pan	W	597

Desantis, George

Title	Pub	No.
Winnie-The-Pooh Meets Gopher	G	D117

Deson, Gus

Title	Pub	No.
Dondi	W	783

Dettmer, Mary Lou

Title	Pub	No.
Little Red Riding Hood	TAT	2507

Dewitt, Cornelius

Title	Pub	No.
Night Before Christmas, The	G	20

Di Ciccio, Sue

Title	Pub	No.
Little Mermaid, The	G	105-85
Quints 'The Cleanup'	G	107-72
Tale Spin 'Ghost Ship'	G	104-62

Di Salvoryan, Dyanne

Title	Pub	No.
Best Friends	G	209-46

Dias, Ron

Title	Pub	No.
101 Dalmatians	G	105-81
Beauty And The Beast	G	104-65
Cinderella	G	103-57
Dumbo	G	104-59
Lady And The Tramp	G	105-72
Little Mermaid, The	G	105-68
Little Mermaid, The 'Ariel's Underwater Adventure'	G	105-68
Mickey's Christmas Carol	G	459- 9
Peter Pan	G	104-60
Pinocchio	G	104-61
Sleeping Beauty	G	104-56
Snow White And The Seven Dwarfs	G	103-58

Dillon, Corinne

Title	Pub	No.
Let's Take A Ride	W	673
Meet The Bobbsey Twins	W	623
Who Will Play With Me?	W	559

Dixon, Rachel Taft

Title	Pub	No.
10 Rabbits	W	648
Bible Stories	G	174
Bunny Hopwell's First Spring	W	614
Heroes Of The Bible	G	236
Kewtee Bear's Christmas	W	867
Kewtee Bear-Santa's Helper	W	652
Nine Rabbits And Another Puzzle For Raggedy Ann And Andy, A	W	845
	W	683
So This Is Spring!	W	844
Three Little Kittens And Other Nursery Tales	W	503

Doane, Pelagie

Title	Pub	No.
Angel Child	Elf	8373
Angel Child	Elf	8715

Doe, Bart

Title	Pub	No.
Roy Rogers' Bullet Leads The Way	TAT	2567

Dolce, Ellen J.

Title	Pub	No.
Busy Saturday Word Book	TAT	2474-42
Little Red Riding Hood	TAT	2461-44

Dorcas

Title	Pub	No.
Circus Train, The	TAT	890
Hippety Hop Around The Block	TAT	924
Truck That Stopped At Village Small, The	TAT	813

Doremus, Hal W.

Title	Pub	No.
Peter Goes To School	W	600

Dottie

Title	Pub	No.
Hide-Away Puppy	Elf	8587

Title	Pub	No.
Hide-Away Puppy	Elf	466
Hide-Away Puppy	Elf	587
Hide-Away Puppy	Elf	8357

Dowd, Vic

Title	Pub	No.
Visit To The Doctor, A	W	733

Dreany, E. Joseph

Title	Pub	No.
Adventures Of Lassie:	G	5012
Annie Oakley Sharpshooter	G	275
Car And Truck Stamps	G	A 20
Dale Evans And The Coyote	G	253
Gunsmoke	G	320
Handy Andy	TAT	2580
Lassie And The Daring Rescue	G	277
Lone Ranger, The	G	263
Train Stamps	G	A 26

Drutzu, Anne Marie

Title	Pub	No.
Lassie Come-Home	W	639

Duga, Irra

Title	Pub	No.
Ernie's Telephone Call	TAT	2452-34

Dugan, William J.

Title	Pub	No.
Animal Stamps	G	A 7
Book Of A, The	G	615
Book Of B, The	G	616
Book Of C, The	G	617
Book Of D E, The	G	618
Book Of F, The	G	619
Book Of G H, The	G	620
Book Of I J K, The	G	621
Book Of L, The	G	622
Book Of M, The	G	623
Book Of N O, The	G	624
Book Of P Q, The	G	625
Book Of R, The	G	626
Book Of T U V, The	G	629
Book Of W X Y Z, The	G	630
Cars	G	251
I'm An Indian Today	G	425
Let's Go Trucks!	G	185*
Machines	G	455
My Magic Slate Book	G	5025
Red Book Of Fairy Tales, The	G	306
Rumpelstiltskin And The Princess And The Pea	G	498
Second Book Of S, The	G	628
Tom Thumb	G	353
Rumpelstiltskin	G	300-56

Dunnington, Tom

Title	Pub	No.
My Little Book Of Birds	TAT	2490
My Little Book Of Boats	TAT	247332
My Little Book Of Horses	TAT	2466-3

Durrell, Julie

Title	Pub	No.
Colorful Mouse, The	G	211-71
Evening Walk, The	TAT	2462-43
Little Mouse's Book Of Colors	G	211-74
Tickety-Tock, What Time Is It?	G	308-51

Eagle, Mike

Title	Pub	No.
Twelve Days Of Christmas, The	G	454-42

Earle, Eyvind

Title	Pub	No.
Peter Pan And Wendy	G	D 24
Peter Pan And Wendy	G	D 72
Peter Pan And Wendy	G	D110

Edwards, Beverly

Title	Pub	No.
Mary Poppins, A Jolly Holiday	G	D112
Ookpik, The Arctic Owl	G	579

Eggleston, Gary

Title	Pub	No.
Aladdin 'The Magic Carpet Ride'	G	107-92

Eisenberg, Harvey

Title	Pub	No.
Beany And His Magic Set	TAT	904
Cindy Bear	G	442
Huckleberry Hound Builds A House	G	376

Title	Pub	No.
Ruff And Reddy Go To A Party	TAT	2567
Tom And Jerry	G	117
Tom And Jerry	G	561
Tom And Jerry In Model Mice	TAT	2509
Tom And Jerry In Tom's Happy Birthday	TAT	2611
Tom And Jerry Meet Little Quack	G	311
Tom And Jerry Meet Little Quack	G	181
Tom And Jerry's Merry Christmas	G	457-42
Tom And Jerry's Party	G	235
Woody Woodpecker, Steps To Drawing	G	372
Ruff And Reddy	G	378
Ruff And Reddy	G	477
Tom And Jerry's Merry Christmas	G	197

Elfrieda

Title	Pub	No.
Gingerbread Man, The	G	182*
Horse For Charlie, A	TAT	2411-1
Johnny Appleseed	TAT	2679
Tommy On The Farm	TAT	2557
What Makes My Cat Purr?	TAT	2425

Elgin, Kathleen

Title	Pub	No.
Little Schoolhouse	W	710

Elliott, Gertrude

Title	Pub	No.
First Little Golden Book Of Fairy Tales, The	G	9
Gingerbread Shop, The	G	126
Happy Family, The	G	35
Little Golden Book Of Words, The	G	45
Magic Compass, The	G	146
Mother Goose	G	4
Mother Goose	G	240
Mr. Wigg's Birthday Party	G	140
Nursery Rhymes	G	59
Two Little Gardeners	G	108
Words	G	A 1
Words	G	A 30
Words	G	A 45

Ellis, Art & Kim

Title	Pub	No.
Barbie 'A Picnic Surprise'	G	107-70
Tawny Scrawny Lion 'Saves The Day'	G	GBL377
We're Busy Charlie Brown	TAT	2541-41
Where's Woodstock?	G	111-63

Elmi, Don

Title	Pub	No.
Wheelie And The Chopper Bunch	Elf	

Ember, Kathi

Title	Pub	No.
Color Kittens, The	G	202-66

Emrich, Sylvia

Title	Pub	No.
My Christmas Treasury	G	144*

Emslie, Peter

Title	Pub	No.
Beauty And The Beast 'The Teapot's Tale'	G	104-70
Pocahontas 'The Voice Of The Wind'	G	104-72
Sorcerer's Apprentice, The	G	100-79

Endred, Helen

Title	Pub	No.
Bunny Tales	Elf	574
Bunny Tales	Elf	8406
Bunny Tales	Elf	8641
Cinderella	Elf	551
Cinderella	Elf	8417
Cinderella	Elf	8644

Ericksen, Barbara

Title	Pub	No.
My Little ABC	TAT	2536

Erickson, Phoebe

Title	Pub	No.
Baby Animal Friends	W	608
Little Peter Cottontail	W	641
Peter Rabbit And Other Stories	W	513

Esley, Joan

Jenny's New Brother	G	596
New Brother, New Sister	G	564
Play Street	G	484

Eubank, Mary Grace

Puppies On Parade	TAT	2476-45

Eugenie

1 Is Red	TAT	2407-2
Good-Bye Day, The	G	209-57
Jenny's Surprise Summer	G	204-39
Lion's Haircut, The	TAT	2519
Moving Day	G	209-57
Too Small Names!	TAT	2614
Two Stories About Lollipop	TAT	2683

Evans, Katherine

Dressing Up	D	206
Jingle Bell Jack	D	219
Jingle Bell Jack	D	DIN 1
Littlest Angel, The	W	755
Peek Fish	D	209

Evers, Helen & Alf

Chatterduck	Elf	8576
Copy-Kitten	Elf	584
Copy-Kitten	Elf	8370
Copy-Kitten	Elf	8689
Crosspatch	Elf	8442
Crosspatch	Elf	8675
Crybaby Calf	Elf	547
Crybaby Calf	Elf	8426
Crybaby Calf	Elf	8606
Day On The Farm, A	Elf	8586
Fussbunny	Elf	530
Fussbunny	Elf	8405
Fussbunny	Elf	8642
Moonymouse	Elf	1021
Moonymouse	Elf	8400
Moonymouse	Elf	8639
Plump Pig, The	Elf	542
Plump Pig, The	Elf	8309
Plump Pig, The	Elf	8592
Pokey Bear	Elf	8451
Pokey Bear	Elf	8720
So Long	Elf	1036
So Long	Elf	8342
So Long	Elf	8622

Ewers, Joe

From Trash To Treasure	G	108-70
I Can't Wait Until Christmas	G	456-10
Little Red Riding Hood	G	300-65
Monsters' Picnic, The	G	109-59

Ewing, Carolyn

Christmas Bunny, The	G	450-13

Fentz, Mike

Garfield 'The Cat Show'	G	110-61

Ferand, Emmy

My First Book Of Bible Stories	G	19

Ferguson, Walter

Birds Of All Kinds	G	380

Fernie, John

Pepper Plays Nurse	G	555

Fisher, Frank

Pinocchio	TAT	2428-2

Fitch, Winnie

Who Are You?	TAT	2521

Fleishman, Seymour

Hop-Away Joey	Elf	8572
Trip In Space, A	Elf	8566

Fletcher, James

Funny Company, The	TAT	2567

One Hundred And One Dalmatians	TAT	2622

Floethe, Richard

Year On The Farm, A	G	37

Florian

Rackety-Boom	TAT	893
Rackety-Boom	TAT	2557
Train Coming	TAT	2556

Flory, Jane

ABC	TAT	896
Dolls Of Other Lands	D	213
Fanny Forgot	TAT	862
Farmer John	TAT	838
Little Caboose, The	TAT	817
Once Upon A Windy Day	TAT	865
Snooty	TAT	851
Surprise In The Barn	TAT	2543
Surprise In The Barn (Second Cover)	TAT	2543
Too-Little Fire Engine, The	W	526

Forberg, Ari

Stories Of Jesus	G	114*

Ford, Pam

Funny Friends In Mother Goose Land	TAT	2647

Foster, Hal

Prince Valiant	T	874

Frame, Paul

Building A Skyscraper	Elf	8552
Turtles Turn Up On Tuesday	Elf	8561

Frankel, Simon

Digger Dan	TAT	2615
Digger Dan	TAT	908
Four Puppies Who Wanted A Home, The	W	530
Jolly Jumping Man, The	W	537
Mr. Mogg's Dogs	TAT	958

Franzen, Jim

Clue Club The Case Of The Missing Racehorse	Elf	
Jabberjaw Out West	Elf	
Josie And The Pussycats/ The Bag Factory Detour	Elf	

Fraser, Betty

That's Where You Live	TAT	2534

Fraydas, Stan

Hoppy, The Curious Kangaroo	W	579

Frees, Harry Whittier

Four Little Kittens	Elf	566
Four Little Kittens	Elf	8336
Four Little Kittens	Elf	8718
Four Little Puppies	Elf	578
Four Little Puppies	Elf	8335
Four Little Puppies	Elf	8597
Little Kittens' Nursery Rhymes	Elf	440
Little Kittens' Nursery Rhymes	Elf	8311
Snuggles	Elf	1005
Yip And Yap	Elf	1022
Yip And Yap	Elf	8380
Yip And Yap	Elf	8690

Freund, Rudolf

Animals Of Farmer Jones, The	G	11
Little Red Hen, The	G	6
Little Red Hen, The (Second Cover)	G	6

Friedel, Violet & Fred

Andy And Betsy At The Circus	TAT	906

Friedman, Joy

Baby Sister	G	306-55
Batter Up!	G	211-68

Friend, Esther

Cap That Mother Made, The	Elf	8579
I Think About Jesus	Elf	8652
In My House	D	212
Mother Goose	Elf	424
Mother Goose	Elf	1028
Mother Goose	Elf	8300
Mother Goose	Elf	8647
Mother Goose	Elf	8723
Old Woman And Her Pig, The	Elf	464
Old Woman And Her Pig, The	Elf	1035
Old Woman And Her Pig, The	Elf	8379

Frost, Bruno

Baby Moses	TAT	917
Beloved Son, The	TAT	825
Captain Kangaroo 'Tick Tock Trouble'	TAT	2610
Loopy De Loop 'Odd Jobber'	TAT	2611
Where Timothy Lives	TAT	2505
W Book Of Bible Stories, The	W	577

Fry, Rosalind

Monster! Monster!	G	808

Gaddis, Rie

Little Friends: Kittens, Puppies, Bunnies	Elf	455
Little Friends: Kittens, Puppies, Bunnies	Elf	593
Little Friends: Kittens, Puppies, Bunnies	Elf	8408
Scalawag The Monkey	Elf	477

Galst, Annie

Around The World Cutout Book	W	826

Gantz, David

Darby O'Gill	G	D 81
Inspector Gadget In Africa	G	107-49
Pink Panther And Sons Fun At The Picnic	G	111-60
Smokey Bear 'Saves The Forest'	TAT	2463

Garris, Norma & Dan

Bingo	TAT	2560
Bingo	TAT	2576
Happy	TAT	2631
How Big Is A Baby	TAT	2601
Toby Zebra And The Lost Zoo	TAT	2505
Two Stories About Wags	TAT	2560

Gaulke, Gloria

Look Who's Here	W	834

Gavy

Let's Play	TAT	907

Gay, Patti

Cats	G	309-72

Gayer, Marguerite

Brave Little Duck, The	W	777
Brave Little Duck, The	T	854
Farm Animals	Elf	467
Farm Animals	Elf	8735
Farm For Andy, A	Elf	448
Farm For Andy, A	Elf	596
Farm For Andy, A	Elf	8358

Gehr, Mary

Little Tweet	TAT	814

Gergely, Tibor

Animal Gym, The	G	249
Animal Orchestra	G	334
Animal Stories	G	5006
Bobby And His Airplanes	G	69
Christopher And The Columbus	G	103
Circus Time	G	31
Circus Time	G	A 2
Daddies	G	187

Horton, Mary
| ABC And Counting Book | W | 823 |

Hoskins, Winfield
| Golden Book Of Fairy Tales, The | G | 9 |

Hubbard, Allen
Bozo And The Hide 'n' Seek Elephant	G	598
Lady	TAT	2552
Lucky Puppy, The	G	D 89

Hudson, Patric
| Circus ABC | TAT | 2505 |
| Circus Alphabet | TAT | 2563 |

Hull, John
| Big And Little | T | 883 |
| How The Clown Got His Smile | W | 566 |

Humbert, Claude
| Littlest Raccoon, The | G | 457 |
| My Word Book | G | 525 |

Hunt, Darren
| Beauty And The Beast 'The Teapot's Tale' | G | 104-70 |

Hunt, Judith
| Maggie To The Rescue | TAT | 2476-39 |

Hurd, Clement
| Race Between The Monkey And The Duck, The | W | 510 |

Hurst, Earl Oliver
| W Book Of Boats, The | W | 580 |

Ike, Jane
| Pamela Jane's Week 'A Story About Days Of The Week' | TAT | 2424 |
| Susan In The Driver's Seat | G | 600 |

Irvin, Fred
ABC Around The House	G	176*
Flying Car, The	G	D 96
Land Of The Lost, The Surprise	G	136*
My Little Book Of Flying	TAT	2414-4
Petey And I, A Story About Being A Friend	G	186*
Superstar Barbie	G	162*
Swiss Family Duck	TAT	2509

Irving, James Gordon
| Animal Stamps | G | A 7 |
| Bird Stamps | G | A 8 |

Irwin, Josephine
| Three Little Pigs, The | TAT | 860 |

Ito, Willy
| Duck Tales 'Silver Dollars For Uncle Scrooge' | TAT | 2454 |

Ives, Ruth
Cinderella	W	660
Cinderella	T	879
My First Book Of Prayers	W	661
My First Book Of Prayers	T	868
Sleeping Beauty	W	635

Jackson, Pauline
| How Peter Cottontail Got His Name | W | 668 |
| Who Lives On The Farm? | W | 518 |

Jackson, Polly
| Out Of My Window | G | 245 |

Jacobs, Raymond
| Mushmouse And Punkin Puss 'The Country Cousins' | TAT | 2552 |

Jancar, Milli
| Bozo And The Hide 'n' Seek Elephant | G | 598 |

Jason Art Studios
Little Lulu And The Birthday Mystery	TAT	2502
Magilla Gorilla Takes A Banana Vacation	TAT	2552
Mister Rogers Neighborhood Everyone Is Special	TAT	2599
Mr. Rogers Neighborhood 'Henrietta Meets Someone New'	G	133*
Pink Panther In The Haunted House, The	G	140*
Pink Panther Rides Again, The	TAT	2628
Remarkably Strong Pippy Longstocking, The	G	123*
Road Runner, The 'Tumbleweed Trouble'	TAT	2466
Tweety And Sylvester 'Picnic Problems'	TAT	2448
Under Dog	TAT	2611
Underdog And The Disappearing Ice Cream	G	135*
Wizard Of Oz, The	G	119*

Jason, Leon
Bullwinkle's Masterpiece	TAT	2594
Heckle And Jeckle	W	694
Mary Poppins, A Jolly Holiday	G	D112
Sparkie-No School Today	T	902
Yogi Bears Secret	TAT	2608

Jean, Zallinger
| Fish | G | 5023 |

Johnson, Audean
| Who Needs A Cat | G | 507 |

Jones, Bob
| Big-Little Dinosaur, The | W | 731 |

Jones, Elizabeth Orton
| Little Red Riding Hood | G | 42 |
| Little Red Riding Hood (Puzzle Edition) | G | 42 |

Jones, Keenan
| Poky Little Puppy's Special Day | G | GBL371 |
| Shy Little Kitten's Secret Place | G | GBL372 |

Jones, Robert
| W Book Of Happy Animals, The | W | 687 |

Jottier, Rik
| Busy Baby Lion, The | W | 737 |

Joyner, Jerry
| Bialosky's Special Picnic | G | 204-55 |

Jules, Mervin
| Famous Fairy Tales | W | 505 |

Justice, Bill
| Bunny Book | G | D111 |
| Donald Duck's Toy Train | G | D 18 |

Kagran Corporation
| Howdy Doody's Clarabell And Pesky Peanut | TAT | 934 |

Kane, Herbert
| Animal ABC Book | Elf | 8658 |

Kane, Sharon
Counting Rhymes	G	361
Farmer In The Dell, The	Elf	8578
Little Mommy	G	569
Time For Everything	Elf	8562

Kane, Wilma
| Little Golden Paper Dolls, The | G | 113 |

| Peter Potamus 'Meets The Black Knight' | TAT | 2506 |
| Tawney Scrawney Lion And The Clever Monkey, The | G | 128* |

Little Golden Paper Dolls, The	G	280
Paper Doll Wedding	G	193
Paper Doll Wedding	G	A 22
Paper Dolls	G	A 3
Paper Dolls	G	A 47

Kantz, Phil
| Valley Of The Dinosaurs | Elf | |

Karch, Pat & Paul
| Goodnight Book, The | TAT | 2487 |
| My Little Book About Our Flag | TAT | 2578 |

Karsten, Lisa McCue
| Bunny's New Shoe | G | 204-60 |

Kassian, Olena
| Day In The Jungle, A | G | 309-56 |

Kaufman, Joe
| My Little Golden Word Book | G | 305-53 |
| Things In My House | G | 570 |

Kaula, Edna M.
| One Two Buckle My Shoe | TAT | 807 |

Kawaguchi, M.
| Yogi Bear | G | 395 |

Kean, Edward
| Surprise For Howdy Doody | TAT | 2573 |

Keane, Bill
| Family Circus Daddy's Surprise Day | G | 111-29 |

Kelsey, Dick
Bunny Book	G	D111
Donald Duck And The Witch	G	D 34
Donald Duck's Toy Train	G	D 18
Little Man Of Disneyland	G	D 46

Kelsey, Richard
Bugs Bunny And The Indians	G	120
Peter And The Wolf	G	D 5
Peter And The Wolf	G	D 56

Kelsey, Richmond I.
| Bugs Bunny And The Indians | G | 430 |
| Mad Hatter's Tea Party, The | G | D 23 |

Kendrick, Alcy
December Is For Christmas	W	776
How The Rabbit Found Christmas	W	866
Little Duck Said Quack, Quack, Quack, The	W	636

Kennel, Moritz
Animal Counting Book	G	584
Big Little Book, The	G	482
My Little Golden Animal Book	G	465
Old Mac Donald Had A Farm	G	400

Ker, Edith M.
| Especially From Thomas | TAT | 2527 |

Kessler, Leonard
Choo Choo Train, The	W	718
Who Has My Shoes?	W	801
Whose Hat Is That?	W	742

Ketchum, Hank
| Dennis The Menace Camps Out | Elf | 1002 |

Keyser, Evelyn
| Let's Visit The Farm | TAT | 876 |

Kicks, Russell
| Beauty And The Beast | TAT | 2455-59 |

Kimbrell, Woody
| Little Lulu | G | 476 |

King, Dorothy Urfer
| Little Red Bicycle, The | TAT | 2585 |

Kinney, Dick

Peter Pan And The Indians	G	D 26

Kirkel, Stephen

Luno The Soaring Stallion	W	831
Minute-And-A-Half-Man	W	758
Muskie And His Friends	W	828
Trick On Deputy Dog	W	830

Knight, John

Woody Woodpecker's 'Pogo Stick Adventures'	TAT	2562

Koehler, Cynthia & Alvin

Insect We Know	W	747
This Magic World	W	723
Wonder Book Of Birds, The	W	757
Wonder Book Of Cottontails And Other Rabbits, The	W	852
Wonder Book Of Fish, The	W	782
Wonder Book Of Flowers, The	W	784
Wonder Book Of Horses, The	W	857
Wonder Book Of Kittens, The	W	786
Wonder Book Of Puppies, The	W	804
Wonder Book Of The Seashore, The	W	785
Wonder Book Of Trees, The	W	827
Wonder Book Of Turtles, The	W	838

Koenig, Jo Anne E.

Ginghams Backward Picnic, The	G	148*

Koering, Ursula

Columbus, The Exploring Burro	TAT	826

Koester, Sharon

Larry The Canary	Elf	8322
Larry The Canary	Elf	8685
My Baby Sister	G	340
My Counting Book	Elf	8399
My Counting Book	Elf	8636
Red Riding Hood	G	A 34

Kohn, Arnie

Donald Duck And The Super-Sticky Secret	TAT	2425-6

Korta, Bob

My Little Book Of Cars And Trucks	TAT	2473

Kostanza, John

Bisketts In Double Trouble	G	111-49
Robotman & His Friends At School	G	110-58
Ronald McDonald And The Tale Of The Talking Plant	G	111-50

Kraus, Robert

All My Chickens	G	200-67

Krehbiel, Becky

Raggedy Ann And The Tagalong Present	TAT	2417-1

Krupp, Marion

Farm Animals	TAT	2464-50

Krush, Beth

Count To Ten	G	A 43

Krush, Bob

Count To Ten	G	A 16

Krusz, Arthur

Crusader Rabbit	W	698

Kudo, Ben

Bugs Bunny At The Easter Party	G	183

Kunhardt, Edith T.

Animal Quiz Book	G	308-44

Kurtz, Bob

Alvin's Lost Voice	W	824

Clyde Crashcup And Leonardo	W	837

Kurtz, Eliane

Aren't You Glad	G	489

La Grotta, J.M.

Roy Rogers And The Lane Ranch	TAT	811

La Mont, Violet

ABC Around The House	G	A 18
ABC Around The House	G	A 44
Let's Save Money	G	A 21
Numbers	G	243
Numbers	G	337
Off To School	G	5015
Reading, Writing & Spelling Stamps	G	A 24

La Padula, Thomas

Look For Trucks	TAT	2473-25
Noah's Ark	G	311-64

Laite, Gordon

Blue Book Of Fairy Tales, The	G	374
Chitty-Chitty Bang-Bang	G	581
Cinderella	G	A 36
My Little Golden Book Of Fairy Tales	G	211-62
Snow White And Rose Red	G	A 49

Lamont, Violet

Little Black Sambo	TAT	2661

Land, Kate

Ginghams, The Ice-Cream Parade	TAT	2619

Langley, Bill A.

101 Dalmatians	G	105-81
Duck Tales 'The Secret City Under The Sea'	G	102-57
Lady And The Tramp	G	105-72
Noel	G	456-16

Lanza, Barbara

Baby's Christmas	G	98785-01
Nutcracker, The	G	460-15

Lap, Pranas

Story Of The Christ Child, The	W	587

Lapadula, Tom

Daniel In The Lions' Den	G	311-62
Lord Is My Shepherd, The 'The Twenty-Third Psalm'	G	311-60

Laqueur, Alys

Fuzzy Mittens For Three Little Kittens	TAT	823

Laslo, Doris

Kittens Who Hid From Their Mother, The	W	529

Latimer, Constance

Teddy The Terrier	Elf	558
Teddy The Terrier	Elf	8308

Laurence, Johnny

Dipsy Donkey	TAT	882

Le Grand

Are Dogs Better Than Cats?	W	56
Boy Who Wanted To Be A Fish, The	W	55

Le Hew, Ronald

Where Jesus Lived	G	147*

Leaf, Anne Sellers

Aesop's Fables	Elf	463
Aesop's Fables	Elf	1019
Aesop's Fables	Elf	8440
Aesop's Fables	Elf	8615

Emperor's New Clothes, The	Elf	8567
Gingerbread Man, The	Elf	8457
Gingerbread Man, The	Elf	8599
Goody: A Mother Cat Story	Elf	470
Goody: A Mother Cat Story	Elf	545
Goody: A Mother Cat Story	Elf	8310
House That Jack Built, The	Elf	8312
House That Jack Built, The	Elf	8681
Jack And Jill	Elf	1001
Jack And Jill	Elf	8395
Jack And Jill	Elf	8625
Jack And The Beanstalk	Elf	8372
Jack And The Beanstalk	Elf	8668
Little Boy Blue And Other Nursery Rhymes		8366
Little Boy Blue And Other Nursery Rhymes	Elf	555
Little Boy Blue And Other Nursery Rhymes	Elf	8711
Little Red Riding Hood	Elf	1037
Little Red Riding-Hood	Elf	8419
Little Red Riding-Hood	Elf	8646
Muggins Becomes A Hero	Elf	8448
Muggins Becomes A Hero	Elf	8702
Muggins Big Balloon	Elf	8447
Muggins Big Balloon	Elf	8701
Muggins Mouse	Elf	8444
Muggins Mouse	Elf	8673
Muggins Takes Off	Elf	8700
Old Mother Hubbard	Elf	1007
Old Mother Hubbard	Elf	8413
Old Mother Hubbard	Elf	8624
Princess And The Pea	Elf	8727
Rip Van Winkle	Elf	8383
Rip Van Winkle	Elf	8671

Leake, Donald

Boo And The Flying Flews	G	803

Lear, Edward

Nonsense ABCs	Elf	550

Lear, Mirian

Bootsy	W	741

Leder, Dora

Jack And The Beanstalk	G	545
Jack And The Beanstalk	G	207-54
Mother Goose In The City	G	336*
My Little Golden Book About Cats	G	309-57

Lee, Jared D.

Roger's Upside-Down Day	TAT	2463-4

Lee, Manning De V

Bugle, A Puppy In Old Yorktown	Elf	8618
Elves And The Shoemaker, The	Elf	8315
Elves And The Shoemaker, The	Elf	8682
Little Lost Kitten: Story Of Williamsburg	Elf	544
Little Lost Kitten: Story Of Williamsburg	Elf	8600
Pocahontas, A Little Indian Girl Of Jamestown	Elf	575
Pocahontas, A Little Indian Girl Of Jamestown	Elf	8601
Story Of David, The	Elf	8725
Story Of Joseph, The	Elf	8724
Twenty-Third Psalm, The	Elf	8698

Lee, Robert J.

David And Goliath	G	110*

Leigh, Tom

Kermit Saves The Swamp!	G	111-84

Leiner, Alan

Longest Birthday, The	TAT	2418-1

Leob, Anton

Storytime Favorites	W	514

Leone, John

Maverick	G	354
Tales Of Wells Fargo	G	328

Leone, Sergio

All In A Day's Work	W	807
Night Before Christmas, The	W	858
Romper Room Exercise Book, The	G	527
Uncle Wiggily And His Friends	W	766
Uncle Wiggily's Adventures	W	765

Lerch, Steffie

Christmas Manger, The	G	176
Heidi: Child Of The Mountain	W	532
Story Of Jesus, The	G	27
Surprise Doll, The	W	519
We Like To Do Things	G	62

Lesko, Zillah

Gingerbread Man, The	TAT	2596
Little Red Riding Hood	TAT	2606
Mother Goose	TAT	925
Night Before Christmas, The	TAT	839
Night Before Christmas, The	TAT	2517
Runaway Ginger	TAT	897
Sunny, Honey, And Funny	TAT	824

Lewis, Jean

Dogs	G	209-53

Lobel, Anita

Pierrot's ABC Garden	G	312-04

Loeb, Anton

Little Train That Won A Medal, The	W	512

Lorencz, William

Beany Goes To Sea	G	537
Pebbles Flintstone ABCs	TAT	2622
Scooby Doo And The Pirate Treasure	G	126*
Touché Turtle	G	474
Tweety Plays Catch The Puddy Cat	G	141*
Wally Gator	G	502

Lougheed, Robert

Puppies To Love	Elf	8565

Love, Mary

Teddy The Terrier	Elf	558
Teddy The Terrier	Elf	8308

Lowe, Richard

Scooby-Doo And The Case Of The Counterfeit Money	Elf
Scooby-Doo And The Haunted Doghouse	Elf
Scooby-Doo And The Headless Horseman	Elf

Luhrs, Paul

Paul Revere	G	D 64

MacCombie, Turi

My Little Golden Book About Dogs	G	309-71

MacLaughlin, Don

Bugs Bunny Gets A Job	G	136
Donald Duck Full Speed Ahead	TAT	900
Tom And Jerry	G	117
Tom And Jerry	G	561
Tom And Jerry Meet Little Quack	G	181
Tom And Jerry Meet Little Quack	G	311
Ugly Duckling, The	G	D 22

MacPherson, Ruth Rosamond

Tag-Along Shadow	TAT	2601

Mack, Brice

Peter Pan And The Indians	G	D 26
Peter Pan And The Indians	G	D 74

Magagna, Anna Marie

More The Merrier, The	TAT	2523

Malvern, Corinne

5 Pennies To Spend	G	238
All Aboard	G	152
Christmas Carols	G	26
Christmas Carols (Second Cover)	G	26
Christmas Carols	G	595
Christmas Carols (Second Cover)	G	595
Counting Rhymes	G	257
Day At The Beach, A	G	110
Doctor Dan The Bandage Man	G	111
Doctor Dan, The Bandage Man	G	295
Doctor Dan, The Bandage Man (Without Band-Aids)	G	295
Doctor Dan, The Bandage Man	G	312-07
Frosty The Snowman	G	142
Fun With Decals	G	139
Happy Family, The	G	216
Heidi	G	192
Heidi	G	258
Heidi	G	470
How Big	G	83
How Big (Second Cover)	G	83
Jerry At School	G	94
Jerry At School (Puzzle Edition)	G	94
Little Golden Book Of Hymns, The	G	34
Little Golden Book Of Hymns, The	G	392
Little Golden Book Of Poetry, The	G	38
Little Golden Book Of Singing Games, The	G	40
Night Before Christmas, The	G	20
Night Before Christmas, The (Second Cover)	G	20
Night Before Christmas, The	G	450*
Nurse Nancy	G	154
Nurse Nancy	G	346
Nurse Nancy	G	473
Nursery Rhymes	G	529
Nursery Songs	G	7
Nursery Songs (Second Cover)	G	7
Off To School	G	5015
Open Up My Suitcase	G	207
Rainy Day Play Book, The	G	133
Robert And His New Friends	G	124
Surprise For Sally	G	84
Susie's New Stove	G	85
Tex And His Toys	G	129
Uncle Mistletoe	G	175
Up In The Attic	G	53
When I Grow Up	G	96
When I Grow Up (Puzzle Edition)	G	96
When You Were A Baby	G	70
When You Were A Baby	G	435

Marge, Elias

Howdy Doody And Mr. Bluster	G	204

Marlier, Marcel

Peter Hatches An Egg	W	772

Mars, W. T.

Old Woman And Her Pig, The	TAT	2610

Marshall, Carol

Hooray For Lassie!	TAT	2503

Marshall, Earl & Carol

Babes In Toyland (Green Background)	G	D 97
Babes In Toyland (Blue Background)	G	D 97

Marshall, James

Pocketful Of Nonsense	G	312-05

Marsia, Robert

Animals Build A House, The	W	817
Donkey Who Wanted To Be Wise, The	W	771

Martin, Judy & Barry

Bunny's Magic Tricks	G	441
Hansel & Gretel	G	A 41

Marvin, Fred

Twelve Dancing Princesses, The	G	310-64

Masha

Bedtime Stories	W	507
Nursery Tales	G	14
Three Little Kittens	G	1
Three Little Kittens	G	225
Three Little Kittens	G	288
Three Little Kittens	G	381
Toys	G	22

Mastri, Fiore & Jackie

Wful Plane Ride, The	Elf	433
Wful Train Ride, The	Elf	427

Matchette, Karen

Dennis The Menace 'Takes The Cake'	TAT	2451-4

Mateu, Franc

Alice In Wland	G	105-77
Rescuers Down Under, The	G	105-70
Welcome To Little Golden Book Land	G	GBL370

Mathieu, Joe

Cookie Monster And The Cookie Tree	G	159*
Cookie Monster And The Cookie Tree	G	109-52
Ernie's Work Of Art	G	109- 5

Matson, Elizabeth

Rainy Day Story On The Farm	TAT	858

Mattinson, Sylvia & Burne

Pixi, Dixi & Mr. Jinx	G	454
Yogi-A Christmas Visit	G	433

Matulay, Laszlo

Alice In Wland	W	574

Mayer, Gina & Mercer

This Is My Family	G	312-02

Mazza, Adriana

Runaway Baby Bird, The	W	748

McCann, Gerald

Let's Play Ball	G	325

McClain, Mary S.

Raggedy Ann And Andy, Five Birthdays In A Row	G	107- 4

McCue Karsten, Lisa

Timothy Tiger's Terrible Toothache	G	209-60
Arthur's Good Manners	G	305-58
Puppy On The Farm	G	304-52
Ugly Duckling, The	G	207-72

McElwain, Diane

We Talk With God	TAT	2404-3

McGary, Norman

Bugs Bunny Hangs Around	TAT	2410
Bugs Bunny In Something Fishy	TAT	2543
Donald Duck And The Christmas Carol	G	D 84
Scamp	G	D 63

Woody Woodpecker, Steps To Drawing	G	372

McKean, Emma C.

Pussy Willow	TAT	873
Snoozey	TAT	853
Snoozey	TAT	2538
Fluffy And Tuffy The Twin Ducklings	TAT	872

McKim, Sam

Toby Tyler	G	D 87

McKimson, Thomas J.

Bugs Bunny 'Party Pest'	G	111-69
Bugs Bunny And The Indians	G	430

McKinley, Clare

Amos Learns To Talk: The Story Of A Little Duck	Elf	446
Amos Learns To Talk: The Story Of A Little Duck	Elf	576
Amos Learns To Talk: The Story Of A Little Duck	Elf	8352
Chester, The Little Pony	Elf	581
Chester, The Little Pony	Elf	8354
Chester: The Little Pony	Elf	452
Misty The W Pony	Elf	536
Misty The W Pony	Elf	8628
Mr. Bear's House	Elf	511
Mr. Bear's House	Elf	8349
Mr. Bear's House	Elf	8707
Penny And Pete's Surprise	Elf	434
Penny And Pete's Surprise	Elf	8396
Penny And Pete's Surprise	Elf	8627
Penny And Pete's Surprise	Elf	1023
Three Bears Visit Goldilocks, The	Elf	445
Three Bears Visit Goldilocks, The	Elf	8401
Three Bears Visit Goldilocks, The	Elf	8620
Wynken, Blynken And Nod And OtherNursery Rhymes	Elf	8367
Wynken, Blynken And Nod And Other Nursery Rhymes	Elf	8714
Wynken, Blynken And Nod And Other Nursery Rhymes	Elf	571

McLaughlin, Birdice

Who Is My Friend?	W	646

McLean, Mina Grow

My Big Brother	D	214
My Gold Fish	D	211

McLean, Sammis

Monsters Come In Many Colors!	TAT	2452-39

McNatt Jr., Rich

Peter Pan And The Tiger	TAT	2616

McNaught, Harry

Emerald City Of Oz	G	151
Howdy Doody's Lucky Trip	G	171
Road To Oz, The	G	144
Tin Woodsman Of Oz, The	G	159

McQueen, Lucinda

Cheltenham's Party	G	201-56
Gull That Lost The Sea, The	G	206-45
Kitty's New Doll	G	210-63
Puss In Boots	G	300-58
Silly Sisters, The	G	204-59
Theodore Mouse Goes To Sea	G	201-45
Theodore Mouse Up In The Air	G	204-57

McSavage, Frank

Flintstones At The Circus, The	TAT	2552
Hey There It's Yogi Bear!	TAT	2602
Pinocchio	TAT	2428-2

Woodsy Owl And The Trail Bikers	G	107*
Woody Woodpecker 'Shoots The Works'	TAT	2439
Woody Woodpecker At The Circus	G	149*

Medvey, Steven

Brave Firemen, The	W	563

Megargee, Edwin

Dog Stamps	G	A 9

Meisel, Paul

Daddies All About The Work They Do	G	301-69
Halloween ABCs	G	313-01

Mekimson, Thomas J.

Bugs Bunny Party Pest	TAT	2607

Merkling, Erica

Baby Goes Around The Block	TAT	2493

Meshekoff, Edward

Little Car That Wanted A Garage, The	W	573

Messerli, Joseph

Bugs Bunny Calling!	G	111-70
Bugs Bunny Calling!	TAT	2453-48
Bugs Bunny Marooned!	G	110-55
Bugs Bunny Rides Again	TAT	2472-35
Tom And Jerry's Big Move	TAT	2451-38
Tweety And Sylvester 'A Visit To The Vet'	TAT	2453-47
Tweety And Sylvester In 'Birds Of A Feather'	G	110-78
Tweety Global Patrol	G	110-82

Meyerhoff, Nancy

Bunny Sitter, The	W	774
Let's Go Shopping	W	693
Ollie Bakes A Cake	W	829

Meyers, Jack & Louise

Ho-Hum	TAT	2510

Michaels, Serge

Hunchback Of Notre Dame, The 'Quasimodo's New Friend'	G	107-36

Michell, Gladys Turley

Little Black Sambo	TAT	2661
Farm ABC	TAT	2468

Miclat, Alex

Poky Little Puppy Follows His Nose Home, The	G	130*

Mikolaycak, Charles

Bremen-Town Musicians, The	TAT	2610

Mill, Eleanor

I Like To Be Little	TAT	2615

Miller, John P.

Brave Little Tailor, The	G	178
Circus ABC	G	222
Day On The Farm, A	G	407
Doctor Squash	G	157
House For A Mouse, A	G	304-63
House That Jack Built, The	G	218
Jack's Adventure	G	308
Jingle Bells	G	458*
Jingle Bells	G	553
Jingle Bells (Second Cover)	G	553
Little Golashes	G	68
Little Golden Funny Book, The	G	74
Little Pee Wee Or, Now Open The Box (First Edition)	G	52
Little Pee Wee, The Circus Dog Or, Now Open The Box	G	52

Little Red Hen, The	G	209
Little Red Hen, The	G	296
Little Red Hen, The	G	519
Lucky Mrs. Ticklefeather	G	122
Marvelous Merry-Go-Round, The	G	87
Musicians Of Bremen	G	189
Puss In Boots	G	137
Puss In Boots	G	359
Rags	G	586
Rags	G	303-44
Tommy's Wful Rides	G	63
What If?	G	130
Wful House, The	G	76

Miloche, Hilda

Elves And The Shoemaker, The	TAT	2561
Little Golden Paper Dolls, The	G	113
Little Golden Paper Dolls, The	G	280
Paper Doll Wedding	G	193
Paper Doll Wedding	G	A 22
Paper Dolls	G	A 3
Paper Dolls	G	A 47
Three Little Pigs, The	TAT	2542

Mitchell, Benn

Zippy The Chimp	Elf	487
Zippy The Chimp	Elf	8306
Zippy The Chimp	Elf	8705

Mitchell, Frances Score

Little Golden Book Of Hymns, The	G	211-57

Mitter, Kathryn

My Kindergarten Counting Book	G	301-68

Miyake, Yoshi

Rudolph The Red-Nosed Reindeer	TAT	2517-2
Seven Wishes, The	TAT	2606

Mode, Nathalee

Buffy And The New Girl	TAT	2526
Parade For Chatty Baby, A	TAT	2562

Mones, Isidre

Mickey Mouse 'Those Were The Days'	G	100-61
Tootle And Katy Caboose 'a Special Treasure'	G	GBL374

Moore, Robert J.

Donald Duck's Christmas Tree	G	D 39
Mickey Mouse Goes Christmas Shopping	G	D 33
Peter Pan And The Pirates	G	D 25
Peter Pan And The Pirates	G	D 73
Terry Bears Win The Cub Scout Badge, The	T	903

Moore, Sparky

H.R. Pufnstuf	TAT	2624

Moores, Dick

Donald Duck And The New Bird House	TAT	2516
Goofy And The Tiger Hunt	TAT	2552

Morel, Eve

Tutu The Little Fawn	W	836

Mortimer, Winslow

Very Busy Barbie	G	107-90

Moyers, William

Horse For Johnny, A	W	754
Monkey See, Monkey Do	W	521
Stacks Of Caps	W	722

Munshi, Carol

Night Before Christmas, The	TAT	2517

Munson, Floyd

Yippie Kiyi	TAT	940

Murdocca, Sal

Grover's Own Alphabet	G	108-46
Grover's Own Alphabet	TAT	2402-6

Murray, Marjorie

Child's Ten Commandments, A	TAT	2624
Tiny Tots 1-2-3	TAT	2615

Murtagh, Betty

I Can Do Anything ... Almost	W	822

Myers, Bernice & Lou

Billy And His Steam Roller	W	557
Brave Little Steam Shovel, The	W	555
Bunny Button	TAT	2526
Bunny Button	TAT	923
Christmas Favorites	W	869
It's A Secret	W	540
Picnic At The Zoo	W	613
Puss-In-Boots	Elf	507
Puss-In-Boots	Elf	513
Puss-In-Boots	Elf	8356
Puss-In-Boots	Elf	8573
Sailing On A Very Fine Day	Elf	497
Trumpet	TAT	931
W Book Of Christmas, The	W	575

Myers, Jack & Louise

Big Whistle, The	TAT	2522
Ho-Hum	TAT	2553
Jasper Giraffe	TAT	898
Lambikin, The	TAT	2617
Oh, Look!	TAT	2672
Peter Rabbit	TAT	2539
Playmate For Peter	TAT	803
Teena And The Magic Pot	TAT	2423
Three Little Pigs, The	TAT	2547

Nagel, Stina

Beware Of The Dog	TAT	2553
Big Bark, The	TAT	2510
I Walk To The Park	TAT	2616
In, On, Under, And Through	TAT	2666
Magic Friend Maker, The	G	137*
Two Stories About Wendy	TAT	2659
Whose Baby Is That?	TAT	2553

Nankivel, Claudine

Barbie, The Baby Sitter	W	849
Jerry And Dr. Dave	TAT	2601
Romper Room Laughing Book	W	808

Nebbe, William

Bunny Tales	Elf	8406
Sergeant Preston And The Yukon King	Elf	500
Seven Wful Cats, The	Elf	8411
Baby Chipmunk, The	D	208
Mr. Meyer's Cow	D	DIN 2
Three Billy Goats Gruff, The	Elf	8368
Big Coal Truck, The	D	203
Bunny Tales	Elf	574
Bunny Tales	Elf	8641
Cinderella	Elf	551
Cinderella	Elf	8417
Cinderella	Elf	8644
Mr. Meyer's Cow	D	220
Sergeant Preston And Rex	Elf	569
Seven Wful Cats, The	Elf	548
Seven Wful Cats, The	Elf	8607
Slowpoke, The Lazy Little Puppy	Elf	582
Snoopy, The Nosey Little Puppy	Elf	509
Three Billy Goats Gruff, The	Elf	583
Your Friend, The Policeman	D	200

Neely, Jan

Donnie And Marie, The Top Secret Project	G	160*

New Friends For The Saggy Baggy Elephant | G | 131* |
| Walton's The 'Elizabeth And The Magic Lamp' | TAT | 2579 |

Neff, George

Squiffy The Skunk	Elf	476

Newell, Crosby

Big Joke, The	W	628
Helpful Friends, The	W	631
I Love You	W	657
Land Of Peek-A-Boo, The	T	901
Let's Go Fishing	W	764
Make-Believe Book, The	W	634
Moppets' Surprise Party, The	W	794
Really Truly Treasure Hunt, The	W	793
Really Truly Treasure Hunt, The	T	891
Surprise Party, The	W	620
Tom Terrific's Greatest Adventure	W	735
What Are You Looking At?	W	792
What Are You Looking At?	T	895

Newton, Ruth E.

Night Before Christmas, The	TAT	839

Nez, John

Baby Brown Bear's Big Bellyache	G	304-64
Look For Boats	TAT	2473-46
Mother Goose Rhymes	TAT	2464-36
My First Book Of Planets	G	308-56
Sesame Street ABC	TAT	2471-43
Tortoise And The Hare, The	G	207-56

Nicklaus, Carol

Mrs. Brisby And The Magic Stone	G	110-38
Puppy Love	G	109-46

Nielsen, Jon

Camping Trip With The Range Rider, A	W	681
Wild Bill Hickok	W	649

Nigro, Joanne

Let's Give A Party	W	752

Nofziger, Ed

Mister Magoo	W	708

Nonnast, Marie

Captain Kangaroo And The Beaver	G	427

Nugent, Alys

ABC	TAT	2658
Alphabet Rhymes	TAT	2430

O'Brien, John

Little Golden Book Of Jokes & Riddles	G	211-45
Snow White	G	D 66
Snow White And The Seven Dwarfs	G	D 4

O'Sullivan, Tom

Big Enough Helper, The	G	152*
Cat Who Stamped His Feet	G	806
Corkey's Hic-Cup	G	503
Hiding Place, The	TAT	2553
I Live In The City ABC	TAT	2554
Pals	TAT	2544
Who Comes To Your House	G	575

Obligado, Lilian

Animals And Their Babies	G	A 29
Charlie	G	587
Charlie	G	302-44
Four Puppies	G	405
Golden Egg Book, The	G	456
Golden Egg Book, The	G	307-69

I Like To Live In The City	G	593
If I Had A Dog	G	205-40
Little Black Puppy	G	804
Little Cottontail	G	414
Little Cottontail	G	304-73
New Puppy, The	G	370
New Puppy, The	G	203-55
Pussycat Tiger	G	362
Reading, Writing & Spelling Stamps	G	A 24
Willie Found A Wallet	G	205-56
Wait-For-Me-Kitten	G	463

Oechsli, Kelly

Great Fort, The	TAT	2564
Peaky Beaky	Elf	8598
Waldo, The Jumping Dragon	TAT	2688

Ohlsson, Ib

Rainy Day Play Book	G	206-35

Oogjen, Barbara & Thomas

Lonely Pony, The	W	645

Opitz, Marge

I Decided	D	204
Ugly Duckling, The	Elf	8327
Ugly Duckling, The	Elf	8590
What Happened To George?	Elf	1006
What Happened To George?	Elf	8409

Oreb, Tom

Once Upon A Wintertime	G	D 12

Oriolo, Joe

Felix On Television	T	904
Felix On Television	W	716
Surprise For Felix, A	W	728

Ortiz, Phil

Rudolph The Red-Nosed Reindeer	TAT	2483-02

Orville, Oliver

And So To Bed	TAT	2462-46
Honey Bear Finds A Friend	TAT	2466-46
Stuck In The Tub	TAT	2463-44

Osborne, Richard N.

Cousin Matilda And The Foolish Wolf	TAT	2530
Little Boy In The Forest, The	TAT	2553

Ostapczuk, Phil

Hong Kong Phooey And The Bird Nest Snatchers	Elf	
Hong Kong Phooey And The Fire Engine Mystery	Elf	

Ozone, Lucy

Pockets	TAT	2616
Robin Family, The	D	215
Surprise!	Elf	562
Surprise!	Elf	8384

Paflin, Roberta

Counting Rhymes	G	12
Good Night 'A Flocked Book'	TAT	955
This Little Piggy Counting Rhymes	G	12
Uncle Remus	G	D 6

Paplo, Bob

Dennis The Menace	Elf	541

Paris, Pat

Lady Lovely Locks Silkypup Saves The Day	G	107-57

Parmalee, Ted

Johnny Appleseed	G	D 11

Parsons, Virginia

Fly High	G	597
Sam The Firehouse Cat	G	580

W Book Of Counting Rhymes,
The W 682

Peet, Bill
Golliath II G D 83

Peller, Jackie
Animal Crackers TAT 837
Animal Jingles TAT 837
Lucky Four Leaf Clover TAT 893
Three Little Pigs And Little
Red Riding Hood W 609
Treasure Book Of Favorite
Nursery Tales T 856
W Book Of Favorite
Nursery Tales, The W 730

Peltier, Phyllis A.
Tabitha Tabby's Fantastic Flavor TAT 2476-44

Perma, Debi
How Does Your Garden Grow? G 308-55

Petruccio, Steven
Dr. Hilda Makes House Calls TAT 2463

Pfloog, Jan
Animals On The Farm G 573
Sly Little Bear G 411
Tiny-Tawny Kitten, The G 590

Pfloog, Piet
Pick Up Sticks G 461

Phillips, Katherine L.
Mr. Punnymoon's Train Elf 449
Mr. Punnymoon's Train Elf 557
Mr. Punnymoon's Train Elf 8415
Mr. Punnymoon's Train Elf 8632
Smart Little Mouse, The Elf 441
Smart Little Mouse, The Elf 8421
Smart Little Mouse, The Elf 8626

Pickett, Helen
Day Downtown With Daddy, A D 205
My Daddy Is A Policeman D 223

Pierce, Alice
Bartholomew The Beaver Elf 471
Bartholomew The Beaver Elf 597
Bartholomew The Beaver Elf 8423
Bartholomew The Beaver Elf 8643

Pinchevsky, Leonid
Hush, Hush, It's Sleepytime G 301-43

Plummer, Virginia
Count The Baby Animals W 702

Poehlmann, Jo Anna
Happy Book, The TAT 2610

Pointer, Priscilla
Baby's Day W 663
Baby's Day T 859
Our Baby D 218
Our Baby D DIN 8
Ten Little Fingers W 714
Ten Little Fingers T 875

Pollard, G.
Freight Train Elf 534
Freight Train Elf 8414
Freight Train Elf 8631

Ponter, James
Henny-Penny W 685
Henny-Penny T 882

Porter, Genevieve
Puffy TAT 819

Powell, Linda
Rabbit Is Next, The G 173*

Pratt, Hawley
Bamm-Bamm G 540
Beany Goes To Sea G 537
Bozo Finds A Friend G 485
Bullwinkle G 462
Dennis The Menace And Ruff G 386
Dick Tracy G 497
Fireball X-L5 G 546
Gay Purr-ee G 488
Hey There It's Yogi Bear G 542
Jetsons, The G 500
Lippy The Lion And Hardy
Har Har G 508
Ludwig Von Drake G D 98
Magilla Gorilla G 547
Peter Potamus G 556
Quick Draw McGraw G 398
Top Cat G 453
Wally Gator G 502

Prebenna, David
Alvin's Daydream G 107-73
Grover's Guide To Good
Manners G 109-66

Prestopino, Gregorio
Pony Engine, The W 626

Prickett, Helen
Goody Naughty Book Elf 572
Goody Naughty Book Elf 8385
Goody Naughty Book Elf 8593
Goody Naughty Book Elf 8693
My Daddy Is A Policeman D DIN 3

Probst, Pierre
Bobby The Dog G 440
Puff The Blue Kitten G 443
Rusty Goes To School G 479

Provensen, Alice & Martin
Color Kittens G 86
Color Kittens (Puzzle Edition) G 86
Color Kittens G 436
Color Kittens, The G 202-28
Color Kittens G 86
Funny Bunny G 304-59
Fuzzy Duckling, The G 78
Fuzzy Duckling, The G 557
Katie The Kitten G 75
Katie The Kitten (Puzzle Edition) G 75
Little Fat Policeman, The G 91
Mr. Noah And His Family G 49
Old Mother Goose And Other
Nursery Rhymes G 300-54

Purtle, John
Land Of The Lost The Dinosaur
Adventure TAT 2607

Pyk, Jan
New Home For Snow Ball, A G 800

Quigley, Ray
Trucks (2 Paper Model Trucks) G A 6

R.O. Fry
Three Little Pigs G 544

Rachel
Cradle Rhymes TAT 894
Little Folks Mother Goose TAT 863

Raw, J. G.
Bible Treasures W 643

Ray, Tom
Tom And Jerry And The Toy
Circus TAT 2509

Read, Isobel
Big Game Hunter, The TAT 869

Chitter Chatter TAT 889

Reed, Veronica
Smoky The Baby Goat TAT 867

Riley, Bob
Counting Book, The W 692

Rinaldi, Joe
Scamp G D 63
Scamp's Adventure G D 70

Robertson, Maurice
Playful Little Dog, The W 562

Robinson
Shy Little Horse, The W 511
Shy Little Horse, The T 880

Robison, I. E.
Matilda, Mac Elroy, And Mary TAT 836
Three Little Mice TAT 836

Robison, Jim
Animals Christmas Eve, The G 154*
Bible Stories From The Old
Testament G 153*
Elves And The Shoemaker, The TAT 2496
Superstar Barbie G 162*

Rockwell, Eve
Mommy Cat And Her Kittens Elf 8317

Rodegast, Roland
ABC Rhymes G 543
ABC Rhymes (Second Cover) G 543

Rodger, Elizabeth
Bunnies' Counting Book, The G 203-58

Rofry
Little Boy & The Giant, The G 536
My Home G 115*

Rojankovsky, Feodor
Animal Dictionary G 379
Animal Dictionary G 533
Big Elephant, The G 206-51
Cow Went Over The Mountain,
The G 516
Gaston And Josephine G 65
Golden Book Of Birds, The G 13
Hop, Little Kangaroo G 558
Kitten's Surprise G 107
Kitty On The Farm G 200-57
Little Golden Mother Goose, The G 390
Little Golden Mother Goose, The G 472
Little Lost Kitten G 302-56
More Mother Goose Rhymes G 317
Mother Goose G 283
Mother Goose G 5007
Mother Goose Rhymes G 5016
Name For Kitty, A G 55
Our Puppy G 56
Our Puppy G 292
Ten Little Animals G 451
Three Bears, The G 47
Three Bears, The
(Second Cover) G 47
What's Next Elephant? G 206-61
White Bunny And His Magic
Nose, The G 305
Wild Animal Babies G 332
Wild Animals G 394
Wild Animals G 499

Rooks, Dale & Sally
Three Little Bunnies Elf 443
Three Little Bunnies Elf 589
Three Little Bunnies Elf 8388
Three Little Puppies Elf 447
Three Little Puppies Elf 598
Three Little Puppies Elf 8363
Three Little Puppies Elf 8745

Rosenberg, Amye

Biggest, Most Beautiful Christmas Tree, The	G	459- 8
I Don't Want To Go	G	208-59
Lily Pig's Book Of Colors	G	205-58
Polly's Pet	G	302-55

Ross, Larry

Circus Is In Town, The	G	168*

Ross, Sharon

Mickey And The Beanstalk	G	103-59

Rossi, Ken

Visit To The Hospital, A	W	690

Rowand, Phyllis

Who Does Baby Look Like?	W	525

Rowland, Helen

Three Bears, The	TAT	909

Ruhman, Ruth

Gandy Goose	W	695
Jingle Dingle Book, The	W	675
My Little Counting Book	TAT	2407-3
Slowpoke At The Circus	TAT	2457
When I Go To Bed	TAT	2542

Ruiz, Art

Barbie 'Soccer Coach'	G	107-71

Rumely, Louise

Brownie Scouts	G	409

Russell, H. R.

Lion King, The	G	107-93
Lion King, The 'No Worries'	G	107-97

Russell, Solveig

Three Bears, The	TAT	2551

Ruth, Rod

Feelings From A To Z	G	200-6
Jumpty Dumpty And Other Nursery Rhymes	TAT	2610
Marvelous Monster	TAT	2632
My Little Book Of Dinosaurs	TAT	2482
Whales	G	171*

Rutherford, Bonnie & Bill

Goby Goat And The Birthday Gift	TAT	2595
House My Grandpa Built	TAT	2530
How Can We Get To The Zoo?	TAT	2660
I Play In The Snow	TAT	2510
Magic Clothes Basket, The	TAT	2544
Once I Had A Monster	TAT	2512
Tuffer	TAT	2672
Under The Saskatoon Tree	TAT	2543

Rutherford, William De

Dinosaurs	G	355

Sagendorf, Bud

House That Popeye Built, The	W	750
Popeye	W	667
Popeye	T	888
Popeye Goes On A Picnic	W	697
Popeye's Big Surprise	W	791

Sahula-Dycke

Hopalong Cassidy And The Bar 20 Cowboys	G	147

Salva, Ada

Tammy	G	A 52

Sampson, Katherine

Doctor Dan At The Circus	G	399
Kobo The Koala Bear	TAT	2521
Tubsy And The Picnic Tree (Ideal Doll)	TAT	2552
Why Do You Love Me?	TAT	2428

Sanderson, Ruth

One Of The Family	G	208-42
Owl And The Pussy Cat	G	300-41
Store Bought Doll, The	G	204-54
When You Were A Baby	G	306-41

Santis, George De

Gumby And Gumby's Pal Pokey To The Rescue	TAT	2552
Gumby And Gumby's Pal Pokey	TAT	2506
Hoppity Hooper Vs Skippity Snooper	TAT	2552
Littlest Snowman, The	W	720

Santoro, Christopher

Cat That Climbed The Christmas Tree, The	G	458-03
Lion's Mixed-Up Friends	G	304-62

Santos, George

Black Beauty	W	595
Loopy De Loop Goes West	G	417

Santro, Christopher

Flying Dinosaurs	G	309-51

Sari

Gingerbread Man, The	TAT	2504
Three Bears, The	TAT	2512
Why The Bear Has A Short Tail	W	508
Yellow Cat, The	TAT	911
Yippie Kiyi And Whoa Boy	TAT	2514

Sarkin, Jack

ABC And Counting Book	W	506

Satterfield, Charles

Bozo The Clown	G	446
Huckleberry Hounds And The Christmas Sleigh	G	403
Mouseketeers Tryout Time, The	TAT	2649

Saviozzi, Adriana Mazza

Farm Stamps	G	A 19
Four Little Kittens	G	322
Four Little Kittens	G	530
Ginger Paper Doll	G	A 14
Ginger Paper Doll	G	A 32
Mike And Melissa (Paper Dolls)	G	A 31
Nursery Songs	G	348
Peter Rabbit	G	313
Peter Rabbit	G	505
Peter Rabbit (Second Cover)	G	505
Peter Rabbit (Third Cover)	G	505

Sayeles, William

First Golden Geography	G	534
Our World	G	242

Scarry, Richard

Albert's Stencil Zoo	G	112
Animals Of Farmer Jones, The	G	211
Animals Of Farmer Jones, The	G	282
Animals' Merry Christmas, The	G	329
Best Little Word Book Ever!	G	312-01
Brave Cowboy Bill	G	93
Brave Cowboy Bill (Puzzle Edition)	G	93
Bunny Book, The	G	215
Busiest Firefighters Ever	G	208-66
Cars And Trucks	G	366
Chicken Little	G	413
Chipmunk's ABC	G	512
Chipmunk's ABC	G	202-44
Chipmunk's Merry Christmas, The	G	375
Colors	G	A 28
County Mouse And The City Mouse, The	G	426
Cowboy Stamps	G	A 11

Cowboys And Indians	G	5019
Danny Beaver's Secret	G	160
Duck And His Friends	G	81
Duck And His Friends (Puzzle Edition)	G	81
Fireman & Fire Engine Stamps	G	A 27
Floating Bananas	G	208-65
Gingerbread Man, The	G	165
Gingerbread Man, The	G	437
Good Night Little Bear	G	447
Here Comes The Parade	G	143
Hilda Needs Help!	G	208-64
Just For Fun	G	264
Little Benny Wanted A Pony	G	97
Little Indian, The	G	202
Mr. Fumble's Coffeeshop Disaster	G	208-67
My Little Golden Book Of Manners	G	460
My Little Golden Book Of Manners	G	205-57
My Little Golden Book Of Manners	G	205-64
My Little Golden Calendar	G	A 39
My Little Golden Dictionary	G	90
My Little Golden Dictionary	G	5001
Naughty Bunny, The	G	377
Nursery Tales:	G	5009
Party Pig	G	191
Pierre Bear	G	212
Rabbit And His Friends	G	169
Rudolph The Red-Nosed Reindeer	G	331
Smokey The Bear	G	224
Smokey The Bear	G	481
Three Billy Goats	G	173
Tommy Visits The Doctor	G	480
Two Little Miners	G	66
When Bunny Grows Up	G	311-71
Winky Dink	G	266
Snow Storm Surprise	G	208-69

Schaar, Bob

Lassie And The Big Cleanup Day	G	572

Schad, Helen G.

Baby's First Book	W	606
I Can I Can I Can	W	676
Timothy's Shoes	TAT	856
Who Am I?	T	864
Who Is That?	T	906

Schaffenberger, Kurt

Buck Rogers And The Children Of Hopetown	G	500*

Schart, Trina

My First Book Of Sounds	G	205-54
Riddles, Riddles From A To Z	G	490

Schlesinger, Alice

Two Stories About Kate & Kitty	TAT	2510
W Book Of Nursery Songs, The	W	619

Schlining Studios, G

Campbell Kids At Home, The	Elf	493
Campbell Kids Have A Party, The	Elf	494

Schmidling, Jack

Playtime Poodles	Elf	501
Playtime Poodles	Elf	8330

Schmidt, Al

Cheyenne	G	318

Schmidt, Edwin

Captain Kangaroo And The Panda	G	278
Captain Kangaroo And The Panda	G	421
Captain Kangaroo's Surprise Party	G	341

Stirnweis, Shannon
Where's Harry?	TAT	2546

Stoddard, Maru Alice
Buster Bulldozer	TAT	834

Stolgerg, Doris
Playtime For Nancy	W	560

Stone, David K.
Jumpy, Humpy, Fuzzy, Buzzy, Animal Book, The	TAT	2488
Manuel's Cat	TAT	2521
My Little Book Of Dogs	TAT	2476-93

Stone, Dick
Baby Bunny, The	W	548

Storms, Robert
Have You Seen A Giraffe Hat?	TAT	2535
Pebbles Flintstone 'Daddy's Little Helper'	TAT	2657
Rubbles And Bamm-Bamm, The 'Problem Present'	TAT	2622

Story, Miriam
Daniel Boone	G	256

Street, T.
Busy Ants, The	Elf	8551

Strobe, Dorothy
Sleeping Beauty & The Fairies	G	D 71
Bugs Bunny At The Easter Party	G	183
Bugs Bunny Gets A Job	G	136
Donald Duck On Tom Sawyer's Island	TAT	2409
Pebbles Flintstone ABCs	TAT	2622
Peter Potamus 'Meets The Black Knight'	TAT	2506
Pluto	TAT	2509
Swiss Family Duck	TAT	2509
Uncle Scrooge 'The Winner'	TAT	2552

Sullivan, Pat
Felix The Cat	W	665
Felix The Cat	T	872

Sumera, Anabelle
What Lily Goose Found	G	163*

Super, Terri
First Airplane Ride, A	G	310-57
Flying Is Fun	G	310-53
Frosty The Snowman	G	451-11
Grandma And Grandpa Smith	G	305-55
Littlest Christmas Elf, The	G	459-00
Patsy The Pussycat	TAT	2475-4
Ten Items Or Less	G	203-54

Suschitzky, W.
Wild Animals	G	5010

Sutton, Judith
Velveteen Rabbit, The	G	307-68

Suzanne
Franky, The Fuzzy Goat	TAT	820
Fuzzy Wuzzy Puppy, The	TAT	915
House That Jack Built, The	TAT	2480
Lazy Fox And Red Hen	TAT	2603
Little Black Sambo	TAT	812
Teddy's Surprise	TAT	809
Three Bears, The	TAT	2512
Too Many Kittens	TAT	2525

Svendsen, Julius
Mickey Mouse And The Missing Mouseketeers	G	D 57
Mickey Mouse Club Stamp Book	G	A 10
Mickey Mouse Flies The Christmas Mail	G	D 53

Seven Dwarfs Find A House, The	G	D 35
Seven Dwarfs Find A House, The	G	D 67
Sleeping Beauty	G	D 61
Sleeping Beauty	G	A 33
Sleeping Beauty & The Fairies	G	D 71

Swanson, Maggie
Big Bird Visits Navajo Country	G	108-68
Big Bird's Day On The Farm	G	107-61
Curious Little Kitten Around The House	G	206-57
"Me Cookie"	G	109-69
Rabbit's Adventure, The	G	164*
Sesame Street 'Mother Goose Rhymes'	G	108-69
Up And Down Book Staring Ernie And Bert, The	TAT	2402-7

Szekeres, Cyndy
Tale Of Peter Rabbit, The	G	307-11
Whispering Rabbit, The	G	313-03

Szepelak, Helen
Busy Book, The (Rhymes & Riddles & Things To Do)	Elf	462
Busy Book, The (Rhymes & Riddles & Things To Do)	Elf	1038
Busy Book, The (Rhymes & Riddles & Things To Do)	Elf	8402
Busy Book, The (Rhymes & Riddles & Things To Do)	Elf	8623
Funland Party	Elf	478
Popcorn Party	Elf	468
Popcorn Party	Elf	8303
Popcorn Party	Elf	8743
Sleepy-Time Rhymes	Elf	8346
Sleepy-Time Rhymes	Elf	8664

Szwejkowski, Adam
Scooby Doo At The Zoo	TAT	2570

Tallarico, Tony
Astronaut And The Flying Bus	W	853
Puff The Magic Dragon	W	851
Soupy Sales And The Talking Turtle	W	860

Tamburine, Jean
Billy Whiskers' Twins	Elf	538
Billy Whiskers' Twins	Elf	8333
Five Busy Bears, The	Elf	498
Five Busy Bears, The	Elf	8404
Five Busy Bears, The	Elf	8629
Fraidy Cat	Elf	8319
Goat That Went To School, The	Elf	469
Goat That Went To School, The	Elf	594
Goat That Went To School, The	Elf	8386
Goat That Went To School, The	Elf	8594
Help Mr. Willy Nilly	T	886
Outdoor Fun	Elf	479
Pillowtime Tales	Elf	552
Pillowtime Tales	Elf	8338
Pillowtime Tales	Elf	8740
Pudgy The Little Bear	Elf	8441
Pudgy The Little Bear	Elf	8674
Scamper	Elf	8326
Scamper	Elf	8716
Three Little Pigs And Little Red Riding Hood	W	609
Treasure Book Of Favorite Nursery Tales	T	856
W Book Of Favorite Nursery Tales, The	W	730

Tedder, Elizabeth
Billy Bunnyscoot - The Lost Bunny	TAT	888
Polka Dot Tots	TAT	864

Poor Kitty	TAT	850

Tellingen, Ruth Van
Bertram And The Ticklish Rhinoceros	Elf	430
Daddy's Birthday Cakes	D	207
Grandmother Is Coming	D	216
Growing Things	D	210
Suitcase With A Surprise, A	D	202

Tenggren, Gustaf
Bedtime Stories	G	2
Bedtime Stories	G	239
Bedtime Stories	G	364
Bedtime Stories	G	538
Bedtime Stories (Second Cover)	G	538
Big Brown Bear, The	G	89
Big Brown Bear, The	G	335
Five Bedtime Stories	G	5002
Giant With Three Golden Hairs, The	G	219
Golden Goose, The	G	200
Golden Goose, The	G	487
Jack And The Beanstalk	G	179
Jack And The Beanstalk	G	281
Jack And The Beanstalk	G	420
Kittens	G	5013
Lion's Paw, The	G	367
Little Black Sambo (42 page)	G	57
Little Black Sambo (28 page)	G	57
Little Black Sambo (24 page)	G	57
Little Trapper, The	G	79
Lively Little Rabbit, The	G	15
Lively Little Rabbit, The (Second Edition)	G	15
Lively Little Rabbit, The	G	551
Poky Little Puppy, The	G	8
Poky Little Puppy, The	G	271
Poky Little Puppy, The	G	506
Saggy Baggy Elephant, The	G	36
Saggy Baggy Elephant, The	G	385
Shy Little Kitten, The	G	23
Shy Little Kitten, The	G	248
Shy Little Kitten, The	G	494
Snow White And Rose Red	G	228
Tawny Scrawny Lion	G	138
Thumbelina	G	153
Thumbelina	G	514
Thumbelina	G	300-66
Topsy Turvy Circus	G	161
Where Is The Poky Little Puppy	G	467

Thomas, Richard
Bugs Bunny's Birthday Surprise	TAT	2421

Thomas, Stephen
Pony Who Couldn't Say Neigh, The	TAT	2543

Thompkins, Kenny
Aladdin 'The Magic Carpet Ride'	G	107-92

Thompson, Riley
Woody Woodpecker	G	145
Woody Woodpecker	G	330
Woody Woodpecker's 'Peck Of Trouble'	TAT	831

Thompson, Robert
Toy Soldier, The	G	D 99

Tierney, Tom
Barbie 'The Big Splash'	G	107-86
Barbie On Skates	TAT	2450-01

Timmins, William
Adventures Of Robin Hood And His Merry Men	Elf	532
Cowboys	Elf	1004
Cowboys	Elf	8341
Cowboys	Elf	8666
Davy Crockett: American Hero	Elf	523

How The Camel Got His Hump: Kipling "Just So" Story	Elf	529	
How The Rhinoceros Got His Skin: "Just So" Story	Elf	540	

Weiniger, Egen
Boy's Friend, A	TAT	916
Child's Friend, A	TAT	2519

Weisgard, Leonard
Indian, Indian	G	149
Just Like Me	W	672
Just Like Me	T	881
Let's Play Train	T	870
Little Eskimo, The	G	155
Little Pussycat	G	302-51
Most Beautiful Tree In The World, The	W	653
Mrs. Goose's Green Trailer	W	633
Pantaloon (Die-cut Window)	G	114
Pantaloon	G	114
Pussy Willow	G	314
Wheels	G	141

Weisner, William
W Book Of Firemen And Fire Engines, The	W	637

Wenzel, Paul
Lone Ranger Desert Storm, The	TAT	2622

Werber, Adele
Animal Alphabet	G	349
Animal Babies	G	39
Good Night Fairy Tales	W	726
Kittens Who Hid From Their Mother, The	W	529

Westelin, Albert G.
Playtime Poodles	Elf	501
Playtime Poodles	Elf	8330
Zippy Goes To School	Elf	489

Westerberg, Christine
Bouncy Baby Bunny Finds His Bed, The	G	129*

Westlake, Laura
Missing Wedding Dress Featuring Barbie, The	G	107-63

Wheeler, George
Cinderella	TAT	964
Cinderella	TAT	2604
Cinderella	TAT	2427-2
Donald Duck's Safety Book	G	D 41
Donald Duck's Toy Sailboat	G	102-41

Wheeling, Lynn
Amy's Long Night	TAT	2512

White, Al
Bozo The Clown: King Of The Ring	TAT	2552
Donald Duck And The Private Eye	G	D 94
Huckleberry Hound Builds A House	G	376
Huckleberry Hound Safety Signs	G	458
Little Lulu	G	476
Mary Poppins	G	D113
Pinocchio And The Whale	G	D101
Rocky And His Friends	G	408
Rocky And His Friends (Second Cover)	G	408
Ruff And Reddy	G	378
Ruff And Reddy	G	477
Sword In The Stone, The	G	D106
Touché Turtle	G	474
Wizards' Duel, The	G	D107

Woody Woodpecker Takes A Trip	G	445
Yanky Doodle And Chopper	G	449

Whitilock, R.Z.
Cow And The Elephant, The	G	304-48

Wickart, Terry
Let's Count All The Animals	TAT	2407-4

Wiersum, Gale
My Christmas Treasury	G	455*

Wilburn, Kathy
Beach Day	G	208-57
Christmas Tree That Grew, The	G	458- 1
Friendly Bunny, The	G	209-61
Little Golden Book Of Holidays	G	209-58
My Own Grandpa	G	204-56
Night Before Christmas, The	G	450-10
Oh, Little Rabbit!	G	304-50
Scarebunny, The	G	209-59
Shoelace Box, The	G	211-56

Wilde, Carol
Davy Plays Football	TAT	2512
Jean Ellen Learns To Swim	TAT	2508
Tip-Top Tree House	TAT	2555
Wrong-Way Howie Learns To Slide	TAT	2523

Wilde, George & Irma
Bronto The Dinosaur	Elf	8575
Christmas Puppy, The	W	585
Corky	G	486
Daniel's New Friend	TAT	2433
Dress Up Parade, The	T	861
Dress-Up Parade, The	W	688
Fixit Man, The	W	756
Fixit Man, The	T	851
Fraidy Cat Kitten, The	W	542
Giraffe Who Went To School, The	W	551
Happiest Christmas, The	TAT	2516
Hiawatha	Elf	442
Hiawatha	Elf	565
Hiawatha	Elf	8307
Hiawatha	Elf	8686
Hide-And-Seek Duck, The	W	568
Hungry Little Bunny, The	W	531
Let's Grow Things Children	Elf	8571
Let's Take A Ride	T	862
Lucinda, The Little Donkey	Elf	465
Lucinda, The Little Donkey	Elf	592
Lucinda, The Little Donkey	Elf	8362
Lucinda, The Little Donkey	Elf	8584
Merry Christmas Mr. Snowman	W	818
Mr. Wishing Went Fishing	W	584
My First Book Of Farm Animals	T	858
Pelle's New Suit	W	803
Polly's Christmas Present	W	819
Puppy Who Found A Boy, The	W	561
Raggedy Ann's Tea Party	W	624
Rocket For A Cow, A	Elf	8458
See It Goes!	TAT	805
Snowman's Christmas Present, The	W	572
Splish, Splash, And Splush	TAT	2526
Story Of Our Flag, The	Elf	8398
Story Of Our Flag, The	Elf	8635
Timothy Tiger	Elf	8324
Timothy Tiger	Elf	8672
Trucks	Elf	8325
Trucks	Elf	8687
Two Stories About Chap And Chirpy	TAT	2526
What's For Breakfast?	W	846
Wful Treasure Hunt, The	T	853

Wildman, George
Casper And Friends 'boo-o-s On First'	G	107-85

Wilkin, Eloise
Baby Dear	G	466
Baby Jesus Stamps	G	A 12
Baby Listens	G	383
Baby Looks	G	404
Baby's Birthday	G	365
Baby's Christmas	G	460-08
Baby's First Christmas	G	368
Birds	G	184*
Birds	G	5011
Boy With A Drum, The	G	588
Busy Timmy	G	50
Busy Timmy	G	452
Child's Garden Of Verses, A	G	289
Child's Garden Of Verses, A	G	493
Christmas ABC	G	478
Christmas Story, The	G	158
Come Play House	G	44
Day At The Playground, A	G	119
Eloise Wilkin's Mother Goose	G	589
First Book Of Bible Stories	G	198
Fix It Please	G	32
Georgie Finds A Grandpa	G	196
Good Little Bad Little Girl	G	562
Good Morning, Good Night	G	61
Guess Who Lives Here	G	60
Hansel And Gretel	G	217
Hansel And Gretel	G	491
Hansel And Gretel	G	207-51
Hansel And Gretel	G	207-65
Hi! Ho! Three In A Row	G	188
Jamie Looks	G	522
Kittens	G	5013
Linda And Her Little Sister	G	214
Little Book, The	G	583
Little Golden Book Of Holidays, The	G	109
Make-Believe Parade, The	W	520
My Baby Brother	G	279
My Dolly And Me	G	418
My Kitten	G	163
My Kitten	G	300
My Kitten	G	528
My Little Golden Book About God	G	268
My Pets	G	5027
My Puppy	G	233
My Puppy	G	469
My Snuggly Bunny	G	250
My Teddy Bear	G	168
My Teddy Bear	G	448
New Baby, The	G	41
New Baby, The	G	291
New Baby, The	G	541
New Baby, The	G	306-68
New House In The Forest, The	G	24
Night Before Christmas, The	G	241
Noises And Mr.Flibberty-Jib	G	29
Play With Me	G	567
Prayers For Children	G	5
Prayers For Children	G	205
Prayers For Children	G	301-10
Prayers For Children	G	301-93
So Big	G	574
This World Of Ours	G	5026
Twins, The	G	227
We Help Daddy	G	468
We Help Daddy	G	305-51
We Help Mommy	G	352
We Like Kindergarten	G	552
Where Did The Baby Go?	G	116*
Wiggles	G	166
Ws Of Nature	G	293

William, Arthur
Mickey Mouse And The Lucky Goose Chase	TAT	2454-45

Master Book Title Index

Legend: * = A different title for a Little Golden Book in the regular numbers.

Title	Num.	Cat.
1 Is Red	2407-2	TAT
1 To 10 Again	2471-47	TAT
10 Rabbits	648	W
101 Dalmations	105-84	LGB DN
101 Dalmations	105-65	LGB DN
101 Dalmations	105-81	LGB DN
101 Dalmations	55	LGB L
101 Dalmations	98069-01	LGB DN
12 Days Of Christmas,The	526	LGB
123 Juggle With Me!	594	LGB
123 Juggle With Me!	201-2	LGB N
123 Juggle With Me!	201-32	LGB N
5 Pennies To Spend	238	LGB
A B C Around The House	A 18	LGB A
A B C Around The House	A 44	LGB A
A B C Around The House	176*	LGB
A B C Around The House	200-5	LGB N
A B C Book	1032	Elf
A B C Book	8364	Elf
A B C Book	8653	Elf
A B C Is For Christmas	108*	LGB
A B C Is For Christmas	454-1	LGB N
A B C Is For Christmas	454-31	LGB N
A B C Is For Christmas	454-32	LGB N
A B C Is For Christmas	454-41	LGB N
A B C Rhymes	200-33	LGB N
A B C Rhymes	200-3	LGB N
A B C A Tale Of A Sale	2658	TAT
A B C	2552	TAT
A B C	808	TAT
A B C	896	TAT
A Picinic Surprise	107-70	LGB N
A Picinic Surprise	107-80	LGB N
Abc And Counting Book	506	W
Abc And Counting Book	823	W
Abc Rhymes	543	LGB
Adventures Of Buster Hood, The	111-72	LGB N
Adventures Of Goat	201-10	LGB N
Adventures Of Goat	201-46	LGB N
Adventures Of Lassie:	5012	LGB G
Adventures Of Robin Hood And His Merry Men	532	Elf
Aesop's Fables	463	Elf
Aesop's Fables	706	W
Aesop's Fables	1019	Elf
Aesop's Fables	8440	Elf
Aesop's Fables	8615	Elf
Airplanes	180	LGB
Airplanes	373	LGB
Aladdin -The Magic Carpet Ride'	107-92	LGB DN
Aladdin	371	LGB
Aladdin	107-88	LGB DN
Aladdin	52	LGB L
Albert's Stencil Zoo	112	LGB
Ali Baba	323	LGB
Alice In Wonderland	105-77	LGB DN
Alice In Wonderland	451	Elf
Alice In Wonderland	574	W
Alice In Wonderland Finds The Garden Of Live Flowers	D 20	LGB D
Alice In Wonderland Meets The White Rabbit	103-1	LGB DN
Alice In Wonderland Meets The White Rabbit	103-21	LGB DN
Alice In Wonderland Meets The White Rabbit	103-31	LGB DN
Alice In Wonderland Meets The White Rabbit	103-41	LGB DN
Alice In Wonderland Meets The White Rabbit	105-40	LGB DN
Alice In WonderlandMeets The White Rabbit	105-50	LGB DN
Alice In Wonderland Meets The White Rabbit	D 19	LGB D
Alice's First Word	LGB F	
All Aboard	152	LGB
All In A Day's Work	807	W
All My Chickens	200-67	LGB N
Alonzo Purr The Seagoing Cat	2569	TAT
Alphabet A-Z, The	3	LGB
Alphabet Rhymes	2430	TAT
Alphabet Walks	8553	Elf
Alvin's Daydreams	107-73	LGB N
Alvin's Daydreams	107-82	LGB N
Alvin's Lost Voice	824	W
Amanda's First Day Of School	204-56	LGB N
Amanda's First Day Of School	204-63	LGB N
Amazing Mumford Forgets		
The Magic Word	108-45	LGB N
Amazing Mumford Forgets The Magic Word	108-5	LGB N
Amos Learns To Talk: The Story Of A Little Duck	8352	Elf
Amos Learns To Talk: The Story Of A Little Duck	446	Elf
Amos Learns To Talk: The Story Of A Little Duck	576	Elf
Amos Learns To Talk: The Story Of A Little Duck	8352	Elf
Amos Learns To Talk: The Story Of A Little Duck	8694	Elf
Amy's Long Night	2512	TAT
Anastasia	98805-00	LGB N
And So To Bed	2462-46	TAT
Andy And Betsy At The Circus	906	TAT
Andy	2543	TAT
Angel Child	8373	Elf
Angel Child	8715	Elf
Animal A B C Book	8345	Elf
Animal Abc Book	8658	Elf
Animal Abc	887	TAT
Animal Alphabet	349	LGB
Animal Babies	39	LGB
Animal Counting Book	584	LGB
Animal Crackers	837	TAT
Animal Daddies And My Daddy	576	LGB
Animal Daddies And My Daddy	208-33	LGB N
Animal Daddies And My Daddy	208-43	LGB N
Animal Daddies And My Daddy	208-53	LGB N
Animal Dictionary	379	LGB
Animal Dictionary	533	LGB
Animal Dictionary	205-1	LGB N
Animal Dictionary	205-31	LGB N
Animal Fair		LGB F
Animal Friends	167	LGB
Animal Friends	560	LGB
Animal Gym, The	249	LGB
Animal Homes		LGB F
Animal Jingles	837	TAT
Animal Orchestra	334	LGB
Animal Paintbook	A4	LGB A
Animal Quiz	396	LGB
Animal Quiz Book	308-44	LGB N
Animal Quiz Book	308-54	LGB N
Animal Quiz Book	309-50	LGB N
Animal Show, The	8748	Elf
Animal Show	8459	Elf
Animal Stamps	A7	LGB A
Animal Stories	5006	LGB G
Animal Train	2556	TAT
Animal's Vacation	839	W
Animals Abc's	202-65	LGB N
Animals And Their Babies	A29	LGB A
Animals Build A House, The	817	W

Book Codes

Activity LGB—LGB A	Big LGB—LGB B	DingDong—D	DingDong G—DD G	DingDong R—DD R
Elf—Elf	First LGB—LGB F	Giant LGB—LGB G	Little Golden Book—LGB	LGB Disney—LGB D
LGB Disney New—LGB DN	LGB New—LGB N	Little LGB—LGB L	Tell-A-Tale—TAT	Treasure—T
Wonder—W				

Title	No.	Type
Animals Christmas Eve, The	154*	LGB
Animals Christmas Eve, The	456-09	LGB N
Animals Christmas Eve, The	456-13	LGB N
Animals Christmas Eve, The	456-1	LGB N
Animals Christmas Eve, The	456-41	LGB N
Animals In Mother Goose	2474	TAT
Animals In The Woods	10271	LGB B
Animals Of Farmer Jones, The	11	LGB
Animals Of Farmer Jones, The	211	LGB
Animals Of Farmer Jones, The	282	LGB
Animals of Farmer Jones, The	13	LGB L
Animals Of Farmer Jones, The	200-42	LGB N
Animals Of Farmer Jones, The	200-52	LGB N
Animals Of Farmer Jones, The	200-87	LGB N
Animals Of Farmer Jones, The	200-92	LGB N
Animals Of Farmer Jones, The	303-23	LGB N
Animals On The Farm	573	LGB
Animals On The Farm	200-41	LGB N
Animals On The Farm	203-33	LGB N
Animals On The Farm	203-3	LGB N
Animals On The Farm	205-55	LGB N
Animals On The Farm	205-92	LGB N
Animals Party, The	790	W
Animals' Merry Christmas, The	329	LGB
Animals' Merry Christmas, The	10290	LGB B
Animals' Playground, The	825	W
Annabelle's Wish	98842	LGB N
Annie Oakley	221	LGB
Annie Oakley Sharpshooter	275	LGB
Another Monster At The End Of This Book	98769-01	LGB N
Are Dogs Better Than Cats?	565	W
Aren't You Glad	489	LGB
Aristocats, The	105-67	LGB DN
Aristocats, The - A Counting Book	2516	TAT
Aristocats, The	D122	LGB D
Around The World Cutout Book	826	W
Arthur's Good Manners	305-58	LGB N
Arthur's Good Manners	305-66	LGB N
Astronut And The Flying Bus	853	W
Babar And Father Christmas	592	W
Babar The King	602	W
Babes In Toyland	D 97	LGB D
Baby Animal Friends	608	W
Baby Animals	274	LGB
Baby Animals	517	LGB
Baby Animals On The Farm		LGB F
Baby Animals	204-2	LGB N
Baby Animals	304-57	LGB N
Baby Animals	39	LGB L
Baby Brown Bear's Big Bellyache	304-64	LGB N
Baby Bunny, The	548	W
Baby Chipmunk, The	208	DD R
Baby Dear	466	LGB
Baby Dear	306-42	LGB N
Baby Dear	306-52	LGB N
Baby Dear	306-67	LGB N
Baby Dear	309-34	LGB N
Baby Elephant, The	541	W
Baby Farm Animals	333	LGB
Baby Farm Animals	464	LGB
Baby Farm Animals	12	LGB L
Baby Farm Animals	200-56	LGB N
Baby Farm Animals	200-66	LGB N
Baby Farm Animals	203-2	LGB N
Baby Farm Animals	203-32	LGB N
Baby Farm Animals	309-46	LGB N
Baby Fonzie Visits The Doctor	111-89	LGB N
Baby Goes Around The Block	2493	TAT
Baby Huey	787	W
Baby Jesus Stamps	A 12	LGB A
Baby Jesus, The	8556	Elf
Baby Listens	383	LGB
Baby Looks	404	LGB
Baby Mickey Plays Follow-The-Leader		LGB F
Baby Mickey's Book Of Shapes		LGB F
Baby Mickey's Book Of Sounds		LGB F
Baby Moses	917	TAT
Baby Raccoon	797	W
Baby Sister	306-55	LGB N
Baby Sister	8443	Elf
Baby Sister	8663	Elf
Baby Susan's Chicken	546	W
Baby's Birthday	365	LGB
Baby's Book	10	LGB
Baby's Christmas	35	LGB L
Baby's Christmas	460-08	LGB N
Baby's Christmas	460-12	LGB N
Baby's Christmas	98785-01	LGB N
Baby's Day	663	W
Baby's Day	859	T
Baby's Day Out	113-01	LGB N
Baby's First Book	358	LGB
Baby's First Book	606	W
Baby's First Book	2422	TAT
Baby's First Book		LGB F
Baby's First Christmas	368	LGB
Baby's First Christmas	738	W
Baby's First Christmas	876	W
Baby's House	80	LGB
Baby's Mother Goose	303	LGB
Baby's Mother Goose	422	LGB
Bambi & The Butterfly		LGB F
Bambi - Friends Of The Forest	101-59	LGB DN
Bambi - Friends Of The Forest	101-50	LGB DN
Bambi - Friends Of The Forest	101-62	LGB DN
Bambi - Friends Of The Forest	106-22	LGB DN
Bambi - Friends Of The Forest	106-42	LGB DN
Bambi - Friends Of The Forest	107-46	LGB DN
Bambi - Friends Of The Forest	107-56	LGB DN
Bambi Friends Of The Forest	D132	LGB D
Bambi's Children	544	W
Bambi	105-9	LGB DN
Bambi	106-1	LGB DN
Bambi	106-21	LGB DN
Bambi	106-41	LGB DN
Bambi	106-60	LGB DN
Bambi	106-61	LGB DN
Bambi	106-9	LGB DN
Bambi	109-09	LGB DN
Bambi	2548	TAT
Bambi	98071-01	LGB DN
Bambi	D 7	LGB D
Bambi	D 90	LGB D
Bamm-Bamm	540	LGB
Bananas in Pajamas		LGB F
Barbie - The Baby Sitter	849	W
Barbie	125*	LGB
Barbie And Skipper Go Camping	2489	TAT
Barbie And The Scavenger Hunt	107-96	LGB N
Barbie On Skates	2450-01	TAT
Barbie, In The Spotlight	98862-00	LGB N
101 Dalmations 'Bark If You Love Santa'	69	LGB L
Barney Sharing Is Caring	98790	LGB N
Barney's Sand Castle		LGB F
Bartholomew The Beaver	8643	Elf
Bartholomew The Beaver	471	Elf
Bartholomew The Beaver	597	Elf
Bartholomew The Beaver	8423	Elf
Bartholomew The Beaver	8643	Elf
Batter Up!	211-68	LGB N
Be Kind To Animals!	10285	LGB B
Be Nice!		LGB F
Beach Day	208-57	LGB N
Beany And Cecil Captured For The Zoo	2551	TAT
Beany And His Magic Set	904	TAT
Beany Goes To Sea	537	LGB
Bear Country	2554	TAT
Bear County	2612	TAT
Bear In The Boat, The	397	LGB
Bears' New Baby, The	306-57	LGB N
Beauty And The Beast	104-65	LGB DN
Beauty And The Beast	2455-59	TAT
Beauty and the Beast	53	LGB L
Beaver Valley	2553	TAT
Beaver Valley	2612	TAT
Bedknobs & Broomsticks	D 93	LGB D
Bedknobs And Broomsticks - A Visit To Naboombu	2541	TAT
Bedtime Book, The	2475-32	TAT
Bedtime Stories	2	LGB
Bedtime Stories	507	W
Bedtime Stories	507	W
Bedtime Stories	507	W
Bedtime Stories	239	LGB
Bedtime Stories	364	LGB
Bedtime Stories	499	Elf
Bedtime Stories	507	W
Bedtime Stories	538	LGB
Bedtime Stories	595	Elf
Bedtime Stories	8355	Elf
Bedtime Stories	8595	Elf
Beloved Son, The	2518	TAT
Beloved Son, The	825	TAT
Ben And Me	D 37	LGB D
Benjamine Brownie and the Talking Doll	2516	TAT
Benji The Detective	2640	TAT
Benji Fastest Dog In The West	111-36	LGB N
Benji Fastest Dog In The West	111-46	LGB N
Benji Fastest Dog In The West	111-6	LGB N
Benji, Fastest Dog In The West	165*	LGB
Benny The Bus	846	TAT
Bert's Hall Of Great Inventions	321*	LGB

Title	No.	Code
Bertram And The Ticklish Rhinoceros	430	Elf
Berts Hall Of Great Inventions	109-23	LGB N
Berts Hall Of Great Inventions	109-3	LGB N
Best Balloon Ride Ever	208-68	LGB N
Best Christmas Eve!, The	98815	LGB N
Best Friends	209-46	LGB N
Best Little Word Book Ever!	312-01	LGB N
Best Little Word Book Ever!	312-13	LGB N
Best Nickname, The	10265	LGB B
Best Of All, A Story About The Farm	170*	LGB
Best Of All, A Story About The Farm	203-4	LGB N
Best Surprise Of All	2601	TAT
Best Surprise Of All	2521	TAT
Best Thanksgiving Day, The	96009-00	LGB DN
Betsy Mc Call	559	LGB
Bettina The Ballerina	211-69	LGB N
Beware Of The Dog	2553	TAT
Bialosky And The Big ParadeMystery	10262	LGB B
Bialosky's Special Picnic	204-55	LGB N
Bible Stories From The Old Testament	153*	LGB
Bible Stories From The Old Testament	409-1	LGB N
Bible Stories From The Old Testament	409-2	LGB N
Bible Stories Of Boys And Girls	174	LGB
Bible Stories Of Boys And Girls	401-1	LGB N
Bible Stories Of Boys And Girls	404-2	LGB N
Bible Stories: Old Testament	491	Elf
Bible Stories: Old Testament	8613	Elf
Bible Treasures	643	W
Big Albert Moves In	2533	TAT
Big And Little	883	T
Big And Little Are Not The Same	2474-33	TAT
Big Bark, The	2510	TAT
Big Bird Brings Spring To Sesame Street	108-57	LGB N
Big Bird Brings Spring To Sesame Street	108-63	LGB N
Big Bird Follows The Signs	2452-4	TAT
Big Bird Meets Santa Claus	89914-01	LGB N
Big Bird Visits Navajo Country	108-68	LGB N
Big Bird's Baby Book	98865-00	LGB N
Big Bird's Busy Day	26	LGB L
Big Bird's Busy Day	LGB F	
Big Bird's Day On The Farm	107-61	LGB N
Big Bird's Day On The Farm	109-58	LGB N
Big Bird's Day On The Farm	109-65	LGB N
Big Bird's Day On The Farm	109-68	LGB N
Big Bird's Day On The Farm	200-50	LGB N
Big Bird's Red Book	157*	LGB
Big Bird's Red Book	108-22	LGB N
Big Bird's Red Book	108-2	LGB N
Big Bird's Red Book	108-32	LGB N
Big Bird's Red Book	108-42	LGB N
Big Bird's Red Book	108-52	LGB N
Big Bird's Red Book	108-54	LGB N
Big Bird's Red Book	108-55	LGB N
Big Bird's Ticklish Christmas	98829-01	LGB N
Big Birds Busy Day	LGB F	
Big Brown Bear, The	89	LGB
Big Brown Bear, The	335	LGB
Big Brown Bear, The	304-41	LGB N
Big Brown Bear, The	304-51	LGB N
Big Cheese Caper, The	105-78	LGB DN
Big Coal Truck, The	203	DD R
Big Elephant, The	206-51	LGB N
Big Enough Helper, The	152*	LGB
Big Enough Helper, The	204-41	LGB N
Big Enough Helper, The	208-5	LGB N
Big Game Hunter, The	2507	TAT
Big Game Hunter, The	869	TAT
Big Joke, The	628	W
Big Little Book Of Planets, The	10279	LGB B
Big Little Book, The	482	LGB
Big Little Golden Book Of Funny Poems	10276	LGB B
Big Little Golden Book Of Knock-Knocks, The	10275	LGB B
Big Little Kitty	2525	TAT
Big Little Kitty	942	TAT
Big Red Pajama Wagon, The	840	TAT
Big Red	D102	LGB D
Big Splash, The	107-86	LGB N
Big Splash, The	107-94	LGB N
Big Whistle, The	2522	TAT
Big-Little Dinosaur, The	731	W
Big-Little Dinosaur, The	731	W
Biggest, Most Beautiful Christmas Tree, The	459-08	LGB N
Biggest, Most Beautiful Christmas Tree, The	459-10	LGB N
Biggest, Most Beautiful Christmas Tree, The	459-8	LGB N
Bill's Birthday Surprise	966	TAT
Billy And His Steam Roller	557	W
Billy Bunnyscoot - The Lost Bunny	888	TAT
Billy Whiskers' Twins	538	Elf
Billy Whiskers' Twins	8333	Elf
Billy Whiskers' Twins	8588	Elf
Billy's Treasure	8560	Elf
Bingity-Bangity School, Bus The	550	W
Bingity-Bangity School Bus, The	550	W
Bingo	2560	TAT
Bingo	2576	TAT
Bird Stamps	A8	LGB A
Birds	184*	LGB
Birds Of All Kinds	380	LGB
Birds	202-1	LGB N
Birds	202-31	LGB N
Birds	309-55	LGB N
Birds	5011	LGB G
Bisketts In Double Trouble	107-47	LGB N
Bisketts In Double Trouble	111-49	LGB N
Black Beauty	595	W
Black Caldron Taran Finds A Friend, The	105-54	LGB DN
Black Hole, The	501*	LGB
Blondie's Family Cookie, Alexander, And Dog, Elmer	666	W
Blondies Family	887	T
Blow, Wind, Blow	740	W
Blowaway Hat, The	554	W
Blue Barry Bear Counts From 1 To 20	203-59	LGB N
Blue Barry Bear Counts From 1 To 20	47	LGB L
Blue Book Of Fairy Tales, The	374	LGB
Blue Book Of Fairy Tales, The	211-60	LGB N
Boats	125	LGB
Boats	339	LGB
Boats	501	LGB
Bobby And His Airplanes	69	LGB
Bobby The Dog	440	LGB
Bongo	D 9	LGB D
Bongo	D 62	LGB D
Boo-o-s On First	107-85	LGB N
Book Of God's Gifts, A	112*	LGB
Bootsy	741	W
Bouncy Baby Bunny Finds His Bed, The	129*	LGB
Bow Wow! Meow! A First Book Of Sounds	523	LGB
Bow Wow! Meow! A First Book Of Sounds	207-33	LGB N
Box Of Important Things, The	2510	TAT
Boy Who Wanted To Be A Fish, The	553	W
Boy Who Wouldn't Eat His Breakfast, The	815	W
Boy With A Drum, The	588	LGB
Boy With A Drum, The	211-41	LGB N
Boy With A Drum, The	211-43	LGB N
Boy With A Drum, The	211-53	LGB N
Boy With A Drum, The	311-35	LGB N
Boy With A Drum, The	311-5	LGB N
Boys Friend, A	916	TAT
Bozo And The Hide'n' Seek Elephant	598	LGB
Bozo Finds A Friend	485	LGB
Bozo The Clown	446	LGB
Bozo The Clown: King Of The Ring	2552	TAT
Brave Cowboy Bill	93	LGB
Brave Eagle	294	LGB
Brave Firemen, The	563	W
Brave Little Duck, The	777	W
Brave Little Duck, The	854	T
Brave Little Steam Shovel, The	555	W
Brave Little Steam Shovel, The	555	W
Brave Little Tailor, The	178	LGB
Bravest Of All	402	LGB
Breezy -The Air Minded Pigeon	870	TAT
Bremen-Town Musicians, The	2610	TAT
Broken Arrow	299	LGB
Bronto The Dinosaur	8575	Elf
Brown Puppy And A Falling Star, A	2560	TAT
Brownie Scouts	409	LGB
Buck Rogers And The Children Of Hopetown	500*	LGB
Buddy, The Little Taxie	456	Elf
Buddy, The Little Taxie	564	Elf
Buddy, The Little Taxie	8351	Elf
Buddy, The Little Taxie	8736	Elf
Buffalo Bill, Jr.	254	LGB
Buffy And The New Girl	2526	TAT
Bugle, A Puppy In Old Yorktown	1027	Elf
Bugle, A Puppy In Old Yorktown	8618	Elf
Bugs Bunny	72	LGB
Bugs Bunny	312	LGB
Bugs Bunny	475	LGB
Bugs Bunny And The Health Hog	10250	LGB B
Bugs Bunny And The Health Hog	110-60	LGB N
Bugs Bunny And The Health Hog	110-77	LGB N
Bugs Bunny And The Indians	120	LGB

Title	Number	Code
Chipmunk's Merry Christmas, The	375	LGB
Chitter Chatter	889	TAT
Chitty-Chitty Bang-Bang	581	LGB
Choo Choo Train,The	718	W
Choo-Choo, The Little Switch Engine	485	Elf
Choo-Choo, The Little Switch Engine	1034	Elf
Choo-Choo, The Little Switch Engine	8394	Elf
Choo-Choo, The Little Switch Engine	8621	Elf
Christmas A B C	478	LGB
Christmas Bunny	450-13	LGB N
Christmas Carols	26	LGB
Christmas Carols	595	LGB
Christmas Carols	469-00	LGB N
Christmas Carols	469	LGB N
Christmas Donkey, The	460-09	LGB N
Christmas Donkey, The	460-41	LGB N
Christmas Donkey, The	460-9	LGB N
Christmas Favorites	869	W
Christmas In Song And Story	586	W
Christmas In Song And Story	586	W
Christmas In The Country	95	LGB
Christmas Is Coming	593	W
Christmas Manger, The	176	LGB
Christmas Mice	LGB F	
Christmas Pageant, The	LGB F	
Christmas Pageant	45	LGB L
Christmas Puppy, The	585	W
Christmas Sled, The	2487-1	TAT
Christmas Story, The	158	LGB
Christmas Story, The	36	LGB L
Christmas Story, The	456-08	LGB N
Christmas Story, The	456-11	LGB N
Christmas Story, The	456-15	LGB N
Christmas Story, The	456-42	LGB N
Christmas Story, The	456-8	LGB N
Christmas Story, The	461-31	LGB N
Christmas Tree That Grew, The	458-02	LGB N
Christmas Tree That Grew, The	458-1	LGB N
Christopher And The Columbus	103	LGB
Christopher's Hoppy Day	2601	TAT
Chritopher John's Fuzzy Mittens	2672	TAT
Churkendoose, The	832	W
Churkendoose, The	547	W
Churkendoose, The	832	W
Cinderella	660	W
Cinderella	A 36	LGB A
Cinderella	103-68	LGB DN
Cinderella	551	Elf
Cinderella	660	W
Cinderella	879	T
Cinderella's Friends	D 17	LGB D
Cinderella's Friends	D 58	LGB D
Cinderella's Friends	D115	LGB D
Cinderella	103-23	LGB DN
Cinderella	103-33	LGB DN
Cinderella	103-3	LGB DN
Cinderella	103-43	LGB DN
Cinderella	103-51	LGB DN
Cinderella	103-57	LGB DN
Cinderella	103-65	LGB DN
Cinderella	2427-2	TAT
Cinderella	2604	TAT
Cinderella	8644	Elf
Cinderella	964	TAT
Cinderella	D 13	LGB D
Cinderella	D 59	LGB D
Cinderella	D114	LGB D
Cinderella		TAT
Cindy Bear	442	LGB
Cinnamon Bear, The	2674	TAT
Circus Abc	222	LGB
Circus Abc	2505	TAT
Circus Alphabet	2563	TAT
Circus Boy	290	LGB
Circus Boy And Captain Jack	2608	TAT
Circus Is In Town, The	168*	LGB
Circus Is In Town, The	201-34	LGB N
Circus Is In Town, The	201-4	LGB N
Circus Is In Town, The	203-43	LGB N
Circus Is In Town, The	203-53	LGB N
Circus Mouse	2466-40	TAT
Circus Time	31	LGB
Circus Time	A 2	LGB A
Circus Train,The	890	TAT
City Boy And The Country Horse,The	850	T
City Boy, Country Boy	810	W
Cleo	287	LGB
Clip Clop	2492	TAT
Clown Coloring Book	A5	LGB A
Clue Club The Case Of The Missing Racehorse	HANNA18	Elf
Clyde Crashcup And Leonardo	837	W
Cold Blooded Penguin, The	D2	LGB D
Color Kittens	86	LGB
Color Kittens	86P	LGB
Color Kittens	436	LGB
Color Kittens, The	202-28	LGB N
Color Kittens, The	202-38	LGB N
Color Kittens, The	202-66	LGB N
Color Kittens, The	205-41	LGB N
Colorful Mouse, The	211-71	LGB N
Colorful Mouse, The	46	LGB L
Colors	A 28	LGB A
Colors Are Nice	4 96	LGB
Colors Are Nice	207-1	LGB N
Colors Are Nice	207-21	LGB N
Colors Are Nice	207-31	LGB N
Columbus, The Exploring Burro	826	TAT
Come And See The Rainbow	43	W
Come Play At Home!	LGB F	
Come Play At The Park!	LGB F	
Come Play House	44	LGB
Come Visit My Ranch	536	W
Cookie Monster And The Cookie Tree	159*	LGB
Cookie Monster And The Cookie Tree	109-2	LGB N
Cookie Monster And The Cookie Tree	109-32	LGB N
Cookie Monster And The Cookie Tree	109-42	LGB N
Cookie Monster And The Cookie Tree	109-52	LGB N
Cookie Monster And The Cookie Tree	109-53	LGB N
Cookie Monster And The Cookie Tree	109-57	LGB N
Cookie Monster's Book Of Cookie Shapes	2402-8	TAT
Copy-Kitten	584	Elf
Copy-Kitten	8370	Elf
Copy-Kitten	8689	Elf
Copycat Colt, The	545	W
Corey Baker Of Julia And His Show And Tell	2506	TAT
Corkey's Hic-Cup	503	LGB
Corky	486	LGB
Count All The Way To Sesame Street	203-56	LGB N
Count All The Way To Sesame Street	203-57	LGB N
Count All The Way To Sesame Street	203-60	LGB N
Count The Baby Animals	702	W
Count To Ten		LGB F
Count To Ten	A 16	LGB A
Count To Ten	A 43	LGB A
Count to Ten	62	LGB L
Count's Poem, The	2402	TAT
Count's Poems, The		LGB F
Counting Book, The	692	W
Counting Rhymes	12	LGB
Counting Rhymes	257	LGB
Counting Rhymes	361	LGB
Counting Rhymes	311-1	LGB N
Counting Rhymes	311-31	LGB N
Country Mouse And The City Mouse		LGB F
County Mouse And The CityMouse, The	426	LGB
County Mouse And The CityMouse, The	207-55	LGB N
Cousin Matilda And The Foolish Wolf	2530	TAT
Cow And The Elephant, The	304-48	LGB N
Cow And The Elephant, The	304-58	LGB N
Cow In The Silo, The	534	W
Cow Went Over The Mountain, The	516	LGB
Cow Went Over The Mountain, The	304-10	LGB N
Cow Went Over The Mountain, The	304-45	LGB N
Cowardly Lion, The	642	W
Cowboy Abc	389	LGB
Cowboy Eddie	8645	Elf
Cowboy Eddie	437	Elf
Cowboy Eddie	599	Elf
Cowboy Eddie	8418	Elf
Cowboy Eddie	8645	Elf
Cowboy Mickey	100-63	LGB DN
Cowboy Mickey	100-70	LGB DN
Cowboy Stamps	A 11	LGB A
Cowboys And Indians	5019	LGB G
Cowboys	1004	Elf
Cowboys	8341	Elf
Cowboys	8666	Elf
Cozy Little Farm, The	749	W
Cozy Little Farm, The	502	W
Cozy Little Farm, The	749	W
Cozy Little Farm,The	878	T
Cradle Rhymes	894	TAT
Creation Story, The		LGB F
Cristmas Mice	50	LGB L
Crosspatch	8442	Elf
Crosspatch	8675	Elf
Crusader Rabbit	698	W
Crybaby Calf	547	Elf
Crybaby Calf	8426	Elf
Crybaby Calf	8606	Elf
Cub Scouts	5022	LGB G
Curious Little Kitten Around The House	7	LGB L
Curious Little Kitten Around The House	206-57	LGB N
Curious Little Kitten Around The House	206-63	LGB N
Curious Little Kitten's First Christmas, The	51	LGB L
Curious Little Kittens First Christmas, The		LGB F
Custume Party, The	800	W
Daddies All About The Work They Do	201-69	LGB N

Title	No.	Series
Dumbo's Book Of Colors		LGB F
Dumbo	104-33	LGB DN
Dumbo	104-3	LGB DN
Dumbo	104-43	LGB DN
Dumbo	104-53	LGB DN
Dumbo	104-59	LGB DN
Dumbo	104-67	LGB DN
Dumbo	D 3	LGB D
Dynomutt And The Pie In The Sky Caper	HANNA02	Elf
Early One Morning	8436	Elf
Early One Morning	8656	Elf
Eeyore, You're The Best!	98765-01	LGB DN
Elephant's Child,The	508	Elf
Elmo Loves You	98846-00	LGB N
Elmo Says...		LGB F
Elmo's 12 Days Of Christmas	98787-01	LGB N
Elmo's New Puppy	98897-00	LGB N
Elmo's Tricky Tongue Twister	98871-00	LGB N
Eloise And The Old Blue Truck	2454	TAT
Eloise Wilkin's Mother Goose	589	LGB
Eloise Wilkin's Mother Goose	300-10	LGB N
Eloise Wilkin's Mother Goose	300-22	LGB N
Eloise Wilkin's Mother Goose	300-2	LGB N
Eloise Wilkin's Mother Goose	300-32	LGB N
Eloise Wilkin's Mother Goose	300-43	LGB N
Eloise Wilkin's Mother Goose	300-60	LGB N
Eloise Wilkin's Mother Goose	307-67	LGB N
Elves And The Shoemaker, The	207-64	LGB N
Elves And The Shoemaker, The	2496	TAT
Elves And The Shoemaker, The	2561	TAT
Elves And The Shoemaker, The	307-56	LGB N
Elves And The Shoemaker, The	307-61	LGB N
Elves And The Shoemaker, The	8315	Elf
Elves And The Shoemaker, The	8682	Elf
Emerald City Of Oz	151	LGB
Emmett Kelly In Wille The Clown	573	Elf
Emperor's New Clothes, The	8567	Elf
Emperor's New Cloths, The	207-66	LGB N
Enchanted Christmas,The	89928-01	LGB DN
Enchanted Egg, The	577	Elf
Enchanted Egg, The	8407	Elf
Enchanted Egg, The	8640	Elf
Ernie The Cave King And Sherlock The Smart Person	2604	TAT
Ernie's Telephone Call	2452-34	TAT
Ernie's Work Of Art	109-25	LGB N
Ernie's Work Of Art	109-5	LGB N
Ernies Work Of Art	109-45	LGB N
Especially From Thomas	2543	TAT
Especially From Thomas	2527	TAT
Evening Walk, The	2462-43	TAT
Exploring Space	342	LGB
Fairy Princess, The	162*	LGB
Fairy Princess, The	111-33	LGB N
Fairy Princess, The	111-48	LGB N
Fairy Tales:	5020	LGB G
Family Circus Daddy's Surprise Day	111-29	LGB N
Famous Fairy Tales	505	W
Famous Fairy Tales	505	W
Fanny Forgot	862	TAT
Farm Abc	2468	TAT
Farm Animals	467	Elf
Farm Animals	514	Elf
Farm Animals	2464-50	TAT
Farm Animals	8337	Elf
Farm Animals	8735	Elf
Farm Babies	539	Elf
Farm For Andy, A	448	Elf
Farm For Andy, A	596	Elf
Farm For Andy, A	8358	Elf
Farm For Andy, A	8741	Elf
Farm Friends	8329	Elf
Farm Friends	8719	Elf
Farm Stamps	A 19	LGB A
Farmer In The Dell, The	8578	Elf
Farmer John	838	TAT
Farmyard Friends	272	LGB
Farmyard Friends	429	LGB
Fat Albert And The Cosby Kids Getting It Together	2598	TAT
Favorite Nursery Rhymes	D125	LGB D
Favorite Nursery Tales	106-34	LGB DN
Favorite Nursery Tales	106-44	LGB DN
Favorite Nursery Tales	106-4	LGB DN
Favorite Nursery Tales	106-54	LGB DN
Feelings From A To Z	200-6	LGB N
Felix On Television	904	T
Felix On Telivision	716	W
Felix The Cat	665	W
Felix The Cat	665	W
Felix The Cat	872	T
Find The Way Home	480	Elf
Fire Dog	2412	TAT
Fire Engines	2	LGB L
Fire Engines	382	LGB
Fire Engines To The Rescue	306-58	LGB N
Fire Engines	210-2	LGB N
Fire Engines	210-32	LGB N
Fire Engines	310-46	LGB N
Fire Engines	310-56	LGB N
Fire Engines	310-88	LGB N
Fire Fighters' Counting Book,The	203-45	LGB N
Fire Fighters' Counting Book,The	203-55	LGB N
Fireball X-L5	546	LGB
Fireman & Fire Engine Stamps	A 27	LGB A
First Airplane Ride, A	310-57	LGB N
First Book Of Bible Stories	198	LGB
First Golden Geography	534	LGB
First Little Golden Book Of Fairy Tales, The	9	LGB
First Times	65	LGB L
Fish	5023	LGB G
Five Bedtime Stories	5002	LGB G
Five Busy Bears, The	8404	Elf
Five Busy Bears, The	8629	Elf
Five Jolly Brothers, The	552	W
Five Little Bears	498	Elf
Five Little Bunnies		LGB F
Five Little Finger Playmates	522	W
Five Little Firemen	64	LGB
Five Little Firemen	301	LGB
Fix It Please	32	LGB
Fixit Man, The	917	W
Fixit Man,The	756	W
Fixit Man,The	851	T
Flash Gordon	905	T
Flash Gordon And The Baby Animals	684	W
Flinstones At The Circus, The	2552	TAT
Flintstones, The	450	LGB
Flintstones: Everyone's Egg	927	W
Floating Bananas	208-65	LGB N
Flounder to the Rescue		LGB F
Fluffy And Tuffy The Twin Ducklings	872	TAT
Fluffy Little Lamb	780	W
Fly High	597	LGB
Flying Car, The	D 96	LGB D
Flying Dinosaurs	309-51	LGB N
Flying Dinosaurs	309-52	LGB N
Flying Is Fun	310-53	LGB N
Flying Sunbeam,The	820	TAT
Forest Babies	435	Elf
Forest Babies	546	Elf
Forest Babies	8328	Elf
Forest Babies	8730	Elf
Forest Hotel	350	LGB
Forest Hotel	201-35	LGB N
Forest Hotel	210-5	LGB N
Four Little Kittens	322	LGB
Four Little Kittens	530	LGB
Four Little Kittens	566	Elf
Four Little Kittens	15	LGB L
Four Little Kittens	203-21	LGB N
Four Little Kittens	302-31	LGB N
Four Little Kittens	302-42	LGB N
Four Little Kittens	302-52	LGB N
Four Little Kittens	8336	Elf
Four Little Kittens	8718	Elf
Four Little Puppies	8335	Elf
Four Little Puppies	578	Elf
Four Little Puppies	8335	Elf
Four Little Puppies	8597	Elf
Four Puppies	05	LGB
Four Puppies Who Wanted A Home,The	530	W
Four Puppies Who Wanted A Home,The	530	W
Four Puppies	19	LGB L
Four Puppies	202-4	LGB N
Four Puppies	303-42	LGB N
Four Puppies	303-52	LGB N
Four Seasons, The	108-24	LGB N
Four Seasons, The	108-25	LGB N
Four Seasons, The	108-26	LGB N
Four Seasons, The	108-44	LGB N
Four Seasons, The	108-4	LGB N
Fox Jumped Up One Winters Night, A	300-53	LGB N
Fozzie's Fabulous Easter Parade	98849-00	LGB N
Fozzie's Funnies	111-87	LGB N
Fraidy Cat Kitten,The	542	W
Fraidy Cat	8319	Elf
Fraidy Cat	8662	Elf
Franky, The Fuzzy Goat	820	TAT
Freddy And The Indian	816	W
Freight Train	534	Elf
Freight Train	8414	Elf
Freight Train	8631	Elf
Friendly Beast, The		LGB F
Friendly Book, The	199	LGB
Friendly Book, The	592	LGB
Friendly Book, The	206-34	LGB N
Friendly Book, The	209-41	LGB N
Friendly Book, The	209-9	LGB N
Friendly Bunny,The	209-61	LGB N
Frisker	2660	TAT
Frisky, The Black Colt	699	W
Fritzie Goes Home	103*	LGB
From Tadpoles To Frogs	8550	Elf

Title	No.	Pub.
Land Of The Lost,The Surprise	136*	LGB
Large And Growly Bear, The	510	LGB
Large And Growly Bear, The	304-1	LGB N
Large And Growly Bear, The	304-42	LGB N
Larry The Canary	8322	Elf
Larry The Canary	8685	Elf
Lassie And Her Day In The Sun	307	LGB
Lassie And Her Day In The Sun	301-33	LGB N
Lassie And Her Day In The Sun	301-3	LGB N
Lassie And The Big Cleanup Day	572	LGB
Lassie And The Cub Scout	2503	TAT
Lassie And The Daring Rescue	277	LGB
Lassie And The Fire Fighters	2462	TAT
Lassie And The Kittens	2503	TAT
Lassie And The Lost Explorer	343	LGB
Lassie Come-Home	639	W
Lassie Finds A Friend	2406	TAT
Lassie Shows The Way	255	LGB
Lassie Shows The Way	415	LGB
Lassie's Brave Adventure	2571	TAT
Lassie's Day In The Sun	518	LGB
Lassie's Long Trip	674	W
Lassie:The Busy Morning	2484	TAT
Lazy Fox And Red Hen	2485	TAT
Lazy Fox And Red Hen	2603	TAT
Lazy Jack	8435	Elf
Learning To Count With Twelve Elves	2555	TAT
Leave It To Beaver	347	LGB
Let Me See	2615	TAT
Let's Be Thankful	96022-00	LGB N
Let's Count All The Animals	2407-4	TAT
Let's Count Our Blessing	LGB F	
Let's Fly A Kite, Charlie Brown	111-62	LGB N
Let's Give A Party	752	W
Let's Go All Around The Neighborhood	LGB F	
Let's Go Fishing	764	W
Let's Go Fishing!	10274	LGB B
Let's Go Shopping	33	LGB
Let's Go Shopping	693	W
Let's Go Shopping!	208-58	LGB N
Let's Go To School	691	W
Let's Go To School	691	W
Let's Go To School	893	T
Let's Go To The Airport	98833-01	LGB DN
Let's Go To The Fire Station	98802-01	LGB DN
Let's Go To The Vet	98804-01	LGB DN
Let's Go, Trucks!	185*	LGB
Let's Go, Trucks!	211-1	LGB N
Let's Go, Trucks!	211-31	LGB N
Let's Go, Trucks!	310-42	LGB N
Let's Go, Trucks!	310-52	LGB N
Let's Grow Things Children	8571	Elf
Let's Play	2601	TAT
Let's Play Ball	325	LGB
Let's Play Indians	538	W
Let's Play Nurse And Doctor	686	W
Let's Play Nurse And Doctor	863	T
Let's Play Peek-A-Boo!	LGB F	
Let's Play Peek-A-Boo	LGB F	
Let's Play Train	870	T
Let's Play	907	TAT
Let's Pretend	680	W
Let's Save Money	A 21	LGB A
Let's Take A Ride	673	W
Let's Take A Ride	862	T
Let's Take A Trip In Our Car	890	T
Let's Visit The Dentist	599	LGB
Let's Visit The Farm	876	TAT
Life And Legend Of Wyatt Earp, The	315	LGB
Lily Pig's Book Of Colors	205-58	LGB N
Lily Pig's Book Of Colors	205-65	LGB N
Linda And Her Little Sister	214	LGB
Linusn A Smile For Grouse	2567	TAT
Lion And The Mouse, The	8569	Elf
Lion King, The	107-93	LGB DN
Lion's Haircut, The	2519	TAT
Lion's Paw, The	367	LGB
Lions Mixed-Up Friends	304-62	LGB N
Lippy The Lion And Hardy Har Har	508	LGB
Little Audrey And The Moon Lady	759	W
Little Audrey And The Moon Lady	759	W
Little Ballerina	1003	Elf
Little Ballerina	8390	Elf
Little Ballerina	8614	Elf
Little Bear And The Beautiful Kite	2548	TAT
Little Bear And The Beautiful Kite	2559	TAT
Little Beaver	935	TAT
Little Benny Wanted A Pony	97	LGB
Little Bitty Raindrop	875	TAT
Little Black Sambo	2661	TAT
Little Black Sambo	57	LGB
Little Black Sambo	2661	TAT
Little Black Sambo	812	TAT
Little Bobo And His Blue Jacket	472	Elf
Little Bobo And His Blue Jacket	1026	Elf
Little Bobo And His Blue Jacket	8378	Elf
Little Bobo And His Blue Jacket	8654	Elf
Little Book, The	583	LGB
Little Book, The	209-3	LGB N
Little Boy & The Giant, The	536	LGB
Little Boy Blue And Other Nursery Rhymes	8711	Elf
Little Boy Blue And Other Nursery Rhymes	555	Elf
Little Boy Blue And Other Nursery Rhymes	8366	Elf
Little Boy Blue And Other Nursery Rhymes	8711	Elf
Little Boy In The Forest, The	2553	TAT
Little Boy With A Big Horn	100	LGB
Little Brown Bear	304-60	LGB N
Little Caboose,The	817	TAT
Little Calf That Couldn't Moo, The	LGB F	
Little Campers	8439	Elf
Little Campers	8660	Elf
Little Car That Wanted A Garage, The	573	W
Little Car That Wanted A Garage, The	573	W
Little Christmas Treasure, A	LGB F	
Little Chuff Chuff And Big Stremline	843	TAT
Little Cottontail	414	LGB
Little Cottontail	304-43	LGB N
Little Cottontail	304-73	LGB N
Little Cottontail	304-9	LGB N
Little Cottontail	476-1	LGB N
Little Cottontail	476-21	LGB N
Little Cowboy's Christmas, A	570	W
Little Cowboy's Christmas, A	570	W
Little Crow	113*	LGB
Little Cub Scout	8445	Elf
Little Cub Scout	8665	Elf
Little Dog Who Forgot How ToBark, The	504	W
Little Duck And The New Baby		LGB F
Little Duck Said Quack, Quack,Quack, The	636	W
Little Duck's Moving Day		LGB F
Little Engine That Could, The	48	LGB
Little Engine That Could, The	305-2	LGB N
Little Engine That Laughed, The	729	W
Little Engine That Laughed, The	857	T
Little Eskimo, The	155	LGB
Little Fat Policman, The	91	LGB
Little Folks Mother Goose	863	TAT
Little Friends: Kittens, Puppies,Bunnies	455	Elf
Little Friends: Kittens, Puppies,Bunnies	93	Elf
Little Friends: Kittens, Puppies,Bunnies	8408	Elf
Little Friends: Kittens, Puppies,Bunnies	8737	Elf
Little Garage Man,The	744	W
Little Golashes	68	LGB
Little Golden Abc, The	101	LGB
Little Golden Book A B C	200-1	LGB N
Little Golden Book A B C	202-53	LGB N
Little Golden Book Of Dogs	260	LGB
Little Golden Book Of Dogs, The	131	LGB
Little Golden Book Of Holdays, The	109	LGB
Little Golden Book Of Holidays	209-58	LGB N
Little Golden Book Of Hymns, The	34	LGB
Little Golden Book Of Hymns, The	392	LGB
Little Golden Book Of Hymns, The	211-44	LGB N
Little Golden Book Of Hymns, The	211-57	LGB N
Little Golden Book Of Jokes & Riddles	211-45	LGB N
Little Golden Book Of Jokes & Riddles	211-55	LGB N
Little Golden Book Of Poetry, The	38	LGB
Little Golden Book Of Singing Games, The	40	LGB
Little Golden Book Of Words, The	45	LGB
Little Golden Funny Book, The	74	LGB
Little Golden Mother Goose, The	390	LGB
Little Golden Mother Goose, The	472	LGB
Little Golden Mother		

Title	No.	Code
Little Golden Mother Goose, The	300-1	LGB N
Little Golden Mother Goose, The	300-31	LGB N
Little Golden Paper Dolls, The	113	LGB
Little Golden Paper Dolls, The	280	LGB
Little Golden Picture Dictionary	369	LGB
Little Golden Picture Dictionary	202-41	LGB N
Little Golden Picture Dictionary	202-51	LGB N
Little Golden Picture Dictionary	202-55	LGB N
Little Golden Picture Dictionary	202-67	LGB N
Little Golden Picture Dictionary	205-2	LGB N
Little Golden Picture Dictionary	205-32	LGB N
Little Gray Donkey	206	LGB
Little Gray Rabbit	2651	TAT
Little Hank	883	TAT
Little Henry To The Rescue	2604	TAT
Little Horseman	8347	Elf
Little Horseman	8649	Elf
Little Indian, The	202	LGB
Little Joe's Puppy	2560	TAT
Little John Little	558	W
Little Kittens' Nursery Rhymes	440	Elf
Little Kittens' Nursery Rhymes	8311	Elf
Little Little Dog	8437	Elf
Little Little Dog	8661	Elf
Little Lost Angel	483	Elf
Little Lost Angel	580	Elf
Little Lost Angel	8376	Elf
Little Lost Angel	8680	Elf
Little Lost Kitten	302-56	LGB N
Little Lost Kitten: Story Of Williamsburg	544	Elf
Little Lost Kitten: Story Of Williamsburg	8600	Elf
Little Lost Puppy, The	528	W
Little Lulu Has An Art Show	2532	TAT
Little Lulu Has An Art Show	2622	TAT
Little Lulu	476	LGB
Little Lulu And Her Magic Tricks	203	LGB
Little Lulu And The Birthday Mystery	2502	TAT
Little Lulu Lucky Landlady!	2437	TAT
Little Lulu Uses Her Head	2552	TAT
Little Mailman Of Bayberry Lane, The	458	Elf
Little Mailman Of Bayberry Lane, The	590	Elf
Little Mailman Of Bayberry Lane, The	8361	Elf
Little Mailman Of Bayberry Lane, The	8729	Elf
Little Majorette	8410	Elf
Little Majorette	8605	Elf
Little Man Of Disneyland	D 46	LGB D
Little Mermaid, The ' Ariel's Underwater Adventure'	105-68	LGB DN
Little Mermaid, The ' Ariel's Underwater Adventure'	105-82	LGB DN
Little Mermaid, The	105-79	LGB DN
Little Mermaid, The	105-85	LGB DN
Little Mermaid, The	105-68	LGB DN
Little Miss Muffet And Other Nursery Rhymes	8302	Elf
Little Miss Muffet And Other Nursery Rhymes	556	Elf
Little Miss Muffet And Other Nursery Rhymes	2483	TAT
Little Miss Muffet And Other Nursery Rhymes	8302	Elf
Little Miss Muffet And Other Nursery Rhymes	8709	Elf
Little Mommy	569	LGB
Little Mouse's Book Of Colors	211-71	LGB N
Little Mouse's Book Of Colors	211-74	LGB N
Little Pee Wee Or,Now Open The Box	52	LGB
Little Pee Wee,The Circus Dog Or,Now Open The Box	52	LGB
Little Peter Cottontail	641	W
Little Pond In The Woods	43	LGB
Little Pony, The	806	TAT
Little Puppy Who Would Not Mind His Mother	515	W
Little Puppy Who Would Not Mind His Mother,The	877	T
Little Pussycat	302-51	LGB N
Little Quack And Baby Ducky		LGB F
Little Raccoon Takes Charge	10254	LGB B
Little Raccoon's Nighttime Adventure	10255	LGB B
Little Red Bicycle, The	2543	TAT
Little Red Bicycle, The	2508	TAT
Little Red Bicycle, The	922	TAT
Little Red Caboose That Ran Away	852	T
Little Red Caboose That Ran Away,The	715	W
Little Red Caboose, The	162	LGB
Little Red Caboose, The	319	LGB
Little Red Caboose, The	210-56	LGB N
Little Red Caboose, The	210-61	LGB N
Little Red Caboose, The	210-86	LGB N
Little Red Caboose, The	306-22	LGB N
Little Red Caboose, The	306-2	LGB N
Little Red Caboose, The	306-32	LGB N
Little Red Hen, The	6	LGB
Little Red Hen, The	209	LGB
Little Red Hen, The	296	LGB
Little Red Hen, The	3	LGB L
Little Red Hen, The	438	LGB
Little Red Hen, The	519	LGB
Little Red Hen, The		LGB F
Little Red Hen	2603	TAT
Little Red Riding Hood	42	LGB
Little Red Riding Hood	2670	TAT
Little Red Riding Hood	232*	LGB
Little Red Riding Hood	1037	Elf
Little Red Riding Hood	18	LGB L
Little Red Riding Hood	2461-44	TAT
Little Red Riding Hood	2507	TAT
Little Red Riding Hood	2606	TAT
Little Red Riding Hood	2651	TAT
Little Red Riding Hood	300-65	LGB N
Little Red Riding Hood	307-45	LGB N
Little Red Riding Hood	307-55	LGB N
Little Red Riding Hood	307-59	LGB N
Little Red Riding Hood	307-66	LGB N
Little Red Riding Hood	309-1	LGB N
Little Red Riding Hood	309-21	LGB N
Little Red Riding Hood	309-31	LGB N
Little Red Riding Hood	937	TAT
Little Red Riding-Hood	8419	Elf
Little Red Riding-Hood	8646	Elf
Little Schoolhouse	710	W
Little Schoolhouse	710	W
Little Sister	10256	LGB B
Little Skater	8389	Elf
Little Skater	8610	Elf
Little Squirt The Fire Engine		LGB F
Little Swimmers	8416	Elf
Little Swimmers	8633	Elf
Little Train That Saved The Day, The	571	W
Little Train That Saved The Day, The	571	W
Little Train That Won A Medal, The	512	W
Little Trapper, The	79	LGB
Little Tweet	814	TAT
Little Yip Yip And His Bark	73	LGB
Littlest Angel, The	755	W
Littlest Angel, The	755	W
Littlest Christmas Elf, The	38	LGB L
Littlest Christmas Elf, The	459-00	LGB N
Littlest Christmas Elf, The	459-12	LGB N
Littlest Christmas Tree, The	625	W
Littlest Christmas Tree, The	625	W
Littlest Raccoon, The	457	LGB
Littlest Snowman, The	720	W
Lively Little Rabbit, The	15	LGB
Lively Little Rabbit, The	551	LGB
Lively Little Rabbit	201-44	LGB N
Lively Little Rabbit	481-31	LGB N
Lone Ranger & Tonto, The	297	LGB
Lone Ranger And The GhostHorse, The	2561	TAT
Lone Ranger And The Talking Pony, The	310	LGB
Lone Ranger Desert Storm, The	2622	TAT
Lone Ranger, The	263	LGB
Lonely Pony, The	645	W
Longest Birthday, The	2418-1	TAT
Look For A Rainbow	8558	Elf
Look For Boats	2473-46	TAT
Look For Trucks	2473-25	TAT
Look Who's Here	834	W
Look Who's Here	834	W
Looking In And Other Poems	8568	Elf
Looking Out The Window	217	DD R
Loopy De Loop Odd Jobber'	2611	TAT
Loopy De Loop Goes West	417	LGB
Lord Is My Shephard, The ' The Twenty-Third Psalm'	311-60	LGB N
Lord's Prayer, The (Catholic)	647C	W
Lord's Prayer, The (Protestant)	647P	W
Lost In The Funhouse'	111-68	LGB N
Lost In The Funhouse'	111-79	LGB N
Love Bug, The	D130	LGB D
Love Letters		LGB F
Lucinda, The Little Donkey	465	Elf
Lucinda, The Little Donkey	592	Elf
Lucinda, The Little Donkey	8362	Elf
Lucinda, The Little Donkey	8584	Elf
Lucky Four Leaf Clover	893	TAT
Lucky Mrs. Ticklefeather	122	LGB
Lucky Puppy, The	D 89	LGB D
Lucky Rabbit	221	DD R
Lucky Rabbit	DIN 7	DD G
Ludwid Von Drake	D 98	LGB D
Luno The Soaring Stallion	831	W
Machines	455	LGB
Mad Hatter's Tea Party, The	D 23	LGB D
Madeline	186	LGB
Maggie To The Rescue	2476-39	TAT
Magic Bus, The	516	W
Magic Clothes Basket, The	2544	TAT
Magic Clown, The	876	T

Title	No.	Series
Magic Compass, The	146	LGB
Magic Friend Maker, The	137*	LGB
Magic Next Door, The	106*	LGB
Magic Pot, The	8433	Elf
Magic Wagon, The	222	DD R
Magic Wagon, The	DIN 6	DD G
Magic Word, The	578	W
Magic Zoo - Or How To Tell Time, The	2565	TAT
Magilla Gorilla	547	LGB
Magilla Gorilla And The Super Kite	707	W
Magilla Gorilla Takes A BananaVacation	2552	TAT
Make Way For The Highway	310-55	LGB N
Make Way For The Thruway	439	LGB
Make-Believe Book, The	634	W
Make-Believe Parade, The	520	W
Manni The Donkey	D 75	LGB D
Manuel's Cat	2521	TAT
Many Faces Of Ernie, The	109-34	LGB N
Many Faces Of Ernie, The	109-44	LGB N
Many Faces Of Ernie, The	109-4	LGB N
Many Faces Of Ernie, The	109-54	LGB N
Martha's House		LGB F
Martha's House		LGB F
Marvelous Merry-Go-Round, The	87	LGB
Marvelous Monster	2632	TAT
Mary Poppins, A Jolly Holiday	D112	LGB D
Mary Poppins	2606	TAT
Mary Poppins	D113	LGB D
Matilda, Mac Elroy, And Mary	836	TAT
Maverick	354	LGB
Max Helps Out		LGB F
Me Cookie!	109-69	LGB N
Me Too!	2616	TAT
Meet My Buddy		LGB F
Meet The Bobbsy Twins	623	W
Merry Christmas Book	820	W
Merry Christmas Mr. Snowman	818	W
Merry Christmas Mr. Snowman	818	W
Merry Mailman Around The World	892	T
Merry Mailman, The	865	T
Merry Shipwreck, The	170	LGB
Merton And His Moving Van	2633	TAT
Mickey And The Beanstalk	103-69	LGB DN
Mickey And The Beanstalk	103-59	LGB DN
Mickey And The Beanstalk	103-66	LGB DN
Mickey Mouse - Those Were The Days'	100-61	LGB DN
Mickey Mouse - Those Were The Days'	100-76	LGB DN
Mickey Mouse And Goofy, The Big Bear Scare	100-34	LGB DN
Mickey Mouse And Goofy, The Big Bear Scare	100-44	LGB DN
Mickey Mouse And Goofy, The Big Bear Scare	100-4	LGB DN
Mickey Mouse And Goofy, The Big Bear Scare	100-54	LGB DN
Mickey Mouse And Goofy, The Big Bear Scare	100-73	LGB DN
Mickey Mouse And Goofy, The Big Bear Scare	D138	LGB D
Mickey Mouse And His Space Ship	D 29	LGB D
Mickey Mouse And His Space Ship	D108	LGB D
Mickey Mouse And Pluto Pup	D 32	LGB D
Mickey Mouse And Pluto Pup	D 76	LGB D
Mickey Mouse And The Best Neighbor Contest	D134	LGB D
Mickey Mouse And The Best-Neighbor Contest	100-3	LGB DN
Mickey Mouse And The Best-Neighbor Contest	100-43	LGB DN
Mickey Mouse And The Great Lot Plot	100- 2	LGB DN
Mickey Mouse And The Great Lot Plot	100-32	LGB DN
Mickey Mouse And The Great Lot Plot	100-42	LGB DN
Mickey Mouse And The Great Lot Plot	100-66	LGB DN
Mickey Mouse And The Great Lot Plot	100-74	LGB DN
Mickey Mouse And The Great Lot Plot	D129	LGB D
Mickey Mouse And The Lucky Goose Chase	2454-45	TAT
Mickey Mouse And The Missing Mouseketeers	105-21	LGB DN
Mickey Mouse And The Missing Mouseketeers	105-53	LGB DN
Mickey Mouse And The Missing Mouseketeers	D 57	LGB D
Mickey Mouse And The Mouseketeers - The Animal Guessing	2631	TAT
Mickey Mouse And The Mouseketeers Ghost Town Adventure	105-21	LGB DN
Mickey Mouse And The Mouseketeers Ghost Town Adventure	105-2	LGB DN
Mickey Mouse And The Mouseketeers Ghost Town Adventure	105-31	LGB DN
Mickey Mouse And The Mouseketeers Ghost Town Adventure	105-42	LGB DN
Mickey Mouse And The Mouseketeers Ghost Town Adventure	D135	LGB D
Mickey Mouse And The Pet Show	2454-2	TAT
Mickey Mouse And The Really Neat Robot	2475	TAT
Mickey Mouse And The Second Wish	2418	TAT
Mickey Mouse And The World's Friendliest Monster	2424-2	TAT
Mickey Mouse Club Stamp Book	A 10	LGB A
Mickey Mouse Club Stamp Book	D 58	LGB D
Mickey Mouse Flies The Christmas Mail	D 53	LGB D
Mickey Mouse Goes Christmas Shopping	D 33	LGB D
Mickey Mouse Heads For The Sky	100-60	LGB DN
Mickey Mouse Heads For The Sky	100-68	LGB DN
Mickey Mouse's Picnic	100- 5	LGB DN
Mickey Mouse's Picnic	100-55	LGB DN
Mickey Mouse's Picnic	100-62	LGB DN
Mickey Mouse's Picnic	100-69	LGB DN
Mickey Mouse's Picnic	D 15	LGB D
Mickey Mouse, The Kitten Sitters	100-21	LGB DN
Mickey Mouse, The Kitten Sitters	100-31	LGB DN
Mickey Mouse, The Kitten Sitters	100-41	LGB DN
Mickey Mouse, The Kitten Sitters	100-51	LGB DN
Mickey Mouse, The Kitten Sitters	100-52	LGB DN
Mickey Mouse, The Kitten Sitters	D133	LGB D
Mickey's Christmas Carol	459-09	LGB DN
Mickey's Christmas Carol	459-11	LGB DN
Mickey's Christmas Carol	459-42	LGB DN
Mickey's Christmas Carol	459-9	LGB DN
Mickey's Christmas Carol	98789-01	LGB DN
Mickey's Walt Disney World Adventure	98842-00	LGB DN
Mighty Mouse	860	T
Mighty Mouse And The Scarecrow	678	W
Mighty Mouse And The Scared Scarecrow	884	T
Mighty Mouse To The Rescue	717	W
Mighty Mouse-Dinky Learns To Fly	677	W
Mighty Mouse-Santa's Helper	896	T
Mighty Mouse-Santas Helper	662	W
Mighty Mouse: Dinky Learns To Fly	866	T
Mike And Melissa	A 31	LGB A
Mimi The Merry-Go-Round Cat	2467	TAT
Minnie's Slumber Party	100-65	LGB DN
Minnie's Slumber Party	100-78	LGB DN
Minnies Slumber Party	100-71	LGB DN
Minute-And-A-Half-Man	758	W
Miss Piggy -Queen Of Hearts	98854-00	LGB N
Missing Wedding Dress Featuring Barbie, The	107-63	LGB N
Mister Dog	128	LGB
Mister Dog	204-27	LGB N
Mister Dog	303-41	LGB N
Mister Dog	303-51	LGB N
Mister Magoo	708	W
Mister Rogers Neighborhood Everyone Is Special	2599	TAT
Misty Makes A Movie	8655	Elf
Misty The Wonder Pony	536	Elf
Misty The Wonder Pony	8628	Elf
Mommies All About The Work The Do	98811-01	LGB N
Mommy Cat And Her Kittens	8317	Elf
Mommy Cat And Her Kittens	8678	Elf
Monkey See, Monkey Do	521	W
Monster At The End Of This Book, The	316*	LGB
Monster At The End Of This Book, The	108-47	LGB N
Monster At The End Of This Book, The	108-48	LGB N
Monster At The End Of This Book, The	108-53	LGB N
Monster At The End Of This Book, The	109-1	LGB N
Monster At The End Of This Book, The	109-31	LGB N
Monster At The End Of This Book, The	109-41	LGB N
Monsters Come In Many Colors!	2452-39	TAT
Monsters Come in Many Colors	66	LGB L
Monsters' Picnic, The	109-59	LGB N
Moonymouse	1021	Elf
Moonymouse	8400	Elf

Title	No.	Line
Moonymouse	8639	Elf
Moppets' Surprise Party, The	794	W
More Mother Goose Rhymes	317	LGB
More The Merrier, The	2523	TAT
Morning Noises	795	W
Most Beautiful Tree In The World, The	653	W
Mother Goose	4	LGB
Mother Goose	424	Elf
Mother Goose	8300	Elf
Mother Goose	106-55	LGB DN
Mother Goose	240	LGB
Mother Goose	283	LGB
Mother Goose	424	Elf
Mother Goose	501	W
Mother Goose In The City	336*	LGB
Mother Goose In The City	200-23	LGB N
Mother Goose In The City	300-3	LGB N
Mother Goose On The Farm	2464-44	TAT
Mother Goose On The Farm	2587	TAT
Mother Goose Rhymes	108-69	LGB N
Mother Goose Rhymes	2464-36	TAT
Mother Goose Rhymes	5016	LGB G
Mother Goose	1028	Elf
Mother Goose	106-35	LGB DN
Mother Goose	106-45	LGB DN
Mother Goose	106-61	LGB DN
Mother Goose	106-62	LGB DN
Mother Goose	2417	TAT
Mother Goose	2511	TAT
Mother Goose	2572	TAT
Mother Goose	5007	LGB G
Mother Goose	8300	Elf
Mother Goose	8647	Elf
Mother Goose	8723	Elf
Mother Goose	925	TAT
Mother Goose	D 36	LGB D
Mother Goose	D 51	LGB D
Mother Goose	D 79	LGB D
Mouseketeers Tryout Time, The	2649	TAT
Moving Day	209-57	LGB N
Moving Day	588	Elf
Mr. Bear Squash-You-All-Flat	523	W
Mr. Bear's House	475	Elf
Mr. Bear's House	511	Elf
Mr. Bear's House	8349	Elf
Mr. Bear's House	8707	Elf
Mr. Bears Birthday	204-26	LGB N
Mr. Bell's Fixit Shop	204-42	LGB N
Mr. Bell's Fixit Shop	204-52	LGB N
Mr. Bell's Fixit Shop	210-34	LGB N
Mr. Ed	483	LGB
Mr. Fumble's Coffeeshop Disaster	208-67	LGB N
Mr. Grabbit	2526	TAT
Mr. Grabbit	816	TAT
Mr. Jolly	868	TAT
Mr. Meyer's Cow	DIN 2	DD G
Mr. Mogg's Dogs	958	TAT
Mr. Myer's Cow	220	DD R
Mr. Noah And His Family	49	LGB
Mr. Puffer Bill Train Engineer	563	LGB
Mr. Punnymoon's Train	8632	Elf
Mr. Punnymoon's Train	449	Elf
Mr. Punnymoon's Train	557	Elf
Mr. Punnymoon's Train	8415	Elf
Mr. Punnymoon's Train	8632	Elf
Mr. Wigg's Birthday Party	140	LGB
Mr. Wishing Went Fishing	584	W
Mr. Wizrd's Junior Science Show	559	Elf
Mr.Rogers Neighborhood 'Henreitta Meets Someone New'	133*	LGB
Mrs. Brisby And The Magic Stone	110-38	LGB N
Mrs. Goose's Green Trailer	633	W
Muffin Mouse On The Go		LGB F
Muggins Becomes A Hero	8448	Elf
Muggins Becomes A Hero	8702	Elf
Muggins Big Balloon	8447	Elf
Muggins Big Balloon	8701	Elf
Muggins Mouse	8444	Elf
Muggins Mouse	8673	Elf
Muggins Takes Off	8700	Elf
Muggsy,The Make-Believe Puppy	537	Elf
Mulan	98861-00	LGB DN
Mumbly To The Rescue	HANNA09	Elf
Muppet -Treasure Island	111-88	LGB N
Mushmouse And Punkin Puss The Country Cousins	2552	TAT
Musicians Of Bremen	189	LGB
Musicians Of Bremen	307-47	LGB N
Musicians Of Bremen	307-57	LGB N
Muskie And His Friends	828	W
My A B C Book	610	W
My A B C Book	610	W
My Alphabet		LGB F
My Baby Brother	279	LGB
My Baby Sister	340	LGB
My Bible Book	8696	Elf
My Big Brother	214	DD R
My Book About God	644	W
My Book Of Dolls	721	W
My Book Of Poems	211-58	LGB N
My Book Of The Seasons		LGB F
My Book Of Words		LGB F
My Christmas Book	298	LGB
My Christmas Treasury	144*	LGB
My Christmas Treasury	455-1	LGB N
My Christmas Treasury	455-31	LGB N
My Christmas Treasury	455	LGB N
My Christmas Treasury	5003	LGB G
My Christmas Tree	10291	LGB B
My Counting Book	8399	Elf
My Counting Book	8636	Elf
My Daddy Is A Policeman	223	DD R
My Daddy Is A Policeman	DIN 3	DD G
My Dolly And Me	418	LGB
My First Book	10	LGB
My First Book Of Animal Sounds		LGB F
My First Book Of Bible Stories	19	LGB
My First Book Of Farm Animals	858	T
My First Book Of Jesus	8555	Elf
My First Book Of Jokes	799	W
My First Book Of Planets	308-56	LGB N
My First Book Of Prayers	661	W
My First Book Of Prayers	868	T
My First Book Of Riddles	745	W
My First Book Of Riddles	745	W
My First Book Of Sounds	205-54	LGB N
My First Book Of Sounds	205-62	LGB N
My First Book of Sounds	28	LGB L
My First Book of Sounds		LGB F
My First Counting Book	434	LGB
My First Counting Book	201-31	LGB N
My First Counting Book	203-41	LGB N
My First Counting Book	203-51	LGB N
My First Counting Book	203-52	LGB N
My First Little Mother Goose		LGB F
My Flower Book	8382	Elf
My Flower Book	8679	Elf
My Gold Fish	211	DD R
My Happy Day: A Word Book	450	Elf
My Happy Day: A Word Book	8332	Elf
My Home	115*	LGB
My Home	206-1	LGB N
My Home	206-31	LGB N
My Home	305-44	LGB N
My Home	305-54	LGB N
My Kindergarten Counting Book	301-68	LGB N
My Kitten	163	LGB
My Kitten	300	LGB
My Kitten	528	LGB
My Little Abc	2536	TAT
My Little Book About Our Flag	2578	TAT
My Little Book Of Big Animals	2466-4	TAT
My Little Book Of Big Machines	2589	TAT
My Little Book Of Birds	2475-50	TAT
My Little Book Of Birds	2490	TAT
My Little Book Of Boats	247332	TAT
My Little Book Of Bugs	24750	TAT
My Little Book Of Cars And Trucks	2473	TAT
My Little Book Of Cats	2626	TAT
My Little Book Of Dinosaurs	2482	TAT
My Little Book Of Dogs	2476-93	TAT
My Little Book Of Farm Animals	2559	TAT
My Little Book Of Flying	2414-4	TAT
My Little Book Of Horses	2466-3	TAT
My Little Book Of Pets	2401	TAT
My Little Book Of Poems		LGB F
My Little Book Of Prayers		LGB F
My Little Book Of Sea Life	2602	TAT
My Little Book Of Trains	2643	TAT
My Little Book Of Words		LGB F
My Little Counting Book	2407-3	TAT
My Little Dinosaur	571	LGB
My Little Dinosaur	209-43	LGB N
My Little Dinosaur	209-53	LGB N
My Little Dinosaur	304-2	LGB N
My Little Dinosaur	304-32	LGB N
My Little Golden Animal Book	465	LGB
My Little Golden Book About Cats	309-57	LGB N
My Little Golden Book About Cats	309-69	LGB N
My Little Golden Book About Dogs	309-71	LGB N
My Little Golden Book About God	268	LGB
My Little Golden Book About God	308-43	LGB N
My Little Golden Book About God	308-9	LGB N
My Little Golden Book About God	311-52	LGB N
My Little Golden Book About God	311-53	LGB N
My Little Golden Book About God	407-1	LGB N
My Little Golden Book Of Cars And Trucks	210-57	LGB N
My Little Golden Book Of Cars And Trucks	210-62	LGB N
My Little Golden Book Of Fairy Tales	211-62	LGB N
My Little Golden Book Of Jokes	424	LGB
My Little Golden Book Of Manners	460	LGB

Title	Number	Type
My Little Golden Book Of Manners	205-57	LGB N
My Little Golden Book Of Manners	205-64	LGB N
My Little Golden Calendar	A 39	LGB A
My Little Golden Dictionary	90	LGB
My Little Golden Dictionary	5001	LGB G
My Little Golden Mother Goose	300-69	LGB N
My Little Golden Word Book	305-53	LGB N
My Little Mother Goose		LGB F
My Magic Slate Book	5025	LGB G
My Own Book Of Fun And Play	885	T
My Own Grandpa	208-56	LGB N
My Pets	5027	LGB G
My Poetry Book	621	W
My Prayer Book	8697	Elf
My Puppy	233	LGB
My Puppy	469	LGB
My Puppy	312-11	LGB N
My Snuggly Bunny	250	LGB
My Teddy Bear	168	LGB
My Teddy Bear	448	LGB
My Truck Book	431	Elf
My Word Book	525	LGB
Name For Kitty, A	55	LGB
Nancy And Sluggo The Big Surprise	2525	TAT
Nancy Plays Nurse	8726	Elf
Natasha's Daddy	60	LGB L
Natasha's Daddy		LGB F
National Velvet	431	LGB
Naughty Bunny, The	377	LGB
Neatos And The Litterbugs, The	515	LGB
Ned's Number Book		LGB F
Never Pat A Bear	105*	LGB
New Baby, The	41	LGB
New Baby, The	291	LGB
New Baby, The	541	LGB
New Baby, The	209-1	LGB N
New Baby, The	306-43	LGB N
New Baby, The	306-53	LGB N
New Baby, The	306-68	LGB N
New Brother, New Sister	564	LGB
New Friends For The Saggy Baggy Elephant	131*	LGB
New House In The Forest, The	24	LGB
New Kid In School - Mc Kids	98886-00	LGB N
New Kittens, The	302	LGB
New Pony, The	410	LGB
New Puppy, The	370	LGB
New Puppy, The	202-5	LGB N
New Puppy, The	203-55	LGB N
New Puppy, The	303-55	LGB N
New Puppy, The	309-42	LGB N
Nibbler	2538	TAT
Night Before Christmas, The	20	LGB
Night Before Christmas, The	241	LGB
Night Before Christmas, The	858	W
Night Before Christmas, The	2517	TAT
Night Before Christmas, The	450- 9	LGB N
Night Before Christmas, The	450-09	LGB N
Night Before Christmas, The	450-10	LGB N
Night Before Christmas, The	450-11	LGB N
Night Before Christmas, The	450-1	LGB N
Night Before Christmas, The	450-31	LGB N
Night Before Christmas, The	450	LGB N
Night Before Christmas, The	68	LGB L
Night Before Christmas	839	TAT
Nine Friendly Dogs,The	622	W
Nine Rabbits And Another	845	W
No Nap Today		LGB F
No Sit-Ups for Porky Pig		TAT
No Stage Fright For Me!	10284	LGB B
No Worries	107-97	LGB DN
Noah And The Ark	2558	TAT
Noah's Ark	109*	LGB
Noah's Ark	461	Elf
Noah's Ark	1020	Elf
Noah's Ark	307-41	LGB N
Noah's Ark	311-64	LGB N
Noah's Ark	8424	Elf
Noah's Ark	8648	Elf
Noah's Ark	D 28	LGB D
Noahs Ark	307-51	LGB N
Noahs Ark	400-1	LGB N
Nobody's Puppy	920	TAT
Noel	456-16	LGB N
Noises And Mr.Flibberty-Jib	29	LGB
Noisy Clock Shop,The	539	W
Nonsense A B C's	550	Elf
Nonsense Alphabet,The	725	W
Not Quite Three	962	TAT
Number 9 The Little Fire Engine	444	Elf
Number 9 The Little Fire Engine	585	Elf
Number 9 The Little Fire Engine	8369	Elf
Number 9 The Little Fire Engine	8708	Elf
Numbers	243	LGB
Numbers	337	LGB
Nurse Nancy	154	LGB
Nurse Nancy	346	LGB
Nurse Nancy	473	LGB
Nursery Rhymes	59	LGB
Nursery Rhymes	529	LGB
Nursery Rhymes	857	TAT
Nursery Songs	7	LGB
Nursery Songs	348	LGB
Nursery Tales	14	LGB
Nursery Tales:	5009	LGB G
Nutcracker, The	44	LGB L
Nutcracker, The	460-15	LGB N
Nutcracker, The	460-16	LGB N
Off To School	5015	LGB G
Oh, Little Rabbit!	304-50	LGB N
Oh, Look!	2672	TAT
Old Friends, New Friends	10257	LGB B
Old Mac Donald Had A Farm	200-43	LGB N
Old Mac Donald Had A Farm	200-53	LGB N
Old Mac Donald Had A Farm	200-55	LGB N
Old Mac Donald Had A Farm	200-62	LGB N
Old Mac Donald Had A Farm	200-65	LGB N
Old Mac Donald Had A Farm	2589	TAT
Old Mac Donald Had A Farm	303-21	LGB N
Old Mac Donald Had A Farm	98806-01	LGB N
Old Macdonald Had A Farm	400	LGB
Old Mother Goose And OtherNursey Rhymes	300-54	LGB N
Old Mother Hubbard	591	LGB
Old Mother Hubbard	1007	Elf
Old Mother Hubbard	300-42	LGB N
Old Mother Hubbard	300-52	LGB N
Old Mother Hubbard	8413	Elf
Old Mother Hubbard	8624	Elf
Old Woman And Her Pig, The	464	Elf
Old Woman And Her Pig, The	1035	Elf
Old Woman And Her Pig, The	8379	Elf
Old Woman And Her Pig, The	2610	TAT
Old Yeller	D 65	LGB D
Ollie Bakes A Cake	829	W
Once I Had A Monster	2512	TAT
Once There Was A House	842	W
Once Upon A Time	700	W
Once Upon A Windy Day	865	TAT
Once Upon A Wintertime	D 12	LGB D
One Hundred And One Dalmations	2622	TAT
One Of The Family	208-42	LGB N
One Of The Family	208-50	LGB N
One Of The Family	208-52	LGB N
One Two Buckle My Shoe	807	TAT
One Two Three	2440	TAT
One Two Three	2616	TAT
One Two Three	926	TAT
One, Two, Cock-A-Doodle-Doo	8570	Elf
One,Two,Cock-A-Doodle-Doo	438	Elf
One,Two,Cock-A-Doodle-Doo	512	Elf
One,Two,Cock-A-Doodle-Doo	8350	Elf
Ookpik,The Actic Owl	579	LGB
Open Up My Suitcase	207	LGB
Ordinary Amos And The Amazing Fish	10269	LGB B
Oscar's Book	120*	LGB
Oscar's Book	108-1	LGB N
Oscar's Book	108-21	LGB N
Oscar's Book	108-41	LGB N
Oscar's Book	108-51	LGB N
Oscar's New Neighbor	109-67	LGB N
Oscar's New Neighbor	109-70	LGB N
Our Animal Friends	563	Elf
Our Animal Friends	8403	Elf
Our Animal Friends	8630	Elf
Our Auto Trip	457	Elf
Our Auto Trip	8339	Elf
Our Baby	218	DD R
Our Baby	DIN 8	DD G
Our Flag	388	LGB
Our Puppy	56	LGB
Our Puppy	292	LGB
Our World	242	LGB
Our World Of Color And Sound	8577	Elf
Out Of My Window	245	LGB
Outdoor Fun	479	Elf
Outside With Baby	2546	TAT
Over In The Meadow	796	W
Over In The Meadow		LGB F
Owl And The Pussy Cat	300-41	LGB N
Owl And The Pussy Cat	300-51	LGB N
Pal And Peter	265	LGB
Pals	2544	TAT
Pamela Jane's Week	2424	TAT
Panda Bear's Paint Box		LGB F
Panda Bear's Secret		LGB F
Pandas Take A Vacation, The	10258	LGB B

Title	Number	Type
Pop-O The Clown	844	TAT
Popcorn Party	8303	Elf
Popcorn Party	468	Elf
Popcorn Party	8303	Elf
Popcorn Party	8743	Elf
Popeye	667	W
Popeye	888	T
Popeye Goes On A Picinic	697	W
Popeye's Big Surprise	791	W
Porky Pig And Bugs Bunny Just Like Magic	146*	LGB
Porky Pig And Bugs Bunny Just Like Magic	110-22	LGB N
Porky Pig And Bugs Bunny Just Like Magic	110-2	LGB N
Porky Pig And Bugs Bunny JustLike Magic	110-32	LGB N
Porky Pig And Bugs Bunny Just Like Magic	110-42	LGB N
Porky Pig And Bugs Bunny Just Like Magic	110-65	LGB N
Porky Pig And Bugs Bunny JustLike Magic	110-75	LGB N
Pound Puppies ' Problem Puppies'	111-61	LGB N
Pound Puppies In Pick Of The Litter	110-59	LGB N
Prayers And Graces For A Small Child	502	Elf
Prayers And Graces For A Small Child	8609	Elf
Prayers For Boys And Girls	918	TAT
Prayers For Boys And Girls	2636	TAT
Prayers For Boys And Girls	2523	TAT
Prayers For Boys And Girls	2520	TAT
Prayers For Children	5	LGB
Prayers For Children	205	LGB
Prayers For Children	301- 9	LGB N
Prayers For Children	301-09	LGB N
Prayers For Children	301-10	LGB N
Prayers For Children	301-45	LGB N
Prayers For Children	301-93	LGB N
Prayers for Children	405-1	LGB N
Prayers For Children	405-32	LGB N
Prayers For Little Children	8557	Elf
Present For The Princess, A	8425	Elf
Present For The Princess, A	8602	Elf
Prickly Tale, A	2519	TAT
Prickly Tale, A	2508	TAT
Priince Valiant	874	T
Prince And The Pauper, The	105-71	LGB DN
Prince And The Pauper, The	54	LGB L
Princess And The Pea, The	207-68	LGB N
Princess And The Pea, The	8455	Elf
Princess And The Pea, The	2610	TAT
Princess And The Pea, The	8727	Elf
Princess Who Never Laughed, The	2610	TAT
Pudgy The Little Bear	8441	Elf
Pudgy The Little Bear	8674	Elf
Puff The Blue Kitten	443	LGB
Puff The Magic Dragon	851	W
Puffy The Puppy	819	TAT
Puppies On Parade	2476-45	TAT
Puppies To Love	8565	Elf
Puppy And Me	504	Elf
Puppy Love	109-46	LGB N
Puppy Love	109-56	LGB N
Puppy Love	109-63	LGB N
Puppy Nobody Wanted, The	10270	LGB B
Puppy On Parade,The	617	W
Puppy On Parade,The	617	W
Puppy On The Farm	304-52	LGB N
Puppy Roundup	LGB F	
Puppy Twins, The	8420	Elf
Puppy Twins, The	8603	Elf
Puppy Who Chased The Sun, The	535	W
Puppy Who Found A Boy, The	561	W
Puppy Who Would Not Mind HisMother, The	679	W
Purrrt	2641	TAT
Puss In Boots	137	LGB
Puss In Boots	359	LGB
Puss In Boots	300-58	LGB N
Puss-In-Boots	507	Elf
Puss-In-Boots	513	Elf
Puss-In-Boots	8356	Elf
Puss-In-Boots	8573	Elf
Pussy Cat's Secret	895	TAT
Pussy Willow	314	LGB
Pussy Willow	302-34	LGB N
Pussy Willow	302-41	LGB N
Pussy Willow	873	TAT
Pussy Willow	98809-01	LGB N
Pussycat Tiger	362	LGB
Put On A Happy Face	107-84	LGB N
Puzzle For Raggedy Ann And Andy, A	683	W
Quasimodo The Hero	98797-01	LGB DN
Quasimodo's New Friend	107-36	LGB DN
Quick Draw Mcgraw	398	LGB
Quiet Book, The	654	W
Quiet Little Indian, The	709	W
Quiet Quincy And The Delivery Truck	2541	TAT
Quiet Quincy And The Delivery Truck	2615	TAT
Quints ' The Cleanup'	107-72	LGB N
Quints ' The Cleanup'	107-81	LGB N
Quiz Fun	5024	LGB G
Rabbit And His Friends	169	LGB
Rabbit And His Friends	209-44	LGB N
Rabbit And His Friends	472-1	LGB N
Rabbit Is Next, The	173*	LGB
Rabbit Is Next, The	474-21	LGB N
Rabbit's Adventure, The	164*	LGB
Rabbit's Adventure, The	471-31	LGB N
Rabbits Give A Party, The	811	W
Rabbits Give A Party, The	811	W
Race Between The Monkey And The Duck, The	510	W
Rackety Boom	893	TAT
Rackety-Boom	2557	TAT
Raggedy Andy And The Jump-Up Contest	2641	TAT
Raggedy Andy's Surprise	604	W
Raggedy Andy's Treasure Hunt	2417-2	TAT
Raggedy Ann And AndyAnd The Rainy Day Circus	401	LGB
Raggedy Ann And Andy And The Rainy Day Circus	107-2	LGB N
Raggedy Ann And Andy And The Rainy-Day Circus	107-42	LGB N
Raggedy Ann And Andy Help Santa Claus	156*	LGB
Raggedy Ann And Andy Help Santa Claus	457-1	LGB N
Raggedy Ann And Andy Help SantaClaus	457-31	LGB N
Raggedy Ann And Andy On The Farm	2596	TAT
Raggedy Ann And Andy The GreyKitten	139*	LGB
Raggedy Ann And Andy The GreyKitten	107-21	LGB N
Raggedy Ann And Andy The GreyKitten	107-31	LGB N
Raggedy Ann And Andy The GreyKitten	107-41	LGB N
Raggedy Ann And Andy, Five Birthdays In A Row	107-34	LGB N
Raggedy Ann And Andy, FiveBirthdays In A Row	107-44	LGB N
Raggedy Ann And Andy, Five Birthdays In A Row	107-4	LGB N
Raggedy Ann And Fido	585	LGB
Raggedy Ann And Marcella's First Day At School	588	W
Raggedy Ann And The Cookie Snatcher	262	LGB
Raggedy Ann And The CookieSnatcher	107-33	LGB N
Raggedy Ann And The Cookie Snatcher	107-3	LGB N
Raggedy Ann And The Cookie Snatcher	107-43	LGB N
Raggedy Ann And The Cookie Snatcher	111-47	LGB N
Raggedy Ann And The Cookie Snatcher	111-57	LGB N
Raggedy Ann And The Tagalong Present	2417-1	TAT
Raggedy Ann's Christmas Surprise	868	W
Raggedy Ann's Cooking School	2498	TAT
Raggedy Ann's Merriest Christmas	594	W
Raggedy Ann's Secret	727	W
Raggedy Ann's Tea Party	624	W
Rags	303-44	LGB N
Rags	586	LGB
Rainbow Brite And The Brook Meadow Deer	107-48	LGB N
Rainbow Brite And The Brook Meadow Deer	107-58	LGB N
Rainbow Brite And The Magic Belt	2451-4	TAT
Rainbow Circus Comes To Town	2474-44	TAT
Rainbow Puppies	98858-00	LGB DN
Rainy Day Play Book, The	133	LGB
Rainy Day Play Book	206-35	LGB N
Rainy Day Play Book	211-51	LGB N
Rainy Day Story On The Farm	858	TAT
Randolph: The Bear Who Said No	509	W
Rapunzel	207-57	LGB N
Rapunzel	98290	LGB DN
Rattle-Rattle Dump Truck, The	656	W
Rattle-Rattle Train, The	655	W
Read Me Some Poems	8574	Elf
Reading, Writing & Spelling Stamps	A 24	LGB A
Ready, Set, Go! A Counting Book	109-71	LGB N
Ready, Set, Grow	308-68	LGB N
Really Truly Treasure Hunt, The	793	W
Really Truly Treasure Hunt, The	891	T
Red Book Of Fairy Tales, The	306	LGB
Red Jacket Mix-Up, The	10267	LGB B
Red Riding Hood	A 34	LGB A

Remarkably Strong Pippy Longstocking, The	123*	LGB
Rescuers Down Under, The	105-70	LGB DN
Rescuers Down Under, The	105-83	LGB DN
Rescuers, The	105-69	LGB DN
Rescuers, The	105- 3	LGB DN
Rescuers, The	105-43	LGB DN
Rescuers, The	2429-3	TAT
Rescuers, The	D136	LGB D
Return To Oz ' Dorothy Saves The Emerald City'	103-55	LGB DN
Return To Oz Escape ' From The Witches Castle'	105-56	LGB DN
Ricochet Rabbit Showdown At Gopher Gulch Bakery	2622	TAT
Riddles,Riddles From A To Z	490	LGB
Right House For Rabbit, The	10268	LGB B
Right's Animal Farm	200-9	LGB N
Rin Tin Tin & The Outlaw	304	LGB
Rin Tin Tin And Rusty	246	LGB
Rin Tin Tin And The Last Indian	276	LGB
Rinty And Pals For Rusty	2571	TAT
Rip Van Winkle	8383	Elf
Rip Van Winkle	8671	Elf
Road Runner , The ' A Very Scary Lesson'	122*	LGB
Road Runner , The ' A Very Scary Lesson'	111-25	LGB N
Road Runner , The ' A Very Scary Lesson'	111-35	LGB N
Road Runner , The ' A Very ScaryLesson'	111-45	LGB N
Road Runner , The ' A Very ScaryLesson'	111-5	LGB N
Road Runner , The ' A Very Scary Lesson'	111-71	LGB N
Road Runner , The ' A Very Scary Lesson'	111-83	LGB N
Road Runner and the Bird Watchers	2408	TAT
Road Runner, The Mid-Mesa Marathon	110-57	LGB N
Road Runner, The 'Tumblweed Trouble'	2466	TAT
Road To Oz, The	144	LGB
Robert And His New Friends	124	LGB
Robin Family, The	215	DD R
Robin Hood & The Daring Mouse	D128	LGB D
Robin Hood And Skippy's Best Birthday	2441	TAT
Robin Hood	D 48	LGB D
Robin Hood	D126	LGB D
Robotman & His Friends At School	110-58	LGB N
Rocket For A Cow, A	8458	Elf
Rocket For A Cow, A	8747	Elf
Rocky And His Friends	408	LGB
Roger's Upside-Down Day	2463-4	TAT
Rolling Wheels	762	W
Roly-Poly Puppy, The	549	W
Romper Room Do Bee Book Of Manners, The	763	W
Romper Room Do Bees	273	LGB
Romper Room Exercise Book, The	527	LGB
Romper Room Laughing Book	808	W
Romper Room Safety Book, The	854	W
Ronald Mcdonald And The Tale Of The Talking Plant	111-50	LGB N

Rootie Kazootie	150	LGB
Rootie Kazootie And The Pineapple Pies	936	TAT
Rootie Kazootie Baseball Star	190	LGB
Rootie Kazootie Joins The Circus	226	LGB
Roundabout Train	2436	TAT
Rowdy	861	TAT
Roy Rogers	177	LGB
Roy Rogers And Cowboy Toby	195	LGB
Roy Rogers And The Indian Sign	259	LGB
Roy Rogers And The Lane Ranch	811	TAT
Roy Rogers And The Mountain Lion	231	LGB
Roy Rogers And The Sure'Nough Cowpoke	801	TAT
Roy Rogers Surprise For Donnie	943	TAT
Roy Rogers' Bullet Leads The Way	2567	TAT
Rubbles And Bamm-Bamm, The 'problem Present'	2622	TAT
Rudolph The Red-Nosed Reindeer	331	LGB
Rudolph The Red-Nosed ReindeerShines Again	452-08	LGB N
Rudolph The Red-Nosed Reindeer Shines Again	452-42	LGB N
Rudolph The Red-Nosed Reindeer Shines Again	452-8	LGB N
Rudolph The Red-Nosed Reindeer Shines Again	460-31	LGB N
Rudolph The Red-Nosed Reindeer	2483-02	TAT
Rudolph The Red-Nosed Reindeer	2517-2	TAT
Rudolph the Red-Nosed Reindeer	37	LGB L
Rudolph The Red-Nosed Reindeer	452-09	LGB N
Rudolph The Red-Nosed Reindeer	452-10	LGB N
Rudolph The Red-Nosed Reindeer	452-11	LGB N
Rudolph The Red-Nosed Reindeer	452-1	LGB N
Rudolph The Red-Nosed Reindeer	452-31	LGB N
Rudolph The Red-Nosed Reindeer	452-41	LGB N
Rudolph The Red-Nosed Reindeer	452-9	LGB N
Rudolph The Red-Nosed Reindeer	98829-00	LGB N
Ruff And Reddy	378	LGB
Ruff And Reddy	477	LGB
Ruff And Reddy Go To A Party	2567	TAT
Rumpelstiltskin	300-56	LGB N
Rumpelstiltskin And The Princess And The Pea	498	LGB
Rumpelstiltskin	8318	Elf
Rumpelstiltskin	8669	Elf
Runaway Baby Bird, The	748	W
Runaway Ginger	2537	TAT
Runaway Ginger	897	TAT
Runaway Pancake, The	2465	TAT
Runaway Squash, The	143*	LGB
Rupert The Rhinoceros	419	LGB
Rupert The Rhinoceros	201-57	LGB N
Rusty Goes To School	479	LGB
Saggy Baggy Elephant No Place For Me	305-59	LGB N

Saggy Baggy Elephant No Place For Me	373	LGB Land
Saggy Baggy Elephant's Birthday		LGB F
Saggy Baggy Elephant, The	36	LGB
Saggy Baggy Elephant, The	385	LGB
Saggy Baggy Elephant, The	4	LGB L
Saggy Baggy Elephant, The	201-42	LGB N
Saggy Baggy Elephant, The	201-52	LGB N
Saggy Baggy Elephant, The	201-54	LGB N
Saggy Baggy Elephant, The	201-88	LGB N
Saggy Baggy Elephant, The	304-34	LGB N
Saggy Baggy Elephant, The	304-4	LGB N
Sailboat That Ran Away	842	TAT
Sailing On A Very Fine Day	497	Elf
Sailor Dog, The	156	LGB
Sailor Dog, The	312-08	LGB N
Sam The Firehouse Cat	580	LGB
Santa's Rocket Sleigh	568	Elf
Santa's Surprise Book	121*	LGB
Santa's Surprise Book	459-1	LGB N
Santa's Surprise Book	459-31	LGB N
Santa's Toy Shop	451-8	LGB DN
Santa's Toy Shop	451-08	LGB DN
Santa's Toy Shop	451-10	LGB DN
Santa's Toy Shop	451-17	LGB DN
Santa's Toy Shop	453- 1	LGB DN
Santa's Toy Shop	453-31	LGB DN
Santa's Toy Shop	D 16	LGB D
Savage Sam	D104	LGB D
Scalawag The Monkey	477	Elf
Scamp's Adventure	D 70	LGB D
Scamp's Adventure	D 88	LGB D
Scamp	D 63	LGB D
Scamper	8326	Elf
Scamper	8716	Elf
Scarebunny,The	209-59	LGB N
Scooby Doo And The Pirate Treasure	126*	LGB
Scooby Doo At The Zoo	2570	TAT
Scooby-Doo And The Case Of The Counterfeit Money	HANNA10	Elf
Scooby-Doo And The Haunted Doghouse	HANNA11	Elf
Scooby-Doo And The Headless Horseman	HANNA12	Elf
Scooby-Doo And The Mystery Monster	HANNA13	Elf
Scooby-Doo And The Old Ship Mystery	HANNA14	Elf
Scuffy The Tugboat	30	LGB
Scuffy The Tugboat	244	LGB
Scuffy The Tugboat	363	LGB
Scuffy the Tugboat	5	LGB L
Scuffy The Tugboat	305-1	LGB N
Scuffy The Tugboat	305-21	LGB N
Scuffy The Tugboat	305-31	LGB N
Scuffy The Tugboat	310-41	LGB N
Scuffy The Tugboat	310-51	LGB N
Scuffy The Tugboat	310-54	LGB N
Scuffy The Tugboat	310-87	LGB N
Sea Shore, The	284	LGB
Secret Life Of Walter Kitty, The	10260	LGB B
See How It Grows	630	W
See It Goes!	2557	TAT
See It Goes!	805	TAT
Sergeant Preston And Rex	569	Elf

Title	Number	Code
Sergeant Preston And The Yukon King	500	Elf
Sesame Street Abc	2471-43	TAT
Sesame Street,The Together Book	315*	LGB
Sesame Street,The Together Book	108-23	LGB N
Sesame Street,The Together Book	108-33	LGB N
Sesame Street,The Together Book	108-3	LGB N
Sesame Streets First Times	2465-43	TAT
Seven Dwarfs Find A House, The	D 35	LGB D
Seven Dwarfs Find A House, The	D 67	LGB D
Seven Little Postmen	134	LGB
Seven Little Postmen	504	LGB
Seven Sneezes, The	51	LGB
Seven Wishes, The	2606	TAT
Seven Wonderful Cats, The	548	Elf
Seven Wonderful Cats, The	8411	Elf
Seven Wonderful Cats, The	8607	Elf
Shaggy Dog	D 82	LGB D
Shake A Leg	LGB F	
Shake a Leg	63	LGB L
Shall We Dance	96002-00	LGB N
Shazam! A Circus Adventue	110-36	LGB N
Shazam,A Circus Adventure	155*	LGB
Sheri Lewis Wonder Book, The	781	W
Sherlock Hemlock And The Great Twiddlebug Mystery	2564	TAT
Shoelace Box, The	211-56	LGB N
Shut the Door!	LGB F	
Shy Little Horse, The	511	W
Shy Little Horse,The	880	T
Shy Little Kitten's Secret Place	302-58	LGB N
Shy Little Kitten's Secret Place	302-68	LGB N
Shy Little Kitten's Secret Place	372	LGB Land
Shy Little Kitten, The	494	LGB
Shy Little Kitten, The	23	LGB
Shy Little Kitten, The	248	LGB
Shy Little Kitten, The	494	LGB
Shy Little Kitten, The	302-22	LGB N
Shy Little Kitten, The	302-2	LGB N
Shy Little Kitten, The	302-32	LGB N
Shy Little Kitten, The	302-53	LGB N
Shy Little Kitten, The	302-87	LGB N
Shy Little Kitten, The	312-10	LGB N
Silly Joe	8434	Elf
Silly Sidney	841	W
Silly Sisters, The	204-59	LGB N
Silver Chief	650	W
Simon Visits The Doctor	LGB F	
Sing With Me My Name Is Ernie	98856-00	LGB N
Sky, The	270	LGB
Sleep-Over Visit, The	10261	LGB B
Sleeping Beauty & The Fairies	D 71	LGB D
Sleeping Beauty	635	W
Sleeping Beauty	A 33	LGB A
Sleeping Beauty	635	W
Sleeping Beauty	104-56	LGB DN
Sleeping Beauty	104-66	LGB DN
Sleeping Beauty	2649	TAT
Sleeping Beauty	8320	Elf
Sleeping Beauty	8683	Elf
Sleeping Beauty	98273-01	LGB DN
Sleeping Beauty	D 61	LGB D
Sleepy Book, The	209-27	LGB N
Sleepy Book, The	209-37	LGB N
Sleepy Book, The	301-41	LGB N
Sleepy Book, The	301-51	LGB N
Sleepy Book, The	301-59	LGB N
Sleepy Book, The	301-62	LGB N
Sleepy Book, The	10	LGB L
Sleepy Puppy,The	2462	TAT
Sleepy Story, A	LGB F	
Sleepy-Time Rhymes	8346	Elf
Sleepy-Time Rhymes	8664	Elf
Sleepytime A B C	202-57	LGB N
Sleepytime For Everyone	612	W
Slowpoke At The Circus	2457	TAT
Slowpoke, The Lazy Little Puppy	582	Elf
Sly Little Bear	411	LGB
Smart Little Mouse, The	441	Elf
Smart Little Mouse, The	1039	Elf
Smart Little Mouse, The	8421	Elf
Smart Little Mouse, The	8626	Elf
Smokey And His Animal Friends	387	LGB
Smokey Bear Saves The Forest	2463	TAT
Smokey Bear And The Campers	423	LGB
Smokey The Bear	224	LGB
Smokey The Bear	481	LGB
Smokey The Bear Finds A Helper	345	LGB
Smoky The Baby Goat	867	TAT
Sneezer	854	TAT
Snoopy, The Worlds Greatest Arthur	10280	LGB B
Snoopy,The Nosey Little Puppy	509	Elf
Snooty	851	TAT
Snoozey	2358	TAT
Snoozey	853	TAT
Snoring Monster, The	208-55	LGB N
Snoring Monster, The	208-92	LGB N
Snow Puppies	98786-01	LGB DN
Snow White	898	T
Snow White And Rose Red	228	LGB
Snow White And Rose Red	8580	Elf
Snow White And The Seven Dwarfs	659	W
Snow White And The Seven Dwarfs	659	W
Snow White And The Seven Dwarfs	103- 2	LGB DN
Snow White And The Seven Dwarfs	103-22	LGB DN
Snow White And The Seven Dwarfs	103-32	LGB DN
Snow White And The Seven Dwarfs	103-42	LGB DN
Snow White And The Seven Dwarfs	103-52	LGB DN
Snow White And The Seven Dwarfs	103-58	LGB DN
Snow White And The Seven Dwarfs	103-60	LGB DN
Snow White And The Seven Dwarfs	103-67	LGB DN
Snow White And The Seven Dwarfs	103-70	LGB DN
Snow White And The Seven Dwarfs	103-87	LGB DN
Snow White And The Seven Dwarfs	2427	TAT
Snow White And The Seven Dwarfs	2578	TAT
Snow White And The Seven Dwarfs	D 4	LGB D
Snow White	D 66	LGB D
Snowball	2670	TAT
Snowman's Christmas Present, The	572	W
Snowman's Christmas Present, The	572	W
Snowstorm Surprise	208-69	LGB N
Snuggles	1005	Elf
Snuggles	8340	Elf
Snuggles	8650	Elf
So Big	574	LGB
So Big	209-26	LGB N
So Big	209-6	LGB N
So Long	1036	Elf
So Long	8342	Elf
So Long	8622	Elf
So This Is Spring!	844	W
So This Is Spring!	844	W
Soccor Coach	107-71	LGB N
Socks	886	TAT
Somebody Forgot	963	TAT
Someplace For Sparky	2659	TAT
Songs To Sing And Play	753	W
Sonny The Bunny	591	W
Sonny The Luck Bunny	848	W
Sonny The Luck Bunny	848	W
Sorcer's Apprentice	100-79	LGB DN
Soupy Sales And The Tallking Turtle	860	W
Space Ship To The Moon	473	Elf
Sparkie-No School Today	902	T
Sparky The Fire Dog	495	Elf
Special Pet, A	2521	TAT
Special Sleepover, The	98808-00	LGB N
Speckles And The Triplets	874	TAT
Speed Buggy And The Secret Message	HANNA15	Elf
Splish Splash, And Splush	2526	TAT
Spoon Necklace, The	2472-41	TAT
Sport Goofy And The Racing Robot	100-57	LGB DN
Sport Goofy And The Racing Robot	105-47	LGB DN
Spotted Little Puppy,The	2560	TAT
Squiffy The Skunk	476	Elf
Squirrel Twins, The	8381	Elf
Squirrel Twins, The	8670	Elf
Stable In Bethlehem, A	LGB F	
Stacks Of Caps	722	W
Star Wars - Adventure In Beggar's Canyon	98879-00	LGB N
Star Wars - Meltdown On Hoth	98202-00	LGB N
Steve Canyon	356	LGB
Stevie's Trycycle	LGB F	
Stop And Go	A 17	LGB A
Store Bought Doll, The	204-54	LGB N
Store-Bought Doll, The	204-44	LGB N
Stories Of Jesus	114*	LGB
Stories Of Jesus	402-1	LGB N
Stories Of Jesus	402-2	LGB N
Stories Of The Christ Child	8612	Elf
Stories Of The Christ Child	484	Elf
Stories Of The Christ Child	8612	Elf
Story Of Babar, The	590	W
Story Of David, The	8725	Elf
Story Of Easter, The	98902-00	LGB N
Story Of Jesus, The	27	LGB
Story Of Jonah, The	311-61	LGB N
Story Of Joseph, The	8724	Elf
Story Of Our Flag, The	8398	Elf
Story Of Our Flag, The	8635	Elf
Story Of The Christ Child, The	587	W
Storybook For Little Tots	1029	Elf
Storybook For Little Tots	8393	Elf
Storybook For Little Tots	8619	Elf

Title	No.	Type
Tickety-Tock, What Time Is It?	308-51	LGB N
Tickety-Tock, What Time Is It?	308-53	LGB N
Tickle Me My Name Is Elmo	98827-01	LGB N
Tiger's Adventure	08	LGB
Tiger's Adventure	351	LGB
Time For Bed	301-55	LGB N
Time For Everything	8562	Elf
Timid Little Kitten, The	98881-00	LGB N
Timothy Tiger's Terrible Toothache	209-60	LGB N
Timothy Tiger's Terrible Toothache	209-63	LGB N
Timothy Tiger	8324	Elf
Timothy Tiger	8672	Elf
Timothy Tinker The Wonderful Oilcan	2522	TAT
Timothy's Shoes	856	TAT
Timothy's Shoes	856	TAT
Tin Woodsman Of Oz, The	159	LGB
Tiny Dinosaurs	308-58	LGB N
Tiny Dinosaurs	308-69	LGB N
Tiny Tots 1-2-3	2615	TAT
Tiny Tots 123	2435	TAT
Tiny-Tawny Kitten, The	590	LGB
Tip-Top Tree House	2555	TAT
Title unknown	894	T
Title unknown	900	T
To Grandmother's House We Go		LGB F
To Market To Market	775	W
To The Store We Go	460	Elf
Toad Flies High	103-44	LGB DN
Toad Flies High	103-54	LGB DN
Toby Bunny's Secret Hiding Place	2465-44	TAT
Toby The Rock Hound	2408-6	TAT
Toby Tyler	D 87	LGB D
Toby Zebra And The Lost Zoo	2505	TAT
Tom And Jerry	117	LGB
Tom And Jerry	561	LGB
Tom And Jerry And The Toy Circus	2509	TAT
Tom And Jerry In Model Mice	2509	TAT
Tom And Jerry In Tom's Happy Birthday	2611	TAT
Tom And Jerry Meet Little Quack	181	LGB
Tom And Jerry Meet Little Quack	311	LGB
Tom And Jerry Photo Finish	124*	LGB
Tom And Jerry's Big Movie	2451-38	TAT
Tom And Jerry's Merry Christmas	197	LGB
Tom And Jerry's Merry Christmas	457-42	LGB N
Tom And Jerry's Party	235	LGB
Tom Corbett's Wonder Book Of Space	603	W
Tom Corbett: A Trip To The Moon	713	W
Tom Terrific With Mighty Manfred The Wonder Dog	703	W
Tom Terrific's Greatest Adventure	735	W
Tom Thumb	8684	Elf
Tom Thumb	353	LGB
Tom Thumb	8323	Elf
Tom Thumb	8684	Elf
Tommy And Timmy	822	TAT
Tommy And Timmy	2644	TAT
Tommy On The Farm	2557	TAT
Tommy Tractor	881	TAT
Tommy Visits The Doctor	480	LGB
Tommy Visits The Doctor	211-59	LGB N
Tommy's Camping Adventure	471	LGB
Tommy's New Bed		LGB F
Tommy's Wonderful Rides	63	LGB
Tonka	D 80	LGB D
Too Many Kittens	2525	TAT
Too Many Names	2614	TAT
Too-Little Fire Engine, The	526	W
Tootle	21	LGB
Tootle	8	LGB L
Tootle And Katy Caboose 'a Special Treasure'	374	LGB Land
Tootle	210-44	LGB N
Tootle	210-54	LGB N
Tootle	210-55	LGB N
Tootle	210-87	LGB N
Tootle	306-1	LGB N
Tootle	306-21	LGB N
Tootle	306-31	LGB N
Top Cat	453	LGB
Topsy Turvy Circus	161	LGB
Tortoise And The Hare, The	207-56	LGB N
Tortoise And The Hare, The	8431	Elf
Touche' Turtle	474	LGB
Town Mouse And The Country Mouse, The	2561	TAT
Toy Party, The	878	TAT
Toy Soldier, The	D 99	LGB D
Toy That Flew, The	2518	TAT
Toys	22	LGB
Train Coming	2556	TAT
Train Stamps	A 26	LGB A
Train Stories:	5018	LGB G
Train To Timbuctoo, The	118	LGB
Train To Timbuctoo, The	210-41	LGB N
Train To Timbuctoo, The	210-51	LGB N
Train To Timbuctoo, The	211-34	LGB N
Travel	269	LGB
Traveling Twins, The	596	W
Treasure Book Of Favorite Nursery Tales	856	T
Treasure Book Of Riddles	855	T
Trick On Deputy Dog	830	W
Trick Or Treat	98838-01	LGB DN
Trim The Christmas Tree	A 15	LGB A
Trim The Christmas Tree	A 50	LGB A
Trip In Space, A	8566	Elf
Truck That Drove All Night, The		LGB F
Truck That Stopped At VillageSmall, The	813	TAT
Trucks (2 Paper Model Trucks)	A 6	LGB A
Trucks	8325	Elf
Trucks	8687	Elf
Trumpet	931	TAT
Try Again, Sally!	2460	TAT
Tubby The Tuba	873	T
Tubby Turtle	8321	Elf
Tubby Turtle	8692	Elf
Tubsy And The Picnic Tree	2552	TAT
Tuffer	2672	TAT
Tuffy The Tugboat	880	TAT
Tuggy The Tuboat	696	W
Turtles Turn Up On Tuesday	8561	Elf
Tutu The Little Fawn	836	W
Tweety And Slyvester At The Farm	2453-35	TAT
Tweety And Sylvester A Visit To The Vet	2453-47	TAT
Tweety And Sylvester In ' Birds Of A Feather'	110-78	LGB N
Tweety And Sylvester Picnic Problems	2448	TAT
Tweety Global Patrol	110-82	LGB N
Tweety Plays Catch The Puddy Cat	141*	LGB
Tweety Plays Catch The Puddy Cat	111-24	LGB N
Tweety Plays Catch The Puddy Cat	111-34	LGB N
Tweety Plays Catch The Puddy Cat	111-4	LGB N
Tweety Plays Catch The Puddy Cat	111-54	LGB N
Tweety Plays Catch The Puddy Tat	111-51	LGB N
Tweety Trap!, The		LGB F
Tweety	901	TAT
Twelve Dancing Princesses, The	194	LGB
Twelve Dancing Princesses, The	301-64	LGB N
Twelve Days Of Christmas, The	651	W
Twelve Days Of Christmas, The	451-16	LGB N
Twelve Days Of Christmas, The	454-09	LGB N
Twelve Days Of Christmas, The	454-10	LGB N
Twelve Days Of Christmas, The	454-42	LGB N
Twelve Days Of Christmas, The	454-9	LGB N
Twelve Days of Christmas, The	49	LGB L
Twenty-Third Psalm, The	8698	Elf
Twilight Tales	8608	Elf
Twilight Tales	426	Elf
Twilight Tales	8427	Elf
Twilight Tales	8608	Elf
Twins, The	227	LGB
Two Kittens	2525	TAT
Two Little Gardeners	108	LGB
Two Little Gardeners	308-59	LGB N
Two Little Miners	66	LGB
Two Stories About Chap And Chirpy	2526	TAT
Two Stories About Kate & Kitty	2510	TAT
Two Stories About Lollipop	2683	TAT
Two Stories About Ricky	2601	TAT
Two Stories About Wags	2560	TAT
Two Stories About Wendy	2659	TAT
Two To Twins, The	2543	TAT
Ugly Daschound, The	D118	LGB D
Ugly Duckling, The	207-72	LGB N
Ugly Duckling, The	8327	Elf
Ugly Duckling, The	8590	Elf
Ugly Duckling, The	D 22	LGB D
Ukele And Her New Doll	102	LGB
Uncle Mistletoe	175	LGB
Uncle Remus	105-66	LGB DN
Uncle Remus	D 6	LGB D
Uncle Remus	D 85	LGB D
Uncle Scrooge, The Winner	2552	TAT
Uncle Wiggily	148	LGB
Uncle Wiggily And His Friends	766	W
Uncle Wiggily And The Alligator	903	TAT
Uncle Wiggily's Adventures	765	W
Under Dog	2611	TAT
Under The Saskatoon Tree	2543	TAT
Underdog And The Disappearing Ice Cream	135*	LGB

Title	Number	Code
Wild Animals	8348	Elf
Wild Animals	394	LGB
Wild Animals	454	Elf
Wild Animals	499	LGB
Wild Animals	510	Elf
Wild Animals	5010	LGB G
Wild Animals	8348	Elf
Wild Bill Hickok	649	W
Wild Bill Hickok And Deputy Marshall Joey	496	Elf
Wild Bill Hickok And The Indians	570	Elf
Wild Kingdom A Trip To A Game Park	2625	TAT
Wild Kingdom	151*	LGB
Willie Found A Wallet	205-56	LGB N
Willy Woo-Oo-Oo	2444	TAT
Willy Woo-Oo-Oo	818	TAT
Wilmer The Watchdog	2627	TAT
Winky Dink	266	LGB
Winnie The Pooh ' Eeyore, Be Happy!'	102-62	LGB DN
Winnie The Pooh A Day ToRemember	101-26	LGB DN
Winnie The Pooh And The Honey Patch	101- 4	LGB DN
Winnie The Pooh And The Honey Patch	101-44	LGB DN
Winnie The Pooh And The Honey Patch	101-53	LGB DN
Winnie The Pooh And The Honey Patch	101-54	LGB DN
Winnie The Pooh And The Honey Tree	98267-01	LGB DN
Winnie The Pooh And The Honey Tree	101- 3	LGB DN
Winnie The Pooh And The Honey Tree	101-33	LGB DN
Winnie The Pooh And The Honey Tree	101-43	LGB DN
Winnie The Pooh And The Honey Tree	101-53	LGB DN
Winnie The Pooh And The Honey Tree	101-63	LGB DN
Winnie The Pooh And The Honey Tree	D116	LGB D
Winnie The Pooh And The Missing Bullhorn	101-55	LGB DN
Winnie The Pooh And The Missing Bullhorn	101-61	LGB DN
Winnie The Pooh And The Special Morning	101-25	LGB DN
Winnie The Pooh And The Special Morning	101-35	LGB DN
Winnie The Pooh And Tigger	101-21	LGB DN
Winnie The Pooh And Tigger	101-41	LGB DN
Winnie The Pooh And Tigger	D121	LGB D
Winnie The Pooh Meets Gopher	101- 2	LGB DN
Winnie The Pooh Meets Gopher	101-32	LGB DN
Winnie The Pooh Meets Gopher	101-42	LGB DN
Winnie The Pooh Meets Gopher	101-52	LGB DN
Winnie The Pooh Meets Gopher	D117	LGB D
Winnie-The-Pooh 'The Blustery Day'	2577	TAT
Winnie-The-Pooh And Eeyore's House	2620	TAT
Winnie-The-Pooh And The Pebble Hunt	LGB F	
Winnie-The-Pooh The Unbouncing Of Tigger	2526	TAT
Wizard Of Oz, The	119*	LGB
Wizard Of Oz, The	543	W
Wizard Of Oz, The	310-22	LGB N
Wizard Of Oz, The	310-2	LGB N
Wizard Of Oz, The	310-32	LGB N
Wizard of Oz	107-69	LGB N
Wizards' Duel, The	D107	LGB D
Wolf and Seven Kids	LGB F	
Wolf And The Seven Kids	2561	TAT
Wonder Book Of Bible Stories, The	577	W
Wonder Book Of Birds, The	757	W
Wonder Book Of Boats, The	580	W
Wonder Book Of Christmas, The	575	W
Wonder Book Of Christmas, The	575	W
Wonder Book Of Clowns, The	638	W
Wonder Book Of Cottontails And Other Rabbits, The	852	W
Wonder Book Of Counting Rhymes, The	682	W
Wonder Book Of Counting Rhymes, The	682	W
Wonder Book Of Cowboy's, The	640	W
Wonder Book Of Favorite Nursery Tales, The	730	W
Wonder Book Of Finger PlaysAnd Action Rhymes, The	627	W
Wonder Book Of Firemen And Fire Engines, The	637	W
Wonder Book Of Firemen And Fire Engines, The	637	W
Wonder Book Of Fish, The	782	W
Wonder Book Of Flowers, The	784	W
Wonder Book Of Fun, The	576	W
Wonder Book Of Fun, The	576	W
Wonder Book Of Happy Animals, The	687	W
Wonder Book Of Horses, The	857	W
Wonder Book Of Kittens, The	786	W
Wonder Book Of Nursery Songs, The	619	W
Wonder Book Of Puppies, The	804	W
Wonder Book Of The Seashore, The	785	W
Wonder Book Of Trains, The	569	W
Wonder Book Of Trees, The	827	W
Wonder Book Of Trucks, The	616	W
Wonder Book Of Trucks, The	616	W
Wonder Book Of Turtles, The	838	W
Wonder Of Easter, The	98796-01	LGB N
Wonderful Animal Band, The	869	T
Wonderful House, The	76	LGB
Wonderful Plane Ride, The	433	Elf
Wonderful School, The	582	LGB
Wonderful Tar-Baby, The	581	W
Wonderful Tony	871	TAT
Wonderful Train Ride	427	Elf
Wonderful Train Ride	427	Elf
Wonderful Treasure Hunt, The	853	T
Wonders Of Nature	293	LGB
Woodsy Owl And The Trail Bikers	107*	LGB
Woody Woodpecker Shoots The Works	2439	TAT
Woody Woodpecker	145	LGB
Woody Woodpecker	330	LGB
Woody Woodpecker At The Circus	149*	LGB
Woody Woodpecker At The Circus	111-3	LGB N
Woody Woodpecker At The Circus	111-43	LGB N
Woody Woodpecker Takes A Trip	445	LGB
Woody Woodpecker Takes A Trip	111-2	LGB N
Woody Woodpecker Takes A Trip	111-32	LGB N
Woody Woodpecker Takes A Trip	111-42	LGB N
Woody Woodpecker's Pogo Stick Adventures	2562	TAT
Woody Woodpecker, Steps To Drawing	372	LGB
Woosy Woodpecker's Peck Of Trouble	831	TAT
Words	202-52	LGB N
Words	A 1	LGB A
Words	A 30	LGB A
Words	A 45	LGB A
Words	202-42	LGB N
Words	202-52	LGB N
Words	205-34	LGB N
Words	205-4	LGB N
Wrong-Way Howie Learns To Slide	2523	TAT
Wynken, Blynken And Nod And Other y Nurser Rhymes	571	Elf
Wynken, Blynken And Nod And Other Nursery Rhymes	8367	Elf
Wynken, Blynken And Nod And Other Nursery Rhymes	8714	Elf
Xavier's Birthday Surprise!	107-64	LGB N
Yanky Doodle And Chopper	449	LGB
Year In The City, A	48	LGB
Year On The Farm, A	37	LGB
Yellow Cat, The	911	TAT
Yes I Love You	LGB F	
Yip And Yap	1022	Elf
Yip And Yap	8380	Elf
Yip And Yap	8690	Elf
Yippie Kiyi And Whoa Boy	2514	TAT
Yippie Kiyi	940	TAT
Yogi Bear	395	LGB
Yogi Bear And The Baby Skunk	921	W
Yogi Bear Mosquito Flying Days	924	W
Yogi Bear Playtime In Jellystone Park	926	W
Yogi Bear, And The Super Scooper	2642	TAT
Yogi Bears Secret	2608	TAT
Yogi-A Christmas Visit	433	LGB
Your Friend, The Policeman	200	DD R
Zip! Pop! Hop! And Other Fun Words to Say	LGB F	
Zipp's Birthday Party	506	Elf
Zippy Goes To School	489	Elf
Zippy The Chimp	8306	Elf
Zippy The Chimp	487	Elf
Zippy The Chimp	8306	Elf
Zippy The Chimp	8705	Elf
Zoo Friends Are At Our School Today!	2423	TAT
Zorro	D 68	LGB D
Zorro And The Secret Plan	D 77	LGB D